The Collected Sermons of

William
Sloane
Coffin

The Riverside Years

The Collected Sermons of

William Sloane Coffin

The Riverside Years

———

VOLUME TWO

———

William Sloane Coffin

Westminster John Knox Press
LOUISVILLE • LONDON

Book design by Drew Stevens
Cover design by Lisa Buckley
Cover photo by Cynthia Johnson / Time & Life Pictures / Getty Images

First edition
Published by Westminster John Knox Press
Louisville, Kentucky

This book is printed on acid-free paper that meets the American National
Standards Institute Z39.48 standard. ∞

PRINTED IN THE UNITED STATES OF AMERICA

08 09 10 11 12 13 14 15 16 17 — 10 9 8 7 6 5 4 3 2 1

Library of Congress Cataloging-in-Publication Data
Coffin, William Sloane.
   The collected sermons of William Sloane Coffin : the Riverside years /
William Sloane Coffin ; introduction by Martin E. Marty.—1st ed.
       p. cm.
   ISBN-13: 978-0-664-23299-3 (v. 2: alk. paper)
   ISBN-13: 978-0-664-23244-3 (v. 1: alk. paper)   1. Presbyterian
Church—Sermons.   2. Sermons, American.   I. Title.
   BX9178.C58C65   2008
   252'.051—dc22   2007039284

Dear Reader,

Before he was unable to do so any longer, Bill always made the morning coffee. He would bring it to me in bed and there we would have our best talks of the day; fresh, sharp, intimate, challenging, and of course, all the "to-dos" that come with living together. Often he would talk around the sermon he was working on, or bring a new quote, like a treasure, that he was going to use to brighten a moment in a sermon. One Valentine's Day morning four or five years ago, he brought me this note with my coffee, and I give it to you, who also try.

> "And we are put on earth a
>   little space
> That we may learn to bear
>   the beams of love"
>   (Wm. Blake)
>
> A serious thought on Valentine Day

It is my hope that you will find courage and hope for your own work in these sermons, that you will see how Bill found his way, and that he may help you find yours.

With all my best wishes,
Randy Coffin

Contents

1983

1984

1985

Contents

1986

1987

Thank You

These sermons could not have been published without first and foremost the dedication of Bill's longtime editor, Stephanie Egnotovich at Westminster John Knox Press, and its former senior editor, Davis Perkins, who encouraged the project at the very beginning, and Julie Tonini, also of WJK. Thanks to folks at The Riverside Church to James Forbes, Thomas Stiers, Victor Jordan, and Robert Lundberg; and at Yale University to Thomas Hyry, William Massa, Diane Kaplan, Nancy Lion, Laura Tatum, and John Lindner. And to David Coffin particularly for help at Yale, to Amy Coffin, Jessica Tidman and Tom Scull, Wil and Jill Tidman, Sperry Wilson, Caroline Steele, Kate Siepmann and Ruth Whybrow for the sustaining encouragement you gave to me throughout . Thank you! I am ever grateful to you all.

Randy Wilson Coffin

Acknowledgments

Copyright © Piet Hein Grook: *The Miracle of Spring.* Reprinted with kind permission from Piet Hein a/s, DK-5500 Middelfart, Denmark.

From *A Thousand Clowns* by Herb Gardner, copyright © 1961, 1962 by Herb Gardner and Irwin A. Cantor, Trustee. Used by permission of Random House, Inc.

From *Guerillas of Grace* by Ted Loder, copyright © 1984 Innisfree Press. Used by permission of Augsburg Fortress.

From *Our Town* by Thorton Wilder Copyright © 1998 by Harper Perennial Classics. Used by permission of The Barbara Hogenson Agency, Inc.

Poem "(Page 31)" from "The Separate Notebooks: A Mirrored Gallery" from *The Collected Poems 1931–1987* by Czeslaw Milosz Copyright © 1988 by Czeslaw Milosz Royalties, Inc. Reprinted by permission of HarperCollins Publishers.

"Shine, Perishing Republic," copyright 1934 by Robinson Jeffers & renewed 1962 by Donnan Jeffers and Garth Jeffers, from *Selected Poetry of Robinson Jeffers* by Robinson Jeffers. Used by permission of Random House, Inc.

The lines from "be of love (a little)." Copyright 1935, © 1963, 1991 by the Trustees for the E. E. Cummings Trust. Copyright © 1978 by George James Firmage, from *Complete Poems: 1904–1962* by E. E. Cummings, edited by George J. Firmage. Used by permission of Liveright Publishing Corporation.

"The Rabbi's Gift," as it appears in M. Scott Peck's Prologue from *The Different Drum* (N.Y.: Simon & Schuster, 1987).

Introduction

"Come off it!" Praise the Reverend William Sloane Coffin too extrav-
agantly, as many did in his hearing, using hyperbole to describe his
works and ways, and they would be dismissed with a smile, a shrug,
and a posture which suggested: "Now that *that's* out of the way, let's
get down to business."

Moved as I am by the Riverside sermons and tempted as I am to
praise the preacher and author lavishly, I hear his virtual "Come off it."
So I will, out of respect and in his honor. This means that hyperbole
will have no place, though here and there I might express some awe.
To get to the point, I will concentrate first on what this chapter is not:

It is not a song of praise. We've already settled that.

It is not a biography. There is a commendable one: *William Sloane
Coffin Jr., A Holy Impatience* by Warren Goldstein (Yale, 2004).

It is not an exegesis of the sermons in this book, though it is an
introduction to the world out of which they issued and a
peephole into the world of the sermons themselves.

It is not a snippet of a personal memoir by the author of this
introduction. While I frequently saw, heard, read, and conversed
with Coffin, hundreds of people who knew him at Yale, Riverside
Church, or elsewhere, have better credentials for reminiscing
than I. So I'll get to the assigned business at hand, introducing a
book of sermons which represent only one element—though an
extremely important one—in his ministry.

It is not a history of Riverside Church, where these sermons
were preached through a decade of Coffin's ministry there. For
the detailed context its numerous authors provide, see *The
History of the Riverside Church in the City of New York*, by Peter J.
Paris and seven other authors—big churches demand big casts of
characters—(New York University Press, 2004). Leonora Tubbs
Tisdale wrote the chapter on the Coffin decade, 1977–1987.

It is remarkable, first off, that anyone cares about sermons preached from one pulpit, far away from all but New York readers, up to thirty years before their publication here, namely 1977 to 1987. There are so many sermons preached each week, and most preachers, however high they aim in faith, are realistic enough to know that most are ephemeral. If we count one homily or sermon per congregation each weekend, almost half a million messages get preached each Friday night, Saturday, or Sunday in the United States. Many of these forms of witness are quite effective, life-giving—some hearers would even say life-saving—alongside the many more that are less effective, vibrant, or memorable. Most of them achieve their goal if they help situate the hearers in the experienced presence of God, are instructive, and inspire the congregation to leave the pulpit and pew behind in order to put the message to work for the next seven days. Only a wildly egocentric preacher could envision seeing all of his or her messages in print, or at least in print that was intended for more than the local membership. Local hearers often can pick up the previous week's messages at the door as they leave the house of worship.

What becomes of these sermons? Are some of them folded and crafted into paper airplanes for children's play; are they piled up on bedroom reading tables; do they nourish passengers on commuter trains or transform the lives of some of those who could not be present for the preaching? If this sounds dismissive of preaching, an act commanded by the Jesus of the Gospels and an honored form of communication through twenty centuries of Christian meeting, it is not intended to be. Rather, it reflects something about the ephemeral character of human achievements, even those which reflect sacred intentions, and also shows awareness of the limits of human memory.

As for the substance of sermons, a British theologian asked an audience of regular worshipers: *Try to bring to mind five sermons you have heard in your lifetime.* Most of those who were challenged to do so were stumped. They might remember a funeral sermon, something said on a special occasion, or an occasional stunner. Most are forgotten. After they came up with a few, the theologian went on: *Now try to bring to mind five people through whom the hand of God was laid upon you.* Instantly, everyone came up with such.

Not a few of those described as God's agents were preachers remembered from childhood or through long years of the pastoral care they offered. From all evidences of his popularity and the demand for published versions after decades, Dr. Coffin would be one of those few whose sermons were remembered and cited by hearers and readers after many years. He would also be one that a generation of Yale students, Riverside members, and guests remember. They could say, "The hand of God was laid upon us" by him. If they would choose to follow up on this metaphor, they would likely go on to say that that figurative hand of God in the case of Coffin's sermons was one that could lift people up when they were down, push them back when they were proud, and impel them into action. I envision a new generation of readers of these works from the Coffin years and ministry feeling that hand of God and hearing whispers of the divine call afresh. Those who might consider that sentence to be hyperbolic and its expectation too extravagant are asked to read a few of the sermons here and see whether my vision is realistic or not.

Regard these sermons first as what Christian sermons should all be: testimonies. One definition of preaching, tired-sounding but full of promise, is that of the great Boston preacher Phillips Brooks: "Truth through personality." The personality of preacher Coffin is evident on every page. That is why the many subscribers to his sermons years ago soon learned that from them they could probe more deeply into biblical texts; learn what Coffin did with a text and how he did it; and pick up a line full of insight here and there. But they soon discovered that they could not simply reproduce and then preach his sermons effectively. I am told that an Episcopal priest in California was caught simply lifting one of his homilies. Such plagiarism was easy to discern.

Truth through personality—the idea pushes us into the realm of a more complex concept: that to understand the act of preaching we have to become aware of the "hermeneutics of testimony." That is a phrase of the French philosopher Paul Ricoeur, who pondered what happens when we reject "absolute knowledge of the absolute," or, in Pauline terms, we recognize that "our knowledge is piece-work" or partial (1 Cor. 13). Yet the preacher who wishes to address and impart the things of God cannot simply surrender all notions that "the absolute," or, in Johannine terms, "the Truth" is accessible and can be partly imparted.

Testimony, for Ricoeur, first involves the "claim to have experienced something." Second, as with testimony in court, we have to judge the truth of the witness. Whoever has been in court is likely to agree that the testimony cannot be grasped absolutely. It does deal strongly with "the probable." Ricoeur recognizes testimony could be false, and some preaching turns out to be such. We call it "inauthentic," if not deceiving. A commentator on Ricoeur puts all this well: "Witnesses must back their beliefs. Commitment does not guarantee the veracity of a belief, but lack of commitment undermines it." In

Ricoeur's terms, this means that "testimony is also the engagement of a pure heart and an engagement to the death." To the death?

Martin Luther King Jr., for instance, was a credible witness because those who testify on the basis of conscience and risk death become especially attractive and believable to those whose consciences are stirred. Members of audiences were aware that enemies of his message might kill him at any moment, and his audiences and congregations knew it. That is why, even when on some occasions and in some modes he preached the gospel in terms that a comfortable suburban pastor might use, his message rang truer and was more compelling. It sealed the relation of the hearer with the speaker and behind them, "the Absolute" or in biblical terms, "the Truth." Lest the reference to the suburban pastor is taken as a slap against preachers who enjoy apparent security, let me say that it does not exclude the witness of those who are not at the edge of the zone where the violent would kill. "Testimony" is compelling when the middle-class, comfortable preacher is fighting a shattering disease, or is facing a psychological battering. Such can come when the preaching parent is frustrated in efforts to be reconciled to an alienated child, or when existential doubt is plaguing.

It is at this point that one can hear a haunting, chiding whisper: "Come off it." Bill Coffin would squirm or kick if he thought we thought that anything he did put him in a "quasi-martyrial" situation. The label "martyr" applies to St. Stephen, or Steve Biko in South Africa or Dietrich Bonhoeffer in Germany, or some murdered civil rights workers in the American South. True, Bill was hated, lividly, by those who could never forget the activities he undertook and instigated at Yale and elsewhere to protest the American adventures in the Vietnam War. It is also true that he was hated for his participation in civil rights and disarmament causes. Many a pastor-preacher will identify with Coffin, who engaged in ominous tangles with some influential membership blocs and even some obstructionist staff members at Riverside Church. Yet whatever the scale of threat and jeopardy a preacher feels, or however nagging the personal and up-close temptations might be, they serve to force the preacher to think through what truth he or she is to convey, and with what degree of self-reference he does so in the sermon.

Coffin retains authenticity because his references to conflicts afar, conflicts near, conflicts within, are always brief, as readers will soon find. They are, if anything, understated and told in such a way that they display no traces of narcissism. I do not mean by that last comment to suggest that Coffin was a virtuoso at self-deprecation, modest to a fault, or someone who felt compelled to remind us how insignificant he is. Part of the "hermeneutics of testimony" in Christian preaching is that the witness manifests enough sense of self-worth—thanks to the genes and Jesus—to show the guts to commend "the Absolute"="the Truth" of God in Jesus Christ and to ask others to join in the wager, the one that deals with the "probability" of the resurrection of Christ, the decisive point of witness for Paul, Paul Ricoeur, and Bill Coffin.

Paul Ricoeur, on a theme that perfectly matches the stand and outlook of Coffin, continued with analysis of the biblical or "sacred" meaning or context for testimony when it uses extraordinary expressions. "What separates this new meaning of testimony from all its uses in ordinary language is that the testimony does not belong to the witness. It proceeds from an absolute initiative as to its origin and its content." To bring testimony, says the philosopher, is different than cinching the deal through philosophy: "To attest is of a different order than to verify in the sense of logical empiricism." (On the hermeneutics of testimony and comment on it see Dan R. Stiver, *Theology after Ricoeur: New Directions in Hermeneutical Theology* [Westminster John Knox Press, 2002], 196–202.)

Whoever wants to test the testimony of Bill Coffin as father need only read "Alex's Death," his most famous and revered sermon from the Riverside years or all his life. Note also the sermons that chronologically follow "Alex's Death." They are cries of the heart, revelations of bewilderment, exorcisms of temptations to turn against God but, significantly, they show that the signals of a more profound faith and impulse to exercise ministry comes from them. After suffering the loss of a child during those Riverside years, all the rest was put in perspective. He faced criticism and rejection even by many Riverside stalwarts. Some of them were reached by adversarial television and newspapers, for his stand against nuclear armament and, after showing some signs of timidity, support for homosexual rights and the enhancement of understandings on this troubling issue. Even further in the background are the nagging tensions over Riverside church administration, which was not his chosen or favorite field of action, or one in which he excelled.

Now for some lower level but perhaps relevant personal testimony of my own: I had not expected to read so much Coffinesque Christian orthodoxy as one finds on so many pages. Before I was personally acquainted with him or had read him, back in his Yale years, I only knew that he was described as the most prominent standard-brand or liberal Protestant. Those were the years when the concept of a Protestant mainline was being marketed. Often it was used invidiously against those who were not in the evangelical/evangelistic or Pentecostal ranks and certainly against those who were forming a religio-political New Christian Right. In polemical portraits of these, "liberal Protestants" were faithless Christ-deniers who got their signals from Soviet communism or secular humanism, and then spoke and acted while applying only a biblical-sounding Christian veneer to their preaching and preachments. William Sloane Coffin was supposed to be "Exhibit A" to represent the faithless.

During the intervening years, when I began to read Coffin's books and occasional sermons, I was jolted into the need to make reappraisals or, should I say, first-time appraisals. Far from muffling the voice of the Gospels and serious Christian theologians through the ages, Coffin was a witness to the acts of God in Christ, one ready to profess faith in the Trinity, one at home with the relevant voices of Christian traditions. True, you will find here no discussions of modalistic monarchianism, patripassionism, or semi-Pelagianism. However, as their author employs fresh language, Coffin's sermons are clear and draw their power from the basics. When it came to politics, he may have seemed to be, to polarizers in the parish and the media, "on the left." My hunch is that his biblical testimony must have sounded as if it was coming not "from the right" but from the mainline of the mainline. I'd call it the "moderate" middle, but Coffin did not believe that Christian prophecy, judgment, or gospel, could ever be "moderate."

The immediate impression one receives from any page of these sermons is that preacher Coffin had internalized a dictum of top theologian Karl Barth, one which had almost been reduced to cliché by the 1970s, but which was still to the point: "Take your Bible and take your newspaper and read both. But interpret newspapers from the Bible." Today I suppose Barth would have to urge preachers to google internet signals in order to know what is going on in the minds of YouTube and MySpace addicts in the pew. Here, again, standard-brand Protestants of the sort who established Riverside Church and many from African-American church traditions that were cherished and assertive on Morningside Heights in the Coffin decade might have expected preacher Coffin in his sermons to become enslaved by a passion for the moment. He certainly did have an awareness of performance and attracting the media. But he did not become addicted to it, and he did not have to become obsessed with a passion for relevance.

Something needs to be said about the situation of Riverside Church. It was founded in the 1920s in a merger of a Baptist and a Congregational Church. With the backing of immensely wealthy John D. Rockefeller Jr., they built cathedral-size modern-Gothic appearing Riverside. It towered and towers over Morningside Heights near Columbia University, Union Theological Seminary, and any number of educational institutions. A succession of great preachers, most notably fighter-against-fundamentalists Harry Emerson Fosdick in the 1920s, led it to become well known for liberal theology and its powerful agencies for making change in New York City. Massive though the walls were, the church with its programs and personalities had always been fragile. Fosdick and Rockefeller, who admired each other, regularly tangled, especially when Fosdick would preach about social policies offensive to the man of wealth.

Morningside Heights became a neighborhood of turmoil, and Riverside had to react to shocks as both rich and poor, black and white, liberal and moderate, and, by Coffin's day, gay and straight people were in tense relations with each other. The cumbersome polity of the church was Baptist-style writ large—it stressed the autonomy of the local congregation. It was heavily bureaucratic, difficult to administer. As years passed, funding itself became a major problem, and Coffin had to attend to financial affairs, not always adeptly. For all the tremors and traumas affecting the foundations of that church and the people who worshiped in it, Riverside became no doubt the most prominent pulpit in American Protestantism. The press and radio and television knew where to focus on issues of the day, and found them in the Coffin pulpit. Tourists and guests knew where to come for great preaching and the music for which the church was also famed. By the time Coffin came to the scene, relations between the large black caucus and some other elements in the membership of the staff were tense. Coffin had to address them.

In addition to the description of the location and the physical circumstances of the church, we need to pay some attention to the place of preaching in such a pulpit, circa 1977. In church and society, a kind of therapeutic revolution was continuing. One of the features of its "feeling movements" was the sowing of distrust of the spoken word. In these years the public was experiencing the high prime of Marshall McLuhan, priest of the media revolution, who called into question messages and even the concept of messages in a critique. The electronic revolution was focused on television and devoted to imagery. Often advocates of this medium dismissed oral communication. Seminaries attracted students who felt a call to ministry, but many of them wanted to avoid anything as drab and boring as preaching, then seen as an outmoded form. They were told that embrace, gesture, drama, and pictures were the ways to communicate the sense-revolution. Preaching, discourse by one to many, was declared to be dying out.

Yet at the same time, new movements were arising. And every one of them—whether they existed in support of civil rights or in causes such as dealing with the environment, war and peace, identity movements of ethnic or interest groups, the understanding of gender—was led by people who used words well. The pioneers of the women's movements possessed no guns, no ships, and meager funds. But they had words, and their speeches rallied newcomers to the cause and fortified those already in it. In other words, they were secular preachers. In religion, there had been new stirrings for twenty years. Heads of the black movement for those two decades had been "Reverends." Among all these activists was Bill Coffin, preaching and gaining followings mainly through sermons. He believed in the spoken word. Without instruments of government, the military, big business, or advertising firms, he had virtually no source of power beyond his spoken words. He had used his feet during protests at Yale and was ready to use them now, but they were relatively unimportant when compared to this voice box and his words that issued from it.

A third event or trend that should have worked against Coffin at Riverside was the relative decline of churches that came to be called "mainline," ironically at the time this putative mainline was seen to be losing its place. Others were on the rise. Barriers which had once set quotas on Jews in the academy were down. Nonwhite Protestants, tending to the city, were producing headlines and celebrities unmatched in the then still prevalent Protestant style. Preaching was being rediscovered, most significantly among African Americans. Significantly, Coffin's successor at Riverside was to be James Forbes, who, like Coffin, was often pointed to as the most prominent preacher of the day.

In the midst of this colorful cast was Coffin, whose very name recalled the days when Anglo-Saxonhood meant so much. The Reverend Doctor William Sloane Coffin Jr., rooted in WASPdom, was now a prophet against some of its practices and an evangelist who would heal people within the old Protestant nexus. Others took confidence from his example.

One learns from the record of Coffin at Riverside how hard it is for even the most eloquent and wisely admired spiritual leaders to move complex institutions. In fact, as one reckons with the causes to which he gave support, it was clear that few were prospering. During those years the electorate took a turn to the right with the election of Ronald Reagan. More and more investment of funds and faith went to armament. Priorities in the nation favored the rich and led to neglect of the poor. In almost every sermon here there is a reference to some in-church or beyond-church matter that needed address, but for which there were no resources in pocketbook, mind, or heart to turn things around easily. So, since the nation and church were losing so much, was Coffin himself a loser? Hardly. Realistic as he was about his own fallibility—his marital record, for instance, had disturbed some on the calling committee at Riverside—he was generous in his appraisal of faults of others. His critical voice was never whiny. He once chuckled during a University of Chicago visit which included a stop in my office where there was a sign "No Whining." I don't think he noticed my other wall decoration, Walt Kelly's Pogo saying: "We have faults we have hardly used yet." His sermons suggest that he would have acclaimed it.

The reason he could be angry but not sullen, disappointed but not despairing, was because he believed in the Christian gospel, with its accent on the triumph that came with suffering, the power that issued from the weak, the victory that was the seal of the loving sacrifice unto death of Jesus on the cross. The theology was moving to those who heard it, and should be so to readers of these sermons. They were not covered by the media as much as were his demonstrations against racism and nuclear armament, or as had been his counseling of conscientious objectors to the Vietnam War draft in the years before he came to Riverside. Yet devotion to that gospel of weakness was the secret of his power, or the power of that in which he believed. To test that, one has to sample the sermons, or, in due course, to read them all with a highlighter or colored pen for underlining in hand.

Pastor William Sloane Coffin, in times of such unrest, tried to "interpret the newspapers" in the light of the Bible. He could preach some landmark sermons, one of which we will sample: The occasion was Martin Luther King Jr.'s fiftieth birthday. Coffin used the occasion to celebrate King's ability to shake things up in general.

> Even as Blacks are breaking up all-white patterns, so women are upsetting the patriarchal structures of America. And this bodes well for the Gay liberation movement, as historically only societies that subordinate women are harsh in their treatment of homosexuality—male homosexuality, that is. Interestingly enough, with the exception of one vague passage in St. Paul, there is not a single mention of lesbianism in all the Bible. (Someday we'll deal with the gross misinterpretations of Scripture on the part of those who, for their convenience, forget that the Nazis put over 200,000 homosexuals to death.)

That is the typical Coffin who loads up several causes within a few lines. A few lines later he pointed to those who put no friendly hand on the shoulders of teenagers in Harlem and other ghetto sites. Still a moment later he could ask: "Isn't the arms race getting ahead of the arms control process?" Old military veteran Coffin almost lost it whenever he came to current military affairs and war:

> As Martin well knew, the church is called to be the Bride of Christ, not the whore of Babylon. She cannot bind herself to the Prince of Peace and go awhoring after the gods of war. She cannot proclaim the gospel of Christ while officiating at the altars of anticommunism. She cannot stand for peace while lying prostrate before the shrine of "national security."

Soon he was announcing Riverside Church's organizing of an anti-arms race initiative, crediting King's spirit.

What is more striking than those comments, which almost became boilerplate among Christian critics of racial injustice and the arms race, is the incidental way Coffin would reach beyond the moment:

> What the prophets teach us to believe and what the world regards as belief are not the same. . . . Prophets recognize that revelation always has to be worked out, that there is a progressive nature to moral judgment. So they criticize what is, in terms of what ought to be. They judge the darkness of the present by the light of the future. And they reject what is narrow and provincial, in the name of what is universal. Prophets know that just as all rivers finally meet in the sea, so all individuals, races and nations meet in God.

Coffin quoted Galatians 3:28 after those lines which summarize as well as any what being prophetic in his time meant, though he was embarrassed when people called him a prophet as he himself was addressing the agenda he had just outlined.

The reader will find many variations on this prophetic theme, which he handles with care. In a sermon preached soon after there was a poignant reference to the presence of the powerful in the case of Nelson Rockefeller, whose funeral at Riverside drew the wealthy and the mighty. Almost immediately in the sermon, Henry Kissinger was the focus. Here was another illustration of a preacher who had that newspaper in his one hand. On the global scene, Iran and Iraq became regular topics in the year when Iranian leaders took some Americans hostage.

Sometimes pastors in large and endowed congregations are envied because their main task is preaching, so they have all week to prepare for the pulpit. It happens that prominent pulpits are usually the main means of outreach of a congregation and the chief means of nurturing the adults, and, one hopes, often the children. This connecting task inevitably forces administrative tasks on the leader of the pastoral staff, usually the preacher. Coffin saw to it that he did set aside plenty of hours for study and the writing-out of his sermons. But anyone who reads the history of Riverside covering his years knows that he was forced to face tensions and crises, sometime financial, sometimes in staff battles, and most of all when his participation off the premises in causes that not all members found congenial took great expenditures of time. He used the tensions as energizers for the act of speaking.

Sometimes his allusions are so dense that the reader, finding it difficult to follow, has to have empathy for the congregation. Still, the people stuck with him, looked forward to his sermons, quoted them, and sometimes testified that they tried to live by what they learned. Here is a sample of an overladen allusion-rich paragraph that is still worthy of unpacking:

> Descartes was wrong. *Cogito, ergo sum?* ("I think, therefore I am.") We are not detached brains, nor do we establish who we are by thinking alone. Self-knowledge through self-contemplation is self-defeating. In his *Memoirs*, the British philosopher A. J. Ayre writes, "The self seethes, and philosophy analyzes. An abacus is substituted for the sinew of human mystery, and wit for passion."

One hopes that the hearers "got it," for it encapsulates so much of what I found to be central to Coffin in Ricoeur's "hermeneutics of testimony." For the French philosopher and here for an English one thrown in, analysis is not testimony. One can stand back during analysis. My teacher of preaching sixty years ago planted an idea that has never left my classmates or me. He posed eighteen questions that dealt with the quest for effective preaching. Coffin would have breezed through such a test. But the eleventh question was elusive and plaguing. We were to read other people's sermons and ask, "Does this preacher *describe* God or *offer* God?" Offering God meant testifying that "the Absolute"—no, translate that to "the Truth" in Jesus

Christ—is an offering of God's presence which expects response. Philosophy, like the abacus, is then on the shelf, while the self seethes and the sinew of human mystery has to be reached.

Coffin moved on to disturb the peace of the antirationalist romantics who were coming to such prominence in the church and world in 1978. These were the romantics who dodged the reach of God by saying *sentio, ergo sum* ("I feel, therefore I am"). If Coffin could have appraised such "feeling" as a mere fad in middle-class therapy and the discourse of the time, he would have dropped the matter; but he found that something was at stake. He feared that people would end their quest for or response to God with nothing but feeling. Those who wanted to be closer to God, he urged, had to go deeper. For deeper than thinking, deeper than feeling, is caring. I care, therefore I think. I care, therefore I feel. I care, therefore I wish, therefore I will. I care, therefore I am. Coffin discerned an ontological and biblical grounding for this depth: "We have passed out of death into life, because we love the [sisters and brothers]" (1 John 3:14). If one was to care, he or she had to get rid of grievances, in the manner of Jesus the "plant from the stem of Jesse," who never allowed his soul to be cornered into despair; who needed no enemies to tell him who he was; who never counted what was unworthy of his suffering.

In a time when people were beginning to be "spiritual but not religious," or who found the church and ministry irrelevant, Coffin found a way to confront them by asking questions, even by quoting questions.

> I have a friend—very successful—who in the fifties toyed with the idea of becoming a minister. When he came to see me at Yale Divinity School I introduced him to my teacher, Richard Niebuhr. . . . Afterwards my friend told me of their conversation. He said to Dr. Niebuhr, "I believe in God all right, and Jesus and the Christian life, but somehow the church and its ministry seem a bit irrelevant, not part of the 'big show'" as he put it. He wanted himself to be part of the big show. Finally Dr. Niebuhr said, "Tell me, Mr. Jones, what is the big show?"

That exchange prompted a new inspection of Nicodemus, the successful ruler who came to Jesus at night. Soon he was speaking against the concept of machismo which did not allow the powerful to have to ask questions or be questioned.

I cannot conclude this beginning of a book without citing a typical Coffin sermon. Typical, you might think? It's the one he preached the Sunday after his son Alex's death in an auto accident in 1983. The agony was more deep, no doubt, than that the preacher felt over the deaths of children far away. His theological blast at people who were too sure they knew the will of God in the accident was more furious than it might have been when other well-meaning people misspoke theologically. But it all comes close to the heart of his preacherly theology:

> And of course I know, even when pain is deep, that God is good. "My God, my God, why hast thou forsaken me?" Yes, but at least, "My God, my God"; and the psalm only begins that way, it doesn't end that way. As the grief that once seemed unbearable begins to turn now to bearable sorrow, the truths in the "right" Biblical passages are beginning once again, to take hold. . . . "The light shines in the darkness, and the darkness has not overcome it" (John 1:5).

Coffin regularly preached about victory over death and the triumph of resurrected life. So he could conclude of this accident, "If a week ago last Monday a lamp went out, it was because, for him at least, the Dawn had come. So I shall—so let us all—seek consolation in that love which never dies, and find peace in the dazzling grace that always is."

Authors of introductions to books don't usually end with an "Amen," but sermons by William Sloane Coffin Jr. make up a different kind of book, so I end with: Amen.

Martin E. Marty
Emeritus, The University of Chicago

1983

Alex's Death

JANUARY 23, 1983
Readings: Psalm 34:1–9; Romans 8:38–39

As almost all of you know, a week ago last Monday night, driving in a terrible storm, my son Alexander—who to his friends was a real day-brightener, and to his family "fair as a star when only one is shining in the sky"—my twenty-four-year-old Alexander, who enjoyed beating his old man at every game and in every race, beat his father to the grave.

Among the healing flood of letters that followed his death was one carrying this wonderful quote from the end of Hemingway's *Farewell to Arms*: "The world breaks everyone and afterward many are strong at the broken places." My own broken heart is mending, and largely thanks to so many of you, my dear parishioners; for if in the last week I have relearned one lesson, it is that love not only begets love, it transmits strength.

Because so many of you have cared so deeply and because obviously I've been able to think of little else, I want this morning to talk of Alex's death, I hope in a way helpful to all.

When a person dies, there are many things that can be said, and there is at least one thing that should never be said. The night after Alex died I was sitting in the living room of my sister's house outside of Boston, when the front door opened and in came a nice-looking middle-aged woman, carrying about eighteen quiches. When she saw me she shook her head, then headed for the kitchen, saying sadly over her shoulder, "I just don't understand the will of God." Instantly I was up and in hot pursuit, swarming all over her. "I'll say you don't, lady!" I said. (I knew the anger would do me good, and the instruction to her was long overdue.) I continued, "Do you think it was the will of God that Alex never fixed that lousy windshield wiper of his, that he was probably driving too fast in such a storm, that he probably had had a couple of 'frosties' too many? Do you think it is God's will that there are no streetlights along that stretch of road, and no guard rail separating the road and Boston Harbor?"

For some reason, nothing so infuriates me as the incapacity of seemingly intelligent people to get it through their heads that God doesn't go around this world with his finger on triggers, his fist around knives, his hands on steering wheels. God is dead set against all unnatural deaths. And Christ spent an inordinate amount of time delivering people from paralysis, insanity, leprosy, and muteness. Which is not to say that there are no nature-caused deaths (I can think of many right here in this parish in the five years I've been here), deaths that are untimely and slow and pain-ridden, which for that reason raise unanswerable questions, and even the specter of a Cosmic Sadist—yes, even an Eternal Vivisector. But violent deaths, such as the one Alex died—to understand those is a piece of cake. As his younger brother put it simply, standing at the head of the casket at the Boston funeral, "You blew it, buddy. You blew it." The one thing that should never be said when someone dies is, "It is the will of God." Never do we know enough to say that. My own consolation lies in knowing that it was *not* the will of God that Alex die; that when the waves closed over the sinking car, God's heart was the first of all our hearts to break.

I mentioned the healing flood of letters. Some of the very best, and easily the worst, came from fellow reverends, a few of whom proved they knew their Bibles better than the human condition. I know all the "right" Biblical passages, including "Blessed are those who mourn," and my faith is no house of cards; these passages are true, I know. But the point is this: While the words of the Bible are true, grief renders them unreal. The reality of grief is the absence of God—"My God, my God, why hast thou forsaken me?" The reality of grief is the solitude of pain, the feeling that your heart's in pieces, your mind's a blank, that "there's not a joy the world can give like that it takes away" (Lord Byron).

That's why immediately after such a tragedy people must come to your rescue, people who only want to hold your hand, not to quote anybody or even say anything, people who simply bring food and flowers—the basics of beauty and life—people who sign letters simply, "Your broken-hearted sister." In other words, in my intense grief I felt some of my fellow reverends—not many, and none of you, thank God—were using comforting words of Scripture for self-protection, to pretty up a situation whose bleakness they simply couldn't face. But like God Herself, Scripture is not around for anyone's protection, just for everyone's unending support.

And that's what hundreds of you understood so beautifully. You gave me what God gives all of us—minimum protection, maximum support. I swear to you, I wouldn't be standing here were I not upheld.

After the death of his wife, C. S. Lewis wrote, "They say, 'the coward dies many times'; so does the beloved. Didn't the eagle find a fresh liver to tear in Prometheus every time it dined?"

When parents die, as did my mother last month, they take with them a large portion of the past. But when children die, they take away the future as well. That is what makes the valley of the shadow of death seem so incredibly dark and unending. In a prideful way it would be easier to walk the valley alone, nobly, head high, instead of—as we must—marching as the latest recruit in the world's army of the bereaved.

Still there is much by way of consolation. Because there are no rankling unanswered questions, and because Alex and I simply adored each other, the wound for me is deep, but clean. I know how lucky I am! I also know that this day-brightener of a son wouldn't wish to be held close by grief (nor, for that matter, would any but the meanest of our beloved departed), and that, interestingly enough, when I mourn Alex least I see him best.

Another consolation, of course, will be the learning—which better be good, given the price. But it's a fact: few of us are naturally profound; we have to be forced down. So while trite, it's true:

> I walked a mile with Pleasure,
> She chattered all the way;
> But left me none the wiser
> For all she had to say.
>
> I walked a mile with Sorrow
> And ne'er a word said she;
> But oh, the things I learned from her
> When Sorrow walked with me.
> Robert Browning Hamilton

Or, in Emily Dickinson's verse,

> By a departing light
> We see acuter, quite,
> Than by a wick that stays.
> There's something in the flight
> That clarifies the sight
> And decks the rays.

And of course I know, even when pain is deep, that God is good. "My God, my God, why hast thou forsaken me?" Yes, but at least, "My God, my God"; and the psalm only begins that way, it doesn't end that way. As the grief that once seemed unbearable begins to turn now to bearable sorrow, the truths in the "right" Biblical passages are beginning, once again, to take hold: "Cast thy burden upon the Lord and He shall strengthen thee" (Ps. 55:22); "Weeping may endure for a night, but joy cometh in the morning" (Ps. 30:5); "Lord, by thy favor thou hast made my mountain to stand strong" (Ps. 30:7); "for thou hast delivered my soul from death, mine eyes from tears, and my feet from falling" (Ps. 116:8). "In this world ye shall have tribulation, but be of good cheer, I have overcome the world" (John 16:33). "The light shines in the darkness, and the darkness has not overcome it" (John 1:5).

And finally I know that when Alex beat me to the grave, the finish line was not Boston Harbor in the middle of the night. If a week ago last Monday a lamp went out, it was because, for him at least, the Dawn had come.

So I shall—so let us all—seek consolation in that love which never dies, and find peace in the dazzling grace that always is.

Loving Your Enemy

FEBRUARY 6, 1983
Reading: Matthew 5:43–48

Nuclear energy is an unforgiving technology; you make one mistake and you've had it. If the world is to survive, we need a new kind of technology, and no end of forgiving people. Americans are told almost daily that we have many enemies, and especially the Russians. Hence this sermon on loving your enemy, with these words of Jesus as a text: "You have heard that it was said, 'You shall love your neighbor and hate your enemy.' But I say to you, 'Love your enemies.'"

At first that sounds like a very straightforward commandment, albeit as easy to follow as for a camel to pass through the eye of a needle. But even as an idea, loving your enemy seems to me difficult to grasp, for love represents both tenderness and judgment. Jesus, who enjoined us to love our enemies, himself passed the harshest possible judgment on all who were cruel, unjust, and indifferent. Is not the Soviet government precisely that to millions within and without its borders? So how are we to love the Russians and, at the same time, oppose cruelty, injustice, and indifference?

The first thing to be said about enemies is trite but true: they are our sisters and brothers. That's what monotheism is all about—one God, one human family. The trouble is, we don't *feel* the relationship.

The other day I heard of a Zen Buddhist monk who came upon a baby abandoned in the road. He picked up the baby, wept, and put it down again. He wept because the baby had been abandoned; he left it there because in his mind no one could replace the mother. It's a haunting and troubling story, and I tell it only to suggest that we might view all our relationships as indispensable and irreplaceable. A mother and a child are not one, but also not two. They are some mystical number in between. So also are lovers, and truly good friends. But spiritually speaking, that's the way we all ought to be together— not one, but also not two. And that includes our enemies.

For all his faults, Oliver Cromwell in the seventeenth century understood the reality of relationships. When it came time to draw up the rules of war for his newly formed revolutionary religious army, he had to confront the question of what to do with a man who was found with a wound in his back. The answer was, find his comrades and drill them out of the army and out of the Church. Why? Because cowardice is more a communal than an individual failing.

Enemies are like cowards: they represent communal failures, breakdowns in sacred relationships. For the initial breakdown itself only some may be guilty, but all are now responsible. And to repair these breakdowns is of such urgency that Christ could say in the Sermon on the Mount, "If when you are bringing your gift to the altar, you suddenly remember that your brother has a grievance against you, leave your gift where it is before the altar. First go and make your peace with your brother, and only then come back and offer your gift" (Matt. 5:23–24). Does this mean that every Sunday, on our way to Riverside, we should swing by the Soviet consulate?

St. Paul said, "All have sinned and fallen short," and St. Augustine elaborated: "Never fight evil as if it were something that arose totally outside of yourself." In other words, it takes a sinner to catch a sinner. If the Soviets have intervened monstrously in the internal affairs of others, so, Lord knows, have we. If they suppress civil liberties at home, we conspire to suppress these same liberties abroad, from Honduras through the Philippines to South Korea and Pakistan. If what the Russians do in Poland is heartbreaking, it is not to be compared with the continuing torture and death we are aiding and abetting in El Salvador, In short, if we are not yet bonded with the Russians in love, at least we are one with them in sin—which is no mean bond, for it precludes the possibility of separation through judgment. That's the meaning of the Scriptural injunction, "Judge not, that ye be not judged" (Matt. 7:1).

So we are not only brothers and sisters, we Americans and the Russians, we are fellow sinners. And there must be at least as many

Russians who know that as there are Americans, even though, for obvious reasons, their voices are muted. I believe the world is sustained by a kind of international solidarity of people who are ashamed of what their governments are doing. Shame is not only a deeply religious but an intensely patriotic emotion, reflecting the determination of citizens to carry on a lover's quarrel with their country, a quarrel that is but a reflection of God's eternal lovers' quarrel with the world.

And let us not forget what hatred does to those who hate. To quote other words of Augustine: "Imagine the vanity of thinking that your enemy can do you more damage than your enmity."

What damage can our enmity, our hatred of others, do us? Among many insights of the Roman Catholic Church, I prize the one that makes the first of the so-called cardinal virtues *prudentia*, or *providential*, which can be translated "darn good thinking." Only if your heart's full of love can you think straight. Love has a limbering effect on the mind, while hatred paralyzes it. Lack of compassion distorts the intellect—maybe not when it comes to examining the stomach of a spider, but certainly when dealing with the hearts of human beings. Far from blind, love is visionary. Only love sees rightly that what is essential is invisible to the eye. It is love that sees that one and one don't make two, but something in between. It is love that sees enemy Russians as sisters and brothers and as fellow sinners. And love sees also as sisters and brothers the homeless and hungry of this city and the poor and persecuted the world around, those overlooked by hearts too busy with hatred or with themselves. Consider the 250 million of the world with no housing, the 300 million who are unemployed, the 550 million illiterate, the 700 million who are undernourished, the 950 million who live on less than thirty cents a day, and the 2 billion who have no access to pure water—which is crucial, because 80 percent of the world's illnesses are related to impure water—are they not victims of callous thinking ("stinking thinking," to borrow a phrase from Alcoholics Anonymous), victims of worldwide hatred and indifference, victims by denial of a world that presently spends $1 million a minute on arms? (We won't even mention other forms of frivolity.)

But the opposite of love is really not hatred, but fear. As it is written, "Perfect love casts out fear" (1 John 4:18). Fear is the enemy that always defeats us, both as individuals and as nations. Wrote Rabindranath Tagore: "The mind, seeking safety, rushes towards its death." Frankly, nothing scares me like scared people, unless it be a scared nation—scared of communists, scared even more of being "soft" on communists, and most of all, perhaps, scared of being humiliated by communists. Don't we always fear most those who have the power to humiliate us? And wasn't Othello right: "Thou hast not half that power to do me harm as I have to be hurt"?

So the first and final enemy is always the enemy within—our own fears and hatreds, which means the first enemy to be loved is ourselves. Have you ever seen anyone who was for higher defense budgets who wasn't personally defensive? (An interesting question!) And would we be so defensive were there not so much that has yet to be forgiven?

Whatever is worthy of censure is, at another level, deserving of compassion. People who are full of hatred are only demonstrating their insecurity and their desperate efforts to secure themselves against their insecurity. But the only road to inner peace lies through the forgiveness that once walked the earth, in whose name we are gathered here today.

And the only road to outer peace lies through our forgiveness of our enemies. To forgive is not to condone. In fact, what we cannot possibly condone, we can only forgive. Forgiveness means to be hard on the issues and gentle with people (confrontation, yes, but also compassion); to have the capacity to lift human beings above their present level. Forgiveness spells reason, not hysteria. Forgiveness means positive Christianity, not negative anticommunism. Forgiveness means the lifting of a mental roadblock, the clear proclamation that the evil act is no barrier to a continuing relationship. Forgiveness to Christians means to outlive, out-love, out-pray, out-suffer, and out-die everyone else in this world, as did our beloved Lord and Savior.

As we begin Black History Month, let us remember words of Dr. King: "Returning hate for hate multiplies hate, adding deeper darkness to a night already devoid of stars. Darkness cannot drive out darkness; only light can do that. Hate cannot drive out hate; only love can do that."

Eyeball to Eyeball with the Devil

FEBRUARY 20, 1983
Readings: Genesis 2:1–7; Luke 4:1–13

In the three gospels that carry it, the story of Jesus' temptation in the wilderness follows hard on the heels of the story of his baptism, a high moment when, as you recall, the heavens opened and a voice was heard: "This is my beloved Son in whom I am well pleased" (Matt. 3:17).

Does this sequence of events indicate that every great vision fades into the light of common day; that after every mountaintop experience comes a return to the valley floor? Perhaps so, and for the reason offered by T. S. Eliot: "'Go, go, go,' said the bird; 'Humankind cannot bear very much reality!'"

But that assessment is beside the point, for here Reality itself, the Holy Spirit, leads Jesus out of the Jordan and into the wilderness, proving that the Spirit is both comforter and *dis*comforter. Pain is an essential part of the religious life, for as the story shows, pain is the breaking of the shell that encloses our understanding.

Heart-searching time that it is, Lent *should* be painful *and* rewarding, a time to be led by the Spirit into our own wildernesses, to have it out, eyeball to eyeball, with the devil, on all the basic issues of our lives. For, like steel, we human beings are uncertain until tested.

Do not be dismayed that the Church personifies evil. The devil is imaginatively portrayed as a person because evil is experienced as an intensely personal power. Its seductions are personally persuasive. Moreover, while evil certainly arises within us, still it is experienced as something greater than us—hence its separate existence. And most importantly, the devil is a fallen angel. How many parents tell their children that evil arises in the so-called lower nature! But notice that the devil never asks Jesus how he feels, for example, about sex, any more than Jesus ever put that question to anybody else. Both know that evil arises in our "higher" nature, in that which is most Godlike— our freedom. Not that our higher nature can't abuse our lower nature, but the source of the evil is always in our freedom. And what does the devil ask us to do with our freedom? In countless subtle, seductive ways the devil whispers, "Sell it!"—which is to say, "Sell yourselves short."

The subtlety comes through in the first temptation: "Command this stone to become bread." After forty days Jesus was of course hungry, desperately so, but I think his own hunger was making him remember hungry people everywhere. After all, he had just been baptized, and he was now wrestling with the meaning of it all—what was his mission to be on this earth? Palestine was plagued by extremes of drought and flood. Bread, a basic necessity, had become a precious commodity, the more so because the Roman taxes, like American taxes today, hurt most those least able to protect themselves. Why then should not Christ become a Messiah of justice, fulfilling God's commands and the hopes, too long deferred, of those whose lives were hard, endless, dirty labor? It would have been a proper, hard-headed, courageous role for him to have assumed, and one that would have met popular messianic expectations. That Christ turned it down simply reminds us how extraordinary—*extra*-ordinary—human lives are. "Give us this day our daily bread": bread is essential, and for that reason, we should never rest until everybody has enough. The rabbis say, "Without material sustenance there is no Torah," and in the *Three-penny Opera* Bertolt Brecht writes, "First feed the face, and then talk right or wronger ("Erst kommt das Fressen, dann kommt die Moral")." What we have to confront in this Lenten season in our wildernesses is the truth of this statement: "When bread has been assured, then God becomes a hard and inescapable reality, instead of an escape from harsh reality" (Berdyaev).

Haven't we set our sights too low—on a secure life that insures us against harsh reality, that assures us bread? In my younger, more obnoxious days, I used to ask tenured professors what they had said that year that they would not have dared to say had they not been given tenure. It was a mean but fair question. Originally designed to protect controversial ideas, tenure now protects uncontroversial professors. But they are not the only noncontroversial people. On that now-famous *60 Minutes* show, the National Council of Churches was criticized only for what it was aiding and abetting abroad. Isn't it doing anything controversial at home? And why should the Council be defensive? Shouldn't every decent church boast at least a few enemies—as did their Lord and master?

There are many things I have done that I repent. But they are as nothing compared to the good things I regret not having done. To me, it's not the lives we've lived, but our unlived lives that stand out, and that poison our existence.

Listen again to the story of our creation: "Then the Lord God formed man of dust from the ground, and breathed into his nostrils the breath of life, and man became a living being" (Gen. 2:7). Obviously we don't all have to be controversial, but all of us have to recall that the breath of life has been breathed into our nostrils. We are nature *plus*. Our hands not only bring food to our mouths, they play the flute; they help us salute one another, and they help us address God. We are *extra*-ordinary. We do not live by bread alone. So in this Lenten season, in our separate wildernesses, we have to ask ourselves whether the devil has not seduced us to sell ourselves short, to live only by the light of the obvious, to grab so greedily at today that we lose all tomorrows. Have we not, like Esau, sold our birthright for a mess of pottage? Clearly we have much to think about, including these words of Jesus: "My food is to do the will of him who sent me, and to accomplish his work" (John 4:34).

If the first temptation was to satisfy the economic needs of Jesus' people, the second temptation seems to have been to satisfy their patriotic passion. Rome was then the oppressor, with a garrison of soldiers in every sizeable town, not only to levy taxes but also to put down revolts. Surely the spiritual descendants of "the boys of '76" can understand Christ's temptation to become the George Washington of Israel, to rally the six million Jews scattered throughout the ancient world; and, perhaps in alliance with the Parthians, to bring defeat to Rome, peace to his people, and glory to God.

Alfred the Great is reported to have said, "Power is never good unless he who has it is good." The devil could have whispered convincingly, "If anybody is good it is surely the Son of God. Wouldn't power in your hands represent love implementing freedom and justice? Why not prove, once and for all, that love and power are not polar opposites?"

That Christ withstood this temptation too should lead us to more painful heart-searching, to question our own American reliance on power—particularly the power to kill—as the best way to protect freedom and peace in the world.

Suppose you picked up the paper this morning and read that Police Commissioner McGuire, tired of conventional means of fighting crime, has come up with a new policy of deterrence. From now on, the police of New York City are going to kill every last member of the family and every last acquaintance of anybody who from now on commits murder within the city limits. You'd be horrified, wouldn't you? To threaten to kill so many innocent people represents power run amok.

Yet that is an analogy for our present policy of nuclear deterrence—except that the hostage system is massive. We—and the Russians—have promised to kill in retaliation every last man, woman, and child in each other's countries, almost none of whom will have anything to say with the decision to press the button. It's madness, obscenity. So go into your wildernesses and search your hearts and see if you can square that policy with the worship of the Lord your God.

And finally we read that the devil "took him up to Jerusalem and set him on the pinnacle of the temple, and said to him, 'If you are the Son of God'" (always that attack at the identity point, where we're always weakest), "'throw yourself down from here, for it is written,

"He will give his angels charge of you, to guard you.'" . . . And Jesus answered him. 'It is said, "You shall not tempt the Lord."'"

The first thing to note—and well—is that the devil quotes Scripture! But what is the temptation? Is this "unfaith clamoring to be coined to faith by proof"? Can't you picture the crowds gathered below: "Look, he's going to jump. He *has* jumped. He's safe. He *must* be the Messiah!" And did Jesus reject the temptation knowing that freedom and proof, religiously speaking, are indeed polar opposites? Or did he think then what he said later in the parable: "If they hear not Moses and the prophets, neither will they be persuaded, though one rose from the dead" (Luke 16:31)?

Or, more subtly, is this the kind of temptation that comes to a person who has finally renounced the struggle for worldly security and the struggle for worldly power and has committed himself or herself to God, but with the secret expectation that God will now do all the work? So much so-called spirituality is superficiality, pure laziness reminiscent of the story of the priest who went golfing with the rabbi. Before putting the priest crossed himself. By the ninth hole he was nine strokes ahead. Said the rabbi, "Father, do you suppose it would be all right if before I putted I too crossed myself?"

Answered the priest, "Of course, rabbi. But it won't do you any good till you learn how to putt."

There are so many lazy people in the churches, people who want to cop out on all the responsibilities that go with freedom, who want selfishly to ask God to take care of them when they are supposed to be out taking care of the world. They come to church, but they don't leave. They do church work, but not the work of the church.

So, dear Christians, we have our work cut out for us. Let us not be afraid in this Lenten season to go out into our own wildernesses and go eyeball to eyeball with the devil on the basic issues of our lives. Let us not be afraid of the pain that is the breaking of the shell which encloses our understanding. Let us remind ourselves that because God has breathed into our nostrils the breath of life, we cannot sell our freedom, we must not sell ourselves short. Besides, who really wants to sell his or her freedom for material well-being? Do we as a nation really want to trade in our power to love for loveless power? And as individuals, do we want God to take care of us when we should be caring for others?

And one more thing: At the end of Matthew's account of this story we read: "Then the devil left him, and behold, angels came and ministered to him" (4:11). There are still angels around ready to do no less for us.

Not Self-Control but Self-Surrender

FEBRUARY 27, 1983
Readings: Isaiah 40:27–31; John 16:31–17:1

I am most grateful to my colleague Russell Davis for giving me John Claypool's *Tracks of a Fellow Struggler*, a book that inspired and gave much substance to this sermon. Preachers are incurable magpies!

Earlier we heard Isaiah claim, "They who wait for the LORD"—or "wait upon" or "hope in" the Lord, as different translations have it—"will renew their strength." Then the prophet suggests three ways in which their strength will be renewed in three quite marvelous metaphors, the first of which is—shall we say—soaring: "They shall mount up with wings like eagles."

Long before it became a patriotic symbol, the eagle was a religious symbol, representing in its body and wings the strength which Isaiah saw that God could renew in each of us, in any time, and in any situation. That is why in so many churches, our own included, this great bird holds on its outstretched wings that book which is at once the most soul-searing and uplifting of all books, the Bible. You'd never know it to look at so many long-faced Christians, but the Christian faith is supposed to make us ten times as exciting and as excited as pagans: exuberant, exhilarated, even ecstatic. The reason so many Christians do not soar like eagles is that they have, alas, missed the secret. They think the secret to the Christian faith is self-control; in fact, it's self-surrender. Self-surrender is really the life, for how can you be "captivated," "enthralled" by anything or anyone—Bach, Beethoven, Brahms, Leontyne Price, or Jesus—until first you surrender? You don't step into love, you fall.

So alike are "waiting for the Lord" and being in love that I want to read you a love poem, which I suspect many of you have not heard—even though I'm sure all of you are still following my prescription to read a poem a day. (I don't know why you laugh; it simply shows how futile these sermons are! How are you going to mount up with wings like eagles without reading poetry?) This poem is by Alfred Kreymborg, and it's called "Image."

> Showing her immortal—
> it's mine to do
> but I can't.
> Shaping her as she is,

a thing to
turn a glance
to an eternity—
it's there,
I can see it
but I can't say it.

If one could transcribe
some infinitesimal phase
of the trillion-starred endowment
which comes tumbling
out of simply trying to look at her,
or out of catching a glance,
slyly pointed,
trying to look at me,
stirring a trillion-starred emotion
vibrating like a bell
across endless tides of endless seas—

I'd do it.
but I can't.

I love her so much
I can't do anything else.

You see the point? You love Jesus so much, you can't do anything else.

Self-surrender is the proper attitude to life in general, simply because life finally can't be earned or grasped with fists clenched, it can only be received with palms open. Such a gift is life itself that each morning we should wake up and say, "My God, another day has been added unto me to see and hear and smell and read and walk and talk and love and glory. Praise the Lord!"

To soar like an eagle you have to remember that the secret is to abandon self-control for self-surrender; you have then to fall in love with God, with Jesus, and with life; you really have to be a little crazy, a "fool for Christ's sake," as St. Paul puts it—after all, "It's the cracked ones who let the light through."

But now suppose you, like Susan Lamb and Simone Wilkinson, are in Britain waging war against war; or you're in America trying to persuade administrations in Washington and New York that justice, not charity, is the answer to the homeless; or you're in the UN trying to persuade the world that poverty, not scarcity, is the cause of starvation.

Suppose the walls of Washington appear trumpet-proof, and the world seems like a place where time between tragedies is spent only waiting for the next. If you're that kind of person, with those kinds of perceptions, and you should be, then obviously you can't possibly stay in a constant state of exaltation, not without being an insensitive escapist. But according to Isaiah, where you can't "mount up with wings like eagles," you can "run and not grow weary."

Many Christians can't run without getting weary because they think life constantly rebuffs them, whereas in fact their problems arise not so much from their experience of life as from their expectations of life. Professors like to believe the world is rational, and all of us want to think it fair. But whoever said the world was either rational or fair? Think of all the undeserved good in the lives of all of us!

Those who are fighting for peace or for human rights like to think battles won should stay won, points proved should stay proved. They like to think that progress is an arrow, not a pendulum. In short, they are easily disillusioned and quickly discouraged. But let me ask you this: if you are disillusioned, whose fault is it for having illusions in the first place? Who ever gave you the right to stay innocent? None of us can any more blame the world for our disillusionment than we can complain about the way the ball bounces when we're the ones who dropped it. The main reason we can't run and not grow weary is self-pity—of all emotions, surely the most exhausting. I'm impressed by how weak and ineffectual we human beings are against the immensities of death and sickness and evil. "In the world you have tribulation"—I believe those words of Christ. So I keep my own expectations very low, which is why I have a lot of gravy in my life.

But I also never forget what we've just sung, "Through many dangers, toils, and snares [we] have already come." If God's grace has been with us in the past, surely God's grace will be with us in the future. There is absolutely no way we can absolutize our answers in favor of cynicism or naive innocence. We can say neither that the darkness swallows up the light nor the light the darkness. In this world, we can only say with St. Paul, "we see in part"; "we see through the glass darkly."

But it is not results, in any case, that secure our capacity to run and not grow weary. Ultimately, we have to do what's right, and penultimately to worry about what's effective. Imagine Socrates, when they handed him the hemlock, asking, "Is Plato going to write me up?" Or imagine Nathan Hale, as the noose settled around his neck, saying, "Wait a minute, fellows, are these thirteen colonies going to win this little revolution and then is every school kid in the new country going to memorize the famous last lines I am now about to utter?" The most effective people in the world are those who don't worry about being effective. And Christians, especially, don't have to "win." It's been said that Christians are the only folk who can afford to lose.

For us, it is enough to know that sense of undeserved integrity that comes from being in the right fight. For us it's enough to hear, "Be of good cheer, I have overcome the world."

With no illusions, with no final dependency on results, and with confidence that grace will see us home, we can indeed run and not grow weary.

But finally, suppose you are today among the hungry, the homeless, the bereaved of Assam or New York, or you're over eighty with a broken hip in St. Luke's, or under forty with terminal cancer in St. Vincent's. In such a situation no one can "mount up with wings like eagles," or even "run and not grow weary." But one can still "walk and not faint."

In many religions the gods seem content to dwell on the other side of the sky, where our affairs are no more theirs than theirs are ours. But not so in the Christian understanding of the ways of heaven and earth. Once, during World War II, a family received that always-feared telegram announcing that their son, their only child, had been killed. Quickly the word spread around the neighborhood, and when their minister heard it he hastened to the home. When he came through the door, the father, in anguish, half out of his mind, rushed toward him screaming, "Tell me, I want to know: where was God when my boy was being killed?" After a long pause the minister answered quietly, "I guess he was where he was when his own boy was being killed."

In every kind of tragedy, those we understand and those we don't, God is a grieving companion. She's there to help us endure when only endurance is possible, to help us be patient when impatience is futile, to help us walk and not faint.

Never think that such suffering is totally pointless, because we never know. Preachers love to compare the Sea of Galilee to the Dead Sea. The fresh waters of the Sea of Galilee sparkle and are full of fish, while in the salty Dead Sea no fish can live. The reason for the difference is that the river Jordan runs *through* the Sea of Galilee but only *into* the Dead Sea, which has no outlet. The obvious point, and a good one, is that life comes through giving as well as receiving. But an exceptionally imaginative preacher, George Buttrick, once went on to identify another truth: The Dead Sea *does* have an outlet, an upward one. Over the centuries, as the sea has surrendered itself to the sun, a residue of potash has built up around its shores. Potash is a main ingredient of fertilizer, and engineers estimate that if the potash around the Dead Sea could be properly mixed and distributed, there would be enough to fertilize the whole surface of the earth for at least five years.

Does life ever come to a complete dead end? When the only outlet open is the sky, let us remember Jesus—"Yet I am not alone, for the Father is with me." And if we give ourselves to God, God will see to it that new life comes from the old.

Who Tells You Who You Are?

MARCH 6, 1983
Reading: Matthew 16:24–26

"Whoever would save his life will lose it, and whoever loses his life for my sake will find it." That these words are found, with variants, in all four Gospels, a total of six times, underscores their place at the heart and center of the Christian faith. These words also describe a general truth of life that certain things are lost by being kept and saved by being used. A talent, for example—be it singing, painting, viola or basketball playing—will develop if used, and if not will atrophy and be lost. If life is, par excellence, a talent to be exercised, to be matured by use, then we have to say that Socrates was wrong: it is the uncommitted, not the unexamined life that is finally not worth living. Descartes too erred: *"Cogito, ergo sum"*—I think, therefore I am? Nonsense. *Amo, ergo sum*—I love, therefore I am.

That being said, we must be careful not to deride the importance of self-examination. Not for nothing has the inscription above the temple at Delphi, "Know Thyself," become famous throughout all history. Losing your life should never be seized upon as an excuse for not finding out who you are. God save us from cocksure Christians, people who never dare to wrestle with doubt, who don't realize that sincerity stammers, who think they have committed their lives to Jesus, that they have put their hand in his and he is leading them on, when it is patently obvious they have Jesus' hand in theirs and are trying desperately to drag him off in some selfish direction of their own. "(People) never do evil so completely and cheerfully as when they do it from religious conviction," observed Pascal.

And "know thyself" applies equally to nations, who are all too prone to do evil cheerfully in the name of national security. After reading on Friday of President Reagan's latest rationalization for torturing still further the poverty-tortured people of El Salvador, I couldn't help thinking of that place in *Macbeth* toward the end of the fourth act, where Macduff asks, "Stands Scotland where it did?" to which Ross answers: "Alas, poor country! Almost afraid to know itself. It cannot be call'd our mother, but our grave."

But how do we get to know ourselves? It is no easy task, for who among us can boast no blind sides? I'm convinced we don't get to know ourselves by trying to find all the answers first and then starting to live. I could easily be persuaded that the great mistake of Adam and Eve—repeated frequently by intellectuals—was that before they lived they wanted to know all the answers, whereas God had ordained that knowledge was to come through and after experience. It is in the light of experience that we try to understand ourselves. We don't know in order to live; we live in order to know. And one of the things we must find out in living is the answer to the question, Who—or what—tells us who we are? Trying to answer that question is a fruitful way of trying to reach self-knowledge. Particularly in the Lenten season, we should continually ask ourselves, "Who—or what—tells me who I am?"

Let me illustrate. In my previous incarnation as a university chaplain, I was frequently asked to write letters of recommendation for seniors going on to graduate school (seniors who had yet to realize that education kills by degrees!). To deans of admission of such illustrious schools as Columbia Law or Harvard Medical I would frequently write: "This student will undoubtedly be in the bottom quarter of the class. But surely you will agree with me that the bottom quarter should be as carefully selected as the top quarter, and for what would you be looking in the bottom quarter if not all the sterling extra-curricular qualities so eminently embodied in this candidate?" Then I would say how sensitive, caring, and conscientious this student was. You won't believe this, but when I showed the student what I had written, invariably the student's feelings were hurt.

"How do you know I'm going to be in the bottom of the class?"

"The evidence is all in, isn't it?"

"Well, you didn't have to tell them!"

You see what I'm driving at: Never mind that the student was already in the ninety-nine-point-something percentile of all students in the nation; never mind that I said that she or he was a super human being. If he or she was not going to be in the top quarter, or half, or three-fourths of the class, he or she was a nothing. Such is the power of institutions of higher education to tell human beings who they are.

In this season in which we are mindful of the IRS, we are also reminded that some people need money to tell them who they are. Long ago, before the days of tax resistance, I used to be impressed by the fact that those most reluctant to pay their taxes were those most able to do so. Oh, they would give to charity, because charity reinforced the notion, "Money talks." But taxes are like Delilah's shears: they cut at the root of the strength, revealing the underlying weakness!

Closely related to money is power, and some people need lots of that to tell them who they are. Still others need enemies—whites need Blacks, and vice versa; Gentiles need Jews and Jews the "Goyim." Communists need imperialists, and anticommunists sure need communists to tell them who they are. Fifteen years ago this very month, in the middle of the Vietnam War, President Johnson announced his decision not to stand for reelection. Instantly half a million people in the peace movement lost their identity. ("Who are we without our enemy?") Fortunately, Richard Nixon came along and rapidly restored it. Some people need their sins to tell them who they are. Why, the way some of us treasure our mistakes, you'd think they were the holiest things in our lives!

And some few—very few, really—allow God to tell them who they are. These are people who believe that God's love doesn't seek value, it creates it. Rather than try to achieve their worth, they receive it as a gift. Rather than try to prove themselves, they seek only to express themselves. You can recognize these few real Christians because at home or in church, at work or in their lives as citizens, they are both vulnerable and fearless. They know that God provides no protection but no end of support. So "captivated" are they by Jesus that they are free to follow him if necessary from Galilee into Jerusalem. Having lost their lives to Jesus, paradoxically, they have found them.

And think of this: these are among the very few Christians who are never bored or boring. No matter how much or how little education they have, no matter how old or how young they are, whether they are rich or poor, in good health or bad, they are alive and well, fascinating folk, fun to be with.

So—what do you say?—let's risk joining them. Let's allow God—not money, not power, not our sins, nor "anything else in all creation"—to tell us who we are. Let's not seek to prove but only to express ourselves by becoming both vulnerable and fearless. It sounds scary, but also rewarding. "For whoever would save his life will lose it, and whoever loses his life for my sake will find it."

Whiners or Fighters?

MARCH 20, 1983
Reading: Matthew 16:13–23

Now when Jesus came into the district of Caesarea Philippi, he asked the disciples, 'Who do [people] say that the Son of man is?'" It was really an easy question. Anyone from an erudite Sadducee to an illiterate camel driver, anyone with ears open and a reasonable memory, could have answered it, because it concerned what other people thought. It was an academic, not a personal question. So, not surprisingly, we read, "And they said"—presumably all the disciples—"'Some say John the Baptist, others say Elijah, and others Jeremiah or one of the prophets.'" Then Jesus asked, "'But who do you say that I am?'" This time only one disciple answered. Simon Peter replied, "'You are the Christ, the Son of the living God.'"

This second question strikes me as at once the hardest and the easiest question to answer. It's the hardest because you can have the ears and memory of an elephant, the research capacity of a Ph.D. in comparative literature or musicology; you can think clearly before the demands of reason and even humbly before the face of God, and all these attributes will not help you answer it. They cannot change the Jesus of history into the Christ of personal faith. To answer, as did Peter, "You are the Christ," takes something more. It takes a leap of faith, a willingness to be wrong, a willingness to plunge in, to go beyond what the mind can reveal into that far richer realm of truth that the mind can defend, but never discover. It's also the easiest question, because you don't so much find the answer as the answer finds you: "Blessed are you, Simon Bar-Jona! For flesh and blood has not revealed this to you, but my Father who is in heaven."

As Peter alone among the disciples takes this leap of faith, on him alone Jesus founds his church—although less, perhaps, on the person of Peter than on the faith of Peter; and "church" less perhaps in an institutional sense than in the sense of the fellowship of faith. It is as if Jesus says to Peter, "Peter, your name means 'a rock'" (which it does, quite literally, in Aramaic; in Greek the word for rock is Petros), "and your destiny, Petros, is to be a rock. You are the first person to recognize me for what I am, and you are therefore the first stone in the edifice of those who will call themselves Christians."

So far, so good—quite lovely and rather moving. Let's go on: "From that time Jesus began to show his disciples that he must go to

Jerusalem and suffer many things from the elders and chief priests and scribes, and be killed, and on the third day be raised. "And Peter took him"—literally, caught hold of him—"and began to rebuke him, saying, 'God forbid, Lord! This shall never happen to you.'"

In other words, Peter's leap of faith, his willingness to risk being wrong, is as nothing compared to Jesus' act of faith in making Peter the foundation of the church! Having declared Jesus to be the Christ, Peter now shows no understanding whatsoever of what that means.

Let's be sympathetic for a moment. Who among us doesn't long to see goodness vindicated and emulated? Not all prophets are slain or exiled. Didn't kings listen to Isaiah? Didn't the Lord deliver Daniel? Didn't the crowds follow Jesus all over Galilee? Besides, I like Peter's protective love—none of the other disciples "caught hold" of Jesus. But protective love is always in part self-protective, as we see in this instance. What a disaster it will be to Peter to lose his friend and mentor! Furthermore, if rejection and death await the Messiah, fame and fortune can hardly be the lot of his disciples.

"From that time, Jesus began to show his disciples that he must go to Jerusalem." All this time he and the disciples have been in Galilee. Peter's words and behavior in this story suggest a distinction between being a disciple, or Christian, in Galilee, and being a disciple, or Christian, in Jerusalem. It's a distinction worth making today, for next Sunday, Palm Sunday, we're going to be asked to follow Jesus into Jerusalem.

What does it mean to be a Christian in Galilee? In dropping his fishing nets and following Jesus, Peter gave up his dependence on money, power, and reputation; he took the question of his identity totally out of the hands of other people and made it a matter strictly between himself and Christ. Christ taught Peter what Christ teaches all of us: that the freedom to make our own decisions is our greatest possession. In other words, in Galilee Peter learned to be autonomous, which in our day is no mean achievement.

Autonomy, let me suggest, is the key word to describe a Christian in Galilee. But following Christ to Jerusalem means you have to surrender this greatest possession, your hard-won autonomy. In Jerusalem you lose control over your life, just as Jesus did, and just as Peter refused to do when he denied Jesus. Peter didn't realize that the key word to describe a Christian in Jerusalem is no longer autonomy, but surrender.

I am, of course, exaggerating the control any of us have over our lives. You who are senior citizens know that sickness and old age rob you of a great deal of your autonomy. So does losing a husband, or losing a son, or for that matter losing a job. But even in the midst of unexpected tragedy, we have a choice—not to whom we attribute the tragedy, but how we're going to respond. We can remain in Galilee and insist with Peter that bad things don't happen to good people: "God forbid, Lord! This shall never happen to you." When tragedy strikes and the light goes out and the darkness falls, we can follow Dylan Thomas's advice: "Do not go gentle into that good night! Rage, rage against the dying of the light." Or we can follow Jesus into Jerusalem, where we don't see God's will any more clearly, but where we learn that we have to surrender our own wills. In Jerusalem people sing, "If thou but suffer God to guide thee, and trust in him through all thy days, / He'll give thee strength whate'er betide thee, and bear thee through the evil days." In Jerusalem senior citizens rejoice with St. Paul, "Though our outer nature is wasting away, our inner nature is being renewed each day." In Jerusalem a bereaved parent turns a broken heart over to a suffering God and asks not that the pain be lessened, but that the quality of the suffering be improved. In Jerusalem the unemployed pray, "Though I be out of work, O Lord, yet still employ me in thy service."

Tragedy forces a choice; Jesus, of course, chose his goal himself. He was no whiner about the sad state of Israel's affairs. He was a fighter, and had to carry the fight to the heart of the political and religious establishment. He knew that in Jerusalem he was going to lose control over his life, because rather than cling to the old illusions of humanity—Peter's illusions that goodness would somehow be vindicated and emulated—Christ faced humanity's ruthless facts. Some people need a blow on the head to bring them to their senses, which may account for the sternness of Jesus' rebuke to Peter: "Get thee behind me, Satan!" In any case, what the events that will take place in Jerusalem teach us is very simple: what most people fear is not the evil in the world, nor even the evil in themselves. What most people fear above anything else is the good in themselves, that good being so demanding and so often unrewarded. They repress the good in themselves, and then repress those who remind them of what they have done. Never would we have crucified the best among us had we not first crucified the best within us. We become Christ-killers because we're scared to death of being Christ-bearers.

There's the choice: to be whiners in Galilee, or fighters in Jerusalem. We can cling to the old illusions that bad things can't happen to good people—"God forbid, Lord! This shall never happen to you"—or we can face the fact that if the world didn't reward Christ for being Christ, it's not going to reward us for being Christians.

Despite the shallow understanding Peter displayed in Galilee and his total collapse thereafter in Jerusalem, Christ never gave up on his disciples. His act of faith in founding the church on Peter was more than vindicated, Petros became indeed a rock—and we must remember this: to whatever degree the church is founded on Peter, it's founded on a second chance. That's good news, for all of us have betrayed Christ far more than three times. Nevertheless Christ wants us to be added stones in the edifice of those he calls his church.

It's no mean achievement to gain autonomy, to be a Christian in Galilee, but the true test of what it means to be a Christian takes place in Jerusalem. The true test comes when, faced with tragedy or overwhelming forces of evil, we give up our claims to autonomy, we surrender our wills to God, and we pray with Jesus, "Not my will but thine be done."

Being a Christian in Jerusalem

Palm Sunday
MARCH 27, 1983
Readings: Zechariah 9:9–10; Luke 19:28–46

The exuberance of the Palm Sunday procession through the streets of Jerusalem puts us in mind of an earlier one described in the sixth chapter of the Second Book of Samuel. Here the procession, equally large, equally boisterous, is outside the city, as the crowd wends its way up the perilously steep slopes of Jerusalem, headed for the distant gates which until recently had guarded an ancient Jebusite fortress. Now in the hands of the Israelites, the fortress has become the City of David. To celebrate the change, the procession goes upward and onward, priests and singers to the fore, the crowd behind struggling up the slopes, and in the middle, perched on a rickety cart drawn by a team of oxen, the centerpiece of the procession, the Ark of God. For the occasion, David—so it is widely believed—wrote the Twenty-fourth Psalm. The procession having finally made it to the top, we can hear the priests and people burst into song, chanting antiphonally, "Lift up your heads, O ye gates; and be lifted up, ye everlasting doors; and the King of glory shall come in. Who is the King of glory? The LORD of hosts, he is the King of glory" (v. 9).

Keep your imaginations at work and you can see the ancient, creaky gates begin slowly to swing open before the multitude. Keep your imagination still working and picture now these gates as the gates of entrenched evil, or as the gates of death, or better yet, as the gates of the heart barred against God's entry. Then remember what is written in the Book of Revelation: "Behold, I stand at the door and knock; if any one hears my voice and opens the door, I will come in to him and eat with him, and he with me" (Rev. 3:20).

But aside from the exuberance and fervor that mark both processions, Palm Sunday is unique: in all Scripture there is no event in which the participants have more confused and conflicting views of what is taking place. Jesus' primary enemies (President Reagan, please take note) were not godless communists or atheists of any stripe; rather they were the religious leaders of his own nation—a sobering thought for the parson. They are there on Palm Sunday not to march, of course, but to try in any way possible to prevent their ideas of law and order from being pounded into dust altogether. The Pharisees think they have a heretic on their hands, and a peculiarly obnoxious one at that, for Jesus is saying, in effect, that the real troublemakers in this world are not the ignorant and cruel, but the intelligent and corrupt—people like the Pharisees (read "parsons") themselves. They resist Jesus as they have resisted him all along, and they will do so more vigorously later in the week when he "cleanses" the Temple, *their* Temple, symbol of *their* power, driving out the money changers who, in turn, symbolize one of the oldest forms of corruption—religion become subservient to profit-making. Yet these religious leaders, who by Thursday will see to it that Jesus is arrested and on Friday crucified, these same religious leaders on Palm Sunday are powerless. In John's account of Palm Sunday we read, "The Pharisees then said to one another. 'You see that you can do nothing; look, the world has gone after him'" (12:19).

Also not marching, but no doubt watching with equal interest, are the scribes or lawyers, men not about to allow any moral excitement to overwhelm their practical judgments. They are full of cunning and realism, these men of the law (there are, of course, no women). For them the real challenge of life is to rise above the rest, to grab the lead; you're tough or you're nothing. Not that they are without humanity, but finding it is a little like looking for that thin line of mercury in some thermometers: you have to get the light just right.

As good counselors listen for what people *don't* tell them, so the Palm Sunday scene is better understood by noting who's *not* there.

What shall we call them—the "count-me-outs"? These are the people whom busyness has taken hold of. You know how it is: when busyness takes hold of you, then religion, art, music, poetry, sports, friends— all the things that give height, depth, and flavor to life—go out the window. Of the genteel poor, we say, "They live in reduced financial circumstances"; of those of whom busyness has taken hold, we can say that they live in reduced emotional circumstances. (They may think they're cookin', but their pilot light has gone out!)

But back to those taking part. "Look," said the Pharisees, "the world has gone after him." If by "the world" the Pharisees meant the great majority of the downtrodden, they were right, for the common folk heard Jesus gladly. We can picture small children charging in and out, charmed-life children running barefoot in the dusty, dog-fouled streets; adolescents ill-assembled and awkward; grown men with sweat bands tied on their foreheads; and women, away for a blessed moment from the grease and garbage of kitchens. Here was the spirit of Jerusalem, the spirit of ancient Israel at Passover time, speaking in its lowest registers, from the very bottom.

But before we sentimentalize the poor, before we cheer this multitude, let us ask whom they were cheering. Was it a religious leader, one who had searched their consciences, convinced their minds, and won their hearts? Or were they following a political leader whose power was proved—as is suggested again in John's account of the day—by the story circulating through the city that Jesus had raised a man named Lazarus from the dead? It is true that they carried palms, which then as now were symbols of peace. But it is also true that the Romans would not allow them to carry spears. It is true that they were praising God. But it is also true that they were hailing the King of Israel. Some no doubt remembered the prophecy of Zechariah: "Lo, your king comes to you;. . . humble and riding on an ass." But I'll bet the majority had Saul and Solomon in mind. I'll bet the majority were hailing a new national leader come to help throw off the hated Roman yoke; and you can't blame them for wanting political independence. But you also can't equate such a political leader with "the lamb of God that taketh away the sins of the world."

With different perceptions go different emotions. The chief priests and scribes are sullen, the people are ecstatic. But the most heartrending contrast is between the emotions of the crowd and those of Jesus. Instead of acknowledging the cheers, as would any political leader, or even the Pope, Jesus quietly sobs. And were he weeping for what he had earlier predicted would befall him, that would be poignant enough. But no, he weeps for what he is sure will befall the very people urging him on, because they did not know the time of their visitation. "And when he drew near the city he wept over it saying, 'Would that even now you knew the things that make for peace.'"

Would he weep over New York today? Of course he would, if only because, as the Irish poet wrote, "When God gives us the truest sight, he does not touch our eyes with love, but sorrow" (John Boyle O'Reilly). Jesus would weep over our ghettos, our prisons, our 36,000 homeless, and, yes, the callousness in downtown Manhattan that makes all those things possible. Would he weep over Washington? Of course he would. Our own capital city, far from being occupied, as was Jerusalem on that first Palm Sunday, has become itself oppressive; the descendants of Thomas Jefferson are making like George III. Here's a sign of our greed: the more harm we do the Nicaraguans and Salvadorans, the more we claim they have done us. We grab everything for ourselves, even the injury. (A devouring person devours all there is.)

But most of all Christ would surely weep over Christians who in hindsight should know better what that Palm Sunday was all about; who, as I suggested last week, should be willing to follow him not only around Galilee but also into Jerusalem, where he confronts the political and religious establishments of every nation. "Would that even now you knew the things that make for peace": We *do* know the things that make for peace, in both the religious and political senses of the word. We know we have to put an end to the madness of the arms race; we know we have to put an end to the arms themselves; to put an end to foreign policies of intervention and domination; to begin the reallocation of the world's resources to meet human needs; to begin to affirm life, to celebrate our common humanity, to love each other, to share the bounty of the earth more equitably.

We know all those things. Our problem is that we only *wish* for peace, we don't *will* it. Like the Pharisees, we're too self-righteous; like the lawyers, too ambitious; like those not there on that first Palm Sunday, we're too busy, too intensely elsewhere; most of all, we have been living so long with our weaknesses that we cannot believe in our own power and strength. But this is the day to take a small step toward a greater faith in him who said on another occasion, "Everything is possible for anyone who has faith" (Mark 9:23). This is the day to swing open the creaky gates that bar our hearts to the King of glory, the day to hear the very stones cry out, "Blessed be the King who comes in the name of the Lord" (Luke 19:38).

We know our situation. The odds against our saving the planet are desperate, but as ancient Aeschylus said, "Desperate odds fling a challenge." Human beings are not made for safe havens; the fullness of life lies in the hazards of life. So come what may—hell or high water—let us this Palm Sunday try to follow our Lord into Jerusalem.

"Would that even now you knew the things that make for peace." Sisters and brothers, let us arise and wish one another the peace of God, and then go forth and really work for it.

Like Him We Rise

APRIL 3, 1983
Readings: Matthew 28; 1 Corinthians 15:17–18, 20

In Haydn's oratorio *The Seasons,* in the section called "Spring," the chorus sings, "As yet the year is unconfirmed, and oft-returning winter's blast the bud and bloom destroy"—an apt description of this blustering day. But no matter: we know that energy soon will be pouring out of the ground and into every blade of grass, into every flower, bush, and tree; we know that soon the robins will join the pigeons, the sky will be full of the thunder of the sun, "the shaggy mountains will stomp their feet, the waves toss high and clap their wild blue hands." Overhead and underfoot and all around we shall soon see, hear, feel, and smell the juice and joy of spring.

But suppose this horrible weather was here to stay. Suppose that April had never come, that the earth somehow had spun out of orbit and was headed for the immensities of space, there forever to be assailed by winter's blasts. Not only would that be a gruesome prospect, but also, according to St. Paul, a proper analogy for the state of human affairs without Easter. Not one to hedge his bets, St. Paul puts all his Christian eggs in one Easter basket: "If Christ has not been raised, your faith is futile." Just as we know that April's coming, despite all appearances, because April's already here, so we know that we no longer live in a Good Friday world because Easter is already here. Or put it this way: The Kingdom of God could never come were it not already present!

God knows it looks like a Good Friday world. What makes the Good Friday story so devastating is that it is still so devastatingly true. In totalitarian countries politicians have but to hear "Thou art not Caesar's friend," and, like Pilate, away they fall like autumn leaves; while in more democratic countries, politicians seek to minimize their responsibilities, washing their hands and thereby plaiting the crown of thorns. Like Peter, most of us disciples follow our Lord halfway, but not the other half; while too many religious leaders today still, like the New Testament scribes and Pharisees, deify not God but their own virtue. As for the majority of citizens, are they not like the crowd that gathered on Calvary, not to cheer a miscarriage of justice, but also not to protest it? Failing to realize that compassion without confrontation is hopelessly sentimental, the crowd goes home beating their breasts, preferring guilt to responsibility.

By all appearances, it is a Good Friday world. But by the light of Easter, through the thick darkness covering the nations, we can dimly discern a "Yes, but" kind of message. Yes, fear and self-righteousness, indifference and sentimentality kill, but love never dies, not with God, and not even with us. The Easter message says that all the tenderness and strength which on Good Friday we saw scourged, buffeted, stretched out on a cross—all that beauty and goodness is again alive, and with us now not as a memory that inevitably fades, but as an undying presence in the life of every single one of us, if only we could recognize it. Christ's resurrection promises our own resurrection, for Christ is risen *pro nobis,* for us, to put love in our hearts, decent thoughts in our heads, and a little more iron up our spines. Christ is risen to convert us, not from life to something more than life, but from something less than life to the possibility of full life itself. As it is written: "The glory of God is a human being fully alive."

We'll come to the actual Easter event, the empty tomb, but first it's necessary to emphasize that Easter has less to do with one person's escape from the grave than with the victory of seemingly powerless love over loveless power. And let us also emphasize this: Too often Easter comes across very sentimentally, like a Nabisco wafer—airy and sweet. But there's nothing sentimental about Easter. Easter represents a demand as well as a promise, a demand not that we sympathize with the crucified Christ but that we pledge our loyalty to the risen one. That means an end to all loyalties to all people and all institutions that crucify. I don't see how you can proclaim allegiance to the Risen Lord and then allow life to lull you to sleep again, to smother you in convention, to choke you with success again. It seems to me that the burden of proof is with those who think they can combine loyalty to the Risen Christ with continuing the arms race or think that we Americans have the right to decide who lives, dies, and rules in other countries; or with an economic system that clearly reverses the priorities of Mary's Magnificat—filling the rich with good things and sending the poor away empty.

True loyalty to the Risen Lord is surely that displayed by Peter, who finally went the second half, who became ten times the person he was before Jesus' death; the loyalty of St. Stephen, who wasn't afraid of confrontation, and who under the rain of death-dealing stones cried out, Christlike, "Father, forgive"; the loyalty of so many early Christian men and women who, like Peter and Stephen, watered with their blood the seed of the church until it became the acorn that broke the mighty boulder that was the Roman Empire.

There is an Easter sunrise service that takes place on the edge of the Grand Canyon. As the Scripture line we earlier heard is read, "And an angel of the Lord descended from heaven and rolled back the stone," a giant boulder is heaved over the rim. As it goes crashing down the side of the Grand Canyon into the Colorado River far below, a two-thousand-voice choir bursts into the Hallelujah chorus. Too dramatic? Not if, despite all appearances, we live in an Easter world.

But let's move on with St. Paul's understanding of Easter. "If Christ has not been raised, your faith is futile, *and you are still in your sins.*" I don't know why sin is such a bad word. Obviously we're all sinners, the more so the more we try to deny it. But that's not the issue. At issue is whether there is more mercy in God than sin in us. And according to Paul, just as love is stronger than death, so forgiveness is stronger than sin. That may be the hardest thing in the faith to believe. The empty tomb is as nothing compared to the fact that we are indeed forgiven. But think again of Peter. Peter denied Christ just as surely as Judas betrayed him. The difference is that Peter came back to receive his forgiveness. The tragedy of Judas is that he never did.

Easter proclaims that forgiveness is offered all of us exactly as it was Peter. Just think: Andropov is forgiven, Arafat is forgiven, Begin too, Reagan, Watt, Jerry Falwell, yes, even the members of Riverside Church, who like their senior pastor always have God in their mouths but not as frequently in their hearts—just think, *all* of us are forgiven! And there's nothing sentimental about that either. What does it mean? It means that we are relieved not of the consequences of our sin, but of the consequences of being sinners. It means we are no longer sinners, but *forgiven* sinners. It means that with the zeal of gratitude we too can become ten times the people we are. It means that instead of trying to prove ourselves endlessly, we can express ourselves—fearless, vulnerable, dedicated, joyous followers of our Risen Lord.

And now perhaps we can deal with the empty tomb. St. Paul was the earliest New Testament writer, and it is clear that his Resurrection faith, like the faith of the disciples, was not based on the negative argument of an empty tomb, but on the positive conviction that the Lord had appeared to him. It is also clear that Christ's appearances were not those of a resurrected corpse, but more akin to intense visionary experiences.

Not only Peter, but all the apostles after Jesus' death were ten times the people they were before; that's irrefutable. It was in response to their enthusiasm (the word means "in God") that the opposition organized; and it was in response to the opposition—so many scholars believe—that the doctrine of the empty tomb arose, not as a cause but as a consequence of the Easter faith. The last chapter of Matthew *may* be literally true—I don't want to dispute it—but I also don't want you to stumble forever over it. Like many a miracle story in the Bible, it may be an expression of faith rather than a basis of faith.

Convinced by his appearances that Jesus was their living Lord, the disciples really had only one category in which to articulate this conviction, and that was the doctrine of the resurrection of the dead. To St. Paul, the events of the last days had been anticipated, and God, by a mighty act, had raised Jesus from the dead—in a spiritual body. To Paul, this living Christ and the Holy Spirit are never clearly differentiated, so that when he says "Not I, but Christ who dwells within me," he is talking about the same Holy Spirit that you and I can experience in our own lives. I myself believe passionately in the resurrection of Jesus Christ, because in my own life I have experienced Christ not as a memory but as a presence. So today on Easter we gather not, as it were, to close the show with Bob Hope's "Thanks for the Memory," but rather to reopen the show, because "Jesus Christ is risen today."

There remains only to say a word about the final consequence Paul draws from the Resurrection. "If Christ has not been raised, your faith is futile, and you are still in your sins. *Then those also who have fallen asleep . . . have perished.*" What then are we to say of those who have died, and how are we to anticipate our own death?

The Bible is at pains to point out that life ends: "All mortal flesh is as the grass." But St. Paul insists that "neither death nor life . . . can separate us from the love of God," that "whether we live or whether we die, we are the Lord's." If death, then, is no threat to our relationship to God, if "made like him like him we rise, ours the cross, the grave, the skies"—then death should be no threat at all. If we don't know what is beyond the grave we do know *who* is beyond the grave, and Christ resurrected links the two worlds, telling us we really live only in one. If love is immortal, then life is eternal, and death is a horizon, and a horizon is nothing save the limit of our sight. Can we not then also proclaim with St. Paul's wonderful freedom, "Now this I say, sisters and brothers, that flesh and blood cannot inherit the

Kingdom of God; neither doth corruption inherit incorruption. For this corruptible must put on incorruption, and this mortal must put on immortality. So when this corruptible shall have put on incorruption, and this mortal shall have put on immortality, then shall be brought to pass the saying that is written, Death is swallowed up in victory. O death, where is thy sting? O grave, where is thy victory? Thanks be to God who giveth us the victory through our Lord Jesus Christ" (1 Cor. 15:50, 52–55, 57).

So sisters and brothers, what are we going to do on this horrible, blustery, glorious Easter Day? God has done God's part: resurrection has overcome crucifixion, forgiveness sin; our departed loved ones are at rest where we too shall be someday. Are we going to continue the illusion of a Good Friday world, or start living the reality of an Easter one? Let's start answering that question by arising and exchanging with one another the traditional Easter greeting: "Christ is risen!" . . . "He is risen indeed!"

Be Angry, but Do Not Sin!

Youth Sunday
APRIL 24, 1983
Readings: Isaiah 1:9; Ephesians 4:26–32

Why do we have Youth Sunday? Because youth is idealistic. But along with youthful idealism goes ambition. Then as we grow older we find the world is not quite as cheerful a place as once we'd thought, and more resistant to change than we had anticipated. So what do we do—abandon our ambition? No, we abandon our idealism and hang on to our ambition, thereby making one of the greatest mistakes of our lives. So the Church celebrates Youth Sunday to warn youth of the dangerous decision that lies ahead, and also to remind their elders that it is never too late to change!

Of course, we also celebrate Youth Sunday to show off. The only reason I don't hand over the pulpit is the fear that I'd never get it back. So God bless all of you—Jason, Carter, Tracey, Adrienne, the Riverside Singers, and all the wonderful youth whom we shall receive into the church later on in the service.

The text for today's sermon is one to which I return with great regularity and pleasure. It is simple, powerful, always fresh and engaging, and you can find it in the fourth chapter of Ephesians, verse twenty-six, where St. Paul writes: "Be angry, but do not sin."

"Be angry." Notice the imperative, which is rather strange, for how can you command anger? We could as well ask, how can you command love? Yet love is commanded. "Thou shalt love the Lord thy God . . . and thy neighbor as thyself." Maybe Biblical writers use the imperative as an extra impetus to do the hardest things in the world to do, and some Christians certainly find it even harder to be angry than to love.

For one thing, many Christians don't associate anger with love, and with some reason. In 1 Corinthians 13, St. Paul writes: "Love is patient and kind; love is not jealous or boastful; it is not arrogant or rude. Love does not insist on its own way; it is not irritable or resentful" (vv. 4–5). One thing Paul does not say is, "Love is angry."

Yet in this same, so often tender, letter, Paul also warmly admonishes the Corinthians: "Do you not know that you are God's temple and that God's spirit dwells in you?" (3:16). (There's a definition of the human race according to its ideals!) Or elsewhere: "Brethren (and sisters), do not be children in your thinking; be babes in evil, but in thinking be mature." And wasn't Christ himself angry a great deal of the time, rebuking both unclean spirits and his disciples, although in dealing with the latter's obstinate stupidity he mixes sorrow with anger: "Do you still not understand? Are your minds closed? Are you as dull as the rest?" "Could you not watch with me one hour?"

Obviously Jesus was furious when he drove the money changers from the temple and no less so when he attacked religious leaders: "Woe to you, scribes and pharisees, hypocrites! for you tithe mint and dill and cummin, and have neglected the weightier matters of the law, justice and mercy and faith. . . . You blind guides, straining out a gnat and swallowing a camel!" (Matt. 23:23–24). This kind of irrelevant righteousness is the bane of the religious community—so concerned, for example, with "free love" and so indifferent to free hate. I remember, at the height of the savagery of the Vietnam War, how some Christians took off, once again, after the public libraries, totally unmindful that all the so-called dirty books that they wanted to purge from libraries across the land were not to be compared, in terms of obscenity, with one minute of the war itself. Or consider the Christians today who demand prayer in the public schools. We shouldn't be praying in the public schools, but *for* the public schools!

"Be angry." Christ was angry because he loved us, because he didn't want us to sell ourselves short, because love simply refuses to tolerate the intolerable.

I thought it a loving act of Derek Bok, president of Harvard and former dean of its law school, to show anger over the fact that we are an overlawyered society, or, more accurately, in his words: "There is far too much law for those who can afford it, and far too little for those who cannot."

And I thought it was a loving act of Dr. Cahill, director of the tropical disease center at Lenox Hill Hospital, to get even more angry, having observed that when a fatal disease struck down veterans attending an American Legion convention, and when women using tampons became ill with toxic shock syndrome, the medical profession instantly marshaled its talent and resources; yet doctors have done next to nothing about AIDS, once it became clear that the victims were primarily drug addicts, Haitian refugees, and homosexual men.

And how can we not become outraged at the fact that if any one of us had spent $2 million a day from the time our Lord and Savior walked this earth to the present, that sum would not equal what President Reagan proposes to spend in the next seven years on arms alone? How can we say we are kind, caring, even civilized, when at the same time we tolerate weapons of a barbarity inconceivable to former generations?

The importance of anger becomes even clearer when we note its opposite. Here's a confession from a Herb Gardner character, one brother talking to another.

> There's the people who spill things, and the people who get spilled on; I do not choose to notice the stains, Murray, I have a wife and I have children, and business, like they say, is business. I am not an exceptional man, so it is possible for me to stay with things the way they are. I'm lucky. I'm gifted. I have a talent for surrender. I'm at peace . . . You can't convince me I'm one of the Bad Guys. I get up, I go, I lie a little, I peddle a little, I watch the rules, I talk the talk. We fellas have those offices high up there so we can catch the wind and go with it, however it blows. But, and I will not apologize for it, I take pride; I am the best possible Arnold Burns. (*A Thousand Clowns*)

The best possible guy who has held on to his ambition and totally surrendered his idealism. To everyone who has made his or her no-questions-asked peace with the world at any price—St. Paul says, "Be angry."

And we should be no less angry with our friends when they sell themselves short. A friend is someone willing to risk her friendship for the sake of her friend. If we don't get angry with each other, how much do we care? Aren't we using our friends for the sake of their friendship and what it does for us?

And finally, shouldn't we at least occasionally get angry at ourselves? Seeing and listening to these wonderful kids leading the service this morning reminds me of my own children, and how occasionally I used to say and do things to get them to obey me that I really didn't believe in at all. I said and did them simply because these same things had been said and done to me when I was a child. Luckily my children protested vigorously, until I came to realize that what I obviously was trying to achieve was only a long-deferred and displaced revenge for the indignities and sufferings I had endured. It was outrageous behavior on my part, and, quite properly, I was furious with myself.

So there are plenty of good reasons to be angry, to which I would add only one more. In these crazy times when we are told that the only way to help the poor is to keep assisting the rich, that the only way to reduce nuclear weapons is to increase them—in these crazy times when almost every weed is called a rose and every rose a weed, anger preserves your sanity. There is a fine story told of an ancient ruler. When informed that the entire crop of the kingdom had been poisoned, and to such a degree that all who ate it would go mad, the ruler ordered the crop distributed as usual, for otherwise all would die of hunger. But the small reserve of last year's crop was to be given to a chosen few whose continual task it would be to remind the others that they were mad. This same task today falls to those who refuse to tolerate the intolerable, whose capacity for anger has preserved their sanity. Isaiah understood the problem: "If the LORD of hosts had not left us a few survivors we would have been like Sodom, and become like Gomorrah."

"But," says St. Paul, "do not sin." We are talking here of a lover's quarrel, not a grudge fight, whether the quarrel be with society, our nation, our friends, or ourselves. We're angry because we care, not because we hate. All anger that stems from hatred is destructive. That is why this Cold War is so bad for warm hearts, why St. Augustine wrote: "Imagine the vanity of thinking that your enemy can do you more harm than your enmity." Anger has to be like prophetic anger— grand, ironic, not petty and vindictive.

Unfocused anger likewise is destructive. Christ never found the whole world unfriendly, nor turned his wrath against all of Israel, nor even all its leaders. Nor did he nurse his anger. No matter against what or whom it was directed, it burst like a thunderstorm and was as quickly spent. The full verse in Ephesians reads: "Be angry but do not sin; do not let the sun go down on your anger, and give no opportunity to the devil."

And speaking of the sun, wasn't it wonderful yesterday, and won't it be out again tomorrow? And what a crime it would be not to draw every drop of strength and pleasure from every sticky leaf in Riverside Park, from meadows and woodlands "robed in the blooming garb of spring." No, Camus was right: "There is in the world beauty, and there are the humiliated, and we must strive, hard as it is, not to be unfaithful, neither to the one nor to the other." And he was also right in observing, "There are more things to admire in people than to despise."

So on this Youth Sunday, let us lay claim to our idealism, which is actually realism, for to Christians the essence of reality is love. Let us reclaim our idealism and sit a bit looser to our ambition. Like Isaiah and all the prophets, St. Paul, and Christ himself, let us carry on a lovers' quarrel with the world, our friends, and ourselves. Let us be angry but keep our anger loving, focused, un-nursed. It's a rough, mean world, full of rebuffs and heartaches, but never mind: "Ever singing, march we onward, victors in the midst of strife; joyful music leads us onward in the triumph song of life."

Neither Do I Condemn You

MAY 1, 1983
Reading: John 8:3–11

On this first day of May, should we not thank our Lord, "enthroned," as we shall shortly sing of her, "in heavenly splendor," for all the arrivals of this last week: each sticky leaf, as Dostoyevsky would say, each lilac, apple, cherry blossom, each shy daffodil waving in the breeze, each forsythia bursting brazenly into bloom, and not forgetting the song sparrow that awakens each day, and the occasional noisily trilling cardinal? And following that prayer of thanksgiving, should not our prayer of petition be, "O God, grant that all thy frozen people may also bloom"? Actually, this sermon has a lot to do with frozen people and how Christ tried to help them bloom.

In both life and literature, less is often more. To write well, or to live well, you have to guard against spattering out in irrelevant directions. In life and literature, you have constantly to relearn simplicity. What always hits me, whenever I reread today's New Testament lesson, is how with a minimum of words the tale of Jesus and the woman caught in adultery tells so much of the story of heaven and earth.

It also tells of prejudices not limited, alas, to Biblical times. Take the phrase, "a woman caught in adultery." Truly stunning—because, if there was a woman caught, most certainly there was also a man caught. You can no more catch one person in adultery than you can catch one person playing tennis, chess, double dutch, or double solitaire. So why didn't the scribes and pharisees bring the man along too? The answer is simple: in Biblical times, sexual sins were held against women. Men were sometimes admonished, but women were punished. Only if a man had sex with a betrothed virgin was he also to be stoned, which sounds like what I'm afraid it is, a property violation.

The same double standard was still in effect in Colonial times: Hester Prynne wore the scarlet letter on her bosom, the capital A for adultery, while her co-sinner, Dimmesdale, went free. But great novelist that he was, Nathaniel Hawthorne used the tale to demonstrate growth through forgiveness and self-acceptance on the part of the public sinner, while we watch Dimmesdale go to his destruction through private guilt.

Like Hawthorne, Jesus refused to assign guilt according to sex. And only the woman—none of the men—hears his words of forgiveness, "Neither do I condemn you." By today's standards, it should have been the men who heard those words, for not only were they guilty of incredible self-righteousness, but also perhaps of conspiracy to murder.

That being said on behalf of the single standard of judgment, which we have yet to reach, let's look now for a moment at that word "caught." As people generally don't allow themselves to be caught in this situation, we have to wonder whether or not some small part of that woman really wanted to be caught. I see this woman as a stand-in for all of us who find ourselves reflected in St. Paul's words of anguish, "The good that I would, I do not, and that which I would not do, that I do" (Rom. 7:19). I see this woman reflecting the fact that a rational mind is no match for an irrational will. Like all the rest of us in this or other situations, this woman found temptation too strong, and part of her, at least, didn't want to go unpunished. Like many people who have extramarital affairs and make excuses that are absolutely transparent for where they have been, or leave notes and letters and telephone numbers all over the place, so this woman made it easy for someone to catch her. And catch her they did: "The scribes and pharisees brought a woman caught in adultery."

Now picture, if you will, the faces of these men, scarcely a panel of her peers. Pretty starched, wouldn't you say? I see faces of men who have disapproved of too many things over too many years. I see faces of men who hate evil more than they love good, so that they have become good haters. I see puritanical faces, haunted by the fear that somewhere someone might be getting away with something. I see the faces of sex-fearing and God-fearing men who know little of the immutable love of a heavenly Father. I see the frozen faces of religious leaders, who can't bear the freedom, joy, and love radiating from the face of Jesus—freedom, joy, and love that contradicts their moralistic, legalistic understanding of life and undermines their authority.

But they are not dumb, these scribes and pharisees. Quite the contrary; in fact, they have constructed what is probably the subtlest trap since the serpent used the apple to go after Eve, except that the scribes and pharisees use one victim to trap another. Listen again: "Teacher, this woman has been caught in the act of adultery. Now in the law Moses commanded us to stone such. What do you say about it?" Should Jesus say yes to the ancient Jewish law, he might well fall afoul of the Roman authorities, who could charge him with illegally inciting to kill. On the other hand, if he denies the validity of Mosaic law, he will certainly be discredited in the eyes of many a devout Jew. So what does he do?

"Jesus bent down and wrote with his finger on the ground." A lot of people are curious about what he was writing. I don't think that's relevant to the story at all; the timing, the gesture is everything. "And as they continued to ask him, he stood up and said to them, 'Let him who is without sin among you cast the first stone.' And once more he bent down and wrote with his finger on the ground."

Having earlier been so harsh on the scribes and pharisees, it's time now we identified with them—which is not hard, for here they represent all those who seek to elevate themselves by separating sheep from goats, insiders from outsiders, good guys from bad guys. The scribes and pharisees are, of course, the faithful, who need the infidel to confirm them in their fidelity. The scribes and pharisees are the insiders who need outsiders to confirm them in their inside status. In this sense, President Reagan, in his public pronouncements at least, is a perfect pharisee. But so too are the outsiders who need the insiders to confirm them in their superior radical position. Where would we anti-Reaganites be without Reagan? Where would the antiestablishment be without the estabishment?

Had you asked Jesus whether he considered himself establishment or antiestablishment, the question would have been meaningless. He didn't need a structure, or enemies, to define his existence. God was his authority, not some authority his God. And beyond that, he recognized that all human beings, if not one in love, are at least one in sin: "Let him who is without sin among you cast the first stone."

Notice Jesus does not dispute the sin with the scribes and pharisees, nor even the sentence of death. Rather, he changes the premise of the whole argument. He simply suggests that it would be questionable for persons condemned by their own standards to condemn another to death. What is so beautiful is the way he takes a conspicuous example of wrongdoing and uses it not to nourish our cherished divisions, but rather to overcome these divisions by pointing to our shared need for repentance. There are no insiders, no outsiders, not in Christ's view. And in Christ's sight our only true failure is failure to love. We already heard the choir sing, "*Ubi caritas et amor, Deus ibi est*"—where charity and love are found, God also is there.

Then something little short of a miracle takes place. Suddenly the scribes and pharisees are no longer exultant. Some of Christ's thinking breaks through their guard. We read, "When they heard it, they went away, one by one, beginning with the eldest." (Whoever said the old tend to be crusty, mean, and selfish? This story bears out Goethe's insight, "One need only grow old to become gentler in one's judgment.") After the oldest lead the rest of the men away, Jesus is left alone with the woman. "He looked up and said to the woman, 'Where are they? Has no one condemned you?' And she said, 'No one, Lord.' And Jesus said, 'Neither do I condemn you. Go, and sin no more.'"

Jesus does not trivialize her wrongdoing, because that would trivialize her as a person. Sin is related to meaning: if nothing counts against you, nothing counts, period. Unlike many hopelessly sentimental people, Jesus never confuses the virtue of compassion for the sinner with the vice of condoning the sin. But if Jesus will not condone our sin, nor relieve us of its consequences, he can and will relieve us of the consequences of being sinners. Where others condemn, Jesus forgives. And if you think you are unworthy of such forgiveness, you miss the whole point of the Gospel. It is the revolutionary premise and promise of Christianity that the lost can be found only by love.

Dear sisters and brothers, we don't so much change our natures as we receive a new way to deal with them. Like the woman caught in adultery, we are always going to be caught in binds, in sin, one way or another. Our struggles toward things worthwhile are always going to be undermined by doubts. At best, we are going to be half saved—but that's the half Christ is going to strengthen, rather than condemning the other. "Neither do I condemn you. Go, and sin no more." With that assurance, we can go on, radiant blossoms in the springtime.

Mary and Jesus

MAY 8, 1983
Reading: Luke 2:41–52

Just as "I'm Dreaming of a White Christmas" aspires to the status of a Christmas carol, to be considered on a par with "Lo, How a Rose" and "Joy to the World," so Mother's Day clamors for religious recognition, to be hailed as an official day on the church calendar. A brave preacher might try to buck the tide; a brave preacher might quote Philip Wylie: "Megaloid Mom-worship has gotten completely out of hand"; a brave preacher such as Fanny Erickson might even have fun reminding her congregation that "I Want a Girl Just Like the Girl That Married Dear Old Dad" is but one of the more naïve expressions of the Oedipus complex. But a smart preacher, rather than buck the tide, will go with the flow. Seeing you can't lick 'em, a smart preacher will join the matriolators, and quote the old Jewish proverb, "God could not be everywhere, and therefore he made mothers." On this Mother's Day I have chosen to be smart.

The relationship between Jesus and Mary is hardly your everyday mother-son relationship, but it struck me this week that three episodes in their life together speak to Mother's Day. The first episode is the story of Joseph and Mary returning to Jerusalem to find their twelve-year-old boy. On Friday I went to look once again at the Heinrich Hofmann painting of this story, called *Christ in the Temple,* which hangs in the Assembly Hall. Sure enough, Hofmann (or his students, there's some question) painted Jesus standing up and speaking to his elders, who give him their rapt attention. But Luke, the only evangelist who recounts this story, writes, "They found him in the temple, sitting among the teachers, listening to them and asking them questions." Hofmann's painting reflects the myriad stories in the apocryphal gospels that never made it into the canon, stories that depict Jesus as a kind of *Wunderkind,* a Wonder Boy. But I personally prefer what might be called Luke's Christian understatement: "And Jesus increased in wisdom and in stature, and in favor with God and man" (or, as we would say today, "with God and his fellow human beings").

Perhaps it's worth underscoring Jesus' popularity. Some prophets don't become unpopular because they say unpopular things; they are simply unpopular to begin with, and then make the best of the situation—for as we all know, there is more truth squeezed from sour grapes than from all the fruits of success. But according to Luke, people liked Jesus from the very beginning. The future Man of Sorrows was probably a boy of joys, one who could have fitted very happily into, let's say, the Sherman clan. He also minded his parents: after describing the episode in the Temple, Luke continues, "He then went down with them and came to Nazareth and was obedient to them."

Describing Mary and Joseph, Luke writes, "They assumed he was with the caravan, and it was only after a day's journey that they went to look for him among their relatives and acquaintances." Clearly, Joseph and Mary gave their son a commendable amount of independence. And it was certainly normal for a mother, having found her son, to burst out, "Son, why have you treated us so? Behold, your father and I have been looking for you anxiously." Personally, I wouldn't have been half that polite, not after looking for three days! But in response, Jesus shows amazing independence for a twelve-year-old. In his answer, there's not a trace of guilt. In fact, it's all their fault! But there is sorrow rather than annoyance in Jesus' voice: "Did you not know"—or, as in the King James Version, "Wist ye not that I must be about my Father's business?" It's as if Jesus is asking, "I've been with you both for twelve whole years, and you haven't noticed anything special? How I love to read and argue about Scriptures? Have you forgotten that I have a heavenly as well as an earthly father?" It's as if Jesus is saying to Mary, "I'm a loaned treasure, Mom. I'm very happy to be on loan to you, but I belong to God, who has in mind for me things beyond any you could dream of."

And Mary, bless her heart, didn't say, "Don't be impertinent; Mother knows better. Hush your mouth!" No, while she didn't understand, she kept an open mind and a good memory. As Luke records, "His mother kept all these things in her heart." How rare is the person who realizes that you can learn more if you don't try to understand too soon. How rare is the parent who can open a discussion without closing it. How rare are parents who lead with a light rein, giving their children their heads. And how rare are children who can voice their expectations for their parents as readily as parents can voice theirs for their children. From this episode we would have to conclude that mother and son are off to a good start.

For the second episode we have to skip eighteen or so years, if, as some scholars believe, Jesus' active ministry began when he was about thirty. At the end of the twelfth chapter of Matthew we read, "While he was still speaking to the people, behold, his mother and his brothers stood outside asking to speak to him. But he replied to the man who told him, 'Who is my mother? And who are my brothers?' And stretching out his hand toward his disciples he said, 'Here are my mother and brothers, for whoever does the will of my Father in heaven is my brother, and my sister, and my mother'" (Matt. 12:46–50).

At first hearing, those words certainly have a chilling effect. They seem to bear out Ernest Renan's contention in his *Life of Jesus* that Jesus "warred against the most legitimate cravings of the heart." But suppose we ask what Mary and her sons were doing outside? Why did they call him out to speak to him, and not themselves go in to listen to him? We know that because of his words and deeds, the Pharisees and scribes were after him. We know from the Gospel of John that even his brothers didn't believe in him. And we know from the Gospel of Mark that at one point his friends tried to stop him, thinking he was "beside himself." So it's probably safe to assume that on hearing of his family's arrival, Jesus knew they had come not to open themselves to what he had to say, but rather to persuade him to stop all this wild-eyed radical preaching and come home! And Mary probably wanted to remind him of the backlog of carpentry orders waiting to be filled in Nazareth.

Poor Mary. Your heart has to go out to a mother who keeps hearing such terrible things about her son. But surrendering to her will was no answer. Had Jesus done what his mother wanted, he would have become the best carpenter in Nazareth, instead of saving the world. It's a familiar story, isn't it, this conflict of visions, these conflicting demands on a heavenly and an earthly parent? If you try seriously to be a child of God, it is almost certain that a protective mother will try to protect both you and herself by pleading, "Play it safe, son (daughter); don't climb out on a limb"—all those protective slogans that constitute, as it were, the eleventh commandment on which are *hanged* all the law and the prophets! Christians in the first decades after Jesus' death and resurrection were so regularly misunderstood by their nearest and dearest that an early martyr exclaimed, "A Christian's only relatives are the saints."

Now if you think about that, you understand better the supposedly cruel statements of Jesus, such as, "He who loves father and mother more than me is not worthy of me" (Matt. 10:37); "Do not suppose that I have come to bring peace to the earth. It is not peace I have come to bring, but the sword" (Matt. 10:34); or, "Let the dead bury the dead," which clearly means, "and not the living." In other words, God could not be everywhere, and therefore he made mothers, yes—but simply having children doesn't make mothers. Home is where the heart is, yes, but home can also be a bondage. Jesus understood these family tensions, so hard on all of us, whether we're parents or children. But they are no harder for us than they must have been for him. Catch again the sorrow in his voice when he says, "A man's enemies will be those in his own household." Moreover, he understood how often family tensions take the form of generational conflicts, for he himself said, "I have come to set a man against his father, a daughter against her mother, and a daughter-in-law against her mother-in-law" (Matt. 10:35).

The greatest mistake children can make is to seek peace through evasion, repression, and unwarranted comprise. Remember what I said about Jesus' legitimate expectations of his parents—they were just as legitimate as his parents' expectations of him. And remember that had all children sought at all costs to avoid all generational conflicts, there probably would never have been an end to slavery nor to child labor; there never would have been school integration, an environmental movement, a women's movement, a gay rights movement, and now a freeze movement.

"He who loves father and mother more than me is not worthy of me." Finally, it makes good sense, doesn't it? Harsh, cruel, but true.

But let's move on now to the third and last episode. Only at the very end of his life does Jesus finally resolve the conflict with his mother, and then only on a cross: "Mother, here is thy son." And to John, his beloved disciple, "Son, here is thy mother." That in this moment of agony Jesus could be so filial is very moving. Apparently Mary is widowed, and Jesus is providing for her economic well-being. But beyond that, he is providing for her spiritual well-being in a very interesting way. Now Mary too leaves her family and goes to John; and by urging her to join his disciple, Jesus includes her in his mission, thereby resolving the conflict between loyalty to her and loyalty to God.

Where do you suppose Mary's other children were—those who had been with Mary that day outside the synagogue, those brothers to whom a dying son would normally commend his mother? Probably they were still in Nazareth, cursing the fool to whom misfortune had related them. But not Mary. What she suspected at the beginning and doubted in the middle, she finally saw in the end. Her son, clearly, had reached her. She is a new person. She is standing, we read, at the foot of the cross, not fainting; perhaps in distress too deep for tears but also, at last, in all the legitimate pride of motherhood. And notice that Jesus is not the least bit protective; he doesn't say, "Take her away, John, this is no sight for a mother's eyes to see." No, Mary has to suffer his sufferings and to translate them into the pangs of childbirth that will result in a new and larger family, for she will take care not only of John but of countless millions who, in many languages, will call her Mother—because they consider themselves sisters and brothers of Christ.

On this Mother's Day let us remember that each of us is born of God, as well as of woman. Each of us, whether we be parents or children, has dual citizenship, here below and in the City of God. Each of us has dual parentage with our earthly parents and our heavenly Father/Mother. Each of us has dual membership in our family and in the world, that larger family so desperately in need of the beautiful love we see in the relationship of Mary and Jesus, mother and son.

Pentecost

MAY 22, 1983
Reading: Acts 2:1–21, 43–47

The other day I saw a cartoon in which a man, having entered the office, was peering across and down the other side of a desk and saying, "Look, Gormly, there is such a thing as being too laid back!" Well, I guess your failure to laugh proves once again that one picture is worth a thousand words! In any case, I would say, "Amen," to the cartoon and its insight: it is possible to be too cool and too laid back. Another example: I saw a young man in Riverside Park last Sunday afternoon. He was seated on a bench. At his side was a veritable apparition of delight and on his knee a pocket calculator. As I passed, I heard him say, "How do I love thee? Let me count the ways." That man simply confirmed a deep-seated suspicion that it's no more than a hop, skip, and a jump from "cool and laid back" to "dead and buried."

In any event, today, of all days, is not one to be cool and laid back, for this Sunday we celebrate the day of the fiery Pentecost. Don't ask exactly what happened on that day, fifty days after Christ's resurrection, for no one knows for sure. Once again, as it is so often the case in the Bible, it is the invisible event that counts. For sure, we know only that the eleven disciples, heretofore waiting and watching for

God, began to be moved and used by God. For sure, we know only that these disciples, thereafter, were ten times the people they were during Jesus' life on earth; and because of the demonstrated power of the Holy Spirit moving through Peter and the other disciples—witness, three thousand converted in one day—Pentecost is widely considered the birthday of the Church.

That's interesting and that's important. For if it is the coming of the Spirit that marks the beginning of the Christian Church, if the Church was founded on a day when Peter stood up to speak with a loud voice of the sun turning into darkness and the moon into blood, and exhorted his hearers, "Save yourselves from this crooked generation," then Christians have no business thinking that the good life consists mainly in not doing bad things; or, that to do evil you have to be a tame tabby—a nice guy, but not a good man or woman. In short, Pentecost suggests that nothing is so fatal to Christianity as indifference. The true infidels are the truly indifferent, the cool and laid back, the spiritually dead and buried. You may remember what Ernest Hemingway wrote of Francis Macomber, "He always had a great tolerance which seemed the nicest thing about him, if it were not the most sinister."

In Paul's first letter to the Corinthians we read, "The Kingdom of God consists not in words, but in power" (4:20). That, I think, is what comes through most of all on that first day of Pentecost. Peter speaks words, lots of them, and good ones, too, but what cuts to the heart of his hearers is the power of the Holy Spirit working through him. Peter energizes his hearers. He warms their hearts, fires up, like a furnace, their imagination; he puts iron in their spines, sufficient to make them stand strong as mountains against the blandishments of the crooked generation into which they were born.

"The Kingdom of God consists not in words, but in power." There's a nice story told of Heinrich Heine, the German—or if you prefer, Jewish—poet, standing with a friend before the great Cathedral of Amiens in France. The friend says, "Heinrich, tell me why people can't build piles like this anymore?" And Heine answers, "Cher ami, it's really very easy. In those days people had convictions, we moderns have opinions and it takes more than an opinion to build a gothic cathedral."

It takes more than opinions to build Christian communities. What it takes is the same energy, the same ignited imagination, the same courage of your convictions, all fruits of the same Holy Spirit that once poured forth in such abundance on Peter and the disciples. For our times are no less perverse than theirs. So to us, as to Peter's hearers, comes his exhortation: "Save yourselves from this crooked generation."

Several years ago John Gardner, founder of Common Cause, wrote of his country, "The nation disintegrates. I use the phrase soberly, the nation disintegrates." Today I see more clearly what he meant. Ghettoes, once considered problems, are now, in effect, solutions. Prisons, once considered problems, are, in effect, solutions. Ghettoes, prisons—that's where we put the expendables of our society. The disintegration is accelerating with our increased neglect of the poor. There's no money today for public housing, no money for Section VIII. There isn't even money to fix the elevators of the old public housing. Reaganomics is today reversing the priorities of Mary's Magnificat, filling the rich with good things and sending the poor empty away. Never have so few taken so much from so many so quickly.

The source of our troubles is once again deeply spiritual. Right after World War II in 1946, when this nation was at the pinnacle of its power, our leading playwright, Eugene O'Neill, in the course of an interview explained that he "worked on the theory that the United States, instead of being the most successful country in the world, is the greatest failure. Its main idea is that everlasting game of trying to possess your own soul by possession of something outside it." He said that we were "the clearest example of 'For what shall it profit a man if he gain the whole world and lose his own soul?'" The other day I read that West Germans look at East Germans with contempt and pity, mixed with a certain yearning, because they wonder if their sisters and brothers to the East, being less materialistic, might be more authentically German.

"The everlasting game of trying to possess your own soul by possession of something outside it." Wherever there are riches, or power, the game is played and souls are lost. This is certainly true even in the churches, even here in Riverside, where some good Christians both on the staff and among the Deacons and Trustees are greedy for power, not to share it, but to possess it, not to create with it, but to exercise it by saying "No" to almost every creative idea that comes along.

So on this day of Pentecost, this one thousand and nine hundred and something birthday of the Christian Church, let me suggest the following: Remembering that the Holy Spirit is a discomforter, as well as comforter, let us not fear the cleansing fire of Pentecost. Truth, after all, is error burnt up. Truth is only possible when our make-believe world lies in ashes. Regarding our personal lives, let us pray mightily to God to pour down upon us the Holy Spirit, whose power can overturn our beloved self-protecting lies, can say no to the secret flatterings of self-importance, can pull the rug from under ambition's tower of blocks, and then make us twice as tender, as only the truly strong can be tender.

Then let us pray that the Holy Spirit in this Church may make of us a community of believers like unto the one formed in Jerusalem on that first day of Pentecost. May we speak in many tongues the one message of Christ's love. May we see to it that the cruelty and greed we see around us find no place among us. When outside these walls we side, as side we must, with the oppressed against the oppressor, may the Holy Spirit guide us to seek only such a world in which there will be no master/slave relationships. When we oppose, as oppose we must, political and religious leaders, may we do so with the clear understanding that if, by God's grace, the Holy Spirit is alive in us, it needs only liberation in them.

Sisters, and brothers, the whole world disintegrates—I use the phrase soberly—the world disintegrates—and we're not going to save it by being cool and laid back. We're not going to save it by opinions alone, not even the right opinions of the Church: nor certainly are we going to save it by continuing to play the everlasting game of trying to possess our souls by trying to possess something outside them. In this nuclear age which threatens to turn every child, woman, and man into a nuclear ash, it is clearer now than ever that only God's heavenly fire, moving and using us, can contain the ever-advancing flames of hell. Playwrights, poets, they always say it best:

> The dove descending breaks the air
> With flame of incandescent terror,
> Of which the tongues declare
> The one discharge from sin and error.
> The only hope, or else despair
>   Lies in the choice of pyre or pyre—
>   To be redeemed from fire by fire.
>   T. S. Eliot

Ahab and Naboth

JULY 3, 1983
Readings: 1 Kings 21:1–19; Colossians 3:12–17

If we survey the long sweep of American history, as well we might on the eve of July 4th, few, I imagine, would conclude that we live in the best of times. In fact, on a continuum between the best and the worst of times—to borrow from Dickens—I would place us fairly close to the worst. There have been other bad times to be sure in our history—the long bleak winter at Valley Forge, the spring of 1862 when American blood North and South flowed like rivers, the long years of the depression during the '30s, that day in infamy, December 7, 1941, and the seemingly endless years of slavery which stretched both before and after the Emancipation Proclamation, and the disenfranchisement of women. But generally, in bad times past, we Americans seemed to have retained some solid sense of who we were and where we were heading. But today our sense of ourselves and our sense of direction seem to be in shambles.

I know this is no way to speak to a congregation in a holiday mood, on a hot July day when the waters are cool, and the hills are leafy, and the sky is divine, and even the air of New York seems rather finely tempered (although every true New Yorker will tell you, "I don't trust any air I can't see"). Still if we are patriotic, if we love our country, we will take the truth without chloroform and I believe on this hot July day that it is February in our national soul.

Consider the following: We are told that the tide of economic recovery is rolling in, but morally speaking, the tide is still out, nothing is visible but mud flats. It used to be that unemployment was called "the scandal of capitalism," and by capitalists, too. But few today seem scandalized by the approximately 11 million men and women who are looking for work and will not find it, because big corporations are relying on automation and workers abroad to aid output in the coming recovery and because neither corporations, with precious few exceptions, nor the government deem it their business to retrain citizens of this land to the new and different industries resulting from technological change. Eleven million men and women are being given, in effect, the back of the hand.

Or this: the President makes political hay by baiting the poor. Everyone knows that the poor have always had their fair share of cheats, sneaks, and rogues, but what Bible reader, or plain old person of conscience, doesn't know that what the poor steal from the rich is not comparable to what the rich rob from the poor!

And in Central America we North Americans seem totally to have forgotten our recent history. It was exactly 60 years ago that Charles Evans Hughes, then Secretary of State (and later member of Riverside Church), announced, "We are seeking to establish a Pax Americana." He served Calvin Coolidge who explained, "We are saving Nicaragua from the Bolsheviks," as he ordered the marines into Nicaragua for the 14th time in Nicaraguan history.

But exactly 50 years ago, 10 years later at Montevideo, Cordell Hull proclaimed Roosevelt's "Good Neighbor" policy which signaled a shift from unilateral action to collective action, and resulted in 1948 in the formation of the Organization of American States. We were making progress but today in Nicaragua, El Salvador, Guatemala and Honduras once again "the North American shark is feeding on Latin American sardines"—to quote a former President of Guatemala; or, in a Biblical image, we are Ahab, bound and determined to have our way with Naboth's vineyard. The story you remember: Ahab, king of Samaria, thinks Naboth's vineyard should be his merely because of its proximity to his palace, and because he wants to turn the vineyard into a vegetable garden. But Naboth replies, "The Lord forbid that I should give you the inheritance of my fathers," which is to say, "that land that belongs not to me alone, but to all the members of my family, members past and those yet to be born."

Now listen to these words from the Roman Catholic bishops of Latin America gathered in Pueblo, Mexico in 1978: "The civilization of love rejects subservience and dependence which undermine the dignity of Latin America. We do not accept the condition of satellite of any country in the world. It is time that we, as Latin Americans, tell the developed countries not to immobilize us, not to put obstacles in the way of our progress, but rather to help us with greater encouragement to overcome the barriers of our underdevelopment by respecting our culture, our principles, our sovereignty, our identity, and our natural resources."

The comparisons are almost too obvious but let's go on. Ahab's wife appeals to his credibility, not in terms of wisdom, not in terms of decency, but merely in terms of might. "Do you now govern Israel?" Then she sends secret instructions to the elders of his city, telling them to proclaim a fast, which was done only in cases of extreme national emergency, and instructs them to trump up charges against Naboth so that he could be stoned to death and Ahab take possession of the vineyard. Now listen to these words: "The national security of all the Americas is at stake in Central America. If we cannot defend ourselves there, we cannot expect to prevail elsewhere. Our own credibility would collapse, our alliances would crumble, and the safety of our own homeland would be put in jeopardy." I am sure you recognize these words of the President. And the equivalent of Naboth's supposedly cursing God and the king—the false charges? The Sandinistas are totalitarian, fanatically Marxist-Leninist, and have sold their destiny to the Soviets as have the Salvadoran guerillas their revolution. These charges are matched only by the inability of administration spokesmen to present convincing evidence, but by sheer repetition these statements leave their mark on U. S. citizens too uncaring of the lives being lost daily to do their homework, which would disclose among other things that in Nicaragua, for example, there are no Communists in the government; the Communist party is infinitesimal, 80 percent of the land belongs in private hands and 75 percent of the industry. To be sure the Sandinistas have nationalized banks, but so have the Mexicans, a long time ago, as well as the oil industry. The President never refers to "Marxist Mexico," let alone "Leninist". . . (I wish some reporter would have the imagination to say, "Mr. President, what do you mean by Leninist?")

Notice that in the story no case is made for Naboth. Was he a good or bad man? We don't know. Nor is there any discussion about whether he and everyone else might not be better served by a vegetable garden in place of a vineyard. The point of the story is that Ahab had no business using his mighty power to intervene massively and unilaterally in the internal affairs of another man. Likewise you don't have to think the Sandinistas are doing anything right to know that the United States is doing everything wrong.

Finally, notice also how many in the story could have stopped the injustice, could have saved Naboth's life if only they had cared. Let's start with the elders and nobles who chose subserviently to serve Ahab rather than God and the truth. Why don't we hear any protests from the elders and nobles of American society, the businessmen and the lawyers? Are they too busy for the main business of life? In Dickens' *A Christmas Carol*, Scrooge at one point is confronted by the ghost of his dead partner, Jacob Marley, who in life had been as stingy as Scrooge. To comfort him Scrooge says, "But you were always a good man of business, Jacob," to which Marley's ghost replies, "Business! Mankind was my business. The common welfare was my business; charity, mercy, forbearance and benevolence, were, all, my business."

Then in the story there were the people who made the false charges, and knew they were false. Where today is there a single resignation from the administration from the State Department, from the CIA or from the White House? And finally, couldn't the crowd have asked Naboth for his side of the story before they proceeded to stone him to death? According to the latest *New York Times*/CBS poll, only 25 percent of Americans surveyed knew that the administration supports the government of El Salvador, only 13 percent knew that it sides with the insurgents in Nicaragua, and only 8 percent knew both alignments (*New York Times* Friday, July 1, 1983).

That's what made me decide to preach this Fourth of July sermon to a congregation in a holiday mood. What this great people of ours does not seem to realize is that the military situation in El Salvador is rapidly deteriorating. What Americans apparently don't recognize is that the President is surrounded by advisors who would love to send in American troops, but if they can't send in troops would love to send in airplanes; and if airstrikes make no military sense in El Salvador they could be devastating in Nicaragua. (I doubt that the administration is willing to lose its "credibility" in two Central American countries at once.) But if we the people of the United States don't stop this immoral killing south of the border, which is in violation of the UN, the OAS and the Boland amendment, we shall never again be able to lift our heads and criticize the Soviets for what they are doing south of their border, we will have richly deserved the ill will we are so rapidly earning, and the blood of another Naboth will be on our hands.

As some of you know, about one hundred of us—almost all church people—will be holding a vigil tomorrow night outside the American Embassy in Managua, and another one on July 6 somewhere near the Honduras border. If you are in sympathy, go to the chapel of the UN opposite the UN at six o'clock on Wednesday where there will be a service from six to seven, followed by a vigil outside the American Embassy at the UN. Whether you do that or not is not really the important thing. I am not here to make people choose sides, I am here only to appeal to you as Americans and Christians to care enough that you will think and pray about what we are doing to poor people in this country and people who are far poorer in countries of Central America. So have a wonderful Fourth of July, but do something too for God and country so that these worst of times may turn toward the best.

Let's listen once again to what St. Paul wrote the Colossians: "Then put on the garments that suit God's chosen people. . .: compassion, kindness, humility, gentleness, patience. . . . To crown all, there must be love, to bind all together and complete the whole. Let Christ's peace be arbiter in your hearts; to this peace you were called."

Death Is More Friend than Foe

JULY 17, 1983
Reading: Romans 8:31–37

I want this morning to talk about death, not because I am feeling morbid, sad, or even old. Although I am the "senior" minister around here, in all senses of that adjective, "old" to me is when you get into your rocking chair and have trouble getting it started; "old" is when you get winded playing checkers; "old" is when you still look at beautiful women but you can't remember why, and when the only glint in your eye comes from the sun hitting your bifocals just right. No, I want to talk about death simply because it is well, from time to time, to contemplate the end towards which, with irreversible steps, we all walk.

Let us take as a text these words of Paul found in First Corinthians 13, "Love never ends." Because love refuses to be imprisoned by time, because love says "forever," love rejects death, which is why when someone really near and dear to us dies, grief renders everything unreal. But when unbearable grief becomes bearable sorrow, we can profitably meditate on certain truths about death.

First of all, death is not the enemy we generally make it out to be. Consider only the alternative, life without death. Life without death would be interminable—literally, figuratively. We'd take days just to get out of bed, weeks to decide what to do next. Students would never graduate, and faculty meetings, deacon meetings and all kind of other meetings would go on for months. Chances are, we'd be as bored as the ancient Greek gods and up to their same silly tricks. Death cannot be the enemy if it is death that brings us to life. You see what I'm after: just as without leave-taking there can be no arrival, without a growing old, no growing up; just as without tears, no laughter, so without death there could be no living. So let us pause to thank, with brief thanksgiving, our Creator that "all mortal flesh is as the grass."

Death enhances not only our individual life but our common life as well. Death *is* the great equalizer, not because death makes us equal, but because death mocks our pretensions at being anything else. In the face of death, all differences of race and class and nationality become known for the trivial things they ultimately are. I love the old Moravian cemeteries which house no pyramids to the ego, all tombstones being flat; and when Mrs. Schmidt dies, her final resting place, though not far from her husband, is next to the person who died before her in the community. What a wonderful thing it would be if the structure of Moravian cemeteries could inform our communal life!

Recently I experienced something else about death, something new to me. Earlier we prayed together, "In our hearts we have despised those who did us wrong," a line which recalls another from Arthur Miller's play *After the Fall*: "Good God, why are grievances the only truths that stick?" That's a truth that most of us know well! What I hadn't realized was that death has a way with grievances, a way quite wonderfully described in a sonnet of John Greenleaf Whittier:

> My heart was heavy, for its trust had been
> Abused, its kindness answered with foul wrong:
> So, turning gloomily from my fellow-men,
> One summer Sabbath-day I strolled among
> The green mounds of the village burial-place;
> Where, pondering how all human love and hate
> Find one sad level, and how, soon or late,
> Wronged and wrongdoer, each with meekened face,
> And cold hands folded over a still heart,
> Pass the green threshold of our common grave,
> Whither all footsteps tend, whence none depart,
> Awed for myself and pitying my race,
> Our common sorrow, like a mighty wave,
> Swept all my pride away, and trembling I forgave!

Last January when my son was killed, sorrow, "like a mighty wave, swept all my pride away," which is to say, swept all my grievances away. And this relationship of death to forgiveness made me see how, in one more way, the death of a loved one can change us, not from what we were so much as toward what we essentially are—loving, forgiving, understanding people.

Which leads us to the next point: What are we to say when someone dies too soon, of an accident, of cancer, of AIDS—and oh, what stories are coming out now of these AIDS victims. One thing we must never say is that it is the will of God. No one knows that, so let no one pretend that he or she does. Why would it be the will of God that one, or some of us, die young while the rest live on? What we can say, with St. Paul, are the words of our text: "love never ends," for as St. Paul says also: "For I am persuaded that neither death nor life . . . can separate us from the love of God." In other words the abyss of love is deeper than the abyss of death, which means that our own loves— pale reflections of God's love—are right to reject death. Moreover the seers, those great women and men who feel ordinarily what ordinary people feel only in rare moments—the seers, those most attentive to God's presence in this world, have always claimed that the best lies ahead. So Bach wrote one of his greatest arias, "*Komm, süsser Tod*" (Come, Sweet Death) and an American slave saw a band of angels coming for to carry him home. So we, immediately after the death of someone we love, can picture in our mind's eye a band of angels descending to carry that dear one home.

Of course life after death can no more be proved than disproved. "For nothing worth proving can be proven nor yet disproven" (Tennyson). As a child in a womb cannot conceive of life with air, life with light—the very stuff of our existence—so it is hard for us to conceive of any other life without the sustaining forces to which we are accustomed. But consider this: If we are essentially spirit, not flesh, if what is substantial is intangible, if we are spirits that have bodies and not the other way around, then it makes sense that at death, just as musicians can abandon their instruments to find others elsewhere, so our spirits can leave our bodies and find other forms in which to make new music. And consider this: It is well said that virtue is its own reward. In other words, goodness, for its inspiration, does not depend on the pay it receives. That is why we have to reject out of hand all notions of heaven as pie in the sky by and by—deferred gratification. I hate evangelists who try to overcome my selfishness by appealing to my selfish motives. But the fact of the matter is virtue does have a reward. The pay for goodness is the opportunity to become better, just as the proper benefits of education are the opportunities for continuing education; and the rewards of loving are to become yet more vulnerable, more tender, more caring, more loving. But it is also a fact that human life aspires beyond its grasp. At best, like Moses to the top of the Mountain, life leads us to where we can view a promised land dreamed of but never reached. Now I ask you: would a loving God create loving creatures aspiring to be yet more loving, and then finish them off before their aspirations are complete? It's hard, isn't it, to conceive of a God of goodness without some life beyond the grave?

But again, we don't know the circumstances; we know only who is beyond the grave, not what. We are like the Swiss child asked by a traveller, "Where is Kandesteg?" The child answers, "I cannot tell you where Kandesteg is, but there is a road." And we are on that road to heaven already if today we walk with God. For eternal life is not a possession conferred at death, it is a present endowment. We live it now, and continue it through death. And that is why belief in life to come should only increase our commitment to life now and here.

Death is not the enemy. If death enhances both our individual and common life, then finally death is more friend than foe. If neither death nor life can separate us from the love of God, if love never ends, if love is immortal, then life is eternal and death is a horizon, and a horizon is nothing save the limit of our sight. The good news of the Gospel is simply this: "Whether we live or whether we die, we are the Lord's" (Rom. 14:8b).

To Set at Liberty Those Who Are Oppressed

JULY 31, 1983
Readings: Amos 5:18–24; Luke 4:14–21

When Archbishop Dom Helder Camara, that often "persecuted, but never forsaken" five-foot two-inch giant of a man from Recife, Brazil, came to Riverside several years ago to address our Disarmament Conference, he was asked at a press conference: "Bishop, aren't you mixing politics with religion?" Smiling broadly at the questioner, Dom Helder replied, "In former days, when the Roman Catholic Church was in bed with almost every right-wing military government in Latin America, no one said, 'You're mixing religion with politics.'"

It's a familiar charge—"You're mixing religion with politics"—generally leveled against those trying to change the status quo—the World Council of Churches—by those who profit from the status quo—The *Reader's Digest*. It's so old a charge that it was probably first leveled at Moses by Pharaoh, who may well have added, "Furthermore, Moses, you don't understand economics. Were I to allow you to remove all those Hebrew slaves from Egypt, what do you think would happen to the Egyptian economy?"

But wisecracking hardly answers the tough question we have constantly to ask ourselves: "What is the relationship of faith to politics?" Some people, of course, think religion should be "above" politics. "Religion should be 'spiritual,'" they say. Churches should limit themselves to praying, singing hymns, listening to beautiful music and "inspirational" sermons, and doing charitable works. Doesn't the love of God make people good and won't good people do better things? So runs the argument. As for the poor, well, as Jesus himself said, "The poor are always with you," and didn't He imply that poverty is the most certain road to felicity? It's a seductive position certainly, and one reflected in many of our favorite gospel hymns, where salvation is almost always a kind of one on one—"me and Thee, O Lord." But ask yourself: Can religion ever be *above* politics without, in effect, being *for* the status quo? And what about the hypocrisy in promoting

love as a personal virtue, while supporting—if only by not oppos-
ing—political and economic institutions that physically and spiritually destroy our sisters and brothers? In Biblical times, the answer to
slavery in Egypt was certainly not a better Pharaoh, anymore than the
answer today to dictatorships is a good dictator. In times of oppression, personal faith has to lead us to political choices; otherwise
Christianity encourages fatalism on the part of the poor, who, to keep
themselves going, have only the promises of a better hereafter, and
cynicism on the part of the rich, who feel they can do almost anything
to the poor as long as they attend church and baptize their children.

Perhaps the crucial question is this: Is charity ever a substitute for
justice? I've listened to many a Marxist accuse the churches of having
a vested interest in unjust structures which produce victims to whom
good Christians can then pour out their hearts in charity. I've listened
and I've shuddered, because so often in history it's been so true. In
other words, if there is a danger in politicizing the faith—danger we
are coming to—there is also a counter-danger, which is depoliticiz-
ing the faith. In times of oppression, if you don't translate choices of
faith into political choices, you run the danger of washing your hands,
like Pilate, and thereby, like Pilate, plaiting anew Christ's crown of
thorns, for, "Inasmuch as ye did it unto the least of these my brethren,
ye did it unto me." In Scripture, there is no purely spiritual answer to
slavery; no purely spiritual answer to the pain of the poor, nor to the
arrogance of tyrants. In Scripture charity is no substitute for justice,
anymore than is ritual, no matter how beautiful. "Take away from me
the noise of your songs; to the melody of your hearts, I will not listen. But let justice roll down like mighty waters, and righteousness
like an everflowing stream" (Amos 5:23–24).

Now we come to the alternate danger which is that of politicizing
the faith; the danger of churches overly committing themselves to
dubious or mistaken political causes. It is one thing to say, "Let justice
roll down like mighty waters," and quite another to work out the irri-
gation system. What we have to realize is that "there is more certainty
in the recognition of wrongs, than in the prescriptions for the remedy
of those wrongs" (Roger Shinn). Clearly, for example, the arms race
has to end, or the human race probably will. Clearly Christ is dead-set
against the arms race. I have no trouble saying that. But just how
worldwide disarmament should proceed—for that there is no Christ-
given program. Clearly American fear of Marxism has blinded most
Americans to the failures of capitalism in Central America. In El Salvador, Guatemala, and Honduras, present economic structures gener-

ously benefit a minority while leaving unattended the most basic needs of the impoverished majority. Clearly in each of these countries the pyramid of society has to be turned upside down—not a new top put on, but the whole pyramid turned upside down—so that the needs of the poor come first. Didn't Mary in her Magnificat praise God saying, "The poor He has filled with good things and the rich He has sent empty away?" But to say that is not to say that the Cubans and the Sandinistas, who have seriously tried to turn that pyramid upside down, have come up with all the programmatic answers.

I think that Peruvian theologian Gustavo Gutiérrez, a fine representative of liberation theology, puts it well when he says that the Church has a "prophetic function of denouncing every injustice," of living in "authentic solidarity with the poor," and making "a real protest against the poverty of our time." Yet Gutiérrez adds, "My personal option for the socialist way is not a conclusion drawn from evangelical premises. It comes from my sociopolitical analysis" (quoted in Roger Shinn's fine article in *Christianity and Crisis*, March 21, 1983).

There are two things about that statement that strike me. In the first place Gutiérrez infers what is true, that the Bible rarely prescribes the specific political and economic patterns required by God's love. The few times the Bible does get specific—as in the Deuteronomic and Levitical laws or in St. Paul's treatment of how women are supposed to behave—it is probably least useful for our present, very different historical situation. Contrary to fundamentalists, I believe God leads with a light rein, giving us our head. I believe the Bible seeks to open a discussion, not to close it. Jesus gives concrete examples of wrong- and right-doing, as in the story of the Good Samaritan, but he speaks in parables precisely because stories have a way of shifting responsibility from the narrator to the hearer. In short, Jesus gives us, if you will, our marching orders—"to set at liberty those who are oppressed"—but he leaves it to us to figure out the route of march. That leads me to the second thing I like in Gutiérrez' statement. He has figured out a march route, a sociopolitical analysis. We may not embrace his, at least not one hundred percent, but we have to have a sociopolitical analysis—I'm more and more convinced, dear brothers and sisters—else our faith will be divorced from action.

Why do I say that? Because our present system, however we label it, simply is not working, and largely because we Christians worship God in our spiritual life and mammon in our economic life. The system is not working when the answer to New York's homeless is not a home, but a shelter or a motel in New Jersey (while the tide of gentrification rolls on up Columbus and Amsterdam Avenues). The system is not working when hunger is on the rise, yes, in the richest nation of the world, because our system is presently filling the rich with good things, and sending the poor empty away. The system is not working when seventy to eighty percent of all released prisoners return to prison and generally for worse crimes. The system is certainly not working abroad when no end to the arms race is in sight, and when throughout Central and Latin America, South Africa as well, the United States has seemingly nothing to offer the millions who are tired of being unemployed, underfed, ill without money to buy medicines—nothing except the prospect of more dead, mutilated bodies in their streets. The *Reader's Digest* shudders at the prospect of Marxist influences in the churches. The editors should go to Vancouver and watch devout Christians from Third World countries shudder equally at words like capitalism, neocolonialism, and transnational corporations. They may not be right, these Third World Christians, in all their conclusions, but they are right to have what Gutiérrez calls "my sociopolitical analysis." Without such an analysis, how are we going to translate the story of the Good Samaritan into New York terms? Without such an analysis, how are we going to set at liberty those who are oppressed at home and abroad?

The separation of Church and State is a sound doctrine, but it talks about an organizational separation. It is not designed to separate Christians from their politics. For our faith certainly should inform our common life, as well as our personal, more private lives.

And it's our common life that's being so neglected. I have a picture of America today that goes something like this: we have one world in which the rich are getting richer and the poor are getting poorer. Then to take care of both the rich and the poor, we have another world: let's call it the therapeutic world. The rich have their psychiatrists and the poor their welfare. Neglected is our common life where true therapy lies for both rich and poor. If we tended to our common life, the rich would not be left at the mercy of their riches, and the poor would not be left at the mercy of their poverty, and both would be better off. More even than our personal lives, our common life today needs to be informed by Christian insights, Biblical and theological. I said God leads with a light rein, giving us our head. But God gave us our heads to use; cool heads at the service of warm hearts to design a better common life. I think it fair to say that we human beings have created a world for some of us. It's time now to create a world for all of us.

Home-Coming, Home-Leaving

SEPTEMBER 25, 1983
Readings: Genesis 12:1–9; Luke 15:11–32

I want to talk this morning of home-coming and home-leaving. Though it is sadly not the case for some few of us, to most of us the word "home" suggests comfort, warmth, acceptance, dignity, identity. Equally positive are the associations evoked by such expressions as "homeland," "home free," and "home run." "Goin' home" is the popular and properly positive understanding of death reflecting the Biblical "man goes to his everlasting home." In fact, so stirring and fine is everything about the word "home"—with the possible exception of "homework"—we have to agree with the poet's contention:

> Breathes there the man with soul so dead
> Who never to himself hath said,
> "This is my own, my native land."

As every citizen needs a homeland, and every family a home, so every Christian needs a particular house of God, an open house, open to members and strangers alike. Every Christian needs a community that works to find love and defeat hate, a place, in short, to make everyone feel "at home." To acknowledge that fact, and in gratitude for having a home church, let us now—members and visitors alike—on this Homecoming Sunday take twenty seconds to turn to our neighbors and say, "Welcome home."

I suppose the most famous home-coming in Scripture is the return of the Prodigal Son. The parable, of course, is really about the prodigal love of the father who just couldn't wait to run and embrace his wayward son. Jesus told the parable to illustrate the unbelivable good news that there is more mercy in God than sin in us.

Wouldn't it be wonderful—a sort of weekly home-coming—if, Sunday by Sunday, as we approached this church (whether from the Claremont side or from Riverside Drive) we saw in our mind's eye at a distance, standing on the steps, a glorious father or mother figure, ready to run, embrace and forgive each one of us our weekly trespasses? And wouldn't it be wonderful if that kind of imaging could take place the world around, for the parable mirrors the plight of the human race, as most recently and horribly exemplified by the reactions to the flight of Korean Airline Number 007. 1 can think of no tragedy which elicited more uncalled-for responses. The Soviet leaders, of course, stand in need of forgiveness for their stubborn refusal to tell the truth for six days, and for their incapacity to share the world's grief at the loss of so many innocent lives. But so, too, does President Reagan stand in need of forgiveness, not only for his continuing failure to tell the full story, but, more importantly, for charging, without facts to prove it, that the Soviets *knowingly* downed a civilian airliner. Members of Congress and the press need forgiveness for being less interested in collecting all the facts than in rushing to embrace the official interpretation of all too few of them. And the rest of us need forgiveness, at least those who, unwilling to give the Soviets the benefit of any doubt, *preferred* to believe that they knowingly took innocent lives. Like the old Baptist minister who deplored, but didn't really regret, the bootlegger, because he needed him, so we secretly seem to be rejoicing at the occasion given us to revive that always horrendous dialectic—"us" versus "them." The American reaction to the Korean tragedy is emotionally satisfying and spiritually devastating. We resemble no one so much as the older brother of the Prodigal Son or the Biblical Pharisees of whom Christ was so critical, because they were righteous with a righteousness that was nourished by the blood of sinners. The victims of Flight 007 deserve better.

Some people think forgiveness is soggy, without backbone. But to me forgiveness signifies first, the reality of evil, and then, in its fullest sense, the destruction of evil. Forgiveness signifies that while sin estranges us from God, sin never estranges God from us. Surely it is to hear this good news, to try to appropriate a love so prodigal, to realize that no matter how self-orphaned we are, we can never render ourselves fatherless. Surely for these reasons we come home to church.

Here also in church those who think they are nobodies find out who they are—priceless. We human beings, hungering after social respect, take our identity out of the hands of God and put it at the mercy of others. They begin to question it, and we fold like a busted hand in poker. Who tells you who you are if, for example, your wife is moving on the fast track and you seem to have reached the limit of your career? Or if you are a homemaker and, as such, seem to be receiving the same harsh judgment society used to reserve for the working mother? Who tells you who you are if you're not living up to the wage earner's expectations? If you are among those, the cruelties of the world lash like a whip, or, on the contrary, if you are rotten with money and achingly dissatisfied?

Come home to church. Stop trying to prove yourself; God has already taken care of that, all you have to do is express yourself, to receive your identity as a gift from God, not as an achievement of your own. Come to church to receive your forgiveness and your identity—priceless in God's sight.

But do not come home for protection. Even the prodigal love of the father could not protect the son from his own temptations, anymore than Jesus could prevent Peter from denying Him three times. Jesus couldn't even take action against Judas, known defector though he was. Because love is self-restricting when it comes to power, and for a variety of other reasons shrouded in mystery, God clearly is not out to protect us: not from ourselves, not from others, not from plane crashes, not from cancer, AIDS, Crohn's disease, crippling arthritis, death itself. I'll never forget how, only weeks after John Kennedy's assassination, his brother, arriving in Dublin, was greeted at the airport by the Lord Mayor who said, "Oh, Bobby, what's the use of being Irish if you don't know that the world sometime will break your heart."

What's the point of being Christian if you don't also know that what God withholds in the way of protection, he more than supplies in the form of support? For the world breaks God's heart too. No pain our spirits endure, no weakness that impairs our bodies, no grief that bows us low fails to find its counterpart in God who, as we see, in Christ suffers with and for us. "He that keepeth Israel shall neither slumber nor sleep" (Ps. 121:4). Sometimes I think it's God's pain, not God's peace, that passes all understanding. So come home to church, not for protection against all the travails of this earth, but rather for all the support that heaven alone can provide. Finally, come to leave. For we come to God's house, to this open house, to find love and to defeat hate, in order that the world itself can become an open house.

If the most famous Biblical home-coming is that of the Prodigal Son, the most famous Biblical home-leaving is probably that of Abraham. What is so remarkable about 75-year-old Abraham picking up stakes and moving is that he was not a victim of change, but an agent of change. Let me explain. Most of us find familiarity a powerful need. We cling to routines; we are tied to rituals. Innovation we greet with the enthusiasm of a baby meeting the new babysitter. Hence it takes a fait accompli to change us: we contract an illness, we lose a job, or a spouse. If we accept God's support, so that we can respond, "I'm not saying I'm lucky, but I'm not devastated either"; if we allow the fait accompli to change us, not from what we were so much as toward what we really are—more profound, loving, sensitive people—that's no mean achievement.

But Abraham, as I said, was not a victim of change, but an agent of change. Nothing happened to him, and he could so easily have said,

"Look, Lord, my decisions are all behind me. This is my life, my home." At seventy-five, doesn't a person have a right to think of his life primarily in the past tense? The answer to that question, according to Abraham, is, "No, not if you are a believer." Believers know that while our values are embodied in tradition, our hopes are always located in change. So even at seventy-five Abraham gambles everything and founds a whole new nation.

In Irishman Hugh Leonard's play, a character who has more pride than charity, yet nonetheless never pretends to see virtue where he finds none—this man, almost Abraham's age, when told that the chapel was packed at the funeral of an acquaintance, responds, "I'd expect no less. He worked hard and lived decently, and by now he'll have given his mind back to the Almighty in the same unused condition as he received it." It's not, like Abraham, that we have physically to move, but we have to get out within our minds, keep stretching our hearts. Sincerity is not enough: it's the mark of the martyr and the executioner. Soul is not enough, either: Hercules had greatness of soul, but he lacked greatness of mind. Soul and mind—both have to keep moving, stretching, growing.

I'm impressed by the role of feminism, a philosophy that has been the most sweeping agent of change for a generation of women. What women have heard is what every Christian should hear: "It doesn't have to be this way; it can be another way." In the Gospel of Thomas, part of the so-called Gnostic writings that never made it into the Bible, Jesus says, "If you bring forth what is within you, what you bring forth will save you. If you do not bring forth what is within you, what you do not bring forth will destroy you." And if we do not bring forth what is within us, we shall destroy the world, for it is true: "Religion without civilization goes to seed; but civilization without religion goes to hell."

It's time to conclude. We have come home to this service, back to this church, to hear the words of reassurance, "We are forgiven"; once again to make our identity a matter solely between God and ourselves; to find such support as scorns protection, and the realization that was Abraham's that we are redeemed to become redeemers, not saved until God makes us saviors, too. Yes, in church we are loved into being lovers everywhere else.

Don't say you're too old, too tired, too busy, too any of those things to keep moving, stretching, growing. For I say to you, the same God which calls forth shoots from dead stumps, a people from dry bones, sons and daughters from the stones at our feet, babies from barren wombs and life from the tomb—this same God daily can call forth in each of us a new creation. Amen.

The Kingdom

OCTOBER 9, 1983
Readings: 1 Samuel 8; Mark 1:14

Let us take as a text today the first recorded words of Jesus, in the book of Mark: "The time has come; the Kingdom of God is upon you; repent, and believe the Gospel." Clearly from the very beginning and throughout his entire ministry, the proclamation of the coming Kingdom of God was central to Jesus' preaching. Yet today, while many preach Christ, few preach the Kingdom. In part this is true because of the privatization of Christianity, which has gradually taken over church after church and left the public sector to be ruled by ideologies alien to Christianity, like Marxism and capitalism; but it is also true because in progressive Christian circles there is little room these days for kings—earthly or heavenly. For kings suggest submission, a word that has overtones of "abject"; kings suggest obedience, with the implication of "blind"; and kings need subjects, whereas nowadays we're all supposed to be independent citizens. People who make these objections have a point. Too many Christians want God to be strong so that they can be weak; too many want God to give all the answers so that they don't have to be plagued by the questions.

Yet what a loss it is to the Church not to hear the Kingdom preached. And what bad theology it is not to see the difference between our heavenly King and all earthly ones. In Sweden there is a proverb: "In every man there is a king and in every woman a queen. Speak to their majesties and their majesties will come forth." That's precisely what God's power does—it empowers. God is a king who brings forth royalty in all of us. Just think for example: God has made the world such that he could not fashion a Stradivarius violin without his human collaborator, Stradivarius himself. They are co-creators!

But a theology far worse than this misrepresentation of God as King is the trivializing of the faith that results from the privatization of Christianity. It is a theme that goes something like this: "Not my father, not my mother, not my city, not my nation, not the world, just me O Lord—me and thee." Is there any greed greater than the spiritual greed to save one's own private soul? "What do I care?" says such a soul, "if the Biblical view of life has marginal significance in the life of my nation? What do I care if weekdays from nine to five I serve the cause of consumerism, stimulating gluttony among those who already have enough? What do I care if the production of goods in my country is governed by the demands of the relatively prosperous, not by the needs of the poor? 'What do I care if it rains or freezes as long as I have my plastic Jesus down on the old dashboard?'"

And that's pretty much what we have—a plastic Jesus—if we separate Christ from the Kingdom. Preaching the Kingdom reminds us that beyond the destiny of our individual souls there is the life of nations. Preaching the Kingdom reminds us that we believe in a Christ-like world, one where Christ will no longer be crucified but where, on the contrary, "he shall reign for ever and ever and ever," yes, "*King* of kings and Lord of lords."

People who want God to be strong so that they can be weak forget that in Christ, "King" Jesus, God became weak so that we could be strong. People who want God to have all the answers so that they don't have to be plagued by the questions forget what Christmas tells us, that the Word of the Lord hits the world with the force of a hint.

In other words, "King Jesus" is simply not like earthly kings. Earlier we heard what earthly kings do; and just as you don't have to be Jewish to be a Jewish mother, so you can be an elected president of the United States and still behave as the Lord warned Samuel that the first king of Israel would behave. "This," said the Lord, "will be the sort of king who will govern you. . . . He will take your sons and make them serve in his chariots and with his cavalry, and he will make them run before his chariots. . . . He will take a tenth of your grain and your vintage to give to his eunuchs and lackeys" (1 Sam. 8:11, 15). In other words, according to the view expressed in the eighth chapter of 1 Samuel, the desire for an earthly king is an act of apostasy from the true Kingship of God. "It is I whom they have rejected," said the Lord, "I whom they will not have to be their king" (v. 7).

What does the Kingdom of God look like? To Christians the Kingdom of God is Christ-like. It is Jesus who gives a name and a face to the Kingdom. And that's why when we preach the Kingdom we are not preaching simply human betterment. Human rights are an essential part of the Gospel, but they do not exhaust the Gospel. And just as we cannot separate the kingdom from the king, so we cannot really divorce the Kingdom from the church. For the church is supposed to be, at its best, a foretaste, the first fruits of the Kingdom. At its best, the church is a community *in* the world but not *of* it. It is a place where God alone tells people who they are—so that all living is dignified, no matter what its form. In the church, members face truths they have fled elsewhere; they seek to know their faults but live their strengths. In the church we refuse to allow among us the fear and greed we see around us, thereby heeding the poet's words:

Be of love
a little more
careful than of
everything.
e.e. cummings

The church then, represents the first fruits of the Kingdom. A couple of days ago I learned that a colloquial Arabic word for first fruits is *arrabon*, which signifies both a payment and a pledge. It's real cash, and there's more to come. That's what the church is—a down payment on the Kingdom of God.

If the Kingdom of God is a kingdom of goodness and mercy, then obviously its proclamation leads naturally to repentance. For if the Kingdom of God represents normal life—that which operates according to the norm—then all of us are a little subnormal, aren't we? And if the Kingdom of God is reality, we all live a little bit unrealistically, don't we? In other words, repentance is designed not to make us gloomy, only to keep us honest—and most importantly, to make room for the forgiveness that alone can heal us.

Of course we must repent of the many sins of our private lives, such as those we earlier confessed. I hope you were listening well when we prayed: "We confess all the goodness of life which we have received without giving thanks, all the beauties of this fair world which we have ignored, all the love coming to us from other human hearts which we have accepted carelessly." I hope all the workaholics, the grim dutiful types among you, registered what you were confessing, that joy is a much neglected virtue in your life. And all of us need to be reminded that in a world where so much makes the blood run cold, there are also so many things that touch the heart. I liked the heavy emphasis in today's corporate prayer of confession on sins of omission, which to my mind generally dwarf those of commission. A priest once told me that among his many assignments was that of listening to the confession of nuns. I didn't want to be indiscreet, but I certainly was curious when I heard this. So I asked him. "What's it like?" And he answered, "It's like being stoned to death with popcorn." Often I think our own sins of commission are no heavier when compared with our sins of omission.

But I think Jesus had something more in mind when he said, "The Kingdom of God is upon you, repent. . ." For as there is danger in seeking personal salvation apart from the salvation God offers the whole world, so there is danger in confessing private sins apart from the sins of the church of which we are members, sins of the nation of which we are citizens, sins of the whole world of which every one of us is a part. When the World Council of Churches met, not this last summer but the time before in Nairobi in 1975, the delegates heard President Potter say, "At Uppsala [where the Council had last met in 1968] the mood was one of Exodus, going out to change the structures of society. Now we find ourselves in the wilderness. . . . A pilgrim people in conflict and penury, we have discovered a need for spirituality—a spirituality of penitence and hope."

A spirituality of penitence and hope. I think Potter had the corporate life of the church in mind when he spoke of penitence. But he could as well have been thinking of the whole world, which today now spends more than a million dollars a minute on arms while two billion of its inhabitants still don't have access to clean water (which is crucial because doctors tell us that eighty percent of the world's illnesses are related to impure water). And surely repentance is in order for our own beloved country that now ranks forty-ninth in literacy, fourteenth in infant mortality, number one in the sale of arms, and is a place where every year some 27,000 people—mostly young people—gas, hang, shoot, cut, or throw themselves to death. I must say I felt rather penitent yesterday when the paper announced that American "experts" had decided that the Soviet Union may not have known, after all, that it was a civilian airliner they shot out of the sky—and meanwhile, nobody in this country could admit: "We're sorry, we may have been a little hasty in our judgments, too." I tell you, confession is good for the national soul as well as for the personal soul.

Yes, if the Kingdom of God is upon us we should repent; but we should also "believe the Gospel." A spirituality of penitence and hope. "Despair," said Reinhold Niebuhr, "is the fate of the realists who know something about sin, but nothing about redemption." It is clear that fear, not hope, is the greatest glue of American politics today; but hope, not fear, should always be the greatest glue of the Christian church.

Christians are full of hope because we are as sure of God's love as we are of the sunlight. We are full of hope because while sin estranges us from God, sin never estranges God from us; we are indeed forgiven. We are full of hope because, as blacks know well, the answer to persecution is to outlive it. We are full of hope because sorrow is a fruit that God does not grow on limbs too weak to bear it. And finally, we are full of hope because we know that we alone are not responsible for ringing in the Kingdom. Without God's grace human strength is insufficient for the task. The Kingdom comes only in answer to prayer: "Thy Kingdom come . . . on earth as it is in heaven."

But we *are* co-creators. The church is a down payment on the Kingdom. Our heavenly King calls forth the royalty in each of us to labor in Jesus' name in all corners of the Kingdom, in the public sector as well as in the private sector. In our final hymn, properly a prayer-hymn, Charles Wesley writes:

> The task Thy wisdom hath assigned
> O let me cheerfully fulfill,
> In all my works Thy presence find
> And prove Thy good and perfect will.

In *all* my works: because the Kingdom is everywhere.

Said Saint Teresa to all her followers (which certainly include me): "Christ has no body now on earth but yours, no hands but yours, no feet but yours; yours are the eyes through which Christ's compassion looks out on the world, yours are the feet with which he is to go about doing good, and yours are the hands with which he is to bless us now."

In Christ's name, dear Christians, go forth to bless this bruised and baffled world. For the time has come, the Kingdom of God is upon us; we must repent, and believe the Gospel.

"In the Midst of You, among You, within You"

OCTOBER 16, 1983
Readings: Psalm 104:1–23; Luke 17:20–21

Last Sunday, as some of you may be kind enough to recall, I suggested in talking about the Kingdom that while Christianity has always been personal, it has never been individualistic. Beyond our individual lives there is the life of the nation, as well as the ever more urgent need for a Christ-like world. I said also that human rights are an essential part of the Gospel but that they do not exhaust it. It's well in this instance to recall the difference between Poverty (with a capital "P") and poor people. In my experience, political radicals tend to handle more easily problems that can be capitalized: Poverty, Racism, the Nuclear Peril. But the Kingdom of God goes beyond problems, goes beyond "isms," goes beyond ideologies and concerns itself with people—people in all aspects of their lives. So, while it embraces politics and economics, the Kingdom of God is first and last a spiritual kingdom, and therefore it cannot be separated from Christ the King; Christ, to Christians, gives a name and a face to the Kingdom. Nor can the Kingdom be separated from the church, because the church, at its best, is a down payment—hard cash, with the promise of more to come—on the Kingdom.

Today I'd like to add a few more thoughts on the same subject. In the seventeenth chapter of Luke, Jesus says, "The Kingdom of God is in the midst of you"—or "among you," or "within you," depending on the translation. All three translations suggest so much that I find I can't ignore any of them, and I've decided to try to say a word about each, starting with: "The Kingdom of God is *in the midst* of you."

The French theologian, Jacques Ellul, writes about something he calls the "duty of awareness." It's a phrase that brings to mind something I once heard, that in previous centuries, in European ghettos, pious Jews were careful never to tread on a piece of paper floating around in the streets for fear the name of God might be written on it. Likewise should we, in this century, take care not to step on any person, from the most down-and-out derelict in the Men's Shelter on 168th Street to the most shining example among Lower Manhattan's skyscrapers of what St. Paul once called "spiritual wickedness in high places." We can restrain and we can rebuke but we can never step on any person, because Christ died for every last one of us and our job, now and always, is to dignify life no matter what form it may take.

But it strikes me that awareness is too rewarding to be called a duty. Perhaps instead of Ellul's notion of "duty" we should talk of the joy of awareness.

> Thy bountiful care what tongue can recite?
> It breathes in the air, it shines in the light;
> It streams from the hills, it descends to the plain,
> And sweetly distills in the dew and the rain.
>
> Robert Grant

I believe every word of that hymn—whose author, by the way, was governor of Bombay when he wrote it—as I believe every word of the 104th Psalm on which the hymn is based. I also believe God had a hand in the creation of every great work of architecture, art, music, and literature; and daily I thank him for blessings like that noble and reassuring river, the Hudson, on which our church stands. In short, and notwithstanding the too-long, unredeemed faces of many self-professed Christians, I believe that God is not out to dampen our spirits. I believe the Kingdom of God in our midst is nothing if not joyful. My problem is simply this: try as I constantly do to see all there is to see of God's glorious Kingdom, I never see enough. I feel like a man driving through life, constantly having to wipe the foggy windshield in front of him.

Consider, if you will, how many things we long and pray for that are ours already, neglected, unappropriated—but ours! Let me give you an example. In the early 1800s a tall sailing ship, headed for China, ran into trouble around the horn of South America. Beaten back by storms that are without parallel in any other part of the world, with its masts down, its lifeboats destroyed, its crew starving and dying of thirst, it lay helpless off the jungle coasts of Latin America. Suddenly, like a mirage, a proud clipper ship appeared on the horizon under full sail. As it came near, a midshipman on the disabled ship struggled to his feet and, grasping two flags, in semaphore began feebly to signal, "Water, water." Back came the answer, in semaphore: "Lower your buckets; you are in the mouth of the Amazon." That's what the Kingdom of God is like—it's in the midst of us.

But the more interesting translation may be the second one: "the Kingdom of God is *among* you." Those of you who have read Alice Walker's *The Color Purple* will recall the ineffable Shug Avery, who at one point says to her boon companion, "Celie, tell the truth, have you ever found God in church? I never did. I just found a bunch of folk hoping for him to show. Any God I ever felt in church I brought in with me. And I think all the other folks did too. They came to church to share God, not to find God."

I like that sentiment. For it is true that whenever we share God, the Kingdom is among us, as once it was among the disciples when Jesus had departed from their midst. When you stop to think of it that's all the disciples had: the shared Kingdom. For Jesus left "no separate synagogue, no special place of meeting, no fixed teaching, no new legislation—not even any organization. The one thing which bound the disciples together was their personal relationship to Jesus and his message about the Kingdom of God" (George Ladd).

And so the Kingdom of God is among us. But to be among us the Kingdom obviously has to be *within* us—and this is probably the most popular, if not the most obvious, translation. Two weeks ago I read the passage from the Gospel of St. Thomas, part of the so-called Gnostic writings, where Jesus says, "If you bring forth what is within you, what you bring forth will save you. If you do not bring forth what is within you, what you do not bring forth will destroy you."

Nothing is more destructive than being all locked up in ourselves, choking on our own hearts. In passivity we deteriorate. We're not supposed to suffer history, we're supposed to make it. And nothing is clearer than the fact that we are as we love. As the First Letter of John says, "We pass out of death into life because we love the brethren" (which includes sisters, of course, 3:14). Every time I stand up here to baptize a baby I think to myself, "Nobody looks more fundamentally fulfilled than this mother and father." And that thought indicates to me that it is not our freedoms which keep us alive, but rather our obligations.

The other day I heard a stranger to this city complain about it, and I heard her companion, a Riversider and a New Yorker to the bone, reply, "You have to put something into the city before you can get anything out of it." And what do we have to pour into the city, the nation, the world, if not the Kingdom of God that is within us, the love of God that he in his turn has poured into every hollow of every heart. So translate it any way you want: the Kingdom of God is in the midst of us, often neglected; the Kingdom of God is among us, urging us, in and out of church, to share God with one another; or the Kingdom of God is within us, not anxious to express itself but *crazy* to do so.

I'd like to add a more personal thought now, but one that's related to the text. For in an unexpected way this summer I experienced the fact that the Kingdom of God not only is within us, but goes on without us. When the time came for our extended family to climb up the little hill in Vermont to the cemetery, carrying with us the ashes of my son Alex, I had the presence of mind to bring along a small and ill-assembled dog, whom my daughter Amy considers an insult to the dog-maker's art. (My position is that a totally useless dog is a sign of great generosity on the part of God. When we reached the grave that my other son David and I had dug the previous day, the dog suddenly jumped in, no doubt hoping to find some kind of animal life inside. It was very comical, and very comforting under the circumstances, to have along someone who was not on our agenda.) It was very comforting that the sun 93 million miles away didn't stop to pay any attention to our grieving little band. Far from leaving me cold, it inspired me to be so reminded that life goes on without us. It helped pull me out of myself. It put everything in perspective again. And I mention it only because we don't usually see this "indifference" as a source of comfort, which I think it really is.

Let me before closing consider briefly one more line about the Kingdom of God, this one written by St. Paul, who at one point informs the Corinthians that "the Kingdom of God consists not in words but in power" (1 Cor. 4:20).

Surely St. Paul was not minimizing the importance of words. After all, he lived by them—his own, those of the Old Testament, those of Jesus, which if not yet recorded were being faithfully transmitted. But words are tricky, as St. Paul knew; they can confuse as well as clarify. How often these days are we reminded of the 55th Psalm:

> Their speech is smoother than butter
> but their thoughts are of war;
> Their words are slippery as oil
> but sharp as drawn swords.
>
> Ps. 55:21

"'This is not Vietnam,' explains the Great Communicator, while naming as head of his new Central American commission the man who gave us the invasions of Laos and Cambodia. 'We are not seeking a larger presence in the region,' he asserts, while U.S. aircraft carriers steam toward the coast of Nicaragua for the largest joint land and sea training exercises in Central American history" (*Sojourners*, September 1983). Their speech is smoother than butter. . . .

Probably it was with such abuses as these in mind that Paul wrote, "The Kingdom of God consists not in words but in power." And whatever he meant by power he certainly included the staying power necessary to continue to preach and fight for the Kingdom. Any great love always works at cross purposes with society. Or to put it another way: society disowns two kinds of people—those who can't pass the test of its ideals, and those who take the ideals too seriously. Said Damon Runyon: "The race is not always to the swift, nor the battle to the strong, but that's the way to bet."

A society that is willing to countenance the largest homeless population, the largest number of poor people it has had in 50 years, and a 1.6 trillion dollar budget for defense—such a society is not going to receive the proclamation of the Kingdom with unrestrained enthusiasm. But just as mothers and fathers don't abandon their own children, no matter how wayward they may become, so we American Christians cannot turn our backs on our churches, on our nation, or on our world. Citizens of the Kingdom just do not give up, although many will be the time when they feel like the old black slave who sang:

> I've been in the storm so long
> You know I've been in the storm so long
> Oh Lord, give me more time to pray,
> I've been in the storm so long.

Citizens of the Kingdom, take time to pray. Pray mightily, "Thy Kingdom come, O Lord," and add "though in my own undoing," for Christians are called upon not to be successful but simply to be faithful. As you pray, remember that the Kingdom of God is *in the midst* of you; that the Kingdom of God is *among* you; that the Kingdom of God is *within* you. And remember, too: the Kingdom of God consists not in words but in power.

Stewardship

OCTOBER 23, 1983
Readings: Psalm 116; 1 Peter 4:8–11

The New Testament lesson today is found in the First Epistle of Peter. "Above all keep your love for one another at full strength, because love cancels innumerable sins. Be hospitable to one another without complaining. Whatever gift each of you may have received, use it in service to one another, like good stewards dispensing God's grace in its varied forms. Are you a speaker? Speak as if you uttered oracles of God. Do you give service? Give it as in the strength which God supplies. In all things so act that the glory may be God's through Jesus Christ. To him belong glory and power for ever and ever. Amen."

Let me begin with a confession. Were I to join all of you in the pews while one of you took my place in the pulpit, and were I to hear this new preacher announce a sermon on the subject of stewardship, I have to confess that my heart would not beat faster nor my eye grow dim. Quite the contrary. For I would immediately have visions of church properties and financial campaigns. I would wonder testily why churches always have to spoil everything by harping constantly on the need for more money. And then of course I would feel pangs of guilt for harboring such blasphemous thoughts. No, as I say, I would not be thrilled by the announcement of a sermon on stewardship. I would pray for brevity on the part of the preacher, so that all of us might the sooner be blessed by the singing of our Jessye Norman, certainly one of God's great gifts to humanity.

Interestingly enough, however, if instead of a preacher an ecologist were to stand up here and start talking about stewardship, I might get excited. "It's nice," I would think to myself, "how this person is able to adapt a Biblical concept to the question of the physical environment." I'm intrigued these days by the fact that environmentalists, who are for the most part secularists, no longer criticize Christians for trying to put the brakes on progress; rather they accuse the Biblical tradition and the churches of promoting the notion of our human mastery over nature. There's truth in this accusation. "Have dominion," said God to Adam; and because the churches are so hopelessly ambivalent about sex, eating, and all the wonderful animality that is part of being human, they frequently overdo the importance of mind over body, spirit over nature. They forget that the church is founded not on the word but on the word made flesh.

What all this says about stewardship is that the churches have demeaned it by trivializing the concept. Were we Christians good stewards of the very idea of stewardship, we would view it not as a means to church life but rather as an end—a goal—of all life itself.

While it's true that God said to Adam, "Be fruitful and increase, fill the earth and subdue it, rule over the fish in the sea, the birds of heaven, and every living thing that moves upon the earth" (Gen. 1:28), these imperatives can hardly be held responsible for creating the present ecological crisis, which is due far more to the separation of nature from nature's God. But neither did the imperatives help solve what we might call the identity problem of Adam and Eve and their descendents. They didn't answer the agonizing question, "What is man that Thou art mindful of him?"—a question which the psalmist could only answer by saying: "Thou hast made him a little lower than the angels" (Ps. 8:4–5). When you stop to think of it, that's a very imprecise position, as varying Biblical descriptions of us human beings bear out. For if one moment we are "a little lower than the angels," in the very next our righteousness is being described as "filthy rags." On one page we are brides and on the next harlots; in one moment lords and in the next slaves; in one breath keepers of the earth and in the next wastrels and prodigals. All we really know for certain is that we must avoid both pride, on the one hand, and sloth, on the other; we must neither claim too much nor sell ourselves short, aspire too high nor sink too low. We have enormous power but we are accountable to God who gave it to us. In short, what are we if not stewards? A steward is an apt description of every human being from Adam to you and me, for while each of us has been given the responsibility for the management of something absolutely awesome—this wonderful, terrible, beautiful world—yet we must recognize at the same time that it belongs to another: for "the earth is the Lord's and the fulness thereof, the world and they that dwell within" (Ps. 24:1). Listen again to the letter of Peter: "Whatever gift each of you may have received, use it in service to one another, like good stewards dispensing the grace of God in its varied forms."

That's what we're here on earth to do: to dispense God's grace in its varied forms. And there's nothing dull about it! Can't you just hear the excitement in these words of St. Paul to the Corinthians: "For all things are yours, whether Paul, or Apollos, or Cephas, or the world or life or death or the present or the future, all are yours; and you are Christ's; and Christ is God's." Stewardship, in short, consists in living a Christ-like life; it is not a part-time affair of a few church-related folk, but a full-time calling for the whole human species.

And what is a church if not a stewarding community, also seeking to dispense the grace of God in its varied forms? Like an individual, a church too must avoid both pride and sloth; must not claim too much by seeking worldly power and by becoming an end in itself, nor claim too little by retreating from the giant social issues of the day into the pygmy world of private piety. First and foremost, churches must be faithful stewards of the Gospel and the sacraments that celebrate it, as faithful as were those early Christians who met secretly in the catacombs of Rome, and without whom—who knows?—all the riches of the faith might well not be ours today. In the so-called Dark Ages, monasteries were stewards of the Word and sacrament, as today churches are stewards in the Soviet Union, in China, in Chile and El Salvador, where time and again, standing with the poor, resisting the temptation of Judas' kiss, they resemble nothing so much as huddled sheep surrounded by wolves.

But churches have also to be stewards of words (with a small "w"), of truths (with a small "t"), whenever it happens that people prefer their prejudices to good solid information; whenever governments, to avoid serious debate, attempt to denigrate or marginalize those who oppose them—think of the role of the church in Poland, for instance; or whenever governments in cavalier fashion disregard the eighth great commandment and bear false witness against their neighbor countries. There was a time when I considered colleges and universities to be special stewards of words and truth, and indeed they are. But now I see more clearly a special role for the churches as well. Three years ago, in Cuba, in a conversation with the minister of education, a very impressive former general who had defended his country at the Bay of Pigs, I asked him where he had gone to school. "With the Jesuits," he replied, "and a very good education it was." "Then you know the problem we Christians have," I said, "in drawing the line between education and indoctrination." "Claro," (yes, clearly) he answered. "How do *you* do it?" I asked him. For a moment, but only for a moment, he looked defensive. And then he said: "Every country's education reflects that country's ideology."

It was a thoughtful answer. And America is no exception to the rule. Most students in the United States are taught that in this country there are rich people and poor people, with no connection between them; most students in the United States are taught that the poor are a problem, and that abroad there are "good rich" and "good poor," as opposed to bad rich and revolutionary poor. Clearly this is an ideological viewpoint at variance with the Biblical truth which insists that there are poor people *because* there are rich people; that the rich, not the poor, are the problem; and that to have blood on your hands, as do so many of the revolutionary poor, is spiritually no worse than having water on them, like Pilate. Archbishop Romero, the martyr of El Salvador, was a good steward of this Biblical truth when instead of referring to the poor as *los pobres* he used the term *empobrecidos*, those made to be poor, those who have poverty imposed upon them by an ideology that says, "What's good for the rich is best for the poor."

The churches have a role as stewards of globalism as opposed to an entrenched spirit of narrow nationalism. They have a role as stewards of peace and of the environment, especially today when we can see the fragility of the world and when we human beings have stockpiled not goodwill but instead enough "kill power" to annihilate every one of God's creations, including Mother Earth herself. We have the power, but clearly not the authority, to do so. Thank God for the millions, in this land and in Europe, who demonstrated yesterday against nuclear weapons; for what clearer symbol is there of unfaithful stewardship than such weapons of death?

A church is a stewarding community seeking to dispense the grace of God in its varied forms. And on a more local plane I would like to think that that is what Riverside is trying to do in its varied programs: in the food pantry, the clothing service, the adult learning center, the women's center; in Riverside's Biblical and theological studies, its Sunday school, its theater, music, and disarmament programs. I would like to think that dispensing the grace of God in its varied forms is the business of the Black Christian Caucus, of Maranatha, of all the programs of the communications department and task forces. I know that the hills are full of people doing the bidding of the Lord, but I would like to think that not a few of them are right here in this church: people who seek to walk before the Lord in the land of the living, people who keep the faith even when they say "I am greatly afflicted," people who hold their heads high because they have never bowed their worn backs to riches and power, people who seek neither to conform to nor to escape this world, but only to save it. It is to them and to the work of this church that I gladly today make my pledge, which I view as a symbol, and part and parcel, of an all-embracing stewardship.

Let's listen one more time to the words of Peter: "Above all, keep your love for one another at full strength, because love cancels innumerable sins. Be hospitable to one another without complaining. Whatever gift each of you may have received, use it in service to one another, like good stewards dispensing the grace of God in its varied forms. Are you a speaker? Speak as if you uttered oracles of God. Do you give service? Give it as in the strength which God supplies. In all things so act that the glory may be God's through Jesus Christ; to him belong glory and power for ever and ever. Amen."

A Mighty Fortress

OCTOBER 30, 1983
Reading: Psalm 46

Were Protestants called on to choose one hymn above all others, I suspect the majority vote would go to "A Mighty Fortress Is Our God." I suspect Roman Catholics would vote the same, for they sing the hymn all the time, Martin Luther having become—to the hierarchy of the Roman Catholic Church—more of an alumnus than an apostate. A gifted flute and lute player as well as a brilliant theologian, Luther wrote the melody and the words to "A Mighty Fortress." This was in the year 1529. Centuries later, the German-Jewish poet Heinrich Heine called the hymn "the Marseillaise of the Reformation," which was a good description, because for the first 100 turbulent years of its life the hymn was an inspiration to German Lutherans and a tower of strength to Swedish soldiers and French Huguenot martyrs, many of whom died with it on their tongues. In 1631 it was sung by the entire army of Gustavus Adolphus before the battle of Leipzig. Its melody forms the central theme in Giacomo Meyerbeer's *The Huguenots*; Mendelssohn used it in his *Reformation Symphony*; Wagner in his "Kaiser March"; and Bach (as we have heard, and will hear again) in one of his sacred cantatas. The hymn is "not polished and artistically wrought," as the critic Louis Benson notes, "but rugged and strong like Luther himself, whose very words seem like deeds."

Everybody knows that Martin Luther started a reformation. What few people realize is that he also initiated a whole new hymnody, by writing hymns in the vernacular to be sung by all the people. And the outpouring of hymns in German since Luther's day has been nothing short of prolific. The fighting spirit of the Reformation, the pain and misery of the Thirty Years' War, the inward-looking mysticism of the pietists and the outward-looking enthusiasm of the Moravians—all have found expression in German hymns, whose number today must total almost 100,000. In contrast, the Calvinistic churches in England, Scotland, and New England rejected all hymns of "human composure" and for 200 years restricted their members to singing Biblical psalms made metrical. It wasn't until 1736, when John and Charles Wesley, onboard a storm-tossed ship bound for the Crown colony of Savannah, Georgia, heard 26 Moravians stirringly outvie the elements with their hymns, that WASP Christians finally began to wake up to what German Protestants had been enjoying all along.

On this Reformation Sunday I propose that we look at the Reformation theology in "A Mighty Fortress." But first, it would be well to recall the hymn's historical setting. As many of you know, we are celebrating this year the 500th anniversary of Luther's birth, which took place on November 10 in a town called Eisleben, in Saxony, which today is part of the German Democratic Republic but which then was a part of the Holy Roman Empire. Luther lived during a time when abuses were rife. Papal taxes were oppressive and unequally levied. The vast land-holdings and treasure of the Church, including monastic houses, were exempted, while hardworking farmers and enterprising burghers paid through the nose. Many monks and parish priests were lazy and corrupt, and some bishops were so crooked that it was said they could have hidden behind corkscrews. Meanwhile, the Inquisition's stern repression of new ideas, which was sweeping north like a tide out of Spain, angered the intellectuals in Germany. Low standards of living with no prospect of relief enraged the peasants, while the Church's sale of indulgences—forgiveness of sins in return for cash—shocked everyone. These conditions, combined with the strivings of a popular religious awakening, called for a leader who could bring the smouldering unrest to a focus of action. On October 31, 1517, Martin Luther, by this time a 34-year-old Augustinian monk and lecturer of theology at the University of Wittenberg, nailed his 95 Theses on the door of the Wittenberg Castle chapel, and announced that he was prepared to defend them against all challengers. Overnight he became famous, and shortly thereafter found himself in deep trouble. In 1521 he was ordered to appear before the Emperor Charles V and the Imperial Diet at Worms. His friends advised against it, but Luther asserted that even if there were as many devils in Worms as there were tiles on its rooftops, still he would go. When, as his friends had predicted, the legislative assembly demanded that he retract his errors, Luther declared: "It is neither safe nor honest to act against conscience. Here I stand. I can do no other. God help me." He was excommunicated, his books were burned. Fortunately for him and for us, his friend Elector Frederick had him arrested—taken into protective custody—and brought secretly to the Wartburg Castle near Eisenach. There Luther translated the New Testament, not from the Latin but for the first time from the original Greek—a translation which to this day is the standard version used by the German people. A year later, Frederick turned his head and allowed Luther to escape, and the controversial thinker returned to lecturing and writing, mostly on the Bible; nor was this the end to his many battles, as the language of "A Mighty Fortress" reflects.

In writing his hymn, Luther used as his primary source of inspiration the 46th Psalm, the psalm that begins, "God is our refuge and strength." When Luther writes, "A mighty fortress is our God," he is saying that a mighty fortress is not the pope, not the church, not the nation-states, not power, not money, not even my conscience, which is a good servant but a bad master; when Luther said it was neither safe nor honest to act against conscience he had just declared, "My conscience is captive in the word of God." No, a mighty fortress is *my God,* the sole bulwark, which faileth never. In other words, all things else are relative to this one Absolute. In declaring God's sovereignty over every institution and individual, Luther states what we all find impossibly hard to do: keep things in their proper order, first things first.

"Our helper he amid the flood"—or as the Germans say, "*Er hilft uns frei aus aller Not,*" he lifts us free from every need—reflects again the sentiments of the 46th Psalm: "a very present help in trouble." Like the psalmist, Luther insists that God does not protect us *from,* but supports us *amid,* "the flood of mortal ills" which sooner or later engulfs us all.

In other words, if your security is with the Absolute, you can, and you must, like Luther, take on all temporal insecurities; for God will not cause any fruit of danger or sorrow to grow on a limb too weak to bear it. Before going to Worms, Luther was asked, "Where will you be, Brother Martin, when church, state, princes, and people turn against you? Where will you be then?" To which Luther answered, "Why, then as now, in the hands of Almighty God."

Let me, on this 500th anniversary of Reformation Sunday, ask you a similar question: "Where will you be, dear brother, dear sister, when this world, governed as it largely is by a strain of idiots, approaches ever nearer the very gates of death and destruction. Where will you be then?"

How many of us, undaunted by so certain a prospect, can answer, "Why, then as now, in the hands of Almighty God"? How hard it is to have the courage to be honest without becoming hopeless!

What makes "A Mighty Fortress" so eternally relevant is that every line is right on the nerve.

> For still our ancient foe
> Doth seek to work us woe
> His craft and power are great
> And armed with cruel hate
> On earth is not his equal.

How right were folk in the prescientific age to believe in the devil; and O what a slaughterhouse of the imagination we make out of the scientific age! Evil *should* be personified if we experience it as personal power. Evil *should* be personified if, although it arises within us, it is experienced as something bigger and stronger than we are—"on earth is not his equal." It's perfectly true that, "Did we in our own strength confide, our striving would be losing." Those who believe in the perfection of human beings simply show how little they have tried to live out their convictions. St. Paul was right: "The good that I would I do not; and that which I would not, that I do." But, as Paul also wrote, "thanks be to God, who givest us the victory through our Lord Jesus Christ" (1 Cor. 15:57). Christ, whom Luther calls "the right man at our side, the man of God's own choosing."

The hymn continues! "Lord Sabaoth his name." Lord Sabaoth was a title ancient Israelites liked to give to Jahweh, the commander of the hosts of heaven. It is not surprising that Luther should turn to all these military symbols and metaphors—God, as fortress, the devil "armed" with cruel hate, Jesus as Lord Sabaoth, "and he must win the battle" for as I earlier suggested, Luther was fighting on many fronts against the church, against some princes, against people and their populist leaders, too, fearing that they would make overly political his religious revolution. Personally I have no problem with military metaphors, for I think that to Christians today, as to Luther then, the world appears more and more as a battlefield, with more and more cowards stealing away when the day goes hard for those who are trying to oppose rampant nationalism, greed, and corruption. Therefore our constant prayer has to be like Luther's, that we continue to be found where the fighting is fiercest.

"And though this world with devils filled should threaten to undo us." I know that that's an accurate description of the way I felt this past week. And what imagery again: the Devil has now spawned little devils to carry out their little devilish schemes—like little invasions of little islands, quick fixes that inevitably become prolonged agonies, designed to distract us once again from the main business of this world. And what is the main business of this world? Why, clearly, not to irritate things still further but to save them—by bringing nuclear arms under control, by reordering the world's priorities in Judeo-Christian fashion, so that the hungry can be fed and the naked clothed, so that the children can be taught to read, and so that we can all learn not to hate but to love one another. And all this is our common task with God, who "hath willed his truth to triumph through us."

"The Prince of Darkness grim, we tremble not for him." Once again the devil, and once again we are back to the old problem of finding the courage to be honest without becoming hopeless. Says Luther, in effect: "If you can't be hopeful at least you can be persistent." And then he seems to redefine hope as a process of keeping the faith despite the evidence, and then slowly but surely watching the evidence change. "For lo, his doom is sure, one little word shall fell him."

But the cause will be won only by "that word above all earthly powers." "The spirit and the gifts are ours *through him* who with us sideth." Luther always ends where he begins, with the wounds and the resurrection of Jesus Christ; and his confidence in human beings stems from his faith that "God can carve the rotten wood, and ride the lame horse."

And then comes the absolutely inevitable ending. Isn't it true that the great attraction of murder mysteries, of "whodunnits," is that the surprise at the end is only the discovery of inevitability? Well, that's true of God's surprises: they too represent the discovery of inevitability. If a mighty fortress is my God, then why do I make an Absolute out of national security? If a mighty fortress is my God, then why make absolutes out of worldly goods, out of family, even out of life itself? Yes, I see it now: if I can sing the first part of the hymn with conviction then I can sing the last part with no less. If "A mighty fortress is our God, the sole bulwark that never faileth," then of course

> Let goods and kindred go
> this mortal life also
> the body they may kill
> God's truth abideth still
> His Kingdom is forever.

Yes, I see it now: what are worldly things compared to the price-less treasures of a Kingdom that shall never end? And I see just as clearly that the task of a reformed and still reforming church is not so much to discover new truth as to rediscover that which has been lost and found, and lost again and again—what Luther in the 62nd of the 95 Theses called "The most Holy Gospel of the glory and grace of God." And that, dear friends, is not for sale. It's a free, a miraculous gift to each and every one of us.

A Present Day Reformation

NOVEMBER 6, 1983
Reading: Matthew 25:31–46

That the churches could better the lot of humanity, even save the world, goes without saying. The only question is whether Christians in sufficient number will find the imagination and dedication, in the coming decades, to effect a reformation comparable in scope and influence to the sixteenth-century one we celebrated last Sunday. Today I'd like to sketch the outline of such a reformation, and then next week continue by filling in some of the details.

The reform in our day should start with what I have often complained of as the "privatization" of Christianity, which severs *homo religiosus* from *homo politicus* and produces, among its unfortunate offspring, a spiritual schizophrenia in the individual, a trivializing of the Christian faith, and the abandonment of the public domain to the toughest powermongers around.

It is interesting to trace our progress to this sorry state of affairs. Over the recent centuries there have been a considerable number of political revolutions, most of them middle class, which in the name of liberty have succeeded in stripping religious institutions of the worldly powers they long exercised and in separating church from state. (A few years ago, when the Pope visited Mexico City, it was interesting to see on television the image of His Holiness in his resplendent white papal robe, being driven up Paseo de la Reforma, a street named for the Constitution of 1861, which among other things forbade the wearing of clerical garb in public!) At the same time that church and state were being separated, universities, long wed to the churches, began divorce proceedings, pleading mental cruelty. Thus there was set in motion a whole process of secularization, which gradually took over everything in the public domain: government, universities, schools, hospitals, businesses—the works. And in many ways this was a good thing, for by and large the churches were too worldly and too reactionary, too tied to an old and passing order.

But today, with the benefit of hindsight, we can see that this process of secularization had as much to do with power as with the freedom in whose name it was undertaken. For now nation-states are free to demand complete loyalty to themselves without regard to Rome, or even to God. Financiers are free to make money without the moral restraints imposed by religion. Universities are free to exalt the right of the individual to think and do anything over any obligation to do good. And the churches, with no real function for society as a whole, have been relegated to the role of comforting people in this world and preparing them for the next. O, they can tell their members to be kind and honest within established structures, but they are no more expected to change these structures than they were expected, during the Middle Ages, to alter the feudal relationships between the nobility and their serfs.

So the churches that once helped keep royalty in power by being themselves too worldly, are today keeping the middle class in power by being too *other*worldly.

Is this good for the middle class? I think not. I think that by supporting—if only by not protesting—the political and economic goals of their middle-class members, the churches are killing them spiritually. The *Reader's Digest* offers a case in point. Here is a publication that has probably warmed the cockles of more bourgeois hearts than any other publication in America, a magazine that is generally viewed as comfy, earnest, optimistic, a patriotic defender of the national faith; yet its November issue features the following five articles:

How to stay slim forever

Five ways to stop feeling tired

How to get your way

How safe are the new contraceptives?

What it takes to be successful

Clearly the editors of the *Digest* have concluded that their millions of readers are—consecutively—fat, lazy, frustrated, lascivious, and unsuccessful. The thought that the editors might be right, that we are indeed a nation of autoerotic stumblebums, is enough to chill the heart.

But even more damaging than the spiritual slaughter of their middle-class members is the churches' neglect of the vast majority of the human race who are anything but middle class, who are in fact wretchedly poor. And so the reformation I envision calls for the churches, which once supported royalty, and then supported the bourgeoisie, to take up today the cause of the poor—for the sake of the rich as well as the poor. I think that the challenge for the churches today is to shake off reliance on privilege, and to heed the invitation offered four years ago by the Roman Catholic bishops of Latin America (meeting in Mexico City at the same time the Pope was there): "We invite all, without distinction of class, to accept and take up the cause of the poor, as if they were accepting and taking up their own cause, the very cause of Jesus Christ." I think that the challenge for Christians today is to learn, as did Dietrich Bonhoeffer in the Nazi prisons, "to see the great events of world history from below, from the perspective of the outcasts, the suspects, the maltreated, the powerless, the oppressed, the reviled—in short, from the perspective of those who suffer."

Believing that the world is going to be changed from the bottom up and from the edges in, I think we have to put an end not only to "trickle-down" economics but to "trickle-down" theology, which has become irrelevant. Thanks to a forthcoming book by Harvey Cox, I recently figured out why it was that I was so distressed with the brilliant lectures delivered five years ago from this pulpit by Hans Küng. Küng set out to answer unbelief, a completely legitimate undertaking for a theologian. But I now realize that the unbelief he was addressing was the sophisticated skepticism of the educated, not the angry agnosticism of so many of the world's maltreated and powerless. I don't denigrate the importance of winning the elite back to the faith, but I do insist on the link between injustice and the unbelief of the poor.

So we need a theology steeped in justice, one which reminds the nations that "Inasmuch as ye have done it unto the least of these my brethren, ye have done it unto me" for the parable is addressed to the nations ("and before him shall be gathered all nations"). We need a theology that knits together *homo religiosus* and *homo politicus*, so that Christians can once again see how theological and Biblical insights relate to public life as well as to private life. We need a theology that sees sin not only in personal but also in institutional form, for the principal actors in today's world are nations, business enterprises, political and economic groups of one kind and another. We need a theology that reminds the universities, in the old Calvinist phrase, that "truth is in order to goodness," that the acquisition of knowledge is second to its use. We need a theology that has good things to say for anger, because if you lower your quotient of anger against oppression you lower your quotient of love for the oppressed. We need a theology that sees Jesus not only as our personal savior and founder of the church but also as saving grace for the whole world. And we need to see the church not only as an institution but as a community of God's people, a community that envisions salvation as an exodus for all humanity in which all forms of injustice will be left behind.

In short, we need a theology of compassion. For a world that is going to be changed from the bottom up and the edges in, we need a theology that starts at the bottom of everyone's heart and works its way up to the top of everyone's head.

When Jesus is Lord, everybody is somebody. In a few moments we shall hear the words of the institution of the holy supper of our Lord Jesus Christ as they are delivered by the apostle Paul: "Take, eat, this is my body which is broken for you." All of you, without exception. And the bread, the body of Christ, is as well a symbol for the church, also the body of Christ. For are not we, its members, brought together in one loaf to be broken to feed the world? That Christians could better the lot of humanity, even save the world, goes without saying. The only question is whether we will.

God Is Love

NOVEMBER 13, 1983
Reading: 1 John 4:7–12

L ast week I suggested that the churches, both Catholic and Protestant, could use a reformation, one as profound and as wide in scope as the Lutheran-Calvinist Reformation of the sixteenth century. The reform, I suggested, should begin by fighting the privatization of Christianity, which is a dangerous trend that produces spiritual schizophrenia in individual Christians, trivializes the faith, and leaves the public domain of life to the biggest powermongers around. I recalled that the churches had once furthered the economic and political goals of royalty by being too worldly; that they had then done the same for the middle class by being too otherworldly; and

This sermon is based largely on Bishop Spong's *Into the Whirlwind.*—WSC

that now the churches must once again become "this-worldly"—only *this* time to take up the cause of the poor, for the sake of the rich as well as the poor. For as Christ himself said: "Inasmuch as ye do it unto the least of these my brethren, ye do it unto me" (Matt. 25:40).

Today let's leave the social justice front for two others, the intellectual and the sexual. (Not that these three fronts are really separate, but for the purposes of discussion let us treat them individually.)

In the fourth chapter of the First Letter of John it is written, "God is love and they who abide in love abide in God and God abides in them" (v. 16). To some ears that sentence may sound sentimental. I myself find it tough-minded. "God is love" suggests to me that the heart has more to say to the world than does the mind, for while the mind continually looks for ways to dominate, to master, the heart seeks always to surrender—to God and to another human being. That's why Paul writes, "And if I understand all mysteries and all knowledge . . . but have not love, I am nothing." "God is love" suggests to me that there are certain regions where the mind, although it can play an all-important legislative role, cannot finally play a creative one. As with a great composer like Beethoven, so with God: he is a truth the mind can defend but never discover, never fully know. Again St. Paul would seem to agree: "O the depth of the riches both of the wisdom and knowledge of God! How unsearchable are his judgments, and his ways past finding out. For who hath known the mind of God?" (Rom. 11:33–34). We seem to know more of the heart than of the mind of God. In fact, "God is love and they who abide in love abide in God and God abides in them" would seem to suggest that the revelation is the relationship. And revelation provides more in the way of psychological reassurance, shall we say, than it provides intellectual certainty. It's my feeling that you can take all the belief systems that rest on absolute intellectual certainty—be that certainty the doctrine of papal infallibility or the concept of the verbal inerrancy of Scripture—you can take those belief systems and you can throw them out the stained-glass windows. For they are more a bane than a blessing. How's that for radical reform?

In truth, it's not all that radical. For there has always been a sort of *sub rosa* pluralism in Roman Catholicism. Since 1870, when the doctrine of papal infallibility was promulgated, the Pope has only twice pronounced infallibly on matters of faith and morals—both times regarding the Virgin Mary—and even then not all Catholics paid that much attention. This week in Michigan, for example, I met a Roman Catholic priest who, in public masses, has prayed mightily that God would forgive the Pope for his misunderstanding and mistreatment of women. Likewise, there has always been a *sub rosa* pluralism even among fundamentalists, who are as guilty as any of us of picking and choosing among the books of the Bible to serve their own purposes. For who can possibly find a consistent authority in a volume that contains 66 books written over a period of 1,000 years?

So all I'm suggesting is that what is *sub rosa* must surface, if genuine reform is to clear the air. The reformation I seek demands that we Christians quite consciously abandon the security of certainty, along with all the power that certainty wields, for the vulnerability and joy of uncertainty. You see, I envision Christians as permanent revolutionaries, who really believe that "the Lord hath yet more light and truth to break forth from his word." The reformation I seek would confront the presumption of certainty, and the cruelty of it too; for isn't it true that people never do evil so cheerfully as when they do it from absolute conviction? Isn't that how the critics get silenced, the prophets stoned? Wasn't Christ himself crucified by a belief system based on absolute certainty? I'm convinced that had we only one religion in this country a lot of us would long ago have been branded as heretics, and killed. Had we two religions, we'd have killed each other. It's only by having 15,000 different religions—God help us!—that the wisdom of tolerance and proper Christian humility has been forced upon us.

Mind you, I'm not trying to get rid of dogma, only to put it in its proper place—which is penultimate, not ultimate. Dogma is a signpost, not a hitching post. "God is love" means that the purity of dogma is second to the integrity of love. "God is love" means that all life is essentially relational, that we derive our strength from our relations with God and with one another. "God is love" means that love is an expression of our aliveness, and that we pass out of death into life only because we love one another and God.

In other words, a new reformation would spell a more spiritual faith, together with a spirit-filled church that proclaims the love of God seen by its followers in the face of Jesus Christ.

But in putting forward such a program we have to realize, as Beverly Harrison suggested last Wednesday night as part of the Liberation Theology series, we have to realize that the key to spirituality is sensuality. What we need is a *sensual* spirituality if we have any hope of ending, once and for all, the dualism that for too long has separated spirit from nature, the dualism that in pridefully exalting spirit over nature sees sex as sinful, and thereby fans the fires both of misogyny and homophobia. How true it is that those who are themselves repressed become themselves repressive!

The church, of course, didn't invent misogyny, it inherited it, and less from the Jews than from those terribly dualistic Greeks, who proclaimed *"soma sema"*—the body is a tomb. But the church, having inherited misogyny, baptized it, and in a big way. According to St. Jerome, marriage was tolerable "only because more virgins are born as the result." I can hardly bear to cite this passage, but actually Jerome's brand of rigid asceticism was not characteristic of the very early church, which was still poor, still no-authoritarian, and which maintained a large role for women. We can surmise this not only from the Book of Acts but also from second- and third-century sources. Tertullian wrote, "It is not permitted for a woman to speak in the church, nor is it permitted for her to teach, nor to baptize, nor to offer the eucharist, nor to claim for herself a share in any masculine function, least of all in priestly office." Would he have gone to such lengths to prohibit these things had not women been speaking in church, teaching, baptizing, offering the Eucharist? It's just so tragic, though, to think how far we slipped so fast, and how long we stayed there—because, sure enough, Tertullian's views prevailed. Women were put down; and they were put down, I'm convinced, largely because they embodied the satanic power that called men to an awareness of the flesh from which their noble souls sought only release! Marriage was not absolution from sexuality, only a compromise with sin.

By now, of course, things have begun to change, and today women are even ordained. Just as here at Riverside we ordained Beverly Thompson-Travis, so tomorrow all over the world, in every single Roman Catholic and Orthodox church, women will be ordained. There is no question about it; for "in Christ there is neither male nor female." What is disappointing, what is so embarrassing, is how long it always takes the churches to implement their own revelation!

Today we are also in the midst of a sexual revolution, which for the first time in history separates sex from procreation and openly links it with recreation. This is a revolution that is the result of a technological innovation—birth control—and also of a change in life styles, of the fact that many people, taking advantage of new educational and career opportunities, are postponing marriage and sometimes even abandoning it. Clearly we are living in an era when yesterday's guidelines have been largely abandoned and tomorrow's have yet to be established. Provisionally, what can the church say?

I think churches have to face the fact that biologically it is nearly impossible to separate puberty from marriage by some ten or fifteen years, as we are now doing in Western civilization, and still limit sexual intercourse to marriage. I think the churches have to ask whether psychologically it is desirable to impose a standard so contrary to the normal drives of normal people. I can't here deal with some of the tough peripheral issues—adultery, postmarital sex—except to say that any ethical system based on the sacredness of life has to embrace the exceptions. But I would like to make three simple suggestions. First of all, I think it would help a lot if premarital sex were viewed in less ultimate ways; it is rather unimaginative, I think, to view it as the best thing in life—as *Playboy* often implies—or as the worst possible form of human activity, as some straitlaced Christians tend to believe. Surely all the so-called dirty thoughts in all the minds of adolescents all over the world are not to be compared with one minute in the mind of an adult racist or warmonger! Secondly, I think we have to recognize that there is a vast gray area between the ideal of married love, on the one hand, and, on the other, the immorality of loveless sex. And that leads to the third suggestion, which is that we try to concentrate more on keeping sex and love together than on limiting sex to marriage. No less a figure than Geoffrey Fisher, the former Archbishop of Canterbury, suggested (after he retired) that the churches develop a liturgical service of dedication for couples who wanted to enter what he called "trial marriages." Needless to say, his conservative colleagues viewed his thoughtful suggestion as a product of incipient senility. But I mention it here as just one of many things for all of us to think about.

Yes, we are living in an era where yesterday's guidelines have been largely abandoned and tomorrow's have yet to be established. But isn't that always the case, everywhere, in all situations? It is reported that Peter Stuyvesant once asked his New Amsterdam colleagues, "Do we really have to accept the Jews, because if we do we'll have to accept the Roman Catholics and those horrid Lutherans." That was New York's first expression of "Dammit, there goes the neighborhood." But as far as I'm concerned neighborhoods are always going, and coming—as are nations, as is life itself. That's what makes life so exciting; that's what I mean by the *joy* of uncertainty; that's what I mean by saying Christians have to be permanent revolutionaries.

But that does not mean that we are without guidelines whatsoever. "God is love" is no sappy phrase, for the love we speak of is not symbolized by Cupid, a blindfolded infant in diapers, but is a love embodied in the person of Jesus Christ, who tells us, as the Word of God, what the humanity of human beings is all about. God be praised that life *is* always changing. And with Jesus Christ as her helper, we may yet see a reformed church help change it for the better.

The Sabbath Belongs to Man

NOVEMBER 20, 1983
Reading: Mark 2:23–28

To guide us through a World Food Sunday sermon I have chosen three texts: the first is from the Gospel of Mark—"The Sabbath was made for man, not man for the Sabbath"; the second comes from Proverbs—"He who oppresses a poor man insults his Maker" (14:31); and the third, also from Proverbs, states the second text more positively—"He who is kind to the poor lends to the LORD" (19:17).

The pharisees turn to Jesus and say, "Why are they (the disciples) doing what is not lawful on the Sabbath?" And Jesus answers them, "The Sabbath was made for man, not man for the Sabbath." I'm sure the pharisees experienced the rejoinder as a put-down, but I detect no note of triumph in Jesus' response, only sadness, and perhaps a touch of anger at the fact that religious leaders should need to be reminded that love, not law, is the final arbiter in the use of worldly things.

I guess all of us, no matter what our professions, occasionally need such reminders. A grade-school teacher once sent a student home with a note informing his parents that the boy had poor habits of personal cleanliness. Before returning to school, she said, he had to be properly washed. Instead of a scrubbed-up kid, however, what the teacher got in return was another note, saying, "Never mind about Joey's face and neck. Joey's no rose. But your business ain't to smell him but to learn him."

That schoolteacher was prissy, as were the pharisees. But worse than that: with their hostile, critical eyes they were actually spying on Jesus. What else would pharisees be doing in the middle of a cornfield? They must have looked as out of place as did those FBI "birdwatchers" on Block Island several years ago, as they closed in on the fugitive Father Daniel Berrigan.

Lest we feel unduly superior, however, let us remember that the pharisees asked, "Why do they do what is not lawful *on the Sabbath?*" Today, in the USA, on any day of the week, a citizen passing by such a scene might be expected to ask, "Why are they doing what is not lawful?"—period. Meaning, simply, why are they stealing corn? But twenty centuries ago, under an economic system that did not seek solely to maximize returns, taking corn, as the disciples did, was not stealing. Listen to this rule from Deuteronomy: "When you go into your neighbor's standing grain, you may pluck the ears with your hand, but you shall not put a sickle to your neighbor's standing grain. When you go into your neighbor's vineyard, you may eat your fill of grapes, as many as you wish, but you shall not put any in your vessel" (Deut. 23:25, 24). And in Leviticus we read: "When you reap the harvest in your land, you shall not reap right into the edges of your field, neither shall you glean the fallen ears. . . .You shall leave them for the poor and for the alien. I am the Lord your God" (Lev. 19:9–10).

The lesson, in other words, is: "When you walk down Broadway and you are hungry, you may eat fruit or vegetables off the last rows of the food stands, but you shall not put anything in a bag."

Wouldn't New York be a better place if the maximization of returns were curtailed just a bit to console both empty stomachs and troubled consciences? Wouldn't it be a better place if sharing one's surplus were viewed as an act of justice rather than as an act of benevolence? Wouldn't it be a better place if all of us could see what the Bible indicates time and again, *that those in need have ownership rights in our surplus*?

"He who oppresses a poor man insults his Maker" (Prov. 14:31). God doesn't make people poor; rich people do. But as life is fundamentally ethical and consequential—"therefore" is one of the great words of Scripture—God makes two promises which sooner or later are always kept: if you are oppressed you will be liberated; if you are an oppressor you will be destroyed. The first of these promises is embodied in the Exodus, and the second in all the "woe to" passages: "Woe to those who lie upon beds of ivory and stretch themselves upon their couches and eat lambs from the flock and calves from the midst of the stall . . .Therefore, they shall now be the first of those to go into exile, and the revelry of those who stretch themselves shall pass away" (Amos 6:4–7). Jerry Falwell thinks Sodom was destroyed because of its homosexuals, but he doesn't know his Bible: "Behold, this was the guilt of your sister Sodom; she and her daughters had pride, surfeit of food, and prosperous ease, but did not aid the poor and needy . . . therefore I removed them when I saw it" (Ezek. 16:49–50).

I said that God makes two promises which are always kept, "sooner or later." Take only a quick look at history and you will see that the empires which lasted longest—the Roman and the British—had far less injustice built into them than did the truly wicked ones. I have in mind the Assyrian Empire, and Hitler, who lasted a bare—if horrible—thirteen years. But even the comparatively civilized Roman and British empires passed away because of their inequities; and for this same reason the Soviet and American empires also will likely prove "short as the watch that ends the night before the rising sun."

"He who oppresses a poor man insults his Maker." But the hard question is, How are the poor to be helped—by charity or by justice, by voluntary contribution or by legislation? In the Book of Acts we read of the first Christian communities: "There was not a needy person among them, for as many as were possessors of lands or houses sold them . . . and distribution was made to each as any had need" (vv. 24–35). It was all voluntary. But those were small communities, charismatic, filled with the Holy Spirit, visited regularly by one apostle or another; their people were poor and far removed from the corrupting seats of power. Should we hold them up as models for churches? Yes, by all means. Should we hold them up as a model for society at large? Alas, no. Human nature, as every Bible reader knows, is sinful, and therefore the virtue of the few will never compensate for the inertia of the many. Rich people and rich nations will not voluntarily open their eyes to see the Biblical truth that the poor have ownership rights in their surplus. This they will see only in retrospect, after their surplus is taken away—by legislation, if not by violence. Given human goodness, voluntary contributions are possible, but given human sinfulness, legislation is indispensable. Charity, yes always; but never as a substitute for justice. What we keep forgetting in this country is that people have rights, basic rights: the right to food, the right to decent housing, the right to medical care, the right to education. Food pantries like the one we have here at Riverside, and shelters for the homeless throughout the city, are only painful reminders of how the richest country in the world still denies fundamental human rights to the poorest of its citizens. This, I'm sure, will be the burden of Congressman Weiss's message. It is certainly the message of our Food and Justice task force, to whom we owe so much for the organization of today's activities.

Not that we can legislate morality, only the conditions conducive to morality. Martin Luther King Jr. used to say, "You can't make them love us, but you can stop them from lynching us." Likewise, we can't force people to love the poor, but we ought to be able to stop starving them to death—some 500 million of them around the world. We ought to be able to see that just as the Sabbath belongs to man so the economy belongs to human beings, not human beings to the economy. Economics are not science, they are only politics in disguise. It grieves me that we in this nation of abundance passively heed economists who assure us that full employment is impossible, that social welfare programs are too inflationary, that taxing wealth will result in "failure to provide sufficient replacement to maintain capital intact." These same economists rarely mention the following statistic: had the world spent one million dollars every day since the birth of Jesus Christ, it would have spent but one-half of what the Reagan administration wants to spend in five years on the U.S. military alone—1.5 trillion dollars. The economy, the national security system, our laws, our institutions, all belong to us, according to Jesus when he said, "The Sabbath belongs to man"; and oh, how his heart must break as he watches us bow down before our various man-made idols.

"He who is kind to the poor lends to the Lord" (Prov. 19:17). Isn't that a wonderful concluding thought? If we voluntarily give of our surplus, and if we fight for justice, we are helping the poor, yes, but much more than that: we are helping the Creator of heaven and earth, we are helping God with a loan! "He who is kind to the poor *lends* to the Lord." And I leave it to your experience and imagination to surmise what the repayment of that loan might be, for "eye hath not seen, nor ear heard, neither have entered into the heart of man, the things which God hath prepared for them that love him" (1 Cor. 2:9).

An Advent Hope

DECEMBER 4, 1983
Reading: Matthew 3:1–12

Then Jerusalem and all Judea and all the region about the Jordan went out to John, and they were baptized by John in the river Jordan, confessing their sins.

No one would accuse John the Baptist of having had a sunny personality. No one would describe him as a fun-loving fellow. It was not a character defect on his part; he was simply so driven by a vision of moral righteousness that he had neither the time nor perhaps the freedom to become a "complete" person. But even if he was not well-rounded, even if he was not a barrel of fun, John the Baptist remains an impressive and important Advent figure—"the voice of one crying in the wilderness, Prepare the way of the Lord . . ."

Why did John choose to live in one of the most terrible deserts of the world? The answer to this question becomes clear when we consider to whom, in Scripture, the Word of God is generally revealed. While occasionally it is to counselors of kings—Joseph in Pharaoh's court, David's Nathan, the prophet Isaiah—for the most part the Word of God is revealed to those far removed from the glitter and glamour, the intensification of life represented by cities, and farther still from those who occupy the seats of power. Think of Moses minding the sheep of his father-in-law Jethro; think of the boy Samuel, the young Jeremiah, Amos among his sycamores, Ezekiel; or in the New Testament think of Elizabeth, Mary, the shepherds, and finally John the Baptist. Listen to this sentence from the third chapter of Luke: "In the fifteenth year of the reign of Tiberius Caesar"—there's power for you—"Pontius Pilate being governor of Judea"—more power—"and Herod being tetrarch (read "prince") of Galilee, and his brother Philip tetrarch of the region of Iturea and Trachonitis, and Lysanias tetrarch of Abilene, and in the high-priesthood of Annas and Caiaphas"— there's religious power joined to secular power—"the Word of God came to John the son of Zechariah in the wilderness" (vv. 1–2).

The point is made: How can we see the star of Bethlehem when it is eclipsed by the lights of the city? And how can the powerful see the truth when their pride-swollen faces have closed up their eyes? The Bible makes it abundantly clear that those furthest from the seats of power are generally nearest to the heart of things. Lord knows, we saw that for ourselves during the Civil Rights Movement of the '50s and '60s, and during the war in Vietnam. And what we learned from the war was that although rulers may have all the facts, as they frequently claim, once all the facts are in, no one has the truth. Which is why we, dear Christians, who could hardly be more removed from power, must not hesitate to speak out what our hearts and our consciences tell us to say—particularly in these days, when silence on the great issues comes close to betrayal.

But back to our prophet, John, who not only lived where none of us would dream of living, who not only wore clothes that he would screen out of our Riverside clothing service, but who also ate the food of the poorest of the poor. How many people's lives deny their message! But not John's; which may be why we read that "Jerusalem and all Judea and all the region about the Jordan went out to John." For in him they saw that rare, rare person whose life was totally consistent with his words. And in him they found a great preacher as well.

What is good preaching? Good preaching is never *at* people, it's *for* people. Good preaching only raises to a conscious level the knowledge inherent in everyone's experience of life. It tells people what in their heart of hearts they already know, what in the depths of their souls they are only waiting to hear confirmed. In short, just as ears need words so do words need ears; and good preaching needs expectant people, people who yearn for something more, people who *know* there's something more, if only they could be told where to find it. Good preaching needs people who understand, as the great Russian theologian Berdyaev put it, that once bread has been assured God becomes a hard and inescapable reality, instead of an escape from harsh reality. Such, I imagine, were many of the people who poured out of Jerusalem and all of Judea to hear John.

Our problem this Advent season in America, however, seems to be that so many of us have come to expect so little. Our souls seem to have shriveled: unlike Mary's they no longer magnify the Lord, they have no appetite for the glory and majesty of a transcendent God. We have come to prefer our mysteries small. Rather than "do what is in us for the succour of those years wherein we are set, uprooting the evil in the fields we know so that those who live after may have clean earth to till," we pursue private goals and desires.

I would judge this privatistic self-fulfillment to be the single most agreed-upon social practice of our day. The psychologist Fritz Perls has hymned its praise:

> I do my thing and you do your thing.
> I am not in this world to live up to your expectations.
> And you are not in this world to live up to mine.
> You are you, and I am I,
> and if by chance we find each other, it's beautiful.
> If not, it can't be helped.

It's all unbelievably petty; for there's no smaller package in this world than that of a person all wrapped up in himself. It's all unbelievably boring; give me John the Baptist in the wilderness any day over Fritz Perls in the Big Sur. And, of course, it's unbelievably dangerous; for all the individual transgressions and all the national sins against which John the Baptist and earlier prophets of Israel inveighed, we Americans today have them in spades. Yet is there anyone seeking to stay the wrath to come? On the contrary, it seems that for every person heading for the Jordan to be cleansed and rededicated to the reign of heaven on earth, these days one hundred are headed for the nearest department store to buy their kid a Cabbage Patch doll.

Friends, we need to expect more—that's the message this second Sunday in Advent. I cannot find until I seek. The door cannot be opened unto me until I knock. Until I say, "I have sinned," God has no chance to say, "And I forgive," and to fill the hollow in my heart once again brimful with the love of life.

We need to expect more. When we seek our own identity we must expect to find a few other people too. When we are married we must expect to give, not just sit back and wait for the dividends to come in. If we have children we must expect them to be different from us, and to cherish and seek to understand that difference. If we have jobs we had better be sure they're useful to somebody else as well. And if we belong to a church we ought not to pretend that we're in a lifeboat trying to save ourselves from a sinking ship; we ought to consider ourselves members of the lifesaving crew. We're here to hit the breakers to save the strangers, the poor, the needy—yes, the whole world—from drowning in a storm that is, after all, a storm of our own making.

Today John Phillips carried in the banner of hope, and as he did so I couldn't take my eyes off of it. For that hope is what the people pouring out of Jerusalem and Judea had. That's what John, in his unique way, demands of us today—an Advent hope, that we might be the readier for Christmas.

On Thanksgiving, as many of you know, we lost a great member of this church, one of the youngest octogenarians I've ever known, Helen Baker. Since that time, I've tried to imagine to myself what Helen's last words to all of us might have been. I can almost hear her saying, "Lots of hope." And if those were her last words, she was only reflecting what St. Paul wished us, too: "May the God of hope fill you with all joy and peace in believing, so that by the power of the Holy Spirit you may abound in hope" (Rom. 15:13).

Christ's Plan

DECEMBER 11, 1983
Readings: Isaiah 35:1–10; Matthew 11:2–11

It was too inevitable: John, who couldn't see evil without rebuking it, and who therefore called to task King Herod himself for seducing and then marrying his own sister-in-law—John the Baptist now sits in Herod's dungeons. He who lived with his face set to the wind and with the sky as his roof, is now confined to four narrow underground walls. The eagle of Israel has been caged. Then, from prison, through his disciples, John sends to Jesus a truly poignant question: "Are you the one who is to come, or shall we look for another?"

Remember that it was only a short time before that John himself had baptized Jesus in the river Jordan, proclaiming to the crowd lining the bank that Jesus was indeed the Messiah. But now the tide has turned against him and against God's justice, the cause to which he had committed himself 110 percent, and now John has doubts—the same doubts that afflict almost all of us in our moments of crisis. For if you yourself have ever been in jail, or been robbed or raped, or have lost a loved one all too early, or a job or reputation unfairly, haven't you, too, thought of denying God's Messiah? And if you are a young mother or father today, don't you sometimes doubt the efficacy of Christ's salvation, when national arrogance and cosmic foolishness seem intent upon dooming not only your newborn child but every baby the world around?

It is possible, of course, that John asked his poignant question not to allay his own fears but for the sake of his disciples, that their doubts might be ended. But it is probable that having predicted "the wrath to come," having claimed that "the axe is laid to the root of the trees," John, the prophet of cleansing judgment, the prophet of holy destruction, was beginning to experience the darkness of impatience that threatens to quench the light of compassion.

There is a Mormon myth according to which Christ and Satan were each requested to submit to God a plan for dealing with the infant human race. Satan's plan was simple (of the kind of simplicity that Secretaries of State and Defense come up with): God has armies of angels at his command; Satan said, "Why not just assign an angel with punitive power to each human being and the race will behave very nicely." But you don't have to be a military, diplomatic, or business leader, you don't have to be a dictator, to believe in the virtues of the hard line. In fact I think that all of us, in our heart of hearts, are potential hard-liners. For isn't it true when things go badly for us personally—or nationally—that we expect God, and not ourselves, to straighten out the mess? Shouldn't God at least keep our children safe and sound, no matter what kind of cars they drive, and shouldn't he keep the human race from annihilating itself, no matter what fiendish weapons we invent and insist on deploying? And if ultimately children and the human race can only be saved by force, then so be it, by force—"But save us, God."

So much for Satan's plan; Christ's was radically different, and more imaginative as well. "Let them have free will and go their own way," he proposed to God, "only let me live and die as one of them, both as an example of how to live, and to show them how much you care, to show them that there is more mercy in you than sin in them." At

Christmas it becomes clear which plan God chose to implement. But if John the Baptist, confined to his cell, had a hard time understanding and accepting Christ's plan for salvation, if Christ himself nailed to the cross could not quiet his own doubts—"My God, my God, why hast thou forsaken me?"—it would be silly to think it easy for us, in our complicated enough personal lives, and in a world in its present parlous state, to believe that a babe in the manger is all it takes to save our souls and the human race.

To grasp better how the plan Christ submitted to God is supposed to work, let us turn now to Jesus' answer to John's question, "Are you the one who is to come, or shall we look for another?" Note first of all that Jesus doesn't become the least bit defensive—as I certainly would have become. What extraordinary personal security there is in allowing God alone to provide your identity! Jesus says simply, and with confidence, "Go and tell John what you see and hear." He does not say, "Tell John what I am saying, give him my message. Take him a few copies of some recent sermons of mine, and a set of resolutions I've drafted on a variety of important subjects." Christ would not be pleased with our form of "resolutionary" Christianity, for he knew full well that the world is not going to be saved by right opinions alone, not even those of the churches. "Go and tell John what you see and hear," Jesus says—in other words, tell him what's being done, what's happening.

And what *is* happening? "The blind receive their sight and the lame walk, lepers are cleansed and the deaf hear, and the dead are raised up, and the poor have good news preached to them." All these things of course are literally true, and better yet, they are figuratively, spiritually, and eternally true. For Christ is fulfilling Isaiah's promise for all time: "Then the eyes of the blind shall be opened, and the ears of the deaf unstopped; then shall the lame leap like a hart, and the tongues of the dumb sing for joy."

But for all this spiritual healing to take place, today as then, people first have to see the need, to acknowledge that the freedom of will that Christ's plan to God insisted upon has been misused. We have to acknowledge our blindness to truths about ourselves, each other, and God; that we are deaf to certain cries of the needy and that at times we are about as paralyzed by choices as was the proverbial medieval donkey placed equidistant between two bales of hay. We have to admit, as St. Paul would say, that "we have sinned and fallen short." But this is not what is spiritually most dangerous to individuals and a threat to the world's survival. Evil is not guilt, as so many pretend, but rather the effort to escape it. Evil is the human soul evading, avoiding, hiding from itself, pretending, for example, that whatever cars and weapons human beings make, God is responsible for their use. Evil is the soul of a nation explaining away its flaws by blaming others. Evil is the kind of self-protectiveness which invariably sacrifices others rather than ourselves. When Cain refused to acknowledge his imperfection it was inevitable that he would seek to wreak havoc on the lives of others. Nations, of course, in defense of their self-image, do this to such an extent that Camus was led to call "legalized murder" the chief characteristic of our age.

When you stop to think of it, the blindness that goes with power is truly breathtaking. For instance, if some private citizen today were to suggest that a young woman should be burned at the stake, in the manner of Joan of Arc, he would be locked up immediately; but let a government official say that perhaps ten million people may have to be incinerated in the national interest, and he is listened to. And one more thing: if evil is a soul hiding from itself, if the primary motive of evil is disguise, then we should not be surprised to find evil people in the churches. For what better way to disguise one's evil from oneself and from others than to wrap it all up in piety and to become a highly visible Christian—a preacher, let's say, or a deacon or trustee?

"Only let me live and die as one of them, both as an example of how to live, and to show them that there is more mercy in you than sin in them." According to Christ's plan for salvation, the world really divides itself between those held in the embrace of God's love who know it, and those so held who do not know it yet. Newton's hymn is so right:

> Amazing grace, how sweet the sound,
> That saved a wretch like me!
> I once was lost, but now am found,
> Was blind, but now I see.

Now I see that God's love does not seek value, it creates it. Now I see that my identity is a gift from God, not an achievement of my own. Now I see that I don't have to prove myself, for God has taken care of that; all I have to do is to express myself in deeds of love and gratitude. Because I am held in the embrace of God's love I can't run away, nor do I want to. How much better to face it all—the imperfections of my soul and my nation. In my hard moments I shall always be tempted, as was John, to seek a new messiah, but I shall pray God to deliver me from the temptation. For now I see that force can only contain evil, not destroy it. Only forgiveness has that power. And, dear followers of Christ, if the abyss of God's love is deeper than the abyss of death, what shall we fear—our own death, the death of our beloved children, of our husbands, wives, friends, even the death of the world? No, we need fear none of these things, although, God knows, we must do all in our power to prevent every death we can.

Perhaps the most realistic hope for our time was once voiced by Abba Eban: "People and nations do act wisely after they have exhausted all other possible alternatives." I submit to you this Advent, 1983, that we have exhausted all possible alternatives. It's time now for Christmas, for Christ's plan. "Let them have their will and go their way, only let me live and die as one of them, both as an example of how to live and to show them how much you care." Come, Lord Jesus, come.

Our Role in the Incarnation

DECEMBER 18, 1983
Reading: Matthew 1:18–25

Every Christmas is a vivid reminder that while the four Gospels all have Jesus as their subject, they represent four distinct portraits of him. Christmas reminds us again that the Gospels are not biographies but testimonials; they are Jesus according to Matthew, according to Mark, according to Luke, according to John. Moreover, they are written according to the audience each evangelist had in mind and according to the special points each wanted to make. So it should be no surprise that the Virgin Birth appears in Matthew and Luke but never in Mark and John, and nowhere in the letters of St. Paul. The latter three were no less convinced that Christ was God's love in person on earth, but they believed that what made Christ the Son of God had more to do with the events of the end of his life—his death and resurrection—than with any miraculous beginnings of it. I know that for many of you who have a Roman Catholic or Protestant background, the question of whether or not there was a Virgin birth is an agonizing one. Personally, I do not believe in the Virgin Birth, in part because the Biblical testimony is so unclear (even to Biblical scholars who have devoted so much time and study to it), and in part because I don't think it should be the thing that, shall we say, makes Christ Christ for people. I can accept the Virgin Birth as an expression of faith but not as a basis of faith, not as proof that Jesus was the Christ.

What do we want—proof, or freedom? I believe there is nothing factual that can make the Jesus of history the Christ of our personal faith. We have to do our own thinking, make our own commitments, each of us in his or her own way. That's why I'm glad there are four distinct portraits of Jesus. Of the heavenly city it has been said that it "lieth four square," with gates to the East, to the West, to the South, and to the North, so that strangers from all points of the compass can enter. Likewise we can say that in the differing interpretations of the four different evangelists, the one Gospel is open to all who seek to give their hearts and minds to Jesus.

Biblical scholars do agree that the special readers Matthew had in mind in writing his gospel were Jews, Jews in Jerusalem and Palestine and throughout the Hellenistic and Roman world. This explains the greater lengths to which Matthew went to show that the Old Testament foreshadowed the life of Jesus. He alone of the four evangelists begins his gospel with a genealogical table tracing Jesus' descent through King David all the way back to Abraham; and throughout his gospel he never misses a chance to show how Christ fulfills Old Testament prophecy and promise. The very names "Jesus" and "Emmanuel" in today's lesson, as Matthew well knew, would have had enormous impact on Jewish ears. After all, "Jesus" is the Greek for Joshua, a name combining two Hebrew words—God ("Yahweh") and salvation. Matthew implies that just as political freedom came in ancient days through Joshua, so now spiritual freedom will come through Jesus, who "will save the people from their sins." The second name, from more recent times, recalls the promise of the prophet Isaiah, who, in the dark days of King Ahaz, foretold the coming of one so wondrous, so rich in goodness, so caring of all humanity that he would be called "Emmanuel," which means "God is with us."

"You shall call his name Jesus for he will save the people from their sins." With only six shopping days left until Christmas we haven't time to go over all of our sins, so I have decided to deal with one only, one from which most of us, I think, need especially to be saved in our own dark days. Christmas celebrates what theologians like to call the "Incarnation," the time when God's love comes to earth in human form. But the Incarnation says as much about what we are to become as it does about what God has become. Christ becomes like us so that we might become like him. He comes to convert us, but not from life to something more than life, rather from something less than life to the possibility of full life itself. "I came that you might have life, and have it more abundantly," says Jesus in the Gospel of John (10:10b), words which the early Christian father Irenaeus translated into these: "The glory of God is a human being fully alive." What I have been leading up to is this: I think the sin from which we are in special need of being saved, these dark days, is the sin of settling for something less. I think our problem is that we do not play our role in the Incarnation story.

John Knowles, author of that wonderful story of adolescence, *A Separate Peace*, once told an interesting anecdote about himself. Immediately after graduating from college he had gone off to Italy to write his first novel, and in his youthful ambitiousness had been bold enough to send an early draft to Thornton Wilder. The elder writer replied, "I am on page 156 and can go no further. I am convinced you are not really interested in what you are writing." Years afterward, but with the exchange fresh in his mind, Knowles commented, "It had not occurred to me that I was supposed to be emotionally involved." Now, isn't that the way we often live our lives?—lives which, Lord knows, are far more important than novels. How passionately involved in your life are you? Is it full of fierce yearnings, of heartbreaking love for the beauty of the world? Or is it pretty much one day after another?

Not that passionate involvement alone is sufficient. The other night I saw *Educating Rita*, a poignant and charming movie, I thought, that had occasional profound moments. In one of them, as those of you who have seen it will recall, Rita, the hairdresser, eager to fulfill herself, wants to know from her once-a-week tutor if an essay she has written is good enough to pass the examination that will get her the degree she is after. Her tutor, Frank, an alcoholic professor-poet, doesn't know how to reply, because, as he explains, for the purposes of the examination her essay is worthless, while in all other respects it is superb: personal, honest, original—all the things organized education doesn't prize! But Rita is single-minded. She crumples the paper, throws it in the fire, and demands of her tutor that he change her thinking in whatever way will allow her to pass the exam. She's passionately involved in her life, all right, but like so many of us for the wrong reason: *she's willing to become less herself for a goal less worthy than that of being herself.* And isn't that what the contemporary—and habitual—pursuit of reputation and material success is all about? "What shall it profit a man if he gain the whole world and become less of a person?" It's funny: many Americans will readily concede they're in a rat race; what they won't admit, however, is that even if you win a rat race you're still a rat!

But God is always trying to make humanity more human. That's what the Incarnation is all about. Christ becomes like us not that we should become less but more ourselves, more like him who showed us that even though we do pass all examinations, and with distinction; even though we do possess all knowledge so as to understand all mysteries, including that of the Virgin Birth; even though we do resemble virtue incarnate, and give all we have to feed the poor and let our bodies be burned; even though we are all those things but have not love, we are nothing. Love alone is the expression of our aliveness. And the Incarnation offers us all the gift of this life of love. But we have to take it, and we have to try to apply it to our lives in all possible ways.

I know how it is with many of you: you're trapped, at least momentarily, in jobs that are dull, jobs in which you find you can't be passionately involved. But there must be some way that even you can move toward the creative edge of whatever it is you happen to do; there must be ways to be more caring of colleagues, ways to make the worst workplace less dreary, more fun and fulfilling for everybody. Similarly, if we are parents and our children are small there is always more bodily warmth that we can give them, a more consistent sense of being loved; and if they are grown we can, with God's grace and a great deal of human effort and care, treat them as equals. As citizens too, which we all are, we should be able to demand housing, not shelters, for the homeless; jobs, not compensation, for the unemployed; and meanwhile do all that is in our power to ease the pain around us. And if we are old, physically limited, sick, even dying—it's rough, no doubt about it, but it is no cause for despair. For, as St. Paul put it, "though our outer nature is wasting away our inner nature is being renewed each day." Next Sunday the Savior comes to the old as well as to the young.

He comes to convert us not from life to something more than life, but from something less than life to full life itself. "I came that you might have life, and have it more abundantly." "The glory of God is a human being fully alive." What a sin it is, then, to live life to the minimum, to be devout but not daring!

We have one last week of Advent to think about this one sin from which we need especially to be saved, and to remember the two names we heard in today's lesson and think about what they might mean for us this year. Perhaps it is something like this: "And you shall call his name Jesus, for he will save his people from ever selling themselves short. And his name shall be called Emmanuel, because if they make room in their hearts for him, he will never, never leave them."

The Christmas Message

DECEMBER 25, 1983
Reading: Luke 2:1–20

L ast week I said that while all the gospels have Jesus as their subject, each represents a distinct portrait of him. Of the four, the French philosopher Ernest Renan preferred St. Luke's, calling it "the most beautiful book in the world." Why quarrel with that estimation? The first two chapters of Luke contain three of the most beloved hymns of the church—Mary's Magnificat, the "Nunc Dimittis" ("Lord, now lettest thou thy servant depart in peace"), and the chorus of the angels, the "Gloria in excelsis Deo"; the last two chapters contain the three most treasured utterances from the cross—"Father, forgive them, for they know not what they do" (23:34), "Verily I say unto you, today thou shalt be with me in Paradise" (23:43), and "Father, into thy hands I commend my spirit" (23:46); and chapters ten and fourteen contain the two best known parables—the Good Samaritan and the Return of the Prodigal Son. On top of all of this, what pastoral narrative ever written has folk poetry more lyrical than Luke's account of the birth of Jesus? Scholars, of course, will forever be busy trying to distinguish the historical—the literally true—from the eternally true, and trying to determine whether Luke was indeed the person tradition holds him to be, the Greek physician and traveling companion of St. Paul. That is the scholarly task. Ours, this Christmas morn, is a little different; our task is to rescue the story from its familiarity. So let's do a little Bible study.

We start with the statement, "In those days a decree went out from Caesar Augustus that all the world should be enrolled." "All the world" is an obvious exaggeration, for although Caesar Augustus was the great-nephew of Julius Caesar and himself a great builder of roads and cities (of Rome it was said, "He found it brick, he left it marble"), even Caesar Augustus could only enroll citizens of the Roman Empire. Still, stretching as it did in those days from the isle of Britain clear across Europe down to Northern Africa and eastward into Asia, the Roman Empire comprised almost the entire known world. The wealth and power concentrated in Caesar Augustus was considerable, so much so that the Romans considered him a god. To support this wealth and power, however, the emperor needed taxes and troops. And so it was that every fourteen years a census was taken, throughout the Empire, to see how much each citizen could pay and who was liable for military conscription.

Thus we read, "And Joseph also went up from Galilee, from the city of Nazareth, to Judea, to the city of David, which is called Bethlehem. . . ." Jews, believing as strongly as they did in their own God, were considered by the Romans too subversive to serve in the army, and so it seems Joseph must have gone up to Bethlehem solely for the purpose of enrolling as a taxpayer. The trip from Nazareth to Bethlehem was eighty miles—a long way in those days—and very arduous. People carried their own food. Inns provided only fodder for the animals and fires to cook over. When Joseph and Mary came to town no one took notice, no one helped them find a place to stay when, as it turned out, there was no room, no room in the inn even for a pregnant woman. The birth itself is recounted in all of one sentence: "And she gave birth to her first-born son and wrapped him in swaddling cloths, and laid him in a manger, because there was no room for him in the inn."

Just think: He who was to be the bread of life for human beings is laid in the feed box of animals! Had there been a Gallup poll in those days, there is no question as to who the more significant figure would have been: Caesar Augustus, the mighty emperor, or Jesus, the babe born in a manger. And yet—and what a hopeful sign for the human race this is!—while the Roman Empire is long vanished, here we are, once again celebrating the birth of Jesus.

But that may be too simple and self-serving a statement. "There was no room for him in the inn," a phrase that is so symbolic of Christ's life, may be as true today as it was then, two thousand years ago. During Christ's time on earth the only place where there was room for him was on the cross. And is there any more room for him today, in our overcrowded hearts, in our cities that can provide only temporary shelters for the homeless, in our nation where planning for nuclear war has become as American as apple pie? It might be more accurate to say that Christ's search for a place to be born, and our rejection of him—the search and the rejection both—go on today as they did then and as they probably always will.

But let's continue with the story: "And there were in that same country shepherds abiding in the fields, keeping watch over their flocks by night." "In that same country." I love the vagueness of it all. We don't know the exact grazing ground of those sheep, nor the exact spot where Jesus was born, nor, for that matter, the burial site of Moses. It is as if God knew that one day there would be Americans intent on commercializing every sacred spot in sight; it is as if he wanted to make sure that no one could ever claim that one spot on his earth was nearer heaven than another. And by the same token, no one can ever claim that one date is more sacred than another, for we don't even know the exact date of Christ's birth! My guess is that it was in the spring, since an efficient government, like the Roman one of old, would not have made people travel in midwinter in order to be enrolled. And what about the words "keeping watch over their flocks *by night*"? Shepherds only stay up all night when there are lots and lots of lambs to protect—i.e., in spring. Why, then, was December 25 chosen? Because, like lambs, Christians in those days were vulnerable. And it made sense for them to choose for their holiday the date of the oldest of Roman holidays, the one that celebrated the birth of Rome—a day when all Romans got drunk and no one would notice the little bands of Christians having their own celebration. But all this is of course only educated guesswork.

A more interesting question than "Why the date?" is "Why the shepherds?" Why should shepherds have been the first disciples? Was it perhaps that God wanted to show that all lives, like all places and all times, are equally close to him, that none is less important than another? This would make sense, for in those days shepherds were not only poor and powerless, but were actually despised by the Orthodox Jews, since, far out in the wilderness, busy with their sheep, they were unable to wash regularly or to observe the other ceremonial laws. Yet at the same time these shepherds were much depended upon by the Temple authorities, who, according to law, twice a day had to sacrifice to God an unblemished lamb. So the authorities owned herds of sheep, and with them went the shepherds. And isn't it a nice twist, that those who looked after the sacrificial Temple lambs should have been the first to see the true Lamb of God, who "taketh away the sins of the world"?

Here's another nice twist. We read, "And suddenly there was with the angel a multitude of the heavenly host praising God and saying, 'Glory to God in the highest, and on earth peace, goodwill toward men' (or, in a new translation, 'and on earth peace among those with whom God is pleased')." Whenever a child was born in ancient Palestine, it was customary for the local musicians to congregate at the child's house to sing God's praises. But when Jesus was born, no Bethlehem musician heard the news, so heavenly musicians had to take over. The first acclamations came from the very sky: a host of angels singing "Gloria in excelsis Deo." And when the angels went away what did the shepherds do? Did they sit around "shmoozing," did they nurse their doubts, did they debate the pros and cons of going to Bethlehem? No, they acted immediately. And maybe that's another reason why the revelation came to them—for their hearts were ready, their hearts were as high as the mountains among which they wandered, those lofty peaks that are always the first to hail the dawn.

Here's what impresses me most, though: when the shepherds found the babe "wrapped in swaddling cloths"—square cloths with a long bandage-like strip on one corner used to wrap the cloth around the baby—when they found the babe "lying in a manger"—probably in a cave adjacent to the inn—did the humble sight shatter their hopes, destroy their faith? No, they understood what so few of us in our day would understand, that greater than Caesar Augustus, the man worshipped as a god, was their God become man. Greater than all the armies of Caesar was this Lamb of God come to bring peace. No longer would a hostile, divided, sinful world have to seek reconciliation with a just God through the sacrifice of lambs, for "God was in Christ reconciling the world unto himself." The shepherds understood, intuitively, that "God so loved the world that he gave his only begotten son that whosoever should believe in him would not perish but have everlasting life."

Do you believe that? It is, after all, the Christmas message. And perhaps it's not so much that it's hard to believe as that it's too *good* to believe, all of us being such strangers to such goodness. But like Mary, let us keep these things, and ponder them in our hearts. Better yet, let's make room, in our overcrowded hearts, that the Christ child may be born in us today. For if we do, we may be certain that our hearts will sing glories, not once, as did the angel chorus, but for ever, and ever, and ever. A wonderful Christmas to all of you.

1984

Epiphany Lessons

JANUARY 8, 1984

Readings: Isaiah 60:1–6; Matthew 2:1–12

Today's New Testament Lesson raises a host of questions. Were they wise men or were they kings—these magi from the East? And who was it who decided their number was three and called them Caspar, Melchior, and Balthazar? Moreover, since Matthew is the only one of the four Gospel writers to record their journey, how sure can we be that it actually took place? The answer to this last question is profound, and goes something like this: "We cannot be sure, but the value of the story hardly depends on its historical accuracy. The story doesn't so much enthrone the Christ-child as the child enthrones the story."

Personally, I see the story as an offering, a work of art presented to Jesus by his disciple, the erstwhile tax collector, who in following Christ left everything behind—everything, that is, except his pen. And what a masterpiece his pen offers! Think of the truths Matthew manages to express in twelve short verses: the truth that people come from afar and by many ways to worship Christ; the truth that no place is too lowly to kneel in; the truth that as knowledge grows so also must reverence and love grow, else doubts will paralyze and too much learning dry the heart. And what of the image of the star, God's sign set high in the mystery of the night sky over Bethlehem? Doesn't it beckon to our deepest longing, which is a longing not for mother or father, or lover, or grocer or doctor, but for a savior—a longing that finally can be answered only from beyond our earth? Yet a sign is only a sign, and the choice remains ours to journey towards it or to stay stuck wherever we are.

That the choice of how to respond to a sign from God is always ours to make—that truth comes through powerfully in Matthew. Notice that although they lived only six miles north of Bethlehem, Herod and "all Jerusalem" (as Matthew refers to the witty, polished, urbane Jerusalemites who surrounded the king) never even saw the star until the strangers from distant lands pointed it out to them. I suppose they were too enamored with and blinded by their own torches and candles to see the heavenly lights. I suppose—to paraphrase Thoreau—that for every truly farseeing, wise person, there are 999 people who are merely clever and unable to see beyond their noses.

And what was the reaction of these people to the announcement of the birth of the new child? Hostility, of course—"Herod the king was troubled, and all Jerusalem as well" (Matt. 2:3). For the last thing in the world most luxury-ridden, power-hungry people want (although it is the one thing they really need) is a savior, someone to release them from their sins. It seems that among people with pretensions, the most common reaction to moral evaluation is violence; last week, those of us spending our Wednesday nights in Bible study saw another example of this phenomenon in Herodias, who demanded the head of her moral evaluator, John the Baptist.

No more surprising than Herod's hostility, though perhaps more disappointing, was the apparent indifference of the chief priests and scribes. You'd think they would have been terrifically excited at the fulfillment of the prophecy they all knew so well; you'd think they would have leapt at the chance to join the wise men on the last leg of their journey—all of six miles. But no, apparently they went back to their books. Like so many learned religious people, they preferred their faith under glass, "in vitro" rather than "in vivo."

Today, as then, there are fundamentally the same three choices before all of us: with Herod and the urbane Jerusalemites we can choose to be hostile to Christ; with the chief priests and scribes we can choose to be indifferent to him, to be devoted, shall we say, to the church but not to Christ; or with the wise men we can choose to fall on our knees and worship, offering Christ our hearts' best treasures.

I think that the adoration scene becomes even more powerful if, following a later tradition which harked back to Isaiah's prophecy— "And nations shall come to thy light, and kings to the brightness of thy rising"—we choose to see the wise men as kings, Caspar representing Europe, Melchior, Asia, and Balthazar, Africa. Picture if you will three kings, with crowns on their heads and rings on their fingers, surrounded by servants with torches leading them through the night; picture them on horseback, old Caspar on a gentle mare, young Balthazar riding a steed as white as milk. Picture three kings with all their worldly power, yet graced with the wisdom of heaven, able to see more beauty in a manger than in Herod's splendid palace, more love in that child than in the hearts of "all Jerusalem"; picture three wise kings who see around the child the shadows of death but within him the light of life.

And what symbolism there is in their royal gifts of gold, frankincense, and myrrh! Gold, of course, represents our worldly substance, our household and national budgets, which cry out these days as much as ever to be handed over, to be dedicated to Christ. Look carefully at our much-heralded economic recovery and you will see that it is accompanied by an ever-widening gap between rich and poor. And how dedicated to Christ are the added millions now requested by President Reagan to shore up the corrupt and murderous government of El Salvador? Thank God for the Salvadoran and American fasters who will be in our Cloister Lounge for the next two weeks, protesting the further torture of an already over-tortured country.

What does frankincense represent? It has come to symbolize our innermost thoughts, which along with our worldly goods need also to be dedicated to the Christ-child. Academics often talk of the "pursuit of truth" as if truth were something evasive, like a rabbit; whereas much of the time it is we who are evasive, dodging and hiding from the personal and national exposure which truth brings. Certainly the truth we see in Christ is one that searches for us, seeking to deepen our innermost thoughts and redirect them from selfish interests towards God and our neighbors.

Finally, because it is used in embalming, myrrh has come to stand for our sorrow and suffering, the hardest things, perhaps, to dedicate to Christ. When we lose someone or something near and dear to us, a child through death, a husband through a divorce, or a long and happily held job, we often turn away from God, forgetting that God's heart is probably as broken as our own. What these moments reveal is something harsh but very important, namely that we have been using God to realize our ambitions—good ambitions but ours nonetheless—rather than making ourselves available to God to fulfill his ambitions through us. If God can use our money, if God can use our innermost thoughts, how much more can he do with our suffering and our sorrow; and in handing over to him our suffering and sorrow, therein lies our best hope for healing broken hearts.

Dearly beloved, today is the last time that we shall see the trees and banners of Christmas until next year. On this Epiphany Sunday I pray that the promise, the hope, the love, and the joy that you see written on these banners may accompany you, may be in your hearts as you go forth from this church. I pray that they may inspire you and your loved ones and indeed the whole world through another year, until once again we gather to celebrate the birth of the Christ-child.

Follow Me!

JANUARY 22, 1984
Readings: Isaiah 9:1–4; Matthew 4:18–22

"Follow me, and I will make you fishers of women and men."

Once again a simple Biblical story produces a rush of complicated thoughts. "Follow me!" It's as if Jesus is saying, "Let me have just a few people, of ordinary background and no great future, and if they give themselves to me, together we'll change the world." Which of course prompts the question, "Why wait? Let's try. Let's live as if the truth were true."

"Follow me!" It's as if the first thing every would-be follower of Jesus has to do is to split from the old family homestead and business, leaving Mom holding the fish heads and Dad a defective net. Is that any way to run a fishing village, let alone to obey the fifth great commandment, to honor your father and mother?

"Follow me!" Just like that. If that's the way to live, then Socrates was wrong; it is not the unexamined but the uncommitted life that finally is not worth living. Equally wrong is Descartes: *Cogito, ergo sum*—I think, therefore I am—? Nonsense. *Amo, ergo sum*—I love, therefore I am.

But we are getting carried away on this torrent of thoughts. Let's slow down, set the scene, and proceed in more orderly fashion. Jesus utters these words "as he walked by the sea of Galilee." It's a small point, but an interesting one, that Luke, the Gentile physician who was more worldly than Matthew, always refers to the Sea of Galilee as a lake. But lake or sea, that body of water was very important, for it gave life to the entire region of Galilee. Thirteen miles long from north to south, and eight miles across, it is surrounded, now as then, by rounded hills and rugged mountains which, as one romantic observer notes, "rise and roll backward and upward to where (Mt.) Hermon hangs the picture against the blue vault of heaven." In Jesus' day there were nine populous cities along the shore. The road joining them also led northeast to Damascus and southwest to Egypt. Josephus, historian of Jews, once counted 330 fishing boats on the water. Fish, not meat, was the staple diet of families in Tiberias and Bethsaida, a town whose name literally means "house of fish" (as Bethlehem means "house of bread"). The fish were caught in two ways—by drag or trawling nets and by casting nets. The latter were circular, up to nine feet across. Around the circumference of the nets were pellets of lead and a draw rope, so that the fish could be brought into a boat or onto shore.

This, then, is the picture; and on the day in question, perhaps before the sun had really gone to work, we can imagine Peter and his brother Andrew, standing in the water, tunics tucked under their girdles, casting their nets with all the skill of cowboys tossing lassos. Passing by, Jesus says to them, "Follow me, and I will make you fishers of women and men."

Now, it is entirely possible that Peter and Andrew, as well as James and John, had heard Jesus before. In fact, in the Gospel of John it is recorded that Andrew had been a disciple of John the Baptist's when he first met Jesus. So the decision to follow may not have been totally impulsive. Moreover, we can't overlook that sense of need and expectation, that feeling inside of so many of us that says, "There must be something more"—the feeling that always is, as it were, the passport to Jesus' presence. I suspect that Peter and Andrew, James and John, were not the docile, obedient citizens whose numbers, as Orwell correctly predicted, continue to increase at a truly stupendous rate. I suspect that in contrast to so many affluent present-day New Yorkers, these four Palestinian fishermen had longings that not even bulging fishing nets could satisfy. A livelihood, after all, is not a life; and so they may have craved wider seas, their combustible hearts may have been awaiting the flame Jesus offered them as he passed by on the shore. Maybe Jesus' eagerness sparked their youth; maybe his tenderness kindled their love, his authority their loyalty. But whatever their reasons—or lack of reason, for love doesn't require a laundry list of reasons—their decision to follow Jesus represents what has come to be known as "the leap of faith." It's a wonderful expression, if understood correctly. As the case of these four fishermen demonstrates, the leap of faith is a leap of action rather than a leap of thought.

Faith is anti-clever, if we mean by cleverness that attitude which vaunts its superiority over the unlearned. But there is nothing anti-intellectual in the leap of faith, for it is not a decision to believe without proof but rather a decision to trust without reservation. Faith is no substitute for thinking, despite what some squirrel-headed preachers may pretend; on the contrary, it is what makes good thinking possible. It has what we might call a limbering effect on the mind; by taking us beyond familiar ground, faith ends up giving us that much more to think about. Certainly Peter and Andrew and James and John, in deciding to follow Jesus, received more to think about than had they stayed at home. And so it is with all of us: if we give our lives to Christ, if we leave familiar territory and take the leap of faith, what we receive in return fills our minds altogether as much as it fills our hearts.

Another point of clarification: the leap of faith, despite what some Christians think, is not a grim decision. What blue-nosed, strait-laced people forget is that, in the Gospel of John, Jesus first visits us human beings in our joy—at a wedding feast in Cana. And whether or not you believe he turned the water into wine, you do have to admit that he comes down firmly on the side of joy. Picture Peter and Andrew, James and John following Christ on his journey of boundless mercy. It would be hard not to believe that they learned not only to love more deeply and see more clearly, but also to live more fully and laugh more easily. In my observation and personal experience, there is less suffering under Christ's yoke—once you accept it, and I admit that's a big "once"—than there is under yokes of our own making: yokes of anxiety, of fear; yokes of prejudice, of hatred; yokes of decadence, of impenitence. It is often said that suffering is the true badge of the Christian, but I would submit that suffering may be more properly the true badge of the heathen, that is, of those who have deliberately cut themselves off from God.

Not that discipleship is not costly—it certainly is—but it is never a solitary suffering, a suffering without Jesus, without grace. Here are sentences of Dietrich Bonhoeffer, a modern-day martyr if there ever was one, sentences to which serious Christians can return with profit time and again:

> Grace is costly because it calls us to follow, and it is grace because it calls us to follow Jesus Christ. It is costly because it costs a man his life, and it is grace because it gives a man the only true life. It is costly because it condemns sin, and grace because it justifies the sinner. Above all, it is costly because it cost God the life of his Son. . . . Above all, it is grace because God did not reckon his Son too dear a price to pay for our life.

If all that is true, dearly beloved, why wait? Let's try. Let's live as if the truth were true. As a new year gets under way, let's once again hear and heed the words, "Follow me," and let Jesus woo and win our hearts anew—that we may live larger, deeper, more reflective, livelier lives.

But what of the second part of our text: ". . . and I will make you fishers of (women and) men"? Does that mean that we're supposed to become insistent evangelists, people who in all kinds of insensitive ways intrude upon the lives of our friends and neighbors in order to demand that they stand up and pledge allegiance to Jesus Christ as Lord? Certainly not. Good fishermen, after all, are known for their patience, their sense of timing. They know when the fish are rising, what bait is appropriate, and most of all how to make themselves as inconspicuous as possible. What, then, is evangelism? The best definition I know of this difficult concept is contained in the following: that it is one beggar telling another where he found the bread. But what does that mean? Here are some words of a wise psychologist, Robert Coles: "In this life we prepare for things, for moments and events and situations. . . . We worry about wrongs, think about injustices, read what Tolstoy or Ruskin . . . has to say. . . . Then, all of a sudden, the issue is not whether we agree with what we have heard and read and studied. . . . The issue is *us*, and what we have become."

That's always the issue, isn't it?—"us, and what we have become." In this life it's finally not what we do or don't do, think or don't think about; it's not whether politically we are conservative, liberal, radical, or whatever. Rather, it's what we have become—more generous or mean-spirited, more thoughtful or slothful, merely clever or truly wise, better company or dull as dishwater. And here's where the faith enters in, for whatever we have already become does not have to be who we might be. Once again, Christ does not seek to convert us from this life to something more than life, but from something less than life to the possibility of full life itself. As the old patriarch said, "The glory of God is a human being fully alive."

And finally, as we have a collective identity (and don't the nations abroad know it!), we have to be concerned with "us and what we have become" as a people. Melville wrote, "It lies not in your power to hang or exile the truth." But an awful lot of people in power these days are trying to do precisely that. St. Gertrude wrote, "Property, the more common it is, the more holy it is." That sounds downright un-American, but it is profoundly Christian. For didn't Christ teach that those who retain what is superfluous possess the goods of others, that the superfluities of the rich are the necessities of the poor? What does that say about our present tax structure? What does it say about an economy that allows the richest country in the world to let so many of its people go homeless, workless, foodless?

One final word. I know how many of you feel much of the time— it is the way I sometimes feel and the way, I am sure, those four fisherman of yore felt, too: "O God, my boat is so small and the sea is so large." But Christ was not daunted by modest beginnings. "Follow me,

and I will make you fishers of women and men." It's as if Jesus is saying, "Let me have but a handful of folks, of no particular background
and no great future, and if they give themselves to me, together we'll
change the world." So why wait? Let's live. The truth is true!

The Nations Are One Blood

JANUARY 29, 1984
Reading: John 8:2–11

On this Sunday, designated "International Sunday" at the request
of certain members of the congregation who have also helped
prepare the liturgy, on this Sunday it is fitting that the sermon text
should be St. Paul's ringing proclamation to the Athenians: "God has
made of one blood all the nations of the earth" (Acts 17:26).

I like the "blood" metaphor, for when you stop to think of it, each
of our bodies is a revelation of the inclusive community Paul proclaims. As the theologian James B. Nelson writes (in his book *Between
Two Gardens*):

> Each of us is made up of more than a trillion individ-
> ual cells, all attempting to work together and main-
> tain one another. Our bodies are communities with
> their own ventilation systems, sewage systems, com-
> munication systems, heating units, and a billion
> miles of interconnecting streets and alleys.
>
> Our bodies are not only communities in them-
> selves but, even more, communities in relationship
> with the earth. Our bodily fluids carry the same
> chemicals as the primeval seas. Quite literally we
> carry these seas within ourselves. Our bones contain
> the same carbon as that which forms the rock of the
> oldest mountains. Our blood contains the sugar that
> once flowed in the sap of now-fossilized trees. The
> nitrogen which binds our bones together is the same
> as that which binds nitrates to the soil.

Likewise, at their best, music, art, and literature proclaim our
human oneness. What could be more quintessentially British and at

the same time more universal than the *King Lear* that moved so many of us to tears last week on television? What could be more quintessentially German and at the same time more universally understood than the cry of Goethe's Faust: "*Augenblick, verweile doch, du bist so schön*"—"Moment, ah, linger on, thou art so fair"? What could be more quintessentially Spanish and at the same time more universally needed than the benediction given each of us by Miguel Unamuno at the end of his book, *The Tragic Sense of Life*: "May God deny you peace and give you glory"—"*Y Dios no te dé paz y si gloria*"?

And of the experience of tragedy, is it not true that when cancer eats at our vitals, when our bones become brittle and break, when genetic diseases deform innocent infants, is it not true that there is still revelation—revelation in the knowledge that this was not the way it was meant to be? Be the tragedy that of illness or of racial prejudice, be it the abuse of women and children, or the terror of war, tragedy always derives its meaning from a vision of unity and harmony. Such is the testimony of the body and the body politic to God's peace—his *shalom*—in the age to come, when "nation shall not lift up sword against nation," when "the wolf shall lie down with the lamb," when "the world shall be full of the knowledge of the Lord as the waters cover the sea."

"God has made of one blood all the nations of the earth." Black, white, yellow, red, smart and stupid, starved and stuffed, from nations large and small, whatever our creed, we all belong one to another. That's the way God made us. Christ died to keep us that way. Our sin is only and always that we are trying to put asunder what God herself has joined together.

Why *do* we? Why do the nations—as Scripture puts it—"so furiously rage together," resisting their God-given unity? The historian Herbert Butterfield gave perhaps the central reason when he wrote: "In the kind of world that I see in history, there is one sin that locks people up in all their other sins, and fastens people and nations more tightly than ever in their predicaments, namely *the sin of self-righteousness*." Certainly it affects all nations, albeit in diverse ways. The Swiss, for example, are inordinately proud of their neutrality—and rather pleased with the money that it has made them. The French still believe in their "mission civilatrice"—which often was accompanied by the Foreign Legion and today seems to include "la force frappe nucléaire." For a while, in the forties, the Germans considered themselves supermen; and in the sixties, Ghana, under Nekruma, thought its solutions were the answer to almost all African problems. The Chinese and Indians are prone to feel that the age their civilizations boast gives them a corner on the world market for wisdom; while the British, the British, well—

In the beginning, by some mistake,
Men were foreigners all created,
Till heaven conceived a nobler plan
And there was born an Englishman.

Conceive the difference, if you can,
Had Adam been an Englishman.

And to be sure, there is something perennial in the American mind which keeps returning to the thought that of all the nations on the face of the earth God smiles the most on ours. "We Americans are the peculiar, chosen people—the Israel of our time; we bear the ark of the liberties of the world. . . . Long enough have we been skeptics with regard to ourselves, and doubted whether, indeed, the political Messiah had come. But he has come in *us*, if we would but give utterance to his promptings." So wrote Herman Melville in *White Jacket*. Nor did the idea of America as God's political Messiah die with the last century. At the beginning of this one Senator Albert J. Beveridge proclaimed to his colleagues that "God . . . has marked the American people to finally lead in the redemption of the world. This is the divine mission of America. . . . We are the trustees of the world's progress, guardians of its righteous peace." Not long thereafter President Wilson assured the citizens of Cheyenne that "America had the infinite privilege of fulfilling her destiny and saving the world." Some of us remember, more recently, President Nixon's insistence during the war in Vietnam that "our beliefs must be combined with a crusading zeal, not just to hold our own but to change the world . . . and to win the battle for freedom." And just this past Wednesday night, after announcing his fourth great goal—a meaningful and lasting peace—President Reagan declared, "It is our highest aspiration. And our record is clear: Americans resort to force only when we must. We have never been aggressors. We have always struggled to defend freedom and democracy." (Tell that to Indians and Blacks, to the Mexicans, to the Nicaraguans, in whose country the Marines have landed no less than fourteen times, to the Philippinos and Puerto Ricans, the Salvadorans, the Black South Africans.)

In any nation, self-righteousness is anathema to God and disastrous to human unity, because it concentrates all attention on the sins of others. It is deaf to St. Augustine's admonition: "Never fight evil as if it were something that arose totally outside of yourself." Moreover, self-righteousness tends toward zealotry, which, by providing a nation with motives that appear to it selfless, can lead in turn to the perpetration of a kind of "redemptive" violence. Recall abolitionist John Brown and his favorite line: "Without the shedding of blood there is no remission of sins" (Heb. 9:22). Recall again last Wednesday night, whose most riveting moment had to be when President Reagan presented Sergeant Stephen Trujillo and every congressman in view of the TV camera stood up to applaud the hero—as if the whole world had not sat and watched in horror this latest example of American redemptive violence, our invasion of Granada.*

The clear and present danger today is not that we will be overcome and overrun by Communists but that we Americans will become like the exultant Pharisees, who were prepared to stone to death the woman caught in adultery. Interestingly enough, in this case, Jesus does not dispute the sin, nor the punishment of death, nor even the condemnation of only the woman when quite obviously more than one person is involved in the act of adultery. No, Jesus simply questions the right of anyone who is himself guilty to pass judgment on another: "Let him who is without sin among you cast the first stone" (John 8:7). He takes an example of conspicuous wrongdoing and uses it not to nourish self-righteousness but rather to heighten awareness of the sin common to all human beings, and of the need we all share for repentance. In repentance lies our hope, the hope that we can see the crisis today before it is validated by disaster tomorrow. Were we Americans to repent of the self-righteousness that fastens us in our predicament we would realize that if we are not yet one with the Soviets in love, at least we are one with them in sin—which is no mean bond, for it precludes the possibility of separation through judgment. That is the meaning of "Judge not, that ye be not judged" (Matt. 7:1). Were we to repent of our self-righteousness, the existence of Soviet missiles would remind us of nothing so much as our own; Soviet threats to rebellious Poles would call to mind American threats to the Sandinistas; Afghanistan would suggest Vietnam, or El Salvador. Soviet suppression of civil liberties at home would remind us of our own complicity in the repression of these same civil liberties abroad—in the Philippines, in Pakistan, in Honduras, in South Africa. Were we to repent we would drop the insidious double standard: they arm, it's evil; we arm, it's for national security. We would

---

*In 1983 President Reagan ordered invasion of Granada, a small island in the Caribbean, when its Deputy Prime Minister seized power in a coup. Along with a perceived threat to American students there, it provided an excuse to eliminate a Marxist regime allied with Cuba's Castro.

cease the self-deluding practice of judging our own motives by our political intentions, and Soviet motives by their military capabilities.

Jesus would never be "soft on communism." But I can hear him saying, "Let the nation without sin among you aim the first missile." And given Christ's far-reaching mercy, I can hear him, at some future and blessed date, addressing a repentant Soviet Union and a repentant United States with words of assurance and admonition similar to the ones he offered that sad and lonely figure a long time ago: "Neither do I condemn you. Go and build nuclear weapons . . . no more."

"God has made of one blood all the nations of the world." Yet our very efforts to deny our unity have only succeeded in making this unity all the more imperative. The present state of affairs is such that if we do not shortly become one in life, we'll all shortly be one in death.

Four hundred years ago Galileo looked into the telescope and saw that Copernicus was right: the earth is not the center of the universe, but only one modest planet revolving around its sun. Today anyone with 20/20 vision, and the humility to match, can see that no one country—no matter how glorious its past, how brilliant its future, how mighty its arms, or how generous its people—no one country is at the center of this earth. This is not the American century, nor is it the Russian century, nor will it be the Chinese century. Today, as eternally in the eyes of God, there is only one century, the human century. So, on this International Sunday, let us pledge ourselves to bringing the vision of God's peaceable Kingdom into international fruition. Let us finally learn to heed the words written so long ago:

> Come, let us go up to the mountain of Yahweh,
> to the house of the God of Jacob,
> That he may teach us his ways
> and that we may walk in his paths.
> For out of Zion shall go forth the law,
> and the word of the Lord out of Jerusalem.
> He shall judge between the nations,
> and shall decide among many peoples;
> And they shall beat their swords into ploughshares,
> and their spears into pruning hooks;
> Nation shall not lift up sword against nation,
> neither shall they learn war any more.
>
> Isa. 2:3–4

The Year of the Human

FEBRUARY 5, 1984
Reading: Matthew 5:13–16

"You are the salt of the earth."
"You are the light of the world."

I'm glad it's the Year of the Rat. Rats generally get a bum rap, especially when they show up in apartments and around small children, where they have no business being and are a genuine nuisance. But, as with so many things, there is another side to the story: rats are prolific, they get around, they move well and fast, they see in the dark as well as in the light, they never complain, they not only survive, they thrive—while eating only garbage!

Now suppose this was also the Year of the Human. Suppose that for twelve months we were to search for, find, and make credible to the world the grandeur that lies neglected within us. Suppose that for twelve months we became what in fact we are: "the salt of the earth" and "the light of the world"?

Why do we hesitate? Well, for one thing, some of us consider ourselves luckless—the kind of people who would receive in the mail two complimentary tickets for a voyage on the *Titanic*. Others consider ourselves trapped in emotional alleys, with all the exits blocked; and when it comes to political matters, we let ourselves believe that every exit from one dilemma is merely an entrance to another. In a world of fast cars and big bombs, crime and worldwide hunger, we throw up our hands and say: "What is the use? What difference can I make? Pop, you're a dime a dozen—and so am I." Sometimes our lives seem little more than litter bins for wasted time.

To feel that way is altogether understandable and just as inexcusable. How dare we so easily forget that we are "fearfully and wonderfully made," yes, set only "a little lower than the angels"? And if God has made us and Christ has redeemed us, then each of us is utterly unprecedented, unrepeatable, and, in the divine dispensation, indispensable.

For Jesus to say to his disciples, "You are the salt of the earth" was like saying, "You are pure gold," for in the absence of ice, salt was the only preservative around. "*Nil utilus sole et sale*," went the Roman saying, "Nothing is more useful than sun and salt." To be the salt of the earth, then, was to be the declared enemy of decay and death.

But salt also seasons, lends flavor to everything it touches. What a travesty of Christianity it is whenever preachers and their congregations represent flavorless mediocrity: the bland leading the bland. Oliver Wendell Holmes once said: "I might have entered the ministry if certain clergymen I knew had not looked and acted so much like undertakers." (No offense to undertakers, who are quite a jolly lot off the job.) And Robert Louis Stevenson wrote in his diary, as if recording an extraordinary phenomenon: "I have been to church today, and am not depressed."

And finally, because it came from the sun and from the sea, and because it lay along the shore glistening white, salt was a symbol of purity; a symbol of the kind of love that no more wants to harm a neighbor than oneself; a symbol of the kind of freedom that is ready, when necessary, to sacrifice possessions and any amount of time; a symbol of a childlike joy in light and color, in all that God is and gives, for God is a pleasure-loving and pleasure-giving God. In Exodus we read that when Moses came down from Mount Sinai, "he wist not that his face shone" (Exod. 34:29). That's the kind of unconscious purity that is the mark of the true believer. "You are the salt of the earth"— its preserver, its seasoning, and its purity.

We need not belabor the symbol of light, "God's first creature." Lights warn, lights guide, lights beckon. When Jesus said, "You are the light of the world," he was stressing the brightness of light, the visibility of a disciple's faith. It has well been said that "there can be no such thing as secret discipleship, for either the secrecy destroys the discipleship, or the discipleship destroys the secrecy."

"Let your light so shine before others that they may see your good works. . . ." But if you stand in your own light you fight your own shadows forever. So Jesus goes on to say, ". . . and give the glory to God who is in heaven." It's wonderful how free you are to enjoy the good things you do when you don't have to take credit for them!

Now I want to mention a few of the many people—some of them here at Riverside—who remind me of what the human heart can do and bear, people who, by their lives, preserve, season, and purify the earth. I start with a young woman lawyer, a recent graduate of the Harvard Law School, clerk of a well-known judge, who has declined an offer to join—shall we call the firm "Airedale, Airedale, Whippet and Pug"?—and instead today defends children through the office of Manhattan Legal Aid. With a caseload of up to one hundred clients at a time, she has chosen a punishingly difficult sphere of activity. And I know another lawyer, an older man, who did join a prestigious law firm (as the world measures these things), but who refuses to tiptoe around, as do so many senior partners, and whose Christian faith has led him to Nicaragua and now leads him to tell all and sundry his opinion about that ill-fated country and our involvement there: Americans can adapt to change or seek to resist it, but even with Marines we can never prevent it. I think of people who work in the Riverside clothing room, in the food pantry, the library, the shelter. And I think of some of the homeless people themselves, who remind me of kittiwakes nesting on a sheer cliff, people who have found a preposterous niche in a hard life and don't complain one little bit. I think of the courage of the Blacks, whose pictures, commemorating Black History Month, can be seen today in the Cloister Lounge, thanks to the Black Christian Caucus. I think of mothers—and some fathers—who like trees live calmly, quietly, silently pouring forth life and bringing forth fruit, mothers who bear out the truth in the slogan, "Every mother is a working mother." I think of a Gay member of this church—another lawyer—who works pro bono long night hours helping AIDS victims draw up wills, often at their bedside, and often holding the pen and guiding it when the victims have become too weak or blind to hold it themselves.

How can we not draw inspiration and support from such followers of Christ? How can we not draw it, too, from some non-Christians, such as a Buddhist monk I know, who vowed for one month to talk about the perils of the arms race to everyone he met—including long-distance operators! I tell you we need more of this kind of spirit if we are going to save the flesh. I tell you our spirits are deflated by having to do too much of what we do not love to do. Inspired by the Holy Spirit, our spirits demand that we do more of those things that are beyond the reach of money and selfish advantage. We are the salt of the earth and the light of the world, and it's just too boring to be anything else!

One final thought: It takes only a pinch of salt to season a dish. It takes only a ray of light to reveal the depths of the surrounding darkness. Had there been ten righteous people the whole of Sodom would have been saved. Eleven disciples sufficed to start the Christian church. So what do you say? Let's preserve, season, and purify this earth of untold beauty and unrelieved grief. Let's make 1984 the Year of the Human as well as of the Rat. Let's search for, find, and make credible to the world the grandeur that lies neglected within us. For we are the salt of the earth and the light of the world. Praise the Lord!

Lincoln's Birthday

FEBRUARY 12, 1984
Reading: Psalm 19

In that rare year when Lincoln's birthday falls on a Sunday, it seems right that in the United States sermons be given recalling the president who, more than any other, stands at the spiritual center of American history.

His official duty as president, Lincoln knew, was to preserve the Union, but his deepest personal wish was that all people everywhere might be free. In his youth he argued against slavery in the light of "self-evident truths," but in his later presidential years he fought it in terms of a Biblical understanding of work. To the Baptists of the Home Missionary Society he wrote:

> To read in the Bible, as the word of God himself, that "In the sweat of thy face thou shalt eat bread," and to preach therefrom that "In the sweat of other men's faces shalt thou eat bread," to my mind can scarcely be reconciled with honest sincerity. When brought to my final reckoning, may I have to answer for robbing no man of his goods; yet more tolerable even this, than for robbing one of himself, and all that he was. When, a year or two ago, those professedly holy men of the South, met in semblance of prayer and devotion, and, in the name of Him who said, "As ye would all men should do unto you, do ye even so unto them," appealed to the Christian world to aid them in doing to a whole race of men, as they would have no man do unto themselves, to my thinking, they condemned and insulted God and His church, far more than did Satan when he tempted the Savior with the Kingdoms of the earth. The devil's attempt was no more false, and far less hypocritical. But let me forbear, remembering it is also written "Judge not, lest ye be judged."

No American president has had a clearer vision of God's will and a more unself-righteous perspective on himself. No American president has been more attuned to the pain and the sorrow tearing at the life of his people. And no citizen of this country—and I bear in mind Jonathan Edwards and Reinhold Niebuhr—no citizen of this country has interpreted more eloquently this sorrow and this pain in the light of the great Biblical motifs of judgment, punishment, justice, mercy, and reconciliation. (Let us remember, when we hear Lincoln referring to the Bible as he so frequently does, that the people of his day read the Bible far more than people do today, and that Lincoln never used the Bible except to be inclusive of all citizens.) Biblical judgment— "The sins of the fathers are visited upon the sons and unto their children's children" (Exod. 34:7)—says that life is consequential, that we cannot escape history, that the world swings on an ethical hinge: loosen that hinge, and all history and even nature will feel the shock; it says that individuals and nations do not so much break the Ten Commandments as they are broken upon them, for, in the words of Saint Paul, "God is not mocked." All this Abraham Lincoln knew better than most, and he said it without that pomposity that has nothing to do with the Christian faith. Rather he spoke with humor, which has much to do with the faith, for while the faith takes care of the ultimate incongruities of life, humor does nicely with the intermediate ones. More than that: by helping to destroy the illusion of our control over life, humor opens us up to the realization of God's governance.

Like so many of you in the '60s and early '70s, I went time and again to Washington to protest the war in Vietnam. It was a duty but not a pleasant one. And while these demonstrations were rightly viewed by many as an exercise in democracy, somehow they left me strangely depressed. To raise my spirits at day's end, I generally stole away for a few quiet moments at the Lincoln Memorial. I didn't know then that Lincoln's relationship to Blacks was not quite what I hoped it was; nor did I know that he never really came to terms with his humble origins, that he was a bit of a social climber, a bit harsh on his father. But those shortcomings would not have mattered to me at that time. For I went to the Lincoln Memorial knowing that when he was in the House of Representatives, Lincoln, too, had protested a war, the war against Mexico, describing it in terms that I felt were proper also for the war in Vietnam, as "unnecessary and unconstitutional"—and I knew that those words had cost him his congressional seat. And I went because of what I felt the memorial itself conveys. Unlike many other American heroes commemorated in Washington, Lincoln is not pictured astride a rearing stallion. Unlike Jefferson, he's not even standing: he's sitting, for heaven's sake—sitting in an old armchair. Yet all the depth and grandeur are there, all the greatness that undoubtedly was his after he had grown from an average self-centered small-town politician—albeit one of unsuspected talents—to a statesman of world stature.

There was a story told in Lincoln's time of a man asking the pilot of a Mississippi riverboat how long he had been plying his trade.

"Twenty-six years," the pilot replied.

"Then," said the man, "you know where all the rocks are, all the shoals and sandbars."

"No," said the pilot. "I just know where they ain't."

And that's where Lincoln consistently tried to steer our ship of state: out there in the deep waters, far from the sandbars of party sectarianism, the rocks of tribalistic chauvinism. That is why in ending slavery he was equally concerned for the slaveholders: "In giving freedom to the slave, we assure freedom to the free—honorable alike in what we give, and what we preserve." That is why, when the Civil War was drawing to a close, Lincoln came out so cleanly for amnesty. Like any sensible man he feared anarchy on the one hand as he did despotism on the other, and his legal training enhanced his respect for the law. Yet he pushed hard against the legal limits when laws seemed to him unjust, and when wisdom, rooted in compassion, revealed to him that human relations are finally just that—human, not contractual. As "the Sabbath belongs to man, not man to the Sabbath," so Lincoln understood the law to be a good servant but a bad master. As a result, not a single soldier or officer who wore the gray—not even those like Robert E. Lee who had once worn the blue—not a single confederate was punished for breaking the law of the land. Of the states that had seceded Lincoln said, "Finding them safely at home, it would be utterly immaterial whether they had ever been abroad."

His ability to keep the ship of state in deep waters, to see big issues in a big way, was aided by an unrelenting willingness to question. I think it fair, and in a church important, to say that because Lincoln doubted the formulation of certain creeds and catechisms he became more deeply aware of the realities they were meant to represent. "Probably it is my lot," he wrote as a young man, "to go on in a twilight, feeling and reasoning my way through life, as questioning doubting Thomas did. But in my poor, maimed way, I bear with me, as I go on, a seeking spirit of desire for a faith that was with him of olden times, who, in his need, as I in mine, exclaimed, 'Help thou my unbelief.'"

Because he refused to be dogmatic, and because he knew how selfish human beings can be even as they claim to be the very opposite, Lincoln abhorred self-righteousness. After reading several dispatches from young General McClellan, all of which began, "Headquarters: in the saddle," Lincoln remarked to the members of his cabinet, "It's strange how the general keeps his headquarters where most people prefer to put their hindquarters." Even more trying than his generals was the self-righteousness of the clergy, who visited him in droves. After the departure of a particularly obnoxious delegation, Lincoln turned to an aide and told him the story of a small boy who sculpted a beautiful church out of mud, a church replete with pews and pulpit. When asked, "Where's the preacher?" the boy replied, "I ran out of mud."

For the most part, the clergy were pressing for an immediate abolition of slavery in all the states and territories. But although he had detested slavery since childhood, Lincoln's dilemma was real: as president he had taken an oath of office to uphold the Constitution, which provided for slavery, at least in the original thirteen states. (Scholars question whether the Emancipation Proclamation was in fact warranted by the Constitution, as Lincoln claimed it was.) Because he was willing to maintain tension, no matter how painful, Lincoln was sensitive to the dilemmas of others, particularly the one tormenting the Quakers. What were they to do, opposed as they were to both war and oppression, when war seemed to be the only way to abolish the oppression?

But although he questioned creedal formulations, and was sharply aware both of the mixture of human motivations and the complexities of history, Lincoln never for a moment doubted the word of the psalmist that "the judgments of the Lord are true and righteous altogether." He doubted whether these judgments could be mechanistically applied from outside, as the clergy frequently suggested, but he was certain that they would always be enacted organically within history, for—once again—"God is not mocked."

To read the Lincoln-Douglas debates is to hear Lincoln expound American history as would a Biblical prophet, the plumb line being morality rooted in the righteous will of God. He appreciates the dilemma faced by the founders of the Republic: unity with slavery, or the abolition of slavery and no Republic—at least not one comprised of thirteen states. Choosing unity, as they did, of course did not solve the dilemma, but left a moral poison in the bloodstream of American life. By prohibiting the extension of slavery to the Northwest Territories in the Ordinance of 1787, our forbears had at least put slavery, as Lincoln saw it, "in course of ultimate extinction," a principle, he argued, that had remained intact despite the Missouri Compromise of 1820, reaffirmed in 1850. But now Senator Douglas was proposing that "popular sovereignty"—the settlers themselves—should decide the question of slavery in Kansas and Nebraska. That, said Douglas, was the democratic way. Answered Lincoln, "This declared indifference, but as I must think, covert real zeal for the spread of slavery, I cannot but hate. I hate it because of the monstrous injustice of slavery itself." As to the argument of self-government, he said, "If the negro is not a man, why in that case, he who is a man may as a matter of self-government, do just as he pleases with him. But if the negro is a man, is it not to that extent a total destruction of self-government, to say that he too shall not govern himself? When the white man governs himself, and also governs another man, that is more than self-government, that is despotism. . . . No man is good enough to govern another man, without that other's consent. I say this is the leading principle—the sheet anchor of American republicanism."

To guard against self-righteousness Lincoln describes the problem as national rather than regional: "They"—southern whites, that is—"are just what we would be in their situation. If slavery did not now exist amongst them, they would not introduce it. If it did exist amongst us, we would not instantly give it up. This I believe of the masses north and south." Because in these debates Lincoln called forth "the better angels of our nature," at least in part for that reason, I like to think he was elected President.

Then came the Civil War, during which he promised, "I shall do nothing in malice. What I deal with is too vast for malicious dealing." The way he interpreted this horrendous event in the light of the great Biblical motifs of judgment, punishment, justice, mercy, and reconciliation confirms his place at the spiritual center of American history. You remember the Second Inaugural; quoting from the eighteenth chapter of Matthew he says:

> "Woe unto the world because of offenses! For it must needs be that offenses come; but woe to that man by whom the offense cometh!" If we shall suppose that American slavery is one of those offenses which, in the providence of God, must needs come, but which, having continued through His appointed time, He now wills to remove, and that He gives to both North and South, this terrible war, as the woe due to those by whom the offense came, shall we discern therein any departure from those divine attributes which the believers in a Living God always ascribe to Him? Fondly do we hope, fervently do we pray, that this mighty scourge of war may speedily pass away. Yet, if God wills that it continue, until all the wealth piled by the bond-man's two hundred and fifty years of

unrequited toil shall be sunk, and until every drop of blood drawn with the lash, shall be paid by another drawn with the sword, as was said three thousand years ago, so it must be said again "the judgments of the Lord are true and righteous altogether."

With malice toward none; with charity for all, with firmness in the right, as God gives us to see the right, let us strive on to finish the work we are in, to bind up the nation's wounds, to care for him who shall have borne the battle, and for his widow, and his orphan, to do all which may achieve and cherish a just and lasting peace among ourselves and with all nations.

I hope many Americans will take time today and tomorrow to think of the pain and sorrow still tearing at the life of our nation. The way we conduct ourselves at home and abroad indicates how far we have strayed from our spiritual center. But if America has lost her way, I feel confident she will find it again. Because we once elected a president who knew so clearly that he stood under the living God of history, I feel certain that the American people will one day again fit the description he gave us—"God's almost chosen people"—if only, like him, we would seek to build our nation life on the bedrock of Scriptural faith.

"Love Your Enemies"

FEBRUARY 19, 1984
Reading: Matthew 5:38–48

Before digging into this most difficult and powerful of Biblical passages, let us pause to note Jesus' audacity, or else his sheer inner authority—one or the other—in daring to reinterpret something as sacred to the ancient Jewish mind as was the Mosaic law. "You have heard it said. . . . But I say unto you." This may just be one of those instances where you have to make up your mind: either Jesus is arrogance incarnate, or he is indeed the Son of God.

But let us then go on to recognize that in reinterpreting ancient laws (laws with either a capital or a small "l") Jesus was in no way discounting their importance. The one thing neither nature nor the human race can tolerate is chaos; to survive we need some semblance of law and order. Said Martin Luther King Jr.: "You can't force them to love us, but you can stop them from lynching us." It is all too true, however, that in recent years the noble concepts of law and order have been demeaned by political officials promoting order for themselves at the expense of justice for others. Several months ago Secretary of State George Schultz declared that we would never allow the Salvadoran rebels to "shoot their way into the government." Not only did his words cause Thomas Jefferson, Benjamin Franklin, and George Washington to raise from the grave a collective eyebrow, but they mistakenly implied that peaceful methods in El Salvador today were synonymous with democracy, while the armed insurrection was somehow undemocratic. Clearly this is not the case; clearly, in that long-suffering country, peaceful methods are instruments of domination, repression, and control. But the case of El Salvador, sad as it is, does not argue that people should do away with laws, only that all laws should seek to incorporate more and more justice. For human beings to survive, law and order are indispensable. Once again: "You can't force them to love us, but you can stop them from lynching us."

But beyond human survival is human well-being, and that is something which demands the very love that Dr. King rightly saw could not be forced. We are talking here of a love that goes beneath the law to address the question of motivation; a love that goes between the law, filling the inevitable cracks; a love that in its unconditional form of forgiveness goes beyond the law and even beyond justice. Maybe that's why, paradoxically, Jesus used the imperative form for the very thing that cannot be commanded—"*Love* your enemies," "*Pray* for those who persecute you." He knew what he was asking for: nothing less than unachievable perfection. He knew that while laws may be irritating, love is far more demanding. Most of all, he knew that we must love our enemies, and not for their sake alone, but for ours as well. Hatred simply has no place in the lives of children of a God as loving as the mother and father of us all. If God has ordained that love is the name of the game, then hate is a wound in the order of being. Better by far that our hearts be broken than that they be hardened.

Obviously, in real life, we can't prevent occasional wicked thoughts about others from coming to mind, and a few such thoughts may actually be healthy. There's truth in the saying, "A thought-murder a day keeps the psychiatrist away." But when wicked thoughts come, we don't have to invite them to supper, we don't have to ask them to spend the night, we don't have to insist that they move in and live with us. If you have any wicked thoughts living in your apartment or home, show them the door. For hate, spiritually speaking, is devastating. It is a diminishing emotion. It shrivels us up, making us inmates in prison-houses of our own spirits.

"Pray for those who persecute you." Persecution is a terrible thing, whether it is deliberate or the result of something as impersonal as the vast carelessness of the rich. Not for a moment did Jesus deny the cruelty and unfairness of persecution, and he fought it at every turn. In the cases of some of us I'm sure he'd wonder if the power of others to do us harm wasn't exceeded by our own capacity to be hurt—but let's leave that discussion for another day. "Pray for those who persecute you" is an admonition that sin can only be cancelled by intercession and forgiveness. It reminds us that whatever cannot be condoned is precisely that which must be forgiven.

"If anyone strikes you on the right cheek, turn the other also." This doesn't mean, however, that we're supposed to be doormats for others to walk on with hobnailed boots. It's my experience that people seldom want to walk over you until you lie down, so it's better to stay standing. Turning the other cheek means, "Be a lightning rod, ground the hostility." When you are insulted, call the other's attention to the hurt, but do not retaliate in kind. Try—and believe me, it is hard—try not even to resent it; for our job is to get *to* each other, not *at* each other. You know as well as I do that when enmities dim, lives glow all the stronger.

I know something about the frenzied longings for revenge. I know how hard it is to put hurts to good use, to turn sighs into songs. And I know it's hard not to be resentful, especially when you've been beaten, mugged, raped, divorced, or fired, and you feel powerless to retaliate. You feel the misery of powerlessness. When Lord Acton came up with his famous maxim, "Power tends to corrupt, and absolute power corrupts absolutely," he should have added: "And by the way, powerlessness too tends to corrupt, and absolute powerlessness corrupts absolutely." And the corruption of powerlessness is bitterness, the hardness of heart we are addressing this morning.

What can you do? Remember that Christ never allowed his soul to be cornered into despair. Remember that impersonating power is the most grueling form of servitude. Remember Othello: "Thou hast not half that power to do me harm as I have to be hurt." Remember St. Augustine: "Imagine the vanity of thinking that your enemy can do you more damage than your enmity." Remember again Jesus: "Love your enemies and pray for those who persecute you"—not for their sake alone; but for ours as well. For either we love or we die.

I meet quite often these days with pastors, and in any group of pastors there's always one who says, "I'm no great prophet, I don't take on public issues, but I'm a pretty good pastor." Every time I hear that I wince, because I know it isn't true. For how can you be a good pastor and not realize how bad the Cold War is for warm Christian hearts? How can you be a good pastor without taking on the homophobia that is a thorn in the flesh of the church?

"Love your enemies, pray for those who persecute you." This certainly includes the Russians, who are our enemies in large part because we make them so. To love them does not mean to ignore Soviet cruelties, for love includes judgment as well as tenderness. But let us not forget what our leaders constantly fail to remind us, that Russians are fellow human beings, that they breathe, they bleed, they mourn their parents and dream for their children, just as we do. What then does it mean to love the Russians? In the first place, love spells reason, not hysteria. Love means positive Christiantiy, not negative anticommunism. Love means the lifting of a mental roadblock, the clear understanding that an evil act is no absolute barrier to a continuing relationship. Dr. King understood what foreign relations should be all about when he said, "Returning hate for hate multiplies hate, adding deeper darkness to a night already devoid of stars. Darkness cannot drive out darkness; only light can do that. Hate cannot drive out hate; only love can do that."

We live in a night lit by so few stars that we are forced to ask: "Will humankind survive?" To which the answer is: "Who knows?" But the more significant, searching question is: "Who cares? Do we care enough for posterity to pay the price of its survival?"

I know how gallantly so many of you deal with the hurts and other hardships of your lives. You remind me of Emily Dickinson's verses:

> To fight aloud is very brave
> But gallanter, I know
> Who charge within the bosom
> The cavalry of woe.

Would that all of us could handle our woe as some of you do. And, as a matter of fact, we all of us could, if we would but "let go, and let God." And we could deal with the woe of the world if we would only take on the love of Christ which is there for the having. But our faith must be lived, not enshrined. The driving force of our lives must be an ardent love for all human beings, including our enemies. "Love your enemies. Pray for those who persecute you." Christians are called on to out-love, out-pray, out-live, and out-die all others, as did our beloved Lord and Savior. The only road to peace within and among ourselves lies through that love which once walked the earth, in whose name we are again gathered here today.

The Transfiguration

MARCH 4, 1984
Reading: Matthew 17:1–9

There are certain stories in the Bible I avoid as I would an eye transplant—at least for purposes of preaching. Reading them, I am reminded of the words of the psalmist: "Such knowledge is too wonderful for me; it is high, I cannot attain unto it" (Ps. 139:6), I cannot make the intellectual and the spiritual come together. Moreover, while most Biblical stories come at you with clear, clean contemporary implications (although the further you wade in, the deeper the water), these other stories seem to recede into the uncertain mists of antiquity. One such story is the raising of Lazarus; another is the transfiguration of Christ.

But the lectionary we have been following since Advent, that is, a fixed selection of readings taken from both the Old and the New Testaments, the inclusive language lectionary of the National Council of Churches rightly places the story of the Transfiguration on the Sunday before Ash Wednesday. So, rather than dive down the nearest rabbit hole, let's see what we can do with it.

Matthew's account begins, "And after six days . . ." What was it that happened six days earlier? In the district of Caesarea Philippi, Jesus had asked, "Who do people say that I am?" To which his disciples had answered, "Some say John the Baptist, others Elijah, and still others Jeremiah or one of the prophets." But when Jesus asked, "And who do you say that I am?" Simon Peter replied, "You are the Christ, the Son of the living God."

It must have been as music to the ear of an anguished Jesus, to hear this confession of Peter's: at last somebody had recognized him for who and what he was!

But before going on with the story, let us note once again that whenever we say with Peter, "You are the Christ," we are not saying that God is confined to Christ, only that God is most essentially defined by Christ. In watching Jesus healing the wounded, empowering the weak, and scorning the powerful, we are seeing transparently the power of God at work. So when we talk of the divinity of Jesus, it is well to recall that what is important is not that Christ is God-like, but rather that God is Christ-like. Moreover, to say of Jesus, "You are the Christ," is to say that he is the Rosetta stone of life, making clear the hieroglyphics of history; or, to use another analogy, that he is the main theme that makes symphonic sense of all the variations we hear about us.

But the music that Peter's confession was to the ear of Jesus soon transposed itself into a melancholy minor key. For no sooner had Jesus predicted his passion, no sooner had he shown his disciples that the Son of God must go to Jerusalem and suffer many things from the elders and chief priests and scribes and be killed, than Peter began to rebuke him, saying, "God, forbid, Lord! This shall never happen to you" (16:22). This misunderstanding of Messiahship on Peter's part, although discouraging, is understandable. For Peter can no more bear the thought that the world will not reward Christ for being Christ, than we can tolerate the prospect that the world will not reward us for being Christian. So the six subsequent days are spent telling Peter and the other disciples something more about the nature of this sinful world. While there is no harm in following Jesus, there is great danger: "If any man would come after me, let him deny himself and take up his cross and follow me" (16:24). The feast to which we, his followers, are all invited on this Communion Sunday, is no picnic. An active faith is sure to arouse official discontent. Faith does not diminish the risks, it engenders the courage to take them on—all of them—recognizing that it is not those who inflict the most (à la American foreign policy) but those who suffer the most, in Christ-like fashion, who will inherit the earth.

Now, having settled with his disciples the meaning of Messiahship and discipleship, Jesus, torn in soul, needs to hear from God that this decision of his to set his face toward Jerusalem and certain death is indeed in accord with divine will. I think that this is a fair reading of Jesus' motives, for in Luke's version it is written, "he went up on the mountain to pray" (Luke 9:28).

The mountain in all likelihood was Mt. Hermon, whose stately slopes rising 11,000 feet above the Jordan Valley can, on a day as clear as this one, be seen from the Dead Sea over a hundred miles to the South. Jesus took with him Peter and James, and James' brother John, and—as we read—"he was transfigured before them, and his face shone like the sun, and his garments became white as light."

Moses too, you remember, went up on a high mountain—Mt. Sinai—and when he returned it is written that "he wist not that his face shone." To enter, as did Moses and Jesus, into the presence of God, to stand "in the white, windy presence of eternity," to hear the word of God from God himself—surely such an experience of divine revelation must awake in a person's face such life as never shone from there before. And we all know how the radiance of a person's face can seem to change the very appearance of his clothes.

"And behold, there appeared to them Moses and Elijah." Is it fact or myth, miracle or metaphor? I don't know. All I know is that Moses and Elijah are the twin peaks in Israel's landscape, the one the greatest lawgiver in her history, the other the greatest of her prophets. Were they there representing benedictions from the past? Were they there to bless Jesus' heartrending decision, to say to him before his death what the Roman centurion said immediately thereafter: "Surely, this was the Son of God"?

And then, even as poor impulsive Peter is making the most inept of suggestions—"Lord, . . . if you wish, I will make three booths here, one for you, and one for Moses, and one for Elijah" ("inept" because moments of transfiguration do not exist for their own sake, but rather to "clothe uncommon moments with a radiance they never had before"; "inept" because high moments in life can only be enshrined in memory, never frozen in place)—even as Peter is speaking, a luminous cloud descends on Mt. Hermon, just as a cloud had overshadowed Moses on Mt. Sinai. And a voice from the cloud says just what the voice said at the time of Jesus' baptism in the river Jordan: "This is my beloved Son, with whom I am well pleased." Only this time the voice addresses the disciples as well, for it adds, "Listen to him."

Truly a wondrous moment. And if the details are elusive, the clarity of direction and the energy released by this intense experience of God's presence are easy to imagine. They carried Christ through his passion and his crucifixion. After his death, the scene must have returned time and again to Peter's anxious mind, returned as a light shining in the dark, disclosing Christ's glory through the shame, his triumph through the humiliation, his crown beyond the cross. For it took Peter as long as it takes most of us to grasp the tragedy that stands at the heart of the Christian faith, the paradox that Jesus of Nazareth, this glorious human being, with God—as John proclaims—from the creation of the world, came to earth to be killed by the very people he came to save. Who wants to believe the world so cruel that our inhumanity to one another is surpassed only by our inhumanity to God? And it took even longer for Peter to find the courage to pay the cost of discipleship to such a Messiah.

The more I think of it, the more convinced I am that the transfiguration of Christ must have helped as much as any other experience to transfigure Peter himself.

The question now is, can the story serve us as well? I think it can; I think it must. The economist/philosopher Robert Heilbroner once defined inertia, as "doing just that thing you know how to do." Late last night I came back from Sheridan, Wyoming—MX missile country—where it is clearer than in most places that for the world to avoid horrors worse than hell people are going to have to do more than just that thing they know how to do; they are going to have to extend themselves. Most of us live in this city, a city of every conceivable form of brutality, where women are beaten by men who once were children beaten by their fathers and mothers; a city demoralized by idleness, where to most people love appears as another form of luxury. Well, for this potentially glorious city to be humanized, people are going to have to extend themselves. Most of us, likewise, are citizens of this country; that is to say, people who in regard to the arms race feel that somehow, somewhere, a fail-safe mechanism will save us, people who in regard to domestic politics consider it more important that entrepreneurs enjoy the fruits of their initiatives than that the widows and orphans be fed. To make our beloved but hard-hearted country more tenderhearted, people are going to have to extend themselves. And who are the people to do God's work and take the risks if not Christians inspired by the radiance that streams from Christ's face as he stands on the slopes of Mt. Hermon; Christians who see in the luminous cloud descending upon Mt. Sinai and upon Mt. Hermon the answer to the cloud mushrooming up from the earth; Christians, people like you and me, who can once again, across the centuries, hear and heed the voice from the cloud saying, "This is my beloved son, with whom I am well pleased; *listen to him*"?

In Christianity you don't surrender your power to Christ; you receive Christ's power from him. Christ became like us that we might become like him. Therefore the miraculous transfiguration of Christ spells the transfiguration of all of us. On this Sunday before Ash Wednesday, let us resolve to preserve and proclaim our faith in the only way possible, by fulfilling her promises. May God grant a transfiguration—miraculous as Christ's—to each and every one of us.

Temptations

MARCH 11, 1984
Readings: Genesis 2:15–3:7; Luke 4:1–13

I was delighted to hear Fanny Erickson end her reading of the story of Adam and Eve with these words: "Thus ends the reading of the Old Testament lesson, in which the woman chooses consciousness." I thought it was a sassy and perceptive bit of feminism. "Perceptive" because in the temptation story of the "Second Adam," as St. Paul in First Corinthians calls Christ, it is the Spirit that leads Jesus into the solitude of the wilderness, into a privation and vulnerability that Eve too must have felt as she was being driven from the garden. Gone now, for both, are the security and comforts of home. Both now are in pain. And where but in deepest pain do we have a better opportunity to come to fullest consciousness? It is well to remember that pain, better even than pleasure, has the capacity to make us fully aware of life; and it might well be said: No cross of pain, no crown of consciousness.

Human beings are the only elements in this world of ours whom the world does not explain. "A rose is a rose is a rose," and a skylark's a skylark, the poet's protest notwithstanding. But who are we human beings? Who are we as a race and as individual members of that race? These, I confess, are questions demanding such painful honesty that I'd just as soon avoid them, were it not for the conviction that in avoiding them, I betray the race and forego my humanity. We are young only once, but we can be immature forever by nourishing a blind life within the brain because we haven't the courage to confront the conflicts of the heart.

It is these eternal conflicts of the heart that constitute the drama to which we return each year at the beginning of Lent. "And Jesus full of the Holy Spirit returned from the Jordan, and was led by the Spirit for forty days in the wilderness, tempted by the devil." Just as the waters of the Jordan divide the Holy Land, so they bisect the Holy Life. Jesus' baptism in the Jordan ends the long peace of Nazareth, which is exchanged for a life of struggle that begins with the devil and is consummated on the cross.

Some of you are going to find this hard to believe, but nevertheless it is true: in every congregation, no matter how devout, there are always one or two people who do not believe in the devil. So allow me, for the benefit of those few, to recall in succinct fashion four facts of satanic life: 1) The mystery of evil is symbolized by a person—the devil—because the reality of evil is experienced as personal power; 2) Satan is given a separate identity, not because evil arises totally outside of ourselves, but because evil is experienced as something bigger than ourselves (as St. Paul said memorably, "The good that I would I do not, and that which I would not, that I do"); 3) because evil does not arise, as our parents taught us, in our so-called "lower" nature but rather in our "higher" nature—in that which separates human beings from roses and skylarks—because evil arises in the realm of freedom, the devil is always pictured as a fallen angel; and 4) rarely does Satan suggest that we do anything bad; Eve, after all, only took the apple when she saw that it was "good for food, pleasing to the eye, and much to be desired to make people wise" (Gen. 3:6).

With those facts firmly in mind, let us now proceed to the first of the three temptations: "And he ate nothing in those days; and when they were ended, he was hungry. The devil said to him, 'If you are the son of God, command this stone to become bread.'"

Some commentators contend that the temptation here is merely to use selfishly the special powers which Jesus must have sensed were uniquely his. The devil is saying to him, in effect, "Look, during baptism, didn't you hear the voice of God telling you that you were his beloved Son? So act accordingly. If God, who rained manna on the children of Israel when they were in the wilderness, who so sent ravens to feed Elijah and even an angel to prepare him a cake, now leaves you to pine and hunger among these heaps of dust, to walk on ground that glows with heat like a vast furnace, then act for yourself! You have the power; why not turn the stone into bread? What's so wrong with that?"

And we might all echo Satan—What *is* so wrong?—we, who spend most of our working hours making bread, in both senses of the word, and aren't even hungry. If it is wrong for starving Jesus to make bread, what does that say about us, who have enough, who have *too much*, some of us, and altogether too many rationalizations for our wealth. (For instance, if the rights of children in the Third World to adequate nutrition conflict with the rights of corporations to choose which crops to grow on which land in that same Third World, we know which rights to acknowledge as overriding—the corporations' rights, of course. At least, that's the way we in this country behave.)

All of which makes me think that the devil's temptation is far subtler. The appeal is not to selfishness, but rather to justice. I think the devil says something like this: "Look, Jesus, you're hungry, and so are a lot of people in this country where only a fifth of the land is arable under the best of conditions. Moreover, there's precious little equity in this nation, plagued as it is by droughts, floods, and Roman legions. Didn't the prophet say, 'Let justice roll down like mighty waters'? How in God's name are you going to stand there and say 'I am the bread of life' to a bunch of starving people?"

Now there's a *real* temptation, to which we can only fervently wish more people would succumb, especially in this country where civil and political rights are accorded a degree of legal authenticity far greater than are the moral rights of subsistence: the right to adequate food, adequate clothing, adequate shelter, clean air, clean water, and minimal preventative public health care.

If it be the will of God that justice roll down like mighty waters, then why is the call to justice a temptation? It isn't, in many cases. And when our society sees that moral rights of subsistence are just that— moral rights—they will become legal rights. But here in Jesus' case, it is; and the temptation, I think, is not to oppose but simply to act independently of God's will. The devil is engaged in an artful effort to throw the will of Jesus out of gear with God's will, to set Jesus' will revolving around its own self-center, a temptation which, in slightly altered form, had been only too successful with the first Adam.

God is not against justice, nor is Christ against feeding the multitudes. We know that. Both are against religion's ever becoming a substitute for justice—"the opiate of the people," as Marx correctly described its misuse. But God is for more than justice; which is why the Son of God has to define his mission in terms greater than bread alone. Christ has to be for more than justice, as does Christ's church. Although the weight and voice of the church should be behind all efforts to make life better for the poor, the final task of the church is to make better people out of everyone, rich and poor alike. Maya Angelou once wrote, "To survive is important, but to thrive is elegant." Without bread, people cannot even survive; but to thrive, as we are made and meant to do, we need the "bread of life." And Jesus, who is the bread of life, consequently answered the devil's challenge on behalf of all of us, saying: "Man shall not live by bread alone."

The second temptation is not unlike the first. The devil, you recall, takes Jesus up to a high place, shows him "all the kingdoms of the world in a moment of time" (what a phrase!), and makes the remarkable claim that all these kingdoms belong to him—or should we say "her," for if God is androgynous and so is the devil! Then the devil offers all these kingdoms to Jesus in return for Jesus' worship. Once again we have a choice of interpretations. We can say that the appeal is to selfishness, to power without measure, to honors without number. We can say that the devil is seeking merely to strike a chord of ambition, something with which all of us can resonate, insofar as we are all constantly tempted to seek status through power. But again I prefer to assume that the devil very subtly is suggesting something that sounds too good to pass up. I can hear him saying, "Look, Jesus, never sacrifice the good for the impossible. Something tangible beats anything wildly utopian. One hundred thousand Israelites have already perished in abortive rebellions against the Roman Legions. Isn't that enough? And haven't their relatives every right to expect a messiah who will implement the word and will of God as prophesied by Zechariah: 'The Lord will set free all the families of Judah . . .' (12:7)? So *be* that messiah. Without a throne, and without a retinue, what kind of a king can you be except a ludicrous one?"

Personally, as a believing Christian, I am convinced that God *will* set free all the captive peoples of the world, whether they live in Poland, Afghanistan, South Africa, El Salvador, or in city slums almost anywhere. God has made people free, and free people will always rise up against tyranny and one day succeed. I'm also convinced that in a sinful world some forceful restraint of violent impulses is necessary. But if I have learned anything else from this sinful world and from my Lord and Savior, it is how limited power is to do good. Two illustrations will suffice. History teaches us that every revolution, no matter how idealistic its initial aims, always ends in the reappearance of a new ruling class; and history teaches that deterrence never deters for long, since power always invites a bigger power.

The invention of the stirrup gave more power to a mounted warrior so armor was fabricated as a rejoinder. Big guns proved able to sink wooden ships, so iron plates were applied to the ships' sides. The machine gun multiplied fire power; tanks were invented. Aircraft begat antiaircraft. Big bombs became superbombs at Hiroshima. And today, more than a quarter of a century and five trillion dollars worth of weapons later, we and the Soviets are not deterred from continuing the arms race. If, as President Reagan proposes, we Americans project our earthly obscenities into the celestial realm, there will surely be a Soviet rejoinder, so that together we may "infect with our evil the unoffending stars" (Joseph Sittler).

The worship of power is Satanic. Sadly enough, the first Adam, when he heard, "Surely you will be as God," jumped at the chance—as most of us still do. But the second Adam, on behalf of all of us, refused the temptation, insisting that God not be displaced but worshipped: "You shall worship the Lord your God, and him only shall you serve."

But to choose love over force means we have to "double the heart's might." A fatalism that takes us off the hook of individual and corporate responsibility has no place in the Christian faith; nor can we expect God to vindicate love by shielding from harm those who practice it. That's what the third temptation is all about. "Surely," says the devil, quoting Scripture (never forget how often the devil quotes Scripture), "surely 'He will give his angels charge over you, to guard you.'" And Jesus, also using Scripture as a sword, to parry the thrust of the devil, answers, "You shall not tempt the Lord your God."

W. H. Auden wrote:

> Nothing can save us that is possible.
> We who are about to die demand a miracle.

God in Christ has given us the miracle of his love and now demands that we use it to save his precious planet and his people. With Christ we can double the heart's might. Using love we can pull together, not apart; we can cooperate, not compete. Never a moral luxury, love today is an absolute requisite for survival.

Let me end with an illustrative story. In Northern Minnesota, a farmer's five-year-old child was playing in the kitchen while his mother was busily engaged in domestic chores. Unnoticed, the child toddled out of the house and into the wheat field. Shortly thereafter, noticing the child's absence, the mother began a frantic search for her baby. When she could not find the child in the immediate vicinity of the farmhouse, she called her husband and together they searched through the heaped-up sheaves of wheat. In desperation they summoned all the farmhands. Several hours later, when the child still had not been found, the townspeople were called in. Those of every vocation, economic level, and religious faith—the minister and the rabbi, the workers and the millowner—beat at the sheaves of wheat, walking and running in every direction, urged on by the entreaties of the father and mother.

When this proved futile, someone suggested: "We seem to be going off in all directions. Why don't we join hands, form one large circle, spread out, and then close in, encompassing every inch of the land?" As a result, the preacher joined hands with the worker, the physician joined hands with the town idler. People of every station of life and of every faith joined hands to form a gigantic circle. Carefully examining every inch of the land, they narrowed the circle until someone reached down, picked up the child, and handed him to his father. As soon as he touched the child, the father knew that his son was dead. And he lifted the tiny lifeless body in his arms and cried out, "My God, my God— why didn't we join hands before it was too late?"

Fellow Christians, fellow human beings: we can no longer afford the luxury of going our separate ways, making bread only for ourselves and our families, seeking status through power, and counting on God somehow to save us all. This period of Lent is designed to help us give up our greed for riches and power and find, in their place, the love of God that can make us all partners rather than rivals. So let us side not with the first Adam but with the second, with Christ, who in resisting temptation showed us the way, and who, we know, has the power to keep us on it. So together, in a gesture of love, let us arise now and wish one another the love of God, which can resolve every conflict of the heart, and the peace of God, which even a sinful world can never take away. May the love and peace of God be with you all.

Young Abraham

MARCH 25, 1984
Reading: Genesis 12:1–5

The Book of Hebrews provides a one-sentence summary of the Old Testament lesson for the day: "By faith Abraham obeyed the call to go out to a land destined for himself and his heirs and left home without knowing where he was to go" (Heb. 11:8). But why, you might ask, why focus on the story of Grandfather Abraham on this Youth Sunday? Possess your souls in patience; all will be revealed.

At 75, Abraham, to be sure, is no Michael Jackson of the Pepsi generation; and with all his possessions and descendants along, he's not exactly travelling light. Yet how many of us half his age would be so willing to pull up stakes and take off for parts unknown? I can just hear the townsfolk in Haran upbraiding him:

"What is this, Abraham—some wild dream?"

"Look, Abraham, the future isn't what it used to be. You don't know where in the world you're going."

"Have you talked this out with Sarah?"

"What about that promising nephew of yours, Lot, who was valedictorian in the school last year; is this fair to him?"

"Although you're probably too humble to realize it, Abraham, to all of us here in Haran you've become indispensable."

To the last observation Abraham gave one of the best answers of his life. It is not recorded in Genesis, but I happen to know it. He said, "No one is indispensable, except to God."

No one is indispensable, except to God. Dig that one out of your eyes, mothers and fathers! How do you like that, senior executives—and senior ministers! Sure they need us, our children, our employees, our parishioners—but not that badly. No one is indispensable, except to God, because God is the eternal Creator and requires every one of us in every corner of this world to continue the work of creation. The Creator's task is to make humanity more human, and so he wants more than that, he needs each of us to protect, to affirm, to dignify life. And when you stop to think of it, who should be better suited to further the work of creation than elders like Abraham? For elders have at their disposal memory, and memory, as Frederick Buechner reminds us, "is more than a looking back at a time that is no longer; it is a looking out into another kind of time altogether where everything that was continues not just to be, but to grow and change with the life that is in it still." Memory, properly used, is like a running broad jump: it takes you back only to launch you further forward. And so the senior years ideally are the formative years. Like Abraham, elders should look out and see and respond to the life that still needs to be protected, affirmed, dignified. If they look back, it should be primarily to remember, as did Abraham, who they were created to be—God's guiltless, cared-for, and caring co-creators of this universe.

The story of Abraham is a powerful one for a year in which, in this country alone, two million citizens will turn 65, bringing the grand total of those over 65 in America to upward of 25 million. From 1900 to 1984, life expectancy has increased from 49 to 74.5 years. And in 1984, science and daily experience are steadily destroying the myths about aging. For example, contrary to popular belief, there is no automatic loss of brain cells in later life. Senility is not a sign of age, it is a sign of a disease. Senility, dementia, Alzheimer's disease—call it what you will—someday, scientists now say, like cancer we'll understand it and we'll cure it. "Age-ism" is therefore shot full of lies—like racism, sexism, and "classism." Only a fraction of "OP"s (as demographers affectionately like to refer to Old Persons) are severely disabled. In short, the expectation of decline becomes a self-fulfilling prophecy. Almost any "OP" who remains socially involved, mentally active, with a personality flexible enough to tolerate ambiguity and to enjoy new experiences, can pull up stakes and take off for parts unknown, exactly as did Abraham, if and when God calls him or her to do so.

All this should be music to old ears, and to young ones as well.

> Grow old along with me!
> The best is yet to be,
> The last of life, for which the first was made:
> Our times are in His hand
> Who saith, "A whole I planned,
> Youth shows but half; trust God: see all nor be afraid!"
> Robert Browning

What can be worse than at 70 to look back on the springtime of your life and say, "Ah, those were the days!"—and be right.

The story of any one of us is in some measure the story of all of us, which makes Abraham's story ours, even on this Youth Sunday. If we think we have no choice, we've made the wrong choice. If we think we're too old or too young to choose, we're wrong again. Karl Barth was right: "Better something doubtful or overbold, and therefore in need of forgiveness, than nothing at all." I recall here a wonderful Jewish story of a man to whom all manner of misfortunes befell. When he prayed to God he asked, "Why me, O Lord, I who have conscientiously and consistently fulfilled all of the 613 laws of the Pentateuch? Why me?" And a voice from heaven replied: "Because God would much rather have us creative than right." When I first came to Riverside Church, Valery Russell gave me a poster whose words, I'm convinced, are as sacred as any in ancient scribal law. They read: "Do not follow where the path leads. Rather go where there is no path, and leave a trail."

Think for a minute, in this last week of Women's History Month, think of the trailblazers among America's suffragettes, many of whose faces were as full as Abraham's of the "credentials of humanity"—as Shaw once called wrinkles. For a century and a half we American males excluded an entire sex from governing what we like to call the greatest democracy in the world. It was only 64 years ago that women finally won the right to vote, and even then, for years, almost all wives voted as did their husbands. Don't protest; my mother voted the way my father did long after he was dead, thereby cancelling her son's votes—and I dare say the mothers of most of you voted the same way. But today, thanks to those trailblazing suffragettes, for the first time in American history there is a recognizable gender gap, a 15 percent difference from men in the way women think and vote on a variety of issues that reflect the values and practices imposed by a white male power structure still in control of both the economy and the government. What an explosion of needs, self-discoveries, and new insights into personal and social relationships we men owe feminists who, in their time, like Abraham and Sarah before them, chose not to follow where the established paths led. Rather they went where there were no paths . . . and left such a wonderful trail!

Too often we picture God as some immovable rock, when in fact it is God and God alone who never rests. I only quote Scripture: "He neither slumbers nor sleeps" (Ps. 121:4). It is God who says, "Behold, I create all things new" (Rev. 21:5). Therefore God's most persistent enemies must be those who are unwilling to move in new directions. Yes, "better something doubtful or overbold, and therefore in need of forgiveness, than nothing at all." Dear Caleb, Monica, Brooke, David, Amy, the youth of this church, remember: if you choose, you're sometimes wrong, but if you never choose, you're always wrong.

One last thought. You don't have to move out, as did Abraham, to be creative, to respond to God's call. You can be born again in place—born of the water, symbol of forgiveness, and of the Spirit, symbol of power. At this moment, in the town of Indiana, Pennsylvania, Mary Katherine Walker, mother of our beloved choir director and organist, is fighting for her life; which is why John is not with us today—except in prayers and spirit. Likewise Kent Toalson, a long-time member of the choir, is fighting for his life in Lenox Hospital—at a much younger age. At his side is Barbara, his wife, also a member of the choir. When I think of these four people, called to go through the deep waters, all four leaning on Jesus and struggling, to live, or die, as God would want them to, I'm astounded once more at what we human beings can do if we have to. In fact, what we can do when we have to is only matched by what we don't do when we think we don't have to. But Christians have to; we're baptized by the water and by the Spirit! And so wherever we are we can take them on, these four enemies of God's creation: racism, sexism, "classism," and "age-ism." Whatever our station, whatever our age, we can be faithful by being constantly creative, by helping God make humanity more human. While Abraham lived through "summer's parching heat," Jesus died young; but didn't both show us that it is by its content rather than by its duration that a lifetime is measured? So let us, like Abraham, yes, like our Savior Jesus, be co-creators with the Creator, who said, "Behold, a whole I planned." It's really quite easy: "Trust God, see all, nor be afraid."

The Raising of Lazarus

APRIL 1, 1984
Reading: John 11:1–44

11:1–5. Now a certain man was ill, Lazarus of
Bethany, the village of Mary and her sister Martha.
It was Mary who anointed the Lord with ointment
and wiped his feet with her hair, whose brother
Lazarus was ill. So the sisters sent to him, saying,
"Lord, he whom you love is ill." But when Jesus
heard it he said, "This illness is not unto death; it is
for the glory of God, so that the Son of God may
be glorified by means of it." Now Jesus loved
Martha and her sister and Lazarus.

How wonderful that the Son of Man who, as Luke records, had
"nowhere to lay his head," could at least rest his weary feet, his
tired mind, and his often broken heart, in this home in Bethany only
two miles from Jerusalem. We all stand in need of a home, a place
where no one laughs at our dreams, where what we say in confidence
is understood, where we are without question accepted and loved.
Obviously Jesus had such a spiritual retreat with these two sisters and
their brother Lazarus. At least that's how I read the statement, "Now
Jesus loved Martha and her sister and Lazarus."

On the other hand, how wonderful for Mary and Martha to know
that it sufficed to send word that their brother was ill for Jesus to
appear. They were wise, these sisters. They had learned what many of
us have learned when those close to us have died, namely that you can
steel yourself against death and in general against the hardships of life,
but that in so doing you wall out the very support you really need.
The one thing a clenched fist can't do is accept a helping hand. In
their distress Mary and Martha extended an open hand, a supplicating hand, and—as he always does—Jesus took it.

But what about the phrase, "This illness . . . is for the glory of God,
so that the Son of God may be glorified by means of it"? It's hardly a
phrase to sit lightly on the hearts of believers who don't like acts of
compassion to be used as means, even as signs of revelation. In many
verses in the Gospel of John there is a surface truth—such as that the

---

This sermon owes a great debt to William Barclay's commentary on John.

cure of Lazarus will show the glory of God in action; and beneath the surface another truth—such as that the raising of Lazarus will hasten Christ's crucifixion, which John always views as the glorification of Christ. Therefore, the phrase, "that the Son of God may be glorified" must be read: "that the Son of God may be *crucified*." And sure enough. If Jesus could dismantle the powers of death, so reasoned the rulers of Israel, he surely could dismantle their own power. In the Gospel of John it was the raising of Lazarus that brought about the crucifixion of Christ; and that's why this story is properly read in the middle of Lent.

> *11:6–10.* So when Jesus heard that Lazarus was ill, he stayed two days longer in the place where he was. Then after this he said to the disciples, "Let us go into Judea again." The disciples said to him, "Rabbi, the Jews were but now seeking to stone you, and are you going there again?" Jesus answered, "Are there not twelve hours in the day? If any one walks in the day, he does not stumble, because he sees the light of this world. But if any one walks in the night, he stumbles, because the light is not in him."

"Are there not twelve hours in the day?" It's a question that points to two experiences with which we are all familiar: the glory of being in time and the tragedy of being too late. There are twelve hours, so what's the rush? There are only twelve hours, so there's no time to spare. What tension there always is in time between haste and waste, as reflected in that wonderful Italian expression "*Festina lente*"—make haste slowly. And it's a fact—you can see it when you read the Gospels—that Jesus never rushed, but was always on time. I wish I knew the secret.

> *11:11–16.* Thus he spoke, and then he said to them, "Our friend Lazarus has fallen asleep, but I go to awake him out of sleep." The disciples said to him, "Lord, if he has fallen asleep, he will recover." Now Jesus had spoken of his death, but they thought that he meant taking rest in sleep. Then Jesus told them plainly, "Lazarus is dead; and for your sake I am glad that I was not there, so that you may believe. But let us go to him." Thomas, called the Twin, said to his fellow disciples, "Let us also go, that we may die with him."

Little did John know in reporting this statement that he was giving marching orders to all of us, Christians past, present, and future: "Let us also go that we may die with him." The disciples were sure he was going to be stoned, as he all but was the last time they were there. I'm drawn to John's courage, because it doesn't represent "expectant faith but (rather) loyal despair." No one need be afraid of fear, only afraid that fear will stop him or her from doing what's right. Courage means being well aware of the worst that can happen, being scared almost to death, and then doing the right thing anyhow.

> *11:17–27.* Now when Jesus came, he found that Lazarus had already been in the tomb four days. Bethany was near Jerusalem, about two miles off, and many of the Jews had come to Martha and Mary to console them concerning their brother. When Martha heard that Jesus was coming, she went and met him, while Mary sat in the house. Martha said to Jesus, "Lord, if you had been here, my brother would not have died. And even now I know that whatever you ask from God, God will give you." Jesus said to her, "Your brother will rise again." Martha said to him, "I know that he will rise again in the resurrection at the last day." Jesus said to her, "I am the resurrection and the life; he who believes in me . . . shall never die. Do you believe this?" She said to him, "Yes, Lord; I believe that you are the Christ, the Son of God, he who is coming into the world."

As in the Gospel of Luke, so in John: it is Martha who acts and Mary who sits still. Martha goes out to meet Jesus and half-reproachfully—how could she help herself?—says, "If you had been here, my brother would not have died." In other words, "Why didn't you come sooner?" And yet with a kind of desperate hope she adds, "I know that whatever you ask from God, God will give you." When Jesus assures her, "Your brother will rise again," she agrees, declaring her faith in the Orthodox Jewish belief of the time in the final resurrection: "I know that he will rise again in the resurrection at the last day." Then Jesus corrects her, with a statement now written on the soft places in every believing Christian heart: "I am the resurrection and the life; he who believes in me, though he die, yet shall he live, and whoever lives and believes in me shall never die." In other words, you don't have to wait for a promised resurrection in an indefinite future. Eternal life begins not at the end of time, nor even at the funeral home, but right now; eternal life exists on both sides of the grave. Death, to be sure, will come, but not the death that separates us from God. "Though he were dead yet shall he live." The abyss of love is deeper than the abyss of death. "Whosoever believeth in me shall never die." He who overcomes his fear of death lives as though death were a past and not a future experience. "Do you believe this?" Jesus asks, and Martha, on behalf of all believers present and future answers, "Yes, Lord; I believe that you are the Christ, the Son of God."

> *11:28–37.* When Martha had said this, she went and called her sister Mary, saying quietly, "The Teacher is here and is calling for you." And when she heard it, she rose quickly and went to him. Now Jesus had not yet come to the village, but was still in the place where Martha had met him. When the Jews who were with her in the house, consoling her, saw Mary rise quickly and go out, they followed her, supposing that she was going to the tomb to weep there. Then Mary, when she came where Jesus was and saw him, fell at his feet, saying to him, "Lord, if you had been here, my brother would not have died." When Jesus saw her weeping, and the Jews who came with her also weeping, he was deeply moved in spirit and troubled; and he said, "Where have you laid him?" They said to him, "Lord, come and see." Jesus wept. So the Jews said, "See how he loved him!" But some of them said, "Could not he who opened the eyes of the blind man have kept this man from dying?"

Mary and Martha, and all the wailing mourners, and now Jesus weeping too. For a moment few words, no deeds, only tears. Why does Jesus weep? Is it with anger at this display of unbelief while in their midst stands one who is the resurrection and the life? I doubt it. Is it with the same sadness with which Jesus viewed the hungry multitudes, the palsied man, or the one born blind? I imagine so. But there is just the possibility that Jesus weeps because he knows from what joys Lazarus will be returning. For here on earth, in life, we see through a glass darkly; but there it is face to face. Here we sit in pews and chairs, but there on thrones. Here there is crying and pain, but there God will wipe the tears from our eyes.

Why he wept I do not know. All I know is that while weeping is not the way of worldly power, which seeks always to maintain control, weeping is the way of God, who in Christ embodies our anguish, and whose "eye is on the sparrow."

> *11:38–44.* Then Jesus, deeply moved again, came to the tomb; it was a cave, and a stone lay upon it. Jesus said, "Take away the stone." Martha, the sister of the dead man, said to him, "Lord, by this time there will be an odor, for he has been dead four days." Jesus said to her, "Did I not tell you that if you would believe you would see the glory of God?" So they took away the stone. And Jesus lifted up his eyes and said, "Father, I thank thee that thou hast heard me. I knew that thou hearest me always, but I have said this on account of the people standing by, that they may believe that thou didst send me." When he had said this, he cried with a loud voice, "Lazarus, come out." The dead man came out, his hands and feet bound with bandages, and his face wrapped with a cloth. Jesus said to them, "Unbind him, and let him go."

"Father, I thank thee that thou hast heard me." Jesus prayed, Lazarus is raised. "Miracles are just so many answered prayers." Was Lazarus literally raised from the dead? How many times we ask the same question of all Christ's miracles, particularly those performed in John! (Did Jesus literally change the water into wine? To that question one factory worker I know answered: "I don't know about changing water to wine. All I know is that in my house he changed beer into furniture, and that's miracle enough for me.")

All I know is that, spiritually speaking, Jesus has raised no end of people from the dead, and I think that to speak spiritually is finally the only significant way of speaking.

What is true of individuals is true of whole peoples. Many of us who were here on Friday night couldn't help but feel hope surge once again, as if the rattling bones of this wonderfully diverse and almost endlessly complicated nation might yet come together, bone knit to bone. If eternal life is on both sides of the grave, then to yearn for the future with no concern for the present is wrong. Heaven—and Hell—begin here and now, both for individuals and for nations, in what theologians call "realized eschatology." So the Spirit of God is always moving, prompting us ever more urgently to disarm the nations and empower the weak.

One final thought: we've just read of a tomb that was a cave. We've read of a stone that was rolled away, of grave clothes. A believer's mind cannot but shift from Lazarus to Jesus' death, burial, and resurrection. As the writer of the Gospel must have had this in mind, we cannot help reflecting on the form of this passage of Scripture. Fred Craddock has written: "A story of a death in a family is told as a narrative about Jesus' own passion, and Jesus' own passion is told as a narrative about a death in a family. When anyone's story and Jesus' story are so interwoven, it is not simply a literary display; it is a presentation of the Gospel."

Acting Our Consciences

APRIL 15, 1984
Readings: Zechariah 9:9, 10; Luke 19:28–48

To the university world Socrates is a hero because he gave his life for what he believed in; he died defending the unarmed truth. Moreover, he didn't worry very much about whether or not he was effective. (It would be difficult to imagine him saying, as they handed him the hemlock, "Wait a minute, fellas, is Plato going to write this up?") Socrates knew that in this world we ultimately have to do what's right, and only penultimately what's effective. He broke Athenian law, but not lightly, and he did so in the name of a higher authority. Furthermore he died full of good will: "I love my city, but I will not stop preaching that which I believe is true. You may kill me, but I will obey God rather than you."

In Holy Week, we see Jesus following a similar road to martyrdom. Although his disciples, in a classic instance of denial, refused to believe it, Jesus had long known that "the Son of Man must suffer many things from the scribes and pharisees, and be killed" (Luke 9:22). He knew that while today—Palm Sunday—the multitudes might hail him, by week's end they would desert him. Abandoned also by his disciples, his sole worldly possession a robe, he too must have wondered about the effectiveness of his mission; from the cross we hear him cry out, "My God, my God, why hast thou forsaken me?" (Matt. 27:46). Like Socrates, Jesus broke the law; the official charge was treason. But his intent was clearly to uphold a higher law, and he died with a heart full of love for those who thought only to heap scorn on his bowed head: "Father, forgive them, for they know not what they do."

How many heroes of today were at earlier points in their lives notorious lawbreakers! Moses was a wanted man and David an outlaw. Isaiah and Jeremiah were both accused of conspiracy and treason. Shadrach, Meshach, and Abednego were known, and known only, for their "divine disobedience." And the disciples, when they finally understood the Christian message—as Peter put it, "We must obey God rather than men"—broke laws with such regularity that the so-called "Acts of the Apostles" could well be retitled "The Arrests of the Apostles."

Add to these Biblical names those of Thoreau, Gandhi, King, and so many others that you could make a list as long as your arm and end up with what has animated the world since the beginning of history: a list of the world's saints, whose individual consciences as opposed to the mass mind, best represent the universal conscience of humanity.

Rarely can majority rule be equated with the rule of conscience. Think, in America alone, of the long years during which the majority of our citizens supported slavery; think of the disenfranchisement of women, of child labor. Democracy is not based on the proven goodness of the people but on the proven evil of dictators. So the law never represents pure justice, but only about as much justice as any given people at any given time will sanction. In other words, the law reflects public opinion as much as it instructs public opinion. Therefore, if the law is to reflect more and reject less, of humanity's highest notions about justice, someone has constantly to provoke change—the change new laws will serve to embody. Civil disobedience, then, as practiced by Jesus—who broke religious as well as civil law—Socrates, and Gandhi, is not only an expression of conscience but a way to move society toward a greater measure of justice and mercy.

Civil disobedience has also been a time-honored community occupation, as a quick reading of American history will show. Seventeenth-century Quakers broke laws in Virginia, Pennsylvania, and Massachusetts. (Said the great Quaker Mary Dyer as she went to her death in Boston, "Truth is my authority, not some authority my truth.") In the 18th century, the followers of Washington, Hamilton, Jefferson, and Adams were strictly speaking traitors, until success crowned efforts and they became great patriots! In the 19th century, abolitionists—black and white—defied the Fugitive Slave Act. In the first half of the 20th century, suffragettes engaged in illegal demonstrations, as did the labor movement with its boycotts and sit-ins, most of which were illegal at the time. And finally, in the second half of our century, in response to continued segregation and to the war in Vietnam, the civil rights and antiwar movements engaged regularly in acts of civil disobedience.

Why rehearse all this religious and American history of individual and community civil disobedience on Palm Sunday? For two good reasons. In many churches Palm Sunday is celebrated as Passion Sunday—a time to wonder whether, as followers of Christ, we too are ready to suffer for what we believe in. And second, Holy Week is full of politics—religious events that took public form. Hence Holy Week is a good time for members of Riverside to start considering whether or not they are ready for civil disobedience, whether or not they want their church to join some 100 other churches in this country who have already declared themselves "sanctuaries" for refugees fleeing El Salvador or Guatemala. Surely we have the facilities to house an individual or family, and the committee promoting the idea of sanctuary, the committee of church members and officers that is sponsoring the discussion after the service today, hopes to see church members do their homework and come to the annual church meeting on May 20 and vote their consciences.

What is the situation? As many of you are aware, over 40,000 people have been killed in El Salvador since 1979, and during the same period, though with less public awareness, another 40,000 have died in Guatemala. In both countries the vast majorities were victims of death squads, government security forces armed and trained primarily by the United States government. The Roman Catholic Bishops Conference of Guatemala has estimated that as many as one million Guatemalans have been made refugees by repression and warfare. And the government of El Salvador estimates that one out of four citizens of that small country now live abroad. The United States Immigration and Naturalization Service (INS) estimates that some 250,000 refugees from both countries have entered the United States.

"Send these, the homeless, tempest-tost to me, lift my lamp beside the golden door." In keeping with the spirit of the Statue of Liberty, the Refugee Act of 1980, passed by Congress, adopted the standards of the United Nations Convention and Protocol on refugees. The law requires the United States to grant asylum, or at least temporary refugee status (and we're not pressing for more than that), to people unable to return to their country because of persecution, or the fear of persecution, for reasons of race, religion, nationality, or membership in a particular political or social group. Furthermore, the U.N. High Commissioner for Refugees has specifically urged the U.S. government to grant asylum to Salvadorans. Yet despite the fact that the Refugee Act and U.N. High Commissioner would classify them as refugees, of the 23,000 Salvadorans who applied for political asylum in 1982, only 65 received permission. It was then, and still is, the position of the INS that Salvadorans and Guatemalans are not political but "economic" refugees, and hence deportable. And the INS does deport them—about 600 a month, mostly from airfields in Texas and Southern California—deporting them to likely torture and death. It is this gross misrepresentation of the facts—that no one has anything to fear in Guatemala or El Salvador—it is this bad interpretation of a good law that the sanctuary movement in this country protests. When the Reagan administration so patently misapplies a law which intends an opposite result, I personally have a hard time viewing the establishment of a sanctuary even as an act of civil disobedience; it seems rather like common sense, like a normal human reaction to an intolerable situation. As Thoreau once said, "They are the lovers of law and order who uphold a law when the government breaks it." Nevertheless I know that should this church choose to be a sanctuary its officers, including the senior minister, could be charged with harboring an undocumented alien, a felony which carries a maximum penalty of $2,000 and five years in jail. Personally, however, I would consider that a small risk compared to the risks run by deported refugees; and a small price to pay for faithfulness to the Gospel when compared to the sacrifices made by our Lord and Savior, sacrifices which we bear witness to this Holy Week.

Officers of a church are called upon to help establish justice and to provide for those in need. They are called to do all they can to keep their church Christ-centered, which means when truth is injured to defend it, and to put obedience to Christ before obedience to government officials. At the same time, of course, the officers of a church must uphold the right of any individual member of the church to dissent from the positions they take, recognizing that in the church, unity is based not on agreement but on mutual concern.

As senior pastor of Riverside, I want to declare my own unqualified support for a sanctuary here. As theologians like to say, it is a human imperative in response to the divine indicative. The establishment of a sanctuary would also tie us to the best in our American heritage: the underground railroad, those who opposed the slaughter of Native Americans, those who protested the Spanish-American War, who marched in Selma, who turned in their draft cards to protest the war in Vietnam. Sanctuary would also bring Central America home, home to our consciences: the rape, pillage, kidnapping, and murder that goes on in almost every Central American country with our money and in our name. It would align us with countless priests, pastors, and laity, fellow Christians pleading with us North Americans to help them stop the carnage in their countries. President Reagan has blood on his hands, but only because too many of the rest of us have water on ours—like Pilate. It is a bleak but realistic assessment to say that our government intends to escalate still further its intervention in Central American countries. Therefore it behooves us North American Christians to realize now what the German churches learned too late some forty years ago: that it is not enough to resist with confession; we must confess with resistance.

As sanctuary provides an opportunity to do just that, an opportunity so clear in the light of the events of Holy Week I am reminded of words of St. Augustine: "I do not say to you, seek the way. The way itself has come to you; arise and walk."

Easter 1984

APRIL 22, 1984
Reading: 1 Corinthians 15:57

*"Thanks be to God who giveth us the victory through our
Lord Jesus Christ."*

What makes Easter so much fun is all the finery: the chickens, the rabbits, the lambs, the eggs, the forsythia, the cherry blossoms in Riverside Park, and now, finally, the warm air—altogether a glorious day! But what makes Easter so exciting is the cosmic quality of it. For Easter has less to do with one man's escape from the grave than with the victory of seemingly powerless love over loveless power. Before we get into that, however, let's investigate this one man's escape from the grave, since it seems to raise in many minds questions which are not easy to answer.

On earlier occasions I have urged my beloved parishioners to read the New Testament gospels not as historical accounts, but rather as four distinct testimonials to the one person of Jesus Christ. For if you read the gospels as testimonials, and remember that they were written decades after that first Easter which we gather today to celebrate, then chances are you will not be puzzled and put off by the obvious differences that exist among them. I urge this approach upon all of us here today. Because in no way can the disparities between the various gospel and Pauline accounts of Easter, and the events subsequent to Easter, be harmonized into one consistent story. There is no agreement as to the people involved; there is no agreement as to the localities where the events took place; and there is no agreement as to the sequence of Christ's appearances.

But that's all right: you don't have to be a fundamentalist to be a Christian. As a matter of fact, it's better not to be one if, with St. Augustine, you "believe in thinking and wish to think in believing." What this means, in our present context, is that you can believe in the truth of Easter without accepting as literally true each and every detail of the Easter stories.

I personally believe in the resurrection of Christ for two reasons, of which the first is the documented enthusiasm of the disciples. A historian may find little objective evidence to support the story of the empty tomb, but no historian will dispute the fact that after Easter the disciples became ten times the persons they were before. Promise-making, promise-breaking Peter, that fearful fellow we remember on Good Friday, suddenly after Easter was so "aflame with faith and free" that he gladly lived and bravely died for the master he had thrice denied. In fact, so great was the enthusiasm of all the disciples—and our word "enthusiasm" comes from the Greek word *entheos* meaning "possessed by God"—that we can say that Christianity really begins with Easter. Had there been no resurrection of Christ, there would have been no gospels, no epistles, no New Testament, no Christian church.

But Easter was not a function of the disciples' faith; their faith was a function of Easter. They were convinced Christ had risen from the dead. And when they proclaimed, "He is risen," it was not like saying "Che Guevara still lives," meaning that his cause lives on. Nor was it like what occurs in Nicaraguan churches, when the names of those who have died defending their revolution and country are read out and parishioners shout "*Presente*," meaning their memory will never die. No, to the disciples the risen Christ was more than a memory that will never die, more than a cause that lives on; to St. Paul, St. Stephen, and many another early Christian, Christ was a real presence. (Though less a physiological than a personal one. Do not worry so much about the molecules in his body, nor about the historicity of the empty tomb: both are far from clear. What is clear is that the disciples recognized Christ's identity, his personality and his character. Instead of death, they beheld a metamorphosis. As is written in the preface of the Roman Catholic Requiem mass: "*Vita mutatur, non tolliter*"—"Life is changed, not ended.")

So the first reason for my believing in the resurrection is a historical one: the documented faith of the disciples. But the historical reason is only a buttress for my second reason, which is that I, like so many people here now and throughout the centuries, have experienced in my own life the presence of the risen Christ, or Holy Spirit. I experience the risen Christ as a mirror to our humanity, showing us what human beings should be about. I experience the risen Christ as a window to divinity, revealing as much of God as is given mere mortal eyes to see. I experience the risen Christ as strength above my own, as joy deeper than the heart's agony. Most of all, I experience the risen Christ as that love which indeed does make the world go 'round, the love that binds us one to another and all to God; for "God *is* love and he who abides in love abides in God and God abides in him."

Thus I see the Easter faith as available to everyone in this church today, to believers and doubters alike, provided our doubts arise out of a need for the truth and not out of a pathological need to doubt. And let's also remember that reason has its limits, that there are truths the mind can defend but never discover. In one of his famous scenes, that great German metaphysical clown, whose name I can never remember, goes frantically searching for something under a bright street light. He is joined by a policeman, who asks him, "What are you looking for?"

"The keys to my apartment," the clown replies.

The officer generously joins in, but after searching vainly for some minutes finally asks, "Are you sure you lost them here?"

"No, I lost them over there," says the clown, pointing to a dark corner.

"Then why are we looking for them here?"

"Because there's no light over there."

We will never find the keys to our heart's true home if we search only by the light readily available to reason. The resurrection of Christ is one of those mysteries—like the B minor Mass, like El Greco's Toledo, like lovers, like starlight and sunset—one of those truths that the mind can defend but never discover, one of those truths in the presence of which the mind plays an all-important legislative, but finally not a creative role.

Now let's get back to the cosmic quality of Easter, to the victory of seemingly powerless love over loveless power. It is perfectly true that Easter celebrates life after death—and we'll get to that part of it—but most of all it celebrates that the good that Jesus did *in this world* was not in vain. Easter proclaims the truth that while you can crucify God's love you cannot keep it dead and buried. "Therefore, my beloved sisters and brothers," as St. Paul wrote the Corinthians, "be ye steadfast, unmovable, always abounding in the work of the

Lord, forasmuch as ye know that your labor is not in vain in the Lord" (1 Cor. 15:58).

We need to hear those words, progress being so painfully slow these days. Three months ago, in New Hampshire, I heard the story of two old codgers who went hunting for moose in the forests surrounding Moose Lake in the northwestern part of Maine. As the pilot of the small seaplane let them off on the shore of the lake he reminded them, "Like I said, I'll be back in three days. But remember, this is a small plane: there's room for the two of you and *one* moose."

When, three days later, the pilot returned and taxied to the shore, he was irritated to see between the two old boys, standing proudly there with their rifles, not one but *two* moose, huge ones at that. "Look," he said, "I told you—the two of you and *one* moose."

The old-timers looked at each other in surprise and answered: "Funny, the fellah last year didn't complain."

The fear of his competition proving greater than all other fears, the pilot relented. Grumbling, he helped them pile both moose into the little plane, and the two old-timers lay on top of them. The plane took forever to get off the lake, barely cleared the trees on the far shore, and about a quarter of a mile further on clipped a high pine and crashed, sending pieces of its wings and moose antlers in all directions. Finally one of the old codgers came to, pulled his head out of the moss, spied his companion a short way off, and asked, "Where are we?"

His companion replied: "Oh, about a hundred yards further than last year."

A quarter of a century and five trillion dollars worth of weapons ago, this planet was a whole lot safer than it is this Easter day. A quarter of a century ago the maltreated and powerless of this world, the oppressed and reviled, the unbefriended children of poverty, were doing just about as well as they are doing today. It's discouraging! We can be optimists only by centuries; by decades we have to be pessimists. But consider this: if Jesus himself rose and saw fit to return to the world that crucified him, rose and saw fit to return to people whose salvability was dubious at best, who are we to complain when in our day we also face religious leaders who can't bear the thought of a new idea; or when we face politicians who have but to hear, "Thou art not Caesar's friend" and away they fall like Pilate, washing their hands and thereby plaiting the crown of thorns; or when we face crowds, like the one on Calvary, that gather not to cheer but also not to protest, failing to realize that compassion without confrontation is pure sentimentality. If Christ rose to return to this world, then *this world*, and not the next, is the primary concern of Christians. "Therefore, my beloved brothers and sisters, be ye steadfast, unmovable, always abounding in the work of the Lord, forasmuch as ye know that your labor is not in vain in the Lord."

But there is also another world. "*Vita mutatur, non tolliter*"—"life is changed, not ended." As it happened to Jesus, so it will be with us. That's the bold claim of the faith: "For since by man came death, by man came also the resurrection of the dead" (1 Cor. 15:21). Said St. Paul also: "As we have borne the image of the earthy, we shall also bear the image of the heavenly" (1 Cor. 15:49). "For this corruptible must put on incorruption, and this mortal must put on immortality. So when this corruptible shall have put on incorruption, and this mortal shall have put on immortality, then shall be brought to pass the saying that is written, 'Death is swallowed up in victory.' O death, where is thy sting? O grave, where is thy victory?" (1 Cor. 15:53–55).

We may not know *what* is beyond the grave, but we do know *who* is beyond the grave; and Christ resurrected links the two worlds, telling us we really live only in one. If Christ is love, and love is immortal, then life is eternal and death is only a horizon—and a horizon is nothing but the limit of our sight.

What makes Easter so exciting is the cosmic quality of it. What is the Easter message? That resurrection has overcome crucifixion, that there is more mercy in God than sin in us, that Christ's work in this world is never in vain, and that our beloved dead are now at peace there where one day we shall be also. What then, dearly beloved, shall we say, but "Thanks be to God who gives us the victory through our Lord Jesus Christ."

Where's the *Love?*

MAY 20, 1984
Readings: Acts 17:1–5; 1 Peter 2:1–10

The Eastertide lectionary readings, of which we have just heard two, tend either to recount stories of how people in the first century responded to the news of Christ's resurrection, or to indicate how we who count ourselves Christians in the twentieth century are to practice Christ's presence in our lives. In the assigned epistle for today, the fifth Sunday after Easter, we read: "Put away all malice and all guile and insincerity and envy and all slander." Why? Because— and I love this phrase—"you have tasted the kindness of the Lord."

But, some of you may well object, a little slander is such fun! How can you get through the day without gossip? And how can you get ahead in life without guile, and at least a touch of insincerity? Furthermore, who can possibly put away so powerful an emotion as envy?—envy which, as contrasted with gluttony and lust, is the only one of the so-called "seven deadly sins" that has no gratification whatsoever. Yet who among us has not envied? When you stop to think of it, envy is proof positive of human perversity! As for malice, you and I are always going to have malicious thoughts about others, for our pride is not accidentally but essentially competitive. I can only go up if you go down; and therefore, as the great philosopher Kant put it, "There is something about the misfortune of even our best friends that is not altogether disagreeable."

"Put away all malice and all guile and insincerity and envy and all slander." Given our capacity for all these things, it's probably a miracle there's not more around! But one more thing needs to be said right away: Peter's command that we not speak ill of each other is not supposed to render us incapable of making critical distinctions. I think you'll all know what I'm talking about if I say that there are too many sentimental slobs in the religious community, people who think they are loving everyone when, in fact, they are suffering from what might be called the "Little Red Riding Hood" syndrome—they can't tell a wolf from their grandmother!

But how do we *try*, at least, to put away malice, guile, insincerity, envy, and slander—the things that tear us apart here in church, in our homes, in the world at large—seeing that we have tasted the kindness of the Lord? The answer, once again, is the one given in the old gospel hymn: "Take it to the Lord in prayer." Are you envious, feeling in the shadow of someone brilliant as the sun on a clear morning? Take it to the Lord in prayer; for while the world may measure the brilliance of our works, God views only the love with which we do them. If we succeed in love we are never failures; while if we fail in love, we fail in all things else. Are you feeling sick as a dog, low—as they say—as a turtle's transmission? Once again, take it to the Lord in prayer, for the hurt of your body and mind can actually cure your soul, if God be your doctor. I know that's harsh advice, but I can testify that in my own life physical and psychological afflictions have been bearable when viewed in the right way, and unbearable only when viewed in the wrong.

In other words, don't suffer alone, suffer with the risen Christ. Don't die alone, die with Christ. Never live alone, but always with Christ in your heart. Pray, and you will learn that "the God of your prayer is the God of your neighbor." If we pray, we are like spokes on a wheel: the closer we come to the hub, to God, the closer we come to one another. Pray constantly, and you will find that prayer is more than simply what you say, but a way of living in which everything you do becomes a prayer. "Where's the beef?" may have won first prize in the 30-second commercial contest, but "Where's the *love?*" is the eternally important question. And love is always there when people truly pray to God. Love is the answer to slander, malice, guile, and envy, and the kindness of the Lord is there for the asking. So let's not stop asking, let's keep talking: to Jesus, to God, everywhere, at all times. And remember, you can do it quietly, for God is much nearer than you think!

Now, turning to the lesson for the day in the Book of Acts, we find sensitive Jews and Greeks opening themselves up to Paul's proclamation of Christ's resurrection, and responding with such revolutionary thoughts and deeds that others less sensitive mount a counterinsurgency against them. (As Christ predicted, "I came not to bring peace but the sword.") Incensed, the counterinsurgents cry out: "These people who have turned the world upside down have come here also . . . they are acting against the decrees of Caesar"—my word, sounds like civil disobedience!—"saying that there is another king, Jesus." (Isn't it amazing how the enemies of Christianity understand its revolutionary nature so much better than do its friends.)

"These people who have turned the world upside down . . ." True Christians have always been world upsetters, because viewed through Christ's eyes the world has always been wrong side up. Perhaps in these crazy times we should draw comfort from the fact that the only thing truly new in our day is our own capacity literally to blow ourselves to kingdom come—but that's all.

The other day a man came into my office and the following conversation took place:

"You remember five years ago I came to see you and I was broke and you helped me and I said I would never forget you?"

"Yes."

"Well, I'm broke again."

Not every five years but every year, nay every week, the world, spiritually speaking, goes broke and needs spiritual renewal. It has always been thus. For every person stimulated and challenged by new ideas there have always been ten people terrified by them. As the great teacher of freedom Alexander Meiklejohn wrote: "The dominant mood has never been the courage of those who dare to think, but rather the timidity of those who fear and hate whenever conventions are questioned." Alas, the world has always been full of violence, resting its security on arms rather than on securing justice and peace. The world has always forced people from their homes and pushed them from their lands.

But the world is also a world of which Jesus is the cornerstone, as St. Peter puts it, placed there by God: a cornerstone on which we are to build a house we will all dwell in. It is a house that cannot be built by us, and at the same time it is a house that cannot be built without us. That is what Paul, Silas, and Jason understood when, despite the counterinsurgency, they continued to proclaim Christ as King. That is what Peter understood when he wrote, in our epistle for the day: "Come to him, to that living stone rejected by men but in God's sight chosen and precious; and like living stones be yourselves built into a spiritual house."

Dear brothers and sisters, *hermanos y hermanas*, we must pray constantly not only for love in our hearts but for iron up our spines, that like Paul, Silas, and Jason we may choose hope over despair, love over hatred, the common need over self-interest, genuine peacemaking over mere peacekeeping. It is our Christian calling. It is our Christian calling to house, not shelter, the homeless; to feed, not starve, the poor; to employ, not corrupt, the young; yes, to pay better wages to the staff of Riverside Church, and to see to it that the three babies we have baptized today have a future other than that of a nuclear ash.

To save this topsy-turvy world we must set it right side up. In place of a house built on the sand we must build one with Christ as its cornerstone. And we can do it, because we have "tasted the kindness of the Lord," because we are indeed "a chosen race, a royal priesthood, a holy nation, God's own people," called to "declare the wonderful deeds of him who called (us) out of darkness into his marvelous light." God grant in this glorious Eastertide that we, like the Lord's disciples, may continue to live in the bright light that shone forth that first Easter morn.

"Let Us Press On to Know God"

JULY 1, 1984
Readings: Hosea 5:15–6:6; Matthew 9:9–13

The text for this morning's sermon comes from the prophet Hosea: "Let us know, let us press on to know God."

A psychiatrist once went fishing with a friend affluent enough to own a small seaplane. Together they flew over that gorgeous lake country in northern Minnesota where lake adjoins lake with only an isthmus between. As there are no villages, let alone industry, the water is exceedingly clear; you can see forty feet down. Flying low over one of these lakes the two friends beheld no fish, but two fishermen happily angling. They thought the only decent thing to do was to land the plane and tell them, "No fish," which they did. As they flew off, the psychiatrist mused to himself, "I had anticipated their disappointment, but not their hostility." But then he went on to think: "But of course, it's not as if we had said to them, 'Come with us, boys, and we'll take you to another lake where you can let down your lines and pull them in like the disciples in the Sea of Galilee'; or 'Come with us, boys, and we'll take you home to your wives and you can take a week off some other time.' No, we left them there where there was nothing else to do but fish. So on they went, doing exactly the same thing, only now twice as angry and frustrated as before."

And there you have the United States today. Everybody knows in their heart of hearts that there are no fish in a foreign policy that seeks to win an arms race all of us clearly are losing, and seeks the Third World over to postpone the empowerment of the poor. In our heart of hearts we Americans know that no longer are we planting, as once our forebears thought they were, "a new heaven and a new earth on our continent." Maybe we are victims of our own success: "A nation which affirms that it lives in the light of the future has become a victim of its past" (Richard Shaull). For whatever reason we now have to call to account a productive system more concerned with production than with people. We have to question an economic system that exhausts the earth's resources, that pollutes its atmosphere, that creates unnecessary wants and induces people to buy worthless products. It's really crazy: we're running around destroying our country! And the destruction and waste in our national life seems to be felt ever more in our increasingly impoverished personal lives. This last week I've been reading Studs Terkel's *Working*, in which he writes: "As the work force in America becomes increasingly younger, so does Willy Loman. Perhaps it is this specter that most haunts working men and women: the planned obsolescence of people that is of a piece with the planned obsolescence of the things they make or sell. It is perhaps this fear of no longer being needed in a world of needless things that most clearly spells out the unnaturalness, the surreality of much that is called work today."

Or the same idea in different words: "The drones are no longer invisible nor mute, nor are they exclusively of one class. Markham's

Man with a Hoe may be Ma Bell's girl with a headset. . . . They're in the office as well as the warehouse; at the manager's desk as well as the assembly line; at some estranged company's computer as well as some estranged woman's kitchen floor."

To sum up: most of our lives seem to serve neither ourselves nor the common good; nor can we say that we are contributing to a better world for our children. And as all this is by choice, not our fate, any American Christian with a heart full of patriotism could well this Wednesday, this 208th anniversary of our country's birth, repeat the words the prophet Hosea addressed to his countrymen when Israel spurned the good, "Come, let us return to God."

But realistically that's no option because, like the Israel of Hosea's time, modern America has lost the knowledge of God so necessary for repentance. Let's face it: misery alone never led a person or a nation to repentance. If misery alone were sufficient for repentance the whole world would be on its knees today. To repent you need an alternative, another place to lower your fishing lines. To know you're on the wrong road you have to know there's a right one. To repent, as did the Prodigal Son, you have to feel both the push of the far country and the pull of the Father's house. Also, as the parable shows, you have not only to wake up to the truth, you have to *get up* to it: "I will arise and go unto my father's house" (Luke 15:18). This same resolve I think we hear in Hosea's words: "Let us know, let us press on to know God." For, as Hosea clearly understood, without this kind of resolution any hope of any repentance, restoration, or renewal is vain. As the prophet laments (speaking for God):

> What shall I do with you, O Ephraim?
> What shall I do with you, O Judah?
> Your love is like a morning cloud,
> Like the dew that goes early away.

Given the fact that the nation as a whole has lost her knowledge of God and thus, rather than repent, continues to do exactly the same thing, only now twice as angry and frustrated as before— given this situation, Americans who take seriously their Judaism and Christianity probably could do nothing more patriotic this fourth of July than to share Hosea's resolve "to press on to know God." Surely our job is to learn ourselves and then to show others fresh ways to manifest "God's steadfast love." It is for us to experience anew in our lives a rebirth of that passion to plant a new heaven and a new earth on our continent. Already the Spirit is moving powerfully across the land, in individuals and communities, pointing us toward new and better ways to self-realization, other sources of satisfaction. I believe the Spirit today is telling us to stop defending values and trends that will leave us more and more deprived as time goes on, to stop looking for jobs that expect less than we can offer. I believe the Spirit is reminding us that being alive is a matter of growth, not accumulation, that being in touch with ourselves and with each other is worth all the worldly positions we gain through ruthless competitive struggle. I believe the Spirit is reminding us that the dollar is not almighty, that we weren't educated to get rich, but rather that we might dedicate our humanity to those who stand in need of our services. And I believe the Spirit is urging us to redistribute more equitably the wealth and power in this land and world and not to fear changes that should be welcomed. Let us remember that if we die to the old order we need not die with it, and that the present is dark only because, as prophets always saw, the future is so bright:

> Let us know, let us press on to know God;
>> God's going forth is as sure as the dawn;
> God will come to us as the showers,
>> As the spring rains that water the earth.

Listen once again to these two sentences from the New Testament lesson: "Passing on from there, Jesus saw someone called Matthew sitting at the tax office; and Jesus said to Matthew, 'Follow me.' And Matthew rose and followed Jesus" (Matt. 9:9).

I'm sure one reason Matthew did so was that he and his fellow tax collectors, at the service of their country's conquerors, were amassing personal fortunes at the expense of their country's misfortune. They too were running around destroying their country. To be sure, Matthew gave up a comfortable job, but in its place he received a destiny. To be sure, Matthew lost a good income, but in its place found integrity. He lost security, but he found the greatest of all adventures. And here's something interesting: the story of Matthew tells us that our most important choices choose us. Jesus said to Matthew, "Follow me"; Matthew's choice was only how to respond. Well, you and I too have been chosen by this same Jesus Christ. So let us "press on to know God."

White Harvests, Few Reapers

JULY 8, 1984
Reading: Matthew 9:35–10:4

The text for today's sermon is taken from the lesson for the day: "The harvest is plentiful, but the laborers are few."

When I was a boy, after a storm like yesterday's, I used to go puddle-gazing, marvelling at how small bodies of water could reflect so much of the sky and earth. Today I still marvel at how so much of the story of heaven and earth can be captured in small Biblical stories: Jesus and the paralytic; Jesus and the woman who bled for 12 years; (who thought she had only to touch his gown and she would be cured—a kind of salvation by ripoff); or Jesus and the Syrophoenician woman, who really, by dint of persistence, won from Jesus the cure of her daughter. (If ever we could rename The Riverside Church, I would suggest: "The Church of the Syrophoenician Woman.") Sometimes even a sentence will suffice to tell the tale: "And Jesus went about all the cities and villages, teaching in their synagogues and preaching the gospel of the Kingdom, and healing every disease and infirmity." He went about preaching, teaching and healing—the story of his life, and a model ministry for all would-be faithful followers. And what about the next sentence: "Seeing the crowds, Jesus had compassion for them, because they were harassed and helpless, like sheep without a shepherd." How many people manage to see an individual with compassion, let alone crowds? In every setting Jesus seems to see others with what we might call the "pain of love," even when they are behaving badly, for he never fails to recognize that what is deserving of censure at one level, at a deeper level is worthy of compassion. And this kind of compassion, of course, is frequently accompanied by righteous indignation, for if you lower your level of anger at injustice you lower your level of compassion for its victims. So anger and compassion go hand in hand.

Let's take just a moment to summarize the things that moved Jesus to compassion. Obviously he was moved by the world's pain—the paralytic, the woman who bled, all the sick and infirm touched his heart. And so did the pain of the poor. Jesus delivered people from paralysis, insanity, leprosy, suppurating wounds, deformity, and muteness. But time and again, in word and deed, he returned to the plight of the poor, whose poverty in true prophetic fashion he considered no historical accident, but the fruit of social injustice.

He was also moved by the world's sorrow: Mary and Martha grieving the death of their brother Lazarus, the widow at Nain. He was
moved by hunger, as we see in the feeding of the multitudes, always by
the vulnerability of children and by the loneliness of lepers living out
their living death. And, as we see in the lesson for the day, he was
moved by bewilderment: "Seeing the crowds, Jesus had compassion for
them, because they were harassed and helpless, like sheep without a
shepherd." Centuries later John Milton wrote: "The hungry sheep look
up and are not fed." And at the turn of our own century a Russian poet,
Mayakovsky, spoke of the pain of bewilderment in these words:

> On the pavement
> of my trampled soul
> the soles of madmen
> stamp the prints of rude, crude words.

And apparently it was the bewilderment of the crowds that
prompted the now famous words of Jesus: "The harvest is plentiful
but the laborers are few."

Note first of all what an incredibly high regard for humanity is
reflected in Jesus' view of crowds as a white harvest. How do we
Christians get away with this idea of an autocratic death-dealing God,
against whose fixed judgments there is no appeal? "The harvest is
plentiful"—the emphasis is not on the destruction of sinners, but on
their salvation. When will we get it through our heads that there is
more mercy in God than sin in us? "The harvest is plentiful"—people
are not chaff to be burned but wheat to be saved. To be sure Christ
knew—who had better reason to know?—that

> Cruelty has a Human Heart
> And Jealousy a Human Face;
> Terror the Human Form Divine,
> And Secrecy the Human Dress.
> William Blake

Still, he knew it was and always will be our destiny to live for God
and neighbor in self-forgetting love.

And if regarding humanity as a white harvest seems a bit high, a bit
risky, what of Christ's view of the reapers? None of the twelve disciples he sent out had any of the so-called "advantages"—education,
wealth, social status. They were as ordinary as they come, which
makes the point that Christ is not looking for extraordinary people,

but for *ordinary* men and women who do ordinary things extraordinarily well.

None of us who count ourselves Christians can count ourselves out—we are reapers, by the grace of God, and God knows the harvest is white, the crowds bewildered. We Christians are sinners, of course, but forgiven sinners. We are inadequate, of course, but as those who remember what Luther taught: "God can carve the rotten wood and ride the lame horse."

Let me suggest that to become reapers in our day, there are at least three requisites. The first is to find in ourselves the peace of God. "Know ye not that ye are a temple of God, and that the Spirit dwelleth within you?" (1 Cor. 3:16). "Behold, I stand at the door and knock: if any man hear my voice and open the door, I will come in to him, and will sup with him, and he with me" (Rev. 3:20). What great peace is implied in those words, the peace within, without which we can do no battle with the turmoil without. Harry Emerson Fosdick once wrote: "Those who cannot rest cannot work; those who cannot let go cannot hang on." He continued: "My consultation hours fill up with men and women who have mastered the techniques of activity and aggressiveness and whose lives are going all to pieces because they have mastered no other techniques at all." He quotes St. Augustine's prayer: "Let my soul take refuge from the crowding turmoil of worldly thoughts beneath the shadow of thy wings, Let my heart, this sea of restless waves, find peace in thee, O God." (And, mind you, no one could accuse St. Augustine of being so heavenly bound that he was of no earthly use.)

People who know the peace of God don't spend their energies defensively. People who know the peace of God don't have defense budgets of their own, they're not interested in personal security. Life to them is not something to be protected, it's an adventure. So they're vulnerable, they're open, they're creative, they're free. They never see themselves as victims, which, in many cases, is an emotional "racket" designed to extort recognition and attention from others. (That's mean, but often true.) To be a reaper you have, like Enoch, "to walk with God"; you have to invite Christ to sup with you; you have to know that peace of God that the world can neither give nor take away.

Secondly you have to see others with Christ's compassion. You have to be moved by the pain of sickness and poverty and grief and loneliness. You don't have to go to pieces, but you have to feel the pain of love. (There are worse things to feel than pain—like no pain.) We should be like good doctors, who don't identify with their patients' diseases, but do identify with their patients—"I know what you're going through." To imitate Christ we have to identify with others, and especially in their bewilderment. I like the line: "Every human being is born a prince or a princess; early experiences convince some that they are frogs." I think most people who are confused about the world are confused about their place in it. They feel like frogs. No wonder they become confused and defensive. They're scared. So to understand their thoughts we have to feel their anxiety. In other words, our basic task as reapers is to reassure: "You are a wonderful human being; God loves you, so do I."

But that is not to mince words. If people are wonderful human beings, then shouldn't we be angry at what dehumanizes them? "My consultation hours fill up with men and women who have mastered the techniques of activity and aggressiveness." I know what Harry Emerson Fosdick was talking about. Sometimes I think New York City is one great big field of ambition where the laborers are many and the harvest is not worth carrying off. And the so-called "gentrification" of New York City is reminiscent of the manic hedonism of Germany under Hitler. As for our government pursuing its ideological phantoms—I thought of it not only when I read Mayakovsky's poem, but also when I read this poem written in 1982 by an Israeli poet:

> They held up a stone.
>   I said, "Stone."
> Smiling they said, "Stone."
>
> They showed me a tree.
>   I said, "Tree."
> Smiling they said, "Tree."
>
> They shed a man's blood.
>   I said, "Blood."
> Smiling they said, "Paint."
>
> They shed a man's blood.
>   I said, "Blood."
> Smiling they said, "Paint."
>   Amir Gilboa

It confuses a crowd, it leaves people helpless and hapless, like sheep without a shepherd, when you call genocidal weapons "Peacekeepers," or when you call kidnappers and rapists "freedom fighters," or when you say that in El Salvador counterinsurgency is called for when, according to all the dictates of justice, the other side probably ought to win. Compassion without confrontation is mere sentimentality. Compassion dictates outrage, for, as I said, if you lower your level of anger at all that dehumanizes people you lower your level of love for humanity.

"The harvest is plentiful, but the laborers are few." Let us first of all strive to hold our fellow human beings in the same incredibly high regard in which they were held by Christ. Then let us not sell ourselves short. "God can carve the rotten wood and ride the lame horse." In Christ's eyes common people are uncommonly able. With the help of the Spirit, ordinary people can do ordinary things extraordinarily well. So with the peace of God in our hearts and minds, with Christ's compassion and indignation, let us swell the number of those laborers, for—"Praise the Lord"—the harvest is still white on this confused and imperilled planet.

The High and Long Road

JULY 15, 1984
Readings: Jeremiah 20:4–12; Matthew 10:28–39

When F. Scott Fitzgerald wrote, "Show me a hero, and I'll write you a tragedy," I'm sure he did not have the prophet Jeremiah in mind. But well he might have, for Jeremiah is heroic and tragic, prophet and psalmist. Like Amos and Isaiah, he thunders against injustice, predicting violence and destruction for the sins of his people. Yet at the same time that he is demanding profound changes in the civic life of Judah, he reveals an intense, intimate and conflict-ridden relationship with God. What more bitter reproach could be lodged against the Almighty than the one just heard, "O God, thou hast deceived me!" recalling the Twenty-second Psalm, whose first line was repeated by Christ on the cross: "My God, my God, why hast thou forsaken me?"

Not only have Jeremiah's predictions failed to come true, they have made him an object of derision: "I have become a laughingstock all the day; everyone mocks me." But when he resolves to speak no more in God's name, "there is in my heart, as it were, a burning fire shut up in my bones . . . I am weary with holding it in, and I cannot."

"Show me a hero, and I'll write you a tragedy." Jeremiah reminds us of two other heroic, tragic figures: one Biblical—

> Why did I come forth from the womb
> to see toil and sorrow
> and spend my days in shame?

and the other, surely the most conflict-ridden of all Shakespearean characters—

> The time is out of joint; O cursed spite
> That ever I was born to set it right.

Hamlet, Job, and Jeremiah remind us that all feelings are valid, even if all behavior isn't.

The time was out of joint for Judah in Jeremiah's time. For forty years he watched horde after horde of Scythians, Chaldeans, Assyrians, and Greek mercenaries, march against his country until finally the capital, the temple, the kingdom and the best people were all gone. And during all these years Jeremiah believed it to be his God-given task to distinguish Judaism as a religion from Jewish national fortunes, to show that they did not stand or fall together; to show, in fact, that the success of one could spell the failure of the other. It was not a task designed to win him popularity. Nor does it make popular today those prophetic rabbis in Israel who present their countrymen with a choice of reclaiming their Biblical lands or reclaiming their Biblical faith. Nor does it make popular those Jews and Christians in America who have decided that it is time our nation chose between its soul and its pride. In these momentous times, so out of joint, will Israel and the United States choose Jeremiah, or will they slip back again to Joshua, the nationalist, conquering hero?

Turning now to the New Testament lesson for the day, we find that the time similarly is out of joint, if only because Jesus promises his disciples no smoother sailing than that experienced by Jeremiah seven centuries earlier. "Behold, I send you forth as sheep amidst the wolves." He adds, "Be wise as serpents and innocent as doves," which is to say, he doesn't ask them to throw their lives away—"Bravado isn't martyrdom"—but he does ask them to give their lives, to risk something big for something good. And isn't that what God asks of faithful believers at all times, times that, alas, are always out of joint because nations always put their damnable pride ahead of their beautiful souls? Like Jeremiah, like the disciples, ours therefore should be a bruised faith, not a coddled one. How can you be devout and not be daring? What true believer could ever have his life summed up as did Tolstoy the life of Ivan Illich: "most commonplace, most ordinary, and therefore most terrible"?

It violates our spiritual selves to tranquilize them with trivia, to lull them with much routine. After the siege of Rome in 1849, Garibaldi offered his soldiers nothing but "hunger and thirst, hardship and death." After the fall of Dunkirk, Churchill offered his countrymen only "blood, toil, sweat and tears." In both instances people rallied to show the world some of the finest hours in Italian and British history. Today the world needs to be inspired by similar hours written in the *world's* history, for the world, in fact, has become one; the world has become a unity—one in death if not in life. The world has become what it is, what it always was in the sight of God, a unity, but for this high destiny humanity is not yet fit. Therefore we in the religious community who have always held that "God has made of one blood all the nations of the earth" must take the high road, the long road; others will follow. I believe it is our ancient God-given task to live astride the visible and the invisible world, so hard because one tends to pull us from the other. (People are either so earthly bound as to be of no heavenly use, or so heavenly bound to do no earthly good!) I believe it is our new God-given task, to humanize the sun and to solarize humanity. I believe it is our most urgent God-given task to remind people in the nuclear age that they are in mortal danger less from their enemies than from their enmity; to remind them that not hunger alone but superabundance also keeps people in a subhuman state; and to remind them that the saddest thing of all in this world is to be duped. Only the truth can make us free; there's a fine Russian proverb that says, "The whole world weighs less than one word of truth."

The "experts" of course will hold us in derision as they did Jeremiah, the disciples, Christ himself. But never mind; experts are right only about what has been, not about what might be. After all, an expert scientist proved with an elegant formula that no machine could ever fly, but two bicycle repairmen went into the air anyhow.

People will also say we are ahead of time. Our reply is that we are on time; everyone else is behind time.

People will say that we are fools, and they will be right. There's a saying in France, *Il faut être bête pour être bon peintre* (you must be a fool to be a good painter). Likewise you have to be "a fool for Christ's sake," as St. Paul put it, which I interpret to mean: you must acquire vulnerability if you are to be a good Christian. I try never to forget that some of the best things in this world were done by people too stupid to know they couldn't be done!

And in the pursuit of our God-given tasks our sole driving force must be the ardent love of others. Now how can you possibly love those who deride, mock, and hate you? The answer is, "You can't." And that's why we need God, as Jeremiah needed God, someone with whom to contend, someone with whom to "have it out." "O God, thou hast deceived me." Remember I said all feelings are valid, even if all behavior isn't. I view heaven as a place to "dump the mud" so that you don't pour it out all over the earth. Watch out for "nice" people who are never quite real. How often of criminals it is said, "He was such a nice boy," which means that a suppressed rebellion seethed beneath an affable facade.

But Jeremiah also knew God as "a dread warrior" (as one translation reads), one who delivers "the life of the needy from the hand of evildoers." Likewise Jesus reassured those he sent as sheep among wolves that God numbered every hair on their head. He reminded them that five sparrows were sold for two pence. What he had in mind was a habit of sacrifice: the rich could afford bullocks, but the poor only sparrows. Sparrows went two for a penny, but if you bought two pennies' worth a fifth sparrow was thrown in. God cares for that fifth sparrow! How much more for each of us!

So heroic and tragic, in the footsteps of Jeremiah, the disciples, let us not hesitate to take the high road, the long road, for the sake of the soul of our nation and of the only world we have, a soul and a world it would be so wonderful to save. "O cursed spite, that ever I was born to set it right." Complain all you want, just as long as, holding fast the master's hand, you keep going. Yes, "O Master, let me walk with thee,"

> In hope that sends a shining ray
> Far down the future's broadening way,
> In peace that only Thou canst give,
> With Thee, O Master, let me live.
> Washington Gladden

Not Peace, but a Sword

JULY 22, 1984
Reading: Jeremiah 6:10–16; Matthew 10:34–39

D o not think that I have come to bring peace on earth; I have not come to bring peace, but a sword." *Y Dios no te dé paz, y sí gloria* (May God deny you peace and give you glory). Christ and the great Spanish philosopher Unamuno certainly would not have opposed the sentiments of Whittier's hymn just sung, nor certainly would they stand against "the peace of God that passes all understanding"—after all, Jesus himself was God's Peace Incarnate. What they are doing in their own way is repeating what Jeremiah said about those priests and prophets who "have healed the wound of my people lightly, saying 'peace, peace,' where there is no peace." In other words, truth is above harmony. In other words, those who fear disorder more than injustice invariably produce more of both.

When on Thursday evening, at the close of the Democratic Convention, Mr. Walter Mondale joined other party leaders in calling for unity, it seemed to most people a right thing to do. But when, during the Vietnam War, President Johnson did the same, calling on the whole country to unite in the name of patriotism, it was wrong. For what patriotic virtue was there in unity if it was unity in cruelty, unity in folly?

Another great philosopher, Nietzsche, said, "I like my truths bloody." All great truths have to be bloody because they brook no neutrality. There is no way that a Nietzsche, or a Beethoven, or a creative genius like Picasso can burst upon the artistic scene without turbulence. They unbalance too many equations. (In one German concert hall, at the end of the last century, they hung signs that read, "In case of Brahms, make for the nearest exit.") Likewise there is no way that a great cause can arise and not divide people. The abolitionist movement, the movement to establish the eight-hour day, the right of women to vote the freeze movement—all make the point. Clearly then, there is no way that the truth of truths—the Gospel—can come peacefully into our lives and still be the Gospel. Human beings always squeeze their eyes against the truth. We resist it because it overturns beloved sheltering lies; it tears us apart. Let's be honest. Even after we Christians accept the Gospel, only about a half of us really repents, the other half remains unrepentant. Half of us really entreats, the other never entreats. We put our best foot forward, but it's the other one that needs the attention.

Or look at it this way: no matter how many wrinkles may adorn our faces, they should always be animated with childlike curiosity and Christlike compassion. Yet too often they show symptoms of that deadly disease, "psychosclerosis," a hardening not of the arteries (as in arteriosclerosis) but of the psyche, the spirit. As a result, our hearts no longer remain vulnerable; our minds cannot see, let alone embrace, new ideas. Clearly the trick in life is to die young as late as possible. But sufferers of psychosclerosis seek spiritually to die old as young as possible. Therefore, to remind us that there is more, far more, not only than the worst but than the best, we need the sharp edge of Christ's truth. Christ came not to bring peace but a sword— Praise the Lord!

Let me read you what to me is one of the most moving opening paragraphs in any book I've read—it's the opening one in Alan Payton's *Too Late the Phalarope*:

> Perhaps I could have saved him, with only a word or two words out of my mouth. Perhaps I could have saved us all. But I never spoke them. . . . For he spoke hard and bitter words to me, and shut the door of his soul on me, and I withdrew. But I should have hammered on it. I should have broken it down with my naked hands. I should have cried out there not ceasing, for behind it was a man in danger, the bravest and gentlest of them all.

(I love what that last sentence implies: small strengths and small weaknesses we understand; what we can't deal with is great strength and great weakness. But that's for another time.)

It's easy—isn't it?—to identify with both people in this opening paragraph, the one who shut the door of his soul, and the one who failed to hammer on it. When marital unpleasantness arises, many husbands are given to what some wives call "the male fade-away." When the going gets tough, these tough men become pussycats, and they quietly close the doors of their souls and withdraw. I think it fair to say that generally men prefer to wait for the turbulences to die down. They never do.

And who hammers resolutely on the shut door of the soul of the boss? When he/she, proving himself/herself to be tough as nails and morally about as sensitive, utters utterly outrageous things, isn't our reaction to deflect rather than to protest, to humor where we should be confronting power? That little game of humoring, with its deadly consequences, is played right up to the top of the nation's political structure. "I should have cried out there not ceasing." May the Lord Christ have mercy upon us who hold our peace where there is no peace at all.

Institutions, like individuals, also need to feel Christ's sword. Show me an organization and I will show you bureaucrats who have learned the advantages of organizational inertia. It's always safer to go on doing what's always been done. Lord knows the media needs to hear the sharpness of heavenly truth—and I don't only mean *Penthouse*. I'm talking about the way the media can be sharply critical of individuals but is totally incapable of transcending the norms, cultural and political, of our society. And of course, local churches, ministers and laity alike, need to be prodded, for we domesticate God's word too soon. Lacking the vigor to deal with big problems, we allow ourselves to become mesmerized by little ones.

In the lesson for today Christ seems most interested in households (which makes the lesson so poignant). "For I have come to set a man against his father, and a daughter against her mother." What are we to make of those seemingly cruel words? St. Benedict wrote: "God often shows what is better to the younger." But, resisting that insight, threatened by what their children say, many parents try to control the thoughts and behavior of their children by undermining their belief in themselves. So there's little harmony in the family anyhow. What I hear Christ asking for is a more honest, courageous confrontation, one that invites all parties to a higher level of understanding and harmony. We heard, "He who loves father and mother more than me is not worthy of me." That's not really cruel. Loving Christ more than our fathers and mothers simply saves the love we have for our parents from corruption and decay. You remember the poem of Lovelace that goes:

> I could not love thee (Dear) so much,
> Loved I not honor more.

Substitute "Jesus" for "honor" and you have the formula for saving God-given mercies—our loved ones—from becoming a Satanic temptation: to think there's nothing more. I don't hear Christ asking us to pull the house down on the heads of our mothers and fathers, husbands, wives and children. I hear him only reminding us that God, as the source of love, is the proper head of every loving household.

And then comes the harsh demand: "He who does not take his cross and follow me is not worthy of me." But this cross-bearing, we are told, is not so much to please Christ as to fulfill ourselves: "He who finds his life will lose it, and he who loses his life for my sake will find it."

I said last week that bravado wasn't martyrdom. But there come these moments in all our lives (and you know what I'm talking about)—there come these moments when it is not enough to reflect the truth; we have to embrace the truth. There come these moments when it is not enough to love the Gospel; we have to live it. And you also know how often these moments come, and we withdraw. We betray those moments, and our self-loathing is only surpassed by our despair. But if we do embrace the truth and live the Gospel, giving ourselves over to that half of ourselves that truly does repent, that truly does entreat, then no longer are we torn asunder. For despair then becomes hope, collapse conversion, and fear a source of action. Said Epictetus of Socrates: "Dying, he was saved, because he did not flee." Had Socrates fled, the real Socrates would have died, for cowardice kills the real self in every one of us.

But—Praise the Lord again—there is resurrection. "Once to every man and nation comes the moment to decide"—nonsense! Twice, three, four, fourteen times to a man and nation comes the moment to decide. It's a beautiful hymn, but theologically unsound. For the God who made us can always remake us. Or think of this: to the degree that the church is founded on Peter, it is founded on a second chance. And that part of us that truly repents and truly entreats never fully dies. So we can still open the door of our souls—live vulnerably, see and embrace new ideas. We can still hammer on the shut doors of those we care for, put truth above harmony, revive our churches, speak truth to power, protest the false assurances of national well-being. By the mercy assured us in the life, death, and resurrection of Jesus we can once again hear:

> Thus saith the Lord:
> Stand by the roads and look,
>   and ask for the ancient paths,
> where the good way is; and walk in it,
>   and find rest for your souls.

May the peace of God that passes all understanding be with you all.

In Praise of Rest

JULY 29, 1984
Reading: Genesis 1:1–2:3

The text for today's sermon is the third verse of the second chapter of Genesis: "God rested on the seventh day and hallowed it, because on it God rested from all his work."

I just know that there's some mean-spirited person out there who's already saying to himself/herself: "That fellow is about to take off on vacation, and he's going to take the text out of context and use it as a pretext to justify his goofing off." Well, Ms. or Mr. Smartypants, you may not be all that wrong, but watch out: theological fireworks are coming your way.

Before we get to them, however, let's first—in a rapid switch to a more serious mood—sympathize with those here in this church, and elsewhere, who have long been on forced vacations by virtue of having been laid off work. If you are unemployed, the chances are you are having an identity crisis, which is to say you are in the middle of a religious crisis. Please, be like a nail: the harder unemployment hits you, the deeper let it drive you into the everlasting arms of the only one to whom you should accord power to tell you who you are. On welfare or off, with or without unemployment compensation, you are God's precious daughter or son, and don't let unemployment tell you differently.

Furthermore, if you are unemployed, chances are you are suffering the effects less of a personal tragedy than of a public scandal, it's a social, not a personal, failure. God grant that one day this nation will come to its senses and see the right to work and the right to food as the moral rights they clearly are, and then accord them the same legal protection we presently guarantee such rights as freedom of speech, press, and religion.

But that's a subject whose elaboration awaits another sermon on another sabbath. Our text today calls to remembrance that first sabbath when none of us were around; when God had an entire sabbath to himself, when after six days of prodigious labor, of wild creativity, God took the seventh day off to catch his breath.

Notice that God did not hallow the day on which God made the beasts of the earth, the birds of the air, the fish of the sea, and "every creeping thing that creeps upon the earth." God did not hallow even that day on which she made you and me, "male and female." No, God hallowed that day and that day only on which God did nothing at all but rest.

There must be more to this business of resting than meets the ordinary eye. This afternoon I'm going to Riverside Park where I love to go because I love to watch the folks rest. It's the most non-competitive scene in the city. With the exception of purse-snatchers and an occasional mean child, no one is trying to take anything from anybody; and only on a see-saw is someone trying to rise by making somebody else go down. And everybody—those reading on the benches, the dog walkers, the frisbee players, the lovers strolling down the paths; and the families sitting on the grass or, more often, on colorful blankets—everyone is receiving something, like a renewed sense of physical and spiritual well-being. It's coming from everywhere, this sense of well-being: from the sky and air, from scudding clouds and singing birds; it's coming from the river and from ice-cream cones, from the sounds of the Riverside carillon and the sight of the Circle Line Ferry on the home stretch of one of the most gorgeous trips a tourist could take any place in this world. But most of all, this sense of well-being is coming from the folks themselves, from each other, *because they have time now* for each other. And it's all free. "Lord, of thy fulness have we received, grace upon grace."

God must have been exhausted by the seventh day, and if God needed to rest, you can count on it, so do we. Our sputtering hearts, our reeling heads, our dragging feet—they all need to rest, and in so doing to receive anew that sense of well-being. If God needed to rest, so do you; it's dangerous theology to think you can improve on God. Yes, there must be something prideful about our reluctance to rest more often. Sometimes I think it's more blessed to receive than to give; at least it takes more humility.

I imagine on that first sabbath God threw a party for himself. He had a lot to celebrate. Read the fifteenth chapter of Luke, as we did in our Bible study earlier this month, and you will find the following: at the end of the parable of the lost sheep, when the sheep was found, the shepherd threw a party; at the end of the parable of the lost coin, when the coin was found, the woman threw a party; and at the end of the parable of the prodigal son, when the son was found, the father threw a party. According to Jesus, God is partying all the time; and once again, it's dangerous theology to try to improve on God.

God rested; God threw a party; I imagine God also took stock. He had a lot to think about, as do we. The other day in the park I passed a person on a bench reading Barbara Tuchman's *Guns of August*. It occurred to me that to go to another place (the park) and to another time (the first decades of our century) was a wonderful way to triangulate on yourself and your own time. "Am I being what I really want to be, doing what I really want to do? Is my church doing all it can to make Christ visible? What more can I do personally about the violence of American life so dreadfully apparent in marginal and expendable people, out of work and on welfare?"

And how fares our relationship with God? Years after the death of Gertrude Stein, her constant companion, Alice Toklas, said of her a wonderful thing: "It wasn't what Gertrude gave me—so much, but it was what she never took away." I often think of God that way: what God gives is no more impressive than what God never takes. Put differently, it's a wonderful thing to be loved by someone who will never be in competition with you; who wants only your exaltation, not his. When you stop to think of it, God is the only person in your life who will never compete with you. That is why it is so restful to be with God, and why God is so readily found in rest. "Be still, and know that I am God." "Come unto me, all ye who labor and are heavy laden and I will give you rest."

As God will never compete with us, so She will never desert us. Many of you, I imagine, know the hymn, "O love, that wilt not let me go." What you may not know is that it was written by George Matheson, famous Scottish preacher, who in his handsome youth was engaged to a beautiful woman. When the doctors determined that Matheson was going blind, she broke the engagement. It was then, in the depths of grief, that he sat down and poured out:

> O Love that wilt not let me go,
> I rest my weary soul in Thee;
> I give Thee back the life I owe,
> That in Thine ocean depths its flow
> May richer, fuller be.

O lovers, never forget that love is greater than the sum of its hearts!

A final purpose of rest seems obvious. While God rested on the seventh day, there is certainly no indication that that was what God had in mind to do for ever and ever. Certainly it wasn't long before rescuing the human race became a full-time job. (God has had a lot of problems, but unemployment has not been one of them.) And saving the human race is our job, too; "The harvest is white but the laborers are few." Success may be far from certain, but where we can't be optimistic we can be persistent. And if, at regular intervals, we rest with God, we can return with God (as St. Paul would say): "to run the straight race, to fight the good fight, to endure unto the end," until with all the saints we are made partakers of God's eternal kingdom.

So get some rest, will you? I'll set you a fine example. God be with you til we meet again.

Homecoming Sunday

SEPTEMBER 23, 1984
Reading: Matthew 27:51–56

W ell, dearly beloved," as St. Paul might say. It certainly is wonderful to be back in the gold field, the oyster bed of talent and kindness that is Riverside Church, and in this sanctuary which seems to remind us, as do all cathedrals, that not only we ourselves, but the whole world is made for more than itself. And I am always ambushed by my emotions when, driving back to New York, I catch that first glimpse of the George Washington Bridge. I guess New Yorkers never outgrow their enchantment with their bridges, and I can't wait to see, once again, the sun glistening off the steel web of suspending girders, cables, stays, shrouds, and lines that hang between the two stone towers of the Brooklyn Bridge. Of course you could say, "Hell of a lot of trouble to go just to get to Brooklyn"—but I wouldn't!

Not that life in Vermont is without its own enchantment. On Wednesday, while driving along some of my favorite backroads of Vermont admiring the early colors, I suddenly spied at the foot of an apple tree, a farmer holding a pig—a large one at that—in his arms so that the pig could eat the apples off the tree. When the pig finished with the apples on one bough, the farmer moved him to another. I couldn't help getting out of the car, walking over to the fence and saying to the farmer, "Wouldn't it be easier, wouldn't it save a lot of time to put the pig down, and then shake the tree until the apples fell off?" The farmer took his time before answering, "Yup, I reckon it would save a lot of time. But then, what's time to a pig?"

I have a "sort of" text for this "homecoming" Sunday. It's a homespun aphorism, and not a very good one at that: "You can't go home again, but you can always go back to church."

The first half of the aphorism, "You can't go home again," is but a variant of the old adage that you can't set the clock back. Just as you can't undo what's done, so you can't become again what you no longer are. "The moving finger writes, and having writ, moves on"— to which we can only cry out, "That's right, *darn it!*" For unless it was misery itself, who wants to leave childhood? You remember the difference between a psychotic and a neurotic: The psychotic thinks 2 and 2 make 5; the neurotic knows they make 4, but oh, how he hates it! Well, most of us leave childhood in a rather neurotic frame of mind, and some of us never do. You've seen them, the middle-aged—ever-older—who have about them incongruous youthfulness. They may be bright or dumb, charming or irritating but above all they are young. Like Dorian Gray, they have never dared to grow up. They have never dared to move into psychological maturity.

"You can't go home again." That truth also spells protection for parents whose children want them to keep their past intact, so that the children, from time to time, can wander through it nostalgically. That desire's unfair, because as much as our children, parents need to keep growing: "Though our outer nature is wasting away, our inner nature is being renewed each day" (2 Cor. 4:16). There is only one house to which you can return expecting to find it unconsumed by moth and rust—incorruptible and unchanged—and that is a doll house. Maybe that explains its lifelong popularity with some people.

But like the moving finger, let's move on. "You can't go home again, but you can always go back to church." Does that mean any old church? No, not if in contrast to Dorian Gray, you have dared to grow up, and now believe in thinking and wish to think in believing. If you have dared to move into psychological maturity, you can't go back to a fundamentalist church that exalts a childhood model of obedience and puts God's power ahead of God's love. You certainly don't want to go back to a church overly conscious of its 2,314 canonical laws. (Said Emerson: "Good men must not obey the laws too well.") Nor should you go back to a church full of esthetes, who love everything about the church except its people; nor to one full of accommodators, arrangers, moral amnesiacs—and there are a few of them around—nor finally to a church that doesn't have the foggiest notion of what the Pope was talking about this week in Alberta, when he warned rich nations that they must change rigid economic systems that give them "imperialistic monopoly" over the world's poor.

A church to which you *can* return on a "homecoming" or any other Sunday is one that sees and embraces the truths set forth in Matthew's story of what happened as Jesus died.

It's a tough passage to explicate, because if we *do* believe in thinking, and wish to think in believing, what are we to make of the sudden rending of the temple veil (by lightning?) and of the earthquake, and of the open graves, which are found only in Matthew's account of Christ's death? Are these "signs" that people in the ancient world would expect to accompany great tragedy? Imagine how inconceivable it would be to someone like Matthew that God could watch his son die on a cross and not immediately write his judgment across a darkened sky and cause the very earth to shake. But whether these things are meant to be taken literally or not, they teach truths central to any church worthy of the name. "And behold, the curtain of the temple was torn in two, from top to bottom." This curtain was the veil which covered the so-called "Holy of holies." It was the veil beyond which no mortal soul was allowed to tread, save only the high priest on the Day of Atonement. It was the veil behind which, in a very special sense, the Spirit of God was believed to dwell.

Suddenly, as Jesus dies, this veil is torn in two. Why? Because the heretofore hidden love of God has now been fully revealed. On the cross of Jesus Christ, "*Deus Absconditus*" becomes "*Deus Revelatus*." On the cross of Jesus Christ, once and for all, and for all eyes to see, the heart of Almighty God is laid bare, teaching us that it is not God's power we are called on to obey, but rather God's love: "When I am lifted up, I will draw all men unto me" (John 12:32). Not "drive" but "draw all people unto me." God does not want our submission to God's power, but for God's love poured out for us on a cross, he wants our own, freely returned.

"The curtain of the temple was torn in two" further suggests that gone now is all but a functional division between priest and worshiper. Gone too is the division between Jew and Gentile, slave and free, male and female. With access to God free to all, gone is every barrier falsely erected between human beings and God, between brothers and sisters which, of course, means every last one of us on this earth. Only a church that sees clearly and embraces those truths of God's amazing love and the oneness of all humanity, is one to which at any hour of day or night, one can return—and must return.

And what shall we say of the empty graves? No church should ever dismiss, demean, or in any way deny the awesomeness of death, nor the fear of it that eats away at the heart of each of us, making us from time to time both insecure and militant—a lethal combination in any individual or nation. Worse yet, because our lives so often cry out for rebuke and forgiveness, we also fear that we may deserve to die. So every church worthy of the name, Sunday in and Sunday out, must proclaim the Good News that Christ is the "lamb of God that taketh away the sins of the world" (John 1:29), that "God was in Christ reconciling the world unto itself" (2 Cor. 5:19), yes, that there is more mercy in God than sin in us. And just as in life, so in death, "nothing can separate us from the love of God." We may not know what lies beyond the grave, but we know who is there. Death is inevitable and death is awesome, but it is the fear of death that is its sting. Remove that fear and there's not a one of us that cannot say with Paul, "O death, where is thy sting? O grave, where is thy victory?" (1 Cor. 15:55). What could better symbolize the defeat of death than those tombs that God caused to open up even before Christ was laid in his own!

And what of the centurion who saw the frightful error of his ways, and risked popularity and perhaps his job by confessing to all around, "Truly, this man was the son of God"? To think that the man who killed Christ became his first follower after death! Indeed, "when I am lifted up I will draw all men unto me."

I suppose one of the most beautiful human acts in the world is the simple, faithful act of commitment to Jesus Christ. It has to be a central act in every church. And it has to be repeated in places as public and sometimes as dangerous as was Calvary to the centurion. For a statement worth making should be heard. And the world needs to hear that you believe in Jesus, and Lord knows the world needs to hear that what you believe is more important than what people think of you.

Finally, the women "watching," Matthew says "from a distance . . . the women who had followed Jesus from Galilee, ministering to him" (Matt. 27:55). Remember, all the disciples forsook him and fled. But the women remained. There's faithfulness despite everything. No doubt their sadness was overwhelming, made all the more so by being mixed with a feeling of helplessness. Yet, "They also serve who only stand and wait." If Jesus saw them, the very sight of them standing at a distance must have lightened his darkness. And who do you suppose gave Matthew his account of the crucifixion? To me these women symbolize that all-important function of a church—the transmission of the faith. Thank God for what God gave them to give to Matthew.

"You can't go home again, but you can always go back to church," at least to one that sees clearly and embraces profoundly the truth that we are all called to respond to God's love, rather than God's power; to one that sees that national discrimination is an evil as prideful as racial; to one that has a nose-thumbing independence of death militant in all its forms; to one whose members rejoice to show forth their faith, not only in words but in deeds, and count faithfulness more important than success.

Is Riverside such a church? It is not for its members to say. But as one of them, I confess to you that I have found the spirit moving here. I confess to you that time and again I have seen the primacy of love here. I confess to you that time and again the courage of my convictions has been renewed here. So I confess to you that I'm glad to be back in my home church. I hope the same is true of all of you.

Religion and Politics

SEPTEMBER 30, 1984
Readings: Exodus 3:1–12; John 7–12

Much is being said and written these days about the mix of religion and politics, yet little, in my judgment, seems helpful. So I want to read to you three statements which seem to indicate that although they are often at sword's points, religion and politics are fundamentally inseparable. The first statement comes from a minister of the gospel who also became the first Black Mayor of Englewood, New Jersey. He was born in Mississippi, one of 14 children, and died in June across the Hudson. Wrote Walter Taylor: "Politics determines the kind of world you will be born in, the kind of education, health care and job you eventually get, how you will spend your old age and even how you die. The church must address itself to, and be involved in, anything that affects life as greatly as this."

The second statement comes from that cheerful hero of Black South Africa, Bishop Desmond Tutu: "If an elephant has his foot on the tail of the mouse, and you say you are neutral, the mouse will not appreciate your neutrality."

And dollars to doughnuts, even the seminary professors among you will not guess the author of the third statement: "Religious distress is at the same time the expression of real distress, and also the protest against real distress. Religion is the sigh of the oppressed creature, the heart of the heartless world, just as it is the spirit of the spiritless conditions." The following, and give away, sentence reads, "Religion is the opium of the people."

I chose that statement to make the point that for Karl Marx, religion was a natural human reaction to oppression and misery, a symptom of an unacceptable state of affairs. But despite what we all hear to the contrary, Marx was in no sense an enemy of religion as such. Nor are all Marxists "godless atheists," as the redundant phrase goes.

If religion and politics are fundamentally inseparable, then the answer to "bad religion" is not "no religion," but "good religion." And to see what that might be let us look once again at the Exodus story. "Then the Lord said, 'I have seen the affliction of my people who are in Egypt, and have heard their cry because of their task masters.'"*

Whatever they do in our minds, it is clear that in God's mind religion and politics *do* mix; economics too. It is equally clear that God chooses sides, siding with those who suffer deprivation and oppression. How could it be otherwise? If God sided with tyrants, God would be malevolent. If God sided with no one, God would be indifferent—which is to say once again "malevolent," because he would be supporting tyranny by not protesting it. It is only by a clear understanding that God sides with the oppressed, that we can say that ours is a God of justice. "I have seen the affliction of my people and have heard their cry." When the elephant has his foot on the tail of the mouse, or, to change the image, when the North American shark is

*The biblical exegesis in this sermon is from Robert McAfee Brown's *Unexpected News.*— WSC

eating Latin American sardines ("*El tiburón norteamericano está comiendo las sardinas latinoamericanas*"), we may try to be neutral, but God is on the side of mice and sardines.*

And that, dear friends, raises an uncomfortable question: Can we ourselves claim to know God if we don't join Her on the side of the oppressed?

In the twenty-second chapter of Jeremiah, the prophet is mercilessly attacking the king of Judah, and meanly so, by comparing him unfavorably to his father:

> "'Did not your father eat and drink and do justice and righteousness? . . . He judged the cause of the poor and needy. Is not this to know me?' says the Lord." (Vv. 15–16)

In churches and church offices throughout Central and Latin America, there are signs that read, "*Conocer a Dios es obrar la justicia*" (To know God is to do justice). Does it not then follow, that to do injustice is not to know God? And if love is more, and not less than justice, then the New Testament lesson makes the same point, "He who does not love does not know God: for God is love."

Incidentally, "Did not your father eat and drink and do justice and righteousness" reminds us that eating and drinking are not antithetical to, but complimentary to justice and righteousness. The first Christians were communists not because they wanted to live ascetically, not because they wanted to raise poverty to the level of a Christian ideal, but simply because they didn't want anyone to go hungry. And the "gentrification" which we see rolling up Columbus and Amsterdam avenues is evil, not so much because of the prosperity it represents, though some of it is tasteless and nauseating, but rather because the means to obtain that prosperity are unjust.

To know God is to do justice. To recognize this implacable moral imperative of the faith represents the kind of good religion that mixes well with politics.

But there is more to be said:

> He has put down the mighty from their thrones, and exalted those of low degree; he has filled the hungry with good things, and the rich he has sent empty away. (Luke 1:52–53)

---

*The shark image is that of a former president of Guatemala.—WSC

As many of you recognize, those are words of the Virgin Mary, who in prayer—God help us!—speaks of politics, and worse yet, of class struggle! I use "class struggle" advisedly to make another point about Marx, that while he may have come up with the term, he did not invent the reality. And for the Vatican to say to Liberation Theologians that if they use Marxist terms they are in danger of becoming secular Marxists is like saying to Thomas Aquinas that because he used Aristotelian categories he was in danger of becoming a Greek pagan. What Vatican nonsense! What gross insecurity!

Had Herod heard Mary's prayer or, better yet, President Reagan, he most certainly would have called her a Marxist, and (let me whisper this) he probably would have been right! The tragedy of the President and of so many Americans, is that they forget that Lech Walesa too is a Marxist—as was Alexander Dubcek in Czechoslovakia, and Andrei Sakharov in Russia. What the President and most Americans fail to realize is that "Stalinism is to Marxism what the Ku Klux Klan is to Christianity; a manipulation of the chief symbols, yet diametrically opposed to the central values" (Cornel West).

Let's summarize: The story of the Exodus teaches us that in the mind of God religion and politics *do* mix, that God understands class struggle, and that God intervenes on behalf of the underdog. No wonder this story has been such a "paradigm passage" (as theologians say) for Blacks here at home, and for millions of Christians of all kinds in the world we call Third, but which should probably be called "Two Thirds," because that represents the number of our sisters and brothers who suffer deprivation and oppression.

But we have to be even more precise and ask, "How does God intervene on behalf of the poor and oppressed?" In Alberta, Canada, two-and-a-half weeks ago, the Pope, in eloquent words, took off once again after the powerful nations of the world, accusing them of maintaining rigid economic systems that represent an "imperialistic monopoly," over the world's poor. In other words, the Pope sought to enlighten the hearts of the pharaohs of the world. But in the Exodus story, God did not seek to enlighten the heart of Pharaoh, God *hardens* the heart of Pharaoh. Whatever else that may mean, it clearly means that waiting around for the rich to feed the poor is not the way to go. The poor must take matters into their own hands. And that, of course, is what must have scared almost to death both Pharaoh and Moses!

Honesty does not come painlessly: The truth will make you free, but first it makes you miserable! So let's press on a bit further. That God is against the status quo is one of the hardest things to believe if you are a Christian who happens to profit by the status quo. In fact, most of us don't really believe it, not in our heart of hearts. We comfort ourselves with the thought that because our intentions are good (nobody gets up in the morning and says, "Who can I oppress today?"), we do not have to examine the consequences of our actions. As a matter of fact, many of us are even eager to respond to injustice, just as long as we can do so without having to confront the causes of it. And there's the great pitfall of charity. Handouts to needy individuals are genuine, necessary responses to injustice, but they do not necessarily face the reason for the injustice. And that is why President Reagan and so many business leaders today are promoting charity: it is desperately needed in an economy whose prosperity is based on growing inequality. First these leaders proclaim themselves experts on matters economic, and prove it by taking the most out of the economy! Then they promote charity as if it were the work of the church, finally telling us troubled clergy to shut up and bless the economy as once we blessed the battleships.

But the prophet did not say, "Let charity roll down like mighty waters"—because giving without receiving is a downward motion. The prophet said, "Let *justice* roll down like mighty waters, and righteousness like an everflowing stream." Therefore, for all his eloquence, the Pope was wrong only to flay the rich; he should have followed the lead of Liberation Theologians and told the poor to organize. For that apparently is the way God intervenes in history. The Exodus story tells us that liberation is primarily the work of the oppressed themselves.

Most of the members of this church are not oppressed. We're not particularly rich, but we're not desperately poor, and neither, I would imagine, are most visitors here today. So that raises the question, "Does all this mean that God is not concerned with the non-poor?" Of course not! God is God not only of the Third World, "He's got the whole world in his hands!" Only his concern for the non-poor is in the context of his concern for the poor, and not the other way around.

Does all this mean there is nothing the non-poor can do? Again the answer is, "Of course not." Last June, as many of you remember, this church voted to declare itself a sanctuary church. If you believe the United States is behaving badly in Central America (as the Soviet Union is certainly behaving badly south of its borders), then come tomorrow night. At 7:30 p.m. we go public with our Guatemalan family—father, mother, and child. With confidence in the right as God gives us to see the right, we take our stand with the mice and the sardines against the elephants and sharks. And we are going to do the same thing with the poor of New York City, for at that same meeting last June, we pledged ourselves to a program of study and action, which this sermon hopefully will serve. There is plenty for the members of this church who are not desperately poor to do. Quite simply, we must allow ourselves to be touched by the plight of our brothers and sisters who are; and as Christians, to strive—hard as it may be—to appropriate the knowledge that to know God is to do justice.

The City

OCTOBER 7, 1984
Readings: Genesis 11:1–9; Revelation 21:9–11, 22–26

I have been asked by the Biblical and Theological Studies Committee to preach on the city, an assignment I gladly accept, but with the wish that none of us forget the hundreds of millions—literally—of our sisters and brothers the world around who with us today, celebrate "Worldwide Communion Sunday." Millions of them too live in cities, which I dare say to them as to us, are problematic and promising.

When we ask, what does the Bible have to say about cities?, we have to answer that the early Hebrews, and many a later prophet, took a very dim view of them. "Come let us build ourselves a city and a tower with its top in the heavens, and make a name for ourselves." Clearly the folks in Babel had in mind to build a once-and-for-all-from-here-to-eternity edifice, reflecting that most fatal of all human inclinations, to try pridefully to live independently of God. Babel was only the first city to prove that God is not mocked. Ezekiel lamented over Tyre, "You corrupted your wisdom for the sake of your splendor . . . All who know you are appalled at you. You have come to a dreadful end" (Ezek. 28:17, 19). And Jeremiah lamented in similar fashion over Babylon, "O opulent city, standing beside great waters, your end has come, your destiny is certain. . . . Worthless now is the thing for which the nations toiled; the peoples wore themselves out for a mere nothing" (Jer. 51:13, 58).

This dim view is an easy one to embrace if you're a New York cabbie working for your PhD degree (PhD meaning Pot hole dodger) and you're undergoing the baptism of venom from determined New York jaywalkers. Or, if you're a rider on New York subways—easily the most dangerous in the world, or you live in a neighborhood where kids

---

This sermon owes much to *Is There Hope for the City?* by Donald W. Shriver Jr. and Karl A. Ostrom.—WSC

are malnourished before they are even born, where the paint is peeling everywhere and people look forever for the key to unlock the help which somebody, somewhere has the power to give them.

But other prophets like Isaiah, and early Christians such as the author of the book of Revelation, saw also in cities a symbol of the hope that God would one day achieve his purposes for his people. "And I saw no temple in the city, for its temple is the Lord God the Almighty and the Lamb."

I think it important that in our proper concern for the humiliated we not miss the constant hope and beauty of this city, the "gestures" as architects like to call buildings like the two that face one another on 116th and Riverside Drive; nor overlook the city's splendid history. How many of you have stopped to take in the fact that with the exception of the second half of the nineteenth century when the ascendency passed to New England, New York City has been the literary capital of the land, and also, perhaps, the single most important factor in American literature? The first Black poet of America, Jupiter Hammon, lived some time ago in Queens, and in this century, almost all the leading Black writers—James Weldon Johnson, Langston Hughes, Ralph Ellison, W. E. B. DuBois, Claude Brown—all lived in Harlem, within a mile or two of Riverside Church.

Ogden Nash once wrote: "The Bronx? No thonks!" But that was not the way Edgar Allan Poe felt in the 1840s when he lived in a little village called Fordham. Nor did Nash express the feelings one hundred years later of Clifford Odets, Herman Wouk, and Sholem Aleichem.

Brooklyn, of course, boasts the greatest city glorifier of them all, the editor of the *Brooklyn Eagle* and perhaps America's most significant poet, Walt Whitman, as well as Henry Miller, Richard Wright, Arthur Miller, Marianne Moore, Maya Angelou, Ossie Davis, and Chaim Potok.

Even Staten Island can claim a poet, Edwin Markham, and also William Curtis, once editor of *Harper's Weekly*. In 1850, he wrote: "God might have made a more beautiful spot than Staten Island but he never did."

As for Manhattan, besides the Harlem writers already mentioned, the Upper West Side alone housed Lillian Hellman, Anais Nin, Susan Sontag, Elizabeth Hardwick, and Isaac Bashevis Singer. The so-called "Beat Movement" was born in the 1940s out of the interaction of Jack Kerouac, William Burroughs, and Allen Ginsberg, all, of whom lived right off Broadway on 114th and 113th Street. J. D. Salinger spent childhood years at 390 Riverside Drive, and at 200 Claremont Avenue, F. Scott Fitzgerald lived for a while in 1919. According to his own testimony, Fitzgerald "had 122 rejection slips pinned in a frieze around his bedroom." I haven't even mentioned the greatest of them all, Herman Melville, because he lived downtown and I haven't mentioned the theatre, I haven't mentioned music, art. Friends this is *some city*!

But enough of the euphoria, let's get back to New York's troubles, and such cures as the Bible and Church history might possibly have to offer them. Last week, as you may remember, I underlined Jeremiah's point "that to know God is to do justice." The other side of that profoundly Hebrew understanding is that spiritual idolatry goes hand in hand with social injustice. To the ancient Jews it was but a hop, skip and a jump, from the worship of Baal to the worship of wealth to the oppression of the poor. To the ancient Jews, God's salvation was, if you will, a package deal that included politics and economics—a package deal that couldn't be untied or negotiated. It was their profound conviction that economic activity, no less than prayer, should tell God's glory. To them a city should always try to organize its entire life around the unfailing love and justice of God.

The early Christians felt much the same way, which is why they refused to perform the annual ritual of putting a pinch of incense on the altar of the god, Caesar, demanded of all citizens of the empire. Many Romans were dumbfounded, saying to them in effect, "Look, your private religious beliefs are your own. Worship whom you will. Just leave politics to us." But like the early Jews, the early Christians refused to separate the public from the private realm. To abandon the public realm to the Emperor would be to abandon God who first saved Israel by intervening in the politics of Egypt. I'm told that in the first century A.D., chariots circulated Rome with stickers on them saying "Rome, love it or leave it!" If you refused to obey Rome (the real meaning of "Love it"), they helped you leave by pushing you into a coliseum full of hungry lions.

Skipping now to the 16th century, the same vision of a holy community was Calvin's when he came to Geneva in the 1550s. To Calvin the world was "the theatre of God's glory," and we are all on stage to bring to completion the divine drama. The "holy community" was to be an ecclesiastical-civil way of life that squared in all respects with a diligent study of the Bible. For that reason Calvin caused a law to be passed forbidding the recruiting of mercenaries in Geneva, and the first dentist to come to that town of 12,000 people was not licensed until Calvin personally tested his skill. Said Calvin to his fellow citizens of Geneva: "We are chiefly to study our neighbor's advantage. No increase is advantageous unless it answers to the needs of the whole body. . . . Let not people be anything for themselves, but let us all be whatever we are for each other."

Such was Calvin's own capacity for self-denial that when he died, his family, following his instructions, buried him without a grave marker.

Finally, three generations later the same pattern was repeated in New England. However, the strain proved too much for the Puritans. Few souls were hardy enough for so strenuous a form of discipleship. Few people really bought the idea of "this worldly asceticism." Besides, as "Protestantism tended toward private enterprise in religion, capitalism tended toward private enterprise in economics." So the Protestant ethic soon succumbed to the spirit of capitalism. The Puritan who denounced the notion that a person might buy as cheap as he can and sell as dear as he can, was subverted by the Yankee trader who made his name doing just that. All that was lacking was the rationalization soon to be supplied by Adam Smith, who said that each seeker of wealth, "is led by an invisible hand to promote an end which was not part of his intention." The market system was now the secular version of God's Providence.

Fellow Americans, let's face it: this great country of ours was built on the old game of taking the money and running. That game wasn't invented in 1967 by gangs that looted in Harlem, Newark, Watts, and the Detroit East side. Ol' Henry Ford took his money and ran to Dearborn a long time before. And let's face the results—quite spectacular! But the game of taking the money and running is winding down. What we are seeing now is the more money, the more needs, and the more complex each new need. Doctors report more visits to their offices by persons suffering from nonphysical complaints than from physical. What we are seeing now is that you can be an economic success and an identity failure.

The psychological effect on the poor is equally devastating. As Dwight MacDonald wrote 20 years ago: "not to be able to afford a movie or a glass of beer is a kind of starvation—if everybody else can." What we are seeing once again is that God is not mocked. I for one don't want to go back to the intolerance of Geneva and Salem, Massachusetts. However, I do want New Yorkers to consider what Calvin said, "that no increase is advantageous unless it answers to the needs of the whole body."

In this city we desperately need structures to help people control their own greed and deny them opportunities endlessly to abuse their power. I want Christians in this city to realize that the day we no longer burn with love, many others die of the cold. That the churches could better the lot of millions of New Yorkers, rich and poor, even save the city we love enough to weep over it as Christ wept over Jerusalem— all this goes without saying. The only question is whether we will. So let us, at least in this church, apply our hearts and minds this fall to New York and the diligent study of the Bible. Who knows, one day instead of a food pantry, we might have food in every pantry. No longer will New Yorkers wake up with stomach pains. No more will children be born with a brain that's not quite right. Who knows, one day some great Latino American may write in Spanglish: "God might have made a more beautiful City than New York, but she never did."

EMC: A Sermon on the Amount

OCTOBER 14, 1984
Readings: Psalm 24; 2 Timothy 4:1–5; Luke 21:1–4

Perhaps you've heard the story of the son who somehow couldn't find it in himself to get out of bed one Sunday morning. Finally his mother appeared at the door and said, "Son, it's high time you got out of bed and went to church."

"Mom, I'm not going."

"Why not?"

"They don't like me and I don't like them. Now give me two reasons why I should go."

"You're 47 years old and you're their pastor."

(I would have said "60" except that some of you might have gotten the wrong idea!)

Why did I think of that story? Because, if you're a member of this church, then like me, you received a letter this week from the esteemed chairperson of the so-called "Every Member Canvass." Today, we will be installing Mr. Thomas Whitley, and his fellow co-laborers in the EMC vineyard, and ask God to bless their outstretched hands. All of which means it is now time to pass from the sublime to the practical, and for me to deliver what might be called "A sermon on the amount."

First of all, I want to try and breathe new life into that much battered phrase, "the joy of giving." Last Sunday afternoon, I left Riverside Church and drove up to Connecticut to perform a wedding. The father of the bride, a very successful and wonderful writer, was so moved by the service, he subsequently sent me a check made out to The Riverside Church for one thousand dollars. (What the father in his generosity did not realize is something every minister comes to know—people really make their own wedding services. The same is eminently true of funeral services.)

You can imagine my happiness in trying to figure out to whom to give this money—Nursery-Kindergarten for another scholarship; Disarmament; the Food Pantry; the Sanctuary committee; or, exiled Bishop Paulos, who now conducts services every Sunday morning in Christ Chapel for exiled Ethiopians, many of whom live on the Upper West Side. Finally, I gave it to Damaris Miranda, head of our Social Services Department. I knew at that very moment she was trying desperately to save a church member and her small child from eviction. You can imagine Damaris' pleasure, and also that of the church member, when I told her that it was precisely because of her plight that the money was going to Social Services and that the money would obviously help far more than just herself.

Without doubt the greatest joy I personally ever had in giving came last year, after my son died. An insurance company called to tell me that Alex, all unbeknownst to me, had taken out a life insurance policy and named me as the beneficiary. Well, I wasn't about to profit by his death, but I could see myself as an agent of his joy, Alex being such a day-brightener to everyone who knew him. Pretty soon a family in Vermont, with no running water, received the Alexander Memorial Well; two hardworking mothers of many children received Alexander Memorial roundtrip tickets to Europe; a cousin, the Alexander Memorial rubber inflated dingy; and a tennis buddy, the Alexander Memorial leaning tower of Wilson tennis balls—cans stacked from the floor to the ceiling. Nothing could have been better for my morale. Money was in my hand as the wand of Cinderella's fairy godmother.

I'm telling you this because such joy in giving can be ours if we truly believe that God is the landlord of ultimate title—"The earth is the Lord's and the fulness thereof" (Ps. 24:1)—and that the Every Member Canvass, therefore, is not asking us to handle well our material wealth on behalf of charity, but rather, to handle well God's wealth on behalf of God. One reason I could so easily enjoy giving away the writer's generous present, and Alex's insurance policy, was because the money didn't belong to me. And my money isn't mine either. As a Christian it is my glory and my humility that I am an agent for God's joy, God being such a day *and night*-brightener to all her people.

If by a miracle of grace, we could get ourselves into that Christian frame of mind, we could indeed know the joy of giving when we fill out our pledge for this year's Every Member Canvass.

However, I said I was going to give a sermon on the amount. How much should each of us give? My answer is simple and I think correct;

it is the preacher's job not to tell people what to do, but rather to remind them who they are, in this instance, agents, or stewards, of God's bounty. Yet some further thoughts may be helpful as you try to decide how much of God's bounty God wants you to keep for yourself, for your family, and how much to give to Riverside Church, and "other good works." There is no mystique of non-possession in the Bible or in most of Church history. The Bible never confuses Lady Poverty, who exalts the ideal of no luxury, with Dame Destitution, who lacks necessities. The Gospels do not distinguish the Haves from the Have-nots, rather the Have-too-muches from the Have-enoughs. Actually, some of the Have-too-muches, clearly wealthy people such as Zacchaeus, Lazarus, and Joseph of Arimathea, receive exceedingly sympathetic treatment. Therefore, we cannot conclude riches are synonymous with corruption, anymore than we can assume poverty produces piety. The goal of Christianity is not detachment from material wealth, but the loving use of it. When trying to decide how much to give, the most helpful story to me is the one about the widow's coins called The Widow's Mite. It seems to say that what counts is not how much you give, but how much is left after you give.

To me, there seem to be at least three compelling reasons for giving far more this year than most Riversiders usually do. A large part of the mission of any decent church is to help those who are not members of the church. We're here for those not here, we're here to remember the forgotten—the aliens, the hungry, and the homeless. If you stop to tally the number of non-members helped by this church, it is really staggering. The food pantry alone has doubled its work in the last year. We now give out 1,000 bags of food a month (approximately fifty per day), and, our policy is to give one bag per family per month. We're talking about literally tens of thousands of people. The cost of the food pantry last year was $127,000. Think also about the wonderful Ethiopians who worship here every Sunday morning; the Chinese who worship in the afternoon; the women who use the Women's Center daily; the men who come every night to the shelter; the scores of immigrants who learn English in several programs here each week; the scores of children who come to our Sunday school; the scores of people who came to our organ recitals last summer; the thousands who will jam the nave in the beginning of December to sing, once again, the *Messiah*; not to mention the visitors who are with us during Sunday worship each week. We are the Inn in the story of the Good Samaritan, and you, the members of the church, are the Good Samaritans who pay the Inn to take care of the people you want to be taken care of. I assume you want us to take care of as many people as possible, which is why the budget was properly raised this year. A reduced budget in the case of an enterprise such as this, in times like these, would be a tragic document.

The members of the church also need the programs of the church—the devotional, the study, the action programs all designed to sustain, comfort, and nurture us in our discipleship. So there's a second reason for being generous.

The third is (sadly) perhaps the most compelling reason of all. Jesus did say that it is harder for a rich person to enter the Kingdom of heaven than for a camel to pass through the eye of a needle. I've been told that there are some rich Americans combing North Africa and the Middle East in search of tiny camels! But most rich, especially rich young Americans, couldn't care less about the Kingdom of heaven these days. They don't pray, "Thy Kingdom come"; they pray, "Lead me not into temptation, I can find it myself." And they do. In New York City and across the country they're spending money as if there were no tomorrow and no poor folks around. God is not mocked, and their economic misdemeanors are anything but rewarded. Instead of becoming free they are getting lost; instead of independence, they're finding isolation; in place of self-discovery, self-obsession. They think they are buying things, but they, themselves, are clearly bought. To prove you are not bought, that your integrity may be battered but is still intact, that you understand material wealth is a means to loving a neighbor and an obligation of stewardship to Almighty God, give generously to the Every Member Canvass. I'm not begging you for money, I'm offering you an opportunity to be useful to others and to save your soul, "for the time is coming when people will not endure sound teaching, but having itching ears . . . will turn away from listening to the truth and wander into myths."

There are some people in this church who give more than they should. To them I say, "You can't give what you do not have. Do not try to improve on the widow. The mite was beautiful then, it's beautiful now. If you think a mite is embarrassingly small to give to a church so large, let me repeat the lesson of that story: it's not what you give, it's what's left after you have given." But there are more people who give less than they might, than people who give more than they should. To them I would offer the simple suggestion that we should give as we have prospered, knowing that "all things come of thee, O Lord, and of thine own do we give."

Money is not grimy or filthy. We wouldn't put it up on the altar if it were not as beautiful as the flowers there. But the beauty of money depends entirely on its use.

Edna Ferber once said:

> Some people make the world, the rest just come along
> and live in it.

Which group do you want to be in?

Stewardship in the Public Realm

OCTOBER 21, 1984
Readings: 1 Peter 4:8–11; 2 Samuel 12:1–7a

Some of you found last Sunday's "Sermon on the Amount" helpful, and were even kind enough to say so. One exuberant church member, obviously a big New York television watcher, said, "It was outstanding, Bill, it glowed like the Trump Casino in Atlantic City." What a comparison for a sermon on stewardship! I could only murmur, "Much obliged." Suddenly I had the title for next year's stewardship sermon!

Actually, one sermon a year on stewardship is not enough, for the Christian understanding of stewardship really affects all of life. To say that is not to detract from the importance of giving generously to one's church, providing that church doesn't grind up its ministers into trivial roles and overwhelm them with administrative trivia, while the basic ministries of the church go unattended. I'm assuming we try not to do that here, that you agree, and therefore can hardly wait to put your generous pledge into the offering plates. I'll only repeat Edna Ferber's words, "Some people make the world, the rest just come along and live in it."

I want to assume all this, because today I want to go on to deal with two other forms of stewardship, that in times like these—neither safe nor sane—demand, if less money, far more time and attention from serious Christians.

I spent the winter of 1976–1977 freezing in Vermont and missing Blacks, Latinos, and Asians—the rich diversity of urban American life. The one Jew in the village was a cabinet maker, but I had heard that he once worked for Bache & Company in New York. So at a New Year's Eve party, where everyone was feeling quite mellow, I asked

Marty Mintz if he felt fulfilled in his new career. To my surprise, he suddenly became quite sober, gave me a long hard look, fairly shouted, "I'm not fouling up any lives, am I?" and stalked off.

What Marty was recognizing was that while every good Jew and Christian may have a God-given calling, it is not always easy to square that God-given calling with ones chosen career, especially in a society with as many entrenched systems of oppression as our own. Are you, for example, if you're working for money, as confident as Marty the cabinet maker that you're not fouling up any lives? Obviously all of us as Christians have an obligation to see to it that our places of work are as humane as possible, and that the work we do does not adversely affect the lives of others. God's stewards have to concern themselves not only with how they spend their money, but also how they make it in the first place. And there, I think, is where we need to dedicate much time and attention these days.

There is a member of this church, a very conscientious person, who is always after me to talk to bankers and other corporate executives. She feels that the way to change society is to change individuals, especially influential ones. Many American Christians share her feelings, and rightly so, for many decent executives working within the system could here and there make significant changes for the better. But there is a fallacy in her position. Suppose I responded to her prodding, spent a lot of time with bankers and actually succeeded in converting a few to the point that they saw clearly their Christian calling to help the needy, and started to provide loans to the poor at little or no interest, while charging higher rates to the rich. Soon they would cease to be bankers; their calling would cancel out their careers. It seems to me that where once the answer to slavery and feudalism was not to make slave owners and feudal lords more moral, but to change the systems of slavery and feudalism, so today it is the system of banking that needs to be converted, not the bankers themselves—and I say that with some feeling. If what we've heard during our Wednesday night series on the city, and what we've read about what banks do in Desmond Tutu's South Africa and all over Latin America—if all these reports are correct, then we have to conclude that the banking system so favors the rich over the poor, and banks over everyone else that Bertolt Brecht was right to ask, "What's robbing a bank compared to owning one?"

I feel the same way about other corporate executives. They are as decent as the rest of us. But if it's true that the 1983 salary of the president of the National Cash Register Corporation was $13 million, and if it's true that last year Exxon, Ford, AT&T, GE, and IBM each cleared over a billion dollar profit, while millions of Americans fell below the poverty line, it would seem that profits have recovered rather than the economy, and that, once again, the system needs to be converted rather than the executives that run it.

I guess what I'm basically trying to say is this. To Christians who pray faithfully, believe joyously, and love ardently, Christ is the Alpha and the Omega, the beginning and end of everything in their lives. But alas, in the vocational life of too many of us, far from the first and the last word, Christ is, at best, *an additional word*. As I said last week, it is not the preacher's job to tell you what to do, but only to remind you who you are: in this instance, "good stewards of God's varied grace." As Peter wrote his fellow Christians: "As each has received a gift, employ it for another . . . ; whoever renders service, as one who renders it by the strength which God supplies; in order that *in everything* God may be glorified."

If we're talking about changing a society that yields most painfully to change, we are really talking about being good stewards not only in our vocations but in the public realm. The important decisions in our time—whether there will be peace or war, freedom or totalitarianism, racial equality or discrimination, homophilia or homophobia, food or famine—all these are political decisions. To Christians, political decisions are not at the center of their faith; they are at the periphery of their faith. But without a periphery there can be no center. A center without a periphery is a contradiction in terms. Together, faith in Jesus Christ and political application of that faith form one unbroken circle. When to stress their distinction and when to stress their unity depend almost entirely on the situation. Not every political issue of the day demands a decision from the churches, and I feel strongly that churches should not pursue political goals that are self-serving or parochial. I hate to see Christians try to legislate their convictions on divorce or abortion into state or federal law. I hate to see Christians fight to establish Sunday Blue laws, or try to keep crèches on public greens or prayer in and evolution out of public schools. But I love to see Christians enter the fray on behalf of the poor and disadvantaged, to fight for housing for low-income families, for decent health care for the aging, for fair treatment for minorities, for peace for everyone—provided they always remember that there are many causes and more than one solution to problems of injustice and war. Most of all, in these times that are neither safe nor sane, I love to see Christians risk maximum fidelity to Jesus

Christ when they can expect minimal support from the prevailing culture. I have in mind what the prophet Nathan did to King David— he spoke truth to power. It is a wise Russian proverb that says, "The whole world weighs less than one word of truth." Two years ago an Israeli poet wrote:

> They held up a stone.
>   I said "Stone."
> Smiling they said, "Stone."
> They showed me a tree.
>   I said, "Tree."
> Smiling they said, "Tree."
> They shed a man's blood.
>   I said "Blood."
> Smiling they said, "Paint."
> They shed a man's blood.
>   I said, "Blood."
> Smiling they said, "Paint."
>   Amir Gilboa

It is wrong, it confuses people, it leaves them helpless and hapless, like sheep without a shepherd, when you call genocidal weapons "Peace Keepers," or when you call kidnappers, rapists, bombers and burners of villages "freedom fighters," or when you contend—as both candidates tonight will—that in El Salvador military, or at least economic counterinsurgency is called for, when all dictates of justice probably indicate that the other side ought to win.

The release this week of the CIA "How to" primer on waging terror in Nicaragua reminded me of what George Orwell wrote: "There is no crime, absolutely none, that cannot be condoned when 'our' side commits it . . . loyalty is involved, and so pity ceases to function."

Not long ago a historian of Columbia University had this to say about events that transpired 50 years ago. "The German people in 1933 did not unanimously choose Hitler, nor did they, as a whole, obey him gladly and voluntarily. But most of them gave up the values of skepticism and freedom for the sake of material benefits, revenge for Versailles, and national greatness."

If Jesus Christ is not just an additional word, but the Alpha and the Omega of all our lives, then surely in the public realm as in our vocational life, in our church life and in our personal life at home, we shall strive to be "good stewards of God's varied grace." We shall not only give generously to our church, but as people of faith we shall be defenders of the truth, bearers of the torch of justice, and weavers of the dreams of freedom. As people of faith we shall make God's promise real for all of God's children. As people of faith we shall show an incredibly patient and loving God that his/her trust in us is not misplaced.

Reformation

OCTOBER 28, 1984
Readings: Isaiah 40:21–31; John 16:20–22, 33

Returning from a panel discussion at Barnard on Friday, I overtook a rather interesting-looking man (about my age) who, as I passed by, gave me a wry sort of warm smile. So I slowed down. "It's not fair," I said. "You apparently know my name and what I do, but I don't know yours nor what you do when you're not walking on Claremont Avenue." He told me his name and that he was a philosopher at Barnard. As we continued to walk along together, he muttered, "Bad times, eh?" to which I rejoined, "At least you philosophers have a lot to philosophize about." At that he stopped and staring at me said, "Look, this country doesn't need philosophy. All it needs is decency, a little common decency, and some common sense." To my surprise tears came into his eyes and quickly into mine too and for a few moments the two of us just stood there—a couple of quiet screamers in a world in which horror is never distant.

But my new philosopher friend, of course, did not mean what he said. As soon as the two of us emerged from our wonderful and valid moment of despair he would have admitted, nay insisted, that what this country desperately needs is precisely philosophy; only not a philosophy that is an adjunct to the mathematics department, not a philosophy that enthrones a heartless reason, but a philosophy based on decency in which the brain doesn't fear to take counsel from the heart.

Likewise, while the church is surely not dogma in search of obedience but love in search of form, to find that form we Christians are going to have to use far more that most precious of all God's gifts— our minds. Love demands tenderness *and* critical judgment. Love in practice is a harsh and dreadful thing; ask any priest, minister, or social worker who, over a lifetime, has flattened his or her feet walking through streets of neighborhoods made of howling families with banshee mothers, drunken fathers, and foul-mouthed children. It's no simple matter to right the poor and suffering world's ancient wrongs.

As Burke said two hundred years ago, most political decisions are between the disagreeable and the intolerable. So Christians need not a will to power, but a will to truth. Faith is no substitute for thought, it makes good thinking possible—thinking undisturbed by fear, thinking unspoiled by pleasures. Faith helps us to think God's good and generous thoughts instead of our own narrow and rather selfish ones.

Bishop Ruiz, I imagine, far more than some of his Vatican superiors, is sympathetic to Latin Liberation Theologians, and probably knows the most scholarly among them, Gustavo Gutiérrez from Peru. Writes Gutiérrez: the church has a "prophetic function of denouncing every injustice," of living in "authentic solidarity with the poor," and making "a real protest against the poverty of our time." Then he adds: "My personal option for the socialist way is not a conclusion drawn from evangelical premises. It comes from my sociopolitical analysis."

The message this Reformation Sunday is that if we Christians want to give relevant form to the love of Christ that dwells within our hearts, we are going to have to develop a "sociopolitical analysis." We may not embrace his, but like Gutiérrez, we'd better struggle to get one, lest our faith become divorced from action. Let's be very clear. This sociopolitical analysis is not at the center of our faith; it's at the periphery. But as I said last Sunday, without a periphery there is no center. A center without a periphery is a contradiction in terms. Why then do I stress what is on the periphery? Because as my philosopher friend on Claremont Avenue sensed so deeply, our present sociopolitical system, however we label it, simply is not working.

If we have learned one thing from our Wednesday night series on New York City it is that we Christians worship God in our "spiritual" life but mammon in our economic life. There are presently in this city 171,000 people on the waiting list for public housing, in which many units already have two families where formerly they had only one. Over 500,000 New Yorkers live in substandard housing, 60,000 are now homeless (of which 20,000 are kids); while over the last two decades, this city has granted a few developers hundreds of millions of dollars in tax abatements to build luxury and super-luxury apartment buildings, mostly in Manhattan. Think of that, and sadness will clutch at your heart. Think of that, and you will have to agree that the system is not working, that God is pained, and that some of those developers in their air-conditioned high towers resemble pilots pressing the button in rarefied cockpits high above the earth. Hunger is on the rise, not only in Ethiopia, but right here in the richest country on earth. We get patted on the head for our food pantry, but folks would say, "Tsk, tsk" were we to push against the system that keeps our food pantry crowded. The prison system is not working when 70 to 80 percent of all released prisoners return to prison, and generally for worse crimes. And certainly the system is not working abroad when, in South Africa and Central America, the United States has seemingly nothing to offer to the millions who are tired of being unemployed, underfed, ill without money to buy medicines—nothing to offer that is, except the prospect of more dead bodies in their streets. American Christians shudder at the prospect of Marxist influences in the churches. They should watch equally devout Christians who come to the altar rail of Bishop Tutu, or to the altar rail of Bishop Ruiz, and shudder at words like "capitalism," "neocolonialism," and "transnational corporations." They may not be right, these Liberation Theologians, in all their conclusions, but they are right to have their "sociopolitical analysis." Without such an analysis, how are we going to translate the story of the Good Samaritan into terms relevant to contemporary New York? How is our love to find form?

But beyond our sociopolitical analysis we must have hope, for the world tomorrow will belong to those who brought it the greatest hope. On Wednesday of last week, at noon, a few of us crossed the street to go and hear Bishop Tutu preach in James Chapel at Union Theological Seminary. Coming into that man's presence is like coming out of dark woods into a clearing splashed with sunlight and littered with flowers. Preaching is "truth through personality" and there is something in Desmond Tutu that is not even in his sermons. He exudes hope. His is an asceticism of cheerfulness in a world which is in a melancholy way.

We too must be full of hope, that hope that believes despite the evidence, knowing that only in so doing has the evidence any chance of changing. Ours must be the hope of the psalmist—"Weeping may endure for a night but joy cometh in the morning" (Ps. 30:5); the hope of the prophet—"They that wait upon the LORD shall renew their strength, they shall mount up with wings like eagles, they shall run and not be weary, they shall walk and not faint" (Isa. 40:31). Ours must be the hope of the evangelist who noted that "the light shines in the darkness and the darkness has not overcome it" (John 1:5). Yes, on this Reformation Sunday we must quicken our resolve to live and walk in that light, following Jesus our first, fast, and last friend who promised: "In this world you have tribulation but be of good cheer, I have overcome the world" (John 16:33).

If we Christians had but one hymn to choose, for many it would be our last hymn today. Luther too was full of hope, hopeful enough to write:

"A mighty fortress is our God, a bulwark never failing." And if that
be true, then who can't sing:

> Let goods and kindred go,
> This mortal life also;
> The body they may kill:
> God's truth abideth still,
> His Kingdom is forever.

Why Christian Education?

NOVEMBER 11, 1984
Readings: Genesis 2:1–9; Romans 12:1–2

In a few minutes we shall be installing the Rev. Patricia de Jong as
Riverside's "Minister of Education for Christian Discipleship."
Quite a mouthful that title, and one which smacks just a bit of conventional piety, wouldn't you say? However, when the search committee got underway and I made that suggestion to the then head of
the Board of Deacons, she snapped back, "It describes perfectly the
job." Mary Ida Gardner was absolutely right. So let me say a word
about "education," another about "Christian," and a final one about
"discipleship."

Three years ago in Cuba I met the Minister of Education, a man of
steady gaze who, in a very different role, had once defended the Bay
of Pigs. I asked him where he had been educated.

"With the Jesuits and a very good education it was."

"So," I said, "You know the problem we have in the religious
community—drawing the line between education and
indoctrination."

"Claro (I understand)," he said with a big smile.

"How do you do it?"

For the briefest of moments, a defensive look flitted across his
face. Then, shrugging his shoulders, he said, "Every country's education reflects that country's ideology."

This sermon owes a great deal to Ann Bennett.—WSC

While hardly answering the question, it was an inciteful reply: "Every country's education reflects that country's ideology." For that reason, Cuban high school students, who often learn in boarding schools built by the government, study in the morning and cut cane in the afternoon. For that reason, Cuban medical students, upon completion of their studies, start practice in the countryside and only gradually work their way back to Havana. And for that reason, civil liberties in Cuba do not flourish as well as the palm trees and lush tropical ferns.

"Every country's education reflects that country's ideology." For that reason, civil liberties fare better in the United States. For that reason also, the freedom of American faculty members and college students to think and do almost anything they please is highly exalted over any obligation to do any good to anybody.

Last year, the Dean of the Chapel at Harvard University said to me, "You know, Bill, back in the '60s when everybody was quarrelling and fighting with everybody else, I had a sense that Harvard had some goals. I didn't know exactly what they were; it was hard to figure out. But today nobody is arguing or fighting with anybody, and Harvard is revealed for what Harvard is—purposeless!" Given the fact that religion is not so much challenged as dismissed, our education is also about as godless as that of Cuba, the Soviet Union, and Western Europe in general. The Moral Majority has a point.

B. F. Schumacher, of *Small Is Beautiful* fame, tells a story of being lost while sightseeing in Leningrad. He was consulting his pocket map when an interpreter stepped up to offer help. When the interpreter showed Schumacher where he was on the map, Schumacher was puzzled. "But these large churches around us—they're not on the map."

"We don't show churches on our maps."

"But that's not so," Schumacher persisted, "that church over there is on the map."

"Oh," said the interpreter, "that's not a church, that's a museum."

Comparably, Schumacher goes on to say that most of the things that most of humanity had considered most important throughout history did not show on the philosophic map his Oxford education provided him. Or, if they did, they showed as museum pieces, things people used to believe about the world but believe no longer.

Peter Berger says, "If anything characterizes modernity, it is a loss of faith in transcendence, in a reality that encompasses but surpasses our quotidian affairs." That is why much of higher education and much of life in general is so dull. It's the strangest of ages because we have lost a sense of the strangeness of things. "God breathed in his nostrils the breath of life, and Adam became a living soul." We think of ourselves as only ascended from savages when we are ALSO *descended* from God.

What is called for is a "rise of soul against the intellect," as Yeats put the matter. There is room, nay, a dire need, for Christian education, but not as seen by the Moral Majoritarians, to whom the word "Christian" connotes dogma, education for certainty a snug harbor of certitudes in a storm-tossed world. I believe just the opposite. I believe Christian education is education for surprise. Why? Because anything less than an ineffable mystery could not possibly be God. By "mystery" I do not mean a definite uncertainty; I mean an indefinite certainty. Let me illustrate.

Chesterton wrote: "The ego is more distant than any star." Yet what could be more real to each of us than our egos? Similarly, God is more distant and greater than all heavenly galaxies combined while at the same time as close to us as breathing, even closer. So Christian education must begin with wonder, continue with wonder, and end with wonder. "The greater the island of knowledge, the greater the shoreline of wonder" (Huston Smith).

As a solid feminist, our new Minister of Education for Christian Discipleship knows that the Church's understanding of God is a history of controversies and constant change and that none of the many theological revolutions of the past can compare to the potential theological revolution implicit in the Christian woman's movement.

If Woman, in the same sense as Man, is "made in the image of God," which is the basic theological tenet of the Christian woman's movement, then who is this mysterious God? Is the all-male Trinity a valid reflection? If the ancient dualism which posits God/Man/Good against Nature/Woman/Evil is no longer tenable, what are the limits, if any, to the interrelatedness, interdependence, and basic mutuality of all creation? If Woman is "made in the image of God," then what must we do about language and imagery which support a sexist, patriarchal culture and a sexist patriarchal God? All of this is included in education for surprise. Now don't run away, men! I see some of you retreating into a kind of bunker mentality. Come on, be manly! Stand up, let's push this a little farther.

Isn't it interesting and surprising that a symbol for knowledge has for so long been a woman with a book or books in her arms and that in statue form she stood on all-male campuses? Isn't it surprising that the traditional figure representing justice was a woman holding the scales, while up until recently there were no women judges?

Isn't it surprising that the figure for wisdom was a woman when the basic pattern for jobs for women was, and still is, non-executive, non-policy making, dead-end and low paying? And most striking of all, isn't it surprising that the figure for freedom was a woman with a torch held high for all men to see and follow when women were not included in the rights so represented? Education for surprise, not for certainty. We do not want to sharpen our minds by narrowing them.

"For freedom Christ has set you free." But freedom is a paradoxical thing and Christian education is therefore also for surrender. It is when I am captivated by the beauty of a poem or the goodness of a person that I most feel free. It is when I am enthralled by the beauty of an anthem sung by the Riverside Choir that I most feel free. It is not when I am alone but when I am in the presence of Jesus that I feel most myself. Free, free at last, free at last, free from self, free for God, "Whose service is perfect freedom." Paradoxical but true, "Whoever I am Thou knowest, O God, I am Thine." That's what we learn through surrender in Christian education. And from the same martyr who wrote those words we learn that "Christians stand by God in God's hour of grieving" (Bonhoeffer).

Such, friends, is the hour in which we meet. The world is become a unity and for this high destiny humanity is not yet fit. The leaders of the world gather like eagles around the carcass of peace. The rich live in splendid indifference to the desperate plight of the poor. God is pained and we who know God's love must share God's grief.

Education for Christian discipleship means that churches can be expected to be sources of moral reflection on the state of their nation's culture. Education for Christian discipleship means Christians must spell out the political consequences of the spiritual demands of the Gospel. It means we must not conform to this world but be transformed by the renewal of our minds, which is to say, we must become what we are not, and do not want to be, but must for God's sake become.

Christian discipleship is costly grace. "It is costly because it calls us to follow. It is grace because it calls us to follow Jesus Christ. It is costly because it costs us our lives. It is grace because it gives us the only true life" (Bonhoeffer).

"Every country's education reflects that country's ideology." That is why we need education for surprise, education for surrender, education for Christian discipleship. Yes, that is exactly what we need. And praise the Lord that in Patricia de Jong we have such a fine educator.

World Food Sunday

NOVEMBER 18, 1984

W hen I think of the ever-escalating nuclear arms race, I think of alcoholics, who know that liquor is deadly, and who, nevertheless, can always find one more reason for one more drink. When I think of the ever-widening conventional arms race, I recall Thoreau's question: "What's the point of having a house if you haven't a tolerable planet to put it on?" And when I think of worldwide hunger, as we all should think this World Food Sunday, I am reminded of the man who, when asked what he feared more, ignorance or apathy, answered, "I don't know and I don't care."

To be sure, the heartrending scenes on television and on the front pages of newspapers depicting stick-like figures huddled in threes on beds in makeshift hospitals and of children with their bloated bellies lying in front of food trucks have prompted a flow of food, medicine, blankets, and tools to the starving millions in Ethiopia. But there are twenty-five other African nations, and Asian and Latin American nations also that are in almost the same dire straits. Worldwide, the situation has gone from bad to worse, and will go from horrible to horrendous unless the consciences of the world unite to shake off their chains of ignorance and apathy.

Ten years ago this month, at the first World Food Conference in Rome, Secretary of State Kissinger proposed the goal "that within a decade no child will go to bed hungry." Today UNICEF reports that forty thousand children die each day from malnutrition and infection. Total up those daily deaths and in one year you have the equivalent of the entire under-five population of the United States.

Instead of a decade of bold initiatives that Mr. Kissinger called for, this decade has seen aid that wasn't, trade policies that discriminated, resources raped, and all to such a degree that I would venture to suggest that famine in Third World countries is now more explosive than nuclear weapons in the hands of the major powers. Soon more and more nations, large and small, will possess these weapons. Desperate people do desperate things. The administration worries about nuclear blackmail from the Soviet Union. It is more likely to come from India.

But let us not succumb to "apocalypse chic." Our sense of responsibility, not our fear or guilt, is what is crucial today. This church owes a lot to its Food and Justice Task Force: constant support of the food pantry, the general confession and the litany in today's service, and the presentation by Arthur Simon after the service. Mr. Simon is the executive director of Bread for the World, a religious lobbying organization founded ten years ago, at the same time as the Rome food conference. To prepare ourselves for what is certain to be a very informative talk (Simon has written a marvelous book called *Bread for the World*), I want to review some basic Christian convictions.

"Thou shalt not steal." "Thou shalt not covet." Implicitly and explicitly, the Ten Commandments sanction private property, and throughout Scripture the legitimacy of private property is affirmed. How, for instance, could Jesus command his followers to give to the poor or to loan without hope of repayment unless his followers had sufficient property and possessions to make such gifts and loans? Even the "redeemed" economic relationships of the first early churches made room for private property. They were not communes in a strictly economic sense.

But "the earth is the Lord's and the fulness thereof," proclaims the psalmist (Ps. 24:1). "Whatever is under the whole heaven is mine," God informs Job (Job 41:11). Because absolute ownership of the land rested with God and not with the Israelite farmers who worked the land, God could demand of them the redistribution of land every fiftieth jubilee year. "The land shall not be sold in perpetuity for the land is mine," says the Lord (Lev. 25:23). In other words, the right to private property is never absolute and the question of ownership is always subordinate to the question of use. Private property reflects a fallen world. In a fallen world we need a little distance from one another. Unlimited intimacy can lead to exploitation. But we are distanced not to keep us apart, but to facilitate our coming together. If private property enhances our life together, it is good. If it keeps us yet further apart, it is evil.

That is why in the United States, "separate but equal" was evil and had to go. And that is why I believe God is once again commanding the redistribution of land in one Third World country after another. Cash crops, be they cocoa in Ghana, peanuts in Gambia, rubber in Liberia, palm oil in Tanzania, bananas and, more recently, beef in Latin and Central America are the business of large estates owned by wealthy families. They are a legacy of colonial times. They destroy a diversified agricultural system that, earlier, more than supported the local population. The cash cropping system, which profits the few rich and punishes the many poor, largely accounts for the paradox of hunger in the midst of possibilities for ample food production. "The earth is the Lord's and the fulness thereof." Can God possibly be pleased with our use of His good green earth?

Worse yet, we Americans are accomplices in the very evil we deplore because we encourage and benefit by it. For instance, we greedy, meat-eating North Americans import from Mexico one million head of cattle every year, half as much Mexican beef as all Mexicans have left for themselves. If we North Americans observed one meatless day a week, it would free up enough grain to feed an estimated 60 million people. A reduction in meat would also reduce the need for corn. Land used for corn could then be extended to wheat and soybean crops, both of which require little fertilizer, an important asset as North Americans also consume far too much energy—twice as much as the average Swede, 191 times as much as the average Nigerian.

Other countries, such as Norway, are way ahead of the U.S. in having a national food policy. That subject, however, I shall leave to Arthur Simon, who knows much more about it. I want only to underline our Christian conviction that the earth is not ours, but God's. Therefore, as regards private property, once again the question of ownership is subordinate to the question of use. Clearly in the field of agriculture we are misusing God's property. In the case of our own country, every report coming out of the U.S. Department of Agriculture insists that the most efficient unit of farming is a family-owned, mechanized, 400-acre farm. What does that say about God and agribusiness?

Let us move on now to our personal attitude toward all our possessions. "Consider the lilies of the field; they toil not neither do they spin; yet I tell you, even Solomon in all his glory, was not arrayed like one of these" (Matt. 6:28–29). Most of us don't like to consider the lilies of the field. They make us downright uneasy. In part the reason is that in each of us there is an emotional pendulum. One moment it swings to the fear of not having enough possessions. Once we have them, it swings to the fear of losing them. Swaying between these two fears makes for an anxiety-ridden life. Jesus, by referring to the lilies, suggests in contrast a joyful life of carefree unconcern for possessions. He is saying that to be dependent upon God is to be independent of everything that is not God. It is hard to have possessions without becoming possessive—the real evil. That is why Jesus said that it is easier for a camel to pass through the eye of a needle than for a rich man to enter the Kingdom of Heaven. The Brazilian archbishop Dom Helder Camara wrote:

> I used to think when I was a child that Christ might
> have been exaggerating when he warned about the
> dangers of wealth. Today I know better. I know how
> hard it is to be rich and still keep the milk of human

kindness. Money has a dangerous way of freezing people's hands, eyes, lips, and hearts.

"Consider the lilies of the field." Let me recommend their consideration to you. Rather than think about guilt because you have so many possessions, consider the unhappiness that goes with being possessive.
Blake said it perfectly:

> He who bends to himself a joy
> Doth the winged life destroy.
> But he who kisses a joy as it flies
> Dwells in Eternity's sunrise.

I tell you, one of the best things about my life now is that I have money enough to give a lot of it away. I am not going to say that giving money away takes the place of going to the movies. But I insist that, like going to the movies, it is fun; many of you will bear me out. It is fun to bring these Thanksgiving gifts up here and put them around the altar. It is fun to think of how much they are going to mean to people who need food more than we do. In other words, when you give, you don't give up, you receive.

We have seen that as regards property the question of ownership is subordinate to the question of use. We have seen that a Christian life is made joyful by a carefree unconcern for possessions. Third, on this World Food Sunday, we must realize that worldwide hunger is a structural evil, a sin of society rather than an individual sin. When one third of the people of the world have an annual per capita income of $100 or less, and another one third of the world eats three-fourths of the world's proteins, systems and structures, power and property relationships are at fault. I would never denigrate changing individual lifestyles; responsible individual consumption is important. But far more important is changing unjust systems and structures. And it can be done. The main cause of hunger is poverty. The greater the poverty the higher the incidence and severity of hunger. Yet China, for all its poverty and its population of one billion people, has virtually eliminated hunger. It is a scandal that the United States has not done the same for its own citizens. We can; we just haven't.

Rapid population growth, a central problem to world hunger, is a symptom rather than a cause of poverty. If you want to reduce the size of the world's families, feed the babies and eradicate poverty. Statistics show that in this country the woman with the least children is a black college professor. Why? Because her life is *not without* issue. In my experience, poor people *do* engage in family planning; they plan big families. They need them spiritually and, in rural areas, economically.

"Let justice roll down like mighty waters." The answer to hunger is justice. India has as much cultivated acreage per person as China— and many more malnourished. Mexico has more cultivated acreage than Cuba—and more malnourished. "Let justice roll down like mighty waters."

Let's eradicate poverty, not just care for it. And, as a matter of fact, to eliminate poverty is cheaper than to maintain it.

"What is the use of a house, if you haven't a tolerable planet to put it on?" Ten years ago, Secretary of State Kissinger also said, "The hopes of development will be mocked if resources continue to be consumed by an ever increasing spiral of armaments." A decade later, world military spending exceeds the total annual income of the poorer half of the world's population. The United States alone spent more last year on arms than the total annual income of the poorest billion people on earth. A peace-loving general said, two months after he became president of the United States, "Every gun that is made, every warship launched, every rocket fired, signifies in the final sense, a theft from those who hunger and are not fed." UNICEF estimates that for every one hundred dollars it spends, one child's life is saved. On this basis, $10 billion spent on the arms race represents the lives of 10 million children.

May God have mercy on our thieving, murdering world.

Born a Child That We Might Grow Up

DECEMBER 2, 1984
Readings: Isaiah 40:1–8; Romans 13:11–14

There are two kinds of Christianity that are so out of step with Advent (whose first Sunday we today celebrate) and Christmas that one of these years Christmas will just have to put them out of business. The first and obvious kind of Christianity opposed to Christmas is joyless Christianity—"Gloom to the world the Lord is come." Joyless Christians fit H. L. Mencken's definition of the Puritan: "One haunted by the fear that somewhere someone might be happy." Usually thin and mean-looking, as if bred by a pair of tomahawks, joyless Christians think being solemn is the same as being serious. They pretend to be upright when they are merely uptight. They are Victorian, never Elizabethan. And they deify virtue which, as we all know, is an unmitigated disaster. Whoever pursues virtue is no longer seeking God or neighbor, as the enterprise is simply too self-absorbing.

The second, and not unrelated, kind of Christianity that comes out all wrong at Christmas is what we might call "authoritarian" Christianity. I have in mind those who put the purity of dogma ahead of the integrity of love, which is why authoritarian Christians always come out divisive rather than inclusive. They are big on rules and commandments, especially the "Thou shalt not's," as if the requirements of religion were satisfied when the prohibitions are not disobeyed. To them God's power seems more important than God's love.

Mind you, I understand why people are drawn to dogmatic certainty, to strict prohibitions. The first thing we all need in our lives is some kind of order and the last thing most of us want is to live with uncertainty. Many of us, in fact, prefer the security of known misery to the misery of unfamiliar insecurity. And I understand the appeal of God's power. I too want protection, supervision, direction—*as do all childish adults*. But clearly at Christmas God comes to us in love, not in power. I think at Christmas God comes to us as a child so that we can finally grow up.

But who wants to abandon childhood? "Freedom," said Nietzsche, "is the capacity to become what we truly are." That freedom, however, is exactly the kind we want to escape. It is an old story. The real slavery of Israel in Egypt was that they learned to accept it. Human beings have always resisted the will of God made so manifest at Christmas. We want God to be strong so that we can be weak, but in the Christ child we see that God wants to be weak so that we can be strong. We want God to protect us and, in the Christ child, God takes such form as demands our protection of him. It's so maddening. I spend half my waking hours sharing the frustration that drove Isaiah to cry out: "O that Thou wouldst rend the heavens and come down . . . that the nations might tremble at Thy presence" (Isa. 64:1–2). But at Christmas the Word of God hits the world with the force of a hint!

God comes to us as a child so that we can finally grow up. A sign of maturity is to reject the protection of dogmatic certainties, strict prohibitions, be they Christian, Jewish, Muslim, or Marxist. It's a sign of maturity to be able to live with uncertainty. It's a sign of maturity to realize that human beings are always called on to live between a past that cannot be retrieved and a future that is barely discernible. A sign of maturity is to realize that all too often we live under seemingly barren skies that refuse all solace—"My God, my God, why hast Thou forsaken me?" In short, we are mature to the degree that we realize that the only security in life lies in embracing its insecurity—just as

God did at Christmas. He comes to earth in the form of a babe in exile. The bread of life for human beings is laid in the feed box of animals. Faith in Jesus, far from diminishing the risks of life, inspires the courage to take on all of them, including intellectual uncertainty and moral ambiguity—just as, growing up, Jesus did himself. What doubts he must have forced himself to live with, and for how long, in order to have the freedom and courage to say to religious leaders twice his age, "you have heard it said . . . but I say to you!"

We shall never grow up as long as we seek to overcome doubt by repression, which is the way of authoritarian religion. We shall never grow up until we see how indispensable doubt is, provided the doubt is prompted by love of the truth and not by a pathological need to doubt. (At many universities the expression "open mind" confuses the virtue of a mind open at one end with the vice of one open at both!) Doubt is not overcome by repression but by courage. As Rollo May writes: "The most creative people neither ignore doubt nor are paralyzed by it. They explore it, admit it, and act despite it. . . . Commitment is healthiest when it is not without doubt, but in spite of doubt."

Have you ever noticed that when you are not pursuing your own goals, you are passively fulfilling the goals of others? That is what I meant by suggesting that the real slavery of Israel in Egypt was that they learned to accept it. That is what Nietzsche understood when he said, "Freedom is the capacity to become what we truly are." But God can't drive us to become the courageous, loving, creative people we truly are; God cannot force us, he can only challenge and teach us, most of all by example. And oh, how God does just that at Christmas! If the sight of that unguarded goodness lying in the manger does not melt your heart, does not teach you something about the importance of vulnerablity, then somewhere along the way you have lost your capacity to become what you truly are. Suppose you had been there at the nativity scene. Suppose suddenly Mary had turned to you and said, "Here hold the child for a minute," and there you were, holding in your arms God's love in person on earth. Wouldn't that have disarmed you? Babies are always disarming because they are so powerless. That is why God came to earth as a child—to disarm us, to make us vulnerable again, so that we might keep on growing into what we truly are: courageous, loving, creative people of God.

That same vulnerability of God which we see at the beginning of Christ's life, we see again at the end. "This is my body broken for you. . . . This is my blood shed for you." Born a child that we might grow up, Christ dies that we might live. What more could we possibly ask of a loving God?

Advent is what St. Paul called the "full time now for you to wake from sleep. For salvation is nearer to us now than when we first believed; the night is far gone, the day is at hand." Sleepers, awake, for God's finest, most tender blessing is coming our way.

Abiding in Love

DECEMBER 16, 1984
Readings: Isaiah 9:1–7; John 1:1–5

Two Sundays ago, the first in Advent, the giant banner preceding the choir read "Promise." The word reminds us that the greatest statements in Scripture are not in the imperative, but in the declarative mode. As Evelyn Underhill wrote, "The primary declaration of Christianity is not, 'This do,' but 'This happened.'" Because that first Christmas "God so loved the world that he gave his only begotten Son, that whosoever should believe in him should not perish, but have eternal life"; because "God was in Christ reconciling the world unto himself" (2 Cor. 5:19); because "the light shines in the darkness and darkness has not overcome it," this world, although like a flower that has yet to burst its bud, is brim full of promise.

Last Sunday it was hope we celebrated. I suggested that if faith puts us on the road, it is hope that keeps us there. Hope reminds us that like the banner preceding the choir, God is altogether as much in front of us as above and within us. Hope, in a metaphor of the Bengali poet Tagore, "is the bird that feels the light and sings when the dawn is still dark." Hope makes us sing, "Awake, awake the night is flying."

Today it's the Alpha and Omega, the be-all and end-all of life that we celebrate. "Now abide faith, hope, and love, these three; and the greatest of these is love." Here are some other great declarative statements: "God is love, and they who abide in love abide in God, and God abides in the brothers and sisters."

Christmas represents God's love come to earth in person. Have you ever been in love? I hope so, and if so, you know that love is not blind but visionary. Behind the armor that, alas, most of us don almost the moment we are out of diapers, love perceives an absolutely totally unique individual. Often, when performing a wedding service, I am moved by the thought that the love the two people standing before me have for one another has probably discovered things in each other that even their parents have not seen. That's what God's love in Christ does for each of us: it celebrates our absolute uniqueness, it confirms our individuality, which is why such violence is done to God's nature and our own whenever we follow the herd like some unthinking beast. We are made to be different and to love it. The beauty of love is that when hearts are one, nothing else has to be one, and nothing else should be one.

God's love not only discovers, and daily rediscovers, our individuality, it creates and re-creates daily our value. One cannot say it enough: it is not because we have value that we are loved, but because we are loved that we have value. If you've ever been in love, and I hope you are still, you have visited "cloud nine." But you didn't get there by ladder, painful rung by painful rung, you got there by levitation, by being borne aloft on the love of the one who loves you, who, in turn, thanks to your love, is walking "on air." So it is with God, thanks to whose love our value is a gift not an achievement. We don't have to prove ourselves because God has taken care of that; we have only to express the unique and loving self that God has made and meant every one of us to be.

I've said enough to make the point that the Incarnation—that is, God's love coming to earth in the person of Jesus Christ—has altogether as much to say about what we are to become as it does about what God became. God became the child of Mary that we might become children of God.

The Bible is nothing if not realistic. "For behold, darkness shall cover the earth" (Isa. 60:2). "The people who walked in darkness have seen a great light: They who dwell in the valley of the shadow of death upon them hath the light shined." Had we pursued further the first chapter of John we would have heard truly poignant words: "He came unto his own and his own received him not" (v. 11). Last week was Human Rights Week, and happily for the world and for those of us who have heard him here so many times, Bishop Tutu was awarded the Nobel Peace Prize in recognition of his part in the struggle for human rights in Africa. A year ago, it was Lech Walesa and Poland, and before that Adolfo Pérez Esquivel and Argentina. And Human Rights Week this year ended in Riverside Church with Chileans fasting in the Cloister Lounge in protest against the violence of the Pinochet government.

The darkness these days doesn't come in patches, does it? While the Chileans fasted on one side of the Cloister Lounge, hungry Americans came to the other, as they do daily in swelling numbers, to the food pantry. Many, including President Reagan, think we're standing tall these days, but I ask you, how can we Americans feel proud when 15 percent of us are "officially" poor, when probably 40 million of us are actually poor, and when half the young Black people in our cities are without employment? And to make matters still more contrary to the Christmas spirit, the president now proposes to reduce the $200 billion deficit by harming still further those least able to defend themselves, by cutting further aid programs already cut in 1981. So in the name of God whose name is love, Christians must once again plead the cause of the needy, become lobbyists for the politically weakest in the land, and remind the president, the Congress, and the nation of the plight of the indigent elderly, the handicapped, the many, many children of poverty-stricken families. If the budget cutting axe falls as the President intends it to fall, those in this country whose lives are already harshest will become even bleaker.

It's strange, isn't it? Most industrialized nations of the world, like Sweden, like Japan, like West Germany, take civilized care of their widows and orphans. Our country could, but doesn't.

> For every boot of the tramping warrior in battle tumult
> and every garment rolled in blood
> will be burned as fuel for the fire.
>
> Isa. 9:5

But not in this country. The military will still be getting a whopping increase this year, even after the highly dramatized cuts take place—never mind the backlog of $239 billion unspent dollars (there were $92 billion in 1980), the fact that the Defense Department is still "a swamp of waste"; and never mind that on the threshold of the space war era a new weapons system can only threaten national and world security, however security is defined.

"Blessed are the peacemakers." But where are they? Those in government still insist on bargaining chips, as they have ever since Sputnik went up, although the argument is long discredited, history showing only chips, no bargains.

Friends, like most ministers at Christmas, I would much rather announce than denounce, but how are we going to do justice to the light until we appreciate the depth of the darkness?

Some of you may recall a report last August from the Census bureau that stated that from 1979 to 1983, nine million more Americans fell below the federally established poverty line, an increase of 35 percent, the largest increase since the poverty figures began being collected in 1960. The only answer to the president's budget is from certain members of Congress who would freeze all spending, freeze in place a disastrous status quo, ratify the very decisions responsible for the resurgency of poverty as a major issue in the United States today.

"For unto us a child is born, unto us a son is given: and the government shall be upon his shoulder: and his name shall be called Wonderful,

Counsellor, The mighty God, The everlasting Father, The Prince of Peace. Of the increase of his government and peace there shall be no end."

I believe that. I believe that "the light shines in the darkness" and that even the darkness that covers this land will never put out the light. I believe all this because I believe the Incarnation can change us. Christ born anew in our hearts can address the intelligent selfless person that dwells in each of us, that self so rarely addressed by our political leaders. I believe the American people will one day see the insanity of the arms race that has the entire world on a countdown to destruction. I believe the people will one day see that in the long run it is cheaper to eliminate poverty than to maintain it. I even believe that today, a lot of American Christians, having applied their minds and hearts to the plight of the homeless, the foodless, and the jobless, will conclude that the president's proposed attack on the federal deficit reflects a moral deficit the likes of which we haven't seen in ages. The New Year might even see busloads of such Christians traveling to Washington dedicated and determined to let their little candle shine in the city's darkness.

Some of you get upset sometimes at anger such as mine in the church. But what else preserves our sanity if not anger? Why should we tolerate the intolerable? Actually, anger, if focused, goes hand in hand with love, because if we lower our quotient of anger against oppression, we surely lower our level of love for the oppressed.

Annunication and denunciation. You cannot announce the light and not denounce the darkness. Christmas is both a melting moment and a tough assignment. But we're ready—I hope—to protect in Christ's name the God-given individuality and infinite value of every human being.

To this day the Orthodox Jew is careful not to step on any piece of paper for fear the name of Yahweh might be written on it. Likewise we don't want to step on any human being, for we know that Christmas reminds us that God's love is for everyone, none excluded.

Joy

DECEMBER 23, 1984
Readings: Isaiah 60:1–5; Matthew 1:18–23

Two weeks ago we praised our hope-giving God for keeping us on the road of faith, arduous and long though it may be.

These days, realism demands pessimism—more famine in Africa and homeless people in New York, more hideous weapons everywhere, including outer space, weapons that can only ruin the weak, enrich the wealthy, give more power to the powerful, but no assurance of world security.

Hope insists that we take a dim view of the present only because we hold a bright view of the future, not a predictable future, to be sure, but a preferred future for which we can work and pray and suffer because hope arouses, as nothing else can, a passion for the possible. Always to be remembered is this: Just as all the water in the sea cannot sink a boat unless it gets inside; so all the despair in the world cannot bring you under unless it seeps into your soul.

Last week, it was love we celebrated—all that unguarded goodness lying in a manger. How God's vulnerability shames our personal and national defenses! I suggested that God's love, as opposed to Cupid's, is not blind, but visionary; and, as opposed to most human love, God's gratuitous love doesn't seek value, it creates it. Which leaves us two days before Christmas to recognize love's first fruit, which is joy. Like hope, like love, joy, Biblically understood, is easy to affirm in these hard times because joy unites most easily with pain.

Five years ago, three of us (a Roman Catholic priest and two Protestant pastors) were asked to go to Tehran to visit the American hostages held there. I suggested to the hostages that the best thing to be said for their worst of all possible Christmases was that it most nearly resembled the first Christmas, which for everyone involved, was misery itself. So, if they were up for it, they were in a unique position to grasp the true meaning of Christmas joy.

We read, "There was no room for them in the inn" (Luke 2:7). But that, of course, is nonsense. There was *all* the room in the inn for them, only no one—so thought the innkeeper—would *make* room for a woman about to give birth. The familiar ox and ass were not picturesque guests (as we so often portray them) who along with the shepherds, had to "come and see." They were not guests at all. This was their home. He who was to be bread of life for human beings was laid in the feed box of animals.

Nevertheless (one of those greatest of Biblical words), nevertheless, "Joy to the world!" because our inhumanity to one another and to God notwithstanding, "the Lord is come."

In Tehran, I reminded the hostages that at the beginning of Christ's life, as at the end, human beings come off badly. But God comes off wonderfully, giving each of us the finest and best Christmas present ever—himself, wrapped in swaddling clothes. As all the joy of Christmas comes from on high, it is only proper that "Joy to the world, the

Lord is come" begins on high D, and gradually works its way down the scale until it finally reaches us a full octave lower. Then, our proper response is to rise and sing right on up the scale, "let earth receive her King," starting on the fifth because God's loving care has already levitated us that far.*

Now, more specifically, how does divine joy unite with human pain? Try to recall in your own life some moment of great pain or terrible confusion, a moment in any case of intense suffering.

You know that at such moments there is nothing more important than the presence of someone who cares. That someone does not have to say anything. In fact, not to speak is often better. Advice, at least, or any attempt to cheer you up, is generally experienced as a refusal to enter into your pain and suffering.

Two years ago in the early morning hours when I received word that my son had been killed, friends, also notified, came to my apartment. I can hardly remember a word of what was said, but I'll never forget the facial expressions. I'll never forget the arms around me. The fact that friends came at all at four in the morning helped prevent despair—not from seeping, but from flooding my soul, drowning me in grief.

And that is exactly the way it is with Emmanuel, "God with us." This child, whose birth we celebrate two days from now, is not a memory but a presence, a constant caring presence of unbelievable sensitivity. Only of Jesus can you say: "He knows exactly what I am going through." As the Spiritual claims, "Nobody knows the trouble I've seen, nobody knows but Jesus—Glory, Hallelujah."

Christ is always with you—as he was with me the days and months following that worst of nights—not necessarily giving advice, nor even saying a word; not easing the pain so much as improving the quality of the suffering. Christ, by his constant, caring presence brings a touch of heavenly joy to every earthly sorrow.

All of this is true, as many of you will attest. But we must guard against being too individualistic and elitist in our understanding of spirituality. Some Christians talk endlessly about the importance of one's interior life and how to develop it more fully, forgetting that Christ is born to bring hope and joy also to whole communities of people—the exiles, the deported, the tortured, the silenced—the vast Latin American and South African majorities, for instance, so dispossessed today as to live as aliens in their own country. Who but

*Cf. the hymn, "Joy to the World," words by Isaac Watts, music by George F. Handel.

Jesus himself can bring any semblance of joy to rural Haitian Christians facing eviction, a group of whom gave this heartrending account of their lives:

> These fields are our entire life, our entire support. They give us food. Thanks to them we can send our children to school. . . .
> Farmhands can no longer find work, even as day laborers. How are we to live? . . . Where can we go? If we move to Port-au-Prince our situation will only be worse, because there is such misery there. If we go to the mountains, what kind of land can we expect to till? Must we, then, leave Haiti—get on a boat to discover the misery in other places? We do not deserve this torture, for sure.

God knows they do not. Jesus is born in utter poverty and exile to be a constant caring presence in their communal sorrow and communal struggle—and that of all oppressed people: "To tear down Satan's kingdom and build up Zion's walls." For, as we sing, "He [Christ] rules the world with truth and grace, and makes the nations prove the glories of his righteousness and wonders of his love."

But Christ is not only a source of joy and comfort in tragedy. Earlier we heard, "You shall call his name Jesus, for he will save his people from their sins" (Matt. 1:21). Perhaps the worst form of psychological pain is the guilt that comes from sin. You know what I mean. Some of you may be suffering some terrible guilt for an action you consider unforgivable. But the very word, "unforgivable" is itself unforgivable, because it is precisely what can't be condoned that must be forgiven.

Emmanuel is "God with us," not only to comfort us in tragedy but to forgive us in our sin. Jesus doesn't approve our sins nor does he relieve us of the consequences of them, for life is nothing if not consequential. But we are relieved of the consequences of being sinners. Through forgiveness, we are given a fresh start, new hope, a new chance to love; and if you've ever had the humility to be forgiven (guilt being the last stronghold of pride), you know that there is no joy like unto it. Forgiveness is pure gift, something for nothing.

So let God make you a Christmas present of forgiveness. And let's hope this whole nation will soon come to its senses sufficiently to seek forgiveness for the harsh way it treats its own widows and orphans, and for the many ways it seeks to thwart the empowerment of the poor—everywhere.

I said that divine joy unites most easily with pain. And what scripture writes of love, we can say of joy. "Many waters cannot quench it, neither can the floods drown it" (see Song of Solomon 8:7). Divine joy is that which still burns brightly when sin and sorrow sweep over us like a sea.

But joy can also unite with happiness. And this is very important to say: Far from denying happiness, joy supplies happiness its true foundation, infusing pleasure with meaning.

How many cartoons are there of the preacher taking off after the happy drunk, saying, "You're not really happy," when clearly the drunk is a helluva lot happier than the preacher. Still, pleasures that are an escape from reality lack meaning, lack foundation.

Sometimes I think a large number of today's affluent Americans are like kids playing "cowboys," running around slapping their thighs, dressed up in chaps, bandanas, cowboy hats. It's all very fine as long as you don't look down and see—"No horse!" In contrast, the joy that is of God is no escape from reality, but rather infuses earthly pleasures of all kinds—drinking, singing, concert-going—with a foundation of meaning.

The Emmanuel we await the day after tomorrow is no John the Baptist eating health food in the desert. Jesus will be called "a glutton and a drunkard." In the Gospel of John, he first meets people not in their sorrow, but in their happiness. He goes to parties. He himself is full of happiness as well as sorrow, making the point that the greater one's capacity for sorrow, the more one is capable of happiness. If you know some gloomy Christians, they are not gloomy because they are Christians. Quite the opposite. They have probably struck some kind of dull bargain: In order not to feel too badly about living, they won't feel too good about it either. And they have the nerve to call this emotional mediocrity "the good life."

All of which suggests that finally joy really has little to do with happiness or unhappiness, and everything to do with meaning and fulfillment. Didn't Paul write of Jesus that "for the joy that was set before him, he endured the cross" (Heb. 12:2)? How paradoxical and true. And that brings us back to the love embodied in the child in the manger, the love that is of God, that "bears all things, believes all things, hopes all things, endures all things" (1 Cor. 13:7). The love that is the name of the human journey. It is in being loved and in loving that we find life's deepest meaning, a meaning that we can affirm in the face of tragedies we cannot fathom and in the face of human stupidities we understand all too well. The highest purpose of the Christian faith is to make people loving—by choice. And the first fruit of love is joy, the joy of meaning and fulfillment.

So, dearly beloved of the Lord, may your Christmas be full of promise, hope, love, and joy. May our Christmas together be one in which we are present to one another in tragedy, sin, and happiness, as God is present to us in Emmanuel—which means, "God with us."

1985

Jesus—Not "Answer" but "Presence"

Epiphany
JANUARY 6, 1985
Reading: Matthew 2:1–6

One of the things I like most about Ann Landers' column—aside from her rare common sense—is the way her correspondents sign off: "Perplexed in Peoria," "Miserable in Memphis," "Hassled in Hackensack," or "Yearning in the Yukon." There is something touching about these signatories, and universal, as well; for in every time and place, people have been perplexed, miserable, hassled, and always, yearning for answers to their problems. They want a Delphic Oracle, a witch doctor, a Merlin or a Messiah to deliver them from whatever undesirable state they are in and, on a different level, to give meaning and purpose to their lives. And we are right, we human beings, to want deliverance from oppression—if only the oppression of a treadmill existence. If life is not an unceasing quest for meaning, forget it. We are just killing time.

It was the same in Galilee in the period between the Old and New Testaments. Colonized by Rome, Israel had been handed over to the absolutist ruler, Herod. Everywhere there was physical pain and fiscal grief. The poor felt the boots of the rich in their faces. All forms of injustice—homes without roofs, fathers and sons meeting untimely ends—all became familiar tribulations. There had been hope that when Herod died, things would get better. But all petitions to Rome for improved conditions came to naught as the colony was subdivided among Herod's sons, and the little district of Galilee got the worst son of the lot. As a result, everyone was looking for deliverance. Messianic expectations had accelerated to a frenzy.

Last month, a movie maker asked a few of us: "If you were to make a movie of Jesus' life, where would you begin?" Without hesitation, a young and imaginative professor of Old Testament replied: "Right away I'd zero in on the Messiah, show him surrounded by his disciples, performing miracles, then five minutes into the movie the audience would realize they'd gotten the wrong one."

This sermon owes much to my good friend, Arthur Brandenburg.—WSC

How, then, did the wise men know enough to get the right one?

"He was despised, rejected, a man of sorrows and acquainted with grief" (Isa. 53:3). If they knew Isaiah's prophecy as they doubtlessly did, the wise men knew the true Messiah would steadfastly refuse to become whatever popular messianism expected him to be. To those looking for a military leader to bring political deliverance, he would say, "Put up your sword; am I not to drink the cup the Father has given me?" (John 18:11). To those seeking easy comfort, he would bring disturbance, while to those whose lives raged like a sea, he would offer calm and tranquility. To those wanting a way out, he would be an invitation to jump in, while to those in over their heads, he would suggest withdrawal to fast and pray.

To those who took the law lightly, he would say, "not a jot or tittle will pass away until the law has been fulfilled" (Matt. 5:18), while to those for whom the law was the ultimate meaning of life, he would demonstrate other priorities by picking grain on the Sabbath (cf. Matt. 12:1).

I said that at all times and in all places people have been perplexed, miserable, hassled and yearning for answers to their problems. The trouble is that too often too many of us yearn not for answers but for The Answer, with a capital A, and we want it delivered in such fashion as to remove all doubt. That is the essence of popular messianism in all its varied religious and nonreligious forms. And to those who have such messianic expectations, Jesus seems to be saying, in effect: "There is no answer, and I'm it. I who refuse to solve your problems, am the solution to your problems. And those of you who believe this will, together, be able to solve your own problems. And furthermore, you will become the solution to the problems of the world."

The true Messiah was an offense to the Jews because instead of taking power, he empowered, and in a special way, by bringing love to life in every expectant heart.

And he would be a scandal to the Greeks because his wisdom did not conform to their "richly odored ignorance," to borrow a phrase from W. H. Auden.

All this, I surmise, the wise men were wise enough to know, though how they knew the babe was the Messiah only God's star can tell.

My concern this Epiphany Sunday is that we be as wise, in hindsight, as were the wise men in foresight. They realized that instead of an answer with a capital A, Jesus represents Presence with a capital P.

So, dearly beloved, the good news this Epiphany is that we not only are empowered to love, but never will we be abandoned, even when wrong. The good news is that no matter how puzzled, miserable, or hassled we are, we can, by God's gracious presence in our lives, act when we cannot be sure. The good news is that we are free to be wrong and not to bear the weight of that forever. The good news is that we are free from the tyranny of timidity that results from having to be right. It is wrong to believe that you can always know exactly what it is that God intends. It is right to believe that you can risk— you can gamble on things that really matter—knowing that both you and the kingdom of God may suffer loss, but that neither will lose their worth, nor ultimately be undone.

Dearly Beloved, I declare unto you, the true Messiah has come— not as an Oracle, nor as an Answer, but as a Presence. The true Messiah who says, "There is no answer and I'm it. I, born in a stable for you; I, who will die on a cross for you; I who refuse to solve your problems am the solution to your problems. And those of you who believe this will, together, solve your own problems; and furthermore, you will become the solution to the problems of the world."

At the end of today's service, the four big Advent banners will be carried out, together, as singly, they were carried in during Advent. Let them go, for they have done their work. The *promise* is fulfilled, and *hope*, *love*, and *joy* are ours forever because of Christ's eternal presence in our lives. "The people who walked in darkness have seen a great light" (Isa. 9:2).

May the blaze of heaven warm and keep your hearts always. Amen.

Life Is a Gift

JANUARY 20, 1985
Reading: 1 Peter 2:1–10

"Bless the Lord, O my soul;
and all that is within me,
bless his/her holy name!"
Psalm 103:1

Let's ask what it means to "bless the Lord," and start by asking what it means just to "bless."

As you have already noticed, we are including a lot of poetry in the service today, and from time to time I will be quoting a few verses myself, though, I assure you, not my own.

This sermon owes a great deal to Father David Steindl-Rast, *Gratefulness, the Heart of Prayer* (Paulist Press, 1984).—WSC

Wrote a poet called Kabir:

> Do you have a body? Don't sit on the porch
> Go out and walk in the rain.
>
> If you are in love
> Then why are you asleep?
>
> Wake up, wake up!
> You have slept millions and millions of years.
> Why not wake up this morning?

I don't know how it is with you, but some mornings, I start right up, even in the coldest of weather. For example, last Thursday, to catch an airplane, I got up early and caught God painting the buildings white.

But generally, before two cups of coffee, I hardly *believe* in God. And some people don't wake up until they have been at work at least an hour; and the dull-witted and bitterly sophisticated close their hearts to all but the most superficial things in their lives. These are the bored and boring adults who never become excited children. These are the people for whom nothing short of a double rainbow in the sky will open "the eyes of their eyes." That's from e.e. cummings, "the eyes of my eyes are opened," and it suggests what I'm after: To bless—just to bless—we need first to wake up—to wake up from taking things for granted.

When I said that I got up early and caught God painting the buildings white this past Thursday morning, some of you probably registered, "He's trying to be poetic himself." Well, I was, but I was also trying to be factual. Let's jump ahead two months. You tell me if it isn't true:

> Black earth becoming yellow crocus
> Is undiluted hocus pocus.
>
> Piet Hein

And there's something in the human world pertinent to the day which is equally incomprehensible: Millions of dollars are spent to build a stadium; hundred of thousands more are spent to buy tickets; and thousands more to pay twenty-two players to dispute possession of a ball that costs $16.95.

In other words, the human heart is made for surprise—not to sleep, but to wake up. God gave us hearts to appreciate "the dearest, freshest, deep-down things," whether those things are expected—

snow in the winter, crocuses in spring, football this afternoon, cups of coffee and each other every morning—or something as unexpected as a double rainbow. God has seen to it that nothing in this world is given, yet everything is a gift. And if that sounds like chirping optimism, let me quickly add that I never saw grass so surprisingly green as amid the ruined buildings of German cities in 1945. 1 never saw water lilies fairer than those that blossomed in Vietnamese craters formed by American bombs. Two years ago, when it became my turn to find in the worst possible way that death can sometimes be gratuitous, I also discovered that life *always* is. "In the mud and scum of things / There, always, always, something sings" (Ralph Waldo Emerson, *Fragments*).

So, the first thing to say about what it means to bless is that you have to have a grateful heart. More than anything else, gratitude tells us whether or not we are aware. It is gratitude that measures our awareness.

The second thing to be said follows naturally from the first. If nothing is given, everything is a gift, then the next thing is to thank the giver. "Bless the Lord, O my soul."

But here, we must be careful. How does the receiver of life thank the giver of it?

All of us have a healthy urge—I repeat, healthy urge—for independence. Without it, none of us would ever outgrow being spoon-fed. But stubborn independence, the machismo of Latinos, the "I can do it alone" attitude of Anglo-Saxon males, not only chokes off gratitude, it masks the fact that within each of us there is a child in a high-chair, with oatmeal from head to toe.

But if self-sufficiency is an illusion, mere dependence is slavery. So, the real choice, as Father David Steindl-Rast, monk and co-author of this sermon, points out, the real choice is not between independence and dependence; it is between alienation and interdependence. Both stubborn independence and slavish dependence alienate us from each other and from God. But interdependence dissolves alienation and we are home free—home where all depend on all and all are free. To bless the Lord, then, is to express interdependence. When my soul blesses the Lord, it not only says, "Thank you," it says, "We belong together, God, you and me. We complete each other. You give me the gift of life, and I give you myself."

And God answers, "That's right. You are loved. There is not a mirror in the world that can show how beautiful you are to me."

When all that is within me blesses God's holy name, all that is within me comes together in a way so wonderfully integrated that I can say to God what the poet wrote of his beloved:

And something else: to bless the Lord is to know communion not only with God, but with each other. Weren't we really together last Sunday when Jim Forbes was preaching the gospel and Clamma Dale and the choir were bringing the message in song? Morover, we so experienced communion with black South Africans that 160 of you signed up to take buses to Washington, D.C., to protest and thus be arrested before the South African Embassy there. (The buses leave a week from Tuesday; more on that later.)

This same communion (with sufferers of this city, for instance, as we cry out for a housing policy), which comes with blessing the Lord, is also at the heart of the sanctuary movement.

Were the U.S. administration today forcibly repatriating Russians to the Soviet Union, forcibly repatriating Poles to Poland, neither the Congress nor the American people for one minute would stand for it. Why then do both sit idly by when innocent Salvadorans are being forcibly returned to a country whose death squads long ago would have eliminated a Lech Walesa? Why do they tolerate the forcible return of innocent Guatemalans to a government widely viewed as the most brutal in the entire Western Hemisphere? And now the administration is out to put nuns and priests, ministers and Christian laity behind bars for doing God's holy work of hospitality. "Thou preparest a table before me in the presence of mine enemies" (Ps. 23:5).

"Bless the Lord, O my soul, and all that is within me, bless his/her holy name" by striving to affirm communion with all God's people whose beauty to God no mirror can reflect. And this means especially communion with "mine enemies." We have, all of us, to learn to be merciful when we live at each other's mercy. We have to learn to be meek or there will be no earth to inherit. I have a motto I'd love to place on the wall of Messrs. Kampelman, Glitman and Tower, our three new arms negotiators. It reads: "When you are in the same boat with your worst enemy, will you drill a hole in his side of the boat?"

We've noted that gratitude measures our aliveness, that you can only bless with a grateful heart. To bless the Lord is to declare our loving interdependence with God and with one another. It is clear that the greatest evils of humanity are due to lack of love and that the New Testament's "miraculous catch" (cf. Luke 5) was not the haddock and shad and whatever else Peter and the rest of them caught that day, but that Peter and the rest were caught up, even as we are, in the net of Christ's love.

This is the miraculous catch: "You are a chosen race . . . God's own people, that you may declare the wonderful deeds of him who called you out of darkness into his marvelous light" (1 Peter 2:9).

Our last thought: The more we bless the Lord, the more God blesses us, and this dynamic growth in holiness and wholeness can go on and on, in each of us. This is what the psalmist meant when he wrote "so that your youth is renewed like the eagle's" (Ps. 103:5).

Oliver Wendell Holmes saw a similar dynamic in the life of the chambered nautilus, that mysterious sea creature which, as it grew, moved from one chamber to another, scaling off the old one it had outgrown as it moved to a new and bigger one.

But soon this new chamber also grew too small, forcing its inmate to build again and move on.

Wrote Holmes:

> Build thee more stately mansions, O my soul,
> As the swift seasons roll!
> Leave thy low vaulted past!
> Let each new temple, nobler than the last,
> Shut thee from heaven with a dome more vast
> Till thou at length art free
> Leaving thine outgrown shell by life's unresting sea!
> Bless the Lord, O My Soul
> And all that is within me
> Bless his/her holy name. Amen

Pray Continually

FEBRUARY 3, 1985
Readings: Isaiah 58:6–10; 1 Thessalonians 5:12–18; Luke 18:1

Recently I heard that Secretary of Defense Casper W. Weinberger had taken a day off to go fishing. To prepare himself, he went into a store and inquired about the price of bait. Said the man behind the counter, "All you can carry out for the price of a dollar."

"Good," answered Cappie, "I'll take two dollars' worth."

I tell this story not only to take a well-deserved swipe at Mr. Weinberger's insatiable appetite for deadly weapons (a recent *New Yorker* cartoon has a king asking a courtier, "Have we enough might to make it right?"), but also to suggest that today's texts offer salient advice in the face of such exaggerated demands.

When you loose the bonds of wickedness, undo the thongs of the yoke, and let the oppressed go free, when you share your bread with the hungry, "*then* you shall call, and the LORD will answer; you shall cry, and he will say, Here I am." In other words, Isaiah makes a connection between our actions and our prayers (cf. Isa. 58).

In the eighteenth chapter of the Gospel of Luke, Jesus tells his disciples to "pray continually"; and in his first letter to the Thessalonians, St. Paul admonishes, "Pray without ceasing."

What does that mean? Is no time to be allowed to eat, sleep, just shoot the breeze?

It helps, I think, to distinguish prayer from prayers. To Isaiah, to Jesus, to St. Paul, what matters is prayer, not prayers. What counts is what we might call "prayerfulness," an all-pervading attitude of heart and mind by which any activity in our lives can become a prayer— anything from eating, sleeping, shooting the breeze, to comforting one another, setting up exhibits for Black History Month, protesting apartheid before the South African Embassy. Prayers, on the other hand, constitute just one activity among others.

St. Teresa said, "There's a time for prayer and a time for partridge." But we can *pray* continually, pray without ceasing.

It helps also to recognize that lazy as we are, we are not prone to this attitude of prayerfulness. Prayer demands concentration and wonderment; a heightening of consciousness and perception. Christian prayer demands that Christ be born in you, that Bethlehem become your heart, Christmas be every day in your life. Christian prayer is the interiorizing of the Incarnation.

No easy process is this, as William Blake understood:

> Unless the eye catch fire
>   The God will not be seen.
> Unless the ear catch fire
>   The God will not be heard.
> Unless the tongue catch fire
>   The God will not be named.
> Unless the heart catch fire
>   The God will not be loved.
> Unless the mind catch fire
>   The God will not be known.

I love those lines, not only because they suggest a Christian (in the words of the hymn) "aflame with faith and free," but also because they suggest that it is more important to see clearly than to behave well, for redemptive action is born of vision. They also suggest that knowledge of God comes more through the heart than the intellect, "Blessed are the pure in heart, for they shall see God" (Matt. 5:8).

All of which is not for a moment to minimize the importance of prayers, only to stress the importance of prayerfulness as an all-pervading attitude. Without this attitude of prayerfulness, prayers become empty husks; spirituality becomes bogus.

As you will not be surprised to learn, my preference is for passionate prayers, prayers that are full of feeling. Let me give you three examples, the first two of which show how impossible it is to be genuinely prayerful without God's grace.

Earlier we heard portions of the fifty-first psalm but it was sung in an Anglican setting so typically antiseptic it could not possibly do justice to the urgency of the psalmist's pleas. (No offense intended to the choir members or director; all musical settings of this psalm, including Brahms', are just the same.) But imagine the feelings of a soiled spirit that produced the lines, "Create in me a *clean* heart, O God, and renew a *right* spirit within me." Imagine the guilty fear of estrangement that prompted, "Cast me not away from thy presence; and turn not thy holy Spirit from me"; and from what depth of sorrow the psalmist pleads, "Restore unto me the joy of thy salvation and uphold me with thy free spirit." How many of us have prayed those prayers because they reflect such prayerfulness! The psalmist surely was a person who prayed continually, prayed without ceasing. He may not have always behaved well, but he saw clearly both God and himself.

The second example, no less passionate, is a seventeenth-century sonnet by John Donne, which begins, "Batter my heart, Three Personed God," and ends with two paradoxical metaphors, the last fiercely sexual:

> Take me to you, imprison me, for I,
> Except you enthrall me, never shall be free
> Nor ever chaste, except you ravish me.

And the third example comes from a friend, Theodore Loder, the minister of the "sanctuary" church in Philadelphia. It comes from a book called *Guerrillas of Grace*, subtitled *Prayers for the Battle*:

Sometimes, Lord,
it just seems to be too much:
    too much violence, too much fear;
    too much of demands and problems;
    too much of broken dreams and broken lives;
    too much of war and slums and dying;
    too much of greed and squishy fatness
        and the sounds of people
            devouring each other
                and the earth;

Too much, Lord,
    too much
        too bloody,
            bruising;
                brain-washing much.

Or is it too little,
    too little of compassion,
too little of courage,
    of daring,
        of persistence,
            of sacrifice;
too little of music
    and laughter
        and celebration?

O God,
make of me some nourishment
    for these starved times,
some food
    for my brothers and sisters
        who are hungry for gladness and hope,
that, being bread for them,
    I may also be fed
        and be full.

As Loder's prayer brings out clearly, prayers are personal, but
never private. They are essentially social and subversive, disaffiliating
us from the powers that seek to gain control over us.

Said Karl Barth, "To clasp the hands in prayer is the beginning of an
uprising against the disorder of the world." Alas, too many churches

fail to understand that. They ban "spirituality," and all that pertains thereto, to the private sector, making spirituality a sort of leisure-time activity having no effect on society as a whole, no effect, for example, on the New York City Medical Examiner's Office, once considered the finest in the world, frequently consulted by Scotland Yard, but this week becoming the latest example of the deterioration of everything in our society not connected with profit-making.

Sisters and brothers, prayers that do not have direct human and social application are not Christian prayer. To love Jesus is not to imprison him in our hearts, but to take him into the streets and subways of New York, into the corridors of power in Washington, D.C., and before every South African embassy in every country of the world.

Nothing so nourishes such an understanding of prayer as the Eucharist, which commemorates the cross, the place where the mercy of God was supremely manifest, where God laid bare God's heart for all to see. Like prayer, the Eucharist is a social and subversive act, the sacrament of equality in an unequal world.

G. K. Chesterton once contrasted *The Rubaiyat of Omar Khayyam* with the Gospel of Christ.

> "Christ," he says, "made wine not a medicine, but a sacrament, while Omar made it not a sacrament but a medicine. Omar drinks to drown his sorrow, Christ to celebrate his joy. Omar says, 'Drink, for you know not whence you come nor why. Drink, for you know not when you go, nor where. Drink, because the stars are cruel and the world is as idle as a humming top. Drink, because there is nothing worth trusting, nothing worth fighting for.'
>
> "Christ, by contrast, says, 'Drink, for the whole world is as red as this wine, with the crimson of love and wrath of God. Drink, for the trumpets are blowing for battle, and this is the stirrup cup. Drink, for this is my blood of the New Testament which is shed for you. Drink, for I know of whence you come, and why. Drink, for I know of when you go and where.'"

Dearly Beloved, may you be comforted and fortified by the Eucharist this morning. And all week, may you pray continually, pray without ceasing—not always behaving well, but always seeing clearly, so that your life may become like a prayer, a wonderful communion with God.

Race Relationships Are Human Relationships

FEBRUARY 10, 1985

Readings: Psalm 96; Romans 12:14–21

This Sunday has been designated by our denominational parents as "Race Relations Sunday." I have some reservations.

In the first place, "Race Relations Sunday" sounds old-fashioned, suspiciously like "Brotherhood Week," which used to roll around about this time of year, prompting such uplifting slogans as "Take a Honkie to lunch" or "Whoop it up with a Wop." I once proposed, in place of Brotherhood Week, "Hate Week"—get it all out, then we will try to practice brotherhood (and sisterhood) for the rest of the year. I was told, "You can't get it all out in one week."

There are other problems. "Race Relations" does not square with Sunday. From a Christian point of view, there really is no such thing as interracial relations, all relationships being strictly interpersonal. Said James Baldwin, "You can't tell a black man by the color of his skin." And who am I, a white man, to talk about Asians, Native Americans or blacks? Don't ask a sword to tell you how a wound feels. Adam Clayton Powell warned, "Beware of Greeks bearing gifts, blacks looking for a loan, and white people who understand black people."

Finally, I have a feeling that national church bodies designated this day for churches who otherwise would not dream of talking about anything so unpleasant as racial discrimination; and they, of course, will be precisely the churches not observing Race Relations Sunday.

But enough of such reservations. Let us take a text that is well-worn, yet wears well, and see where it leads us. Wrote St. Paul to the Galatians: "There is neither Greek nor Jew, there is neither slave nor free, there is neither male nor female; for you are all one in Christ Jesus" (Gal. 3:28).

"For you are all one." The essence of monotheism is one God and one human family. Most of us might prefer to pray, "*My* Father, who art in heaven," but the "*Our*" makes us all sisters and brothers, children of one God who is like unto an unbelievably loving mother or father. Sin may fracture the vision, but not the fact of unity.

The trouble is, even though we see the vision, we do not feel it. I know that each of you is my sister or brother, as precious in God's eyes as ever I will be, but I do not always feel that way, and neither do you. You and I can at least see and hear each other, but how are we going to feel brotherly and sisterly about those afar off whom we shall never see, those our government calls "the enemy," and those a big-oted culture deems inferior?

I fear the trouble lies even deeper. In this land of atomized individuals, most people are not even trying to see each other, let alone feel about each other as if we were all brothers and sisters. We North Americans seem barely to believe anymore in communal relations. We view society as a figment of the socialist imagination. "Go for the gold" is not a communal objective.

In saner societies, this is not the case. I am frequently haunted by a story of the Zen Buddhist monk who came across an abandoned baby in the road. He picked up the baby, wept, and put it down again. He wept because the baby had been abandoned; he left it there because, in his mind, no one could replace the mother. I think the monk was a good man who did the wrong thing for the right reason.

It was wrong to leave the baby in the road, but the monk was right to see the indispensability and irreplaceability of a mother-child relationship, and by extension, of all relationships. Wrote Anaïs Nin: "We are always giving birth to each other." A mother and child may not be one, but they are not two. They are some mystical number in between. So also are lovers, and truly close friends. And spiritually speaking, which is the only significant way of speaking, that is the way we all ought to be together—not one, but also not two, nor three billion. "You are all one in Christ Jesus."

Oliver Cromwell reflected that view of human relations in the seventeenth century when in drawing up the code of conduct for his new revolutionary army, he had to deal with the question of what to do about cowardly behavior. Specifically, "What do you do with a man who is found with a wound in his back?" The answer, he decided, was to round up the man's closest friends and drum them out of the army and the church; for, in his view, cowardice is not an individual, but a communal failure. That is an understanding of brotherhood that seems now, three centuries later, to push us back to square one. Our race relations are today deteriorating because our human relationships are frequently so inhuman.

Bernard Goetz is a good case in point.[*] From what we are told, he is a lonely man, nursing—probably alone—his grievances and especially his humiliation of four years ago at the hands of muggers. Certainly last December on that fateful day in the subway, he was not

[*]Bernard Goetz, a white man, shot four young black men who he said were intent on robbing him on a Manhattan subway. The incident created a furor and became for many a symbol of New Yorkers' frustration with the high crime rate.

reciting to himself, "'Vengeance is mine; I will repay,' saith the Lord," or "Be not overcome with evil, but overcome evil with good" (cf. Rom. 12:19 and 21).

He certainly was not feeling at one with all humanity, and it should be pointed out that in that subway, he was not in an environment conducive to fraternal feelings and sane thinking. As opposed to Paris, Moscow, or Washington, D.C., New York subways are violence looking for a place to happen. With those lethal dum dum bullets in his pistol, Goetz was programmed for murder; otherwise his first, and—we might hope—last shot would have been fired into the air.

Why did he not become an object of anger and pity, instead of a hero, to so many New Yorkers? Was it because they identified with his loneliness and his humiliation, his insecurity, his lack of charity, his narcissism? I say narcissism because I believe the original Greek mythological figure, Narcissus, staring endlessly at his image in the pool, was less enamored with what he saw than defiant in the face of his own sense of inferiority. Freud had a lot to say about narcissists like Bernard Goetz and his admirers. He wrote, "It is a good thing people do not love their neighbors as themselves; if they did, they would kill them."

Was Goetz racist? If he was not, as his lawyer contends; and if the members of the grand jury who held him innocent of manslaughter were not racist, anymore than the mayor who this week upheld their findings; then, at least, all of them appeared to be winning friends mostly by the passion of their prejudices or by the consistent narrowness of their outlook.

Maybe sin does not destroy the fact of human unity, but it surely fractures the vision of it. Until one of them sued, no one knew the name of any of Goetz's four victims. And had Goetz been black and his victims white, the crowd that hailed him hero would certainly have been different in makeup, and, I would hope, far smaller.

You remember the pictures we used to see in school of legionnaires leading their captives in chains through the cheering streets of Rome? Well, in the streets, subways, stores, and offices of New York City, we too often see shackled reason led in triumph by prejudice.

Prejudice never dies, it only passes itself off for reason. But race relations can and will improve if we improve our human relationships. Only the weak are prejudiced. That is why we need each other—for strength. Anais Nin was right, "We are always giving birth to each other." (Twice born is not enough. We have to be born a hundred times anew.) We are each other's harvest. This city is full of people who can function with grace and confidence only as long as they keep their world small enough. They need no end of support to widen their horizons. This city is full of people who have no more than a slippery toehold on the American ladder of success, people who will tell you, "The world is a dangerous place full of evil people." They need help. So do white folk who, when black families move into the neighborhood, find nothing better to do than to long for the torpid stability of homogeneous suburbs. They need to hear that the answer to the oppression they feel is not to get a larger piece of the ever-growing American pie, but rather to ask why the pie never gets recut, or how it gets baked in the first place. Long before Reagonomics increased the disparities, 1 percent of all North Americans owned 35 percent of the country's wealth, while the bottom 45 percent owned all of 2 percent, and the bottom 61 percent owned only 7 percent of the country's wealth.

To talk these days of race and not of class is dishonest. Only class divisions can explain the violence in the subways, the lack of low-income housing, the structural unemployment of the poor, the fact that decent education is increasingly available only to an elite, defined not by ability but by bank balance.

Most of all, we need—all of us—to recapture the vision of St. Paul, shared by the Zen Buddhist monk and by Cromwell. With Cromwell, we have to see that cowardice is not an individual but a communal failure. With the monk, we have to see the indispensability and irreplaceability of all relationships. A mother and child may not be one, but they are not two. They are some mystical number in between. So, all of us in this world are not one, but also not two, nor three billion; for one God broods over one family.

Yes, sin may fracture the vision, but not the fact of human unity. "There is neither Greek nor Jew, there is neither slave nor free, there is neither male nor female; for you are all one in Christ Jesus."

Let the whole church say, "Amen."

Vengeance and Violence

FEBRUARY 17, 1985
Readings: Genesis 11:1–28; Luke 15:11–32

Earlier this week I asked some colleagues, "What shall I preach about on Sunday?" Replied one, "Say something more about vengeance and violence."

It was a provocative suggestion. Why do so many citizens of color still die in police custody? Why do so many New Yorkers rate the results of the Goetz and Sullivan grand juries by the race of their targets? Why, in an important mayoral race, cannot those who used to pick cotton join hands with those who used to cut cane? What is the mysterious power of those ancient grudges? Why is grievance the only truth that sticks?

I don't know why my mind went to the Old Testament, which is hardly bloodier than the New. (What could be more violent than Herod's massacre of the innocent unless it be humanity's crucifixion of the Son of God?) But, I thought first of King Saul, who, returning from battle a conquering hero, had but to hear the women singing, "Saul has slain his thousands, and David, his ten thousands" (1 Sam. 18:7), to eye David from that day on with envy. And on the morrow, "an evil spirit rushed upon him," and he tried, not once, but twice, to pin David to the wall with his spear.

I also thought of Joseph, whose older brothers, jealous of their father's love for their younger brother, sold him into Egyptian captivity when he was all of seventeen years old. I thought, still further back, of Cain's envy of Abel. How discouraging that the first murder recorded in the Bible is a fratricide. How arresting, the symbolism. Vengeance is not only sweet, it is old.

Then my mind turned to the New Testament and to another set of brothers about whom we read in what has been termed "the greatest short story in history." Fortunately, the violence of the Prodigal Son's older brother was only verbal, which may be one reason it is easier for us to identify with him, rather than, say, with Cain or with Saul. But there is another reason. We heard how the elder brother was "in the field." He was a worker, this young man, which is more than can be said about his younger brother.

Roman Catholics and Jews know as much as do the rest of us about the Protestant work ethic. Think of the citizens of "Little Italy" and "Polish Hill" who constructed the skyscrapers, operated the railroads, worked on the docks, and in the factories, steel mills, and mines of our country. Almost every red-blooded American can identify with this hard-working, first-born son, without whom the farm would probably have become a shambles, and the father a wreck. Yet, no fatted calf was killed for him—ever!

So, why use him as an example of vengeance and violence? All he wants is a little justice. What is so wrong with that? On the surface, nothing at all is wrong with that. But if we dig deeper into the story, we find out, as so often is the case, that the demands of justice are but a modification of envy: "Yet you never gave me a kid, that I might make merry with my friends."

Then comes the verbal violence: "But when this son of yours came. . . ." Notice, not "my brother," but "this son of yours." Then, more envy: "who has devoured your living with harlots. . . ." Up until now, there has been no mention of harlots. It is as if the older brother were accusing his younger one of sins he himself would like to commit.

Truman Capote once observed, "Great fury, like great whiskey, requires long fermentation." Let's guess that the envy of the older son had a long history, that in earlier years he had envied his younger brother's easy good looks and high spirits. Feeling himself to be inferior, he had decided that the father's love for him must also be inferior. If so, this older son resembled Cain and Joseph's brothers and, in some respects, Saul, who thought his popularity was slipping away toward David. He also resembled the folk in Little Italy and on Polish Hill whose labor was demanded, but who, themselves, were not accepted by the Yankee patricians who ran so much of the show in those days.

In other words, Cain, Saul, Joseph's brothers, Italians and Poles in nineteenth-century America—all these suffered hurting experiences, feelings of loss and humiliation. In all of them, we sense the power of the ancient grudge.

Many times you have heard me say what I want now to repeat: All feelings are valid. It is perfectly natural to feel envy, hatred, and resentment, which are inevitable responses to rejection, humiliation, and injustice, whether real or imagined. Freely to acknowledge hatred and resentment is the best way to avoid becoming hateful and resentful. If you deny these feelings, then, just as surely as today is Sunday, you will act them out on others, on surrogates like the Prodigal Son, like Abel, like Joseph, like David.

Hatred is basically pain denied. Physical violence is a clash between one person's spirit and another's body. The subconscious has no digestive tract. What goes down has to come up again. And, generally, it does, in the form of displaced violence. The vengeance solution is, "Don't get mad, get even." But the alternative to vengeance is, "Get mad, not even."

Envy is proof perfect of the perversity of human nature. Unlike the other, so-called deadly sins, envy—as opposed to gluttony and lust—has no gratification whatsoever. Yet, which of us has not envied? If we are free to acknowledge the pain of envy, we will not seek to deny it by vengeance.

Sure, the Prodigal Son had the power to harm his older brother just as Joseph had the power to harm his older brothers: as Abel, Cain, and as David, Saul. But the stories of them all bear out Othello's claim, "Thou hast not half that power to do me harm as I have to be hurt."

There is something else in the story, in addition to envy, that helps explain vengeance and violence: You remember that the older son says to his father, "Lo, these many years I have served you, and I never disobeyed your command." Instead of trusting his father's love and becoming himself loving, the older brother seeks to become virtuous, to do the right thing: "I never disobeyed your command." Instead of expressing himself in love, he tries to prove himself in virtue.

We can say categorically that whoever seeks virtue no longer seeks God or neighbor. The enterprise is simply too self-enclosing, self-seeking, self-justifying. How clearly we see this in the story when we compare the father's attitude toward the Prodigal Son to that of the brother. The father sees the wayward lad from afar, the older brother, from above. The father wants him restored, the older brother wants him punished. The father sees what is good in the situation and tries to develop it, while the older brother has clearly decided what is evil in this world so that he will not have to come to grips with what is really good—like love and forgiveness.

If we dig deeper into the story, we find this hard-working young man insecure, self-righteous and harsh in his judgments. How his hard line is reflected in a contemporary form of American patriotism that combines a love of country with a moral duty to hate! How his sanctimoniousness is reflected in national egotism, the anesthetic that dulls the pain of mediocrity.

Almost twenty years ago, LeRoi Jones (Imamu Amiri Baraka) wrote, "God has been replaced . . . with respectability and air conditioning." Leaving air conditioning aside for the moment, we recognize a tendency in all of us to seek to develop an ethic rooted not in wickedness but in respectability and virtue; yes, in respectability and virtue, but not in God and in love. Like the elder son, we do not trust God whose prodigal love is what the parable is all about. So, instead of expressing ourselves in love, we try to prove ourselves in virtue. Violence is inevitable. We can only prove ourselves by disproving someone else, pride being not accidentally but essentially competitive. And, let's face it, in the final analysis, none of us is all that virtuous anyway. The profile of a virtuous person is like the silhouette of a giraffe—lofty up front, but dragging a bit behind.

We are talking about the very heart of the Christian faith. St. Paul wrote, "No one lives unto himself alone, and no one dies unto himself alone. If we live, we live unto the Lord, and if we die, we die unto the Lord. So, whether we live, or whether we die, we are the Lord's" (Rom. 14:7–8).

Whether we are mugged or not mugged, we are the Lord's. Whether we are raped or not raped, we are the Lord's. Whether we were loved by our parents, or not loved, we are the Lord's. And whether those who rob and rape, love or do not love us, are black, white, yellow or red, they too are the Lord's. And Christ died for Goetz and Sullivan, the mayor, and for the coalition for a just New York; for Russians and Cubans—and even for you and for me.

No one said it would be easy; the claim is only that it is true. God is around not to mollycoddle us, but to make us freer, larger, more loving. The greatest compliment to sinning humanity is found in this story, in the little phrase, "when he came to himself."

When we come to ourselves, we see that the church is "a hospital for sinners, not a museum for saints." When we come to ourselves, we realize that the vengeance and violence we see all around us should have no place within us, that God may be subtle but never bloody-minded, that religion should never become an alibi for cruel means, and that the price of hating others is loving ourselves less.

Don't get even, get mad—and get God, who "is our refuge and strength, a very present help in trouble" (Ps. 46:1).

Don't get even, get mad—and get God, whose Son promised, "In this world you shall have tribulation. But be of good cheer. I have overcome the world" (John 16:33).

The Conversion of St. Paul

First Sunday in Lent
FEBRUARY 24, 1985
Reading: Acts 9:1–20

Flying home this week to New York in a swollen 707, every seat of it squashed full with one of us, I had time, if not ample space, to ponder St. Paul's famous conversion experience on the road to Damascus. What are we to make of his falling to earth and hearing a heavenly voice, of his seeing a bright light, and his subsequent blindness?

St. Paul was not exactly what most modern physicians would wish their patients to be. But, then, think of earlier seers like Amos and

Ezekiel, or later ones like Martin Luther and Søren Kierkegaard. Rarely is the world changed by commonplace people with supremely average experiences. It is the "cracked" ones who let the light through.

Those of us attending the Emily Dickinson seminar yesterday heard:

> Much madness is divinest sense
> To a discerning eye.
> Much sense, the starkest madness.

What makes Paul's conversion unusual, if still unclear (there are five accounts, diverging in detail), is that his was not that of a profligate (like St. Augustine) converted to a life of virtue, but the conversion of an exceedingly devout person from one set of convictions to another. Within him, two sets of convictions were in such radical opposition that he had to "burn what he had adored, and adore what he had burned."

Paul (Saul) had grown up with a deep attachment to the Temple, to the Law, and to the People. To a Jew of such intense, unswerving loyalties, Christianity among Jews—and all the first Christians were Jews—could only appear as an insidious form of national apostasy. How could any serious Jew believe that God's Anointed One was to be found in the person of a criminal, handed over by the religious authorities of the nation to the Romans to die what could only be regarded as an accursed death? But the more Paul dragged off those Christian men and women to prison and breathed "threats and murder against the disciples of the Lord," the more he himself seemed to be led into tortures of self-examination. He must have asked how his religious faith could, indeed, justify the pain he inflicted upon his victims. And almost as painful must have been this question: "Why does not my unremitting obedience to the Law that Moses brought to Israel bring peace to my soul?"

To the latter question, Paul's best answer is given in the seventh chapter of his letter to the Romans. There, he says that the Law, though good in every respect, was paradoxically the condemnation of such as he knew it. None could observe its every precept. By its prohibitions, and in particular by its prohibitions of certain desires, it stimulated those very desires. The Law, far from saving us, could only underscore how far we had fallen short. So the Law was, as he wrote, "holy, just and good," and at the same time, it spelled death, not life, to the human race.

He agonized for every human being when he wrote, "The good that I would, I do not, and that which I would not, that I do" (Rom.

7:19). The solution, in modern pietistic parlance, is to "let go and let God," to recognize, as did St. Paul, quoting Habakkuk, that "the righteous shall live by faith."

Stop striving endlessly to be more and more virtuous, to separate yourself from the impurities of the world. It won't work; human beings are not perfectible. Those who are convinced that human nature is perfectible simply show how little they have tried to live out their own convictions. Actually, the more you strive to be perfect, the more you realize your shortcomings. The more you realize your shortcomings, the more you dislike yourself. The more you hate yourself, the less you can love others, for love is a gift of yourself. How will you make a gift of that which you hate?

"The righteous shall live by faith." The righteous, as Paul came to see, will accept their acceptance at the hands of God. What converts a sinner to a saint is sheer forgiveness, which is always there; for while we never succeed, "there is no failure in Christ," as the gospel song goes.

Forgiveness alone makes love possible. As long as we feel rejected by God, we cannot love God or anyone else. For God appears oppressive—as one who judges according to his commandments and condemns according to his wrath. But if we receive what God offers without condition—that is, forgiveness—then God's power enters into us like a healing stream of fire, reaffirming us, igniting our gratitude and our love for God, for one another, and for all of life. Remember, to love God is not to hate life, but to try to bring love to life everywhere in life.

When you know you are loved by God, you can love others without being sure of their answering love. When you know you are loved by God, you can accept yourself, warts and all. If you reject God's love, and try to be righteous, not by faith but by virtue, listen carefully, and you too will hear the voice of Jesus, saying, as to Paul, "Bill, John, Molly, Anne, why do you persecute me?"

The righteousness of virtue is cold, unwarmed by love, self-assured, like that of Paul before his conversion. The more you are forgiven, the more you love. The less you are forgiven, the less you love. And if you feel no need of forgiveness, God help all the rest of us.

Walter Wink is a wonderful New Testament professor from Auburn Seminary, across the street. Frequently, when he conducts weekend retreats, he asks people when in their lives they most felt the love of God. Many answer, "When I was going through a divorce."

That was not the case with me when I was divorced in 1968. So pharisaic was my understanding of God that, as a Christian minister, I felt I could never be forgiven. One evening, months later, after a meeting of Clergy and Laity Concerned about Vietnam, I walked along this city's Claremont Avenue with Rabbi Abraham Joshua Heschel. (Heschel, with his white hair and an imperfect beret sitting somewhere on top of his head, was then in his seventies, had had a heart attack, and was holding on to my arm.)

"My friend, " he said, "I understand you have been through much suffering."

"Yes, I have, Father Abraham," I answered. (I called him Father Abraham because he looked to me both patriarchal and ecumenical.)

"Why didn't you call me?" he asked.

"Well, you were in Los Angeles, and there were others I could talk to."

"That was a big mistake, I could have helped you."

So insistent was he about his help that finally I stopped, faced him, and said, "OK, how could you have helped me?"

He put his hand on my arm, looked up into my face, and answered, "I would have told you about my father, blessed be his memory, who was a rabbi and who was also divorced. I would have told you it was all right to be a minister and divorced. You Christians are so vexed by perfectionism."

As I listened, tears coursing down my cheeks, I realized how right he was. He could have helped me. I should have called him. And I realized further that you don't have to be a Christian to have Paul's conversion experience. You have only to believe Habakkuk: "The righteous shall live by faith."

There is another aspect to Paul's conversion experience that should not be overlooked. Paul converted from pharisaic Judaism to universal Christianity. Prophetic Judaism, which Heschel certainly embodied, as opposed to pharisaic Judaism, was universal as well as national. But at the time of Christ and Paul, the adherence to the Law, the Roman occupation, and the legacy of hatred that the Maccabean struggle bequeathed to posterity, all these caused the national aspect to predominate.

But something in Paul must have longed for conversion to a larger vision. He, of course, knew these words of God delivered to Isaiah: "I have been found by those who did not seek me; I have shown myself to those who did not ask for me," as well as God's condemnation of Israel: "All day long I have held out my hands to a disobedient and contrary people" (Rom. 10:20, 21).

If it is hard to be converted from the fear of God to the love of God, it is no less difficult to be converted from "God loves me and mine, but not them and theirs," to Paul's understanding that God loves all as if all were but one.

Perhaps the hardest thing of all is to recognize the particularity in every universal claim. Liberation theologies claim to offer liberation to all humanity, yet how much Black theology is sexist, and how much Feminist theology is racist? Every liberation movement tends to make its liberation the priority even while claiming to seek the liberation of all. But of far greater danger today is pharisaic Americanism, so characteristic of American Christians, a form of patriotism that combines love of country with a moral duty to hate all Marxists, a form of patriotism as self-righteous as the pharisaic Judaism that St. Paul abandoned when he was converted to universal Christianity. When every day we remain alive is a day of grace, when all humanity is as a prisoner in the death cell awaiting the uncertain moment of execution, for the United States government to spurn the arbitration of the world court in matters Nicaraguan, to turn its back on the Contadora nations offering mediation in Central America, and on the five continents' initative—the six nations' offering daily to mediate in Geneva—is the height of national pharisaic insolence. "All day long I have held out my hands to a disobedient and contrary people."

"America, America, why do you persecute me?" Sin may fracture the vision of our oneness but not the fact of it. And only by the acknowledgement of it has hope in our day a chance to prevail over terror.

I said on Ash Wednesday evening that the greatest compliment paid sinning humanity was in that little phrase from the Parable of the Prodigal Son, "when he came to himself." My Lenten wish was, and remains, that we might all, like the Prodigal Son, come to ourselves, that we might, like Paul, regain our sight and be filled with the Holy Spirit, realizing that our individual salvation lies not in being sinless but in accepting the forgiveness God always offers in Christ; and that the salvation of this planet lies in understanding that just as God loves each as if God had naught else to care for, so God loves all, as if all were but one.

Two Cheers for the Rich Young Ruler

MARCH 3, 1985
Reading: Mark 10:17–22

If not three, then at least two cheers for the man often referred to as the rich young ruler, whose story, just heard, appears in almost identical form in Mark, Matthew, and Luke. Although a person of great possessions, he came running to kneel before the penniless prophet who was on his way to becoming a crucified outlaw. Although young and rich, he was old and wise enough to know that affluence cannot buy morality, let alone salvation. Although a ruler, he realized, before Lord Acton told the world, that "power tends to corrupt, and absolute power corrupts absolutely." Yes, two cheers, at least, for the rich young man who was miles ahead of his modern American Yuppie counterparts whose lives seem to represent little more than step ladders set up against the New York Stock Exchange.

Of course, greed is not new. Said Jeremiah, "From the least to the greatest of them, everyone is greedy for unjust gain" (6:13). Nor is greed today restricted to the young of the United States. Nevertheless, greed is peculiarly American. In 1946, when the United States was the number one power of the world—there was not even a number two around—Eugene O'Neill, the nation's leading playwright, in the course of an interview, said that in his view "the United States, instead of being the most successful country in the world, is the greatest failure. Its main idea is that everlasting game of trying to possess your own soul by possession of something outside it." O'Neill added that we were "the clearest example of 'For what shall it profit a man if he gain the whole world and lose his own soul?'"

Predictably, nearly forty years later, many Americans have lost their shirts—their farms and food stamps—while others have lost far more than their souls. Recently, the *Reader's Digest*, that comfy, optimistic, patriotic defender of the national faith, featured the following five articles: "How to Stay Slim Forever," "Five Ways to Stop Feeling Tired," "How to Get Your Way," "How Safe Are the New Contraceptives?" and "What It Takes to Be Successful." It would appear that the editors had concluded that their millions of readers were—consecutively—fat, lazy, frustrated, lascivious, and unsuccessful. The thought that the editors might be right, that we are indeed a nation of auto-erotic stumblebums, is enough to chill the heart.

In short, the story of the rich young ruler may be a good one for all of us on this second Sunday in Lent. Personally, I am drawn to the man's restless discontent. I don't read him as an indulgent lover of grand agonies. I think he was a person of wealth and power who saw through both, a man not afraid of his own pain. And I like the way he called Jesus, "Good Teacher." It is important to feel grateful, the more so in unhappy times when feelings of gratitude are hard to come by; and I think it important to express gratitude to those we admire. A compliment, after all, is not flattery, just encouragement, something we all need.

Even so, I understand Jesus' response, "Why do you call me good? No one is good but God alone." That is the natural attitude toward God of every devout believer; and every good teacher points beyond him/herself, true teaching demanding a certain degree of self-obliteration.

Then, you remember, Jesus goes on: "You know the commandments: 'Do not kill. Do not commit adultery. Do not steal. Do not bear false witness. Do not defraud. Honor your father and mother.'"

These words are a good reminder that just as we can miss the essence of Christianity by identifying it with conventional morality, so we can miss the essence of Christianity by minimizing its moral commandments.

Yes, indeed, "Do not kill"—Mr. Mugger or Mr. Goetz. "Do not bear false witness"—against Nicaragua, Messrs. Reagan, Bush, and Schultz. Not for nothing is one of the Ten Commandments: "Thou shalt not bear false witness against thy neighbor." (Last week, President Reagan compared those trusty arsonists, kidnappers, and rapists, the Contras, to "freedom fighters" the likes of Simón Bolívar. This week, they became the moral equivalent of our founding fathers. I guess Simón Bolívar was right, over one hundred and fifty years ago, when he said, "The United States seems destined to plague Latin America with miseries in the name of liberty.")

We are approaching both the heart of the story and the essence of Christianity when the rich young ruler replies, "Master, all these have I observed from my youth." In effect, the man is saying, "All my life I have never done harm to anyone." Maybe he is right, but the question is, "What good has he done?"

He has observed all the commandments—and all but one are negative—but that you can do with a heart as cold as March waters in New England streams. He has been a respectable man, respectability consisting in not doing things. But Christianity consists in doing things. "For it is in giving that we receive; it is in pardoning that we are pardoned; and it is in dying that we are born to eternal life."

To follow Jesus, you have to see that life is made for more than itself, you have to risk something big for something good. All of which the rich young ruler must have known; hence his malaise, his running up and kneeling down before Jesus; hence Jesus, looking upon him and loving him, as Scripture records. But, what the man wanted, he did not want enough to pay the price; so, while he ran up full of expectancy, it was only minutes before he walked sorrowfully away. We can be sure that when he turned away, God's eyes closed against a rush of grief. For nothing so pains God as to see people choose not to be what they have it in them to be. Spiritually, it is a matter of life and death.

In a gospel that never made it into the Canon, Jesus says, "If you bring forth what is within you, what you bring forth will save you. If you do not bring forth what is within you, what you do not bring forth will destroy you."

Like Hamlet, the rich young ruler wavers for all of us. His restless discontent is ours and, too often, his sorrow as well; for like him we can bear neither the restless pain in our own hearts nor the remedy that could cure it. Remember, it is not the man's wealth but his heart that concerns Jesus. When he says, "Give to the poor," he knows that it is the heart that gives; the fingers only let go. Jesus is concerned for all our hearts. He wants us all to have treasure in heaven, not on earth, be that earthly treasure wealth or power, athletic ability or scholarship, good looks or young looks.

This brings me to the last thing I want to say this morning. Last week I spent a day in Southern California. Never have I seen more people trying to possess their soul by possession of things outside it. It is the United States of Shopping out there, one mall right after another. It is enough to give you "mall-aise," not to mention "mal de mall." But in that sea of consumerism, there is an island of brains and integrity. It is a retirement home for church-connected people, about three hundred of them. It is called Pilgrim Place, and it takes a while to get accustomed to palm trees waving over "Mayflower Road" and "Alden Way."

A lot of Riversiders retire there, which is why I always visit when I can. This time, I was there for lunch, the common meal, and for a talk afterwards; so I saw everyone. In that crowd I felt like youth incarnate. What moved me was the way those folk—their faces lined with "the credentials of humanity," as Shaw once called wrinkles— embodied Tennyson's familiar challenge (from *Ulysses*):

> 'Tis not too late to seek a newer world
> . . . .
> Tho' much is taken, much abides.

They read books, they review books, they write books. They bombard the Congress with letters, their dander higher than any I have seen in a long time. (It is a good thing for Reagan his ranch is at some distance.)

In true Christian fashion, they watch the erosion of their bodies by time, as a woman would watch, from a corner, a thief at her jewelry box, her treasures being elsewhere. When they all said grace before lunch, I pictured their morning prayer, "Lord, help me to remember that nothing is going to happen to me today that you and I cannot handle."

The Riversiders there put me in mind of Riversiders here who are also willing to say, with Browning's *Rabbi Ben Ezra*,

Grow old along with me!
The best is yet to be,
The last of life, for which the first was made:
Our times are in His hand
Who saith, "A whole I planned,
Youth shows but half; trust God: see all nor be afraid!"

I mention these Riversiders because when they were young, they too ran up to Jesus and knelt down. They too heard the same advice: Go, sell, give, come, follow.

And they did! God bless them. And may we, too.

"Not unto Us, O Lord, but unto Thy Name Be the Glory"

MARCH 17, 1985
Readings: Psalm 115:1–11; 2 Corinthians 4:1–2

If you walk through the world, as Karl Barth suggested, a Bible in one hand and the day's newspaper in the other, you quickly realize how everlastingly right Jesus and the prophets were in their reading of life. The passing parade brings daily testimony to the truth that compassion is more important than ideology—be it communism or anticommunism; that we should live by our dreams, not by our fears; that gentleness takes more courage than machismo; that nonviolence may be a flop but violence is a bigger flop.

Yes, the passing parade tells us we should rise each day with the psalmist's prayer on our lips, "Not unto us, O Lord, not unto us, but unto thy name be the glory." For either we learn to love the Lord our God with all our heart, mind, and strength, and our neighbors as ourselves, or one day the streets all over the world will be empty.

"Not unto us, O Lord, not unto us, but unto thy name be the glory." The sad fact to be confessed on this fourth Sunday in Lent is that, far from glorifying God, we Americans are idol worshippers, with one idol numbing millions of minds. Despite the fact that adding to overkill is irrational, that the Pentagon does not refute the nuclear winter, but actually confirms it; despite the polls that now indicate that 80 percent of the American public believes that a nuclear war cannot be limited, won, or survived, this nation is on its knees to the

Bomb. Say what you will about our being a Judeo-Christian nation, the truth is that in our heart of hearts we believe our only safety lies in the Bomb—not God, not Jesus Christ, nor any of the prophets, saints, or angels—but the Bomb and only the Bomb.

To the Soviets, too, the Bomb is the ultimate power, greater than any other. I once tried to persuade some Soviet arms control people to take a unilateral initiative for bilateral disarmament. This was several years ago when in exchange for no deployment of Pershing IIs and cruise missiles, the Soviets, at Geneva, had offered to scale back their SS-20s, -19s, and -18s to the level of the French and British intermediate range missiles. I urged them to stop talking and just do it—publicly, verifiably. It was just what we needed, a "Sadat-like" initiative. (You remember how the Egyptian President went in peace, for peace, alone to Jerusalem?) Such a move, I said, would easily be our best hope to stop American deployment. While they saw the point, they could only rejoin, "Dear friend, it would be viewed by your government as a sign of weakness."

They, of course, were right, and therein lies the tragedy, and my point about our worship of power. For years already, and as far as I know, today, the Geneva negotiations represent two competing denominations trying to agree on a Service of Common Worship to the Bomb.

"Star Wars" is no less idolatrous. If the Soviets had come up with it, we would see it for what it is: not a defense system, but an undermining of deterrence by refusing to be deterred. Only an idolatry of power can account for the fact that war-making institutions have been given control over:

the largest single block of industrial resources in the country,

the largest single block of research and development laboratories and talent,

the largest single labor force under one management, and above all,

the largest single block of finance capital in the American economy.

All this is controlled by the world's largest industrial administrative office, a staff of fifty thousand people, headquartered in the Pentagon, which continues to demand ever more financial devotion, even though it has, right now, upwards of $100 billion in unspent funds, of which, we can be assured, not one penny will be spent on the homeless or the 60 million Americans we now learn are functionally illiterate.

"Not unto us, O Lord, not unto us, but unto thy name be the glory."
Listen to what happens to those who worship man-as-god through
man-made works. Psalm 115 goes on:

> Their idols are silver and gold,
>   the work of men's hands.
> They have mouths, but do not speak;
>   eyes, but do not see.
> They have ears, but do not hear;
>   noses, but do not smell.
> They have hands, but do not feel;
>   feet, but do not walk;
>   and they do not make a sound in their throat.
> *Those who make them are like them.*

If we turn again from the Bible to see what the daily newspaper has
to say about the passing parade in Central America and about the role
of the United States there, we learn something else about violence. It
lives in symbiotic relationship with lies. Violence needs lies to justify
it, while lies need the protection of violence.

Without a single major smokestack industry, our nation's capital
has the worst pollution problem in the country—an air of deceit. The
paper tells us that Archbishop Rivera y Damas of El Salvador accuses
the White House of misrepresenting the views of the Central American bishops, that a bipartisan congressional report states that the
Administration is giving Congress "insufficient, misleading and false
information" about the nature of our aid to El Salvador. And whenever I read the latest absurdity about the Sandinistas "falling behind
the Iron Curtain," their country "a totalitarian dungeon" (What other
country but Switzerland gives arms to its people?), or about the Contras being "the moral equivalent of our founding fathers," I think of St.
Paul's condemnation of such rhetoric by his statement, "We refuse to
practice underhanded, disgraceful ways" (2 Cor. 4:2). I think, also, of
that great hymn of G. K. Chesterton's:

> O God of earth and altar, bow down and hear our cry,

(especially its second verse, which goes)

> From all that terror teaches, from lies of tongue and pen,
> From all the easy speeches that comfort cruel men,
> From sale and profanation of honor, and the sword,
> From sleep and from damnation, deliver us, good Lord.

Let me read you some testimony gathered in June 1984 in Nicaragua by "Witness for Peace," a group of North American Christians:

> Mr. Mejia got on his knees and pleaded with the Contras that they let his wife and children go free. "My husband said they could do what they planned with him, but to show mercy for the women and children. So they let us go—but, as we fled into the woods, they threw a grenade at us. It wounded me slightly on the shoulder, but, thank God, none of the children were hurt.
>
> "Then, as we hid in the woods, we could hear my husband scream and we knew they were torturing him. About 12:30 p.m. we heard an explosion. We saw smoke rising and knew that they had torched our house.
>
> "About an hour later, as the Contras were retreating, they stopped at my mother's house (which is located one-quarter mile from the Mejia farm) and kidnapped my two younger brothers, Jose Antonio, 13, and Emilio Ubaldo, 14, as well as my sister, Reina Riveras Amador, 16. Neither my parents nor brothers nor sister were involved in any popular organization or in politics. They were kidnapped 22 days ago and we have not heard of them since.
>
> "After the Contras left the area," Mrs. Mejia continued, "we went to our house to find my husband. We found him lying in front of our totally burned house. They had cut his arms with a knife and had completely smashed in his head until it was not recognizable. They used a big knife to cut a large cross in his back," she said with a trembling voice.

If you wonder why the cross in the back, remember the Ku Klux Klan. Remember what history teaches, that never do people so cheerfully do evil as when they do it from religious conviction.

"From sleep and from damnation deliver us, good Lord." And this, from a great rabbi, Leo Baeck: "A spirit is characterized not only by what it does, but no less by what it permits, what it condones, and what it beholds in silence."

Christians simply cannot stand by and allow a super power to rake with violence a poor, small country like Nicaragua whose citizens not only breathe and bleed, but worship, sing to, pray to, and love the same Lord Jesus as do we. Christians in Nicaragua divide in their feelings about the Sandinista government. Some are upset, some very upset, while others believe the revolution allows them to live their faith more fully. But almost to the last sister and brother, they want us North American Christians to stop the carnage, the violence and its lies, all those accompanying "easy speeches that comfort cruel men."

In response to their pleas, I urge you not to leave this church, or at least not to let today's sun go down without writing your congressional representatives to stop funding this war—by covert aid, overt aid, "humanitarian aid," or any use of a third world country.

You should know that the following bodies have called on our government to stop funding this war: the American Baptist Convention, the United Methodist Church, the Presbyterian Church (U.S.A.), the Episcopal Church, the Unitarian Universalist Association, the United Church of Christ, the Moravian Church, the Mennonites, the Church of the Brethren, the Jesuits, the U.S. Catholic Conference of Bishops and almost all Catholic orders.

Thank God that in this dark hour we celebrate a bright one—"One Great Hour of Sharing," a timely reminder of what we could do the world around with our money if only we believed what we ourselves inscribed on it: "In God we trust."

Just think: For $10, two blankets; for $50, an eight-pound package containing thirty-two different kinds of vegetable seeds that can produce vegetables enough to feed an entire community plus seeds for the next planting. Take the special envelopes and stuff them with the good things others so desperately need, and let your gift be a reminder of how important it is these days that each of us make a difference in the way described by St. Paul, "We have renounced disgraceful, underhanded ways; we refuse to practice cunning or to tamper with God's word, but by the open statement of the truth, we would commend ourselves to everyone's conscience in the sight of God."

To Run and Not Grow Weary

Fifth Sunday in Lent
MARCH 24, 1985
Readings: Isaiah 40:28–31; 2 Corinthians 4:8–10

This has been an exhilarating, unhappy week for me. It started with a funeral I was asked to take in Blue Hill, Maine, the funeral of an eleven-year-old boy, son of very good friends, who drowned in a freak accident in a motel swimming pool. Being myself the father of a drowned son, I knew exactly what the family was going through: a time when the only line of Scripture you can remember is "My God, My God, why hast Thou forsaken me?"; a time when you are convinced that "the world has nothing to give like that which it takes away."

When the boy was in the ground, notes from his schoolmates lying beside him in the casket, and we had all thrown in our handful of dirt, with a parting prayer or two, and when I was again on the plane, I read of the 55–45 Senate vote to deploy twenty-one more of those vulnerable, destabilizing, wretchedly expensive MX missiles. These are the missiles which last year the president told us were not really missiles, after all, but only bargaining chips to get the Soviets back to the Geneva conference table, a table, which, last week, the president turned into a bargaining chip to get himself more missiles. Last year we were told we had to have these missiles because there were no talks going on in Geneva; this year we are told we must have them because there are talks going on in Geneva. Oh, how we have to mock the fools, brave the wicked, and force ourselves to laugh at everything for fear of having to cry about it all! (That's Beaumarchais: "*Me moquant des sots, bravant les mechants, je me presse de rire de tout de peur d'être obligé d'en pleurer.*")

In the next two days I managed to read Jonathan Kozol's *Illiterate America,* a book sixty million of his adult compatriots could not for the life of them read even if they wanted to. (Twenty-five million American adults cannot read the poison warnings on a can of pesticide, a letter from their children's teacher, or the front page of a newspaper.)

Finally at week's end we concluded here at Riverside a highly successful conference on economic justice, made exhilarating by the amount and variety of straight talk, such talk being so rare in this time and land of smoke and mirrors.

But what we heard was not exhilarating:

that rural America is swamped with depression (42 percent of all farms in Iowa and other north-central states alone are sliding rapidly toward insolvency);

that 40 percent of all black children live today below the poverty line;

that for uneducated Americans, jobs available pay so little that they can no longer be called an alternative to poverty (How right was Archbishop Romero to call the poor not "*los pobres*," but "*los empobrecidos*"—those made to be poor!);

that corporations that used to pay 25 percent now only pay 6 percent of all tax revenues;

that retirement pay for the military is three times that of civilian pensions, and the average military retiree is all of forty-one years old.

All this is not to mention what we heard about the swampland of waste that is the Pentagon, what we heard Friday night about South Africa and Nicaragua, and this morning from Sister Donovan about her experiences in Central America.*

As I say, it has been an exhilarating, unhappy week. So how do we continue to fight the good fight, to endure unto the end, until with eleven-year-old Ben Holloway we are made partakers of God's eternal kingdom? How do you keep going when you feel like a fly in the evening of its only day in life—tired from the struggle?

How much worse it would be if we experienced nothing; if we were indifferent! I used the word "exhilarating" because so often we are so much more alive when we are in pain. Those six hundred mourners packed into that little Congregational church were throbbing with life—parents and children singing and weeping their hearts out as they affirmed with Noel Stookey ("Paul" of Peter, Paul, and Mary), "All will be well when the day is done." It was so wonderful to feel so vulnerable, so defenseless, to realize anew that the only arms we need—and that the whole world needs—are the two God gave us to embrace one another.

Likewise, the conferees of the last two days were vibrant with life as were we all just now listening to Sister Donovan insist on truths that cannot be denied.

I prayed a lot this week, because in prayer you do not so much hear a voice as acquire a voice—your own—to speak comfort to those in distress and truth to those in power. I pray a lot these days in order not to lose my ability to believe in a better world, to keep striving for peace, defending justice, informing good people so remarkably ignorant. It is hard. It is tiring. I remember a socialist complaining, "The only thing most Americans know about socialism is that they don't like it." And whenever I try to speak truth to power, the answer I receive from power recalls a line from Ring Lardner Jr.: " 'Shut up,' he explained."

*Sister Donovan, a Roman Catholic nun, was briefly kidnapped by the Contras in Nicaragua. She was attending Riverside on this Sunday as a participant in the Conference on Economic Justice sponsored by the Riverside Church. She spoke during the morning worship service in observance of Central America Week and the fifth anniversary of the assassination of Archbishop Oscar Arnulfo Romero of El Salvador.

But "they that wait upon the Lord shall renew their strength; they shall mount up with wings as eagles; they shall run and not grow weary, walk and not faint."

I am confident that the Maine family of little Ben Holloway will learn, as I did, to improve the quality of their suffering by offering it up to God, as one would offer one's money, in order to ask God to use our pain to put us in touch with the pain of others. And I am confident that yesterday's conferees will continue to identify these situations of injustice that call for change; that they will, in the words of John C. Bennett, former president of Union Theological Seminary, "press the socialist questions even though they do not accept ready-made socialistic answers." I am confident that they will seek solutions beneficial to those least favored in our society, solutions that will never permit justice and freedom to destroy each other. And I fervently hope that the American people will soon say loudly and clearly that they have had enough of the wars in El Salvador and Nicaragua. On that day those wars will cease.

Faithfulness is more demanding than success. But Christians are saved from self-pity, that most debilitating of all emotions, by the remembrance that Christ never allowed his soul to be cornered into despair. Although he knew the disciples would desert him, that we would all let him down, still he keeps hoping that, like Peter and unlike Judas, we will return for our own forgiveness. He needs us to speak comfort to those in distress and truth to those in power.

And blessed are those who so speak. They die in glory as the stars die at sunrise.

So, hard as it is sometimes, let us take our stand with St. Paul: "We are afflicted in every way, but not crushed; perplexed but not driven to despair; persecuted but not forsaken; struck down, but not destroyed; always carrying in the body the death of Jesus, so that the life of Jesus may also be manifested in our bodies."

Praise the Lord.

God Was in Christ

Palm Sunday
MARCH 31, 1985
Reading: John 12:9–19

As any writer will tell you, the essence of good writing is drama, and the essence of drama is conflict. And that is what makes the Palm Sunday story so dramatic. In the whole of scripture, Calvary not excepted, no scene depicts more conflicting ideas about what is going on than this one. The Pharisees think they have a heretic on their hands, and a peculiarly obnoxious one, for Jesus is saying, in effect, that the real troublemakers in this world are not the ignorant and cruel, but the intelligent and corrupt, people like the Pharisees themselves. (Pascal once said, "the world divides itself between saints who know themselves to be sinners and sinners who imagine themselves to be saints.")

Quite naturally, the Pharisees resist Jesus, and will do so all the more vigorously after he "cleanses" the temple by chasing away the money changers, symbols of that oldest form of corruption—religion become subservient to profit-making. Yet for all their power, they are today powerless: "The Pharisees then said to one another, 'You see that you can do nothing; look, the world has gone after him'" (John 12:19).

Indeed, in the form of the Jerusalem multitudes, the world did go after him that day. That is why Palm Sunday is so festive an occasion. Yet were they cheering a religious leader, these multitudes? Were they praising a man who had searched their consciences, convinced their minds, and won over their hearts? Or were they following a political leader whose power had been proved by the story circulating through the streets of the city that he had actually raised a man named Lazarus from the dead?

To be sure, they were carrying palms, symbols of peace, but then the Roman authorities forbade the carrying of spears. To be sure, they were praising God, but they were also hailing the King of Israel. Some of them no doubt remembered the prophesy of Zechariah: "Behold, your king is coming to you, humble, and riding on an ass" (Zech. 9:9; Matt. 21:5). But I'll bet the majority had Saul and Solomon in mind. I'll bet the majority were hailing a new national leader come to help throw off the hated Roman yoke. And you can't blame a one of them for wanting political independence. "Give me liberty or give me death." On the other hand, you cannot equate such a political leader with "the lamb of God that taketh away the sins of the world" (John 1:29).

With these differing perceptions went differing emotions. The Pharisees were sullen, the multitude ecstatic. But the greatest contrast was between the crowds and Jesus. While the crowds shouted wildly, "Hosannah, blessed is he who comes in the name of the Lord, even the King of Israel," instead of smiling and acknowledging the cheers, the King wept: "And when he drew near and saw the city he wept over it, saying, 'Would that even today you knew the things that make for peace! But now they are hid from your eyes'" (John 12:12–13; Luke 19:37–42).

Had Jesus wept only for what he had earlier predicted would befall him, that would have been poignant enough. Instead he wept for what he was sure would befall the very people who today were urging him on, and who tomorrow, because of their blindness, would be shouting, "Crucify him!"

There is something so special about this scene in which Jesus, amid a sea of smiling, cheering humanity, rides totally alone with God, weeping. He will disappoint the expectations of the thousands milling and marching around him, but in so doing he will acknowledge the author of his being, the appointee of his spiritual fate. He has so much more to say, so much life still to live and give: Why didn't he stay in Galilee where it was safer? Instead, he chose to bring his words and deeds into the very heart of entrenched political and religious power. He could have entered the capital on a horse, as a wartime king, but chose instead to come in peace, for peace. Rather than inflict suffering, he chose to take suffering upon himself. He could have lived to save Israel; he chose to die to save the world.

Dearly beloved who have come here on this Palm Sunday, I hardly need remind you that the world he died to save still resists its salvation. Even more than his, ours is a world of reprisals (think of the Middle East, think of South Africa), a world of injustices and invasions (in Central America and elsewhere), a world of moral horror in which common sense and prudence are swept away by fears too elemental to master.

I do not need to remind us all that amid the epochal events of these agitated years, we have to define a position, make a difference—every one of us. Amid a swirling sea of voices urging us to ease our lots, to curry favor, to get power, to consider money of vast and overwhelming importance, every one of us has to choose to walk alone with God. Every one of us has to discover that which has been lost, and found, and lost again and again—the reality of self-sacrifice and love that shines so radiantly in the words and deeds of Jesus Christ our Lord.

I have a friend who, years ago, upon losing a race for the House of Representatives, called to ask if he could visit me at Yale Divinity School where I was a student. He told me he was reconsidering the possibility of entering the ministry. (Nothing like a little failure to teach a little wisdom!)

Among other things, I arranged for him to meet Richard Niebuhr, a man who spent a lot of time alone with God. After explaining the reasons for his renewed interest in the church and ministry, he went on, "But you must understand, Dr. Niebuhr, I am a man interested in public life, I want to be a part of the big show."

After a considerable pause, Dr. Niebuhr asked quietly of my friend, "What *is* the big show?"

We all want to be part of a show of some significance. None of us wants to be an outsider; we all want to be insiders. But we shall always be outsiders until *we are inside ourselves*, until with Jesus we acknowledge the author of our being, the appointer of our spiritual fate. To follow Christ may not be part of the big show (as the world measures size), but it is part of the only show that counts, for if we fail in love, we fail in all things else.

And we must make love count. This city, hemorrhaging at one end and health-clubbing-it at the other, needs desperately our love. Without love, all humanity will come to judgment, not before God, but before the Bomb. Unless we all learn to love here and everywhere, the poor will get poorer, the rich richer, and the military more powerful. With love we may yet see, the world around, "alabaster cities gleam, undimmed by human tears." We may hear again the words of the Pharisees, "look, the world has gone after him."

Some people, knowing how confused the scene was and how the story ends, find it difficult to celebrate Palm Sunday. But look at it this way: With a better understanding of what was going on, we have even more to cheer about. The cross of Christ says something terrible about us, but something wonderful about God. It symbolizes not only the triumph in defeat of a good man; it also represents the merciful action of a loving Mother/Father; for "God was in Christ reconciling the world unto himself" (2 Cor. 5:19). Therefore, with the kind of joy that shines through tears we can sing:

> Ride on, ride on in majesty;
> Thy last and fiercest strife is nigh;
> Bow thy meek head to mortal pain,
> Then take, O Christ, thy power and reign.
> Henry H. Milman

Despite Appearances, It Is an Easter World

Easter Sunday
APRIL 7, 1985
Readings: Zechariah 9:9–10; 1 Corinthians 15:51–58

It is so wonderful to know that despite today's chill and yesterday's bluster spring is here. Energy is pouring out of the ground and into every blade of grass, every crocus, magnolia bush and cherry tree.

Soon the robins will join the pigeons, the sky will be full of the thunder of the sun, "the shaggy mountains will stomp their feet, the waves toss high and clap their wild blue hands." Overhead and underfoot and all around we shall soon see, hear, feel, and smell the juice and joy of spring.

Likewise, it is wonderful to know that despite appearances to the contrary, this is an Easter world. It looks like a Good Friday world when, as in Jesus' time, politicians have but to hear, "Thou art not Caesar's friend," and away they fall, like Pilate, washing their hands and thereby plaiting the crown of thorns. It feels like a Good Friday world when we, Christ's disciples, follow him like Peter—halfway, but not the other half. It feels like a Good Friday world when so many crowds are like the one that gathered on Calvary, not to cheer a miscarriage of justice, but also not to protest it. Failing to realize that compassion without confrontation is sentimental, the crowds went home, we read, beating their breasts, preferring once again guilt to responsibility.

As Harvey Cox wrote in Friday's *New York Times*, "[Christ's] death tells us nothing in particular about Jews or Romans, but it speaks volumes about the human propensity to prop up teetering positions of privilege with the pain of innocent people."

God knows that continues. Still, it is an Easter world and for this reason, fear and self-righteousness, indifference and sentimentality can kill, but love never dies, not with God and not even with us in whom God's love abides. The Easter message says, "You can kill God's love, but you cannot keep it dead and buried." All that tenderness and strength, which on Good Friday we saw scourged, buffeted, stretched out on a cross, all that beauty and goodness is again alive, and with us now, not as a memory that inevitably fades, but as an undying presence in the life of everyone of us.

Christ is risen. He is risen indeed. And Christ is risen *pro nobis*, for us. The point of his resurrection is to produce our own, by putting love in our hearts, decent thoughts in our heads, and a little more iron up our spines. Christ is risen to convert us, not from this life to some other life, but from something less than life to the possibility of full life itself. As it is written: "The glory of God is (a human being) fully alive" (Irenaeus).

But the choice is ours, whether or not to live the Easter truth in a world of Good Friday illusions. Will we choose to be Easter people—human beings fully alive—or elect to be as that government official riding a bus, so vividly described by the French poet-aviator, Saint-Exupéry, in his book *Wind, Sand and Stars*:

Old bureaucrat, my comrade, . . . you, like a termite, built your peace by blocking up every chink and cranny through which the light might pierce. You rolled yourself up into a ball in your genteel security, in routine, in the stifling conventions of provincial life, raising a modest rampart against the wind and the tides and the stars. You have chosen not to be perturbed by great problems, having trouble enough to forget your own fate as a [human being]. You are not a dweller upon an errant planet, you do not ask yourself questions to which there are no answers. You are a petty bourgeois of Toulouse. Nobody grasped you by the shoulder while there was still time. Now the clay of which you were shaped has dried and hardened, and naught in you will ever awaken the sleeping musician, the poet, the astronomer that possibly inhabited you in the beginning.

To be a citizen of a Good Friday world, you do not have to be a monster, an out and out crucifier. You do not have to be a Bengal tiger; it is enough to be a tame tabby, a nice guy but not a good person; to inhabit a Good Friday world, it is enough to be half alive. It is as if we settled for March weather, forgetting the riotous beauty that lies just ahead. It is as if, listening to Liberace, we thought we were hearing Horowitz. It is as if, in reading the unchastened optimism of the *Reader's Digest*, we thought we were approaching the heights of Dante's *Divine Comedy*.

Good Friday people crucify Christ for a simple reason. We crucify Christ, the best among us, because first we crucify the best within us, and we do not want to be reminded. Then when Jesus grasps us by the shoulder, forcing us to face the bitter fruits of caution, the vacant years, the ugly altars to ourselves, our nation's lunatic lust for place and possessions, we crucify the prophet in the time-honored tradition of ancient kings who killed the bearer of bad news—in Jesus' case, the good news that we can be human beings not half but fully alive.

I mentioned Peter who denied our Lord just as surely as Judas betrayed him. The difference is that Peter came back to receive his forgiveness. The tragedy of Judas is that he never did. Like Judas, we too can stay stuck in our sins, paralyzed by guilt, treasuring our mistakes as if they were the holiest things in our lives. Or, with Peter, we can realize that there is more mercy in God than sin in us. The church is founded on Peter because he moved from a Good Friday to an Easter world; he accepted his forgiveness; he overcame his fear of confrontation and death; he went the second half of the way; he became ten times the person he was before Jesus' death. Our lives run from God in God to God again; death is only a horizon, and a horizon is nothing but the limits of our sight.

"Made like him, like him we rise, ours the cross, the grave, the skies."

And that's the truth, friends, the Easter truth: We are forgiven, and death has no dominion.

Now, wouldn't you rather be an Easter person if only because it is dull to be half-alive in a Good Friday world? It is boring to be a petty bourgeois, whether in Toulouse or in New York. It is boring to live a life to the minimum, to retreat from the mysterious to the manageable, from freedom to bondage.

By contrast, it is exciting to live the Easter truth, but not easy in a world of Good Friday illusions. For Easter demands not sympathy for Christ crucified, but allegiance to Christ risen. And loyalty to the resurrected Christ means an end to all loyalties to people, organizations, institutions, and movements that crucify. I fail to see how you can combine loyalty to the risen Christ with MX missiles or with the notion that the United States, the Soviet Union or any other power has the right to decide who lives, dies, and rules in small Third World countries—with apartheid or with economic systems that fill the rich with good things and send the poor empty away.

Senator Hubert Humphrey was asked once to discuss the relationship of compassion to politics. He held up a brand-new pencil. "My friends," he said, "compassion is to politics as this eraser is to the rest of the pencil. And as with the eraser, so with compassion: it is only used when you have to correct mistakes."

That's in a Good Friday world. Easter people must expand compassion, fan the spark of imagination, revive integrity, and above all cast out fear, for as Eleanor Roosevelt once observed, "Those who 'view with alarm' never build anything."

Tolstoy tells the story of a peasant who refused military service and, while being transported to jail, managed to convert his guard, Sereda, whom Tolstoy quotes as saying, "I do not want to be with the tormentors, join me to the martyrs." That is how Christians should practice gentle subversion of the existing order.

On Friday morning, at five minutes before eleven o'clock, six thousand disc jockeys played a disc cut by forty outstanding musicians. Many of you must have heard it. Tears glistened as I listened to the singers insist that the day is dark, that we have to save our lives, and can only do so by recognizing that every dweller on this errant planet is a child of God and therefore a brother or sister of every other inhabitant.

We are the world, we are the children
We are the ones who make a brighter day
So let's start giving. . . .

It is so true. We all belong one to another. That is the way God made us. Christ died and rose again to keep us that way. Our sin is always and only that we are constantly trying to put asunder what God has joined together.

So, sisters and brothers, what shall it be? What shall we choose: to live half alive and preserve the illusions of a Good Friday world, or live fully alive the Easter truth that Christ is risen, love never dies, not with God, not even with us, and because Christ is risen we too are risen?

Let's start answering that question by arising and exchanging with one another the traditional Easter embrace and greeting: "Christ is risen." He is risen indeed!

Parable of the Sower

APRIL 21, 1985
Reading: Matthew 13:1–8

Parables are not to be looked at, but to be looked through. When you do look through a parable, you see Jesus, and when you look through Jesus, you see, transparently, the power of God at work.

I love parables—earthly stories with a heavenly meaning. They start with the here and now—a sower, a woman baking bread, a torn garment, a lost sheep or coin or son—but they begin with the here and now only to get us to there and eternity. And I love the way parables make us think by shifting the responsibility from the narrator to the hearer. Christians tend to forget that God leads with a light rein, giving us our heads. It has been said that you cannot tell people the truth; you can only put them in a position where they can discover the truth for themselves. That is what a parable does; and a nice thing about a parable (as opposed to an argument, which seeks to win) is that a parable never puts down anybody. Finally, parables are a lively reminder to preachers that dullness is a failure, perhaps even a breach in love, and therefore a sin. But, let's hasten on!

Before getting into this particular parable, let me quickly set the scene. In the thirteenth chapter of Matthew we find a special turn in Jesus' life. The doors of the synagogue are beginning to close on him because he has offended the religious authorities; and as we all know, hell hath no wrath like that of a bureaucracy scorned. But the people are glad to hear him, in their homes, in the village streets, on the open road, or by the seashore where, in this chapter, they find him.

"That same day Jesus went out of the house and sat beside the sea, and great crowds gathered around him. So he got into a boat and sat there; and the whole crowd stood on the beach." Then, looking over their heads he saw this man going out into the field to sow, and he was off: "A sower went out to sow and as he sowed, some seed fell along the path and birds came and devoured it." Already, if we had been listening carefully (as we should have been, God having given us two ears to one mouth) we would have guessed that this parable was not about a sower but about the soil, as it turns out, four different kinds of soil.

The first kind is hard. In effect, what Jesus is saying is: If you are hard-hearted or hard-nosed (wherever that expression comes from); if you play only hardball with other people, and hard to get with God; if your spirit is unreachable and your prejudices such as to blind you to anything you wish not to see, then you are like that path beaten hard by many feet, that right-of-way that leads through the narrow strips of land, which in ancient Palestine were the fields in which the seed were sown. O yes, one more thing, "you're for the birds!'" I only quote scripture! "And as he sowed, some seed fell along the path and birds came and devoured it."

Going on, "other seed fell on rocky ground where they had not much soil and immediately they sprang up, since they had no depth of soil." It was common in ancient Palestine to find a thick layer of earth just above a ledge of lime rock. In such ground, speedily warmed by the sun and by the rock beneath, absorbing the heat of the sun, the seeds would sprout quickly; but as soon as they sent down roots in search of moisture, in search of nourishment, they hit bedrock, and the seeds would wilt. As Jesus said, "but when the sun rose, they were scorched, and since they had no roots, they withered away."

We are talking now of soil that was not hard but shallow, of people who are not hard, but shallow, of people who, in the manner of today's surfers, are afraid of not catching the next social wave as it forms, and thereby (the ultimate nightmare for Americans) being left out of the action.

Scholars, too, can be shallow. There are those who know a lot but experience little; scholars who had rather read a map than be there; scholars who live from the neck up.

And a lot of religion is shallow. Just because a painting has a religious subject, it is not necessarily a religious painting, not if it is sentimental and shallow. And, likewise, all who say, "Lord, Lord," are not thereby profoundly Christian. What, for instance, in our day, could be more shallow than for Christians to insist upon prayer in the public schools, as if that is all it takes to make people Christian? We don't need to pray in, we need to pray for the public schools!

There is a Peter De Vries character who confesses for quite a few of us when he says, "Deep down, I'm shallow."

After hard soil and shallow soil comes what farmers call "dirty soil," that is, rich soil, but cluttered. In Jesus' words, "other seeds fell upon thorns and the thorns grew up, and choked them."

While in Nicaragua last week, I was reminded that in revolutions the people most afraid are the rich. In revolutions, it is revealed that to those who have lots of it, money generally means a lot more than does social justice. It's very hard to be rich in things and rich in the freedom to know how to use those things. As it is written, "expenditures rise to meet income."

In Faulkner's *Intruder in the Dust*, there is a wonderful moment when the sixteen-year-old black lad is being asked to go out into the cemetery and dig up a corpse to prove that the person accused could not possibly have shot the dead person. The young man, understandably, is reluctant. He is assured that money is involved and he blurts out, "I ain't rich. I don't need money." Thus there are two ways to be rich: One is to have lots of money and the other is to have few needs. If all of us could say, "I ain't rich, I don't need money," we'd be in a new land.

But of course you don't have to be rich to live a cluttered life. It is enough to be busy. Too busy. I have a friend, perhaps my oldest, whom I see so rarely that one day he suggested, "Coffin, let us be buried side by side and the epitaph on our common grave will read, 'In death united, in life, too busy!'"

As they say in the journalistic trade, that statement had a "chilling effect."

Finally, after hard soil and shallow soil and dirty soil, comes good soil. "Other seed fell on good soil and brought forth grain, some a hundredfold, some sixtyfold, and some thirtyfold."

Maybe good soil is the soil that the plowshare of tragedy has broken up. Maybe it is soil made rich by love, carefully weeded by tender, loving care. To be soil that is rich and deep, you don't have to be well educated, although education helps. To be soil that is good and rich, you don't have to travel, though travel helps. I say this because experience is not what happens to you, it is what you do with what happens to you. To be good soil, you can doubt the quality of the bread, but you cannot kid yourself that you are not hungry. You can doubt the truth, but only out of love of it; you can be skeptical, but only from a depth of commitment. To be good soil, you have to know that "*Cogito, ergo sum*," "I think, therefore I am," is shallow. And that "*Amo, ergo sum*," "I love, therefore I am" is profound.

I think we all know what good soil is. It is not hard, it is not shallow, it is not cluttered. But I think the parable is finally about something else. The world may mock the labor of a sower, but there is always a harvest.

If Jesus, seated in the boat, did indeed point to a man sowing seed, chances are, that man looked like the one in the painting by Jean Paul Millet—weary, alone in a very wide field. But, never mind, the harvest is sure. "Some seed may indeed fall by the wayside and be snatched away by the birds; some seed may fall on shallow ground and never come to maturity; some seed may fall among the thorns and be choked to death; but in spite of all that, the harvest does come" (William Barclay).

I read this parable as pro-spring, anti-despair, a good parable for Youth Sunday, a Sunday full of handbells (at four o'clock this afternoon) and baptisms (this morning) and new members who prove once again the truth of St. Benedict's remark, "God often shows what is better to the younger."

So, I was wrong. This parable is about a sower after all. I think God wants us to be both good soil and tireless sowers. God wants us to chuck despair and pitch tents of light in the darkened valleys of this world. God wants us to be hopeful, which is to say, to believe despite the evidence, knowing that only in so doing has the evidence any chance of changing.

So, on this third Sunday of Eastertide, what do you say? Let's get off the path, steer clear of the rocks and thorns, and be good soil and cheerful sowers for our Risen Lord. Amen.

Peace within Our Walls—and Without

Peace Sabbath
APRIL 28, 1985
Readings: Psalm 122; Matthew 5:1–12

It was wonderful this week to watch on television those vintage GIs hugging those rotund Russians, both sides laughing and weeping as they celebrated the fortieth anniversary of their war-ending encounter on the Elbe River in East Germany. But the week also brought news of another reunion, this one in Bandung, Indonesia. There, representatives of eighty Asian and African countries declared the world to be in worse shape now than it was at the first meeting of non-aligned nations thirty years ago. From Allan Boesak we have heard today of South Africa's agony, and in the days ahead we had better all pray for President Reagan, that somewhere between Bitburg and Johannesburg he may find his way.

At 12:30 sharp in the ninth floor lounge, I will give a half-hour report on my week's trip to El Salvador, Nicaragua, and Guatemala. But in this service I have elected to talk not of peace on our errant planet, but of peace within the walls of Riverside Church. There are two significant issues troubling Riverside's peace, and that is good. My tendency is to believe that where there is perturbation someone must be doing something right. Two years ago, the Dean of the Chapel at Harvard said to me: "in the sixties when people around here were arguing and shouting at each other, I figured Harvard had a purpose. I wasn't sure what it was, but I felt certain it was here somewhere. Today, no one is arguing, no one is shouting and Harvard is revealed for what it is—purposeless."

That, by the way, is true of most higher education in this country, and for a simple reason: every country's education reflects that country's ideology. So, in institutions of higher education all over America today, the freedom of faculty and students to say and think what they will is vastly exalted over any obligation to do any good to anybody. That is why we should rejoice at what Columbia students have sparked on so many campuses.

But back to Riverside where we are pretty much in agreement, I think, on the wisdom of divestment by universities and churches, at least, if only to bring further pressure on American companies in South Africa to do more than they have done to date to subvert the evil system of apartheid.

What troubles and divides us here at Riverside are two other significant issues: sexist language—or let us call it more positively inclusive language; and the Gay/Lesbian statement the church is being asked to vote on at the annual meeting. The latter issue I will address another time. Meantime, however, I want to commend to every member's attention Gene Laubach's column in the latest "Carillon." Indeed we must "resist the impulse to turn away," we must "not vote, or even talk, out of our own ignorance or fear or prejudice." We must, as he says, "understand clearly what is involved and think concretely about what is the response our *faith* calls us to make."

Like so many of you in the congregation and choir and collegium, I have been troubled by the issue of inclusive language. In matters liturgical, I am a traditionalist. I do not find it easy or fun to change words in hymns, let alone Scripture. And I know—or thought I knew—a fair amount about language, enough to know that when I read that first sentence of the first psalm—"Blessed is the man who walks not in the counsel of the wicked"—"man" includes woman. Man can refer to one male person or to everyone. In the latter case, it is gender free, simply a feature of grammar.

But over the years I have seen the pain in the eyes of women—intelligent, secure, whole women—as they have heard Scripture read, sermons preached, hymns sung, church meetings conducted—all in the masculine gender. These women have persuaded me that my former understanding that masculine language can incorporate women is not far removed from another understanding—that the male world can incorporate and subordinate women.

I can see now that there must be something wrong with a gender-free language that claims to be inclusive, but uses only male, never female, terms to express the inclusiveness. I can even see that we may be denying the Gospel by the very words we use to proclaim it if these words hurt members of, and thereby disrupt, the inclusive community that the Gospel is at pains to create and affirm.

If we, who are whites, were, and still are, willing to let blacks call things to our white attention for reconsideration in the name of justice, then we who are men must stand ready to allow women to call things to our male attention for reconsideration in the name of justice. How can we men say that we are for justice and community, that we believe in pastoral care, and not care about inclusive language?

Let me tell you some other things I have learned at the not always tender hands of Council I's committee on inclusive language. When I boasted about being a traditionalist, what I really meant was, I was "stuck in a rut." Five times out of ten, tradition is a euphemism for habit: "I've always said (or done) it that way and I like it that way."

Once lifted out of that rut, by the grace of God working through this relentless committee, I have found it interesting, provocative, refreshing to think about inclusive language and all its implications. It has made me realize that while I have preached about Abraham and Isaac and Jacob, I have hardly mentioned Sarah, Hagar, Rebecca, Rachel, and Leah, although a lot of the action in Genesis revolves around them. God works through the mothers of Israel as well as the fathers.

I am also beginning to see that while social change creates language change, the reverse is also true: language change can help social change. The word, "Black," instead of "Negro" helped a lot of whites to move a little further down the road. And inclusive language is feasible and practical. Instead of congressman we can say congressional representative (it is only a little longer). Instead of policeman, we can say police officer; instead of fireman, firefighter (which is actually more exciting). And how about this: "Blessed are they who walk not in the counsel of the wicked, nor stand in the way of sinners, nor sit in the seats of scoffers; but their delight is in the law of the Lord, and on this law they meditate day and night" (Psalm 1:1).

That wasn't too bad was it? In lieu of "Faith of our fathers," we can sing, "Faith of the martyrs, holy faith" (that is what the hymn is all about anyhow); in lieu of "This is my father's world," "Our God has made this world" (although that is a bit more banal). And could you not without too much stress and strain sing, "Good Christian folk rejoice," and "Rise up, O Saints of God"?

I find that where earlier a change of language called attention to itself and therefore was awkward, now sexist language calls attention to itself even more. Where that happens, we have no choice but to press on. But mindful we must always be that our task is to correct language, not history—that is, "he" is appropriate to the historic Jesus if not always to the Cosmic Christ who is present and with us now; and some language should probably not be changed, tradition being important if not all-important. At this point on the journey, I have in mind the Lord's Prayer and the Twenty-third Psalm.

Most of all, I think none of us should seek to feel always comfortable in the church of Jesus Christ, who had no place to lay his head. The Holy Spirit is after all a discomforter, as well as a comforter.

It is well said, "God must afflict the comfortable before comforting the afflicted."

And that leads to a last suggestion. Inclusive language is part and parcel of the struggle to build an inclusive community throughout the world. Ultimately, justice is a seamless robe, and if you can see the pain in the eyes of women assaulted by sexist language, chances are you can also feel the pain of the poor, and recognize the very existence of nuclear weapons as an assault on the human heart.

If you can break habits long ingrained, see your favorite proven fact disproved before your eyes; if your security with the eternal God is such that you can live with all manner of temporal insecurity, then chances are you will not write off inclusive language as ridiculous, nor be blind in your loyalty to your country, nor be hasty in moving toward military solutions.

Everywhere on God's earth, peace is in search of makers, of people whose more inclusive thoughts lead them to more inclusive language, to more inclusive communities. For God's sake, and for the sake of our children, that they may walk the same earth, under the same sky, as do we this glorious spring day, won't you too become a peacemaker within and without the walls of this church?

The Fundamental Injunction: Love One Another

MOTHER'S DAY, MAY 12, 1985
Reading: Luke 2:41–51

As this is the 113th annual celebration of Mother's Day I hope there is not a single soul in this church, who does not agree with the author of the Yiddish proverb that says: "God could not be everywhere, so God made mothers."

But before turning to mothers to whom every one of us owes our very existence, I want to say a few words about my beloved colleague's sermon of last Sunday and the subsequent intervention in the service that the sermon prompted.* You can be sure the collegium has thought of and dealt with little else all week.

I can only begin to imagine the hurt and anger felt by those of you who thought you had found here at Riverside what you had almost despaired of finding anywhere: a church where, despite the misinformation, superstitions, and prejudices of our culture, not only black and white could feel at one and at home, celebrating and affirming each other's existence in the name of Jesus Christ but also gay and straight. I can also understand the pain of others who thought they had heard confirmed their moral apprehensions about homosexuality (and divorce) only to have these apprehensions then questioned by a demonstration—in church yet!—albeit a demonstration called, I believe genuinely, in the name of healing and love. If it did not come

---

*May 5, 1985: After much public study and prayer, the church was one month away from voting up or down, the use of inclusive language in all public preaching and praying. Without any forewarning or intimation before hand of his disagreement with a new language, collegium member Channing Phillips preached that day (Coffin was preaching out of town) that to deviate from the gospel pronouncement on the evils of divorce and the sanctity of heterosexual marriage was a sin. After Communion was served, a graduate student stepped forward and protested the sermon and asked that all who disagreed with what they heard from the pulpit that day come forward, in love, around the Communion table during the singing of the last hymn. Hundreds of people did come forward. For the following week the collegium met daily and invited theologians to help them think through the mess that had been created on many levels. May 12 sermon is Bill's response.

through to you as healing and love, then simply say to yourself that pain often makes people jump the gun.

Dearly beloved in the Lord, we now have a sharply divided church, one divided by homosexuality, or should we call it homophobia—the fear of, or contempt for homosexuals, the belief that their sexual orientation is "unnatural"? However we label it, it is the most divisive issue the churches of America have encountered, or evaded, since slavery.

What are we going to do? It is simple, although about as easy as for a camel to pass through the eye of a needle: We are going to behave as those who believe in the Lord Jesus Christ. Christianity has not been tried and found wanting; it has been tried and found difficult, as we are about to find out. Let us be clear: At stake are not our thoughts, clouded or clear; at stake are not even our lives, whatever their sexual preference; at stake is the Gospel, nothing less, the Gospel that alone—so we believe—can clear our thoughts and liberate our lives.

If we now obey the simplest, most fundamental, and difficult injunction of Scripture, we will love one another, gay and straight. If we are of one heart, we can, as the collegium has discovered this past week, be of two minds. But, if we are of one heart, we will also resolve not to retreat either from one another or from the issue, until misinformation has been sorted from fact, superstition and prejudice separated from the truth.

Dear Riversiders, if not us, who? If not now, when? May we anticipate a day, not too distant when others will say, "See how they love one another," and "My Lord, how much they have learned!"

During the talk-back, which will come after the service, you may want to make suggestions as to how best now to proceed. Here I want to say only two things more: The best way to talk of these matters is confessionally, that is, with sentences that begin, "I feel . . ." or "I used to feel, but now . . ." or "When I was small I was taught. . . ." Second, it is important that you know where I stand.

Some years ago Professor James B. Nelson suggested that there are basically four stances a person can take vis-à-vis homosexuality: reject and punish; reject and not punish; accept conditionally; accept unconditionally. After some struggle, because of my understanding of the Gospel and because of the witness to it borne by gay and lesbian friends, whose same-sex relationships were clearly vehicles of God's humanizing intentions, I moved from conditional to unconditional acceptance. I believe that just as the "Negro" problem, as we used to call it, turned out to be a problem of white racism, just as the woman's problem turned out to be a problem of male chauvinism, so the homosexual problem will turn out to be one of homophobia on the part of heterosexuals.

I know that St. Paul called homosexual acts "unnatural," but he was referring to heterosexual people (cf. Rom. 1:26ff. and 1 Cor. 6:9); he also called "unnatural" men wearing their hair long and "shameful" women speaking in church (cf. 1 Cor. 11:14 and 14:34). I know that in certain books of the Old Testament there are laws that forbid homosexual acts, again on the part of heterosexual people. I also know that the Old Testament considers prostitution quite natural and necessary as a safeguard of the virginity of the unmarried and the property rights of husbands (cf. Gen. 38:12–19 and Josh. 2:1–7), an idea as foreign as can be to the minds of contemporary Bible readers. But I read the Bible most, not for its ancient laws, but for its ancient wisdom, not for what is literally true but eternally true. Most of all, I read it because it once told me enough to change the Jesus of history into the Christ of my personal faith. So, the problem, to me, is not how to reconcile homosexuality with scriptural passages that condemn it, but rather how to reconcile the rejection and punishment of homosexuals with the love of Christ. I don't think it can be done.

I do not see how Christians can define and then exclude people on the basis of sexual orientation—not if the law of love is more important than the laws of biology. Not that I myself am free of homophobia; the journey from the head to the heart is the longest in the world. But I am on my way, guided as I see it by the Gospel, prodded and encouraged by gay and lesbian friends.

Believe it or not, all this leads quite directly to mothers and to families that owe them so much. As parents know well, traditional family values are under siege. All around us we see divorce and remarriage, single parents and premarital sex. This instability, without doubt, intensifies homophobia, as do the many gays who demand a kind of carte blanche legitimation of a lifestyle that includes all the dehumanizing effects of promiscuity. But let parents remember that other gays, and especially Christian gays, share their "I've had it" exasperation with that kind of attitude; and let parents resist the seductive temptation to seek sanctuary and a renewed sense of righteousness in the self-deceptions of a frightened "moral majority."

It is hard—how I know—to love our children rightly. I know parents who love their children in a way that cuts their breath and stops their hearts, and others who take their children to their bosom in a passion of love, only in the next moment to push them away, cursing and covering them with blows. I like Margaret Mead's idea of lots of body warmth and consistent discipline. I like the way Fanny Erickson of our own staff here at Riverside talks of the need in this world to nurture children and challenge adults. It is a good family where parents nurture their children and the children challenge their parents.

We see both in the story of Jesus in the Temple. Mary is worried and properly so. She wants to protect Jesus, to smother her boy in love. Yet she allows him to challenge her when he says, "Wist ye not that I must be about my father's business?" Mary doesn't say, "O yeah?" "Mother knows better," or "Hush your mouth," or any of those things. No, we read, "and his mother kept all these things in her heart," a line reminiscent of the one in the Christmas story, "Mary kept all these things, pondering them in her heart." We learn more if we try not to understand too soon.

Let me read you two passages, one about a mother, the other from a mother:

> No one had told her what it would be like, the way she loved her children. What a thing of the body it was, as physically rooted as sexual desire, but without its edge of danger. . . . Once they were in the house, the air became more vivid and more heated: every object in the house grew more alive. How I love you, she always wanted to say, and you can never know it. I would die for you without a thought. You have given to my life its sheerest, its profoundest pleasure. But she could never say that; instead, she would say, "How was school?" "Was lunch all right?" "Did you have your math test?" . . . She loved that, that her children were not tabulae rasae, but had been born themselves. She loved the intransigence of their nature, all that could never be molded and so was free from her. She liked to stand back a little from her children—it was why some people thought her, as a mother, vague. But she respected the fixity of her children's souls, what they were born with, what she had from the first months, seen. . . . (from *Men and Angels*, by Mary Gordon)

And the second one by a mother:

> If the doctor had told me, when Troy was born, that he was a homosexual, that he'd grow up to be one, I could not have loved him any less than I did, nor than I do now, not any less than I love all my other sons. I can't understand any mother that would turn her

back on her children because they are homosexuals. It is hard to stand by them at first and hard not to feel ashamed because at first it is hard for them not to feel ashamed. But that shame is just being afraid of what others feel or think and that's plain silly when it comes down to it. But if you accept them and they accept themselves, then you can really learn the true meaning of love and family. I know. I did.

I get good feelings from both those mothers. I think their families are in good shape. Families are arenas of love and learning, no matter what form the family may take. Families must be places where children are nurtured and parents are challenged. That is something on which all of us can agree. And as we all have mothers, alive or sainted, let us take a silent moment to thank them for our very existence, and for so much more.

One closing thought. I said that today was the 113th annual celebration of Mother's Day. More accurately, in 1872, Julia Ward Howe, author of "The Battle Hymn of the Republic," founded the Women's Peace Association, the parental precursor of Mother's Day, as a protest against the institution of war, specifically the American Civil War and the Franco-Prussian War, which, between them, took two-thirds of a million lives. Let that remembrance be ours as we struggle to end our warfare here in this church. Most of all, let us remember him of whom Howe wrote:

> In the beauty of the lilies Christ was born across the sea
> With a glory in his bosom that transfigures you and me
> As he died to make (us) holy, let us die to make (all) free
> Our God is marching on.

The Flame of Creativity vs. The Fires of Sin

MAY 26, 1985
Readings: Genesis 11:1–9; Acts 2:1–21

You have often heard me say that a lot of people have only enough religion to make themselves miserable. All they recall from the Bible are the great "Thou shalt not's." In their minds, religion is what you don't do. It is important, especially today, to remember that the Christian faith seeks as much to fan the flame of creativity as it does to quench the fires of sin.

Today is the day of the fiery Pentecost, which celebrates the flame of creativity, symbolized by what the book of Acts described as "tongues as of fire distributed and resting on each" of the disciples, on those about to become Christians, about to be infused with the light and power of the Holy Spirit (Acts 2:3).

The flame of creativity versus the fires of sin: That is the way St. Peter portrayed the choice. "Save yourselves from this crooked generation" (in case you thought ours was the only one), he cried out to his hearers. "Repent and be baptized, every one of you, in the name of Jesus Christ" (2:40, 38).

Almost two thousand years later, T. S. Eliot pictures the choice posed by Pentecost in much the same way:

> The dove descending breaks the air
> With flame of incandescent terror,
> Of which the tongues declare
> The one discharge from sin and error.
> The only hope, or else despair
>   Lies in the choice of pyre or pyre—
>   To be redeemed from fire by fire.
>
> . . . .
>
> We only live, only suspire
> Consumed by either fire or fire.
> *Four Quartets*, "Little Gidding," Part IV

Fire or fire: The fires of sin or the flame of creativity. Let's say a word about the first, for sin was certainly a subject that came up repeatedly during the talk-back after the service two weeks ago. Then I suggested, and today wish to spell out, that sin need not be viewed morosely and negatively, but rather realistically and even positively, this in at least two ways:

In the first place, sin affirms meaning. If nothing counts against you, nothing counts, period. All of us fear all sorts of things in life—its end, for example, the fact that "like as the waves make towards the pebbled shore, so do our minutes hasten to their end" (Shakespeare, *Sonnet 60*).

We also fear fate—where will it strike next, upsetting once again our cherished notions of order and fairness? Likewise we are afraid of guilt and of the possibility of final condemnation. But most of all, perhaps, we fear a world devoid of meaning.

Tomorrow and tomorrow and tomorrow
Creeps in this petty pace from day to day
To the last syllable of recorded time.
And all our yesterdays have lighted fools
The way to dusty death. Out, out brief candle.
Life's but a walking shadow, a poor player
That struts and frets his hour upon the stage,
And then is heard no more. It is a tale
Told by an idiot, full of sound and fury,
Signifying nothing.

Shakespeare, *Macbeth*

Sin, in contrast, signifies something. It is the reverse side of the coin of meaning. When we defy the purpose of life we are reminded that life has one, which is "*lieben und arbeiten*" (to love and to work). Freud was absolutely right—but he forgot to add "*Ad majoram gloriam Dei*" (to the greater glory of God). To live means to live and to work to the greater glory of God.

When Jesus said, "Neither do I condemn thee, go and sin no more" (John 8:11), he was saying to the woman that loyalties, including marital, are for real, that in fact, it is our obligations, rather than our freedom, that give our lives their meaning. Had Jesus said, "Neither do I condemn thee, go and sin some more," it would not have been sin, it would not have been anything, and that is the point—no sin, no nothing. If nothing counts against you, nothing counts. Sin, positively viewed, realistically accepted, reaffirms meaning.

Now, a word about "original sin," or better termed, "constitutional" sin—the sin that inheres in every one of us. That too can be viewed positively, for surely it is of no small comfort to learn that in the sullied stream of human life, it is not innocence but holiness that is our only option.

Sin is absolutely inevitable. Why? Because at the very heart of life lies a quandary: Sin is basically self-centeredness, but the same self-centeredness that is a sin is also a necessity. Say the Buddhists, "With the ceasing of craving, grasping ceases; with the ceasing of grasping, existence ceases." If the two children who were baptized this morning were not self-centered they would not survive. But once "grown up," they will have to realize that self-centeredness is an intellectual error because no one of us, in truth, is at the center of the universe. Self-centeredness is also a moral error because no one of us has the right to act as if he or she, or his or her nation, were at the center of the universe. But if we cannot assert too much for ourselves, we also cannot renounce ourselves. We have, in effect, to sail between Scylla and Charybdis, between the suicide of self-assertion and the euthanasia of self-renunciation. The channel is too narrow, none of us can make it. We remain self-centered in plenty and in want, in joy and in sorrow, for "the egotism of those who suffer is probably even more all-embracing than the self-regard of those who are happy" (Eugenia Ginzburg).

So, St. Paul was right, "All have sinned and fallen short." But now comes the real sin! Instead of realistically accepting our original sin as a fact of life, instead of allowing it to point us toward the beauty of forgiveness, the true meaning of life which is to be God-centered rather than self-centered, we continue to try to make it on our own. Instead of "taking to the Lord in prayer" all our fears about death and fate and guilt and meaninglessness, we try vainly, stupidly, to secure ourselves against our own insecurities.

Take, for example, those descendants of Noah, down in the Tigris-Euphrates valley. Did they really think that by dint of furious activity they could build a from-here-to-eternity edifice, defying gravity, chance, human error, human sinfulness, even God herself—and finally secure for themselves a sunny and safe perch on top of their world? Apparently they did, and if so, they proved no crazier than we. For don't we also seek to arrest the course of history, to build from-here-to-eternity edifices, be they of brick or of ideas or of conquest, like the Roman or British empires or the Third Reich, which Hitler boasted "will last a thousand years"?

Ambition is a good servant but a bad master. It invites destruction, its own included, as the Third Reich and the Tower of Babel prove. For God is not mocked. Whenever we say, "Come let us build ourselves a city and a tower with its top in the heavens, *and make a name for ourselves,*" just as surely as this spring has been gorgeous, the enterprise will end in confusion and a scattering of the people. Activity rooted in pride can only divide, never unify, for pride is not accidentally but essentially competitive. You would think, realizing all this, that we would douse with water these fires of sin, or at least walk away from them. Ah, but they warm our hearts—especially pride, the most heartwarming of sins!

Let's turn now to the fire of creativity, which we celebrate on this day of Pentecost. Do not ask exactly what happened on that day, fifty days after passover, seven weeks after the day of Resurrection, for no one knows for sure. Once again, as is so often the case in the Bible, it is the invisible event that counts. For sure, we know only that the disciples heretofore waiting and watching for God began to be moved and used by God. As the book of Acts shows us, after Pentecost, they became ten times the people they were during Jesus' life on earth. And because of the demonstrated power of the Holy Spirit moving through Peter and the other disciples—witness three thousand converted in one day—Pentecost is widely regarded as the birthday of the church.

Contrast those two stories, that of the disciples at Pentecost with the tower builders at Babel. Instead of trying to storm the ramparts of heaven, the disciples allowed heaven to take them by storm. Their zeal was no less than that of the tower builders, only their creativity stemmed not from ambition based on insecurity but from gratitude for forgiveness and the love of God in whom they now lived and moved and had their being.

Shortly after Pentecost, the converted St. Paul was to become as zealous as ever was Saul, only now he was to insist, "not I, but Christ who dwells within me." William Blake is reported to have murmured, centuries later, as he backed away from a just-completed and awesome painting, "Not I, not I." (How much easier it is to enjoy your successes when you don't have to take credit for them!)

Someone—Norman Brown, perhaps?—said, "Truth is error burnt up." Certainly the cleansing fire of Pentecost leaves our make-believe world in ashes, overturns our beloved self-protecting lies, and pulls the rug from under ambition's tower of blocks. But most of all, the Holy Spirit is experienced as love, a love outpassing human telling, a love more heartwarming by far than the fires of sin. It represents in the words of a nineteenth-century theologian, "the expulsive power of a new affection" (Horace Bushnell). And because the Holy Spirit is love, it does not divide as does pride; it unifies.

Friends, the deepest human need in each of us is to be in relationship both with God and with each other. And Jesus is our model. He excluded no one, not the poor, not the rich, not the many groups of social outcasts of his time. Therefore, we in our time must be no less inclusive.

I pray that the Holy Spirit may visit our church and every church this Pentecostal Sunday. May we speak in many tongues the one message of Christ's love for all humanity. May the cruelty and greed we see around us find no place among us. And when, in the world, we side, as side we must, with the oppressed against the oppressor, may we do so with the clear understanding that if, by God's grace, the Holy Spirit is alive in us, it needs only liberation in those we oppose.

Babel or Pentecost. The fires of sin or the flame of creativity. There is hardly a choice any more in such a world that the ethics of perfection are fast becoming the ethics of survival. We have to be merciful when we live at each other's mercy. We have to be meek or there will be no earth to inherit. So it is truer than ever this Pentecost:

The only hope, or else despair
    Lies in the choice of pyre or pyre—
    Consumed by either fire or fire.

Dearly beloved in the Lord, have a heartwarming, fiery day!

The Pharisee and the Publican

JUNE 2, 1985
Reading: Luke 18:9–14

L ast Sunday those of you on hand will recall that it was fire against fire. We pitted the fires of sin against the flame of creativity. It was the builders of the tower of Babel versus the disciples at Pentecost; storming the ramparts of heaven or allowing heaven to take you by storm. In a similar vein today let us contrast the prayer of the Pharisee—"Lord, I thank thee that I am not as other people are"—with that of the Publican who said: "God, have mercy on me, a sinner."

Every circus in the world has to have two kinds of performers, because without the one you have too much of the other. There are of course what you might call the virtuosi—the high-wire artists, the gravity-defying acrobats who catapult and somersault themselves off the ground to the top of a human pyramid; there are the heroic lion and tiger tamers, and bareback riders astride magnificent galloping steeds.

And there are the clowns. They are not center stage. They come between the acts. They fumble and fall. "Clowns don't have it together. They do not succeed in what they try. They are awkward, they are off balance but they are on our side. Of the virtuosi we say, 'How can they do it?' Of the clowns we say 'They're like us.' With a tear and a smile we are reminded that we share the same human weaknesses" (Henri Nouwen).

I think there is something of the virtuoso and something of the clown in each of us. In certain areas of life we succeed in what we try, in others we fumble, we fall, we don't have it together. It's fine to be a virtuoso. For that you need a healthy self-confidence, a realistic sense of self-worth. In Jesus' parable, the Pharisee is, you might say, a virtuoso in virtue. He's no lion tamer, he's an appetite tamer. He fasts not once a year, but twice a week. He also tithes beyond any demands of the law, which is more than can be said for a few members of Riverside—well, I don't want to get into that!

But it's hard to picture this Pharisee clowning. It's hard to picture him smiling or weeping; he's probably too tight-lipped for either. And while he's virtuous, we have to ask how religious is he. True he goes into the Temple, but maybe he goes into the Temple the way so many good Christians go into church—to make their last stand against God (not to allow heaven to take them by storm). I suggest that, because, while the Pharisee prays, he seems to be praising not God but his own virtue, worshipping not the Lord, but himself worshipping. I think this Pharisee sees God as some kind of corporation in which he has earned sufficient stock to warrant the expectation that any day now he will be asked to join the board of directors.

"God, I thank thee that I am not as other people are." That's not healthy self-confidence, a realistic sense of self-worth; that's overweening pride, arrogance, what Martin Buber calls "affirmation independent of all findings." We see this pharisaical spirit on a national level—"God, we thank thee that our nation is not as other nations are: atheist, communist, imperialistic, understanding only force." We Americans are prone to judge other nations by their actions and our own by our ideals.

But let us stay on the personal level and see the crux of what Jesus is saying. You remember Jesus spoke the parable to "some who trusted in themselves that they were righteous and despised others." Can you be righteous and not despise others? I think it is fair to say that if you acknowledge in yourself the virtuoso but not the clown, if you see in yourself virtue only, no sin, if you deny your own inadequacies, then you will project them on to others. As I said last week, pride is not accidentally but essentially competitive. Notice only the Pharisee compares himself to others. The Publican doesn't compare himself to anyone. And notice this: it is in the very act of praying, the most religious thing anyone of us can do, that the Pharisee sins by breaking the God-given unity in which we all share. I say "God-given," for according to the faith we are together before we come together. According to the faith there is unity prior to unifying action. According to the faith, community is not made by us but given by God. So it is the sin of the Pharisee, and of the Pharisee in each of us, that we seek to put asunder what God has joined together. I mean not only races and nations, rich and poor, members of all religions and both sexes; I mean also gay and straight. We all have much to learn in this area of life, and have therefore to live with one another in the tension of having and not having the truth. But I ask you once again to consider: can we call "sin" feelings that are as unchangeable a part of a person as the color of that person's skin? Can we call "sinful" relations that manifestly reflect the mutual concern and love to which God beckons all humanity?

Here is the kind of prayer that I want to pray today:

> God, I thank thee that I *am* as other people are, that in me dwells both the virtuoso and the clown, for without the one there would be too much of the other. I thank thee that in me dwells both the Pharisee and the Publican, virtue and the knowledge of sin, that I may know thee who both bruises my ego and mends my heart. God, be merciful to me a sinner, that I may show like mercy to others who share my same weaknesses. Yes, dear God, bless me with guilt, grant me the strength to tolerate the pain of self-reproach, that I may be free from pretense and pride, "affirmation independent of all findings."

Dearly beloved, what the world always needs and what Riverside Church needs today is not more blood on the floor, but the saving blood of our Lord on the Communion table. We need to remember what St. Paul never forgot: "God was in Christ reconciling the world unto himself" (2 Cor. 5:19). Christ our Passover is sacrificed for us; therefore let us keep the feast. As the psalmist said, "O taste and see that the Lord is good. Blessed is the one who trusts in God" (34:8).

No Vengeance

JULY 7, 1985
Readings: Hosea 2:18–20; Luke 9:46–56

Occasionally, when I get down on myself, exasperated by the church (any deacon will tell you that "budget process" is an oxymoron around here), or even angry at ol' Deus Absconditus, I think that Riverside Church is a beehive without honey. But I have only to calm down, or better yet go away, and I quickly realize how, indeed, we are in the words of the hymn, "with milk and honey blest." In short, it is great to be back.

At 12:45, in the Assembly Hall, I'll have a few things to say about the possibilities of peace amid the shifting sands of the Middle East. Now I want to reflect on the hostages, safely home, thank God, all but the seven still alive and the one, alas, dead.

As in 1979, so again last month, the taking of American hostages quickly seized the minds and hearts of all Americans.* But in 1979, we blew it, we learned little. Our suffering led to self-righteous postures, not to increased sensitivity. I want us to do better this time, both for our spiritual health and for the sake of the world, for like it or not—and most of the time I don't—"The United States," as a Palestinian put it to me a couple of weeks ago, "is not somewhere, it's everywhere."

It was absolutely right of President Reagan to say to the 39 liberated men and women, and through them to us: "Kidnapping is a crime, murder is a crime, and holding people prisoner is a crime." We all join him in grieving the brutal death of 23-year-old Robbie Stethem, and in deploring the continued incarceration of seven other Americans.

My concern is that our outrage and sorrow *widen* our hearts, deepen our understanding of ourselves and of the people in the Middle East. The dead body of young Robbie Stethem must remind us that also prostrate and bleeding lies an entire nation. Today, almost every inch of Lebanese soil is soaked with the tears and blood of people altogether as innocent as was Robbie Stethem.

Christians in particular must feel and bewail the suffering that even strange and hostile people have to endure. And God forbid that we should ever forget that kidnapping is kidnapping, whether it be Americans in Lebanon or Shiites held in Israel in violation of the Geneva Convention; forget that terrorism is terrorism, whether it be bludgeoning Americans on an airstrip in Beirut, or mining the waters of Managua.

I liked the way the president called Robbie Stethem "a son of America"; every nation is a macroscopic family. But Robbie isn't our only son. The homeless and hungry, the hard-pressed elderly, today's victims of our ever-growing structural unemployment, the 22 percent of American children now living below the federally established poverty line—they too are not to be forgotten sons and daughters of America.

---

*On June 14, 1985, TWA Flight 847 was hijacked while flying from Athens to Rome by Organization for the Oppressed of the Earth; the hijackers killed a US Navy diver, Robert Stethem. The last hostages were released on June 30.

Not only should we rejoice at their safe return, we should also celebrate the restraint that freed the hostages in Lebanon as it finally did the 52 held in Iran. Force is not always wrong. But what is wrong—always wrong—is the desire to use it. This is what I fear today—our desire to show a little muscle, to get even, to get revenge, to strike back. But, "'Vengeance is mine, I will repay,' says the Lord."When the fabric of civilization is coming apart not only in Lebanon (Abba Eban speaks of the possible "lebanonization" of Israel) and when dangers of the greatest magnitude are bearing down on the whole green earth, we must pray God to eradicate from our hearts this desire to use force. Of course we want justice; foul play was done. But justice doesn't come by the sword alone. In fact, history shows that the sword has delayed and perverted far more than it has fulfilled the demands of justice. The sword of justice often is but a symbol of the age-old temptation to use wrong means to attain right ends.

In the Bible, and especially in the Old Testament, we hear lots of horses neighing, shields clashing and trumpets blaring. But even in the Old Testament the central imperative is clear—to nourish the life God brings into being. Listen to the prayer of Hannah, mother of Samuel: "The bows of the mighty are broken and they that stumbled are girded with strength. God will keep the feet of his holy ones, but the wicked shall be put to silence in darkness, for not by strength shall man prevail" (1 Sam. 2:4, 9).

Consider the condemnation of violence in the story of Cain and Abel, and how God thought it punishment enough to leave the murderer, Cain, at the Bar of history. (Oh, how I wish the Israelis, having once again put before the world the whole horrible story of the death of six million people in concentration camps, could then have turned to Eichman and said "Okay, that's it, you can go.") Consider Abraham's intercession on behalf of the doomed Sodomites. Contrast Isaac, the man of peace, with Ishmael whose hand is raised against all around him. Remember the inefficacy of the contemplated violence by the brothers against Joseph and their final reconciliation.

David, Israel's greatest warrior, was also its sweetest singer, who in his songs never boasted of his prowess, but only of God, his rock and strength:

> "For I trust not in my bow
> Neither can my sword save me."
>
> Ps. 44:6

The prophets hated the love of force. We've already heard from Jeremiah—"Let not the mighty man glory in his might" (9:23); and from Hosea—" 'And I will break the bow and sword and the battle out of the earth' says the Lord." Hear now from Isaiah, not only a prophet, but a counselor to kings: "Woe to them that go down to Egypt for help, and rely on horses, and trust in chariots, because they are many, and in horsemen, because they are exceedingly mighty; but they look not unto the Holy One of Israel, neither see the Lord." And finally hear these words of Zechariah, words faithful Jews always read at Chanukah, the festival that celebrates the military victory by the Hasmoneans over the Seleucid Greeks: "Not by might, not by power, but by my spirit, says the Lord of hosts" (4:6).

The Old Testament message is clear: immeasurable is the merit of those who preserve God's handiwork, incalculable the retribution against those who destroy it. In the Gospel lesson were two stories on the duty of tolerance—tolerance based not on indifference but on conviction. According to Jesus, we are tolerant not because we couldn't care less, but because we couldn't care more—for one another. According to Jesus, we destroy our enemies when we make them our friends.

Surely, the message to the United States today is: "Do not be overcome by evil, but overcome evil with good." It is not us against them, but them and us together against all that is tearing Lebanon and the Middle East apart. If we retaliate, neither we nor the Shiites will win. Only hatred will win, and keep on winning.

It is the duty of the religious community to see that force lose its suggestive power. The desire for its use, be it in the Middle East, Central America—wherever—must go, driven out by a desire for peace, a desire above all other national desires.

We destroy enemies when we make them our friends. And we do this when we extend our sense of kinship beyond the limits of the macroscopic family that is our nation, when we see the whole world under God as home.

Let me end with a homely illustration: All of you, I imagine, remember Pelé, the greatest soccer player of the century. Pelé was the superstar of the Brazilian Santos, who in his last years came to play for the New York Cosmos. The last match of his career was between his new team and his team of many years. For the first half, Pelé played his heart out for the Cosmos, then he went over to the Santos and played just as hard for them. There was no "versus" in his mind, no home team against the visitors, for both were home teams for him.

Thirsting for Righteousness

JULY 14, 1985
Reading: Matthew 5:1–12

The Sermon on the Mount has been accorded all manner of laudatory titles—"The Magna Carta of the Kingdom,""The Ordination Address to the Twelve,""Message From the Messiah," all names to indicate that these 107 verses in Matthew constitute the very essence of Christ's teaching. The most famous verses are chapter 6, verses 9–13, The Lord's Prayer. After that, I guess, would come the first verses of chapter 5, the so-called Beatitudes. And of the Beatitudes the most powerful, certainly in imagery, is the 4th: "Blessed are they who hunger and thirst after righteousness for they shall be filled."

As righteousness is a heavy word, let's deal with it first. Probably all of you will remember that in the parable of the Prodigal Son (which is really the story of the Prodigal Father), after the father embraced the wayward lad, he immediately ordered, "Bring a ring to put on his hand, put a robe on him and kill the fatted calf." There is practical love, the kind of love embodied in Christ, the love that goes right to work and asks questions afterward. Righteousness is not a straitjacket we put on, it's one we take off. Righteousness is something we expose rather than impose. It is not a characteristic of the acid reformer, nor is it the icy faultlessness of the prim and proper. (Give me faulty warmheartedness any day!) Righteousness is exposition, the revealing of God's heart and the revealing of our own vulnerable response. Like Christ who wept over Jerusalem, we too can no longer bear to see what human beings do to one another and thereby to God. So this Beatitude could read: "How blessed are they who long with their hearts for right to prevail."

Only "long" is too tame. I mentioned the power of the imagery; it's primitive. Few of us have ever been in a situation where our bodies so craved food that only the strongest mind could think of anything else. But in Jesus' day, day laborers—and a lot of his listeners were just that—day laborers lived never far from the border separating hunger from actual starvation. So they knew what it meant to hunger. And you had only to look around at the Palestinian landscape to begin to get thirsty. Probably all Jesus' listeners had, at one time or another, been caught in a sandstorm where all you could do was bury your head in your burnoose, turn your back to the wind and wait it out, while the swirling sand so filled your nose and throat that you thought you were going to suffocate. Those people knew what it meant to have a throat parched with an imperious thirst. So the Beatitude came through to them with a force we're not likely to get. Let's say it went like this: "Blessed are those who long for right to prevail as a starving man craves food, and a man dying of thirst water."

We've said enough for two things to be clear. If only a few of us cared that much for goodness, we could save this world hell-bent for self-destruction. We might even right some of its ancient wrongs. But the second thing, equally clear, is that such fervor displayed on behalf of righteousness would be widely viewed as an activity about as deviant as foot fetishism. Our generation has so organized apathy, has developed so mechanistic a view of such things as the arms race and the economy, that ancient sun-worshippers and African animists would have regarded us as strangely fatalistic.

I worry about a lot of things these days. I worry about the vengeful "who can we stick it to next?" mood that seems to dominate the congress and the country; it certainly doesn't help stem the pitiless onslaught of open violence in the world. I worry also about fundamentalism, be it Christian, Jewish, or Muslim; intolerance is never the answer, as history has revealed—how many times? But I spend a lot of time worrying also about what Robert Louis Stevenson called "the malady of not wanting." It's sick to hunger and thirst for nothing more than food and drink, cars and condominiums. It is sick to pretend that God has not seen to it that goodness be an "implacable hunter" always on our heels. It's sick to deny that even the worst among us is "condemned to some kind of nobility." It is the malady of not wanting that makes so many of us so pallid and sickly.

Last Sunday afternoon I flew to Bangor, Maine, to take part in a march and to speak at a rally commemorating the death, a year ago, of Charlie Howard. He was the gay man thrown off the bridge in the middle of the night by three teenagers. They threw him into a deep canal, both sides of which were sheer concrete walls. There was no way to escape, especially as his last words, shrieked into the night were, "No, no, I can't swim." Like Robbie Stethem, the lad brutally murdered on the airstrip in Beirut, Charlie Howard was a victim of terrorism. Like Robbie Stethem he was also twenty-three years old; and the words President Reagan used to describe Robbie also described Charlie: he too was "a son of America."

As the two hundred or so people—mostly Gay and Lesbian—dropped their flowers from the bridge into the slow moving waters below, some cars, moving barely faster started to pass by behind. And then the shouts began, "Anybody want a lift?" "Heave-ho," "another homo over the bridge." That wasn't really surprising. It's not that Bangor is a lumber town with a lot of redneck types. No, Bangor is part of Maine, which is one beautiful state which just happens to have some very special prejudices which it shares with forty-nine other states. The only state in the Union that has civil rights legislation protecting Gays and Lesbians is Wisconsin.

What was sick was the absence of the straight community. Where were the ministers of the standard-brand Protestant denominations, the Catholic priests? Where were the representatives of the respectable business community, the intellectual community? Where were the editors of the *Bangor Times*? To take part, you didn't have to think homosexuality was right, only that murder was wrong. But precious few showed up and probably for the same reason that Abraham and God couldn't find ten righteous people in Sodom: fear that the majority would view their righteousness as deviant activity.

Dearly beloved, what has happened to the spiritual health of this nation when common integrity is made to look like courage? Where is freedom of speech when silence prevails, imposed by fear? What good is freedom of choice when you've lost your capacity to choose, and follow instead the path of least resistance?

Norman Thomas, that perennial Socialist Party candidate for the presidency, once told a large audience, "If you people insist on behaving like sheep, don't blame your leaders for treating you like mutton."

The only salvation for humanity, as this Beatitude points out, lies in our concerning ourselves with everything, everywhere. Father Zosima in *The Brothers Karamazov* says, "All are responsible for all." That doesn't mean that all of us are guilty, but that all of us are responsible.

A new member of Riverside Church wrote me last week: "What a great world Riverside is helping to make. A world where everyone belongs. A world where everyone bends and cups his hands to give the soul next to him a boost toward heaven. I look forward to being a member of Riverside Church."

It's a beautiful image. Were it true of all the members of Riverside Church, we single-handedly could save New York—or at least the Upper West Side and parts of New Jersey and Westchester. But, alas, too many Christians, even in Riverside Church, think they can be holy people without being moral people. But listen again to the Beatitude: It does not say "blessed are they who hunger and thirst for God," but simply "hunger and thirst for right to prevail"—another reminder that God's people dwell outside as well as inside God's churches.

The fourth Beatitude is not only demanding but hopeful, because it implies that the true wonder of human beings is not that we are sinners, but that even in our sin, we are haunted by goodness. Even in the mud we can't forget the stars. King David, some of you remember, wanted to build a temple, but because of his sin, his ambition was denied him. But God said to him, "You did well that it was in your heart" (1 Kings 8:18).

"Blessed are they that hunger and thirst after righteousness, for they shall be filled." Actually, the Greek word is rather pastoral, used for the feeding of sheep as they move from one bit of lush grass to another. It suggests a kind of lasting satisfaction, a lot of nosh, rather than a weight watcher's diet. Or look at it this way: is there anything quite like that sense of undeserved integrity that comes with being in the right fight? Don't they look wonderfully fulfilled—those people in whom we clearly see truth alive?

I love the hymn we just sang, "Send Down Thy Truth, O Lord." In his 1970 Nobel Prize lecture, which he wrote but never delivered, Solzhenitsyn wrote of the close kinship that exists between violence and lies: "Violence has nothing with which to cover itself except the lie, and the lie has nothing to stand on but violence." Solzhenitsyn went on to point out that in this violent world you and I are always being asked to take the "oath of the lie," as he puts it, to participate in the lie. "And," says Solzhenitsyn, "simple is the act of an ordinary courageous human being of not participating in the lie, not supporting false actions. So be it that this takes place in the world, even reigns in the world—but never with my complicity."

That's something all of us can do as a start. To fulfill this Beatitude, we can battle the lies. We can refuse to take the oath of the lies that so many powers want us to do. We can remember the Russian proverb: One word of truth outweighs the whole world. Last month, when a group of us were in Tel Aviv interviewing the mayor, he said, "Israel is a peaceful nation. All we want is a piece of Syria, a piece of Jordan and a piece of Egypt!" There's one way to destroy the lie that stands between Israel and peace. Couldn't we Americans not participate in a similar lie by remembering that we sell twice as many arms to more countries than any other country in the world? And blessed are those Americans who refuse to say, "The economy prospers" when 15 million are lastingly unemployed, when one out of three Americans is functionally illiterate, and when 22 percent of our beloved children live below the federally established poverty line.

The world is too violent and deceptive, and life too short and dull not to do God's will with all our heart, mind, and strength. So let me suggest that each day this week we ponder and be moved anew by the power of the fourth Beatitude: Blessed are they who want right to prevail as a starving man craves food and one dying of thirst water, for they shall be filled.

On Suffering Persecution

JULY 21, 1985

L ast Sunday I suggested that of all the Beatitudes, the most powerful one, certainly in terms of imagery, was the fourth: "Blessed are those who hunger and thirst after righteousness" or, as the New English Bible says, "How blest are those who hunger and thirst to see right prevail." That beatitude has a companion, the last beatitude, "How blest are those who have suffered persecution for the cause of right; the kingdom of Heaven is theirs." Then Jesus goes on addressing directly each of his hearers there on the side of the mountain: "How blest you are, when you suffer insults and persecution and every kind of calumny for my sake." Then this astounding imperative: "Accept it with gladness and exultation"—not, mind you, with stoicism, not with courage, but "with gladness and exultation"—"for you have a rich reward in heaven; in the same way they persecuted the prophets before you."

I suppose the first thing we ought to say is that opposition alone is no sign that you are right. There are a lot of dedicated screwballs in the world. And the number who occupy pews and pulpits must tax the patience of even our long-suffering and merciful God. Some are downright wicked. As the French philosopher Pascal observed, "Human beings never do evil so cheerfully as when they do it from religious conviction."

Moreover, it's fine to want to see right prevail. But who's to say what's right? The physicist Werner Heisenberg asked, "What's the opposite of a profound truth?" and answered, "Another profound truth." One thing I have learned about solutions is that they cause problems. Therefore Christians should not only answer questions but also question answers; all the answers, for instance, of all the "isms"—capitalism, communism, nationalism, socialism, and let's throw in "scientism," because when all the scientific answers are in, the most important questions of life have not been touched. It is wrong to seek safety in some preordained social order, especially when we are supposed to be surrendering ourselves to the anarchic splendor of the Holy Spirit. So, as Cromwell enjoined, "Remember, by the bowels of Christ, you may be wrong."

But the Beatitude is after something else: if you are a loyal keeper of the flame, if, as a follower of Jesus, you try to live in one world, belong to a second world, and be faithful to both; if you "wake up in the morning with your mind stayed on Jesus," you're in for trouble. It is clear that Jesus came not "to make life easy—but to make us great." He became like us that we might become like him. And if Christ was persecuted for being Christ, why should not Christians expect to be persecuted for being Christians?

The early Christians certainly were persecuted. We heard the story of Stephen, the first martyr, who under a rain of stones fell on his knees and cried aloud, "'Lord, hold not this sin against them' and with that he died" (Acts 7:60). The whole world knows of the Christians who were flung to the lions. But those were kindly deaths. "Nero wrapped Christians in pitch and set them alight, and used them as living torches to light his gardens. He sewed them in the skins of wild animals and set his hunting dogs upon them to tear them to death. Early Christians were tortured on the rack—their hands and feet were burned while cold water was poured upon them to lengthen the agony. These things are not pleasant to think about, but these are things people had to be prepared for" (William Barclay).

And why the persecution? Because a Christian stone mason would have no part in building a temple to a heathen God; a Christian tailor would not sew the robes for heathen priests. That's something to think about in a city where a stone mason, carpenter, contractor or an architect would hardly think twice about taking part in the building of a super-luxury condominium high-rise, with a tax abatement to boot, to the glory of mammon, the heathen God of greed. Think again of Stephen, who died with love on his lips; how wonderfully he compares with the preachers in our day who are out to stir up intolerance, which is so emotionally satisfying and so spiritually devastating. These preachers, of course, are never persecuted. You don't get persecuted for giving people what they want. You get persecuted for giving them what they need and do not want.

The great ground of persecution, however, was political. As empires go, the Roman Empire wasn't really all that bad. It cleared the roads of brigands, the seas of pirates, and many a tin-hat provincial dictator was banished by impartial Roman justice. But it was hard to hold all those diverse folks together, and to avoid the corruption of power. So while the Emperor Claudius was dead set against divine honors being paid any human being, his successors, supported by some portly Roman senators, came to view emperor worship as the one thing that could unify so vast an empire. At first voluntary, the worship of the emperor became mandatory. Once a year a person had to go to the altar, burn a pinch of incense and say, "Caesar is Lord." This, many Christians refused to do. So they died by the thousands; their only crime being Christ.

Then, gradually, the Church moved from the periphery of society to the center. Centuries after those first Christian stone masons were persecuted, it was the Church that was building temples. It was the Pope, not Caesar, who was deciding whether someone was damned or saved, and cardinals like Richelieu and Wolsey not only crowned kings, they made them. In other words, the Church was at the center of power, an institution to which attention had to be paid.

That's no longer the case. In Europe, it seems, the average citizen goes to church three times in his life: to be baptized, to be married, and to be buried, which means that two out of three times he has to be carried in!

In parts of the world—I think of South Africa, I think of Central and Latin America—heroic Christians are maligned by malicious-minded people. But more frequently, people take little notice of us. And it's not only because we Christians are powerless. It's because we signify so little. For people outside the Church, it's hard to come to grips with us to see what we're all about, and then to give us hell if they're of a mind to do so. The early Christians gave distinctiveness and clarity to the Gospel. We modern Christians have the miraculous ability of turning wine into water.

I don't mind Christians slipping into the minority position. The majority position is really anomalous. Moral majority is a contradiction in terms. In the Bible, majorities generally stone the prophets. A prophetic minority always has more to say to a nation than a moral majority, a "silent" majority, or any kind of majority. Democracy is not based on the proven goodness of majorities but on the proven evil of dictators. But the minority *has to be prophetic*. It has to stand for something, or it will fall for anything. And who will dispute the fact that the landscape in this nation is strewn with Christians in the prone position? "How blest are those who have suffered persecution for the cause of right." Christians are expected to speak up clearly and to pay up personally. We are expected not only to answer questions, but, as I suggested earlier, we're expected to question answers. When we are told, "The economy is recovering," we must ask, "For whom?" Profits may be rising, but losses are also on the rise for the hard-pressed elderly, the diseased, the disadvantaged. We are told that force is the answer to the Soviet threat in Central America. When I was in Central America the week after Easter, I asked a fellow minister, a rural Salvadoran, what he wanted me to tell my people upon my return. He said, "You can tell them that this conflict has nothing to do with East and West, it's between misery and opulence and misery is losing out everyday." "And," he added, tears welling in his eyes, "you can tell them that your American-supplied Air Force has now replaced the death squads as the chief agent of civilian destruction."

Does silence aid our Baptist brother? Should we not minimally be sure that our fellow Americans know what we are doing; know that we are putting a million dollars a day into El Salvador—one hundred thousand dollars per guerrilla a year—while almost a quarter of our children are malnourished, mal-housed, mal-educated—mal about everything! Should we be silent when through tough talk delivered in speeches around the country or through a much publicized letter delivered in Managua last Thursday, the Administration is seeking to soften American opposition to airstrikes against Nicaragua, as if the Contras didn't represent unfocused violence enough?

Shakespeare wrote of mercy:

> Tis mightiest in the mightiest: it becomes
> The throned monarch better than his crown.

Shakespeare recognized that appeals to angered prejudices are the stock-in-trade of monarchs, presidents, political leaders of every kind while the plea for understanding and restraint is often a lonely voice. But that voice is ours to raise whenever others are eagerly creating the mayhem of self-perpetuating violence.

"How blessed are those who have suffered persecution for the cause of right; the kingdom of heaven is theirs." There has to be some reward else life is robbed of meaning. But the reward of the kingdom is here, the reward of the kingdom is now, even in the midst of persecution. A hundred years after Stephen, history records another martyr, Polycarp, the aged bishop of Smyrna. When he was dragged to the tribunal for refusing to put his pinch of incense on the altar and say, "Caesar is Lord" (and you can imagine how many people said, "Come on, Polycarp, it doesn't mean anything anyhow"), Polycarp said, "Eighty and six years have I served Christ and he has done me no wrong. How can I blaspheme my King who saved me?" And when they strapped him to the stake, he prayed: "Oh Lord God Almighty, the father of thy well-beloved and ever blessed son by whom we have received knowledge of thee—I thank thee that thou hast graciously thought me worthy of this day and hour."

Stephen, Polycarp, the prophets before them—Elijah, Amos, Jeremiah, Isaiah—and the prophets after them—"our fathers chained in prison dark" they knew that something worth living for was also worth dying for. The enemy is not pain, nor even death. The worst foe of each of us is a life devoid of meaning.

But can we really accept suffering "with gladness and exultation"? Isn't that just a little much? Not if we wake up in the morning with minds "stayed on Jesus." For Jesus can make a way out of no way. Consider the joy in Black religious music shaped in the very crucible of slavery. Snatched from their homeland, raped of their culture and language, Blacks held tight the music of their souls. They who came to trust the Lord who looks beyond our faults and sees our need, they never forgot the cloud and fire and they never stopped singing the Lord's song in a strange land.

The song we all know, "We Shall Overcome," is based on an old prayer meeting hymn of C. A. Tindley:

> The world is one great battlefield
> With forces all arrayed,
> With the Lord, a sword of mine,
> I'll overcome someday.

> Refrain: I'll overcome, I'll overcome
>   I'll overcome someday
>   If in my heart I do not yield
>   I'll overcome someday.

Listen again: "How blessed are those who have suffered persecution for the cause of right; the kingdom of heaven is theirs. How blessed you are when you suffer insults and persecution and every kind of calumny for my sake. Accept it with gladness and exultation, for you have a rich reward in heaven; in the same way they persecuted the prophets before you."

Salt of the Earth

JULY 28, 1985
Reading: Matthew 5:13–16

Imagine Jesus calling his hearers on the Mount, and us, his readers of that sermon—folk who generally stone the prophets (or ignore them, which hurts worse); folk who, on the national level, tend to do the right and wise thing, but only after all other alternatives have been exhausted; folk who are spent arrows, smoking lamps, empty vessels, and fruitless vines—imagine him calling us "the salt of the earth" and "the light of the world"! Has ordinary humanity ever received such a compliment from so high and *so informed* a source?

"You are the salt of the earth": Christians are to life what salt is to food—that which preserves and seasons life. I want to underscore the flavoring role. A young woman once told me that she was in love with two men and couldn't make up her mind which to marry. The first was charming, witty, and consistently good company, but not too reliable in a crisis. The second was a little on the dull side, but always a rock of Gibraltar. I heard myself ask her: "How often are you going to be in a crisis?"

This is not often said in church, but I want to suggest that the first fellow may have been as Christian as the second. Proverbs 17:22 states: "A cheerful heart is a good medicine, but a downcast spirit dries up the bones." Well, who wants to be Mrs. Dry Bones? If you can handle the crisis yourself, why not marry someone who can keep you entertained?

Oliver Wendell Holmes remarked: "I might have entered the ministry if certain clergymen I knew had not looked and acted so much like undertakers." (That's unfair to undertakers, who, I have reason to know, off duty look and act very differently.) And Robert Louis Stevenson wrote in his diary, as if recording an extraordinary phenomenon, "I have been to church today and am not depressed."

All of which is to remind us, dear Christians, that our God is no frowning deity. Even in a world as depressed as our own, we should be full of the joy of life. When the earth offers us its fullness, we are wrong not to desire it, we are wrong again not to take it, and we are three times wrong not to share it as widely as we can with as many human beings as possible. Finally, on this score, just as a pinch of salt seasons far beyond its proportion, so a handful of really joyful Christians can radiate gladness in all directions.

Christ also calls us "the light of the world." Whether it be to guide or to illumine, the point of any light is to be seen: "A city set on a hill cannot be hid. Nor do people light a lamp and put it under a bushel, but on a stand, and it gives light to all in the house."

With rare exceptions, secret discipleship is a contradiction in terms. Either the secrecy destroys the discipleship, or the discipleship destroys the secrecy. The term "evangelism" is in ill repute these days, thanks largely to self-proclaimed TV evangelists, whose exhibitionism is the best argument against evangelism. So what else is new? Christians have always been the best argument against Christianity, albeit never the central one. (The question is not "What do you think of Christians?" but "What do you think of Christ?") Moreover, as the Catholics would say, *Abusus non tollit usum*—misuse does not negate right use. The answer to bad evangelism is not no evangelism, but good evangelism. What does that look like?

When Christ said "You are the salt of the earth," he recognized how quickly greed and indifference lead to decay. Like teeth, friendships and marriages are generally lost through decay. Cities too: Consider in New York the present decay of just about everything not connected with profit making. Visitors from other cities do not need to be reminded that New York is a moveable famine. And if on the national and world scene "gross darkness seems to cover the people," it is only because too many have wearied of carrying torches. Kurt Vonnegut was right to note in the preface of an early novel: "We do good too covertly and evil too overtly."

But "you are the light of the world." You are witnesses to that "light which shines in the darkness and the darkness cannot overcome it." You are flaming ambassadors of that love which streams from the cross, spotlighting every single soul on this earth, a love "so amazing, so divine" as to demand "my soul, my life, my all."

The agonies of South Africa, which are spread all over the front pages of our newspapers these days, remind us of the fifties and sixties when, in this country, Lord knows we were doing good too covertly. It seemed then that nothing was more difficult for White folks to bear than the feeling of not being identified with the larger group. So ministers betrayed the Gospel, senators temporized, and the Supreme Court earned the label "controversial" only because lower courts didn't have the courage to make the tough decisions. Fortunately, the inner light kept shining brightly in Black faces.

"Let your light so shine before people that they may see your good works." Those good works (incidentally, the Greek word for "good" is *kalos*, which means beautiful, attractive, even winsome) are not limited to works of social justice. For example, what a lovely small lamp of the Lord was that first hymn: "When Morning Gilds the Skies." Beyond the fact that he or she was German—"*Beim frühen Morgenlicht*"—and clearly a nature lover, we know nothing about the author. But thanks to another little light, a nineteenth-century translator, the lamp lit long ago in Germany today adorned our service and, I dare say, lit quite a few hearts here in this church. From overseas also came the second hymn, another beautiful lamp lit to the Lord, one of Charles Wesley's 6,500 hymns that have encouraged the saints, inspired sinners, raised up and put on their feet how many millions! And Wesley too, in England, was probably inspired by another German, the Moravian leader Peter Böhler, who, within earshot of Wesley, happened to remark: "Had I a thousand tongues, I would use them all to praise my Lord."

And speaking of Germans, the greatest of them all, Johann Sebastian Bach, died this very day, July 28, in 1750. Those of you who were here last night will remember for a lifetime how, in honor of his birth three hundred years ago, we heard the B minor Mass sung by two hundred voices, played by an orchestra of fifty, and conducted by one of the brightest lights of the musical world, Robert Shaw, who makes the best seem so easily credible. For two and a half hours there was no darkness at all in this church, as one lamp lit another, then another and another, all to the glory of Almighty God.

But just as you don't have to be a drum major for justice, you don't have to be an artist or a musician to be a lamp of the Lord.

> If I can stop one heart from breaking,
> I shall not live in vain:
> If I can ease one life the aching,
> Or cool one pain,
> Or help one fainting robin
> Unto his nest again,
> I shall not live in vain.
>
> Emily Dickinson

"No one is useless in the world who lightens the burden of it for anyone else." And those who carry their burden with grace—what shining lights to the rest of us they are! Helen Keller said of her light-denied, sound-denied life: "The greatest calamity may be God's gateway to the Promised Land."

"Let your light so shine before people that they may see your good works and glorify your father who is in heaven." It's not a question of being humble, just a question of fact. As all light streams from the sun, so all goodness stems from God. If you can accept your goodness not as an achievement but as a gift, you are, in fact, much freer to enjoy it. When someone appreciates your good works, you don't have to get all flustered and say, "Aw, shucks." You can just say, "Thank you," both to the person who appreciated them and to the Holy Spirit who inspired them.

St. Paul writes: "Though our outer nature is wasting away, our inner nature is being renewed each day" (2 Cor. 4:16). It is the experience of religious people that even as their sight grows dimmer their light can shine more brightly. Inspired by Isaiah's statement of this experience—"They that wait upon the Lord shall renew their strength" (40:31)—Isaac Watts, another prolific hymn writer, wrote one ending with these two verses:

> Mere human power shall fast decay
> And youthful vigor cease,
> But they who wait upon the Lord
> In strength shall still increase.
>
> They with unwearied feet shall tread
> The path of life divine;
> With growing ardor onward move,
> With growing brightness shine.

Last week I went to Philadelphia to see a woman I had not met before and in all likelihood shall not meet again. She is in her late seventies and has cancer of the liver. Through her son, she had asked if I might be willing to take her funeral service. I said, "Of course, but I'd like to meet her." Not wanting to tax her limited strength, I got to important matters quickly: "How are you and cancer getting along?" She answered in a very even tone, "Cancer is an unwelcome intruder I have made at home." I thought of Maya Angelou: "To survive is important, but to thrive is elegant." Here was one elegant lady. We had a wonderful exchange of views on life and death, and life hereafter. When I got up to leave, she kissed me tenderly. Prompted by a strong desire, I said, holding her two hands, "Maybe we'll meet again." She smiled. "Not as I am," she said. To which I could only reply: "Then not as I am either."

"You are the light of the world." Dearly beloved, if God so loved this world as to send his only son to brighten our darkness, let us not fear to carry the torch, even down to the very gates of death itself. Let us comfort the poor, shelter the weak, and with all our might fight for that which is right against that which is wrong. We cannot do everything, but we can all do something. For faith can place a candle in the darkest night.

I Will Do You Good

SEPTEMBER 22, 1985
Readings: Genesis 32:9–31; Romans 12:1, 2, 9–11

Had I known what Chinese citizens take with them from the States, or what Chinese Americans bring with them when they visit relatives in their ancient homeland, I would better have understood why from the San Francisco airport the plane took off like a New Hampshire blue heron from a log—wings flapping and barely making it. I thought the excess weight was due to the fuel necessary to fly a wall-to-wall packed aircraft non-stop from the States to the People's Republic. I was unaware of the iceboxes, the stoves, the fans, the cartons of books that were also on board—unaware, that is, until from the bowels of the baggage delivery machine in the Beijing airport they emerged and started to ride grandly around the carousel. It was wonderful to contemplate what joy these purchases were to bring a still poor, if incredibly industrious, people.

With similiar joy, I contemplate the recent spiritual purchases that you members of Riverside Church bring to your spiritual home this homecoming Sunday. Like me, many of you have memories of far-off places; others have renewed relationships nearer at hand. All of us must have read some good books this summer, acquired suntans, gone white-water canoeing, backpacking, or at least picnicking, and gone at least once to watch Dwight Gooden on the mound or the Czechs making a clean sweep of it out in Queens. Who can't say, "Lord, of thy fullness have I received grace upon grace"?

Still, no one truly comes home to God without thinking of, and sorting out, things a lot more complicated than those I have just mentioned. A few minutes ago we heard the story of Jacob's homecoming—a really rough one. Years earlier, leaving home, Jacob crossed the Jordan river with nothing more than his staff. Now, coming home, he's rich. He has he-goats, she-goats, ewes and rams. He has bulls and cows. In his train he brings handmaidens with their children and, of course, his two wives, Rachel and Leah, with theirs. But Jacob also carries excess baggage—guilt-laden memories. He'd give the world to deny it, but he cannot: he knows he has cheated his brother Esau out of his birthright; he knows that he has fooled his blind father, Isaac, and conned his father-in-law, Laban, out of just about everything that couldn't be nailed down. But to Jacob's credit, he also knows that the truths he has long evaded have to be faced if he is to enjoy a homecoming not only with his brother Esau, but, more importantly, with God.

Friends, hell is truth seen too late. If this day, this week, we are to enjoy a heavenly homecoming, we have to face rather than flee those memories that won't stay buried. Like Jacob, we can't be blessed without being wounded. No laming, no naming. No struggle, no homecoming.

As many of you know, China today is a phoenix reborn from the ashes of the Cultural Revolution. From about 1965 to 1975 the fire seared everyone. Monstrous numbers were falsely accused and unfairly punished. It was a national disaster, a humiliation for the whole nation. But rebirth has come through confession. "No more lies!" cry the people. And I heard Party members say, "We can no longer blame colonialism, the outside world, imperialism, or the Kuomintang for what has happened. We must interrogate our own souls. The fault is there, in ourselves."

It is a sober and hopeful thought that the largest nation in the world, led by a Marxist-Leninist party, can overhaul itself by airing its recent mistakes.

To straighten things out with God, Jacob has to be alone. It makes sense: think of Jesus in the wilderness or alone in the Garden of Gethsemane. All of us, finally, are solitudes. We are born alone, we die alone, and in between we stumble along in the footsteps of lonely prototypes like Abraham, Ulysses, and Faust. That night, alone on the banks of the river, Jacob wrestled his demons as long as it took to bring them to light, as long as it took to make them yield him a blessing. For as in the ancient myths dragons turn out to be princesses, so assailants in the night—those guilt-laden memories—can prove to be angels. God does not want us to carry excess baggage. God wants us to travel light, all parts reconciled and working together. God doesn't want us to be sinners, God wants us to be forgiven sinners. In a wonderful line that recalls Jacob wrestling with his assailant, Calvin wrote, "God becomes in us stronger than the power by which God opposes us." We can come home today, this week, limping like Jacob, so that like Jacob, never again will we try to run away from ourselves.

Let us not fear to be alone with God. Let us not fear to wrestle with God so that, like Jacob, we can be at one with God, at one with the serenity that lies not on this side, but on the far side of conflict.

Having wrestled with God, Jacob is given a new name denoting larger responsibilities. What is so heartening about so many Old Testament characters is that although real heels, they are capable of great visions and awesome achievements. Jacob is renamed Israel, a name his descendants will carry as proudly as most of us carry the name American. To be sure, "God has made of one blood all the nations of the earth." We should be "earth chauvinists." Still, we cannot escape our heritage, our national identity and its responsibilities.

Let me speak personally. Each trip abroad renews my love of America and my appreciation of its democracy. My dream for America is to see economic justice established in an atmosphere of democratic freedom. But I am old enough to have seen how corruption works in a democracy, how the taint of it spreads bit by bit, touching one person and then another, until it is carried by a whole culture. I have seen how painfully and degradingly simple it is for leaders to deceive the people. Foreigners, for example, are often struck at how many Americans, even poor Americans, think privilege is something earned or deserved. Rarely do Americans see privilege as a form of theft. So they are taken aback by questions such as that asked by Bertolt Brecht: "What's robbing a bank compared to owning one?"

And Americans would have been taken aback, as I was last week, by these words, spoken ever so softly at supper by a Chinese scholar who was also an Anglican priest: "Truly you Americans are a remarkable lot. By supporting the right wing of the Israeli government you have discredited yourselves in the eyes of over 100 million Arabs. By constructive engagement you have alienated hundreds of millions of Africans. By arming the Contras you have antagonized more millions of Latin Americans. And by rearming Taiwan and lecturing us on birth control, a problem whose dimensions you are barely aware of, you have angered one billion Chinese. That's quite a record."

If, as a Palestinian said to me last June, "America is not somewhere, it's everywhere," we who bear the name American (or *norteamericano*) cannot seek to come home to God without asking, "Has what little I can do been done to bring my country closer to the will of One who does not wish to see the powerful do as they will and the poor suffer as they must, but rather proclaims, 'Let justice roll down like mighty waters and righteousness like an ever-flowing stream'?"

Actually, most of us here have three names: our own name, our national name, and a religious name. And as mightily as we have to struggle to determine these days what it means to be American, we have to struggle to determine what it means to be Christian. Do we, like some fundamentalists, want to espouse all Scriptural passages *except* those dealing with compassion, understanding, and forgiveness? Do we, in the fashion of so many liberals, want to be like clouds floating back and forth across the sky, unable to form the rain so desperately needed to nourish a parched and thirsty land? What do we want Riverside Church to represent in the religious community of America today?

I suggest we put off the attempt to answer that last question until next week. Still, it behooves us this homecoming Sunday to recognize the possibility that many of us Christians who feel so at home in our churches may, in fact, be miles away from God.

But enough of these grim possibilities. God assures Jacob: "Return to your country and to your kindred and I will do you good." There's the promise, as sure today as it was of old. If, like Jacob, we wrestle with those memories that wake us up in the still of the night, and if we struggle mightily for a vision of what it means to bear the name American—or Chinese or Palestinian—and that awesome name that goes with being followers of Christ, then, whatever evil the world may bring, God will do us good. "Return to your country and your kindred, and I will do you good."

Flying in Unity

SEPTEMBER 29, 1985
Readings: Isaiah 40:28–31; 1 Corinthians 12:4–13

Dearly beloved, on this gorgeous day, when the sky is high and the air so clear, and a promising autumn season of events stretches before us, let's take a few moments to talk about the church. As many of you know, there are in the Bible many images of the church, the most famous being St. Paul's "body of Christ": "For just as the body is one and has many members, and all the members of the body, though many, are one body, so it is with Christ. For by one Spirit we were all baptized into one body—Jews or Greeks, slaves or free"—deacons or trustees, men or women, Black or white, starved or stuffed, all in one body—"and all were made to drink of one Spirit." That image of the church prevails in St. Paul's letters to the Corinthians, the Romans, the Ephesians, and the Colossians.

In the book of Hebrews, however, the prevailing metaphor is the tent. To the writer of Hebrews—and no scholar seems sure who that was—to be a disciple of Christ meant living in tents because Christians are refugees and aliens, foreigners and sojourners in a strange land. "Strange land" is a metaphor that strikes closer to home than we might like, while "tent" seems an excellent image for those who work and worship in a building like this. (I once heard of a sociologist who, every year, gave his entering freshman class the assignment to write for half an hour on the differences between a church, a hospital, and a university. He would then collect the papers and very ostentatiously deposit them in the wastebasket next to his desk. "You are wrong," he would say. "The primary purpose of all three of these institutions is the preservation of the institution. The fact that one dispenses religion and another learning and a third medical care is purely secondary." Incomplete, perhaps, but provocative.

This week I read a fine book by my former preaching professor, from which I'd like to offer a third image of the church—non-Biblical, but highly appropriate to the fall season.* Professor Brown Barr likens a church at its best to a flock of high-flying geese, because—for a starter—they fly with unity, grace, and purpose, and because geese flying in formation fly 70 percent faster than a single goose!

I like that. I like the image of members of Riverside Church not crawling but flying high; not bickering, but flying in unity; maybe not in the fearful cohesion necessary only when the flock passes through a heavy fog bank, but still flying in formation with intention, verve, and glory.

Here's something else I was happy to learn: the lead bird does not necessarily have the most strenuous position. I had always identified with that leading goose or gander out front. I thought of her as a long-suffering martyr, catching the cold blasts of strong countercurrents. But not at all. Apparently all those wings flapping in formation, create an upwash whose benefits are shared by all, the birds, including the leader.

You have to admit this is a terrific image! Let's consider for a moment ordained ministers. They may be "a breed apart" (to mix the metaphor for a moment), but the setting apart is functional; it is not based on spiritual or moral superiority. There are lots of church members who just love to sacrifice the vicar on the altars of vicarious goodness! But consider this: To believe that the ministry represents a spiritual rather than a functional category undercuts function, for then the validity of the Gospel and the efficacy of the sacraments seem to depend upon the moral superiority of the ordained person. Seminarians remember: the question is not who is good enough to preach the Gospel and celebrate the sacraments, but whether anyone could be so wicked as to nullify the grace of God set forth therein.

Professor Barr recalls a cartoon of a flock of geese flying in a V-formation. They look strange, but it's not clear why. When you look

*See *High Flying Geese*, Brown Barr (Seabury Press).

more closely you realize they are flying with the "V" reversed. One goose is saying, "I have a nagging feeling we're doing something wrong." Now a minister in a church has many tasks—to teach, to counsel, to help right things happen—but her main function is to get the flock off the ground and to keep them flying in the right direction. Her main function is, in season and out, to preach that the goal of life is to glorify God and to sanctify humanity.

That's a tough task, and many fail. Søren Kierkegaard, who took a gloomy view of geese, wrote of a flock to whom a gander preached each Sunday:

> The sermon was essentially the same. It told of the glorious destiny of geese, of the noble end for which their maker had created them—and every time (the maker's) name was mentioned the geese curtsied and all the ganders bowed their heads. They were to use their wings to fly away to the distant pastures to which they really belonged; for they were only pilgrims on this earth. The same thing happened each Sunday. Thereupon the meeting broke up and they all waddled home, only to meet again next Sunday for divine worship and waddle off home again. They throve and grew fat, plump and delicious—and at Christmas were eaten—and that was as far as they ever got.

Dearly beloved, the worst thing a congregation can do to its ministers is to domesticate them. The result is always the same: the bland leading the bland!

But enough of ministers. Let's talk now of the other flying geese who, incidentally, in good Protestant fashion, keep rotating positions with that lead bird. As Professor Barr points out, a lot of things fly— insects fly, bats and airplanes fly. But only birds have the comfort and glory of feathers, which come in two kinds.

Down feathers, as we all know, are for warmth, for insulation. When Unamuno, the Spanish philosopher, first heard the famous dying words of Goethe, "Light, light, more light," he is reported to have objected: "Goethe should have said, 'Warmth, warmth, more warmth.' We die of cold, not darkness. It is not the night that kills but the frost."

All of us in this church feel the chilling effects of living in this world. Many of us have joined Riverside because we were baffled and dazed by what life was doing to us. City folk in particular are beset by frustrations, unsatisfactory compromises, and insecurities. Few churches can adequately meet all the hurts and needs of their members, especially of those who belong in therapy as well as in church. But of the increase of love there must be no end. Church members must constantly remember that the whole Gospel is summed up in the three-word imperative, "Love one another." And in church we should concentrate our love not only on the lonely and unloved, the failing and the fallen; we must also love those with whom we disagree. Creative tension is good for a church. We can take disagreement; friendship, after all, includes salt and vinegar as well as sugar. But discord and distrust corrode. So too do church politics. Alas, in every church, too many members are too busy cooking their political pies. When all of us are immigrants in God's mighty empire, it does not behoove us to make like minor vassals in charge of our own little fiefs. Above all, we must root out enmity; for didn't St. Augustine warn, "Imagine the vanity of thinking that your enemy can do you more harm than your enmity"?

Birds have down feathers to keep them warm, but the point of having warm bodies is to provide energy for flight. To give them lift, birds have contour feathers. Contour feathers are what make a bird a bird, what allow a bird to fly.

Church members must see to the increase of love and remind the body of Christ that it is not a redemptive community simply for the spiritual health of its own, but for the whole creation of God and all the separated and separating persons and powers in it. "They who wait upon the Lord shall mount up with wings." We are not here to feel better, but to be better. We are not here to do our thing, but to do Christ's thing. We are here not for ourselves alone, we are here for those not here—the hungry, the thirsty, the imprisoned, the sick.

Riverside Church can never rest easy as long as thousands of homeless children are relegated to sleep without shelter. We have a moral obligation with other churches and synagogues to forge a moral commitment to shelter the homeless and house the poor in New York City. We cannot stand above the battle of our friends Desmond Tutu and Allan Boesak. We have also to internalize the blemish and anguish of the crackdown on compassion in the Sanctuary movement and the atrocious policies being promulgated today in our name and with our money in Central America.* We must love one another, we must study, we must pray, but we must also ponder

*In the 1980s, U.S. citizens contested the Reagan administration's policy of sponsoring wars in Guatemala and El Salvador by housing refugees from those countries in American churches illegally. Riverside housed a family for many years.

these startling words of a former Archbishop of Canterbury, William Temple, who said: "This world can be saved from political chaos and collapse by one thing only, and that is worship."

Maybe those words are not so startling if we remember that George Washington in his farewell address called religion and morality the "indispensable supports of political prosperity."

Geese fly faster in formation than one by one. The upwash from their flapping wings benefits all of us. They have down feathers for warmth and contour feathers for flight. Dearly beloved members of Riverside Church, as we start a new fall season, let us see if we cannot fly in unity with grace and purpose, intention and verve, and all to the end that we may do as Christ would have us do, glorify God and sanctify humanity.

The Liberty of the Restored

OCTOBER 6, 1985
Readings: Psalm 103:1–5, 8–12; Luke 7:36–47

In tribute to his glorious life, which ended this week, at the age of 83, let's hear again these words of E. B. White:

> If the world were merely seductive, that would be
> easy. If it were merely challenging, that would be no
> problem. But I arise in the morning torn between a
> desire to improve (or save) the world, and a desire
> to enjoy (or savor) the world. This makes it hard to
> plan the day.

This calls to mind a comment by another great observer of the human condition, Albert Camus: "There is in the world beauty and there are the humiliated. And we must strive, hard as it is, not to be unfaithful, neither to the one nor to the other."

The real trick is both to savor *and* to save. Look out for those who want only to save; and God save us from those who only savor!

Those here last Sunday will remember that I borrowed a non-Biblical but seasonally appropriate image from Professor Brown Barr. He likened the Church at its best to high-flying geese who, because of the upwash from all those flapping wings, fly 70 percent faster in formation than when alone; who have down feathers for warmth, and contour feathers for flight. I hoped all of us this fall would fly with comparable grace, unity, intention, and verve.

This morning, Worldwide Communion Sunday, I want to talk about what we do in church, all of us the world around, every Sunday. For what we do when we gather determines who we are when we scatter. All life should flow from the common experience we are now having of worship—a word derived from "worthship."

What do you see when you enter the humblest of churches? Always the same three symbols: the lectern on which the Word of God is read; the pulpit where the Word of God is, in the old term, "divided"; and the altar, or Communion table, where the Word of God is sacrificed. The Word of God in the person of Jesus tells us that God's love does not seek value but rather creates it; that in our anxiety and guilt, as creatures and sinners, we are groundlessly and infinitely loved—thus free both to savor and to save the world.

I haven't mentioned the organ, but you tell me what it symbolizes to you. "Ear's deep sweet music, and heart's deep-sore wounding"? Does it symbolize the beauty of holiness? Does it mean that the Word of God, which is a compass not a road map, is a mystery that cannot be definitively analyzed, only infinitely celebrated?

The first hymn, for which the congregation rises to face the altar as the choir and ministers process toward it, is always one of thanksgiving and praise: "O praise ye the Lord," we sang today; we might as well have sung, "The God of Abraham praise," or "Immortal, invisible God only wise," or "Joyful, joyful, we adore thee." Not always, but usually, the opening hymn is in a major key, and a bright one at that— D, G, or A, not D flat or G flat—and the opening line naturally rises.

"Joy is the serious business of heaven," and a much-neglected virtue on earth. The Hassidic Jews, who have known centuries of persecution, state their commitment to "joy in the world as it is, in life as it is, in every hour of life in this world, as that hour is." And the psalmists, who knew every affliction that life had to offer, never ceased to proclaim, "I will sing of thy steadfast love, O Lord"; "Sing aloud to God our strength" (Ps. 81:1); "Bless the Lord, O my soul, and all that is within me bless his holy name" (Ps. 103:1).

Wesley wrote of being "lost in wonder, love and praise." Emily Dickinson said: "Eternity is composed of nows. The ecstasy of mere living is enough for me." We *have* to savor the world—it's God's! I know there are times when God's presence is hard to feel. As George Santayana once put it: "A lion must feel more secure that God is on his side than a gazelle." Still, a gazelle instinctively works against its own fragility, moves always toward life, not toward its death. And so the Spirit works in each of us, renewing and restoring. "Whenever we think of the suffering of the innocent—and I hope it's often—we must always ask ourselves whether it is God's will, or of human making. (I'm thinking of famine, war, racial discrimination, abuse of women and children, brown-lung disease.)

And we must also never forget the unmerited good each of us enjoys. What did you and I ever do to merit a day like this? What did you and I ever do to merit the birds, the beasts, the streams that gush forth and flow between the hills? What did you and I ever do to merit fall foliage, wind, sun, and stars, art and music—and, yes, a series like that between the Mets and the Cardinals? What did you and I ever do to merit the friend we have in Jesus who gladdens the heart, stretches the imagination, and pulls us up to our full stature? (That's the way to stand tall—to be stretched by Jesus!)

> For why? The Lord our God is good,
> His mercy is forever sure;
> His truth at all times firmly stood
> And shall from age to age endure.
> William Kethe

Isn't that the reality Christians come to church to recall Sunday by Sunday the world around?

At Barnard and Columbia and Teachers College, scholars worry about the uncertainty of human knowledge. But the more vexatious problem is the insecurity of human life. Because of it, underneath the blandest of exteriors lurks the universal anxiety, the "worm at the core"—death and the dread of it. Heroism is first and foremost a reflex against the terror of death. But the more typical reflexes are less heroic—cowardice, greed, the manifold ways we try to secure ourselves against our insecurities. Even in the more rational, more optimistic year of 1775, Abigail Adams wrote her husband, "I am more and more convinced that man is a dangerous creature, and that power, whether vested in many or a few, is ever grasping, and, like the grave, cries, 'Give, give.'"

Anyone who has looked deeply into life has seen too much to deny the existence of sin. Anxiety is the precondition to sin, and the essence of sin is a denial of love, cutting ourselves off from God, alienating ourselves from each other and from ourselves. Just as when you see the distant mountaintop you become acutely aware of the floor of the valley on which you stand, once you have sung of God's truth, proclaimed the reality of God's love, you become acutely aware of so much that is unreal in our corporate and individual lives. In other words, there is a natural progression from praise to confession. Worship of God and self-understanding are but two sides of the same coin. Thus it is that in every church service the General Confession follows hard on the opening hymn and opening sentences, the first prayer or invocation (and in this church a choral introit) being the very short bridge that connects the two.

Confession is good for the soul, evasion and repression are not. Yet how hard it is to confess! Pascal said, "Our wounds are too deep, we cannot examine them." Confession also undergirds meaning: how many times have I said, If nothing counts against you, nothing counts? Remember too that we are confessing the sins of the nations, and especially those of the church. At home, alone, is a good place to talk to God of our own personal failings, but here in church we make corporate confession of corporate sins. Most of all, let us remember that the purpose of confession is to point us toward forgiveness, to renewal and restoration.

I am always stunned by people who get all flustered about the Immaculate Conception, the Virgin Birth, the physical resurrection of Jesus, his changing the water into wine, and yet, without, batting an eye, can stand up and say, "I believe in the forgiveness of sins," as if it were a piece of cake! And I am also stunned by those who think it takes a lot of humility to say the General Confession. Don't they realize that guilt is the last stronghold of pride? The Assurance of Pardon is what takes humility, because it means giving up your opinion of yourself and accepting someone else's opinion of you. It means allowing someone else to do for you what you cannot do for yourself. It means that you recognize that finally your value is a gift, not an achievement. How many of us are that humble?

But forgiveness is crucial. As the New Testament lesson made clear, they who are forgiven much, love much, and conversely, they who are forgiven little, love little. It is easier to be guilty than to be responsible. But forgiveness demands that we be responsible, "response-able," able to respond to God's love. Forgiveness lifts us up, it sets us free: "For freedom Christ has set you free." In place of the license of the fallen, we have been accorded the liberty of the restored.

I have long held that the most exciting moment of the service should be the Assurance of Pardon. It is the core and substance of worship. As I said earlier, the Word of God in Christ is that we human beings in our anxiety and guilt, as fragile creatures and rugged sinners, are groundlessly and infinitely loved, for there is more mercy in

God than sin in us. That is the good news by which Christians the world around are restored Sunday by Sunday. In response to it, the whole church should just stand up and shout, "Amen!"

As for the rest of the liturgy, let's leave that for another time. It is enough if today we see the thesis—God is good, the antithesis—we are sinners; and the all-important synthesis—we are *forgiven* sinners. That is enough to enable us once again to savor and to save, to be faithful in this world to its beauty and to its humiliated, and to number us, when we scatter, among the thankful, forgiven, and dedicated. On this Worldwide Communion Sunday may God so bless all our fellow Christians the world around.

Worthy of Our Steeple?

OCTOBER 13, 1985
Reading: Matthew 5:14–16

You are the light of the world. A city set on a hill cannot be hid."

Centuries ago, John Donne asked of "Christ's spouse," as he called the church, this question laden with anguish:

> Doth she, and did she, and shall she evermore
> On one, on seven, or on no hill appear?

And with no anguish, only scorn, a later poet writes, "I could believe in Christ if he did not drag behind him his leprous bride, the Church." The inconsistency is clear: while professing to believe in Christ, the later poet is totally unable to love those whom Christ himself loved.

But there is integrity in Donne's anguish, for time and again it appears that while the Gospel is the solution, the church is the problem. Any Christian has to have some ambivalence about the church, an ambivalence similar to that expressed by a Chinese writer who, in the preface to his short stories, wrote, "I am very familiar with these mountain people and I have put all of my love and hatred into describing them."

A Spaniard once claimed that if you want to see the soul of Spain, you have but to look at Goya's paintings. But you have to look at *all* of them, from the nightmarish sketches to the formal court portraits. Likewise, if you want to see the soul of the church, you have to look at the churches, all of them, from the frightened enclaves of suburban bourgeois values to those affirming liberty and justice for all amid the oppressions of Central America and Eastern Europe, and especially Black and some White Christians of South Africa who, today, lift up their heads knowing their redemption is drawing nigh.

This week, in preparation for a new class of members and in anticipation of our annual Every Member Canvass, I have been rereading the hopes of Harry Emerson Fosdick for this particular church. In 1947, the last year of Dr. Fosdick's ministry, this church, then solely a Baptist church, had 3,000 members, of whom 900 were Baptists. The rest were everything else. That statistic raises a question: How are we, in being faithful to Christ, to realize Christian unity?

Within Protestantism there are two basic ways. One is for denominations to merge—a long, painful, and often, yes, farcical process. Years ago, the Episcopalians wanted to merge with the Methodists. After a spirited debate the Methodist bishop said to his Episcopal counterpart: "I am persuaded that no serious theological issues divide us. But it is painfully difficult for me, who have taken an oath of abstinence, to consider becoming one with you, who love your cocktails. I think I'd rather commit adultery than take a drink."

The Episcopal bishop replied: "My dear fellow, wouldn't we all? But I think our solution is better."

Later, the Episcopalians tried again, this time with the Presbyterians, and in a year when my uncle, Henry Sloane-Coffin, was moderator of the Presbyterian church, and his good friend Henry Sherrill was presiding bishop of the Episcopal church. At the last minute the Anglican wing threatened secession, and no deal was cut. Fit to be tied, my uncle Henry called Bishop Sherrill to say, "Sherrill, I've got the text for you." (It comes from Luke.) "'Do not bother me; the door is now shut and my children are in bed with me; I cannot get up and give you anything.'"

Some attempts, of course, have succeeded. In this country the Evangelical and Reformed churches merged with the Congregationalists to become the United Church of Christ. After a hundred years the Northern and Southern Presbyterians are again one, and The United Church of Canada has replaced, I believe, four denominations. Chinese Protestants today are in what they call their "post-denominational period." From what I was told at the seminary in Nanking last month, it is really working. In 1949, at the time of the Revolution, there were 700,000 Protestant Christians in China. Today there are 3,600,000, and a new church opens on the average of one a day. Praise God for our brothers and sisters in China.

The second way to affirm unity is for an individual church simply to assume the irrelevancy of sectarian divisions and to act on that assumption. Today, thirty-nine years after Dr. Fosdick's retirement, Riverside has approximately the same number of members from the same diversity of religious backgrounds. At the same time, we maintain relationships with the Christian church as a whole through national ties with two denominations—the United Church of Christ and the American Baptists—and by financially supporting the National Council of Churches and the World Council of Churches. This year's Riverside budget allocates $76,000 to our two mother church denominations and the three Councils of Churches—City, National, and World, to two homes for the aged; and to three seminaries—Colgate Rochester (Baptist), Andover Newton (UCC), and Union Theological Seminary, our neighbor to whose faculty and students we owe so much.

I share Fosdick's hope that Riverside will always be the kind of ecumenical church that illustrates the possibility and value of Christian unity.

As there are basically two ways of affirming unity in the Protestant fold, so there are two distinguishable types of Protestant churches. At one extreme, a church conducts a program centered in worship and preaching, with little else going on. In revolt against this self-contained type of congregation, another goes to the other extreme, minimizing worship and preaching, and glorifying practical expressions of Christian service to the underprivileged and unchurched.

No one entering Riverside Church, especially the nave, could suppose for a moment that we minimize worship and preaching. Visitors may be unaware of other chapels or other services, including every Sunday morning a service for Ethiopians and every Sunday afternoon a service for Chinese Christians. At the same time, the only justification for so magnificent a building is to make sure its roof is hospitable to all manner of people who need what we can offer seven days a week.

Personally, I couldn't survive without this service, Sunday by Sunday. It nourishes me, and I need it for the rest of the week. But I'd be ashamed if we didn't feed the hungry two hours a day, five days a week, at a budget cost of $100,000 this year. I'd be ashamed if, in New York City—where the freedom of anonymity is, alas, matched by the indifference that goes with anonymity—if we did not offer a multifaceted program for older adults, if we did not have a clothing service or a shelter, and if we did not offer to literally hundreds of immigrants two English-language programs (one voluntary and the other professional).

In short, I hope Riverside Church will always be an ecumenical house of worship maintained with all the impressiveness we can put into it, and at the same time a center of public concern. I agree with Dr. Fosdick: "Our building must be used to the utmost; it is wicked to have it otherwise." I am happy to report, Dr. Fosdick, that this church's conscience is untroubled by unused space.

Buell Gallagher, for many years a member of Riverside Church and president of City College of New York, has written: "If conscience does not erase the color line within the Christian churches, there will be no conscience left in their membership."

Were Riverside not one-third Black, it would not be one-half the church it is today. We needn't boast, for we have unfinished work to do, but we should be grateful that we are in a place that supports an interracial membership with minimum difficulty and maximum advantage to all concerned.

Like all churches, we have membership classes. But as our new members about to enter will tell us, it is one by one that people are brought to Christ and to God. And, in a church as large as ours, we need *ecclesiola in ecclesia* (little churches within the church). We have house churches. We also have prayer groups, spiritual growth groups, a women's center, a Mother's Workshop, the Business and Professional Women's Association, task forces like the Prison Task Force, an arts and crafts program, and a formidable array of Biblical and theological study groups, all based on the understanding that faith, far from substituting for thought, is what makes good thinking possible. And I haven't mentioned Joan Kavanaugh's Pastoral Counseling Center or Damaris Miranda, who, as head of the Social Service Department, somehow finds time to counsel some 600 individuals and families a year.

In a church, nothing matters except what happens to individuals. But let us not forget how often the better way to serve individuals is not to provide, but to ask for service: "He who loses his life shall find it"; "It is in giving that we receive." I am impressed by the time, energy, and money so many of you pour into this church and by what it does for you as well as for the church. I am equally impressed by so much unused ability in this congregation. Mind you, it's not *church work* I have in mind, but the work of the church—the outreach, the witness of church members wherever they live and work, a witness that can call from them more beauty and love and devotion than they ever dreamed were there. To quote Dr. Fosdick again: "As an apple tree may grow large but still be futile if it does not bear apples, so a church's bigness means nothing unless it bears fruit in transformed and dedicated individuals." This personal result is the primary purpose of any church.

To see people as individuals, however, is not to be indifferent to the environment that either makes or breaks so many of us. I simply cannot imagine God being interested only in my sins and yours, and not being interested in the sins of the nation and the world. I cannot imagine God concerned for the poor but unconcerned about how they got that way. Nor can I imagine God untroubled by the happiness experienced by so many Americans this week because the United States is no longer being "pushed around" by terrorists from small nations —or by terrorists who *wish* they had a nation—while the same citizens remain blissfully unaware that American banks and American companies and the U.S. government are pushing people around every day all over the world and all over the United States. To think that this newfound means of dealing with terrorists is going to bank rather than fuel the flames of political terrorism is naive in the extreme.

Last April, Bishop Paul Moore said,

> We once had a war against poverty; it is said to have failed. It failed only because the people of the United States lost their nerve and lost their way in the swamps of Vietnam and Watergate. If the war on poverty had been continued, restructured where necessary, monitored for corruption where appropriate, and encouraged with resources where successful, hunger would not have reappeared on the American scene, the homeless would not now walk the streets, and the schools would not fail to prepare youths for jobs. Do not say that the war against poverty failed because poverty cannot be defeated by money. Rather, say that the war against poverty failed because the people of America quit.

It is said that if you feed the poor you're a saint; if you ask why they are poor you're a Marxist. But if all church members in this country, wherever they live and wherever they work, had the courage to echo Bishop Moore's sentiments, bearing the criticism that would in all likelihood follow, we Americans would have a society we could show the world with pride.

A Norwegian pastor, so the story goes, was called into Gestapo headquarters during World War II. Before the interrogation began, the Gestapo officer pulled his Luger out of its holster and laid it on the desk between himself and the pastor. The pastor reached into his satchel, pulled out his Bible, and placed it on the desk beside the Luger. "Why did you do that?" the Gestapo officer asked. The pastor replied, "You have put your weapon on the table and I have put mine."

It must be God's highest hope that one day the weapons of the churches will put the weapons of the world out of business. To realize that hope is the primary task these days of every single church in this world.

> You are the light of the world.
> A city set on a hill cannot be hid.
>
> Doth she, and did she, and shall she evermore
> On one, on seven, or on no hill appear?

By striving to be ecumenical, interracial, international, and supportive of the rights of all, whatever their sexual preference; by being both a worshipping community and a center of public concern; by recalling that nothing matters except what happens to individuals, and that all God's children need and deserve an environment that sustains rather than ruins them, may the tallest building on this hill be worthy of its steeple. For, warts and all, we are still "Christ's spouse."

Converting the Purse

OCTOBER 20, 1985
Readings: Proverbs 30:7–9; Luke 19:1–10; Mark 12:41–44

A Vermont farmer one day appeared at the bank, where he requested a one dollar loan. He was told that it could be arranged, but that it was usual to have collateral. The farmer produced a $10,000 government bond and asked if that would be enough. He was assured that it would, and he went off with his dollar. Exactly a year later he came back and said he wanted to renew the loan. It could be done, he was told, but as a rule the bank asked 7 percent interest. The farmer produced a nickel and two pennies, and his loan was renewed. This went on year after year. Finally the bank manager got wind of it. He asked his staff to bring the farmer to see him the next time he came in to renew the loan. When the farmer stood before him the bank manager said, "We have nothing against this one dollar loan for which you pay seven cents interest every year, but I'm curious. Why do you need this dollar loan?" The farmer said, "Do you know how much they charge for a safe-deposit box these days?"

We can readily admire the cunning of the farmer, because there's no need to sympathize with the bank. I tell the story because that's the way some (not all) treat Riverside. This is no bank that makes money for you and more for itself; this is a church, where we are asked to put our belief not in the money, but what's written on the money—"In God we trust."

On this annual Pledge Sunday, I have decided not to be diffident. I want to talk straight about money this morning, about you and me and money, and then about Riverside and money. In 1844 Ralph Waldo Emerson observed, "Money is hardly spoken of in parlors without an apology." In a hundred-odd years we have made progress, but we've a way to go. This week I read the confessions of a young man who said he was brought up by very progressive parents, both of them psychiatrists. When he was a child they talked openly of violence and sex, but whenever they talked of money they went into the bedroom and closed the door.

Oscar Wilde quipped: "Nothing succeeds like excess." But, of course, he was wrong. Surely one of the most pathetic figures in modern American history is Howard Hughes, who turned his inheritance into a fortune worth more than a billion dollars. But look what the fortune turned him into: a recluse and a hypochondriac who devoted most of his life to avoiding germs and people. The point is clear: If God is the source of life, it is self-destructive to put our trust elsewhere.

Dr. Karl Menninger once asked a very rich patient, "What are you going to do with all that money?" Replied the patient, "Just worry about it, I suppose." "Well," the doctor went on, "do you get that much pleasure out of worrying about it?" The man sighed. "No, but I feel such terror when I think of giving any of it away." Stinginess is a symptom of sickness. Menninger concludes, "Generous people are rarely mentally ill."

The Bible never attacks wealth per se, and we have just heard Jesus praise the rich and generous Zacchaeus. But the Bible does consistently attack idolatry. Idolatry is an obsession with created things instead of devotion to the creator. Idols are false gods, and it is truly amazing how money takes on the attributes of deity for both rich and poor. Money promises security, a promise it generally can keep up to a point. It didn't provide much security for Howard Hughes once mortality crept into his bones to take up lodging and an endless darkness began to press against the windows. But then, money promises prestige, money promises power, and money tempts us to believe that we and other people are as we earn, until a whole society begins to measure human worth by yardsticks of economics.

Archbishop Dom Helder Camara, who spends his life seeking justice for the poor, has written, "I used to think when I was a child that Christ might have been exaggerating when he warned about the dangers of wealth. Today I know better. I know how hard it is to be rich and still keep the milk of human kindness. Money has a dangerous way of putting scales on our eyes, a dangerous way of freezing people's hands, eyes, lips, and hearts."

Thirty years ago, when West Germany had recovered from World War II and was becoming rich, and was ruled by a multiparty system, East Germany was still poor and under one-party rule. An East German pastor wrote Karl Barth comparing the two Germanys and pleading with the great theologian to denounce publicly what was going on in East Germany. Karl Barth wrote back, "Is it worse to be in the wilderness or back in the fleshpots of Egypt?" We have all heard of the thousands who flee East to West, but it was only last year that I heard of the hundreds who go in the other direction. One came to see me to explain that in his opinion the simpler, saner life in East Germany was safer for the human soul. Being a fierce civil libertarian, I was not persuaded, but I was intrigued.

A modern Passover ritual says, "In every generation it is our duty to imagine that we ourselves have come forth from Egypt." Perhaps the best thing about the annual Every Member Canvass is that it gives each of us a chance to see if we have come forth, if we are indeed free, no longer in slavery, neither to Pharaoh nor to the fleshpots of Egypt. It gives us a chance to see if our heads are screwed on right, to examine the degree to which we measure our worth and the worth of others by what we earn instead of by what we have received from God.

I worry about some of you. You are not wealthy, but you have good incomes. What worries me is not only that you *do not* give to Riverside in a manner proportionate to your income, you *do not* give in a manner proportionate to the keenness of your awareness of the suffering of others and of how much this church means to you and to them. This tells that money is bidding for your hearts, that you may be trusting the coin rather than what is written on it, and that your life may be transforming you into someone you most definitely are not.

Martin Luther said, "There are three conversions necessary: the conversion of the heart, of the mind and of the purse." How hard it is to have open minds, open hearts, and open purses!

Here in America we believe that our ability to make nuclear weapons is tantamount to a right to make them. We also believe, in this land of Adam Smith, that our ability to make money is also tantamount to a right to make money. But we have only the ability, not the right, to end life on this planet—only God has the authority to do that; and we have only the ability and not the right to gain more and more possessions for ourselves, not if "the earth is the Lord's and the fulness thereof," and not if we believe in a Lord who proclaims, "Let justice roll down like mighty waters."

Here's another Vermont story: A Texan drove up to Vermont in his Cadillac and spied an old farmer working in the field. He stopped the car, lowered the window, stuck out his head, and called to the farmer, "Hi, friend, how much land you got?" The farmer came up and leaned on his hoe. "You see that birch tree over there?" he said. "Let your eye go along the hedge until you come to the wall, and then you come down along that wall and along the spring that runs beside this road and back to where we are, and that's my land." The Texan said, "Friend, what would you say if I were to tell you that I can get into my car before sunup, and by sundown I still haven't driven around all my land?" The farmer said, "Yep, had a car like that myself once."

I'm not sure the farmer wasn't right to find it inconceivable that one person could be so totally uncreative as to have to have all that land. Here in the city, Tiemann Place, two blocks down on Claremont Avenue, is surely no playground of the gods, but oh, the ingenuity and flexibility manifested by those kids playing football! I listened to them in a huddle the other day: "OK, Alvarez, take ten steps down the hill, cut to the left, and I'll throw you one behind the red Toyota."

Most of us here don't need more and more things to enjoy life; we need rather to develop more and more our ability to enjoy what we have.

Once again: God is the source of life; it is self-destructive to put our trust elsewhere. If giving causes more pain than pleasure, it is not our money but our faith that is insufficient.

Now about Riverside and money. As inflation has offset the gains of the higher salaries that many of you have been receiving over the years, so inflation and higher costs have caught up with the endowment of Riverside. Then, too, we have added programs—a food pantry, a shelter, an English-language program for immigrants, a pastoral counseling center, and a disarmament program. We have taxed our staff. We have put heavy pressure on our facilities, true to Dr. Fosdick's philosophy: "Unused space in this building, when real needs can be met by its use, ought always to trouble the church's conscience."

But we have also begun to cut into capital, and that's not good. We have to cut costs— carefully; it's hard work—and we have to do it from top to bottom. You don't need two 60-watt light bulbs behind every exit sign burning 24 hours a day; two 9-watt fluorescent lamps will do just as well. And we have to raise more money, first and foremost from ourselves, and then from friends who believe in what we are trying to do.

"Generous people are rarely ill." They can also help cure Riverside. Some of you with little income are already inordinately generous. You are like the widow who gave her mite, understanding that what counts is not how much you give but how much is left after you give.

You may be rich like Zacchaeus or poor like the widow, but be generous as were both of them. Receive your Every Member Canvass worker as you would a wonderful opportunity. Help the staff and all the terrific volunteers who labor in this church to "redeem the time," to "claim the high calling angels cannot share," to bring the Gospel gladness to young and old. Don't wait til the battle's over—help us right now to find the lost and lonely hearts, to heal the broken soul with love, to free the prisoner from all chains, to feed the hungry children with warmth and good food, to make music in the hearts of the old, to care for the earth below and for the sky above.

Coming to Terms with Death

NOVEMBER 3, 1985
Readings: Psalm 46; Romans 8:31–39

All Saints' Sunday can be a painful time for those who have had occasion to wonder if it's possible to love again when one who was loved is lost forever. (Does the world have anything to give like that which it takes away?) But pain in this life is as natural as breathing, and often in moments of pain we feel more alive than in happiness. "God is our refuge and strength, a very present help *in* trouble." The trick is not to pray to God to rid you of your pain, but to ask for grace to improve the quality of your suffering.

I want to get back to that notion, but first, on this All Saints' Sunday, let us reaffirm what the mind grasps but the heart resists: *death is*

I am grateful to Robert Veninga, author of *A Gift of Hope* (Little, Brown & Co.).—WSC *not the enemy*. Just think: If we didn't move on, who could move in? There'd be no new poets, artists, or composers. It would be all Bach, Telemann, and Scarlatti—no Beethoven, Brahms, or Hindemith. If there were no death, life would be interminable! Deacons and Trustees meetings would never adjourn; graduate students would stay in school forever (which they seem to do anyhow). We'd be as bored as the old Greek gods, and probably up to their same silly tricks. Death cannot be the enemy if it's death that brings us to life. Just as without leave-taking there can be no arrival; without growing old, no growing up; without grounds for despair, no reason for hope, so without death there can be no life. Therefore, let us thank our Creator God that she has so organized things that "all mortal flesh is as the grass."

Let us also reaffirm that death enhances our common life as well as our individual lives. Death is properly called the "great equalizer" not because death makes us equal, but because death mocks our pretensions to being anything else. In the face of death, differences of race, class, and nationality become known for the trivial things they ultimately are.

Now let's get back to the need to improve the quality of our suffering. I am convinced that everything in life represents an opportunity, but alas, when opportunity knocks, most people complain about the noise! Many of you, through your own experience, know that when someone you dearly love dies, your soul goes through many more seasons than the four we ascribe to nature. There is a season of shock, there is a season of sadness. There is also a season of anger when all you want to do is to beat your bloody fists against the bronze doors of heaven, throw another futile appeal over the wall. Then there's a season of peace, and one of hope, and another of despair. And they do not come in orderly fashion, these seasons, they come in a terrible jumble: one day you're sure you're going to make it, the next you're sure you aren't; one hour your heart is light, the next it weighs you down like an anchor.

But if you make it through all these seasons (don't suffer miserably— suffer well, even proudly!) you gradually come to realize that Camus had it right: "In the midst of winter, I finally learned that there was in my heart an invincible summer." You learn to say with Nietzsche, "If it doesn't kill me, it will make me stronger." You understand why Dietrich Bonhoeffer wrote these words that Roger Shinn thoughtfully sent me when my son died:

> Nothing can make up for the absence of someone whom we love. . . . It is nonsense to say that God fills

the gap; he doesn't fill it, but on the contrary, he keeps it empty and so helps us to keep alive our former communion with each other, even at the cost of pain. . . . The dearer and richer our memories, the more difficult the separation. But gratitude changes the pangs of memory into a tranquil joy. The beauties of the past are borne, not as a thorn in the flesh, but as a precious gift in themselves.

"Love bears all things, believes all things, hopes all things, endures all things" (1 Cor. 13:7).

When someone you love dies, remember that the pain you feel is because you have lost someone you want and love—not because the world is unkind and unlovely. And when the world *is* unkind and unlovely, as it is today in Central America, the Middle East, South Africa, and parts of the United States, remember it is *we*, not God, who make it that way. Of all the reactions to the evil and horror of the Holocaust, the one I like best was that of the Jew who insisted there would be no greater mistake, no deeper tragedy than to give up on God and thus do for Hitler what he could not do for himself— destroy Judaism. No posthumous victories for Adolf Hitler!

It's comforting to be bitter about evil—not creative, but comforting. It's also easy to blame everything on a tragedy. But in my experience most people give up on life not because of a tragedy, but because they no longer see joys worth celebrating; they do not see that human life, under any circumstances, never ceases to have meaning. Tragedy offers the opportunity to find new meaning and most of all to reevaluate what's important.

Nan-in, a Japanese Zen master, was visited by a university professor who wanted to learn about his religion. After a while, Nan-in graciously brought tea to his guest. He poured until his visitor's cup was full—and then kept on pouring.

Finally, the professor couldn't restrain, himself. "It's full!" he shouted. "Stop pouring!'

"Like this cup," said Nan-in, "you are full of your opinions. How can I show you Zen unless you first empty your cup?"

Death empties the cup. It renders us available again to all kinds of new truths. A man was consumed by a career that left him lifeless. When his wife died, he finally slowed down. He consciously decided to see and savor all the other wonderful people he had neglected.

It's not what happens that matters, it's how you take it. It's not death that is the enemy, it's resentment and fear of death—mostly fear. To quote Camus again: "There is only one liberty—to come to terms with death." Once the fear of death is put aside—be it the death of someone we love or our own—then, and only then, are we free to engage in life. Fear casts an awfully long shadow, but it shortens as we realize that "whether we live or whether we die, we are the Lord's" (Rom. 14:8), when we realize that "neither death nor life can separate us from the love of God" (Rom. 8:38–39).

So, on this All Saints' Sunday, let us refuse the easy comfort of bitterness. On this Communion Sunday let us bring our wounds to our wounded Lord and healer. Let us remember that those we have loved and lost we can remember with something better than grief. Therefore let us pray God to fill the hollow in the heart with that joy that can absorb all sorrow, that hope that transcends despair, that love that joins all mortal and immortal life, so that we may do as all the saints would have us do: fight the good fight, endure unto the end—yea, become "more than conquerors," until with them we are made partakers of God's eternal Kingdom.

The Noneconomic Uses of Money

NOVEMBER 10, 1985
Readings: Luke 16:13–15; Luke 19:45, 46

I have seen many people die, and some die exceedingly well. Last Sunday—All Saints' Sunday—I wanted very much, because it seemed so appropriate, to read a description of a beautiful death. But there wasn't time. So I thought I would read it today—not to extend our discussion of death, but to focus our attention on life.

> Carolyn Smith returned home. Not to repair relationships, which were in good order. She wanted to say good-bye.
>
> As Carolyn approached her house for the final time she quietly gazed at the surroundings, the landscape, the swing tethered to a large tree. It was a place of serenity. A place of love. A place of quiet strength.

I am grateful to Richard J. Foster, author of *Money, Sex & Power* (Harper & Row), and Donald Krayhill, author of *The Upside Down Kingdom* (Herald Press, 1978).—WSC

She arranged flowers and with the help of a daughter prepared a family meal. She sat in a favorite chair and reread a favorite book. Then she asked to be alone.

Sitting at the kitchen table, Carolyn wrote letters to each of the children, telling them of her love and how happy they had made her. She instructed them to work hard, but to have fun. She wrote to her husband and in the most tender of ways thanked him for a friendship that had spanned twenty-three beautiful years.

The letters were neatly placed in the middle drawer of a desk. A note was attached: "To be read after my death."

An hour later there was a searing pain and a call for help. An ambulance was summoned, and an oxygen mask was placed over her face as the vehicle made its way to the hospital.

With siren blaring the ambulance moved down Highway 12 and onto Interstate 94. But at some point between home and hospital, Carolyn Smith made a decision to die.

Before death came, Carolyn made several requests: The siren was to be turned off. The vehicle was to slow down. The oxygen mask removed. Then she reached out for her husband's hand and grasped it firmly.

In that silent embrace a lasting friendship was affirmed. And in that moment of grace and with an understanding that all business had been completed, she died.*

A lot of people die with regrets, bitter about the past and distraught about the future. And despite what this author says, none of us finishes life with no unfinished business. But we can come close— close enough so that we find, as did Carolyn Smith, that death is not an enemy, or even a stranger, but actually quite friendly.

Much, obviously, depends on how you've led your life, and to lead a good one, you must be tough-minded, prayerful, and exceedingly gentle in handling three things—money, sex, and power. Although the three are distinct, they are closely related. "Money manifests itself

*A Gift of Hope, Robert Veninga (Little, Brown & Co.).—WSC

as power. Sex is used to acquire both money and power. And power is often called the best aphrodisiac" (Richard Foster). Compulsive extravagance is a modern mania; still, it's an old story. The monastic vows of poverty, chastity, and obedience were a direct Christian response to the properly perceived threats of money, sex, and power. What might a modern Christian response be? Maybe three sermons are in order. In any case, here's one on money.

I have been dwelling on money this fall because I am trying to reflect the views of my beloved Lord and Savior, who spent more time talking about money than about any other subject except the Kingdom of God. How to possess money without being possessed by it? Can unrighteous mammon serve the kingdom of righteousness? These questions are terribly hard to answer, because money has power out of all proportion to its purchasing power. The noneconomic uses of money far outweigh the economic ones. Consider, for instance, the fears we all share connected with money. Some people fear not having enough—not only poor people, but people with a car and a house, which puts them immediately in the 98th percentile of the world's citizens. Often their fears are inherited from their parents, who grew up during the Great Depression. Their fears have become their children's fears, without any relationship whatsoever to their children's situation.

Others fear being thought too rich. They fear being too privileged in a world that calls for sacrificial giving.

Keeping up with the Joneses is certainly a noneconomic use of money. And every April we witness the spectacle of those who can best afford to pay taxes being most reluctant to do so. They will give to charity—some of these rich people—because they are generous, and also because charity reinforces the notion that their money is power—whereas taxes are like Delilah's shears, cutting at the root of their strength to reveal the underlying weakness.

It's the noneconomic uses of money that make money so complicated, even demonic. Jesus saw the demonic side when he personalized and spiritualized money, when he saw money as a rival god capable of inspiring great devotion. "You cannot serve God and mammon"—the Aramaic word for wealth, money, profit, and property. Note that only money is put on a par with God. Not knowledge, not family nobility, not reputation, not talent: only money is elevated to divine status. No wonder Jesus talked more about money than about any other subject except the Kingdom of God. ("Woe to you who are rich" [Luke 6:24]; "it is easier for a camel to pass through the eye of a needle than for a rich [person] to enter the Kingdom of Heaven"

[Matt. 19:24]; "Take heed, and beware of all covetousness" [Luke 12:15]; "Do not store up treasure on earth . . . but store up treasures in heaven" [Matt. 6:19, 20].)

If you've ever watched a child at Christmas become totally absorbed with a new toy, you've seen a wonderful sight. But it's not so wonderful when adults become so captivated by material pursuits that these begin to dominate their lives. Then you can see that God and wealth are not bed partners. Wealth can be used to serve God—witness in the New Testament the stories of Zacchaeus, Nicodemus, and Joseph of Arimathea—but an addict to material things is no servant of God. And in case you don't think this addiction common, consider this: None of us wants to go broke, but "the reason we find being broke so unthinkable is because our culture finds it unthinkable, not because it's unchristian. After all, Jesus was himself completely broke, and he told the rich young ruler to go and get himself the same way" (John F. Alexander).

I'm not suggesting we go broke, although doing it in the right way has proved liberating to many more than St. Francis of Assisi. But we must break with a culture that's gone bananas over money. It's a deeply religious matter. "No servant can serve two masters; for either he will hate the one and love the other, or he will be devoted to the one and despise the other. You cannot serve God and mammon."

In the second Gospel story, the merchants in the temple were exchanging money for offerings and selling animals for sacrifice at a profit. They were doing nothing illegal. Yet Jesus found the practice immoral, and called them robbers for concocting a system that bilked the poor—and in the name of religion to boot. Once again we see cultural values inversely related to the ways of God. What is exalted among people is an abomination in the sight of God.

So, dearly beloved, what do we do in order not to become as seed that fell among the thorns—not to grow up choked by the cares and riches of life? How are we to be as the lilies of the field—beautiful and carefree, with property perhaps, but with no excessive concern for its protection and value? When will we learn that our pocketbooks have more to do with heaven and hell than our hymnbooks? And finally, when will the churches give social justice the same due accorded charity? (Marxists have long accused Christians of having a vested interest in unjust structures, which produce victims to whom we then can pour out our hearts in charity.)

In the bosom of our families, in our house churches, with our close friends—and, I would suggest, on a church-wide retreat—the first thing to do is to talk together about our noneconomic uses of money. We must be able to air and not suppress our fears. That's why we have to be tough-minded, prayerful, and gentle—gentle because these fears are very real, and gentle because there's no reason to be more sympathetic to someone seduced by sex than to someone seduced by money.

Then we must call on our Christian convictions. The choir has twice sung today from Mendelssohn's *Elijah*: "Cast thy burden upon the Lord; and he shall sustain thee"; "For he will give his angels charge over thee . . . lest thou dash thy foot against a stone." Do we believe those reassuring lines or do we say of our money, our pocketbooks, and our property, "My refuges and my fortress; my God, in whom I trust"?

And what about "our" property? If you've ever agreed to house-sit (or apartment-sit), you know how aware you are at all times of the absent person. Every picture, every plate, and every pot calls the owner to mind. Likewise, every stick of property we own should remind us—gratefully—of the ultimate owner of everything. Then our property makes us more aware of God, not less aware. Then, and only then, are we truly free to enjoy, because we have no fear of losing. You've heard the William Blake quatrain:

> He who bends to himself a joy
> Doth the winged life destroy.
> But he who kisses a joy as it flies
> Dwells in Eternity's sunrise.

So free from possessiveness was John Wesley that when he heard fire had razed his house to the ground, he exclaimed, "The Lord's house has burned. One less responsibility for me." If our heads are screwed on right, if we are straightened away on the question of ownership, we never ask, "How much of my money should I give to God?" but rather, "How much of God's money should I keep for myself?"

Despite its outrageous prices, New York City is a great place to experience what St. Paul described as "having nothing, and yet possessing everything." I told this story last summer, but it's too good not to repeat. Paddy Chayefsky of blessed memory was a neurotic urbanite if there ever was one, and a passionate lover of this crazy city. On first meeting Arthur Miller he said, "Now let's see, Mr. Miller. You live in the country, right?"

"Yes, in Connecticut."

"Do you like it?"

"Yes, I like it fine."

"Tell me—what do you do when you want to take a walk?"

Chayefsky knew that no sights and sounds in the Connecticut countryside could be compared to those seen and heard of a Sunday afternoon in Central Park; he knew that no neighborhoods in Connecticut topped Little Italy, Little Russia, Harlem, Chinatown, or Greenwich Village; and he knew that nowhere in the world was there a 25-cent view comparable to that seen at sunset from the Staten Island ferry looking back at lower Manhattan. "Having nothing, and yet possessing everything": There is so much that is so wonderful and costs so little in this sink of iniquity, this adrenalin capital of the world, that New York is also a kind of Garden of Eden.

Comparisons are odious, we are told. Not true! Only the wrong comparisons are odious; the right ones are healthy. You and I may have trouble balancing our budgets, but as world citizens we are among the wealthiest. We should never forget that—and always be grateful. That comparison should also help us to see the irrationality of so many of our fears. That people who earn twenty times the average income of a citizen of Kenya should be afraid of being on the brink of starvation is crazy! And Kenyans and other Third World folk—like the poor, the bruised, and the broken at home—should also remind us that our charity, for all its importance, is no substitute for God's justice. It's not the Golden Mean but the Golden Rule we are summoned to obey. If our education is important to us, and God grant that it is, we must at least make it available to others. If hospitals have saved our lives, health care must do no less for everyone. If giving is life-saving, then poor folk everywhere must be accorded the same life-saving opportunity. If Jesus attacked economic systems that rob the poor, it is not our job to promote such systems.

In this country, that means two things. First, as Christians, we must not hold jobs that serve injustice, including jobs that take precious resources away from the needy and use them for military aims or trivial pursuits. (I wish I could inscribe on half the offices in this city Bromily's law: What's not worth doing is not worth doing well.) Second, as William Blake sought to eliminate the "dark Satanic Mills" of 19th-century England, so we, with like fervor, must seek the elimination of all that's unjust in our own country. I love these verses of his:

> Bring me my bow of burning gold,
> Bring me my arrows of desire,
> Bring me my spear, O clouds unfold,
> Bring me my chariot of fire.
>
> I will not cease from mental fight
> Nor shall my sword sleep in my hand

Til we have built Jerusalem
In England's green and pleasant land.

As earth chauvinists, we must mean what we just sang:

Earth shall be fair and all her people one
Nor til that hour shall God's whole will be done.

The more we do God's will, the less unfinished business we leave behind when we die. If our lives exemplify personal charity and the pursuit of social justice, then death will not be the enemy, but rather the friendly angel leading us on to the One whose highest hope is to be able to say to each and every one of us, "Well done, thou good and faithful servant; enter into the joy of the Master." "Whoever clings to me in love, I will deliver. I will protect the one who knows my name." "No servant can serve two masters. . . . You cannot serve God and mammon." Friends, what choice have we but to return God's love with our own?

The Love of Power

NOVEMBER 17, 1985
Readings: Genesis 1–9; Luke 18:9–14

On my more depressed days I occasionally think that this beloved city has about as much future as the man who, acting upon instructions, called his doctor to get the results of his tests. There was a hesitation on the other end of the line; then the doctor said, "There's bad news and worse news."

The man said, "Well, give me the bad news first."

"The tests gave you 24 hours to live."

"Oh, my God, what news could possibly be worse than that?"

"I tried to reach you yesterday."

But why pick on New York? The whole country seems bent on making Isaac Bashevis Singer's point: God was frugal in bestowing intellect, but lavish with passions and emotions. Anywhere you can

I am grateful to Richard J. Foster, author of *Money, Sex & Power* (HarperCollins), and Jacques Ellul, author of *Money & Power* (InterVarsity Press).—WSC

see the horrors as well as the glories of that holy/unholy trinity of money, power, and sex. Everywhere you can observe the noneconomic uses of money, its power far out of proportion to its purchasing power. Still, our money and property can make us more, not less, aware of God if they keep recalling to our minds our banker and landlord of ultimate resort. As it is written, "The earth is the Lord's and the fulness thereof" (Ps. 24:1).

Last Wednesday I was visited by my former preaching professor, Brown Barr, who recently retired from a seminary on the West Coast. He said he wanted to return to the soil that had so nourished his childhood, so he and his wife bought a small farm north of San Francisco. Now, in times of harvest, Professor Barr puts all the produce from the farm beyond the needs of himself and his wife in the back of his pickup truck and drives it 70 miles south to a small Christian commune, whose members then distribute it to the needy in the inner-city neighborhood where they live and work. In his retirement, Professor Barr has simplified his life in order to enjoy the luxury of doing good. Praise the Lord!

Today, as Ronald Reagan and Mikhail Gorbachev prepare to meet one another, it seems appropriate to talk of the uses and abuses of money's kissing cousin, power.

The sin of Adam and Eve had nothing to do with sex and everything to do with power. It all took place, you remember, at the foot of the tree of knowledge. But it was not for the sake of knowledge that Adam and Eve took the apple—they wanted power: to know more, to have more, to be more. "Surely you will be as gods," tempted the serpent, and they jumped at the chance, just as the Adam and Eve in each of us jumps at the chance to seek status through power.

King Saul had boundless power, but power cannot command the hearts of the people; their hearts went out to David. Furious, Saul twice tried to pin David to the wall with his spear. Don't we all feel something akin to Saul's anger when we hear something similar to the chant that came to his ears: "Saul has killed his thousands and David his ten thousands"? And this is true even though we know that of the so-called seven deadly sins, only envy has no gratification whatsoever. Gluttony and lust have immediate if not ultimate forms of gratification, but envy—nothing.

In the wilderness, Satan tempted Jesus with three variants of power: material power, imperial power, and the power of magic. We should probably add another. Malcolm Muggeridge once suggested that if Christ were to go into the wilderness today, Satan would have for him a fourth temptation—an appearance on national television.

Think of the disciples. Could any scene in Scriptures be less edify-ing than that of them arguing bitterly among themselves as to who would be greatest in the Kingdom of God? There's a comparable but more dangerous spectacle to be seen today, that of the nations vying to be number one, only not in the Kingdom of God but in the eyes of Satan. They are not vying to be number one in terms of wisdom or decency, which would have some merit—no, solely in terms of mil-itary power, and this at a time when we live between two holocausts, when all the people on the planet live on the target of World War III, when the whole world is as a prisoner in a cell awaiting the uncertain moment of execution.

In collective form, the love of power is lethal. The hatred of the Ku Klux Klan is so much greater than the sum of its parts. You remem-ber how the power of racism joined with the power of imperialism in the Third Reich, which Hitler predicted would last a thousand years. Like the builders of the tower of Babel, the Nazis sought to construct a from-here-to-eternity edifice. Both the builders of Babel and the Nazis, lusting for power, tried to storm the ramparts of heaven. Com-pare them with the disciples, now chastened, gathered at Pentecost allowing heaven to take them by storm.

It's Babel versus Pentecost: the power of love versus the love of power. Do not say that love is powerless, or that powerless love is no match for loveless power. The Third Reich lasted all of thirteen years. God is not mocked, and people will not passively endure a govern-ment that is in fact unendurable. Rather believe what is written in the Bible: "Many waters cannot quench love"; "Love is stronger than death" (Song 8:6); "Love never ends" (1 Cor. 13:8); "For I am persuaded that neither death nor life, nor principalities, nor power, nor things pres-ent, nor things to come, nor height, nor depth, nor any other creature can separate us from the love of God which is in Christ Jesus our Lord" (Rom. 8:38–39). And Christ Jesus our Lord in Gethsemane could have summoned ten thousand angels to his aid, but he chose instead to suffer an ignominious death on the cross. Yet all the armies that ever marched, all the navies that ever sailed, all the nuclear weapons stock-piled today the world around have not so influenced humanity as did that one human being whose sole possession at death was a robe.

Let's turn now from the destructive to the creative uses of power, from the love of power to the power of love. Of course this power is never pure in our sullied lives. I don't think any of us does anything for one reason alone. I know a preacher who once stood at the door of the church in what we call "an ecclesiastical hold-up" at the end of the service. One parishioner as he went by murmured, "Oh, Reverend, it was such a wonderful sermon." The preacher murmured back, "Yes, I know, the devil just told me."

I also know a man who was awarded an honorary degree. During the commencement address (Emily Dickinson once termed them "the sophistries of June"), the speaker noted how small was the number of truly great people. That night, as our new "doctor," *causa honoris*, was preparing for bed, he mused aloud to his wife, "I wonder how many truly great people there are." To which she replied, "One less than you think."

Humility means objectivity, a realistic sense of worth, and above all a recognition that just as all light streams from the heavens, so whatever is good is of God. I remember reading of William Blake backing off from a completed picture insisting, "Not I," reminiscent of St. Paul's "Not I, but Christ who dwells within me" (Gal. 2:20).

The difference between creative and destructive power is apparent in relationships. Creative power enhances all relationships, destructive power destroys them. The parable of the Prodigal Son is really the story of a loving father who used his power to wait for, rather than dominate, his son. All parents naturally want to shape the will of their children, but loving ones do so without breaking their children's spirit. Loving teachers prod without demeaning; they cultivate growth, not inferiority. Christ used power to nurture confidence in his disciples, not subservience. Likewise employers should promote in their employees feelings of competence, not of inadequacy. You remember that Jesus said, "You know that the rulers of the Gentiles lord it over them. . . . It shall not be so among you." Any boss who promotes feelings of inadequacy displays a need to control. When you seek power over others, you're losing it over yourself. Aren't you always stunned at Jesus' utter lack of need to control? He healed with no strings attached.

Here's something else that's amazing. In the book of Acts we read that in the town of Joppa, Tabitha, a woman "full of good works and acts of charity," fell sick and died. The disciple Peter was summoned and raised her from the dead. Then we read that Peter "stayed in Joppa for many days with one Simon, a tanner," a man who was practically an outcast, as Jewish law considered his practice defiling.

I don't know about you, but were I to raise someone from the dead, I'd be on national television, I'd take a speaking tour and write a book; that is, unless—and this is a very remote possibility—I remembered St. Augustine's warning, "Anyone who needs more than God as his witness is too ambitious."

What if someone—a parent, your boss—is running roughshod over you? Do you bleed silently? If you possibly can, do not let others abuse or misuse you. Subservience is no service to anyone. Only don't "stand up for your rights"—you've already got them, given by God. Nobody can take them from you; God tells you who you are. All you have to do is to ask for the same respect due any child of God. And from time to time, check yourself out with this line from *Othello*: "Thou hast not half that power to do me harm as I have to be hurt."

Earlier I said harsh words about nations vying with one another to be number one purely in terms of military power. Christians, all of us, are called, in the old Quaker phrase, to speak truth to power. But alas, "many are called but most are frozen." Silence in these matters in these days in the workplace is inexcusable. I personally am tired of hearing pastors say, "Well, I don't involve myself in things controversial. I'm not a prophet, but I'm a good pastor"—as if the Cold War weren't chilling warm Christian hearts, as if homosexuality, or rather homophobia, wasn't a thorn in the flesh of the churches.

For years, the Cold War has been an unmitigated disaster for warm Christian hearts. Let me give you an analogy: Suppose you picked up the *Times* this morning and read that the Police Commissioner of New York City, tired of conventional methods of fighting crime, had come up with a new form of deterrence—to wit, the Police Commissioner announced that hereafter the Police Department was going to round up and kill any relative and every last friend and acquaintance of anyone who committed murder within city limits from now on. You'd be appalled. Crime in the streets is bad enough, but such a response is equally immoral, particularly when you wonder how many friends, how many relatives and acquaintances would have anything to say about the decision to commit murder. That is an analogy for deterrence, except that in deterrence the hostage system is massive. We have not said (nor have the Soviets) that we will kill only those who push the button. We have not said we will kill only Party members, we have not said we will kill only those in uniform. No, we've announced loudly and clearly that we will wipe out every last father, mother, and child in the Soviet Union—and if the wind happens to be blowing north to south, watch it south of the border. Imagine thinking that's a civilized way of doing the world's business!

The Cold War has been an unmitigated disaster for warm Christian hearts, breeding in them twin evils, self-righteousness and fear. We heard how the Pharisee in Jesus' parable prayed, "God, I thank thee that I am not as other [people] are, extortioners, unjust, adulterers." The Cold War has taught American Christians to pray, "God, we thank thee that our nation is not as other nations are, atheist, Communist, imperialist." Could anything be more atheist than a Trident submarine, which in one hour can kill many times over the six million Jews exterminated in the course of the six years of World War II? We Americans tend to judge other nations by their actions, ours by our ideals. They arm, it's evil; we arm, it's necessary for national security.

The Cold War is a disaster because fear is a disaster. It's not for nothing that Scripture insists, "Perfect love casts out fear." I don't mean reasonable caution but irrational fear, the kind that produces ever more hideous weapons, that produces more insecurity, not less; that causes a nation to sacrifice its freedom for the sake of its security, its poor for more and more arms, God for the sake of Satanic power, visionary love for blind hatred. As if anticipating Soviet-American relations, Yeats wrote:

> We fed the heart on fantasies,
> The heart's grown brutal from the fare;
> More substance in our enmities
> Than in our love.

For those reasons and many more, we must pray hard this week for President Reagan and Secretary Gorbachev, that they may take to heart the words of the poet—and these too of St. Augustine: "Imagine the vanity of thinking your enemy can do you more damage than your enmity!" We have to pray mightily that the power of love will overcome the love of power.

The Ultimate Optimism

DECEMBER 8, 1985
Readings: Isaiah 11:1–10; Luke 1:46–55

St. Paul wrote the Romans, "May the God of hope give you joy and peace in believing, so that by the power of the Holy Spirit you may abound in hope" (15:13). Two things, I suspect, keep most of us going: a healthy will to live, which surely is one of the finest of animal instincts; and a confidence, naive or informed, that life has meaning. Many people cannot define the meaning of life, but simply live in

---

This sermon owes much to Reinhold Niebuhr's "Optimism, Pessimism, and Religious Faith," found in *The Essential Reinhold Niebuhr* (Yale University Press, 1986).—WSC

trust that it's there. They don't think much about the larger issues. Theirs is a simple optimism.

But the more people do think, the more they find their simple optimism challenged. Thinking people can see the grand nobility in a mountain range, the beauty in the human body; but they also see "nature red in tooth and claw." Thinking people appreciate the school and courthouse—symbols of reason, knowledge, and individual freedom—not to mention the New England meeting house on the town common symbolizing a fusion, not of church and state, but of politics and ethics. But thinking people can't help suspecting that the story of their lives and the history of the race could be more honestly described if the stomach, rather than the head, were taken as the point of departure. And whose faith doesn't waver when she surveys and analyzes the chaos, death, destruction, and misery that seem to deny our simple trust in the harmony and meaningfulness of life? In short, the more people think, the more they tend toward pessimism. Here is a famous expression of such pessimism.

> Brief and powerless is man's life. On him and all his race the slow sure doom sinks pitiless and dark. Blind to good and evil, omnipotent matter rolls on its relentless way. For man, condemned today to lose his dearest, tomorrow himself to pass through the gates of darkness, it remains only to cherish ere yet the blow falls, the lofty thoughts that ennoble his little day, proudly defiant of the resistible forces which tolerate for a moment his knowledge, and his condemnation, to sustain alone, a weary and unyielding Atlas, the world that his own ideas have fashioned despite the trampling march of unconscious power. (Bertrand Russell)

Hope—the word emblazoned on the banner we carried on high above and before the choir at the beginning of the service—the Christian hope we so want once again to celebrate this Advent season must be seen as an ultimate optimism that takes into account all the evil and sorrow which make people tend to the pessimism expressed so movingly in the above words of Bertrand Russell.

We need, of course, always to remember how much of the evil we suffer is the price of freedom, which makes it possible for us to sin. Living as we do under the heavy hammerings of history, we are tempted, like the long-suffering ancient Israelites, to lift our eyes to heaven with the psalmist's anguished question, "How long, O Lord, how long?" At those moments, we must remember that is precisely the question the Lord is addressing to us: "How long, O my wayward children, how long?"

That almost every inch of the earth's surface is soaked today with the tears and blood of the innocent is not God's fault, it is our own. God doesn't make people poor; rich folk do that. God doesn't discriminate against Blacks; that's the work of white heartlessness. God doesn't go around with his foot to the floorboard, his fist wrapped around knives, his finger on triggers. God doesn't abuse women and small children, any more than God builds Trident submarines.

"God is love," proclaims the Gospel, and love remains the law of life even when people refuse to live by the law of love. So it has always been. The Creation story tells of a God who, when she made the world, "saw" that it was good," and loved it. The Incarnation we await reaffirms the goodness of the earth and the sanctity of humanity. The Annunciation announces the good news that there is more mercy in God than sin in us. Our sin is covered—nothing is unredeemed or unredeemable. And the Magnificat repeats the promise of the prophets that justice will roll down like mighty waters; that "the wolf shall lie down with the kid. . . . They shall not hurt or destroy in all my holy mountain, for the earth shall be full of the knowledge of the Lord as the waters cover the sea" (Isa. 11:6, 9).

Still, there is much evil in the world that we cannot explain. The bubonic plague of 1348, the influenza pandemic of 1918, the AIDS of the eighties, crib death, the birth of retarded children—name your own particular form of unexplained evil that you yourself have had to endure. The inexplicable suffering of innocent people assails, like nothing else, our faith in the goodness of God. We can only trust where we cannot see, refuse to condemn what we don't comprehend, remembering that Christ stood by the sufferers and healed wherever he could. And never, never, in all honesty, forget the other side of the equation—the unmerited grace that fills each day. What did you and I ever do to merit the blue of today's sky, the purity of God's air unpolluted by human greed, the vase of flowers on the kitchen table, and a pot of fresh, strong coffee?

What we can hold against God is freedom itself. Sometimes I think it's more than we can handle. If you give a small child an expensive watch and the child smashes it, who is at fault? But the answer from the Lord always comes back: "Love is the name of my game, and I cannot play it without giving you your freedom."

The fact of death we cannot hold against God. That we want so much to live is a tribute to the goodness of the life that God has given us. And the very brevity of life exalts the glory of God—at least that's the way the psalmist saw it when he wrote: "For a thousand years in thy sight are but as yesterday when it is past and as a watch in the night" (Ps. 90:4).

Our hope is based on our faith that "neither death nor life can separate us from the love of God in Christ Jesus our Lord." But Christian hope is primarily for *this* world. It is the hope of the ancient Israelites who could still believe in God though Judah be carried off into captivity. It is the hope of Mary who had to bring her child into a world where the rich were greedy and nations were crazed with power. (Not much really changes.) And she could bring Him into the world in a place dingier than a New York men's shelter, still recognizing the infinite possibilities with which divine life is fraught.

> He has shown strength with his arm,
> he has scattered the proud in the imagination of their hearts,
> he has put down the mighty from their thrones,
> and exalted those of low degree;
> he has filled the hungry with good things,
> and the rich he has sent empty away.
>
> Luke 1:51–53

Mary was not wrong to expect so much from the child in her womb. And we were not wrong earlier to sing, "Come, thou long-expected Jesus, born to set thy people free," any more than Bishop Tutu is not wrong to say, "There is no doubt we are going to be free— whether you help us or not—for the God we worship is the Exodus God who leads his people always out of bondage into freedom."

Hope is the certainty that God will make good the promise of life. Hope is an acorn dreaming its future. Wrote Meister Eckhart: "Pear seeds grow into pear trees; nut seeds into nut trees; and God seeds into God." The seed of God was in the womb of Mary, and Jesus grew into God. The love of God is implanted in the heart of each of us, assuring us that love is the law of life. It is what gives us our image of reality. Hope is an image of the ultimate potential in any particular form of life. Hope is the reflection of the future while the future is still in the womb of potentiality. So hope, understood by Christians, is no mere mist hanging over a marshy land. Hope is the ultimate optimism.

So, friends, let us view our finitude as something acceptable and good. It is death that after all brings us to life and exalts the life of God. With St. Francis let us say, "Praised be my Lord for our sister the death of the body from which no one escapeth."

Let us see further that the tortures and agonies through which our generation is only the latest to go represent the inevitable judgment upon people and nations that refuse to live by the law of love.

Let us see that hope does not prevent tragedy, but prevents tragedy from being pure tragedy. In every misfortune there is a miracle of grace sufficient to enable us to say with St. Paul, "perplexed, but not driven to despair, struck down, but not destroyed."

And let us allow hope to fulfill its intention to stimulate ethical vigor. May it nerve us to exhaust all our resources in building a better world, in overcoming human strife, in mitigating the fury of our inhumanity one toward another, and in establishing a society with minimum security for all: "May the God of hope fill you with all joy and peace in believing so that by the power of the Holy Spirit you may abound in hope."

God Bless the Cheerful

DECEMBER 22, 1985
Reading: Matthew 1:18–25

Well, preacher, having talked of hope and love over the last two weeks, today you're going to tell us that our hearts should thrill and rejoice; you're going to talk to us of joy—yes, in a world almost doubled over with hunger and with violence."

If any of you have been harboring that suspicion, you are absolutely correct: God bless the cheerful, for they cheer everyone else! But not for a moment am I suggesting that anyone become a "chirping optimist" (as Carlyle once called Emerson). There's no point in saying "All's well" in an unwell world; that may make for pleasant dreams but also for a rather rude awakening. My point is simply to remind us all that two days hence in English-speaking countries, millions of Africans, Indians, Austrians, New Zealanders, British, Canadians, and Americans—millions of us will sing Isaac Watts' great hymn (music attributed to Handel), "Joy to the world, the Lord is come." When you sing it, remember the words do not go climbing up the octave, rather, they come tumbling down. It is not earthly, but heavenly joy we will be celebrating on Christmas Eve. Like heavenly hope, heavenly joy can absorb all the evil and the sorrows of this world that turn people's hearts and minds to pessimism and despair. Heaven is only heaven if it can be found and affirmed in the depths of hell.

We are what our most cherished thoughts make us. If what you treasure most are thoughts heavy laden with anxiety, you're really not available for much joy of any kind. Worry is interest paid on trouble before it is due. Think of it that way, and it's really dumb to worry.

It's also hard to be joyful if you're running around like a squirrel when the acorns come, about to suffer from burnout. Intensity that burns for a long time can make charcoal out of you. Prayer, rest, contemplation, fun are the called-for remedies.

You can't be joyful if you are too demanding—that is, if you demand more than you love. If you can bring yourself to love more and demand less, you'll be a lot happier.

Obviously you can't be joyful if you're a whiner, one of those who whimper away their gift of laughter, who nurse a lurking anger at the whole world, on the razor's edge of enjoying their own misery.

The same is true of grievance-nursers. You know how it is: You're barely awake in the morning, your eyes are still shut, and the first thing that comes into your mind is your garden of grievances. You reach for the rake and you reach for the hoe, and before you've even opened your eyes all those weeds are just doing fine.

I mentioned the possibility of disillusionment. The disillusioned eat too much bitterness. These are the folk who were taught—and must have wanted to believe—that if you sow courtesy, you reap friendship; if you plant kindness, you gather love; when people speak ill of you, you have only to behave in such a manner that others won't believe them. But that's not the way it works much of the time. Goodness of heart can't blunt cold steel. If we're disillusioned, it's our fault; no one gave us the right to have illusions in the first place.

And, finally, it's hard to be joyful if you have what we might call a roadblock mentality, if you're always fighting change and growth. Here are some sentences written over one hundred years ago: "New times demand new measures and new people; the world advances, and in time outgrows the laws that in our fathers' day were best; and doubtless after us, some purer scheme will be shaped by wiser ones than we, made wiser by the steady growth of truth."

If those words have a slightly familiar, ring, you're right. Their author, James Russell Lowell, translated them later into a famous hymn whose second verse includes the sentence:

New occasions teach new duties,
Time makes ancient good uncouth;
They must upward still and onward,
Who would keep abreast of truth.

I repeat, we are what our most cherished thoughts make us. If you are not feeling joyful, examine your thoughts. Perhaps you might even change them. For instance, in place of worry you can find joy in the uncertainty of things. I think it's wonderful that we never know for certain what a day has waiting for us. We are never quite safe from being surprised until we are dead. And what surprises, what wonders there are in store for us every day! Say the mystics: "Open your eyes and the whole world is full of God" (Jacob Boehme).

"When I consider the heavens, the work of thy fingers, the moon and the stars which Thou hast ordained . . ." (Psalm 8).

O world invisible, we view thee.
O world intangible, we touch thee.
O world unknowable, we know thee.
. . . .
The angels keep their ancient places;
Turn but a stone, and start a wing.
'Tis ye, with your estranged faces
That miss the many-splendoured thing.
                              Francis Thompson

Should not such heaven-sent joys return us daily to the one fixed point to which we cling: God is good? To the heart full of gratitude the world is full of beauty. All of which is not for a moment to deny that the world is almost doubled up with hunger and with violence, but only to reiterate that the fault is ours, not God's. And if we were to do God's bidding, the benefits of civilization could today be made available to the whole human race. That, I submit, is one of the most important characterizations of the world in which we live.

But how does divine joy unite with human pain? Try to recall some moment of confusion and agony, some time in your life when you suffered intensely. In such moments there is nothing more important than the presence of someone who cares. (Not for nothing do they say, "A joy shared is a double joy, a sorrow shared is half a sorrow.") It's not important that the person say anything. In fact, often it is better if they do not speak; any effort to cheer you up or give you advice you will probably experience as a refusal to enter into your suffering.

Emmanuel—which means "God with us"—is just such a presence, a constant, caring presence of such sensitivity that only of Jesus can you say, "He knows exactly what I'm going through." "Nobody knows the trouble I've seen, nobody knows but Jesus"—to which we can only respond, "Glory, halleluia."

And Emmanuel—God with us—comes to earth because God so loved the world that he wanted to send his hope and love not only to us as individuals, but to whole communities of people like the homeless, whose numbers, we read, are now growing in the suburbs. (This city is beginning to resemble the Middle Ages, with half the people walking around wrapped in furs and the other half wrapped in newspapers.) God is trying at Christmas to send His hope and love to the homeless and the exiled, to the tortured, to the deported, to the silenced; to the vast Latin American and South African majorities so dispossessed as to live as aliens in their own countries. Who but Jesus, a homeless child about to be exiled, could bring them any semblance of comfort, a touch of heavenly joy in their earthly sorrow?

Christ's presence is comfort itself in tragedy; it is also forgiveness in sin. "And His name shall be called Jesus because he will save [us] from [our] sins" (Matt. 1:21). Let God make you a Christmas present of forgiveness. Let God give you a fresh start, new hope, a renewed capacity for laughter and for love.

Christ's presence is also felt in happiness, undergirding earthly joys with heavenly meaning. The Emmanuel we await is no John the Baptist eating locusts in the desert. Jesus will be called a glutton and a drunkard. He parties. He changes water into wine. He is a man of happiness as well as a man of sorrows and acquainted with grief, because the greater the capacity to grieve, the greater the capacity for happiness. Gloomy Christians are not Christian at all. They are people who have struck some kind of dull bargain with life: in order not to feel too badly about some things, they won't feel good about anything. And they have the nerve to call this emotional mediocrity "the good life!"

Heavenly joy really has little to do with happiness or unhappiness and everything to do with meaning and fulfillment. Didn't Paul write of Jesus that "for the joy that was set before him, he endured the cross despising the shame" (Heb. 12:2)? It's paradoxical and true. Jesus knew joy because he knew that the great purpose of life was to spend it for something that outlasts it. (And aren't saints only sinners who keep on trying?) That brings us back to the love embodied in the child in the manger, the love that is of God, the love that "bears all things, believes all things, hopes all things, endures all things" (1 Cor. 13:7). It is in being loved and in loving that we find life's deepest meaning, a meaning we can affirm in the face of tragedies we cannot fathom and in the face of human stupidities we can understand all too well. Love, and you are a success whether or not the world thinks so. The highest purpose of Christianity—which is primarily a way of life, not a system of belief—is to help people love one another. And the first fruit of love is joy, the joy that represents meaning and fulfillment.

So God bless the cheerful, may their tribe increase! They cheer everyone else. Dearly beloved of the Lord, may your Christmas be full of promise, of hope, of love, and of joy past compare. And may our time together always be one in which we are present one to another in tragedy, in sin, and in happiness, as God was, is, and always will be present with us. For his name is Emmanuel, which means "God with us."

December 22, 1985

1986

"The Tooth That Nibbles at the Soul"

JANUARY 5, 1986
Reading: Matthew 2:1–12

If we ask "What made the wise men wise?"—which is not a bad question to ask in a world preoccupied with what makes tough men tough—one possible answer is, "Because they knew that wisdom and worship are inseparable, they go hand in hand." When they saw Jesus, the wise men "fell down and worshipped him."

I can understand people who find the idea of joining a church infinitely resistible. (In a world already too full of restrictions, who needs a cramped version of Christianity?) I can understand people who doubt the quality of the bread. (When people say they don't believe in God and you ask them to describe the God they don't believe in, they generally describe an omnipotent, loveless God you wouldn't believe in either.) What I cannot understand is kidding yourself that you are not hungry. Isn't life more than a brief transition between two oblivions? Both wisdom and worship start from the conviction that there must be something more. Both recognize that mystery is a fact of life, that time, space, life itself, like God, are wonders and miracles in and of themselves. Moreover, wisdom and worship recognize that if we do not look for something above us, we soon sink to something below us, for it is hard to believe in the dreams and powers that we hardly suspect ourselves to possess.

So we need to worship, we who rush around like squirrels when the acorns fall. We need to worship, we who subordinate our lives to our jobs and thereby condemn our souls, we who are lonely to the point that our loneliness devours such little faith as we have. This nation that refuses to recognize mutual vulnerability as an irremovable condition of our existence and considers such acknowledgment to be simply an inadmissible loss of nerve—this nation, and every nation and every individual that tries to go it alone in this world is in need of worship. God is, we are, and in that relationship is the basis of all life.

Whom do the wise men in their wisdom seek to worship? The other day I heard someone say, "I only come to church to hear that

Jesus loves me." That certainly is a good reason to come to church; we all need reassurance. But faith is not the same as reassurance, and to find the truth of God the wise men had to take a long journey through a world as muddled and confused as our own. How often we pray, "O God, guide my footsteps"—then never move our feet. Faith spells seeking, sincere, arduous seeking. The manger, after all, was the last place in the world anybody expected to find the truth of God. We can't go to church just to be reassured. The poet warned:

> Much gesture from the pulpit,
> Strong hallelujahs roll.
> Narcotics cannot still the tooth
> That nibbles at the soul.
> Emily Dickinson

Christians cannot buy the whole rag-bag of Christianity. Like a mighty river, the history of the church carries with it the silt of its past. One reason why so many people do not believe in God is that so many of us Christians believed in crusades and inquisitions, the burning of books by Puritans, the blessing of bombs by bishops. Christians still believe horrendous things, and not so much because the Bible says them as because all religions find their form within existing cultures and have constantly to be set free of them. And the Bible is not God, the Bible is not absolute. We worship the Word made flesh, not the Word made words. Nor is the greater truth we find in the person of Jesus honored by ignoring truth we find elsewhere.

Of course, we come to church to be reassured that God loves us. But we also come, as did the wise men to the manger, to reassure God of our love, and to bring to the Christ child our best gifts. We come to church because it is so hard, in a muddled, confused world seemingly set on a certain and devastating end, to know and to do the will of God. We all know how hard it is not to rush around like squirrels, not to subordinate our lives to our jobs, not to sink to something below us. But try we must, if we are going to make God believable and desirable for others, and if we are to become what God so wants us to be—simply, beautifully, radiantly, friends and followers of Jesus.

Fortunately, we have the example of the wise men who, in their wisdom and perseverance, followed the star until they found the Word of God lying in a manger. And there, "They fell down and worshipped him."

After Christmas

JANUARY 12, 1986

Reading: 1 Corinthians 1:25–31

At the beginning of the service we sang one of Charles Wesley's six thousand hymns, so many of which are prayer hymns addressed directly to God or to Jesus. One line we sang went, "Dayspring from on high, be near; Daystar, in my heart appear." We've also heard an anthem that recalls Christmas, not because we want to go back to Christmas—that poor sacred season has become an exhausting secular marathon—but because we want to go forward *from* Christmas, forward to see how the incarnation of Christ says altogether as much about what we are to become as about what God has already become. So we sang:

> Visit, then, this soul of mine;
> Pierce the gloom of sin and grief;
> Fill me, Radiancy divine,
> Scatter all my unbelief.
>
> Charles Wesley

Let's start with unbelief, by pondering for a moment God's way of appearing to be less than God really is. What could be more ordinary than a child born in poverty and obscurity? What could be more common than a young man growing up unrecognized, than a man entering an ancient city on a donkey, than a prisoner standing with a cauliflower ear and a split lip refusing to answer the false accusations of a judge? What, alas, could be more commonplace than a prophet adored by some but misunderstood, silenced, and finally executed by the majority? I mean, "Who has believed what we have heard? And to whom has the arm of the Lord been revealed? For he was despised and rejected by men; a man of sorrows, and acquainted with grief; and as one from whom men hide their faces he was despised, and we esteemed him not" (Isa. 53:1, 3).

Why does God do something like that? Why does God choose "what is low and despised in the world, even things that are not, to bring to nothing the things that are"? Is Paul right? Is God, in his weakness, stronger than we in our strength?

This sermon owes a great deal to Bryan Rippin's *The Christian Juggler* (Epworth Press, London).—WSC

Could it be that God does this because all saving ideas are born small—like a mustard seed rather than a clanging cymbal? Could it be because we want God to be strong so that we can be weak, while God wants to be weak so that we can be strong? Could it be that while we want God to declare, to prove Herself, God knows that the unknown is the mind's greatest need? Could it be that while we want evidence with which to make intelligently selfish decisions, God figures that it wouldn't be a good idea to leave such evidence lying around?

It's interesting how we insist on making God commander-in-chief when God has already discarded that role. I think it is our need for authority that makes God commander-in-chief. It is this need for authority that makes Roman Catholics believe in papal infallibility and Protestants believe in scriptural inerrancy. If I say to you, "I believe in the Bible as the sole infallible, inerrant source of authority on all matters," that reflects the sincerity of my convictions less than it reveals the depth of my fears that I have not learned the right password, kept the rules. Biblicism, after all, is unbiblical. Scriptural writings themselves do not support the inerrancy of Scripture. As I said last Sunday, Christians believe in the Word made flesh, not the Word made words. You can't tell me that God closed up shop when, in the year AD 382, church authorities decided to close the pages of the New Testament to further writings about Jesus. Nor do we honor the greater truth found in the person of Jesus by ignoring truth found elsewhere. Finally, and crucially, we do not have to diminish our own stature in order to enhance the stature of him who came to expand, not limit, experience, who came that we might have life and have it "more abundantly."

It is interesting how we insist that God be commander-in-chief when that is a status God has already thrown away. It is also interesting that we put such stock in Holy Writ, in creeds and laws, when for doing just that Jesus criticized the Pharisees. It's not that the Bible, creeds, and laws are unimportant; they are all-important—but as signposts, not hitching posts. They are not the essence of Christianity any more than power is what is essential about God. Christ is not the Christian's guru waiting to be asked the right question so he can supply the right answer. What did we learn at Christmas if not that God doesn't give answers, God gives Himself? Then with God's presence within us, we are supposed to search for the right questions and the right answers. Read the Gospels. You remember how it is: Jesus evokes rather than explains. He suggests more than he spells out. He doesn't give us an exact description of the Kingdom of Heaven. He says it's like finding a ring you thought you'd lost forever—like winning the Irish sweepstakes or the New York lottery. He doesn't tell the world how to order its economic activity. He simply insists that the poor no longer be denied their rightful inheritance. In contemporary terms, he says it's harder for a rich person to enter Paradise than for Donald Trump to squeeze through the night deposit slot of the Chase Manhattan Bank.

You who are about to join the church are joining a movement rather than endorsing a manifesto. You are committing yourselves to a way of life rather than to a rigid set of beliefs. You have serious hunches rather than absolute certainties. You read the Bible for the faith it liberates in you rather than for the truth it precisely defines. To you faith is not believing without proof but trusting without reservation. I hope you do not believe in salvation through mutilation. I hope you want God to free yourselves so that you can be yourselves.

Of course, you look to the past to learn from it, to be especially grateful for the courage of the saints, their gentleness and spiritual generosity. Learn from the past, but do not be subject to the past. "Let the dead bury the dead!" means "and not the living." Let not memory limit in you the movement of God's spirit. The past can preserve but not provide the faith. "Christianity is too often like the experience of a child in a large family who constantly has clothes handed down by an older brother or sister; the clothes never properly become your own" (Bryan Rippin). Only a contemporary personal response to Jesus can create a living, burning faith. Your prayer must be deeply personal: "Fill *me*, Radiancy divine . . . Glad my eyes, and warm my heart."

What is faith? Faith is being grasped by the power of love. Faith is recognizing that what makes God God is infinite mercy, not infinite control; not power, but love unending. Faith is recognizing that if at Christmas God became like us, it was so that thereafter we might become more like God. We know what that means: watching Jesus heal the sick, empower the poor, and scorn the powerful, we see transparently the power of God at work. Watching Zacchaeus climb the tree a crook and come down a saint, watching Paul set out a hatchet man for the Pharisees and return a fool for Christ, we know that our lives too can become channels for divine mercy to flow out to save the lost and the suffering.

But just as Christ was not rewarded for being Christ, we can't expect to be rewarded for being Christian. This week and next Sunday we remember another prophet, gifted prince of the Black church, adored by some but misunderstood, silenced, and finally executed by a white majority. His life reminds us that what Jesus and the prophets teach us to believe and what the world rewards as belief are rarely the same. In good Christian fashion, Martin Luther King Jr. preached that gentleness takes more courage than violence. How many in the world are ready to be that courageous? In true Christian fashion Martin preached that compassion is more valuable than any ideology. Tell that to rigid communists and equally rigid anticommunists! Martin preached that we should be governed by our dreams, not our fears. The largest peacetime buildup of military power in the history of the planet belies that belief. What then shall we say? That we love our martyrs only after we have slain them as prophets? Yes, but say also that the drama of redemption continues, enhanced or spoiled by human deeds. Say also that God is waiting for us to "show the heavens more just," to help love prevail. If Christ bled for you can't you bleed just a little for Christ? Rather than feel sorry for ourselves, can we not feel sorrow for God, whose greatness lies precisely in her compassion, her capacity to suffer for and with us? Sometimes I think it's not the peace of God but the pain of God that passes all understanding.

Most church boats don't like to be rocked; they prefer to lie at anchor rather than go places in stormy seas. But that's because we Christians view the church as the object of our love instead of the subject and instrument of God's. Faith cannot be passive; it has to go forth—to assault the conscience, excite the imagination. Faith fans the flames of creativity altogether as much as it banks the fires of sin.

All saving ideas are born small. God comes to earth as a child so that we can finally grow up, so that we can stop blaming God for being absent when we ourselves were not present, stop blaming God for the ills of the world as if we had been laboring to cure them, and stop making God responsible for all the thinking and doing we should be undertaking on our own. I've said it before and will probably say it many times again: God provides minimum protection, maximum support—support to help us grow up, to stretch our minds and hearts until they are as wide as God's universe. God doesn't want us narrow-minded, priggish, and subservient, but joyful and loving, as free for one another as God's love was freely poured out for us at Christmas in that babe in the manger. Let's listen once again to Wesley's words:

> Christ, whose glory fills the skies;
> Christ, the true, the only Light,
> Sun of Righteousness, arise,
> Triumph o'er the shades of night;
> Dayspring from on high, be near;
> Daystar, in my heart appear.

Fill me, Radiancy divine,
Scatter all my unbelief;
More and more thyself display,
Shining to the perfect day.

AIDS

JANUARY 26, 1986
Readings: Psalm 91:6, 9–16; 1 John 4:16–21

O ne of the good things about this century is that the work and writings of psychiatrist Elisabeth Kübler-Ross (author of *On Death and Dying*) and the efforts of the Hospice movement, which first took root in England and has flowered in the United States, have brought to light the special needs of the terminally ill and the privileged experience it is to take care of such folk. In a world none of us can embrace with unrestrained enthusiasm, it is really nice to think of the hundreds of homes that have been started by the Hospice movement, the people trained in pastoral care, the support groups established. Lives that once would have been sad and anxious are today comforted by group discussions among the terminally ill themselves, by visits from family and friends, and by music, flowers, and prayers. Death is a lonely business, but we do not have to die alone. It is grace itself to have a God who is "my refuge and fortress," a God to whom we can sing praises, praying as we shall later:

When I tread the verge of Jordan,
Bid my anxious fears subside;
Death of death, and hell's destruction,
Land me safe on Canaan's side.
William Williams

It must be wonderful to approach the riverbank holding the hand of someone who loves us.

Now contrast that care with the treatment still common today of those dying of AIDS. First, many of them are evicted from their apartments, fired from their jobs, and refused service at restaurants. Then, from their hospital beds, they watch their food being left outside the door, even when they themselves can no longer walk. They watch their IV medication go unmonitored, their pain medication too. They lie helpless as their calls for the nurse go unanswered, sometimes for hours on end, and often they die alone. In the words of the psalm, AIDS is "a destruction that wastes at noonday" (Ps. 91:6)—the average AIDS victim being 35 years old. It is also, "a pestilence that stalks in darkness," shrouded in secrecy, fear, ignorance, and prejudice.

Recently, in beautiful Highland County in western Virginia, nestled between the Shenandoah and Allegheny mountains, Elisabeth Kübler-Ross tried to establish a hospice for children dying of AIDS. Her neighbors rose in protest. "Why here?" they asked. "Because I live here," she answered. They would not allow her to go forward. "You'll turn this place into a ghost town," they said. Similiar confrontations have taken place in Queens and in Manhattan. In the four or five years of the disease's existence, people have been acting out their fears based on misinformation.

None of us can blame parents who want to protect their young. In Mary Gordon's *Men and Angels* one woman asks another, "What do you think having children does to your moral life?" Answers the other woman, "When you're a mother you think with your claws." I understand that; I even like it. But how many mothers and fathers, ignoring the opinions of the American Academy of Pediatrics (representing 28,000 pediatricians), continue to insist that AIDS is contagious so they can continue to blame the disease on people they have never liked anyway: drug addicts and gay men.

God is calling out all our hearts for review. They are too full of the fear that love is supposed to cast out. God is warning us—once again—that the cost of ignoring the truth is higher than the pain of seeing it, that human beings who blind themselves to human need make themselves less human. God is getting mighty impatient with our unsurrendered souls—souls we hold so tightly that they shrink to the size of our hands.

What is the truth all of us need to know? Its victims, and those who search for a vaccine and an eventual cure, know that AIDS is a medical mystery with death its silent partner. It compares in virulence with the cholera that struck New York City in 1832, claiming, in the month of June alone, 12,000 victims. It compares with the bubonic plague of Europe in the 14th century. But AIDS is far less transmissible than the great plagues of past centuries. All the evidence—and there is a lot of it—points to its transmission solely through blood and semen. The virus is not airborne, nor is it carried by food, water, drinking glasses, toilet seats, or any casual contact. Nor is AIDS a "gay plague" simply because in this country it started in the gay community, any more than

AIDS is an African plague simply because today the incidence of AIDS in Kinshasa is higher than it is in San Francisco and New York. Nor, surely, is AIDS divine retribution on homosexuals, if only because most patients in Zaire are heterosexual—half of them are women— and because the lowest risk group in this country is lesbians. If doctors don't know the cause of AIDS, ministers don't either. To jump from agnosticism to God's sure judgment, overlooking all the uncertainties in between, is (to say the least) dangerous. Beware of ministers who offer you the comfort of opinion without the discomfort of thought! To picture a God of love rooting for a virus that kills people, to picture a God of justice waging germ warfare on sinners and not going after war makers, polluters, slum landlords, drug dealers—all of whose sins affect others so much more profoundly—that's not distortion of the Gospel, that's desertion.

Actually, like the threat of nuclear war and so many other tragedies in the world, AIDS is a catalyst that raises heavy-duty questions for which many of us are not quite ready. One example: We now know that children discover, rather than choose, their sex preference. Along with straight children, gay children need to be taught that promiscuity is dangerous to their health, psyche, and morality. If, as most of us still think, example is the best form of teaching, then gay children have the same need as straight children to see loving, stable couples. If gay and lesbian couples demonstrate the same deep and abiding love for one another as do straight couples—and demonstrably they can, the evidence is all about us in this city—then why shouldn't the State offer the same civil marriage available to straight couples, offer in exchange for a public commitment, a public contract with all the benefits that marriage entails, including (all-important these days) death benefits? Why shouldn't the Christian church do the same? Is John Fortunato, an Episcopal psychotherapist, wrong to formulate the issue in this fashion: "As evidence increasingly emerges that homosexuality is a natural biological variation in the human species, is it not time for the smug heterosexual majority to give up its self-image of monochromatic normality and acknowledge *God's* right to a pluralistic creation?"

More than anything else, AIDS reminds us of our own mortality, knowledge we aggressively seek to avoid. It is our need for control, for an orderly, manageable world, that is so threatened by AIDS. So "we project our deepest feats of vulnerability on to those who are suffering the most and who least deserve to be abandoned" (Lee Hancock).

It is the abandonment that is so heart-wrenching and wrong. Lord knows in this city, it's all too easy to find IV drug users, but to persuade them to kick the habit, or at the very least not to use bloody, dirty needles, is almost impossible; most have reached such a point of despair in their lives that they couldn't care less. And most of us couldn't care less either. Still, addiction and rehabilitation centers, such as the one represented here this morning, continue in this city and elsewhere to carry out their hard Samaritan task. God bless them!

Over recent months I have watched the gay community, a community drenched in grief, reaching out to AIDS victims. The Gay Men's Health Crisis has instituted hot lines, put together wonderful educational packages, organized buddy systems so that no one is alone, developed legal resources to protect their members against eviction and loss of medical insurance and care. I have watched gay members of this church be one to another shining examples of pastoral care. To you members of this church who have AIDS—you, Jim; you, Scott—I want to say, I have seen the grace of God shining in your dear faces.

Grace is manifest in your lack of bitterness. Can anyone doubt that if the primary group of victims had been upper middle-class heterosexual whites, funding from the government—which has never been substantial for illnesses of minorities (sickle-cell anemia has never received much attention)—from the very beginning government funding would have been ten times what it is today. And that would still be a pittance in relation to what is needed for education and hospice care.

But the concern today is with ourselves. How are we as Christians—all of us—going to abide the unknown, possess ourselves with patience, while asserting our solidarity with those who suffer and with those who study the disease? Scientists have yet to find a cure for AIDS, but all of us know the cure for AIDS hysteria. When asked in Highland County what she was going to do now, Dr. Kübler-Ross said, "I remain an absolute optimist that someday love will conquer fear." She knew her Bible: "There is no fear in love, but perfect love casts out fear" (1 John 4:18). It is love that banishes fear and prejudice, that allows us to grow in understanding, freedom, and compassion. It was love that made Jesus draw to his bosom those whom the world had abandoned. We who live in his name can do no less.

Now I ask Jim Johnson, a member of Riverside Church, to finish this sermon with his own testimony of faith.

Jim Johnson:

I have AIDS, and I'm not alone. More than 16,000 people in this country have come down with this illness, and more than half, 8,200, have died. It is not now and never has been a "gay" disease; in fact, the proportion of persons with AIDS who come from the heterosexual community is rising.

There are AIDS patients throughout our society; for example, right here in this church this morning there are those ill with AIDS, their lovers, care partners, families, and friends. Thirty thousand cases are anticipated by the end of this year, with 15,000 deaths. The number of cases and the number of deaths are expected to double each year for the foreseeable future. AIDS and its victims *will* touch your lives, if that has not already occurred. There is no cure for AIDS. No one diagnosed with AIDS has ever recovered.

Many victims of AIDS have lost homes and jobs, life and health insurance; their families have abandoned them. So in addition to the great discomfort, pain, and suffering the disease brings, there's also the opprobrium laid on by society. *That's* something we can and must alleviate.

I was diagnosed in November 1984 with Pneumocystis pneumonia. I spent 30 days in the hospital at that time, went back to work for three months, and then started using my accumulated sick leave. I was on full pay for almost 10 months and am now receiving a federal disability retirement pension. Last June I had a second bout of Pneumocystis pneumonia that required three weeks of treatment. I also have Kaposi's sarcoma—a cancer of the blood vessels—which is spreading. In addition, there are assorted gastrointestinal and skin problems. I don't feel well a lot of the time.

Some good things have happened in my life as a consequence of AIDS. I'm no longer working; that's benefit number one! Also, I've learned a lot about loving and being loved, lessons I perhaps could not have learned without this illness. My lover, Tom, is not only staying with me and by me, he's taking care of me despite the strain that is inevitably going to cause in his life. My family is fully loving and supportive. I'm not going to lose my apartment or my insurance. I have lots of caring friends, especially Barry, who is there for me *all* the time. And I've found a sanctuary here at Riverside, where I come a couple of days a week for the succor only this place can provide.

There are some things I've learned from being terminally ill, although, all things considered, with respect to AIDS I would have to agree with W. C. Fields: "I'd rather be in Philadelphia."

To be a Christian is to be in a community, and more so here at Riverside than elsewhere. Those of us who have AIDS can be open to what this community offers us. And for those who are not ill there is an opportunity to reach out to the ill to make their final days more comfortable, to help bring about spiritual acceptance with respect to death, to make this church a haven of love and support in Jesus Christ.

I want to share with you one of the great comforting psalms of my faith.

> The Lord is my shepherd, I shall
>   not want;
> He maketh me to lie down in green
>   pastures.
> He leadeth me beside still waters;
>   he restoreth my soul.
> He leadeth me in paths of righteousness
>   for his name's sake.
>
> Yea, though I walk through the valley
>   of the shadow of death,
>   I fear no evil;
> for thou art with me,
>   thy rod and thy staff,
>   they comfort me.
>
> Thou preparest a table before me
>   in the presence of mine enemies;
>   thou anointest my head with oil,
>   my cup runneth over.
> Surely goodness and mercy shall
>   follow me all the days of my life;
> and I will dwell in the house of the Lord
>   for ever.
>   Psalm 23

Guardian Vessels of the Spirit

FEBRUARY 2, 1986
Reading: Luke 9:49–55

It's easy to understand why so many people in his day rejected Jesus. The champions of law and order, particularly those who thought the letter of the law mattered more than its purpose, saw in him a threat to the system. Revolutionaries couldn't go along with his non-violence. He offended the world-forsaking ascetics with his uninhibited worldliness, while being too uncompromising to the devout who made too easy a peace with the world. "For the silent majority he was too noisy and for the noisy minority he was too quiet, too gentle for the strict and too strict for the gentle. He was an obvious outsider in a critically dangerous social conflict in opposition both to the prevailing conditions and to those who opposed them" (Hans Küng).

It is easy to see why so many rejected Jesus. What is hard to understand, and so dismaying, is how those who loved him and were with him so constantly could misunderstand him so consistently. In the ninth chapter of Luke alone, there are six breathtaking examples.

In the first instance, the disciples could not believe that Jesus could feed five thousand people with five loaves and two fishes—and who could blame them for that? Of course, it just may be that all those folks came with their own food—after all, they were a long way from home—but they hid it for fear of having to share it, and it was not until the disciples put before everybody their tiny store that the others were moved to produce and share theirs. In other words, the miracle may have been changing determined self-interest into generosity. But all of that is wild speculation; Who knows?

In the second instance, Jesus asked the disciples, "Who do people say that I am?" They all answered without any trouble because it was an easy question, an academic question, demanding of them only that they report what they had heard. But when Jesus insisted, "But who do you say that I am?"—a personal question—only one answered, "The Christ of God." No sooner had Peter gotten it right then Jesus told him, "Get behind me, Satan!" Peter simply could not believe that the "Son of man must suffer many things, and be rejected by the elders and chief priests and the scribes, and be killed" (vv. 18–22). ("My God," Peter must have thought, "if they could do that to him, what's going to happen to me?" At least Peter was less naïve than modern disciples of Jesus, who know that Christ was not rewarded for being Christ, but who still think they should be rewarded for being Christian.)

Then comes the Transfiguration story, when Peter, James, and John go on the mountain with Jesus. His countenance is altered as he prays, and his raiment becomes dazzling white. And the disciples' reaction is to build booths (the Christian edifice complex!) until they hear a voice from the clouds saying, "This is my Son, my beloved, *listen to him*" (v. 35).

Then an argument arises among them as to which of the disciples is the greatest—totally inappropriate. Then John says, "Teacher, we saw a man casting out demons in your name, and we forbade him, because he was not following us," and Jesus answers, "Do not forbid him. . . . For he that is not against us is for us."

And finally, when the messengers return saying that the villagers up ahead, reflecting a centuries-old quarrel between Samaritans and Jews, are not ready to receive him, James and John say, "Lord, do you want us to bid fire come down from heaven and consume them?" (Now we are lured by the power of "redemptive" violence when the righteousness of the cause overcomes revulsion at the bloodshed!) And Jesus says, "You do not know what manner of spirit you are of; for the Son of man came not to destroy but to save them."

At least we can appreciate the honesty and humility that prompted these disciples later on to recount all their mistakes. But at this stage of their learning, what do they say to us, these bumbling, fumbling followers of Jesus who are so moved by his kindness and so confused by his demands?

The nation today is beginning to dry its tears in the wake of Tuesday's horrible tragedy (and how well the President spoke at the memorial service for the *Challenger* crew in Houston). On Friday we grieved, as we had all week. But today we are also beginning to wonder how all of us could have concurred in the delusion that riding on rocket power wasn't working pretty close to the edges of death. Exploring space is a wonderful human venture—I eagerly await the invitation for the first parson to go up—if only we could keep the military out of it. What did Churchill warn? "The stone age may return on the gleaming wings of science. . . . Beware, I say, time is short." But Tuesday's tragedy is a reminder of the always present need to put a brake on our ambitions and on our vanity, which leads us to believe we know so much more than we do.

In like fashion, the misunderstanding of those who knew Christ best remind us Christians how dangerous it is to claim to know too much. Christians too often display a terrible need to be absolutely sure about Jesus and about God. And I don't mean Fundamentalists alone, but apologists also, dogmatists, all who try to get a fix on Jesus. Truth for them is not a way to live and believe, but a particular description of belief. "This is the true Jesus; this is the correct understanding of God. Accept my prescription of faith, or I will condemn you according to my description of heresy." These people fear confusion, when the greater danger lies in too much precision. "Jesus defies categories. Christ is beyond christologies. He is outside the dogmas of neat religious minds. He is free" (Bryan Rippin). As Matthew Arnold said of Shakespeare: "Others abide our questions, thou art free."

We ourselves can be truly free only when we allow Jesus to be free. Cage him, and you imprison yourself. Categorize him, and you find yourself in a pigeonhole—another religious clone, not a real human being. Maybe the image we need in our churches is not an immobile Jesus, a statue or a stained glass window, or even Jesus on the cross, but rather the image of the empty tomb with the inscription, "He is not here, but has gone on before you."

Clarity, yes; certainty, no. Let us restore the blessed gift of the imagination to its rightful place at the center of the faith. Let us not fear life's confusion, but rather embrace its profusion, give ourselves to the search rather than repeat endlessly what others have found. And let us give ourselves to each other, which is what living in the Spirit is all about. Our unity is not based on agreement, but on mutual concern—when all hearts are one, nothing else has to be one. Let us keep the faith not by being intellectually dogmatic, but by becoming guardian vessels of Christ's loving spirit. Hatred waters what should be allowed to dry up. It puts in charge of our lives what we should rule over if we want to grow better, not worse, happier instead of more miserable.

"Lord, do you want us to bid fire come down from heaven and consume them?" No doubt the disciples felt rejected by the Samaritans and wanted to strike back. Shakespeare had yet to come along with that line which should be inscribed over every pastoral counseling center: "Thou hast not half that power to do me harm as I have to be hurt" (*Othello*). Just as all the water in the ocean cannot sink a ship unless it leaks in, so all the rejection and hatred in the world cannot pull you down, for no hatred can seep into a guardian vessel of the Holy Spirit.

"Lord, do you want us to bid fire come down from heaven and consume them?" The disciples had yet to appreciate that there is enough fire built into the system: they who take up the sword shall perish by the sword; what shall it profit a man if he gain the whole world and lose his soul? Affluence cannot buy morale. James Baldwin called it "a terrible, an inexorable law, that one cannot deny the humanity of another without diminishing one's own." Respect, nay, reverence for life is where all religions meet and where humanity must go or face a death like the one we beheld on Tuesday, only in a final desecration without reprieve.

So whether you're young or feeling "the fading of the bloom in the blood," whenever you feel like bidding fire come down from heaven to consume someone, or some group, or some nation, remember Christ's words: "You do not know what manner of spirit you are of; for the Son of man came not to destroy lives, but to save them."

Remember that the only fire that comes down from heaven is the Pentecostal fire of the Spirit.

We are guardian vessels of that Spirit. How do you become a disciple of Christ? By allowing Christ to be in your heart when you think of others; by allowing Christ to be in your mouth when you speak to others; by allowing Christ to be in your eyes when you see them, and in your ears when you hear them.

> Salvation is of the Lord
> Salvation is of the Christ
> May your salvation, O Lord, be ever with us.

The Point of Lent

FEBRUARY 16, 1986
Readings: Ezekiel 28:11–19; Matthew 4:1–11

On the first Sunday of Lent, a congregation as informed and alert as this one would naturally expect the preacher to ring the changes on sin. It is a proper expectation, for the point of Lent is to arouse contrition for our less-than-wonderful ways, which, in turn, is a good thing, provided we remember that the point of contrition is to mitigate our pride, not eliminate our hope. Well has the poet written:

> Hope . . . perches in the soul and sings . . .
> And never stops at all.
>   Emily Dickinson

It is a proper expectation as well because the Christian understanding of sin makes more sense out of more facts than any other doctrine of evil, and because the preacher's role is not only to set before the congregation personal and national ideals—"A map of the world that does not include Utopia is not even worth glancing at," said Lewis Mumford—but also to expose the realities camouflaged by those ideals.

How often do conservative ideals mask unjust privileges, just as Marxist ideals hide the absolute inevitability of that sin which arises not in the environment but in the depths of the human heart. (Have you ever heard of a revolution that didn't produce a new ruling class?)

"Then Jesus was led up by the Spirit into the wilderness." Why into the wilderness? Because, said the philosopher Whitehead, "Religion is what people do with their solitude." It is in solitude that instincts for self-preservation oppose those of self-sacrifice. In solitude you discover that your life is not a possession to be defended but a gift to be shared. It is the solitary consciences in history that best represent the universal conscience of humanity. ("Compassion is the fruit of solitude," wrote Henri Nouwen.) But such discoveries come only after long, arduous wrestling with the devil, who, you can be sure, has other things than compassion on his or her mind.

Some of you do not believe in the existence of the devil, which, of course, is precisely what the devil wants you to believe. Football fans remember Big Daddy Lipscomb, a tackle of awesome proportions who used to play with the Colts when they were still in Baltimore. When asked how he could make so many tackles in spite of the many blockers in front of the ball carrier, he replied, "I riffle through the pack until I find the one with the ball and then I keep him." How much easier it is for Big Daddy Devil to keep you when you don't even have blockers, because you think the devil doesn't exist!

Allow me once again to explain that the devil is pictured as a person because evil is experienced as an intensely personal power. The devil is given a separate existence not because evil exists outside of us, but because evil is experienced as something greater than us. St. Paul put it classically: "The good that I would, I do not, and that which I would not, that I do" (Rom. 7:19). And never to be forgotten is the fact that the devil is an angel, albeit a fallen one. That means evil does not arise in our so-called lower nature, which, despite what our mothers may have taught us, is just fine; evil rather arises in our higher nature, in the realm of the Spirit where the devil seeks constantly to corrupt our freedom by seducing us into making wrong choices. That's what the Devil was about when he said to Jesus, "Command these stones to become loaves of bread."

Preachers preach a lot on these passages; I have done so often. There are subtler and better interpretations than the one I offer today. I'm going for the cruder interpretation because it is somehow more powerful. Some things have to be said powerfully and, hopefully, with more veracity than venom, if this country is finally going to bring its spiritual house into order.

With that first temptation, "Command these stones to become loaves of bread," the devil was tempting Jesus to use his powers selfishly for materialistic gain. I think one of the great sources of the president's popularity is his ability to make us comfortable with our prejudices. He never dwells on them, but rather says such things as, "The heart of America is strong and good and true"; "How can we not believe in the goodness and greatness of America?"

If that represents a calm moral verdict arrived at after a penetrating study of inexorable facts, I'll eat my hat. And if it is the role of preachers, particularly in Lent, to be troublers of the national conscience rather than composers of Te Deums in praise of America, then we have to lament over our beloved land as did Ezekiel over Tyre: "Your heart was proud because of your beauty; you corrupted your wisdom for the sake of your splendor." In our beloved land extravagance becomes ever more compulsive even as the lot of the poor worsens. There is in this city a fearful symmetry: 30,000 millionaires and 30,000 homeless—whose plight represents what we might call the continuing "space tragedy" of America. There are, as Senator Daniel Patrick Moynihan points out in James Reston's column in today's *New York Times*, 13.8 million Americans under the age of 18 presently stranded in poverty, while the Head Start program, 20 years old this year, is showing the same signs of deprivation seen so often in the kids it has served so well. We don't need to pray *in* the public schools, we need to pray *for* the public schools, and for the private ones as well—especially the colleges, where the humanities no longer humanize but have become a cultural icing on an economic cake, as college graduates outdo each other in their quest for material success. Where does the heart go to school in America? Whatever became of the notion that the purpose of education was to make us better people? How high is the ideal of free speech when it is so exalted over any obligation to do any good to anyone?

Jesus, who was poor and, in the wilderness, hungry, resisted the blandishments of selfishness, saying to the devil, "[Human beings] shall not live by bread alone, but by every word that proceeds from the mouth of God."

Let those words arouse our contrition, and let contrition mitigate our pride but not eliminate our hope. For even as at home and abroad the situation goes from bad to worse, more and more churches are beginning to see that pocketbooks have more to do with Jesus than hymnbooks. Marxists no longer believe that religion is the dying remnant of an old capitalist system, not when they see that the growing persecution of the churches is the result of their defending the poor. And God is not mocked: great wealth alone cannot buy fulfillment, which is why the Russian theologian Nikolai Berdyaev wrote: "When bread is assured, then God becomes a hard and inescapable reality instead of an escape from harsh reality."

Just being angry isn't going to do any good; we must also be imaginative. I mentioned the 30,000 millionaires for whom bread is most definitely assured. Why not bring them together with the 30,000 homeless, asking every millionaire to contribute the $40,000 or $50,000 necessary to rehabilitate a city-owned apartment, and ask the city to contribute a modest sum beyond the building itself? Let the top and the bottom of the economic ladder get together, let the private and the public sectors do something dynamic and creative for New York, and let Riverside be the catalyst. If you think the idea has merit and can help implement it, please let me know.

"Then the devil took him to the holy city, and set him on the pinnacle of the temple, and said to him, 'If you are the Son of God, throw yourself down; for it is written, "He will give his angels charge over you."'"

Perhaps this is an entirely different kind of temptation, the kind that comes to people who have renounced materialism and the struggle for worldly security. Instead, they have committed themselves to God, but with the secret expectation that now God will do all the work. So much that passes for spirituality is pure laziness, reminiscent of the story of the priest who went golfing with a rabbi. Before putting, the priest crossed himself. By the ninth hole he was nine strokes ahead. Asked the rabbi, "Father, do you think it would be all right if, before I putted, I too crossed myself?" Answered the priest, "Sure, Rabbi. But it won't do you any good until you learn how to putt."

Jesus didn't ask God to take care of him when he was supposed to be taking care of the world. In the repressive state that was Palestine under Roman rule and that of orthodox Jewry, Jesus spoke out, he suffered, he died for his beliefs. We don't live in a state anywhere near as repressive, yet too many people are afraid to speak out openly. There may be no official censorship here, but there is a great deal of self-censorship.

Two weeks ago John Wray, a former judge in Maryland, sent me a book of his poems entitled *Songs from the Heart*. One quatrain reads:

> You called me, Lord?
> I tell no lie;
> I hope you meant
> Some other guy.

Many Christians come to church, but they never leave. They do church work, but they leave the work of the church—out there—to some other guy. The nails will never graze the palms of their hands, because they never speak up.

"Jesus said to [the devil], 'Again it is written, "You shall not tempt the Lord your God."'"

Again, let contrition mitigate, this time, not so much our pride as our laziness, our self-indulgence, but let it not eliminate our hope. We can do better. At the Ash Wednesday service I suggested that rather than give up something for Lent, we add something. Maybe we could add our voices to those who are pleading for more love and peace in the world. I had a friend who resolved for one month to ask everybody he met what they thought about the arms race—on the bus, on the subway, in the office, even telephone operators ("Operator, I want to make a long distance call, but first I want to ask you . . ."). That's not a bad Lenten resolve, and it brings us to the third and last temptation.

"Again, the devil took him to a very high mountain, and showed him all the kingdoms of the world and the glory of them; and he said to him, 'All these I will give you, if you will fall down and worship me.'" (What's so fascinating is that the devil thinks they are his to give!)

The temptation, clearly, is to seek status through power. What does that say to superpowers with their nuclear arsenals bursting at the silos? Haven't we become like alcoholics who know that liquor is killing them, yet can always find a reason for just one more drink? Are these weapons deterring war or merely *deferring* it until the results are guaranteed to be cataclysmic?

And what about the effort to refurbish a tarnished Vietnam war, symbolized by Rambo, a maniacal hero confronting life's problems with weapons and brutality, his message to his eager hearers, "Long before all else fails, resort to violence"?

Listen again to Ezekiel: "In the abundance of your trade you were filled with violence, and you sinned. . . . Your heart was proud because of your beauty; you corrupted your wisdom for the sake of your splendor. . . . All who know you among the peoples are appalled at you; you have come to a dreadful end."

The United States is fast becoming an outcast among its allies because of its war policy in Central America. Not one of our allies believes our national security is threatened by tiny Nicaragua. All are appalled at the proven atrocities of the Contras. None has a serious illusion about the distinction between humanitarian and military aid. Not a single country in the world joined President Reagan's embargo—which even Mexico called counterproductive and harmful. Since the embargo began, Canada, Spain, France, and other allies have replaced the United States as buyers of Nicaraguan products. Even China now trades with Nicaragua. Never in American history has the president veered so radically from the modest admonitions of the country's closest allies. Our world prestige suffers as our war policy inspires aversion virtually everywhere. Congress must vote neither military nor humanitarian aid to the Contras. It must end a war that never should have started.

"Then Jesus said to him, 'Begone, Satan! For it is written, "You shall worship the Lord your God and him only shall you serve."'"

Suppose we were all to say the same thing all this week. Whenever the devil tempts you to use your power selfishly for material gain, say, "Begone, Satan!" When he tries to pass off passivity or ecclesiastical trivial pursuits as some kind of spirituality, say, "Begone, Satan!" And when you see this superpower seeking status through more power, shout it so that all your fellow citizens and even the federal government hear it: "Begone, Satan!"

The point of Lent is to arouse contrition, and the point of contrition is to mitigate our pride, not eliminate our hope. "Then the devil left him, and behold, angels came and ministered to him." It is our sure hope that there are still angels around ready to do no less for us, whenever we are ready to emulate and not betray the example of our Lord and Savior wrestling in solitude with the devil.

Unfriendly, but Loving

FEBRUARY 23, 1986
Reading: Mark 8:31–36

When St. Teresa, that great Spanish saint, finished St. Augustine's *Confessions*, she is reported to have sighed, "I see myself there reflected." And who wouldn't see herself reflected in the prayers of one who prayed, "O God, make me a Christian, but not quite yet"!

To reveal us to ourselves is, of course, a characteristic of all great literature, so it is hardly surprising that we find ourselves mirrored on almost every page of the Bible. We see ourselves, for example, reflected in Adam's excuses: "The woman whom thou gavest to be with me, she gave me the fruit." We see ourselves reflected in Jacob, donning his Gordon Liddy-like disguise in order to deceive his father, the first rung on the ladder of his financial success. And can't we see ourselves in the jealousy of Saul when the chant goes up from the crowd, "Saul has slain his thousands, and David his ten thousands"? Or in Jonah, who, the moment he hears the voice of God commanding,

"Arise, go to Nineveh," hotfoots it for Joppa to take a slow boat to Tarshish?

In the New Testament we see ourselves reflected in the pathetic figure of the paralytic, quite literally scared stiff. Whose hand is free to be extended to anyone? Whose feet are free to tread in any walk of life? Whose eyes are not fixed on some status symbol or another? And who doesn't see himself or herself time and again reflected in all the saintliness and unsaintliness of St. Peter? In his enthusiasm (and the word means "in God"), Peter is always the first to take the plunge, whether it is springing out of the fishing boat to meet his risen Lord, as described in the last chapter of John, or whether it is walking on the water as we find him in Matthew's Gospel: "Lord . . . bid me come to you on the water." But no sooner does Peter take the plunge than he finds himself over his head. Beginning to sink, he cries, "Lord, save me," and Jesus does (vv. 28–30). Jesus probably called him "the Rock" then not for his foundational but for his sinking properties!

In the story we just heard from Mark, I'm touched by Peter's obvious concern for the safety of his Master. Moreover, although only a fool would deny the fact of sin, still, along with Peter, I keep hoping Jesus will be wrong in his predictions of his death; I yearn to see goodness vindicated and emulated. I yearn to see human hearts, however sinful, stilled in the presence of holiness. Such yearnings are not without some justification. Not all prophets are slain; greatness is recognized in some before their death. Didn't the crowds follow Jesus? Doesn't every Palm Sunday raise the hope that there need not be a Good Friday? But clinging to the age-old dreams of humanity is no excuse for not facing the ruthless facts of humanity. Better than any, Jesus knew the fear lodged in every heart, knew that what we humans fear above all is not evil in the world around us, nor even evil within us. There is nothing more feared and less faced than the good in every one of us, that good being so demanding. So we repress it, we deny it. Never would we have crucified the best among us if we had not first crucified the best within us, precisely that best which Jesus is always seeking to resurrect.

The story reveals a lot not only about Peter but also about the meaning of love. Let us examine first how Jesus treated his close friend and disciple Peter, then what he had to say to the multitude of his followers, and finally how he went about loving his enemies.

"And he began to teach them that the Son of man must suffer many things, and be rejected by the elders and the chief priests and the scribes, and be killed, and after three days rise again. And he said this plainly. And Peter took him, and began to rebuke him. [In Matthew's version Peter says, "God forbid, Lord! This shall never happen to you."] But turning and seeing his disciples, [Jesus] rebuked Peter, and said, 'Get behind me, Satan! For you are not on the side of God, but of men.'"

Now that is not a friendly thing to say. But if you stop to think of it, it is a deeply loving thing not to withhold the telling blow when only the telling blow will serve. A true friend is one who will risk his friendship for the sake of his friend.

A more modern example: Leon Howell, the new editor-in-chief of *Christianity and Crisis*, told me of meeting a long-lost friend the other day on Broadway and 108th Street. The friend said to him, "I just heard that you're now the head of a small Christian magazine. How's it going?" As subscribers to the magazine know, the "crisis" in *Christianity and Crisis* is fiscal as well as political, social, and religious. They walked up to about 116th and Broadway, Leon telling his friend all about his financial woes. As they separated, his friend shook his head and said, "You know, Leon, you used to be interesting."

Now some of you may think that such a tongue belongs only in a sandwich, but I'm not sure. When Rita Mae Brown was a child and bad things happened to her, her mother used to reassure her by saying, "Don't worry, honey, worse things have happened to nicer people." The virtue of these jarring remarks is that they knock the self-pity right out of you. Peter must have been feeling self-pity; his concern for his beloved Master was certainly in part concern for himself: "God forbid, Lord! If this happens to you, what in the world is going to happen to me?"

Ossie Davis has many white friends, but that didn't stop him from pointing out—almost 20 years ago—"that in *Roget's Thesaurus of the English Language* the word "whiteness" has 134 synonyms, 44 of which are favorable and only 10 of which are negative in the mildest sense, synonyms such as "gloss over," "whitewash," "gray," "wan," "pale," "ashen," etc. On the other hand, "blackness" has 120 synonyms, 60 of which are distinctly unfavorable, and none even mildly positive. Ossie Davis concluded, "If you consider the fact that thinking itself is subvocal speech (in other words, one must use words to think at all), you will appreciate the enormous trap of racial prejudgment that works on any child who is born into the English language. Any creature, good or bad, white or Black, Jew or Gentile, who uses the English language for the purpose of communication is willing to force the Black child into 60 ways to despise himself, and the white child, 60 ways to aid and abet him in the crime."

Strong medicine is frequently the balm love prescribes for mistaken, not to say sin-sick souls. Watch out for the sweetness of character that backs off from the pain of confrontation; it's unworthy. What a difference between the faith that seeks to liberate us and the churches that seek to tame us! Love never justifies attitudes that evade reality, and certainly not the reality of inequality that is reinforced, because masked, by an ideology of equality. In this Lenten season, let us confess what masters and mistresses of evasion we are:

> I was hungry and you blamed it on the communists
> I was hungry and you circled the moon
> I was hungry and you told me to wait
> I was hungry and you said, "So were my ancestors"
> I was hungry and you said, "We don't hire over thirty-five"
> I was hungry and you told me I shouldn't be
> I was hungry and you told me machines do that work now
> I was hungry and you had Pentagon bills to pay
> I was hungry and you said the poor are always with us.
> Lord, when do we see you hungry?
>
> Anonymous

"And he called to him the multitude with his disciples, and said to them, 'If any man would come after me, let him deny himself and take up his cross and follow me.'" Jesus denies us peace, but gives us glory! "'For whoever would save his life will lose it; and whoever loses his life for my sake and the gospel's will save it. For what does it profit a man, to gain the whole world and forfeit his life?'"

Clearly Jesus did not believe that better jobs and bigger houses, color televisions and expensive cars all add up to the abundant life. No, "He that cometh to me shall never thirst" (John 6:35). What an answer to our matchless thirst! "I am the living bread which came down from heaven; if anyone eats of this bread, he will live forever" (John 6:51). Doesn't that satiate our deepest hunger? We sing it here so often:

> Cure Thy children's warring madness,
> Bend our pride to Thy control;
> Shame our wanton, selfish gladness,
> Rich in things and poor in soul.
>
> Harry Emerson Fosdick

It was moving when the AIDS service we had last month was opened by the gospel choir of ex-addicts from the Addicts Rehabilitation Center. They sang their hearts out, "Let My People Go," and you knew that to them Pharaoh was the dirty little needle from which they had finally liberated themselves. Well, what is Pharaoh for the nonaddicted and the nonpoor of America if not a sensate and materialistic culture that has almost all of us bound in captivity? Christ so loved the rich that he talked to them of their poverty of soul and spirit. Why don't the churches do the same? I am convinced that just as the poor should not be left at the mercy of their poverty, so the rich should not be left at the mercy of their riches, and that it is an unfriendly but loving thing to say, "For what should it profit a man, to gain the whole world and forfeit his life?" That's why the redistribution of wealth should be at the head of the agenda of every church in this country.

How did Jesus go about loving his enemies? "And he began to teach them that the Son of man must suffer many things, and be rejected by the elders and the chief priests and the scribes, and be killed, and after three days rise again." In setting his face toward Jerusalem, Jesus knew he was walking into the lions' den. Confronted with the evidence of their corruption, the religious and political authorities would have no way out but to eliminate the prophet. To Jesus it was never a matter of not having enemies; what mattered was not excluding them from his love. So he met their violence with nonviolence, which always takes more courage and love than violence. He hated their sin but loved them as sinners. He died for those who gloried in their might and in their riches and in their justifications for both, just as surely as he died for the millions who still starve and die in squalor, victims of the oppression of the rich and the mighty.

And so finally did Peter, in whom Jesus never ceased to believe. Peter was ten times the person after Christ's resurrection he was before Good Friday. And after Peter came a great cloud of witnesses, all of whom through the centuries came to believe that there are greater tragedies than the tragedy of death but no greater victories than the triumph of love. They braved the lions, endured trials and tribulations, faced hate-crazed mobs, were attacked and beaten, burned at the stake, and lynched in the woods.

On this last Sunday of Black History Month let us call some few to mind: Richard Allen, David Walker, Nat Turner, Henry McNeil Turner, Sojourner Truth, Harriet Tubman, Frederick Douglass, W.E.B. DuBois, Marcus Garvey, Paul Robeson, Fannie Lou Hamer, Malcolm X, and, of course, Martin Luther King Jr. They were not all nonviolent, but of them this world was not worthy, except for the spirit that can at any moment redeem any one of its inhabitants.

To the degree that the church is founded on Peter, it is founded on a second chance. So let us avail ourselves of God's grace and strive again to love one another with that tough and tender love with which Jesus loved his disciple Peter. Let us remind ourselves and our fellow Christians that the church Christ calls us to build "demands justice politically, equality racially, love religiously, international vision nationally, and mutuality in the relationship between men and women." And by God's grace we shall have the courage to make enemies, and the decency never to exclude them from our love.

A Spiral of Joy

MARCH 2, 1986
Readings: Psalm 104; John 19:30

The text for today's sermon is St. John's "description of the last moments of Jesus' life: ". . . and he bowed his head and gave up his spirit."

I want to start at a very different time and place. It's a bar scene in a short story of Carson McCullers. It's closing time—close to dawn. A shrunken, seedy, frail old man has pulled his head out of his beer mug long enough to collar a 12-year-old on his paper route. He starts to philosophize to the boy: "Men fall in love for the first time. And what do they fall in love with? A woman . . . with nothing to go by, they undertake the most dangerous and sacred experience in God's earth. They start at the wrong end of love. They begin at the climax. Can you wonder it is so miserable? Do you know how men should love?"

The old man reaches over and grasps the boy by the collar of his leather jacket. He gives him a gentle little shake, and his green eyes gaze down, unblinking and grave.

"Son, do you know how love should be begun?"

The boy sits small and listening and still. Slowly he shakes his head. The old man leans closer and whispers: "A tree. A rock. A cloud."

That's a truth as pure as gold. Probably no human enterprise starts with such high expectations, and fails with such regularity, as love. And the reason is simple: people think it easy to love; the only hard

This sermon was written after reading *A Listening Heart: The Art of Contemplative Living* by David Steindl-Rast (Crossroad, 1983).—WSC

thing is to find the right object. That's like saying it's easy to play the organ; the only hard thing is to find the right music.

"Son, do you know how love should be begun? . . . A tree. A rock. A cloud." "Look at the birds of the air." "Consider the lilies of the field."

Love begins where life is most daily, when something catches you unaware and touches your heart. Love starts with something simply there for us to enjoy. Love starts with a gift. Love starts with gratitude.

It is grateful people who keep the world on its unsteady progress toward love. It is the ungrateful ones who have made what our new poet laureate, Robert Penn Warren, calls "this maniacal century." In a world that bristles with injustices, where you have to be kind if only because everyone you meet is fighting a hard battle, it can't be said too often: It is gratitude that produces happiness, not happiness gratitude.

Love begins with gratitude. And gratitude begins with listening. Obedience originally did not mean doing what you are told to do. *Ob-audience* means listening with a heart tuned to life's deepest meanings. *Ab-surdus* means absolutely deaf. It is not life that's absurd; it is we who are deaf.

And gratitude takes time. Properly understood, leisure is not the privilege of those who have time; it is the virtue of those who take time, who give to everything they do the time it deserves to take.

It took time, and listening with a heart tuned to life's deepest meanings, and seeing with eyes that are "the windows of the soul," to produce the gratitude that expressed itself thus:

> Bless the Lord, O my soul!
> O Lord my God, thou art very great!
> Thou art clothed with honor and majesty,
>   who coverest thyself with light as with a garment,
> who hast stretched out the heavens like a tent,
>   who hast laid the beams of thy chambers on the waters,
> who makest the clouds thy chariot,
>   who ridest on the wings of the wind,
> who makest the winds thy messengers,
>   fire and flame thy ministers.
>
> Psalm 104:1–4

Seeing and listening and taking time produce gratitude, and gratitude produces thanksgiving, and thanksgiving does not primarily address the gift but the giver. And in all this process there is what we might call "a spiral of joy" in which the giver receives thanksgiving, and so becomes herself receiver, and the joy of giving and receiving spirals higher and higher.

Let me give you a homely analogy. "The mother bends down to her child in his crib and hands him a rattle. The baby recognizes the gift and returns the mother's smile. The mother, overjoyed with the childish gesture of gratitude, lifts up the child with a kiss. . . . Is not the kiss a greater gift than the toy? Is not the joy it expresses greater than the joy that set the spiral in motion?" (Brother David Steindl-Rast).

Is that not something like the gratitude, love, and joy we who are children of God share with our most loving Mother/Father? Is it not a spiral of joy, which, like Jacob's ladder, stretches all the way from earth to heaven with traffic going both ways?

And it all begins with a tree, a rock, a cloud, a violet, a child catching a minnow in a tidal pool. It all begins where life is most daily, when something catches you unaware and touches your heart.

This is a universal religious understanding. Here are some words of a Japanese Zen Master:

> The other day I was walking along the river. The wind was blowing. Suddenly I thought, oh! the air really exists. We know that the air is there, but unless the wind blows against our face, we are not aware of it. Here in the wind I was suddenly aware, yes, it's really there. And the sun too. I was suddenly aware of the sun, shining through the bare trees. Its warmth, its brightness, and all this completely free, completely gratuitous.
>
> And without knowing it, completely spontaneously, my two hands came together, and I realized that I was making gassho. And it occurred to me that this is all that matters: that we can bow, take a deep bow. Just that. Just that.

And that brings us to our text—"and he bowed his head and gave up his spirit"—for this second bowing of the head comes so naturally from the first.

Jesus would do anything for God—out of sheer gratitude for all the good things, and deep meaning, and sense of purpose, and love and joy that God had put into his life. He who died, his sole possession a robe, knew that there are two ways to be rich: one is to have a lot of money, the other to have few needs. Jesus didn't need all things to enjoy life; he had been given life to enjoy all things. He exemplified the truth that gratitude produces happiness, not happiness gratitude.

And then the paradox: "For the joy that was set before him," we read in Hebrews, "he endured the cross, despising the shame" (12:2). How can crucifixion be the joy of a grateful heart? Because whatever is worth living for is worth dying for. Because "neither death nor life can separate us from the love of God" (Rom. 8:38–39). Because if we fail in love we fail in all things else.

Clearly Christianity is not an enterprise you hope to win on a scoreboard; victory is recorded in the heart. But it is the greatest of victories, this triumph of love.

Asks the psalmist: "What shall I render unto the Lord for all his bounty to me?" Answers the hymn-writer:

> Were the whole realm of nature mine,
> That were a present far too small;
> Love so amazing, so divine,
> Demands my soul, my life, my all.
>
> Isaac Watts

So, friends, let us not be anxious about tomorrow. Worry does not eliminate tomorrow's woes; it empties today of its strength.

There is a Hassidic saying: "A whole Jew is one with a broken heart"—a heart broken by the sorrows of the world, but also by a weight of gratitude that all God's mercies outnumber even our manifold sins.

So let gratitude give us strength to do, even as Olof Palme did, and so many others who hover, a cloud of witnesses, about us. Let us heal debilitating divisions, whether in this church, this city, or among the nations. Let us open our eyes, hearts, and doors to those the world around who ask for aid and receive repression. And let us not hesitate to protest the continuing spiral of arms, the insanity of defending ourselves against what we've already done by doing more of it.

"And he bowed his head and gave up his spirit," and left us an example without parallel. Whether all too soon, as with Olof Palme, or whether in the fullness of time, whenever we are called to bow our heads for the last time, may it still be with gratitude to Almighty God for all the blessings of this life; may it be with a spirit worthy of Him/Her who gave it to us with such hope and love.

Hand-Washers or Foot-Washers?

MARCH 9, 1986
Readings: Matthew 27; John 13

This sermon has two texts. The first is from the twenty-seventh chapter of Matthew: "So when Pilate saw that he was gaining nothing, but rather that a riot was beginning, he took water and washed his hands before the crowd, saying, 'I am innocent of this man's blood'" (v. 24).

The second text comes from the thirteenth chapter of John: "Then he [Jesus] poured water into a basin, and began to wash the disciples' feet" (v. 5).

The names John Dillinger and Pretty Boy Floyd can still tingle the spine of those old enough to remember the great gangsters of this century. The most fearsome of them all was Al Capone. When Capone was on the hoof in Chicago, it was said that the cops did not look the other way, they went in and did the burglaring. When Capone had the whole law-enforcement structure of the city eating out of the palm of his hand, his constant refrain was, "We don't want no trouble."

That's what makes Capone so memorable: he was so like us. We may go to college and clean up his grammar, but our sentiments remain much the same—"We don't want no trouble." We want peace at any price, so long as the peace is ours and someone else pays the price.

I want to bring this text to bear on our life here at Riverside, but first a few observations on the larger scene. Twenty-five years ago a small band of Freedom Riders stood up for sentencing in the Montgomery, Alabama County Court House. Judge Marks leaned over the bench and admonished, "Remember, boys, when in Rome, do as the Romans do." Someone should have had the nerve to say, "Unless, your honor, you're a Christian."

The main reason the Supreme Court under Justice Warren was later labeled "controversial" was that so many judges in the lower courts were so fearful of doing anything in Rome the Romans weren't doing already. And in wanting peace at any price they were hardly alone. Pastors temporized, so did bishops. Had lawyers behaved like lawyers, judges like judges, bishops like bishops, and senators like senators—had everyone simply done their job—the country would have been spared years of agony and several deaths. As it was, time and again, as ten years earlier in the era of McCarthyism, common integrity was made to look like courage.

Today in Congress there are many members who believe, as do millions of church people all over this hemisphere, that $100 million for the Contras will make more of a cemetery than a democracy out of Nicaragua. Yet fearful in an election year of being labeled "soft on communism," Pilate-like members will this week vote for the president's graveyard policy. Peace at any price as long as the peace is theirs and the ultimate price is paid by some of the poorest people in one of the poorest countries of the world.

"So when Pilate saw that he was gaining nothing, but rather that a riot was beginning, he took water and washed his hands before the crowd, saying, 'I am innocent of this man's blood.'"

In this moment, Pilate is a tragic rather than a villainous figure. He could tell a revolutionary when he saw one, and clearly Jesus was no revolutionary. Jesus' irenic demeanor, his dignified silence, must have made Pilate feel in him a finer moral fiber than his own. He must have felt that it was he who was on trial, not Jesus. In short, he felt the innate authority of Jesus, but was too fearful to acknowledge it. Isn't that what makes so many of us so like him?

In the second text, the scene takes place the evening before Jesus' appearance before Pilate; it is the time of the Last Supper. In Luke's version we read that a dispute arose among the disciples as to which of them was the greatest. It may have been in response to their quarreling that Jesus did what he did. In any case, Jesus washed the feet of his disciples.

I can never get over the number of things Jesus did. He enlightened the blind, he cleansed the lepers, he healed the palsied, he drove devils out of human beings, and he raised the dead; he rebuked the winds and walked on the waves of the sea dry-shod. Yet, short of his death, I doubt that any action of his so revealed his character and so perfectly showed his love as the washing of his disciples' feet.

Even disciples weren't expected to do this for their master, let alone the master for his disciples. And remember, he is about to be betrayed and crucified. In his place wouldn't you have been seething with bitterness, trembling with fear? But the knowledge of his imminent betrayal and death made Jesus more loving than ever. The more people hurt him, the more he loved them. To injury and betrayal he responded with humility and love. That's not a memory any of us wants to let die.

As some of you know, and the rest of you will soon learn, this church is undergoing considerable financial difficulties, hard as that may be to believe. For the leadership of the church—the deacons, the trustees, the ministers, and of course the staff—it is a trying, frustrating time. At a recent board meeting our frustrations got the better of us. Some exploded in anger; others, myself included, brooded in sulkiness. After four hours, Pilate-like, we voted for a proposal primarily because it would allow us to get out of the room and go home.

How wonderful it would have been (I thought afterwards) had we, instead of standing on our hurt dignity, been able to kneel at each other's feet and engage in the Maundy Thursday ritual of foot-washing. It would have brought us nearer to Christ and hence closer to each other. It would have reminded us that those who wash each other's feet never wash their hands of responsibility.

But hard times are instructive times. As Rita Mae Brown says, "Human beings are like tea leaves. You never know how strong they are until they get in hot water." I want to pay tribute to the strength of our leadership and staff. For several months they have suffered and persevered, and they will pull us through with your help. The promise of Riverside life will prevail over its frustrations.

I said hard times are instructive. Let's recognize how hard it is when you're hurt and frustrated not to lash out or back off—the classic fight/flight syndrome. It's not so hard to admit we all have faults (not to say gross imperfections). Nor is it that hard to recognize when we feel betrayed. What is hard is to see how our imperfections contribute to our sense of being betrayed, and to recognize how others can feel exactly the same way we do—also betrayed.

There is an unacceptability about unpleasant truth. So our natural instinct is to become hand-washers, to go for peace at any price.

To justify my hand-washing actions, I have a rich repertory of quotations. For example, I have over the last weeks been repeating, almost like a mantra, words of T. S. Eliot: "For us there is only the trying; the rest is not our business," and "Teach us to care, but not to care." They are fine quotations, but the time and place are wrong. I should have been quoting Alan Paton: "Perhaps I could have saved us, perhaps I could have saved us all, with only a word, two words, out of my mouth. But I never spoke them. For he shut the door of his soul on me, and I withdrew. But I should have stayed there, hammering without ceasing, for behind it was a man in danger, the bravest and gentlest of us all."

We don't want to be hand-washers. We want to be foot-washers. And to be transformed we must ponder how the knowledge of Jesus' imminent betrayal made him more loving than ever; how the more people hurt him, the more he loved them.

We have to pray, "O God, I cannot become a foot-washer unless you enable me to do so. O God, I cannot find you in others unless you in me find yourself in them. O God, I who am gross by nature want to be made delicate by grace."

And, you know, all things are possible if one believes, if one hopes, if one loves, and most of all perseveres in the practice of these three virtues.

In Jesus' time a great water pot stood at the door of every house. It was needed to wash away the dust and mud accumulated from the unpaved and unclean roads of ancient Palestine. The washing might be called "the washing of entry" into the house. It was a little like baptism, which is the symbolic washing away of the dirt and mud of life before entry into the household of faith.

As we near the end of the Lenten season, let us not fear to confess how like Pilate we are, how often we want peace at any price, as long as the peace is ours and someone else pays the price. But then let us recall the meaning of our washing, our baptism, and how through God's forgiveness we are always given a new chance. Let us remember how Jesus, by washing the feet of his disciples, showed us how much glory there is in what the world views as humiliation. That should help us become foot-washers instead of hand-washers.

I still can't get over how the knowledge of his imminent betrayal made Jesus more loving than ever; how the more people hurt him, the more he loved them; how he returned injury and disloyalty with humility and love. Far from a memory I want to let die, that's an example I want to emulate.

The Eternal Rider

MARCH 23, 1986
Readings: Zechariah 9:9–10; John 12:12–19

It could have been a day as resplendent and fair as today. Certainly, it was a joyful day for the Jerusalem multitudes that hailed and followed Jesus. But for Jesus himself, Palm Sunday must have been painful. Any soul as sensitive as his must have sensed the conflicting vibrations in the air. For in no day described in Scripture did those taking part have more differing views about what was going on.

From the sidelines, the Pharisees stare sullenly at the heretic who insists, "The Sabbath is made for man, not man for the Sabbath," and, worse yet, that the true troublemakers in this world are not the ignorant and cruel but the intelligent and corrupt, civil and religious leaders like the Pharisees themselves. Later in the week their anger will heat up when Jesus "cleanses" the temple by throwing out the money changers, symbols of that oldest form of corruption—religion become subservient to profit making. Yet today, for all their power, they are powerless. To one another they say, "You see that you can do nothing; look, the world has gone after him."

And indeed, in the form of the Jerusalem multitudes, the whole world does go after Jesus on Palm Sunday, which is what gives us cause for some hope and makes the day so festive. But are they cheering a man who has searched their consciences, convinced their minds, and won over their hearts to God? Or are they following a political leader whose power has been proved by the stories circulating the streets of Jerusalem that he raised a man named Lazarus from the dead? Had some reporter asked them why they were carrying palms, half might have replied, "Because they symbolize peace," and the other half, "Because the Romans forbid our carrying spears." Who can blame those who have in mind Saul and Solomon, rather than that phrase of prophecy, "Lo, your King comes to you . . . humble, and riding on an ass" (Zech. 9:9). What Filipino, Black South African, or American who still has the courage to dissent from the popular wisdom of the moment can't understand their desire, in Whitman's phrase, "to walk free And own no superior"? But you can't equate a political revolutionary with "the lamb of God that taketh away the sins of the world."

What do you suppose Jesus had in mind? Why did he come riding into Jerusalem? More importantly, what does he have in mind today, this eternal rider into the great cities of the world, of which New York City is surely one.

I think we should not be too sure, we Christians today, who like Jesus' disciples are moved by his kindness but confused by his demands. It's terrible the way everyone wants to get a fix on Jesus. But it is a matter of history that he is viewed in vastly different ways by differing groups of Christians. So let's go for clarity, not absolute certainty, remembering that the greater danger these days lies not in confusion but in too much precision. The danger to the United States these days lies less in becoming a secular humanist society than in becoming a repressive, reactionary religious one.

On Saint Patrick's Day, so goes the saying, "They march up Fifth and they fall down Third." I think Jesus would start his New York Palm Sunday procession on neither of those two avenues. I think Jesus would start somewhere in the Bronx, or in Brooklyn, or in Harlem, somewhere among the abandoned buildings that are such concrete symbols of abandoned people. Jesus always sides with those who are left out and left behind. How could it be otherwise? If the son of God sided with tyrants, God would be tyrannical. If the son of God sided with no one, God would be indifferent. Only by a clear understanding that God sides with the bruised and broken, the poor and powerless, can we Christians claim that ours is a God of justice.

It is shameful that the "Biblical passion for social justice has been turned into a teaching about individual salvation, which has the net effect of rationalizing and perpetuating social inequity" (Tom Driver). I think the Christ who today enlightens our minds and inflames our hearts, who gives us hope where without him we would tend to lose it—I think that Jesus Christ rides into New York City today to say that the eye cannot say to the foot "I have no need of thee," to insist that those who leave out and leave behind their fellow human beings diminish their own humanity. He sides with the poor, yes, but for the sake of the rich. He sides with the weak, yes, but for the sake of the powerful. Judgment on the rich and powerful finally spells mercy for the rich and powerful as well. For in the words of St. Paul, "we are all one in Christ Jesus." I think Jesus Christ rides into New York City today to proclaim that life and relationship are synonymous, that goodness cannot occur in isolation, that now, as always, we need to affirm a community of mutual need and love.

For that reason, I picture Christ riding on in majesty, leaving the abandoned buildings for some great church or cathedral. There he asks us Christians to recall all the people who have suffered at the hands of the other people who claimed they were acting in the name of Christ. I am thinking of people of different faiths, and of course there are dilemmas. But we can live with dilemmas.

The worst thing we can do with dilemmas is to resolve them prematurely because we haven't the security to live with uncertainty. God save us from what psychiatrists call "premature closure."

The dilemma is this: It is simply not possible for me to be a Christian, *and* a Jew, *and* a Muslim. But the only way for me to be a good Christian is to focus on the difference between myself and my God, not on the difference between myself and other people. Muslims cannot be both Sunni and Shi'ite any more than Jews can be both Reform and Orthodox. And when we consider how, on any number of questions—from the number of sacraments to the ordination of women, pacifism, abortion, homosexuality—Christians cannot arrive at universal agreement, then we have to be impressed how much people of all faiths need to recognize a divine incomprehensibility so vast that no human being dare speak for the Almighty. Instead of trying to prove each other wrong, let people of different faiths attempt to see that none has a full grasp of the truth. Let us remember that all our faiths are not so much proclaimed as experienced, experienced when we experience not "the war of all against all," but the love of all for all, when we experience that community of mutual need and love not only between rich and poor, but also between people of all religious faiths.

As all of us are too painfully aware, we live in a crisis so extreme as to threaten the continuation of the human race. In such a time could Christ ride into this city without stopping before the UN?

In Saint Luke's version of Palm Sunday we read, "And when he drew near and saw the city he wept over it, saying, 'Would that even today you knew the things that make for peace!'" (Luke 19:41–42).

When I speak of a community of mutual need and love, I don't mean by "need" to awaken a sense of paltriness. I mean what Chinese writer Wang Meng wrote recently of America: "I wish Americans would be aware not only of what they know, what they have, and what they will do, but also of what they don't know, what they haven't achieved, and what they will never achieve. Only then can they be truly mature."

"Would that even today you knew the things that make for peace." Wouldn't it be mature behavior on the part of the United States and the Soviet Union to accept mediation in Geneva, for the United States to accept mediation in Central America, for all nations to heed Olof Palme's last signed wish, a wish so widely shared, that all nations forswear further nuclear testing? Can you imagine Christ arguing that the Cold War is good for warm Christian hearts?

Saint Paul proclaimed, "God has made of one blood all the nations of the world" (Acts 17:26). So true is that unity that every effort to deny it only succeeds in making it all the more imperative. The present state of affairs is such that if we do not shortly become one in life, we'll all be one in death.

Four hundred years ago, Galileo looked into the telescope and saw that Copernicus was right: The earth is not the center of the universe, but only a modest planet revolving around its sun. Today any truly mature person can see that no one country—no matter how glorious its past, how brilliant its future, how mighty its arms, or how generous its people—no one country is at the center of this earth. Today, as eternally in the eyes of God, there is only one century, and it is not the American century, nor the Russian nor the Chinese century; there is only a human century. So Christ rides into the city today through abandoned buildings, past the Cathedral and on to the UN, to affirm a community of mutual need and love between rich and poor, between people of all faiths, and between all nations.

With Palm Sunday begins Holy Week. So the day is both festive and heavy laden. That's why at the end of the service we are going to sing both "All Glory, Laud, and Honor" and "O Sacred Head, Now Wounded." When we do, and later, let us ask ourselves, have we the courage to dissent from the popular wisdom of the moment? Will the churches reinforce a heartless world by caring for its casualties but not challenging its assumptions? Will all of us learn from this most public day of Jesus' ministry to go more public ourselves—knowingly, tellingly? For otherwise we have no public conscience, we become playthings of evil forces, taking no hand in the game and allowing Christ to be crucified all over again.

These are things for us to ponder, we who so want to follow him who comes today in the name of the Lord.

Christ *in Vivo*

MARCH 30, 1986
Reading: Luke 24:1–12

It is wonderful to think that across 28 states, from sea to shining sea, the air today is bone dry, the sky is an uninterrupted blue, and the sun is beaming light and warmth upon millions of grateful people, not to mention their cats and dogs and myriad other forms of animal and plant life. Now all we have to do is to beautify what lies below—a nation and world which, compassionately organized, could feed, clothe, and house its inhabitants. That, I suspect, is why we are all here, we who are still Christ-haunted, if not Christ-centered, in our lives. We are here to celebrate love, that great beautifier of life, and pray for more of it. Not the love symbolized by Cupid, an infant in diapers, blindfolded to boot; but rather that love which has moved us so consistently all our lives, which we see in the Word made flesh, God's love in person on earth, a love not blind but visionary, a love that doesn't seek value so much as creates it, a love which, like William Cullen Bryant's truth crushed to earth will rise again. We are here to rejoice in the Easter message that we can kill God's love, but we cannot keep it dead and buried.

> The powers of death have done their worst,
> But Christ their legions hath dispersed: . . .

The three sad days have quickly sped;
He rises glorious from the dead:
All glory to our risen Head!
Alleluia!

Trans. Francis Pott

But that sounds like stupendous nonsense. It prompts a blizzard of questions, and certainly the Resurrection of Jesus Christ cannot be proved, if only because, as Tennyson noted, "Nothing worth proving can be proven, nor yet disproven." The story begs for interpretation, yet at the same time it defies any final interpretation. And that is what makes all of Scripture Scripture—the impossibility of arriving at a definitive interpretation. To say that is not to limit Scripture, only to limit our understanding of it.

Let two things be noted: (1) Christ came to forge, by love, a community that excluded no one; and (2) it is acknowledged ignorance that unites us, while acknowledged possession of The Truth divides us. Only seekers of the truth can create a community for all; those who have The Truth seem to have only a bottomless enmity for those who do not have it, or have another. Beware of Truth-possessors. They don't believe in human rights for everyone, they believe their Truth is right for everyone, regardless of the opinions we may have for our own lives. Possessors of The Truth don't believe in the Word made flesh, they believe in the Word made words.

We cannot prove the Resurrection, but we can believe in it, and underwrite it with our lives as the only way to experience the truth of it: that Christ is a presence, not a mere if inspiring memory. There is plenty of historical evidence for that experience. Millions have shared it, starting with Christ's disciples who were dispirited at his trial, deserted him in his hour of greatest suffering, and then, after his death, became ten times the people they were before, convinced of his continued presence in their lives.

On that first Easter, at the first streaks of dawn, Mary Magdalene, Joanna, Mary the mother of James, and all the other wonderful women who had accompanied Jesus from Galilee came to the tomb expecting to anoint Jesus' body with their spices. It was not customary to bury the body of criminals; usually they were left to the vultures and dogs. But a member of the Sanhedrin, Joseph of Arimathea, at odds apparently with the conclusions of the council, had saved Jesus' body from this indignity. With Pilate's permission, he had buried Jesus in a tomb; the tomb was then closed by a great circular stone which, like a cartwheel, ran in a groove across the opening.

Years later Joseph went to Britain—so goes the legend—bringing with him to Glastonbury the chalice that had been used at the Last Supper, and in it the blood of Christ. The chalice became the Holy Grail that King Arthur's knights sought so hard and vainly. The first church in Britain was built in Glastonbury, and some of you may have heard of St. Joseph's thorn that blooms at Christmas. To this day slips of it are shipped around the world. The flower originally sprang from the staff of Joseph of Arimathea when he plunged it into the ground to lean on it in his weariness. But I digress.

Arriving at the tomb the women are startled to see (in Luke's version) two men in dazzling apparel, who ask them a question that has altogether as much relevance today as it had then: "Why look among the dead for someone who is alive?" or, in the King James version, "Why seek ye the living among the dead?"

Too many Christians don't look for the living Christ. They don't want to see him *in vivo*, they want to keep him *in vitro*—under glass—embalmed in creeds, dogmas, and rituals, as well as in the King James version of the Bible, which they call a monument to English prose. (Wrote T. S. Elot: "Anyone who calls the King James version of the Bible a monument to English prose means a monument over the grave of Christianity.")

Where, then, would one look to find Christ *in vivo* at Easter time 1986? Saint Paul once dictated a ringing phrase to the Galatians: "For freedom Christ has set you free." I would look for My Risen Lord—and mind you who are properly sensitive to language, they called him "Lord" to make the point that Caesar is *not* Lord—among people free enough to recognize that creeds, dogmas, rituals, and the Bible in all its versions are all-important signposts but not hitching posts. Because I believe spirituality and creativity are kin, I would look for Jesus among those who do not follow where the path leads, but rather go where there is no path and leave a trail. If you march to someone else's drum, you get out of step with yourself. When approval or disapproval regulate what you say and do, freedom dissipates. Besides, anybody who needs more than God as his witness is too ambitious!

"For freedom Christ has set you free." We need to be free to be all we are capable of becoming; only so, deep down, can happiness ripple. But let us be clear. The apex of life is not individuality but personality—that which allows a person to love another person. The aim of individual life, like that of social life, is community life—a life that unifies, not one that fragments. Love is the measure of our freedom, for we are as we love. Let us be clear about this too: *We* cannot find God in other people. It is God in us who finds God in others.

So I would look for the Risen Lord where people are free to give rapt attention to one another's existence. Not where they try to *get* attention, where they *give* it. For giving our attention to one another's humanity is our constant Christian calling.

"Treat your friends as you do your pictures; place them in their best light" (Jennie Jerome Churchill). Treat your enemies as if Christ had died and risen for them too—which, most certainly, Christ did.

"Why seek ye the living among the dead?" My mind keeps returning to those women, who on Good Friday had watched it all from a distance, and in agony of mind and spirit. But pain is the root of knowledge. We learn of necessity. We are not naturally profound, we have to be forced down. You can learn more from ten days of agony than from ten years of contentment. Pain stretches us, it pushes us toward others. It could have been of those women around the cross that Dorothy Dix wrote: "It is only the women whose eyes have been washed clear with tears who get the broad vision that makes them little sisters to all the world."

Do you realize how important it is these days to get the broad vision, to become little sisters and brothers to all the world? The other day I heard of a 75-year-old man whose broker called him to say he had bought some stock that in five years would make him a millionaire. "Five years!" exclaimed the man. "I don't even buy green bananas anymore."

Had he been thinking of more than his own life, the man would have had a point. For time has taken wings and is hastening our world toward an inferno that even the mind of Dante could never imagine.

Only God has the authority to end life on this planet. We have only the power. I have no trouble hearing the voice of the Risen Christ pressing us to be sisters and brothers, not only to each other, but to all the world. I can hear Christ calling us to God's broad vision and in its name to oppose the arms race, the hatred that so frequently becomes a patriotic virtue, and all acts of exasperated imperial violence. To support mediation in place of confrontation, the test ban treaty, the UN, the international income tax, Black freedom (which makes White freedom possible)—all those good and necessary things could also fill the wrinkled bellies of millions of God's children who go to sleep hungry every night in a world which, organized in a brotherly/sisterly fashion, could feed them all.

The Son of God was more than a prophet but not less than one. Therefore, we can expect to find the Risen Christ not only with those who individually love one another, but also with those who work passionately, unrelentingly, for that day when "the last chariot will be burned in the fire, the wicked shall cease from troubling and the weary shall be at rest."

"Why seek ye the living among the dead?" Let us ask finally if we can expect to find the Risen Christ in the Christian church. The answer has to be a qualified yes. Yes, if the church remembers that the integrity of love is more important than the purity of dogma. Yes, if the church remembers that she cannot bind herself to the Prince of Peace and go awhoring after the gods of war. Yes, if the church remembers that she cannot proclaim the Gospel of Christ while officiating at the altars of anticommunism. Yes, if the church remembers that she cannot stand for peace while lying prostrate before the shrine of national security. Yes, if the church remembers that "the greatest of these is love," that Christ came to forge by love a community that excludes no one.

It is wrong that Christ should be used as a divisive symbol when Christ himself crossed every boundary to end all divisions. We say that death is the great equalizer, and so it is; not because death makes us equal, but because death mocks our pretensions at being anything else in the face of death, all differences of race and class and nationality become known for the trivial things they ultimately are. And so it is with Christ, the conqueror of death. As Saint Paul wrote: "There is neither Jew nor Greek, slave nor free, male nor female, for you are all one in Christ Jesus." In the Gospel of John, Christ says, "No one comes to the Father, except by me." That is not as is so often thought, a statement of resolute particularism. That means no one comes to the father except those willing to come with everyone else. *That* is "the way, the truth, and the life."

Do we wish to be Christ-centered, not just Christ-haunted? Do we wish to find Christ *in vivo*, not just *in vitro*? If so, let us pray that Christ today be resurrected in the heart of each of us, that we may give rapt attention to each other's existence, become sisters and brothers to all the world, and help the church draw a circle of love that includes everyone.

> The powers of death have done their worst,
> But Christ their legions hath dispersed:
> Let shouts of holy joy outburst. Alleluia!

"Do You Love Me?"

APRIL 13, 1986
Reading: John 21:1–17

S imon Peter said, "I am going fishing." After Passover in Jerusalem, the disciples are back in Galilee; back among the boats lying on the beach, back among their companions, mending their nets exactly as they had done for years before being summoned away by Jesus. They stand together in the evening light watching boat after boat push off—the women wishing the men good luck, the men getting their tackle in trim and probably casting a look or two of pity at the disciples. Peter can bear it no longer and makes for his boat with the words, "I'm going fishing." The rest need only to hear the suggestion: "We will go with you."

The disciples have beheld the Risen Lord, so there's nothing more to see. For two years they have been listening to everything they needed to hear. The whole Christian church is waiting to be brought to life, midwifed by these disciples, and all the earthly hope of the church can think to do is to fall back into the old routine—six oars flashing in the setting sun. "You gotta make a living."

Nighttime was best for fishing. With torches blazing, the boats glided over the flashing sea. The men gazed into the water until the fish were sighted. Then, quick as lightning, they flung their nets, which belled out in the air, falling so precisely on the water that the small lead weights hit the lake at the same moment, making a thin circular splash. It was also hard work. And often, as on this particular morning, fishermen came into the harbor having toiled all night in vain.

When Jesus told them to cast their nets on the right side of the boat it may have been because from the shore, in the dawn's early light, he could see better than could the disciples in the boat. The catch does not have to be read as a miracle. What is striking, though, is this: we who live so much for the world and so little for God, on the grounds that "you gotta make a living," don't realize that just as Jesus did for the disciples that morning, so the Lord can provide what we need better than we ourselves can provide.

"Cast your net on the right side of the boat." At this time of year I always think of the students who come to universities with both ambition and ideals, encouraged in their ideals by their parents. I'm not knocking ambition per se; it's a splendid servant, albeit a terrible master. Just before graduation students see their ambition and ideals in conflict as they realize that what our society teaches us to believe, and what our society rewards as belief, are very different. Which, then, to put aside—ambition or ideals? Initially their parents had cheered their ideals, but now they tend to urge the fulfillment of ambition: "We spent a lot of money on your education." So, for one reason or another, students tend to go with their ambition. They take their ideals, find a closet to park them in, and there they stay until a few years later these students marry and have children. Then suddenly they remember, open the closet door, pull out the ideals, and say to the children, "Here, play with these." That's how we keep our ideals going in this society.

When Jesus told the disciples to cast their nets on the right side, he was making the point, once again, that "man does not live by bread alone, but by every word that proceedeth out of the mouth of God." We are much safer letting our ambition be a servant to our ideals, much safer to follow our consciences, much safer to do God's bidding rather than to struggle anxiously to make a living. Jesus was very insistent on this point. "Consider the lilies of the field, how they grow; they neither toil nor spin; yet I tell you, even Solomon in all his glory was not arrayed like one of these. But if God so clothes the grass of the field, which today is alive and tomorrow is thrown into the oven, will he not much more clothe you, O men of little faith? Therefore do not be anxious, saying, 'What shall we eat?' or 'What shall we drink?' or 'What shall we wear?' For the Gentiles seek all these things; and your heavenly Father knows that you need them all. But seek first his kingdom and his righteousness, and all these things shall be yours as well" (Matt. 6:28–33).

Then comes breakfast: bread, fish—and Jesus. I love this scene. Breakfast usually represents the same food, in the same place, with the same people, and generally all three are not at their absolute best. I'm reminded of another breakfast scene. In Thornton Wilder's *Our Town*, Emily Webb, who has died, is told that she can go back to earth to relive one day. She chooses her twelfth birthday. She has hardly finished chewing her bacon when she turns to the Stage Manager, who has arranged her return, and says, "I can't. I can't go on. It goes so fast. We don't have time to look at one another." She breaks down sobbing. The lights dim on the left half of the stage. Mrs. Webb disappears. Emily goes on: "I didn't realize. So all that was going on and we never noticed. Take me back—up the hill—to my grave. But first: Wait! One more look. Good-by, good-by, world. Good-by, Grover's Corners . . . Mama and Papa. Good-by to clocks ticking . . . and Mama's sunflowers. And food and coffee. And new-ironed dresses and hot baths . . . and sleeping and waking up. Oh, earth, you're too wonderful for anybody to realize you." She looks toward the Stage Manager and asks abruptly, through her tears: "Do any human beings ever realize life while they live it?—every, every minute?" Stage Manager: "No. . . . The saints and poets, maybe—they do some." To me bread, fish, and Jesus symbolize the routine redeemed. Any affair with Jesus is full of wonder. Everything gets noticed. There's plenty of time for everyone to look at one another. That's why I so love that breakfast scene.

"When they had finished breakfast, Jesus said to Simon Peter, 'Simon, son of John, do you love me more than these?'" Which he probably asked with a sweep of his hand that took in the boats and the nets and the equipment and all the fish. In other words, "Am I more to you than your old life, more to you than your sole means of gaining a livelihood?" And he asked the same question three times, as if to give Peter the same number of chances to affirm Peter's love for Jesus that Peter had taken to deny it before the cock crowed before daybreak on Good Friday.

Jesus is testing not Peter's conduct, but his heart—which I find wonderfully encouraging. All of us who count ourselves Christians can no more doubt our love for Jesus than we can doubt our denial of that love by our conduct. But Jesus is less interested in our conduct than in our hearts. How strong in them is our love for him? "Do you love me more than these?" Do you love me, or is it simply some passing fancy, some momentary impulse, some kind of sense of duty? He asks so insistently because love alone has the power to carry us out of ourselves and make other interests than our own supremely important to us. Jesus tests our hearts rather than our conduct. "Do you love me?" is the only question Jesus asks Peter—and us. Jesus is on the point of leaving the world and leaving the future of the sheep he so loved in the hands of Peter. Does he draw up a creed, some binding articles of faith or conduct? Does he set forth a method by which to govern the future church? Does he ask for oaths and signatures? No, he rests the whole future of the work he had begun at such cost on Peter's love for him.

The apostolic commission is three times the same: "Feed my sheep." In other words, "Be helpful to those for whom I died. Show them my love! My love has attracted you, my disciples; make that love attractive to all humanity. That's all. All the rest is commentary."

God is love, so God presents humanity with goodness in human form. Jesus' goodness is perfect; it is complete. Not to love him is not to love goodness; it is to be out of sympathy with that which can regenerate our wills, make us better people, and help us to better the world. Let the love of Christ possess any soul, and that soul cannot avoid being a blessing to the world around. Wherever the love of Christ exists, sooner or later Christ's purposes will be understood and his goals for justice and peace implemented.

Most of us probably love Jesus more than we know. We probably sang with considerable conviction: "Jesus shines brighter, Jesus shines purer than all the angels heaven can boast." We're set in old ways— routine ways that promise pleasure and profit to self, but little more. For that reason alone we're readier than we think to respond to this absorbing, educating, impelling, irresistible power of love which can carry us beyond our boring selfish ways.

So, this week, whenever you have to make decisions about how you're going to think and act in this world, whether it be with your parents, your children, your spouse, your lover, your colleagues at work, or with friends; whenever you have to decide how your country should respond to terrorism or to invitations to stop nuclear testing, to the plight of the elderly poor and young poor too, don't let your heart contract, let it expand. Let your heart hear that insistent question that Jesus addresses to each of us. "Robert, Sarah, Ruth, Andy"—fill in your own name—"do you love me more than these? Do you love me? Do you love me?"

I suspect a lot more of you than think you can are able, willing, and eager to answer, "Yes, Lord. You know that I love you." And if that's the case, then we know God's precious, hungry sheep will be fed.

The Only Commandment

APRIL 20, 1986
Reading: John 13:31–34

Before exploring the lesson of the day, let's go back and pick up on Judas.

> When Jesus had thus spoken, he was troubled in spirit, and testified, "Truly, truly, I say to you, one of you will betray me." The disciples looked at one another, uncertain of whom he spoke. One of his disciples, whom Jesus loved, was lying close to the breast of Jesus; so Simon Peter beckoned to him and

said, "Tell us who it is of whom he speaks." So lying thus, close to the breast of Jesus, he said to him, "Lord, who is it?" Jesus answered, "It is he to whom I shall give this morsel when I have dipped it." So when he had dipped the morsel, he gave it to Judas, the son of Simon Iscariot. Then after the morsel, Satan entered into him. Jesus said to him, "What you are going to do, do quickly." Now no one at the table knew why he said this to him. Some thought that, because Judas had the money box, Jesus was telling him, "Buy what we need for the feast"; or, that he should give something to the poor. So, after receiving the morsel, he immediately went out; and it was night. (John 13:21–30)

"And it was night"—the night that falls so suddenly after a twilightless sunset in the Middle East. And, of course, it's night anywhere when a man turns his back on Jesus. It's a night devoid of stars when hate puts out the light of love.

In my thirty years of ministry, I have never baptized a child or adult named Judas. It's a name nobody wants. Judas accepted Christ's love, shared his bread, pressed his hand continuously with assurances of fidelity—and then sold out. When a person professes friendship for you, then uses the information gained to slander your character, ruin your peace, injure your family, and damage your business— that's treachery. It's treachery that makes Judas so much worse than the Pharisees, Jesus' declared opponents from the very beginning. It's treachery that makes Benedict Arnold worse than General Howe. It's treachery that makes so moving Julius Caesar's dying question: "Et tu, Brute?"

The trouble with Judas' extraordinary capacity for evil is that it makes us overlook what must have been his more than ordinary capacity for good. After all, he was one of the disciples and must have been so for some time, because he was their treasurer. They must have trusted him. I can see not entrusting the common fund to impulsive Peter, or to dreamy John; but why not to Matthew, the tax collector? He must have had a faculty for finance. Notice also that while other disciples incurred Jesus' displeasure, there is no record of Judas saying or doing anything wrong until he walked out the door that Maundy Thursday night, apparently taking with him the common fund.

It occurs to me that many of us are Christians to the same degree Judas was: we're willing to go along with Christ as long as that proves exciting or consoling, as long as it does something for us. I suspect Judas sought to use Christ, but was not willing to be used by him. I suspect Judas wanted Christ *and* the world, and in trying to get the best of both, he got neither worldly goods nor spiritual attainment. So he became bitter and resentful, the stuff of which traitors are formed. How much better it would have been for Judas if he had never followed Christ, if he had ended up, say, a small trader with false weights in some small town in Galilee. Maybe a lot of us would be better off not trying to follow Christ, if, like Judas, our love for money is greater than our love for others. It's something worth thinking about in a day when the love of money is so easily gratified.

In any case, I'm sad never to have baptized a Judas. And it's sad to think that instead of standing forever on the pinnacle of infamy, Judas could have been one of the twelve foundations of the eternal city.

Now let's get into the lesson for the day. "When he [Judas] had gone out," Jesus begins his farewell discourse to the remaining disciples. He predicts his imminent death—"Now is the Son of man glorified"—and that word "glory" reminds us once again that death is not the great tragedy we so often make it out to be. What is tragic are the "little deaths," the good things that die in us while we yet live. How many otherwise healthy people walk around with dead hearts!

"Now is the Son of man glorified." It is history's simplest lesson that those who have made the greatest sacrifices have always been accorded the greatest glory. We have only to think of Socrates, Joan of Arc, Nathan Hale, Abraham Lincoln, Sandino, Aquino, Martin Luther King Jr., Archbishop Romero: they were selfless people; they never withheld their love simply because there was no guarantee that their love would be honored and returned.

"Now is the Son of man glorified." Look at the cross. Is it not an "I," a capital "I," the symbol of a big competitive ego, to use the kids' well-chosen phrase—is it not a capital "I" crossed out?

"Now is the Son of man glorified." Christ is a mirror to our humanity, showing us, as do all the lives of all the martyrs, that what's worth living for is also worth dying for. Remember: "Love bears all things, believes all things, hopes all things, endures all things."

"Now is the Son of man glorified *and in him God is glorified*." Christ is not only a mirror to our humanity; he is also a window to divinity showing us God's invincible mercy. When the Son of man is crucified upon a cross that his murderers might live, we see God's unconquerable and universal benevolence even toward those who break her laws and hearts. There is a rabbinic tale according to which when the Egyptians were drowning in the Red Sea, some angels began a hymn of praise and thanksgiving. But God said sorrowfully, "The work of my hands are sunk in the sea, and you would sing before me."

Peter, you remember, denied Christ just as surely as Judas betrayed him. The difference is that Peter came back to receive his forgiveness. The tragedy of Judas is that he never did.

Look again at the cross. See in it this time not a capital I crossed out, but our "minus" turned by God's forgiveness into a "plus."

"Now is the Son of man glorified and in him God is glorified." Then follows what Christ calls a new commandment—"A new commandment I give you"—which is new only in the comparison it makes. The old commandment was "Love your neighbor as yourself." The new commandment is to love one another *even as I have loved you.*" And that's the only commandment Jesus gives his disciples. He doesn't say, "You have to go to church every Sunday"; "You must never touch a drop of alcohol"; "You've got to believe in the Virgin Birth, the Immaculate Conception, and every word in the Bible." No, if you love, you can do what you like. But *you have to love*, "even as I have loved you."

It is said that when Voltaire lay dying, some self-styled religious folk crowded around his bed urging him to renounce the devil and all his ways. The old philosopher thought about it, then answered, "This is no time to be making enemies."

We can say that again for ourselves: This is no time to be making enemies. God has not given us hearts to hate and hands to destroy one another.

"That you love one another, even as I have loved you." Many of us have had a lot of schooling. We've had our heads stuffed with literature, science, and philosophy, but we know precious little about getting along with others. Few of us are passionately convinced that love of others is more important than love of money. We haven't learned that love, among other things, is listening. If we can't listen to each other, and, for that matter, to people from all over the world, it isn't long before we aren't listening to God either.

We Americans think we are unqualifiedly the best country in the world. We think we don't have to listen to anybody. And, of course, some other countries think exactly the same way about themselves. The nations of the world are so unequal in their eyes and so equal in God's!

How can we so easily forget the children, as obviously we did last Monday night? The raid on Libya recalls *Macbeth*, Act IV, Scene III:

> *Ross*: Your castle is surprised; your wife and babes savagely slaughtered. . . .

April 20, 1986

Macduff: My children too?

    Ross: Wife, children, servants, all that could be found.

Macduff: And I must be from thence! My wife killed too?

Then Malcolm, who thinks all this should be a whetstone for the sword, chimes in.

    Malcolm: Be comforted: let's make us medicines of our great
            revenge, to cure this deadly grief.

    Macduff (pointing at Malcolm): He has no children.

The death of Qaddafi's 15-month-old daughter is as terrible as the death of the baby blown from the TWA plane by a terrorist's explosive. One does not avenge the other. By fighting fire with fire, Libya and America are producing only more ashes. The more we Americans bomb, the more we are shaped by our actions into the very image of those we profess to oppose and seek to destroy. That is why the attack on the soil of Libya was an assault on the soul of America. As Arie Brouwer, General Secretary of the National Council of Churches, wrote the president, "Justice is not achieved by the vengeful flexing of military muscles. Justice requires us to address the deep underlying issues of injustice, primarily, in this instance, the denial of Palestinian national rights." We must back off from this brink, lest we fulfill the prediction: "And so, to the end of history, murder shall breed murder, always in the name of right and honor and peace, until the gods are tired of blood and create a race that can understand" (*Caesar and Cleopatra*, by George Bernard Shaw).

Youth of Riverside Church: On this your Sunday, let me urge you to consider this new commandment, that you love one another—and everyone else in this world—even as Jesus has loved you. This is no time to be making enemies. This is no time even to be making money—at least not more than you need. This is a time to listen and learn and to remember, as St. Paul says, "Love never ends." It's sometimes hard to believe, but love outlasts sarcasm, put-down, misunderstanding, vanity, thoughtlessness, flippancy, insensitivity, heavy-handedness, snobbery, and all the other misuses of life that foul up relationships and lead to destruction and death.

St. Benedict said, "God often shows what is better to the younger." I believe that. I believe in you. Believe in yourselves. Believe in Jesus. Save this gorgeous world so prone to self-destruct. Love it to life. God will bless you, and those of us still around, you can be sure, will sing your praises.

The Great Bequest

ARIL 27, 1986
Reading: John 14:23–27

St. John's language is often so mystical as to sound almost foreign to Protestant ears. But to Orthodox Christians—Greek, Russian, Syrian, Indian—and to the Orthodox Ethiopians who worship here every Sunday in Christ Chapel, St. John is the best. They love his understanding of mystery—"In the beginning was the Word and the Word was with God, and the Word was God"—mystery defined not as a definite uncertainty, but as an indefinite certainty, which God, Christ, and even we most certainly are. And they are deeply moved by John's insistence that love is the basis of everything: God loves Jesus and Jesus loves God; God loves humanity, Jesus loves humanity; we are to love God through Jesus and also one another. To the Orthodox, the relationship of heaven and earth is like a mystical isosceles triangle with God at the apex, you and me at the base angles (which, you remember, are equal in an isosceles triangle), and all around the triangle courses love—if only we would turn on the circuitry.

But God's love, whose mystery is so wonderfully celebrated by the words in St. John's Gospel and the Orthodox Churches in chant and incense—this love does not pamper. It does not mollycoddle us. It brought St. Stephen to his knees, bruised and bleeding, under a rain of death-dealing stones. It was God's love for him and his love for God that kept St. Paul going when he was driven from one city and dragged lifeless from another, when he clung to a spar in a wild sea and was arraigned before magistrate after magistrate. To his sisters and brothers at Corinth, St. Paul described the Christian life in this fashion: "We are afflicted in every way, but not crushed; perplexed, but not driven to despair; persecuted, but not forsaken; struck down, but not destroyed; always carrying in the body the death of Jesus, so that the life of Jesus may also be manifested in our bodies" (2 Cor. 4:8–10).

In short, this love of God coursing around this mystical isosceles triangle is no tranquilizer. It inspires before it consoles. It shames us and it fires us up. It doesn't relieve our burdens, it piles them on, because, as St. Paul, St. Stephen, St. John, and all the evangelists realized, a moral affinity with Christ is necessary to receive Christ's love. All this is summed up in John's report of Jesus' words: "If any love me, they will keep my word."

After which comes the promise of everlasting comfort in the form of a wonderful mystical thought: "If any love me, they will keep my word . . . and we"—that is, God and Christ—"will come to them *and make our home with them.*"

Mystics often talk of what they call a "wilderness experience," an experience of solitude. Father Thomas Merton once said, "Alas, in America there's no wilderness, only dude ranches." What he was getting at is this: Americans are afraid of being alone for fear of having to pay a call on themselves and finding no one at home! But imagine finding at home not only yourself, but God and Jesus too. Wouldn't that take care of just about everything from a clear direction for your life to the best possible company along the way?

Already I can read the thoughts of some of you: "Why in the world would Jesus ever want to come to my home? That's worse than being born in a manger. My home, which is my heart, is one crummy abode."

I have a story for you self-deprecating folk. Thornton Wilder's earthly home was in New Haven, Connecticut, although occasionally he would go off on a wilderness experience of his own, which he once described as "writing in Arizona in a remote spot equidistant between two bars." In the 1950s, while a seminarian in New Haven, I was invited to listen to Mr. Wilder read his latest play in the company of about 20 older people. Needless to say, I was honored, but not sufficiently intimidated. When he finished reading, which he did with great gusto, he asked if there were any reactions. I allowed as I thought the ending was a bit thin. As no conversation whatsoever ensued from that remark, I quickly concluded that I would not be reinvited—which proved correct. As I was going out the door, Mr. Wilder detained me, and when the others had gone, he asked, "Billy boy, would you like to throw down a few thimblefuls?" Once again I was honored, and this time resolved only to listen.

Mr. Wilder never claimed to believe in God. (He left that to his theologian brother, Amos.) But after two or three thimblefuls, he looked very hard at me and said, "Remember, Billy boy, God has a hard time loving those who do not love themselves."

An astute observation, and here's how, over the years, I've tried to interpret it. It is no easy matter to love yourself because that means loving all of yourself, the miserable, unlovable parts along with the lovable, the "shadow" side, as the Jungians would say, along with the bright. Freud, too, recognized the problem: "It's a good thing people do not love their neighbors as themselves; if they did, they'd kill them"—which is exactly what we're doing a large part of the time.

What we're facing here is a paradox, two things that cannot be reconciled but must be kept together. On one hand, we have morally to recognize that those unlovable parts are intolerable and burdensome, and must change. On the other hand, we have lovingly, laughingly, to accept them just as they are. On one hand we have to try hard, on the other to let go; to judge harshly and to join gladly, because each side has only one side of the truth.

When you think about it, that's the way God loves each of us, and we should love our neighbors, if that's the only way to make the unlovely parts more lovely. So let us not decline the gracious invitation of God and Jesus. Let us gladly make them at home in our crummy little abodes. Pretty soon—just watch!—there will be new slipcovers, carpets, books, and music. And most of all, the windows will be so clean you'll have an entirely new view of life.

> If any love me, they will keep my word, and we will come to them and make our home with them. (John 14:23)

> These things I have spoken to you, while I am still with you. But the Counselor, the Holy Spirit, whom the Father will send in my name, he will teach you all things, and bring to your remembrance all that I have said to you. (John 14:25–26)

We need to be reminded more than we need to be informed. As Christians, we need to be reminded of Jesus' words which, though familiar, are like the seed that fell on the hard ground. They fall on minds too preoccupied, on consciences grown dull, on egos too compulsive, too intentional, too intent on their own way. The ancient writer Homer saw this truth. Ulysses had to best the giant of the hungry eye, the single-minded demon of compulsion, before he could proceed on his way. Likewise, if we are to proceed in Christ's way, we have to defeat our compulsions and constantly find the time to listen again to Jesus *with maximum attention and minimum intention.* Only then can the Holy Spirit of love guide our thinking.

And push us to think further. Christ cannot be both text and exposition. He is the truth, but we have to discover the meaning of that truth for ourselves and for our time. It cannot be said too often: Faith is no substitute for thought; it is what makes good thinking possible. Maybe the Holy Spirit of love is not necessary to dissect and correctly analyze the stomach of a spider, but it certainly is necessary when it comes to the affairs of the heart of human beings and the affairs of God. If your heart's full of hate and icy cold you cannot think straight—not about human affairs. Cold-blooded intellectualism will never force the lock on the temple of learning. Only those who love and long for goodness are wise scholars in the Holy Spirit's school of international affairs, political science, history, philosophy, and literature.

Finally, let's turn to what is often called "the great bequest," which is found only in the Gospel of John and which we recall each Sunday with the passing of the peace. Jesus says: "Peace I leave you; my peace I give to you; not as the world gives do I give to you. Let not your hearts be troubled, neither let them be afraid" (John 14:27).

These words are consoling to hear at funeral services, where they are often read. They are also comforting when, in older age, you feel the sting of transiency, when at your back you hear "time's winged chariot hurrying near."

These words were not originally addressed to old or grieving people, but rather to young disciples soon to be bereft of Jesus' visible presence and facing a future full of uncertainty. Jesus doesn't say, "My house I leave you," or lands, clothes, or money, for he had none. At death his sole possession was a robe. He leaves them to enjoy only that which so characterized his life: the same serenity in danger (he lived, after all, among bitterly hostile people); the same equanimity in troubling circumstances; the same freedom from anxiety about results; the same quiet strength, when reviled, not to revile in turn.

"My peace I give you." I confess I have a hard time with that word peace. I cannot listen to peace-talk from people too shallow to know that it is finally only in the depth of hell that heaven is affirmed and life is sanctified. I cannot listen to peace-talk from scared people who give me quick Biblical answers because they are too frightened to confront tough personal questions. I cannot listen to peace-talk from a lot of folk in the so-called peace movement because they are manifestly hostile.

But when Jesus tells me to pray "Our father who art in heaven," I listen. He can talk convincingly to me, and I suspect to all of us, about a father in heaven because he took so seriously the homeless orphans of the earth. He can talk convincingly to us about living in peace in the hands of love because he knew that the world lives at war in the grip of hatred. "My peace I give you." It is the reliability of the source that gives such authority to the words.

"Not as the world gives do I give to you." Most of us seek our peace in worldly things—comfort, ease, reputation, knowing the right people. But such peace is finally no peace; it is short-lived. Worldly desire gratified is like a beggar to whom you give a dollar—soon he's back with a request greatly enlarged rather than curtailed. And worldly peace is a delusion because it represents the beginning of bondage of the worst kind. ("Woe to those who are at ease in Zion.") Worldly things can no more bring peace of mind than a soft bed can give rest to a fevered body. Peace must arise from within.

Naturally we would love to see peace rise and shine upon us as the sun, without any effort of our own. When Jesus promises us his peace, it's like a father promising a daughter a good education, or a general promising his men victory. It is a demand as well as a promise. We have to put out for the promise to come true.

We have come full circle, or, should we say, gone once around the mystical isosceles triangle. It takes a moral affinity with Christ to receive Christ's love: "If any love me, they will keep my word." If we do love Christ, he and God will make their home in our hearts, making all the unlovely things so much lovelier. The Holy Spirit, the spirit of love, will guide our thinking and push us to further thought until eventually we come to know the peace that the world can neither give nor take away.

Dearly beloved of the Lord, in the midst of turmoil—and we all live in it these days, not to say death and destruction—let not your hearts be troubled, neither let them be afraid. Let us rise and wish one another that oh so mysterious, but oh so real, peace of God.

For the World to Survive

MAY 4, 1986
Readings: Amos 6:1–7; Colossians 3:8–17

There is an ancient rabbinic saying that for the world to survive, it must hold fast to three things: to truth, to justice, and to peace. No one of these has the world ever held in anything approaching a white-knuckled grip. So while nature, displaying gorgeous spring fashions, moves gracefully and inevitably toward summer, the world careens toward nuclear war. We can only hope that the tragedy caused by the Soviet reactor will prove the disaster necessary to validate the nuclear crisis—the crisis of both energy *and* nuclear weaponry. (Why is a crisis never a crisis until it is validated by disaster?)

For the world to survive, it must hold fast to three things: to truth, to justice, and to peace. The three, of course, are related. Lies need violence for protection, just as violence needs the rationalization of lies. And peace is not the absence of tension but the presence of justice.

Still we can distinguish if not separate the three. Let's see, on this Peace Sabbath, if we can say something significant on the subject of each.

What kind of truth did the ancient rabbis have in mind?

Some seven or eight years ago I was invited to address several hundred clergy gathered in Enid, Oklahoma. I like talking to clergy. None of us knows anymore what it means to be a successful minister, priest, or rabbi. The death of certainty is the birth of need. We're needy, we clergy—far more vulnerable and more sensitive than we were thirty years ago. That's good.

For a couple of days I inveighed, in my usual fashion, against the madness of the arms race; I compared sexism and homophobia to racism, and attacked an assortment of other personal and social ills. During the question and answer period after the last session, just before I was scheduled to return to Riverside, one brother rose to make a very astute observation: "Coffin, you're a true prophet. You blow in, blow off, and blow out." Then another asked, "How do you get away with saying the things you say? They'd run you out of town in Tulsa."

I replied, "First of all, I never said Tulsa was leading the nation. But the answer to that question lies not primarily in the difference between New York and Tulsa, or between liberal and conservative churches. How many of you have read two books on homosexuality and the church?" I asked. About four hands went up. "How many have read two books on the arms race?" This time there were about twenty hands—but that was out of several hundred.

"Now you've got the answer," I said. "Most of you would bite your tongues purple rather than speak out on a controversial issue; you wouldn't know what to say. And to make matters worse, to the degree that your ignorance stems from your complacency, it is an ethical and not an intellectual default."

It was a mean but fair remark. And it got at the truth the ancient rabbis had in mind—the truth we would all rather deny, but must confront, for our personal salvation and the world's survival. There is a certain unacceptability about unpleasant truth. Said Amaziah the priest about Amos the prophet, "The land cannot bear his words." But the land must bear his words, dark and awesome though they be. For if there's a way to the better, it lies in taking a full look at the worst. No pain, no gain. No judgment, no hope. Without repentance there's no salvation. There's no other way.

In his book *1984*, Orwell warned of a regime that would control through pain and hate. In 1986 I worry less about the American people being controlled through pain and hate and more about their becoming passive through their appetite for distractions. Instead of freedom-loving, people-loving, truth-seeking—that, is, God-fearing people, I fear we shall become a nation of entertained slaves. I fear our becoming hired applauders for smooth-talking religious and political leaders, an ignorant people because complacent.

Two years ago, when the TWA plane was hijacked, before finally landing at Beirut the terrorists let some hostages go. (I believe it was in Tripoli.) When questioned by the press about their captors, one of the released hostages said, "For some reason they seem to hate New Jersey."

What could young Lebanese terrorists possibly hold against the Garden State? What the hostage had forgotten (if she ever knew) was that the *New Jersey* was the battleship that all too recently had lobbed one-half-ton shells into the mountain villages of Lebanon, killing hundreds of innocent civilians.

There is a nonrabbinic saying: What you don't know won't hurt you. That's nonsense. What we Americans don't know will kill us, as it has already lots of other people.

St. Paul wrote the Colossians: "You must live your whole life according to the Christ you have received." Your whole life—not only your family life, your vocational life, your life as a citizen. Anyone who has received Christ has experienced the death of certainty and the birth of need. Such a person is vulnerable, sensitive, with lots of love in her heart and her mind all stirred up. It is inconceivable that a caring Christian could be ignorant through complacency.

The ancient rabbis were right. For the world to survive, it must hold fast to truth.

Also to justice.

We all know of Rip Van Winkle and how he slept twenty years. What few people realize is what years those were. When Rip Van Winkle went up the mountain to sleep, the picture on the sign below was of King George III. Twenty years later, when he came down, the picture was of George Washington. In other words, Rip slept through a revolution.

Two hundred years later, his compatriots are doing the same. Most Americans are peacefully sleeping through, or are having positive nightmares about, what Adlai Stevenson called "the revolution of rising expectations." It is a revolution of human rights defined in terms of social justice. It is sweeping Third World nations, supported by a theology of liberation that sees justice as central to, not ancillary to, salvation, revelation, sacramentalism, and spirituality. It is a revolution not made by communists, nor even by revolutionaries. Like all revolutions, it is made by unjust, repressive regimes for the simple reason that you can't have a revolt without revolting conditions. The fire won't spread unless the wood is dry. Only when the economic oligarchs are few do the freedom fighters become many. And armed guerrillas they do become, because governments that make peaceful evolution impossible make violent revolution inevitable. As Amos warned, "You think to defer the day of misfortune, but you hasten the reign of violence."

And don't think that this reign of violence is not coming to cities whose ghettos have become breeding grounds for terrorists. Injustices stunt growth in developing countries. They also endanger prosperity in developed ones. In New York City, we live amid great bridges that span the rivers and buildings that kiss the sky. But the economic outlook is bleak and growing bleaker for the hundreds of thousands of poorly educated, low-income residents in our area. The world does not belong to the great and powerful alone. When will they remember the rest? When will they hear the prophet's prediction:

> They drink wine by the bowlful . . .
> but about the ruin of Joseph they do not care at all.
> That is why they will be the first to be exiled;
> the sprawlers' revelry is over.
>
> Amos 6:6–7

The longer we Americans persist in making the rich richer, the poor poorer, and the military more powerful, the shorter the fuse on the time bomb. We must find alternative forms of abundance.

I said justice was central to, not ancillary to, spirituality. When the spiritual life is strong, it creates world history; when weak, it suffers world history. As Christians, let us awake from our sleep and rise from the dead, and Christ will shine upon us so that we can assert the primacy of the spiritual over the material in an increasingly secular world.

For the world to survive, it must hold fast to truth and justice.

And finally to peace, which is hardly a present-day habit of humanity.

Many of us cherish the words of President Eisenhower, spoken shortly before leaving office: "I like to think that people want peace more than governments. In fact, they want it so badly that one of these days governments had better get out of their way and let them have it."

Here are some other words of his: "Down the long lane of history, yet to be written, America knows that this world of ours, ever growing smaller, must avoid becoming a community of dreadful fear and hate, and be, instead, a proud confederation of mutual trust and respect."

Let Christians seek to break down the dividing walls of hostility. Let's not allow the long and chilling silence of the Soviet government about their nuclear calamity to whip up anti-Soviet hysteria in our hearts. As I recall, accurate information was not exactly forthcoming from Three Mile Island. And let us never self-righteously say that the greatest danger to the world is atheistic communism. Atheistic communism declares there is no God. Self-righteousness says that we do not need God. What's the difference? Moreover, I share the view that whenever and wherever the day of reform dawns in the Soviet system, religion will be a part of it.

In the meantime, it's not them and us; it's just us. And all of us, as I said at the outset, are careening toward nuclear war. In World War II, six million Jews were herded into boxcars, stripped, shot or gassed, and incinerated in ovens all over Eastern Europe. But on the trains the great majority never guessed their destiny. We're on such a train to an even greater incineration and haven't the eyes to perceive it.

Peace does not come rolling in on the wheels of inevitability. We can't just wish for peace. We have to will it, fight for it, suffer for it, demand it from our governments as if peace were God's most cherished hope for humanity, as indeed it is. Let's end with words from St. Paul: "To crown all, there must be love, to bind all together and complete the whole. Let Christ's peace be arbiter in your hearts; to this peace you were called" (Col. 3:15).

Our calling, in the ancient vision of the rabbis, is to save the world by holding fast to truth, to justice, and to peace.

"Mother o' Mine"

MAY 11, 1986
Readings: Hosea 11:1–9; Matthew 12:46–50

We pray "Our father who art in heaven," but "Mother is the name for God in the lips and hearts of little children," wrote Thackeray in *Vanity Fair*.

And how about these words from Edgar Allan Poe:

> The angels . . . singing unto one another
> Can find among their burning terms of love
> None so devotional as that of "Mother."

I think that's the way a lot of us feel as we recall the beauty in what Alice Walker calls the "so nearly undefeated faces" of our mothers, so many of whom we see today only in vivid memory.

Nor should we overlook the old Jewish proverb, according to which "God could not be everywhere, and therefore he made mothers."

The proverb is of course sexist, not only because God is referred to as "he," but also because fathers too are supposed to mother. Just as the woman most in need of liberation is the woman in every man, so the mother most in need of recognition is the mother in every father. And we have to mother/father not only children—run to help them when they fall, kiss the place to make it well—but all the incredibly tender lives among which we pass each day.

But let's start with the babies, and with the words (translated from the French Reformed Service) we heard earlier when we baptized little Evanda: "Little child, for you Jesus Christ came, he struggled, he suffered; for you he endured the darkness of Gethsemane and the agony of Calvary; for you he triumphed over death; and you, little child, know nothing of all this. But thus is confirmed the word of the apostle, 'We love God because God first loved us.'"

To be a mother is first and foremost to be a vessel of grace: to love a child before the child can love back; to pour out one's heart to a child before the child can even say, "Thank you." "We love God because God first loved us." Our children will one day love only because they first were loved. If not loved, children become like those young birches we see this time of year in the woods of New England—all bent over because the storms of winter hit them before they were ready, and now no amount of sunshine will ever straighten them out again. If a child is not offered love, or for some reason can't accept love, that child may well end up in a mental hospital more accurately called by the Russians "hospital, for the soul sick," because the mental changes are only an effect; the lack of love is the cause.

It's a heavy responsibility to be a parent. But we kid ourselves when we treasure our freedoms, not realizing that it is our obligations that give our lives their meaning. Children are the anchors that hold us to life. Chubby children hanging to our necks keep us low and wise!

Simply having children, however, does not make mothers. Nor, as I suggested, do you have to have children in order to mother. "Whoever does the will of God is my brother and sister and mother." All of us are called to love each other into all God made and meant us to be.

Let's refine that statement. To love is surely to support and to encourage—but not necessarily to approve. Quite the contrary! If we love one another we will help one another fight against our evil dreams.

When through despair or self-pity we become dead to rapture, friends are needed to remind us that God made the rift of dawn, the reddening rose, Plato and the Pleiades, to give us solace when life becomes rough. A friend is not one who puts her friendship before her friend, but rather one who risks her friendship for the sake of her friend.

So love—mother love at its best—is not always approval. Nor is it sweetness and light. Rather, love has a bitter flavor, like the distilled juice of some wild berry, which makes the idea of sweetness bland and disagreeable by contrast.

But if love is not necessarily approval nor sweetness and light, it is acceptance, always acceptance, keeping love up front no matter what. Isn't that what we heard just now from the prophet Hosea? Isn't that what the story of the Prodigal Son is about? Didn't Kipling write:

> If I were hanged on the highest hill
> Mother o' mine, O mother o' mine
> I know whose love would follow me still
> Mother o' mine, O mother o' mine.

In other words:

> Years to a mother bring distress
> But do not make her love the less.
> William Wordsworth

Here's another distinction: to mother is not to smother. Mother love—like God's love—provides maximum support and minimum protection. Except for small children, I'm really against protection. Protection makes cowards of everyone, which is probably why God provides so little of it. Consider again the father of the Prodigal Son. He could have protected him, he could have kept him at home, he could have kept him from getting into trouble, but he could not have kept him filial. Without freedom, there is no love. So the father has to release the son into the vicissitudes of life, and then stand on the road and wait and long with a mother's longing for the son to return to himself and to his spiritual home.

I had a friend in college who was in full-blown revolt against his father, a well-respected bishop. The son hardly studied at all. He was boozing and carrying on almost every night. At four o'clock one morning he woke me up to tell me, with tears pouring down his face, that he understood what a father's love was all about: "No matter what I do," he said, "I know my father will always love me."

The bishop was not approving but accepting, giving support, not protection. He was mothering, not smothering.

Why is it so hard for parents who believe in God to do as God does? Even as she holds us, she lets us go.

As his chaplain, I was particularly fond of a college freshman. He was eighteen but liked to think of himself as twenty-two. His parents liked to think of him as fourteen. They were having a hard time getting together. One day I tried to explain to him that many parents are sure we have made so many mistakes in bringing up our children that we are quite convinced that once they no longer need us, they will no longer love us. So, quite naturally, we try to keep them dependent. He could appreciate the dynamic.

Then I asked him if he had ever used some of his hard-earned money to take his parents out to dinner. The thought had never occurred to him. But he could see the point: the only way for a kid to attack his parents' no-more-needed-no-more-loved syndrome was to use his independence to demonstrate his affection. He promised to take them out.

A few days later he reported the results: "It was awful, the most embarrassing experience of my life. My old man just sat in the middle of the restaurant blubbering away, 'He loves us, he loves us.' I'll never do that again."

But it doesn't always turn out that well, does it? I think on Mother's Day we may as well recognize that some of you have been badly hurt by your mothers and fathers. Your grief is deep, your tears are real—there's no use pretending differently.

Remember: it is precisely what you cannot condone that you can only forgive. Nothing less *needs* forgiveness. Remember also that scars are all right. Scars are wounds that have healed, not without a trace, but have healed nonetheless. Finally, think of all the scar tissue around Christ's heart, Jesus our wounded healer.

One last thought. Often it seems wrong to me to be narrowly introspective as opposed to broadly contemplative. Likewise in thinking about our families—even on Mother's Day—it would be wrong to be too narrow in our perspective. We have sisters and brothers in extended families, and extending across the world are people with whom we are called to struggle to make the world a more complete and peaceful place. This is the point Jesus makes in the seemingly cruel passage we read at the end of the fourteenth chapter of Matthew. Is Jesus warning against the legitimate cravings of his heart—of all our hearts? Or is he simply insisting that each of us is born of God, as well as of woman? Each of us has dual parentage, with our earthly parents and our heavenly Mother/Father. Each of us has dual membership in our family and in the world, that larger family so desperately in need of stronger family ties.

So let us this Mother's Day recall our mothers whether in mortal or immortal life. Let us remember the beauty in their so nearly undefeated faces. Let us remember them at their maternal best, the way they accepted when not approving, supported rather than protected us, loved us no matter what distress we brought them, and what they taught us about this world and about God. And let us pray for grace to mother one another even as does dear God, Mother of us all.

Accepting Our Acceptance

MAY 18, 1986
Readings: Psalm 104:24–34; Acts 2:1–21

Don't ask exactly what happened on that first Pentecost nineteen-hundred-odd years ago, fifty days after Christ's Resurrection. As is so often the case in the Bible, it is the invisible event that counts. For sure we know only that the disciples, heretofore at best waiting and watching for God, began to be used and moved by God. After Pentecost, they became ten times the people they were during Jesus' life on earth. And because of the demonstrated power of the Holy Spirit moving through Peter and the other disciples—three thousand converted in one day—Pentecost is widely considered the birthday of the church.

What does it mean to be filled with the Holy Spirit? It means, first of all, to recognize with the psalmist,

> O Lord, how manifest are thy works
> In wisdom thou hast made them all . . .
> living things both small and great.

It means to recognize that we are in this world but not of this world.

> The soul that rises with us, our life's star,
> Hath had elsewhere its setting
> And cometh from afar;

Not in entire forgetfulness
And not in utter nakedness
But trailing clouds of glory do we come
From God who is our home.
William Wordsworth

Our lives run from God, in God, to God again. And all the time we are on earth there is stamped on every soul the three words "Made in Heaven."

Consider once again that among the billions born on the face of the planet no two human beings have ever been alike. God has chosen to make each of us unique. So what are we doing trying to be like everyone else? We're not rubber stamps. We're free. Nobody owns anybody. Did you know that the word "gusto" comes from the Latin "to choose"? You can't live with gusto if you let others make your choices. We are chosen, we can choose and live with gusto. For we are not indefinite, half-designed afterthoughts, but children of a heavenly Mother/Father, wanted, welcomed, invited to share in the ongoing glory of creation. That's the joy that should make our hearts beat faster and our eyes grow dim and fire up our imaginations like a furnace when we are filled with the Holy Spirit.

And what is our typical reaction to this Good News?

A first-century rabbi noted that God deals more strictly with the thief than with the robber. The robber, he reasoned, operating in broad daylight, shows no respect for either God or human beings. But the thief, working under cover, or at night, thinks that God doesn't see or hear. This shows less respect for God than for human beings, for while the thief works hard to avoid discovery by people, he takes no precautions against God. So grave an insult, avers the rabbi, makes the thief more punishable than the robber.

Since Adam and Eve people have thought to outwit God. But God is no befuddled ruler of the universe who has lost her glasses. "The eyes of the Lord are in every place, beholding the evil and the good" (Prov. 15:3). "Thou art acquainted with all my ways" (Ps. 139:3). And furthermore there is no need, in thief-like fashion, to hide our sins, because God's mercy is as sure as his eyesight. His concern is endless. His eye is on the sparrow. God is the most beautiful, powerful, intelligent, loving force in the universe, so concerned for the well-being of each of us that nothing can happen to take us out of the focus of his caring eye.

All of which is to say that if God sees all our dirty little secrets and still wishes us well, loves us warts and all, then we should be able, with steadfast gaze, to examine ourselves without despair. We can live amid our earthly imperfections because we live in the fullness of heaven.

Several years ago, a book appeared entitled *I'm OK, You're OK*. It made me want to write a better one entitled *I'm Not OK and You're Not OK, and That's OK*. We are not supposed to be Boy Scouts and Girl Scouts, and that's OK. For to acknowledge sin is not to settle into sinfulness but to grow in grace.

So to be filled with the Holy Spirit is not only to know that we come to earth trailing clouds of glory from God who is our home; it is to know the forgiveness of God. In the words of Paul Tillich, it is to "accept our acceptance."

What I now want to say is for the men in this church. If you women and children want to listen that's fine, but I want to talk directly to the men.

From an early age, gentlemen, we have been taught not to accept our acceptance. We have been urged to hide our warts, to repress our many insecurities, to fear only being called "sissy," "chicken," yes, "faggot." We're told to prove ourselves, to prove that we're men, not mice. Let no one doubt our masculinity. We can cut it. We're tough! Our heroes are Teddy Roosevelt, who talked softly and carried a big stick—and we don't need Dr. Freud to explain that stick. Our heroes are John Wayne, the man who invented the horse; and Clint Eastwood's Dirty Harry—hard, daring, disciplined, fearless, a weapon of destruction all by himself. The genetic code says we're warriors first, human beings second. From childhood on we have been taught not to love but to compete, to compete with each other in endless ways, and endlessly too: "A quitter never wins and a winner never quits." The result is an unmitigated disaster. When I think of the never-ending arms race, and of the Soviet Union and the United States, I think of two macho-warrior superpowers who compare, compete, and duel as to who can piss the farthest with the greatest accuracy.

That's how lack of harmony within contributes to discord without. And do you want to know the price tag of our masculine refusal to accept God's acceptance of us? Here it is: A Trident submarine costs $1.7 billion. But that's only one submarine. Let's talk a trillion. For one trillion dollars, you could build a $75,000 house, place it on $5,000 worth of land, furnish it with $10,000 worth of furniture, put a $10,000 car in the garage—and give all this to each and every family in Kansas, Missouri, Nebraska, Oklahoma, Colorado, and Iowa. Having done this, you would still have enough left to build a $10 million hospital and a $10 million library for each of 250 cities and towns throughout the six-state region. After having done all that, you would still have enough money left to build 500 schools at $10 million each for the communities in the region. And after having done all that you would still have enough left out of the trillion to put aside, at 10 percent annual interest, a sum of money that would pay a salary of 425,000 dollars per year for an army of 10,000 nurses, the same salary for an army of 10,000 teachers, and an annual cash allowance of $5,000 for each and every family throughout that six-state region— not just for one year, but forever.

And to think that one trillion dollars is only about one-half what we are planning to spend on military expenditures alone over the next five years!

I'm talking now to everyone. Friends, if we didn't have so many faults we wouldn't be so eager to find them in others. But if we receive our forgiveness from God, and accept our acceptance, we accept others too, warts and all. If we believe that we ourselves come to earth trailing clouds of glory from God who is our home, then we see a derivative sanctity in everyone. The ancient Jews were careful never to walk on a piece of paper for fear the name of God might be written on it. Likewise we should never tread on each other, for on everyone is that stamp, "Made in Heaven."

To be filled with the Holy Spirit is to speak each other's language. It is to pray for each other's well-being until there is no skin left on our knees. It is to yield to sympathy. It is to love, not blame, to compete only when appropriate. It is to have a new vision of *e pluribus unum*—to be loyal to the United States of the World.

I said Pentecost is widely considered the birthday of the church. That's important, for if it is the coming of the Spirit that marks the beginning of the Christian church, then to Christians it is the Spirit that counts. Love is everything; all the rest is commentary.

And finally, the passion of Pentecost makes it clear that nothing is so fatal to Christianity as indifference. The true infidels are the truly indifferent, the spiritually dead and buried. The cool and laid-back— they're washouts, no fire there. Ernest Hemingway wrote of Francis Macomber: "He always had a great tolerance, which seemed the nicest thing about him, if it were not the most sinister."

Talent is cheap, dedication is expensive; it can cost you your life. But what life is worth living other than a Pentecostal one, used and moved by God, dedicated to the glory of God and to the sanctity of life? So I pray God that the Holy Spirit may fill every nook and cranny of our being this Pentecost Sunday. May it remind us that

Not in entire forgetfulness
And not in utter nakedness,
But trailing clouds of glory do we come
From God who is our home.

William Wordsworth

May the Holy Spirit help us, men in particular, to cease and desist from trying to prove ourselves, convince us to accept our acceptance, and so to accept and not deny others. May the passion of Pentecost persuade us all to rejoice, and teach us how to praise.

Sounding Through

MAY 25, 1986
Readings: Psalm 139; Matthew 28:16–20

In a Protestant wedding service there are three central parts: the declaration of intent—the "I will" in answer to "Jean, wilt thou have this man to be thy husband?"; the exchange of vows—"I, James, take thee, Jean, to be my wedded wife"; and the exchange of rings—not made these days, it is hoped, from South African gold. (Maybe every minister, priest, and rabbi should refuse to bless any ring of South African gold.) "In putting the ring on each other's finger," I explain to the prospective bride and groom, "you can do one of the following: say your own words; say 'With this ring I thee wed, in the name of the Father, and of the Son, and of the Holy Spirit, one God, Mother of us all'; or 'This ring I give thee, in token and pledge of our constant faith and abiding love.'" No longer do I hold my breath. The answer I know ahead of time: "What do you think, honey? I like the last one better."

It is an exceptional Christian who still understands that no oath is more binding nor any protection more effective than the words of the blessed Trinity. Back in the fourth century, against the wiles of the Devil, against venom and vices, enemies and demons, Saint Patrick wore the Trinity as a breastplate:

I bind unto myself this day
The strong name of the Trinity,
By invocation of the same
The Three in One, the One in Three.

Once radical, the Trinity became conventional, then arcane, and finally ridiculed by practical and rational people too blind to see that imagination is even more important to the human race than knowledge.

So on this Sunday, traditionally designated Trinity Sunday, let us, in the manner of Ezekiel, call upon the wind to breathe upon these dry doctrinal bones that they may live. It's important, because the Trinity is not only a conception of God, but an understanding of humanity. Trinitarian thought leads to communitarian life, to a realization that life is essentially relational: we are as we love. There is more of you in your face when you're in love and in the company of the one you love, than when you're not in love and without the company of those you love.

Earlier we sang "God in three persons, blessed Trinity." The primary author of the doctrine, "Trinitas," was Tertullian, full name Quintus Septimus Florens Tertullianus. He lived in the late second and early third centuries. Like St. Augustine after him, he was a native of Carthage and a convert to Christianity. From all accounts he was eloquent and witty, an argumentative debater who tended to see two sides to every question—one clearly right, the other absolutely wrong. (In their defense, we should point out that the intolerance of some people derives less from a fault of character than from the fact that they are driven by a vision of Truth. It's hard to be a visionary and not dogmatic.)

I mention Tertullian's debating because all doctrines really are born in debate. They are correctives, a way of saying "No, no, it's this way, not that!" "God in three persons" is a corrective to a monotheism too narrow to take in Christ, and a corrective to all forms of dualism that seek to divide the world between spirit and matter, or appearance and reality, or the forces of good versus the forces of evil. "Three in One" says "One God, one world."

"God in three persons." The Latin noun *persona* derives from the Latin verb *personare*, which means to sound through (*sonare*, sound; *per*, through). Masks were called *personae*, and they were designed to amplify the voice so that all the spectators in the amphitheater could both see and hear what was being portrayed. Far from disguising, masks were an essential part of a dynamic reality. They helped a person sound through.

The point of the doctrine was not to name the three persons—Father, Son, and Holy Spirit—for the New Testament had already done that. It was to throw light on their nature by defining their relationship as co-equal, co-divine, and co-eternal. We'll get back to that.

I said imagination is more important even than knowledge. Obviously God is not literally our father (or mother) any more than God was literally the father (or mother) of Jesus. But just as the imaginative

Spanish Renaissance painter El Greco deliberately distorted physiognomic detail, elongating fingers and waists and necks to get at the mystery of human personality, so Christians have deliberately to distort human relationships to portray the mystery of an immortal, invisible, yet loving God, one we call holy because merciful as well as mighty.

I said the doctrine of the Trinity was originally radical. To call God "Father" (or Mother) was to describe not God *per se* but God *pro nobis*. It was to say "God is love," and they who abide in love abide in God and God abides in them. That was an understanding of God that broke with Greek philosophic thought and, in fact, remains pretty radical in the eyes of most philosophers today.

I said Trinitarian thought leads to communitarian life. We can now see why. To personify God means the personification of all life. It means we become who we are by personifying—and never depersonalizing—everyone we meet, and those we never meet. It means that love must become all in all in this world. It means nations are to be judged by their treatment of the poor. It means our economic life should be as loving as our prayer life. It means Christians should speak out when those least able to defend themselves are made to suffer the most. And a lot more.

But wait, hold on. There's an important question to be asked. How can anyone talk of God as a loving Father/Mother when, as everyone knows, almost every inch of the earth's surface is soaked with the tears and blood of the innocent? And why tell us to mend our ways and redeem the times when individually most of us feel like bits of rock embedded in the glacial forces of historical process?

To answer those questions we have to move on to the second person of the Trinity. According to a Mormon myth, at Creation's start Christ and Satan were each requested to submit to God a plan for dealing with the infant human race, which was already showing signs of delinquency. Satan's plan was simple (the kind that secretaries of state and secretaries of defense frequently come up with): God has armies of angels at his command; why not assign an angel with punitive power to each human being? That should keep the race in line, and things will move along nicely.

In other words, Satan was the first hard-liner, urging upon God the virtues of force. And don't we all urge upon God the virtues of force?

When things go badly for us personally—or nationally—don't we expect God, rather than ourselves, to straighten out the mess? Shouldn't God at the very least keep our children safe and sound, no matter how fast they drive; and shouldn't God keep the human race from annihilating itself, no matter what fiendish weapons we invent and insist on deploying? If ultimately children and the human race can only be saved by force, then so be it, by force—"But save us, God."

In contrast to Satan's, Christ's plan was imaginative, implying a regard for humanity so high that Satan must have mocked it. "Let them have free will and go their own way," Christ proposed to God. "Only let me live and die as one of them, both as an example of how to live, and to show how much you care for them. The only answer to their delinquency is to persuade them that there is more mercy in you than sin in them."

Each Christmas we are reminded which plan God chose to implement. There really was no choice for a loving God, because love cannot exist without freedom. It is precisely because God is so loving that there is so much suffering. But God shares the suffering. In the second person of the Trinity, God suffers with and for us with a love that Saint Paul properly understood "bears all things, believes all things, hopes all things, endures all things."

Don't be confused by all the complicated metaphysical arguments about the divinity of Christ. What is important is not that Christ be God-like, but that God be Christ-like. What is important is that when we see Christ empowering the weak and scorning the powerful, healing the sick and supporting the lonely, we know that we are seeing transparently the power of God at work. We know that God loves us with a love that will not let us go, "through Jesus Christ our Lord." His is the voice that sounds through: "O'er the tumult of our lives' wild restless sea, day by day his sweet voice soundeth, saying 'Christian, follow me.'"

And when Jesus left us, he left more than a memory, he left us a presence. In the writings of Saint Paul, the resurrected Christ and the Holy Spirit are never clearly differentiated, so that when Paul says, "Not I, but Christ who dwells within me," he is talking about the same Holy Spirit—the third person of the Trinity—that you and I experience in our own lives.

It is the Holy Spirit that keeps us, and keeps us going. History is an education in humility: "Age after age their tragic empires rise." But the Holy Spirit tells us, "Earth shall be fair, and all her people one." The Holy Spirit makes us believe that here on earth a better society is always possible, and holds out hope for what lies beyond:

> Oh, walk together children
> Don't you get weary
> There's a great Camp Meetin'
> in the Promised Land.

The Holy Spirit takes the task of building the Kingdom and turns it into a gift. Within each of us, the Holy Spirit answers death without fear and life with works of kindness and deeds of praise.

The Three in One, the One in Three, all three co-equal, co-divine, co-eternal. If you must view the Trinity hierarchically, then see the second and third persons pulling the first downward, rather than the other way around. For intimacy is what we need, intimacy with God to give expectancy to life. We cannot presume, but we must not despair. We stand, as always, between good and evil, sharing in both, quicker to exercise our freedom than to act on our responsibilities. But the three persons of the Trinity, Father (or Mother), Son, and Holy Spirit, never cease to sound through, ever striving to keep our lives passionate and lyrical with a vision beyond the world that is to what it yet might be.

So when on this Memorial Day weekend you pray that those brave men and women who died in war died not in vain, and when thereafter you feel beseiged by venom and vices, enemies and demons, do as Saint Patrick did:

> I bind unto myself this day
> The strong name of the Trinity,
> By invocation of the same
> The Three in One, the One in Three.

"And Now Abide Faith, Hope, Love . . ."

JULY 6, 1986
Readings: Isaiah 61:1–4; 1 Corinthians 13:8–13

Well, my fellow Americans and dear visitors from other lands, I think we survived July 4th—just barely, perhaps—the hype, the hyperbole, and the hoopla. I think our beloved lady in the harbor, mother of exiles, kept her head and lamp above the rising tide of commercialism that threatened to engulf and drown her. (The merchants all but put a T-shirt on her!) When you stop to think that the number of boats in New York Harbor was forty times the number gathered for the evacuation of Dunkirk, it is no small miracle that no self-appointed sea captain went down to Davey Jones' Locker, taking with him a cooler or two of beer. When I saw the heavens ablaze on

Friday night, and heard our own Clamma Dale singing *Porgy and Bess*; when last night I saw 600,000 people in Central Park listening to Bizet and Beethoven's Ninth; and when wandering in the streets as fat with people as the rivers were with boats, I thought the whole affair was dynamite—or at least a resounding string of firecrackers. Most of all I liked the immigrants. Native-born Americans are impressed by the things that inconvenience them; immigrants record the things that move them deeply.

This morning let's consider some abiding things that move us deeply and start by asking, "In what form do these things abide?"

You cannot *not* know history. We are too conditioned by it—"The past is never dead, it's not even past" (Faulkner). And, if we don't know our history, we are doomed, as warned Santayana, to repeat its mistakes.

But blind imitation of the past, even of the past at its best, is no way to deal with the present. "Let the dead bury the dead"—and not the living. Imitation of the past is impossible. About the same time as Dunkirk, in the early 1940s, musical editions began to appear with that hallmark of purity, *Urtext* (original edition), written across the cover. Inside you might find Beethoven's 32 sonatas replete with indications from Beethoven himself regarding dynamic changes, changes of tempo, and even the fingering necessary to accomplish the desired effect. It was all very impressive. But although each player thought he or she was faithfully executing the wishes of the master, no two pianists ever sounded alike. Imitation was impossible, interpretation inevitable.

Likewise, no two Shakespearean actors have ever sounded exactly alike, and no two readers of the Declaration of Independence, or of the Constitution of the United States, or of the sixty-six books of the Bible, will ever understand those documents in exactly the same way. Let Protestant fundamentalists claim, "The only safe interpreter of Scripture is Scripture itself." It's a fine-sounding claim, but, it is pride masquerading as humility to believe that one can see so plainly revealed the mind and will of God. Search for the truth we can and must, but own it—never. Fundamentalists are no different from the rest of us. Just as often as do we, they use a Bible as the drunk uses a lamppost: for support, not illumination. And consider this: Perhaps God *approves* the struggles of the human mind to try to interpret God's designs. "The unknown is the mind's greatest need, and for it no one thinks to thank God" (Emily Dickinson). So far from being a danger to it, difference of opinion is an essential ingredient of religious life, just as difference of opinion is no danger but an essential ingredient to a healthy political life. So interpretation is not only inevitable, it's desirable.

And one more thought along these lines. Great ideas, like liberty and equality, have no fixed historical context, for they are goals, ideals, aspirations of a nation, and as such belong as much to the present and to the future as they do to the past. A sober warning of this festive weekend is that either we restore and extend our understanding of liberty, or the liberty that is the essence of the United States will be swept into the sea as were pieces of the statue before its restoration. Christians can help by insisting that moral judgment is embedded in the fabric of history by bringing ethics to the forefront of politics, and by renewing our commitment to the three abiding things in our tradition—"And now abide faith, hope, love, these three."

Who today breathes the air of freedom in our land? How about those who are born hungry and homeless and stay hungry and homeless, all the quiet and easily forgotten children for whom today the poverty rate is consistently higher than for the general population— for the first time in American history? And how free are those who have God on their lips and profits on their minds, the opulent who speak of freedom even as they demonstrate their slavery to wealth?

De Tocqueville noted that Americans want self-government but not the ideals that would enable them to govern the self. "Americans are free," he said, "but they are not virtuous." To some degree in his time we could get away with it. For ours then was a society still largely agricultural. A piece of land provided not just sustenance, but the means of economic independence necessary for political independence and expression. To be sure there was economic oppression, but then the answer to economic oppression was to move 200 miles west. Now, in urban America, millions of people live their entire lives with no real prospect of the dignity and autonomy that ownership of property confers. Abroad, we must note that malnutrition, disease, illiteracy, and incredibly primitive living conditions fail today to win from the United States government the kind of attention that is repeatedly lavished on places with a few thousand communist guerrillas. What a tawdry war we are waging against Nicaragua! It's not part of the promise of American life, it's part of the frustration of American life. And what a golden opportunity we are forfeiting to help save South Africa from a horrendous bloodbath! Said Thomas Jefferson, "I tremble for my country when I recall that God is just."

"And now abide faith. . . ." The abiding faith this country needs for its spiritual restoration and future health is the faith of the prophets, the prophets who loved Israel, but whose love for their country was often measured by their disgust with it. Prophetic faith is full of anger, yet it is always anchored in the greatness and goodness of God, not in hatred of enemies. Prophetic faith recognizes that economic tyranny can be as great as political tyranny. Prophetic faith sees justice as central, not ancillary, to salvation. It recognizes that God's unconditional concern for justice is not an anthropomorphism (a projection upon God of our human attributes), but rather that our concern for justice is a theomorphism: to the degree that we embody justice, God takes form within us.

For American liberty to be restored and extended, American Christians need to carry on with their country the same lovers' quarrel that the prophets of old carried on with Israel, and that God consistently carries on with the whole world. We must say "Yes" to what we can, and "No" to what we must. We must see that when a government betrays the ideals of a country, it is an act of loyalty to oppose the government. We must take the road less traveled and be more concerned with our country saving its soul than with it losing face. "I tremble for my country when I recall that God is just."

The point of God's judgment, however, is to mitigate pride, not to eliminate hope. The point of contrition is to get beyond hype, hyperbole, and hoopla to honesty—to see ourselves as individuals and to see our nation in perspectives other than our own, essentially in the divine perspective of God's judgment and mercy. (Isn't it strange how so unscientific a concept as confession can best help us approach the scientific goal of detachment and objectivity!)

No one was more hopeful than the prophets of Israel. They preached judgment, but only up to a point. When the people were willing to remember what they would sooner forget or repress, when the people announced their readiness to meet the challenge rather than to wish it did not exist, at that moment the prophets preached, in place of judgment, hope. We heard it read: "beauty for ashes, the oil of joy for mourning, the garment of praise for the spirit of heaviness." "Violence shall no more be heard in thy land, wasting nor destruction within thy borders; but thou shalt call thy walls Salvation and thy gates Praise" (Isa. 60:18). And in the New Testament the Good News began when a coward stood up to eulogize the man he loved above all others, the one he openly admitted he had betrayed.

The hopeless are poor recruits for any cause. And Christians should be the last people on the face of the world to forget that Pharaoh could not destroy the Jews, Pilate could not kill Jesus, the racists couldn't wipe out Martin Luther King Jr. nor the death squads Archbishop Romero. And we all know that Botha and company will never destroy Tutu, Boesak, and Beyers Naude. And let me also remind any purveyors of gloom here present that the civil rights movement, the women's liberation movement, and the freeze movement emerged not because the United States was becoming more racist, more sexist, and more militaristic, but because it was becoming significantly less so.

So let's put prophetic hope up there alongside prophetic faith. And finally, let's say that a heart is Christian if it beats against all reason with a love not bounded by place or time. If Jesus Christ is God's love in person on earth, then the church should be God's love organized on earth. The church is not dogma in search of obedience, but love in search of form. Let's say that the pursuit of happiness represents the hope that as we grow older we will become more intensely alive and that love will absorb our ardent souls. For love never ends; it is as long as life is short. It is what binds us to God and to one another, and against it the powers of death cannot prevail. Love is what each of us and all of life is all about.

"And now abide faith, hope, love." We keep the faith because God keeps us, and hope springs eternal because God's love is forever. "And now abide faith, hope, love, these three," to help this nation enrich its understanding of life, liberty, and the pursuit of happiness. The one miracle all Americans can ask of God is that by God's grace we may become good people. Let us pray for that miracle.

Three Saving Truths

JULY 20, 1986
Reading: Amos 5:18–24

The text for today's sermon is a fine family motto: "*In tempestate floresco*"—In time of storm I flourish.

When someone asked Gandhi what he thought of Western civilization, Gandhi replied, "I think it would be a good idea." Declared Ralph Inge, Dean of St. Paul's in London, "Civilization is a disease from which nations seldom recover." That remark was no grim foreboding on the part of a man often referred to as the "gloomy dean." Rather it was an undeniable fact. We speak of the glory that was Greece, the grandeur that was Rome, because in both these empires the mind and spirit became subservient to the tyranny of things. Material aggrandizement leads to spiritual impoverishment. So seemingly constant and so sorry is this state of affairs that Helmuth von Moltke, the great German historian, remarked, "Without war, the world would be swamped in materialism." (What would he say now, when war would make the world a swamp?)

It's pretty discouraging, isn't it? Study history and you read of the plundered poor, of the riches of the world profaned. Study history and you get the impression that violence is permanent and peace is fleeting. Human beings do good all right, but they do good too covertly, and evil too overtly. Of the universe that God made, God could say that it was good. But of no period of the history we have made could God say the same thing.

As I said, it gets discouraging: defeated today, tomorrow we die. We develop an emotional investment in cynicism. So where do we turn to be saved?

To the universities, I used to think—but now less frequently. If a little education is dangerous, a lot is lethal. You have to be a Ph.D. to invent and engineer a nuclear warhead. The tragic failure of the modern mind is that it can't prevent its own destruction. Every country's education reflects that country's ideology, which is why freedom of speech in our universities is so highly exalted over any obligation to do any good to anyone. We are free to speculate, but speculative prosperity is no answer to moral bankruptcy. Scholars like to present themselves as pursuing truth, but a more accurate image might be that of truth, "saving" truth, pursuing them. And they are proving to be as elusive as the legendary Scarlet Pimpernel.

For "saving" truth, I find myself turning more and more to the prophets of Israel. They spoke an octave too high, they were strident—you wouldn't want to invite most of them to dinner—and today we would probably call them hysterical. But if such deep sensitivity to evil be hysteria, what name shall we call the abysmal indifference to evil that the prophets bewailed?

To the prophets the world was not devoid of meaning, only deaf to meaning. We bemoan God's dreadful silence, but the prophets were stunned by God's mighty voice, so they cried out:

> O land, land, land,
>   hear the word of the Lord!
>   Jer. 22:29

Here's another comparison. Academics generally recognize as worthy of study only that which is capable of explanation. Not so the God-intoxicated prophets. They had imagination, they knew all knowledge begins in wonder and ends in the same, which is why their utterances are so unacademic, so powerful, so poetic.

For lo, he who forms the mountains, and creates the wind,
    and declares to man what is his thought;
who makes the morning darkness,
    and treads on the heights of the earth—
the Lord, the God of hosts, is his name!

Amos 4:13

"The world does not lack for wonders, only for a sense of wonder" (G. K. Chesterton).

But even more than in nature, the prophets found God in history, which they considered humanity's true home. History to them was first and foremost what people do with power, and to them it was clear: we human beings have choice, but not sovereignty.

The earth is the Lord's and the fulness thereof,
the world and those who dwell therein . . .

Ps. 24:1

Therefore, "Not unto us, O Lord, not unto us but unto thy name be the glory."

The prophets couldn't say "people" without thinking "God." To them the root of all evil was our false sense of sovereignty. From it stem our pride, our arrogance, our presumption, and our destruction.

The Israelites cherished above all else three things: wisdom, wealth, and might. Twenty-seven hundred years later, not much has changed, has it? But to the prophets such infatuation was ludicrous.

Let not the wise man glory in his wisdom, let not the mighty man glory in his might, let not the rich man glory in his riches; but let him who glories glory in this, that he understands and knows me, that I am the Lord who practice steadfast love, justice, and righteousness in the earth; for in these things I delight, says the Lord. (Jer. 9:23–24)

This isn't geopolitics; this is "theopolitics," a new kind of patriotism. In no other people was national pride so inextricably bound up with religion. The Israelites believed that God had delivered the Twelve Tribes from Egyptian slavery. Through Moses, God had made the tribes a nation. The Israelites were convinced that God approved of them. None of the prophets agreed, and to make clear their disagreement they were prepared to be a scandal, a stone of stumbling, a bone in the throat of their people. Listen to Amos:

> Proclaim to the strongholds in Assyria,
>   and to the strongholds in the land of Egypt,
> and say, "Assemble yourselves upon the mountains of Samaria,
> and see the great tumults within her,
>   and the oppressions in her midst."
> "They do not know how to do right," says the Lord,
>   "those who store up violence and robbery in their strongholds."
>   Amos 3:9–10

It's as if some American prophet were to stand up today and say, "Proclaim to the leaders of the Kremlin and to the Sandinistas in the land of Nicaragua. Assemble yourselves on the slopes of the White Mountains, in the high pastures of the Rockies, and on the slopes of the Sierra Nevada, and see the violence in the land and the oppression in its midst. They do not know how to do right, says the Lord!"

As I say, this is theopolitics. It is a new kind of patriotism, a fresh understanding of national security to put the spiritual claims of religion above the material interests of the nation, to insist, as did all the prophets, that God's judgment of human conduct is the main issue—all else is marginal.

To me, theopolitics is a saving truth for a nation. It's realistic—it accords with reality. In the long run it's cheaper to eliminate poverty than to maintain it, and in the very short run, we had all better learn to be meek, or no one will inherit the earth. (I'm talking today of the Old Testament prophets, but we could as well be considering the Sermon on the Mount, for the so-called ethics of perfection are today the only ethics of survival. We have to learn to be merciful when we live at one another's mercy.)

Here's another saving truth. The psalmist wrote:

> Then I will go to the altar of God,
>   to God my exceeding joy;
> and I will praise thee with the lyre,
>   O God, my God.
>   Ps. 43:4

But Amos—speaking for the Lord—said:

> Take away from me the noise of your songs;
>   to the melody of your harps I will not listen.

> But let justice roll down like waters,
> and righteousness like an ever-flowing stream.
>
> Amos 5:23–24

The prophets did not say that justice was more important than worship. They said the worth of worship depended entirely on moral living. Where immorality prevails, they said, worship is detestable. They knew that Satan's subtlest ploy was to separate ritual from righteousness. That's the way the world seeps into the churches.

I said humanity's true home is history. It's God's home too. God's home-away-from-home in heaven. People may not realize it, but when they act as they darn well please, doing what is vile, abusing the weak, they are affronting the divine in her own home. They don't realize that in oppressing human beings they are humiliating God.

> He who oppresses a poor man insults his Maker,
> but he who is kind to the needy honors him.
>
> Prov. 14:31

It is saving truth to know that ritual cannot be separated from righteousness, that there can be no personal conversion experience without a change in social attitude.

To Riverside Church, and to all the churches represented here by you, their visiting members, the message is clear; it is written on parish walls throughout Central and Latin America. The words are from the prophet Jeremiah: "*Conocer a Dios es obrar la justicia*"—to know God is to do justice. What Christians should yearn for in the night is not mystical experience but historical justice.

I said at the beginning that it gets discouraging when ill follows ill, and woe succeeds woe, when what must not happen does. I said we develop an emotional investment in cynicism to spare ourselves the pain of being deeply human. But the prophets never did. They had attacks of despondency, but they were really the most hopeful people around. Why?

The prophets knew that God provides minimum protection but maximum support. They knew that God is tough but supportive, and that tough *is* supportive.

> You only have I known
> of all the families of the earth.
>
> Amos 3:2

That verb "to know" is charged with meaning. "Adam knew Eve, his wife." The prophets compared God's love to married love. They knew

God was so tough because God so cares. We talk about the peace of God; they talked about the pain of God. It is so much greater than ours, for finally what is so unbearable is not what breaks the body but what breaks the heart. To know that God is heartbroken is to be saved from self-pity.

And it is to live in hope. It is saving truth to know that "He who keepeth Israel neither slumbers nor sleeps"; to know that a loving God is closer to each of us than our own breathing.

In tempestate floresco—In time of storm I flourish. It is a good motto for every Christian family. The pain of seeing the truth is not as high as the cost of denying it. (Isn't sunlight the best disinfectant?) So let us not fear to see and ponder these three saving truths granted us by God's prophets of old: Let the nation contemplate theopolitics, which insists that God's judgment of human conduct is the only issue; all else is marginal. Let those who worship God remember that ritual cannot be divorced from righteousness. And let none of us forget the depth of God's love for all of us.

To Receive a Child

JULY 27, 1986
Reading: Mark 10:13–16

When I was a young pastor just starting out, sickness and death depressed me far more than they do currently. I guess I've learned since that pain in this life is as natural as breathing, and that death is not the enemy we too frequently make it out to be. In any case, after visiting sick and dying parishioners in the hospital, I would frequently stop by the maternity ward to check out the latest arrivals. It was a good reminder that life can be as deliriously happy as it most certainly can be sad. And it reminded me that we all have to move on, if only so that others can move in to enjoy a life we are understandably loath to leave. It's not death that's so bad, it's life that's so good!

This week was a sad one for Riverside. Two splendid members moved on: Jim Johnson, who testified at our special AIDS service in January to all he was learning from being terminally ill (although, as he had us all weeping, he said, "I don't want to exaggerate; all things being equal, with W. C. Fields, I would rather be in Philadelphia!"); and that grand old doctor, Sylvester Carter, who surmounted racial discrimination to become one of the greatest hand surgeons in the world. It was a special pleasure to visit him in the hospital. He was always the hero of the ward, and when he got out of the hospital and came back to church he was always in the company of several gorgeous nurses. "I just wanted to show off my church," he would say.

So there's reason for mourning, but also for rejoicing. Didn't we just now baptize a baby made all the more radiant by the presence of her two Ivory Coast grandparents? And I have to tell you that on the other side of the continent, a dynamite tot is momentarily going to appear who one day will leap over high buildings in a single bound or at the very least discover the formula to turn lead into gold. You see, when she/he appears, I'll have my first grandchild, and don't think I haven't been in sympathetic labor, suffering all week from abdominal cramps and pains in my lower back. So don't laugh, just understand why the text for this morning's sermon is from the tenth chapter of Mark: "And [Jesus] put his arms around [the children], laid his hands upon them and blessed them."

Jesus is so wonderfully physical: he wraps his arms around the kids' wobbly limbs, he lays his hands on their chubby cheeks. It's something more men should try. And more are trying. The popularity of the movies *Kramer vs. Kramer*, *Tootsie*, *Mr. Mom* signals a softening of sexual stereotypes. Men are beginning to release their nurturing instincts, to show a more tender, less aggressive and competitive side. It wasn't so long ago that men saw their real job as making money and supporting the family—a view that neutralized the nurturing father in every man. In his memoirs, Russell Baker wrote of going to the hospital to be confined to the "father room" for his "third attempt to win an Academy Award for playing fifth wheel at a parturition." Today as many as 62 percent of all births are attended by fathers. It's right to involve them so early, to hook them for good from day one. Let's do away with the father room and call the maternity ward the "maternity/paternity" ward. Fathers are parents in their own right, not substitute mothers, not babysitters.

"He put his arms around them." Have you hugged your kid today? What kid doesn't need all the body warmth he can get? (What adult too?) And I'll bet Jesus didn't treat the boys much differently from the girls. I'll bet if he were a father in America, he would teach his son how to cook and his daughter to play baseball. Surely he wants us to encourage our children to be strongly feminine, tenderly masculine, and, above all, abidingly human.

"And he put his arms around them, laid his hands upon them, *and blessed them.*"

Baptism repeats Jesus' blessing. It says that every child bears the invisible stamp, "Made in Heaven." Our children belong to God before they belong to us. They are ours on loan. And as God has made each unique, they are ours to guide in the paths of righteousness, not ours to mold or sculpt in our own image. It's nice to see yourself in your children—and scary too—but let us not fail to rejoice in what makes them different from us.

I know it's hard not to control children. Once I met a law professor who, among other subjects, taught wills. I asked him what guided most people when they drew up their wills. "A will," he said, "is a person's last crack at earthly immortality. It is a way, through property bestowed under certain conditions, to extend one's power and influence beyond the grave. A will is a dead hand reaching out one last time for the child's ear."

But Jesus "put his arms around them"! And note how he healed their elders with no strings attached.

"I tell you, whoever does not receive the Kingdom of God like a child shall not enter therein." Jesus makes it sound as if children remind us altogether as much as we teach them. For sure, they remind us of our dependency. A small child has little sense of achieving anything; life's still all gift. A child is also vulnerable, a reminder to take off the armor most of us don almost the moment we're out of diapers. Children are spontaneous. Their impulse to act at once on what they understand is not strangled by calculation and timid skepticism. There is evangelical wisdom in the injunction, "Don't look before you leap. If you do, you will decide to sit down." He may have said it cynically, but Talleyrand was profoundly right when he remarked, "Distrust first impulses. They are nearly always right."

It's interesting how the Gospels seem to talk more about children than any other sacred literature in the world. Elsewhere in Matthew we read: "And he took a child, and put him in the midst of them; and taking him in his arms [once again] he said to them, 'Whoever receives one such child in my name, receives me'" (18:5).

What does it mean to receive a child in Jesus' name? Among other things, it means to recognize that it is our obligations rather than our freedoms that give our lives their meaning. It means that if we can forget ourselves by giving ourselves to those from whom we can expect no benefit in return, at least no benefit in kind—then praise the Lord, Christ dwells within us, because we can do that only by the grace of God. And by giving ourselves to our children, I don't mean money, I mean time and ears and arms when the feelings come pouring out. Another word for the fathers: When Yale went co-ed in the early

1970s, the women were almost instantly besieged by the men who wanted to tell them their troubles. Why? Because as small boys these men had poured out their hearts to their mothers rather than to their fathers, who were less involved.

Parenthood is a common cause, even—and especially—when the parents are divorced. I don't care how bitter the divorce, neither parent should try to evict the other from the lives of their children. I wish we could do away with "visitation," a most unsatisfactory word, and, even more, change a welfare system that devalues and degrades the father by giving financial assistance more generously to families when he is gone, thereby making him feel that the single best thing he can do for his family is to leave it. Surely that's no way to receive a child in Jesus' name.

Equally deplorable—and there are many women who deplore it— is that so much of the modern women's movement has been not only anti-men, but also anti-children, anti-motherhood. Wives, mothers, single women, lesbians—none are inferior, just different. Babies are not incompatible with liberation, poverty is; and the feminization of poverty is no joke. Did you know that over half the children in female-headed households live below the federally established poverty line? That one out of five children in this richest country of the world is poor?

"Whosoever receives one such child in my name receives me." I don't understand some of these pro-life, pro-family forces whose concerns are so restricted as to make you believe that life begins at conception and ends at birth. Reaganomics is no way to receive children in Jesus' name, particularly poor children. Reaganomics trickles not down but up. It gives more food to the overfed while promising the hungry that more crumbs will fall from the table.

A. J. Muste used to say, "We need a foreign policy fit for children." We need domestic policies fit for children too, including maternity (or paternity) leave for something like six months with, say, 75 percent of salary up to three months and job and seniority benefits throughout. We need to erase the wage gap between women and men; in many places it's growing. We do not need to pray *in* the public schools, we need to pray *for* the public schools, that their teachers be properly paid, that they receive all the assistance they need, that the prejudice be ended against men teaching grades earlier than the fifth, that sex education be expanded to family care classes (Bank Street School down the block has model courses), that drugs be eliminated, and that it be drilled into boys, "If you can't be a father, then don't make a baby."

I said poverty is incompatible with liberation. So too is aggressive Yuppieism, which insists you *can* have it all, and raises the question, "Is that all there is?" It's a rotten bargain to trade the very stuff of life for nothing more than dollars. And it's bad for children.

"And he put his arms around them, laid his hands on their heads and blessed them." Let's not blow it with our kids. They come from God, and each one born reminds us that it is God's will that the world go on, the earth not be destroyed but be made more beautiful for all its inhabitants, particularly the smaller ones. I read this week that through a mistake in the records in Houston, Texas, a child two years old was summoned for jury duty. It was a mistake divinely inspired. For the child is the final jury before whom the world must be tried.

"Let Me Receive My Sight"

SEPTEMBER 21, 1986
Reading: Mark 10:46–52

It's good to be back in New York City, this adrenaline capital of the world, and even better to be back in Riverside Church where "all the women are strong, all the men are good-looking, and all the children are above average." It's always good to be in God's house— where, it is to be hoped, we take time to love one another, trust in God, hope for the future, enjoy our victories, and find strength for our burdens. It is always good to be in God's house where—we hope—we voice ideals and expose realities camouflaged by ideals, where our dissent is grounded in affirmation and where—hopefully—we blend reassurance and reproof, for God knows we are workers of iniquity, killers of the prophets, and enemies of the cross, *but also* heirs of the promise of Abraham and Sarah, citizens of the commonwealth of heaven, and members of the glorious body of Christ. Put differently, it's good to be among those who, knowing their blindness, wish to see. For this reason, as a text for today's sermon I have chosen the story of blind Bartimaeus, the beggar who was healed and became a follower of Christ; Bartimaeus the outsider, who stands in sharp and favorable contrast to the insiders in the Gospel of Mark. I would like to dedicate this sermon to the members of the

This sermon was inspired and greatly informed by another preached by Barbara Brown Taylor.—WSC

congregation who are blind, or near blind, who have been such an inspiration to me.

Let's visualize the scene. We're on the outskirts of Jericho, fifteen miles from Jerusalem, where Jesus is going to celebrate the Passover. He is surrounded by a crowd of fellow pilgrims to whom he is talking even as he walks, a common way in those days for rabbis to teach. Another crowd, unable to go to Jerusalem, lines the road to cheer the passing pilgrims and perhaps to get a glimpse of the young Galilean who has pitted himself against the assembled might of religious orthodoxy. Suddenly from the roadside crowd comes a hoarse shout: "Son of David, Jesus, have pity on me!"

It is hard enough for the devout pilgrims to hear what Jesus has to say without this noise from the sidelines, so they try to hush the beggar up, and those who know him probably even try to make him feel guilty: "Shame on you, Bartimaeus, trying to hustle a rabbi for change!"

But Bartimaeus, they quickly find out, is not easily cowed. Moreover, he has that insight so characteristic of the blind: he who, in all his life, has never met Jesus and cannot now even see him, recognizes in him the Messiah and calls him "Son of David." Once again, and this time perhaps with almost ungovernable emotion, he cries out, "Son of David, have mercy on me!"

Now if there is one thing most rabbis and ministers do not appreciate, it is to be interrupted when they are talking. But Jesus, inspired talker though he was—he said more in three years than anyone else has said in a lifetime—Jesus knew when speech must end and action begin. He calls for Bartimaeus, who jumps up and throws off his mantle, the faster to respond to an opportunity he must have had the sense to recognize would not present itself again. Then, when blind Bartimaeus stands before him, all anticipation, Jesus asks, "What do you want me to do for you?"

You may consider that question rhetorical. After all, the man didn't want sunglasses! But let me recall that earlier in this same chapter of Mark Jesus had put the same question to two disciples, insiders, James and John, the sons of Zebedee, and they had answered, "Grant us to sit one at your right hand and one at your left, in your glory." When that kind of remark comes from insiders, we simply have to hope that in every church there is that invisible church of those who have died to self. Besides, maybe the beggar did want to hustle the rabbi for change; a lot of people do pray to Jesus for money. Most likely, though, Jesus wanted Bartimaeus simply to say precisely what he wanted and what he believed Jesus could do. The beggar's answer comes in six words: "Master, let me receive my sight."

"And Jesus said to him, 'Go your way; your faith has made you well.' And immediately he received his sight and followed him on the way."

That's the last miracle recorded in the Gospel of Mark, the last story with a happy ending (with the exception, of course, of the Resurrection).

But let's probe deeper. This week I read of the first people in the world who, blind from birth, underwent successful cataract surgery. You can imagine the wonder with which, for the first time in their life, they saw a climbing rose, a birch tree, a sunset. One girl was so stunned by her first glimpse of the radiance of the world that she kept her eyes shut for two weeks. She reminded me of what Edna St. Vincent Millay wrote of this time of year in New England.

> Lord, I do fear
> Thou'st made the world too beautiful this year.
> Prithee, let no leaf fall,
> Let no bird call.

When the girl finally opened her eyes again she could only say, over and over, "O God! how beautiful!"

But not everything was beautiful for these patients. The world turned out to be bigger and more complex than they expected. Unable to judge distances, they reached for things a mile away and cracked their shins on furniture they perceived only as patches of color. Seeing themselves for the first time in the mirror made many of them unhappy and self-conscious; they wouldn't go outside. The father of one young woman wrote her surgeon that his daughter had taken to shutting her eyes when she walked around the house and seemed happier pretending again to be blind. A fifteen-year-old boy demanded to be taken back to the local home for the blind. "I can't stand it any more," he said. "If things don't change I'll tear my eyes out."

I tell you all this to make the point that if sight is problematic on a physical level, how much more complicated it becomes on a spiritual level. We happily sing, "I once was lost but now am found, Was blind but now I see." But how many of us do you suppose would share Bartimaeus' manifest desire to receive his sight if by sight we meant spiritual sight, seeing ourselves through the eyes of Jesus, seeing our country through the eyes of Jesus, seeing our world, our God, as did Jesus?

Wrote Elizabeth Barrett Browning:

> Earth's crammed with heaven,
> And every common bush afire with God

But only he who sees takes off his shoes
The rest sit round and pluck blackberries.

It's not that we're evil, we're just a little dull. Or maybe it's not that we're dull, only very much in the grip of life and circumstances. So we don't see "earth crammed with heaven." Like some of the cataract patients we prefer the familiar dark where you can't hurt yourself. We prefer to be concerned only with what is within our reach, to stay with what we know if not in perpetual night, at least in unending gray, in never-ending dawnless day.

What would it mean to receive our spiritual sight? If we saw nature through the eyes of Jesus, we wouldn't see scenery, we would see theophanies, the Creator in creation. We'd see that

> The world is charged with the grandeur of God.
> It will flame out like shining from shook foil.
> Gerard Manley Hopkins

If we saw human nature through the eyes of Jesus, we'd see that profound sorrow and great happiness have the same root. It is because pain and joy have the same root that it is quite impossible to make happiness the sole end of life. "The very capacities which make for happiness also subject the soul to greater grief and more poignant pain" (Reinhold Niebuhr). Happiness is episodic, so the proper aim of life is not happiness but the giving and receiving of love. If we saw life through the eyes of Jesus, we would be as vulnerable as he, our hearts would open up like a morning glory to everything in this world that is good and true and beautiful, and we would hear and understand, as did Jesus, the faintest whisper of pain.

If we saw the nations through the eyes of Jesus the prophet we would see that they are ruled by a lust to rule, promoting policies harmful to the legitimate aspirations, not to say inalienable rights, of millions of our brothers and sisters. Yet justice is no wave on an inland lake, but a sea tide, oncoming.

If we saw God as did Jesus, our hearts would melt and our eyes fill with tears at the sight of such unconditional love—suffering love, not triumphant love. We would understand that the same love which moves the sun and the other stars is the flame that sets our wills on fire to put God's world aright, that God's job is not to make only good things happen in our lives, but rather to help us respond in a loving, creative way to whatever happens, good or bad.

And if we saw the church through the eyes of Jesus—this church, our church, the church we serve—we would see Riverside not only as the object of our love, but essentially as an instrument of God's love, a place to witness within our ranks and abroad, to peace, justice, freedom, love, and all the other good things God believes in and which we see so beautifully incarnate in the person of Jesus.

If you didn't exactly jump up and run to church this morning, as did Bartimaeus to Jesus, still you came with some sense of need and some kind of expectation. So picture Jesus standing before you asking, "What do you want me to do for you?" Then consider the possibility of giving the same six-word answer as did Bartimaeus, "Master, let me receive my sight."

It's hard to live a sighted life, to feel the pain of the world, to love what others fear, to walk in ways that others shun. But then, who wants to pluck blackberries all their days? Who wants to leave another generation to reap the whirlwind, and not see every common bush afire with God?

"What do you want me to do for you?"
"Master, let me receive my sight."

Nourishing Ourselves

SEPTEMBER 28, 1986
Reading: Psalm 103

What precisely do we need for our daily spiritual fare? We need, first thing each new day, to reestablish in our minds that life is a gift of God granted moment by moment. Life is to be held in awe. It is something to be wondered at and then reveled in, even if we have scarcely two dimes to rub together. Even when we know that the rope of the final curtain is in singularly incompetent hands, still we say, "Bless the Lord, O my soul, and all that is within me bless His holy name"—for our misuse of the gift of life should only enhance our gratitude to the giver, who, far more than we, is heartbroken by what we have done with his gift.

"Bless the Lord, O my soul!" When Jesus said, "Whoever does not receive the Kingdom of God like a child shall not enter therein"

(Mark 10:15), he was not calling for the childlikeness of primitive ignorance. (Yesterday I saw a wonderful sign: "Jesus came to take our sins away, not our minds!") Rather, Jesus had in mind the childlikeness of a wisdom that approaches life and ends life—and in between lives life—with wide-eyed wonder. Doubts are important, but wonder is all-important. Approach life with doubt, and you will have to whistle up your spirits. Approach life with wonder, and your youth will be renewed like the eagle's. The one thing that depressed me during my seminary days was how often the zest for life seemed to be dimmed by long immersion in Biblical studies. If only one-tenth of the things we believed were actually true, we students and professors should have been ten times as excited as we were—that is, if we truly possessed, not merely professed, our faith.

"Bless the Lord, O my soul!" You will never be spiritually nourished by nursing a lurking anger against the world. You will never be deeply nourished by using piety as a poultice for your sores. And you will surely never be spiritually nourished by living on the razor's edge of enjoying your misery. But you *will* be spiritually nourished—and daily—if in the midst of misery, in the thicket of your uncertainties, when the woes of suffering people settle down on your soul as a burden you are helpless to lift, you can still rejoice in the Lord, saying, "Bless the Lord, O my soul!"

Here in translation is a poem of Czeslaw Milosz, an exiled Pole who, more years than most of us here have lived, has rowed into the teeth of one gale after another.

> Pure beauty, benediction: you are all I gathered
> From a life that was bitter and confused,
> In which I learned about evil, my own and not my own.
> Wonder kept dazzling me, and I recall only wonder,
> Risings of the sun in boundless foliage,
> Flowers opening after the night, universe of grasses,
> A blue outline of the mountains and a shout of hosannas.
> How many times I thought: is this the truth of the earth?
> How can laments and curses be turned into hymns?
> Why do I pretend when I know so much?
> But the lips praised on their own, the feet on their
>   own were running,
> The heart beat strongly; and the tongue proclaimed
>   its adoration.

Life is a gift granted moment by moment. Actually, everything is a gift of God if we know how to make use of it. "Bless the Lord, O my soul, and forget not all his benefits." Let each day begin with the prayer: "O Lord, who lends me life, grant me a heart replete with gratitude."

Only after such a sumptuous spiritual repast—"O taste and see that the Lord is good"—are we ready for the day. But around ten-thirty, whether at home or in the office, some of us find ourselves questioning our capacities, our strength, our world. By ten-thirty some of us are beginning to feel left behind, left out; we're the kid with her nose pressed against the pane looking in at the party to which she was not invited. Far more than a coffee break, we need a prayer break. We need to hear that God has made each of us a "little lower than the angels," and has crowned each of us with "glory and honor."

Hearing those words from the eighth Psalm should not send us running to the bathroom to adore our image in the mirror. Actually, looking at yourself endlessly in the mirror, like Narcissus at the pond, is responding to a sense of unworthiness with defiance. Better to accept it. Two weeks ago in Zimbabwe, when I chanced upon a giraffe, I thought to myself, "How that animal's silhouette resembles my moral profile: high in front, but dragging a bit behind." Not all guilt is neurotic guilt. Some guilt is a sign of a healthy moral life.

To hear that God has made us "little less than the angels" is to realize that just as life is a gift, so is our value not an achievement of our own, but a gift of God. Only the giver has the right to tell us who we are. And if despite our manifold iniquities God loves all of us, and we are forgiven equally, then all of us are of equal value—there are no up-fronts, no behinds, no insiders or outsiders. Said Eleanor Roosevelt, who often suffered from an inferiority complex, "No one can make you feel inferior without your consent." That consent should never be given, for it is not ours to give, not if our value is a gift; only the giver can tell us who we are.

So during that ten-thirty prayer break, ask God to remind you that your value is a gift just as life is a gift. You might want also to repeat that old prayer, "Help me to remember, Lord, that nothing is going to happen that you and I can't handle together."

Prayer is first and foremost an act of empathy, not of self-expression. Prayer is essentially thinking God's thoughts after God. You remember last week I said that Jesus was asking every one of us the question that he put to the blind Bartimaeus, "What do you want me to do for you?" I suggested we each consider Bartimaeus' answer, "Master, let me receive my sight." Jesus, let me see through your eyes myself, my neighbor, my country, my world, my God. That's an act of empathy, seeing through Christ's eyes. That's prayer.

And through God's eyes not only is life a gift, and my value a gift, so is every other human being a gift, for all bear the stamp "Made in Heaven."

So for an afternoon prayer break, let me suggest the following: part of spiritual growth is not to have enemies. You may be their enemy, but they must not be yours. Jesus was adamant: "If you are offering your gift at the altar, and there remember that your brother has something against you, leave your gift there before the altar and go; *first be reconciled to your brother*, and then come and offer your gift" (Matt. 5:23–24). You cannot have a relationship vertically until you've straightened out your relationships horizontally. Husbands and wives know that reconciliation renews the spirit like nothing else. That is why we are devoting the entire month of October to the process of reconciliation within the church as a part of its spiritual renewal.

I know some older folk in this church who hoard ancient grudges. Holding grudges seems to stimulate the adrenaline—which is good for arthritis and, Lord knows, is cheaper than cortisone—but spiritually it is devastating. The decay of nature should be accompanied by an increase of grace. "Though our outer nature is wasting away, our inner nature is being renewed each day" (2 Cor. 4:16).

"First be reconciled to your brother"—or sister. Said Augustine: "Imagine the vanity of thinking that your enemy can do you more harm than your enmity!" Enmity is a diminishing emotion; it shrivels the soul, it makes you mean-spirited.

"First be reconciled to your brothers and sisters"—as through his good deed the Samaritan was reconciled to his Jewish enemy—which makes the point that peoples, as well as individuals, need reconciliation for their spiritual health. Think of all the wounded spirits in the Promised Land today. How devastating to Judaism is the hatred certain Jews bear toward Muslims; how devastating to Islam is the hatred certain Muslims bear toward Jews—not to mention the devastation to Christianity by Christians who hate both. Friends, let us not think that the Cold War is good for warm Christian hearts. Fanatic anti-communism, in its temper of hatefulness, shows a similarity of spirit, if not of creed, to fanatic communism.

Love "*does not rejoice at wrong*, but rejoices in the right." But it is so hard to be reconciled with those we feel have wronged us. It helps to remember that people would probably not have hurt you were they not wounded themselves. It helps to remember that line from *Othello*: "Thou hast not half that power to do me harm as I have to be hurt." It helped this week when I endorsed an invitation to Kim Phuc of Vietnam to visit the United States. Many of you will remember the photograph of Kim as a young girl, naked, covered with napalm burns and screaming in agony as she ran down a Vietnamese road. Last year when she was interviewed on American television, she spoke simply and eloquently in terms that Bob Simon of CBS News summed up as follows: "To survive is to forgive in the world of Kim Phuc." What beauty of spirit to transcend narrow nationalism, sectarian politics, and third-degree burns!

Most of all, it helps to remember that Jesus, the victim of the greatest miscarriage of justice in the history of the world, asked God to forgive his killers, which is why St. Paul wrote: "Love bears all things, believes all things, hopes all things, endures all things. Love never ends" (1 Cor. 13:7–8a).

But a sermon must, and let's end it with the hope that we shall all nourish ourselves daily this week. Let us start the day with the remembrance that life is a gift granted moment by moment, something to be wondered at and reveled in. Let us continue the day with prayer breaks whenever necessary in which to recall that our value too is a gift and not an achievement—we have only to express ourselves, not prove ourselves. And then let us seriously seek to be reconciled with someone with whom today we are at odds. Reconciliation is the key to spiritual health. It is carrying on the work of our Savior, for "God was in Christ reconciling the world unto himself."

Why I Became a Minister

OCTOBER 5, 1986

Teaching in the early sixties at Yale was a distinguished scholar who was something of a racist. His mother-in-law, also from the South, but a thoroughgoing integrationist, explained the situation to me in these words: "You see, he was born conservative and has never had an important experience."

I was far more fortunate. Since the death of my father when I was nine years old, I've had many important experiences and have tried not to miss their meaning. None was more formative, I suspect, for my faith than World War II. Like many another 18-year-old American in 1943, I was an enthusiastic member of the military. Already it had become clear that not since God created the earth had any group been responsible for as much suffering and for as many deaths as the Nazi Party of Germany. As far as I was concerned we were sweeping away the filth of Satan, we were renewing the earth. Never did it occur to me that fighting fire with fire would produce more ashes than anything else. I stood with the French poet Péguy, who wrote, "People who insist on keeping their hands clean are likely to find themselves without hands."

But by war's end, and especially after two more years as a liaison officer with the Russian Army in Czechoslovakia and Germany, I had heard enough to convince me that on occasion Stalin could make Hitler look like a Boy Scout. I had had an important experience. Four years in the service had ended my boyhood innocence. I had lifted my head out from under five feet of sand. World War II was the worst in the history of the world; the fields and cities of Eastern and Western Europe had run with enough blood to float a fleet. Fifty million human beings had died. The mind simply could not grasp it—not the gas chambers of Hitler, nor the atomic victims of Hiroshima. In 1947, all I knew for sure was that human life was not as pure as I had thought, and that in the sullied stream of human life our only option is not innocence but what we might call holiness. Although I didn't know it, I was ready for a religious experience. I was asking all the right questions— Could the human race improve, change? Did it show any evidence of a divine touch?—questions that are so important because nothing in this world is as irrelevant as the answer to an unasked question.

Entering college, I quickly found myself torn. Because they too were asking my questions, I was drawn to the French existentialists— the most sensitive atheists of the time—people like Sartre and Camus. But I couldn't help feeling their answers lacked weight. Their despair over the human condition was real, but the stoicism with which they met it—trying to be "saints without God"—struck me as romantic, lacking strength. By contrast, theologians like Richard and Reinhold Niebuhr and Paul Tillich seemed in touch with a deeper reality. They too knew what hell was all about, but in the depths of it they found a heaven that made more sense out of everything, much as light gives meaning to darkness.

But for a long time I remained in the dark. For one thing I hadn't realized that Christians are always the best argument against Christianity, albeit not the central argument (it's not what you think of Christians, but what you think of Christ that is crucial). So I allowed myself to be put off by the churches, which were just then beginning to desert the cities in droves, following their middle-class constituents to such costly Siberias as Scarsdale, Bronxville, and Greenwich. It offended my understanding of the Gospel to see the churches become protected and withdrawn islands of piety in a sea of social ills. Also, I was eager to disassociate myself from certain fundamentalist fellow students whose ideas seemed too pat, their submission too ready. It seemed to me that as with parents, so with God: too easy a submission is a facade for suppressed rebellion. I sensed a deep, unresolved hostility and had the impression these students wanted Christ to take away not only their sins, but their minds as well.

But Jesus had me hooked. Never had I read or heard anyone who, from the outer periphery to the inner core and back again, was so totally of a piece. Jesus was tender as only the truly strong can be tender. He was in everyone's corner, seeing through everyone and empowering them at the same time. When in my own doubting moments I asked myself, "Who knows more about the existence of God, Coffin, you or Jesus?" I found it pretty hard to answer with any degree of confidence, "I do." As for the Good Friday story, I was overwhelmed by its pain and sorrow, beauty and courage. Such suffering love on God's part was too good to believe.

I can't omit the role of music. Bach's Mass in B-minor, *St. John Passion*, *St. Matthew Passion*, Brahms's *Requiem* and Verdi's too—all these great religious works, many of which I had sung, searched my heart in ways that words could not. They made me realize that religious truths, like those of music, are always apprehended on a level deeper than they are comprehended. There are moments of grace in this world so deep and true and painful that tears come to the eye not for grief, but because the universe is so true at that moment. So the leap of faith, I began to see, was not a leap of thought, but rather one of action. Faith is not believing without proof, it is trusting without reservation. It represents a truth the mind can defend but never discover, a truth the mind can never fully grasp, but one to which the heart can totally surrender. So, following the lead of Alcoholics Anonymous, I committed as much of myself as I could to as much of God as I believed in. It seemed an honest road to conversion.

It took a conference for a hundred or so college seniors at Union Theological Seminary to convert me to the possibility of becoming a minister. I will never forget how Reinhold Niebuhr urged us to go into the ministry only if we lost the battle to stay out. But an hour later—after he had painted a picture of the woes of the world, including American racism and poverty, and had spoken of the need for church people to protest injustice in the name of God and human decency, and said that ministers who knew what they were about, had the courage of their convictions, and were good pastors probably had greater freedom to say and do what they wanted than people in any other vocation—I'm sure mine wasn't the only soul crying out, "Take me!" Niebuhr was followed by Professor James Muilenberg, who looked and sounded like Jeremiah as he alternately thundered at and wailed over the human condition.

By noon I was pulverized. And by evening, after we had been bussed to various sites of the very woes Niebuhr had described and decried, I had to confess that the events of the day had made mince-meat of my contention that the churches had abandoned the histori-cal quest for social justice. On Monday I signed an application to attend Union Theological Seminary the following year. There I stud-ied happily under the leadership of professors who, in Augustine's phrase, "believed in thinking and wished to think in believing."

The Korean War interrupted things for three years, and because of my mother's illness I returned to New Haven, finally graduating from Yale Divinity School in 1956.

Since then I have had more important experiences. My faith, I think, has deepened, but not significantly altered. I hope I haven't mellowed but have grown more compassionate. More than ever I am convinced that we serve God poorly, but because God is merciful, we always have grounds for hope, if none for complacency.

I am a little clearer now on the issue of hypocrisy. Of course we all pass ourselves off as something we are not, but not *anything* we are not. Generally we try to pass ourselves off as something that is spe-cial in our hearts and minds, something we yearn for, something beyond us. That's rather touching.

I am daily impressed that we are but a tiny dot on the edge of a star cluster in a universe that has millions of star clusters just like it. But that leads me to dwell less on our unimportance than to marvel at a God who cares for each of us as if He/She had nothing else to care for.

I know that Jesus walks with us along our pilgrim journey, but doesn't have us in harness or on a leash, for God tenders maximum sup-port but minimum protection. When our journey ends on the verge of Jordan, while we do not know what lies on the other side, we know for sure who is there. "For neither death nor life can separate us from the love of God which we see in Christ Jesus our Lord" (Rom. 8:38–39).

I have a special fondness for the Communion service we today cel-ebrate. Food is the most basic affirmation of life, and the bread of heaven feeds my soul. But the bread is not only a symbol of Jesus, it is also symbolic of the church that calls itself "the body of Christ." I believe that as members of Christ's church, Christians are brought together in one loaf to be broken to feed the world. I believe Chris-tians could make an enormous difference in this world; and maybe, by God's grace, even save it. The only question is whether we will.

A Church like It Oughta Be

OCTOBER 12, 1986
Readings: Psalm 31:9–12; Colossians 3:12–17

Psalm 133 begins: "Behold, how good and pleasant it is for brothers and sisters to dwell in unity." Indeed it is. But behold how hard it also is. It's hard because, unlike a political party, church unity is based not on agreement but on mutual concern. A church is a single but very diverse community built on the sound grounds that when all hearts are one nothing else has to be one—not clothes, not age, neither sex nor sexual preference, race nor mindset.

In fact, a decent church ought to be the darndest collection of people you ever saw, and in that respect we don't do too badly. Actually, the unity of the church is not an ideal to be realized but rather a reality to be recognized. "Behold how good and pleasant it is for *brothers and sisters* to dwell in unity." We do not choose our family, it is God who has made us one. So in church we have, in the old pietistic phrase, to "let go and let God," let go our manifest prejudices and manifold insecurities, our ineffectual feuds and feeble hates, and let God's grace lead us into the freedom and intimacy in which God has ordained us to live. Christianity has not been tried and found wanting, it has been tried and found difficult, and abandoned again and again. Because it is so hard, behold how doubly good and pleasant it is when sisters and brothers do dwell in unity.

I'll tell you another reason why it's so difficult. Doing an evil thing does not make a person evil. But doing an evil thing and seeing that it is evil—calling evil good and believing your own lie—makes an evil person. If the essence of evil is disguise, and the cloak of religious piety the best possible disguise, where else would you look for evil people if not in the church? This is no new idea. Centuries ago Pascal wrote, "people never do evil so cheerfully as when they do it from religious conviction." And didn't Jesus himself warn, "Not all who say 'Lord, Lord' shall enter the kingdom of heaven"?

If Christian unity is so difficult, and the church such a perfect hiding place for evil people, we'd better ask, "Why the church? Why is the physical presence of other Christians such a spiritual necessity?"

Well, there's merit in the old comparison of the church to Noah's Ark: no one could have stood the stench within were it not for the storm without.

Life is a storm. Some of you know the spiritual that begins, "Been in the storm so long, You know I've been in the storm so long, O

Lord . . ." Hopefully not now, but at some time or other most of us have felt our lives to be as the psalmist described his:

> My eye is wasted from grief,
> my soul and body also.
>
> . . . .
>
> I have passed out of mind like one who is dead;
> I have become like a broken vessel.
>
> Ps. 31:9–12

Have you ever held in your cupped hands a bird with a broken wing? If so, you know that if you open wide your hands the bird will flutter its wings, fall out, and die. But if you close your hands the bird will be crushed. Are there not times when all of us need just such an intimate place where our wounds can heal and where we can grow?

Why is the physical presence of other Christians such a spiritual blessing? Because America's got it wrong—you don't win through competition, you win through love.

Prime time televison shows us people driven by personal ambition and consumerism. The message is clear: "If you've got the money, honey, do your thing. Do it for you and yours. Take your particular segment of life and make of it a world large or small, but make it all your own." When J. R. Ewing finally dies (and doesn't get resurrected like brother Bobby), I'm sure he will be buried according to his own instructions: "Embalm me behind the wheel of my latest sports car." And when the giant crane lowers into the grave the streamlined vehicle with J. R. sitting upright, eyes open, hands at ten minutes to two, half the viewing audience will exclaim, "Man, that's livin'!"

Luckily we are seldom as selfish as our therapeutic culture urges us to be. But we need the church to help us not to be swept up in promotions and financial success, to remind us that we cannot possess our souls by possessing things outside of them, to recall that the only truly renewable resources are spiritual, that human beings are defined not by what they have but by who they are, and that we are as we love, for as St. Paul reminds us, if we fail in love we fail in all things else.

Most of all we need the physical presence of other Christians for common worship, to "sing psalms and hymns and spiritual songs with thankfulness in our hearts to God," whose greatness is so much greater than our words can ever describe. We need the church to tell "the old, old story of Jesus and his love."

And that brings us to the heart of our difficulties in this or any other church. Evil people are not the problem; they are too few. As for personal ambition and consumerism, they are more an effect than a cause of America's shortcomings and those of the church. Henri Nouwen writes: "The agenda of our world—the issues and items that fill newspapers and newscasts—is an agenda of fear and power. It is amazing, yes, frightening, to see how easily that agenda becomes ours." To see how the world seduces us into accepting its fearful questions, Nouwen asks us to consider the enormous number of "what if" questions that occupy our minds. What is going to happen if I don't find a spouse, a friend, an apartment, a job? What if I get sick, or get fired? What if my marriage doesn't work out? What if I am mugged, or raped?—not to mention what is going to happen if we can't curb existing conflicts and end the arms race. (I sure hope those folk in Iceland realized that the world may have begun with a big bang, but no one vested a handful of mortals with the right to decide that it should end that way.)

As Father Nouwen notes:

> The trouble with fearful questions is that they never lead to love-filled answers. Fear cannot give birth to love, only to more fear. So for a community of faith to become a true church, its members must strain to hear the voice to which we have become all but deaf, the voice that says "Do not be afraid, have no fear." This voice was heard by Zechariah when Gabriel, the angel of the Lord, appeared to him in the temple and told him that his wife, Elizabeth, would bear a son; this voice was heard by Mary when the same angel entered her house in Nazareth and announced that she would conceive, and bear a child, and name him Jesus; this voice was also heard by the women who came to the tomb and saw that the stone was rolled away. "Do not be afraid, fear not, do not be afraid." The voice uttering these words sounds all through history as the voice of God's messengers, be they angels or saints. It is the voice that announces a whole new way of being, of being in the house of love, the house of the Lord.

A church is a place where we can think, speak, and act in God's way, not in the way of a fear-filled world. A church is a home for love, a home for brothers and sisters to dwell in unity, to rest and be healed, to let go their defenses and be free—free from worries, free from tensions, free to laugh, free to cry. I said at the beginning we had to let go and let God's grace lead us into the freedom and intimacy in which God has ordained us to live. Fear destroys intimacy, it distances us from each other; or fear makes us cling to each other, which is the death of freedom. Fear has so many doors to let life out. Love alone can re-create life. Only love can create intimacy, and freedom too, for when all hearts are one nothing else has to be one—not clothes, not age, neither sex nor sexual preference, race nor mindset.

Look, if we at Riverside are close to being the darndest collection of people you ever saw, we are not doing that badly. And the early returns from the annual canvass show that we are in a generous, giving frame of mind. That's good. But "never enough" describes the best of us. Today God is calling out our hearts for review. They are still too full of the fear love is supposed to cast out. God wants our unsurrendered souls, souls we squeeze so tightly that they shrink to the size of our hands.

Unsurrendered, our souls are fearful. Surrendered, they fill us with the love that only God's grace can provide.

Behold, how good and pleasant and absolutely necessary it is for brothers and sisters to dwell in unity. Sisters and brothers, we can quarrel, but we are a family. That is why the physical presence here of every one of us is such a spiritual blessing to all the rest. Look around you, and behold how good and pleasant it is!

Yesterday, in the bottom of the ninth, the Mets proved true the saying that is written high above the bleachers of Shea Stadium: "Baseball like it oughta be."

We're nowhere near the bottom of the ninth, and we don't need to hang out any sign. But let's be a church like it oughta be.

What the Lord Requires of Us

OCTOBER 19, 1986
Reading: Micah 6:6–8

On the first Sunday of this month, following the service, three hundred of us gathered in the Assembly Hall and told one another something of our pilgrimage of faith. Returning last Sunday, we struggled with the difficulties of a faith community as diverse as

I am much indebted to Walter Brueggemann, Sharon Parks, and Thomas H. Groome for their book *To Act Justly, Love Tenderly, Walk Humbly* (Paulist Press, New York, 1986).—WSC

our own trying to make itself into "a church like it oughta be"—and remember, we are always undefeated as long as we go on trying. Today, we are asked to remember the graffiti slogan of the sixties, "Nostalgia isn't what it used to be," and, in the language of that first great day of Pentecost, to dream dreams and to see visions. Only by so doing can any church be worthy of its past. For to insist that there can be nothing in our future unless it was in our past (as does the Roman Catholic Church on the question of the ordination of women) is to misunderstand the role of tradition in the religious community by ignoring the role of the Holy Spirit.

And how does all this dreaming dreams and seeing visions tie in with Pledge Sunday? Not to worry. Let us approach the subject by what philosophers call the *via negativa*: by seeing what dreaming dreams is not.

Recently a rabbi told me of an old Jewish antique dealer who took a sudden liking to a young customer. Reaching under the counter, the dealer pulled out a lamp the like of which you might find in Turkey. "This is a special lamp," he told the young woman, "but you may have it for a special price. All you have to do is make a wish and then rub the lamp, and your wish will come true." Deeply skeptical, the customer asked the dealer, "If this lamp is so special, how come you're willing to sell it?" The old dealer sighed. "What good is it to me? My daughter is married, and my son calls me once a week." You see what I'm getting at. If God is the sole and direct author of the created order; if we human beings are the conscious work of God's love, the object of God's sustaining and redeeming activity, if God continues to love us when we are least lovable—which is frequently—then we should expect a lot. We should have great expectations—of God, of ourselves, of each other, of our church. Let me put it this way: If the Word of God can call forth shoots from dry stumps, a people from dry bones, sons and daughters from the stones at our feet, babes from barren wombs, and life from the tomb, then this Word, mightier than any power, can call forth from each of us a new creation, and no one of us should rest comfortably with anything less.

I expect great things of Riverside Church and of its members: no more nor less than the requirements set forth by Micah, the last of the four great prophets of the eighth century BC (the others being Amos, Hosea, and Isaiah).

> And what does the Lord require of you
> but to do justice, and to love kindness,
> and to walk humbly with your God?
> Mic. 6:8

There's no point in dwelling on what must be obvious to most members of this congregation. To do justice is not the same as to practice charity. The prophet Amos did not say, "Let charity roll down like mighty waters," but rather, "Let justice roll down like mighty waters." The distinction is important. Marx was in fact quite Biblical in his criticism of the Christian churches when he said that we Christians have a vested interest in unjust structures that produce victims to whom we can then pour out our hearts in charity. So conceived, charity is giving without receiving—a downward motion.

I like Walter Brueggemann's definition. "Justice," he writes, "is to sort out what belongs to whom, and to return it to them." Lincoln didn't give freedom to the slaves, he returned to them the freedom of which they never should have been deprived. Great Britain in 1948 didn't grant independence to India, it returned to Indians the same independence that was always theirs to enjoy, just as much as any citizen of Great Britain. When in the future Americans see food and a roof over one's head as moral rights worthy of the same legal protection we today afford free speech and freedom of the press, it will signal that American social awareness, presently so uninformed and naïve, is reaching a level more nearly that of Amos, Hosea, Isaiah, and Micah 2,600 years ago. Seeing the world through the eyes of God, the prophets recognized power relationships where some folks do not have what belongs to them because others have, use, and enjoy what is not theirs.

"And what does the Lord require of you but to do justice . . ." "Justice is to sort out what belongs to whom, and to return it to them." Justice then is to redescribe the world. And to do justice as God does justice is to intervene in the social order as did Moses in Pharaoh's court when he insisted on freedom for the Hebrew slaves, as did Nathan in David's court when he protested the king's rapacious action against Uriah the Hittite, as did Elijah when he thundered against Ahab and Jezebel for having done in Naboth in order to take his land.

I envision a future in which all members of Riverside Church, in their own unique and wonderful ways, will become shaping souls of society. Wherever they live and work they will redescribe the world to fit the description given them in the faith of the prophets, in Mary's Magnificat, and in the parables of justice and judgment that meet us on every page of the Gospels. In this city, nation, and world, they will be messengers of God's justice: in all their doings they will act justly, for what does the Lord require of each of us but to do justice, to sort out what belongs to whom, and to return it to them?

But all that I imagine must be fairly obvious, at least to members of this congregation. What is less so is why, 2,600 years after Micah, so many people not only still have blind spots, but will do almost anything in their power to keep those spots blind. What are their blinding fears? And if by God's grace we have a clearer vision, then what are the fears that prevent us from acting as did Moses, Nathan, Elijah, and all the seers and saints we so revere in our tradition?

More and more I am convinced that anxiety is the serpent in the garden of life. Let me read you some words written in 1902 about the fear of poverty among educated people, which the philospher William James termed "the worst moral disease from which our civilization suffers."

> We have grown literally afraid to be poor. We despise anyone who elects to be poor in order to simplify and save his inner life. If he does not join the general scramble and pant with the money-making street, we deem him spiritless and lacking in ambition. We have lost the power of imagining what the ancient idealization of poverty could have meant: the liberation from material attachments, the unbribed soul. . . .
>
> Think of the strength which personal indifference to poverty would give us if we were devoted to unpopular causes. We need no longer hold our tongues or fear to vote the revolutionary reformatory ticket. Our stocks might fall, our hopes of promotion vanish, our salaries stop, doors close in our faces; yet, while we lived, we would imperturbably bear witness to the spirit, and our example would help to set free our generation.

If we are to be that example, before we even think of seeing and doing justice in the world, we must first heed Micah's second requirement, which is "to love kindness," or, as in the translation in the Jerusalem Bible, "to love tenderly."

Without a doubt, our culture overvalues the virtues of autonomy, the strength to stand alone, the capacity to act independently. Far too little attention is paid to the virtues of dependence and interdependence, and especially to the capacity to be vulnerable. Learning, and especially unlearning, can take place only in the absence of defensiveness. When we drop our defenses, we can learn. And we can drop our defenses only when we love and are loved. So I envisage Riverside Church as a place where we live more deeply than elsewhere, a place where we talk to each other so that we can begin to see ourselves differently from how the world defines us. I picture us gathering in the Assembly Hall below in order to own up, and so to own our fears, to get in touch with our pain, to feel and so help ease the pain of others. I envision Riverside Church as the most nurturing, confirming community in our lives, a place where we can love tenderly, fiercely, and tenaciously. Only so will we find the freedom to become the examples to set free our generation. Only so will we find the courage "imperturbably to bear witness to the spirit." Let's face it: the realm of grace is a realm of danger.

What does the Lord require of us but to do justice, to love tenderly, and to walk humbly with our God?

When you stop to think of it, that's the only way to walk with God. Humbly is how God has chosen to walk with us, in the person of Jesus Christ.

In his time on earth Jesus stood tall, but not by making others cringe. He had power, but used it solely to empower others. He healed, but with no strings attached. He competed with none, loved all, even when we were least lovable, even to the point of dying for us on the cross. Walking with Jesus we can no longer be heartless, heedless in our haste to "join the general scramble and pant with the money-making street." Scales of heedlessness fall from our eyes. We see ourselves walking not alone with our Lord, but with all the peoples of the world, whom we now view as fellow walkers, not as those who fall in behind. And all are marching to Zion, to the mountain of God, where—can anyone doubt it?—God will cause the nations to beat their swords into plowshares and return to the people the peace that only God could give and no nation had the right to take away.

I believe all this, because I believe "when anyone is united to Christ, there is a new world; the old order has gone, and a new order has already begun" (2 Cor. 5:17). I also believe that by tithing—giving to the church 10 percent of what we receive—we are helping to sort out what belongs to whom, and returning it to them. We are overcoming our fear of being poor, keeping at bay the anxiety that is the serpent in the garden of life. And by tithing to Riverside Church, we are supporting not only our church—the church we serve, the church we love— but also (I have heard it too often now to deny it any more) one of the most significant communities of faith in the religious life of this country.

While my fellow members of Riverside Church contend with God's supernal grace, they will achingly long to do justice, to love tenderly, and to walk humbly with their God. That's why I love Riverside Church.

Spirituality

OCTOBER 26, 1986
Readings: Psalm 46; Galatians 5:16–26

Today, the two questions before our final congregational meeting of the month are: What is the center that pulls us together? and, What is the mission and ministry of Riverside Church? The answer to the first—what is the center that pulls us together?—is obviously "the Spirit to whose recovery the whole fall series is dedicated." The answer to the second question—what is the ministry and mission of Riverside Church, or any church for that matter?—could be, in St. Paul's language, "to live by the Spirit" or "to walk in the Spirit," or "to become a communion of the Holy Spirit."

But that's not very helpful, is it, given the many and often contradictory understandings of the word *spirituality*. What is spirituality anyhow? Let me offer a few starters.

Spirituality is not striving to be godly but trying to be deeply human. People who strive to be godly tend to conceit. They tend to feel, if not actually say, with Jesus' Pharisee, "I thank God I am not as others are"; which, of course, leads others to say with considerable relief and gratitude, "There but for the grace of God goes God." I think of it this way: if you attempt to ascend to heaven in a godly fashion, you may just pass God's son headed in the other direction. We don't have to be heaven-bound when God is earth-bound. Hence spirituality is not striving to be godly but rather trying to be deeply human.

Another way of saying much the same thing is to say that spirituality is not striving to be perfect, but trying to be whole, remembering that the adjectives *whole* and *holy* have the same root. To be deeply human is to be whole. So understood, spirituality is not inhibiting, but freeing. The Spirit frees us to be all God made and meant us to be. Repression is the Devil's work, liberation the Spirit's. Spirituality attracts us to the spirit of religious life, not the letter of religious life ("for the letter killeth, but the Spirit giveth life"). The Holy Spirit prompts us to put the integrity of love ahead of the purity of dogma. And I suspect it was the Spirit that inspired Einstein to say that imagination was more important than knowledge.

Finally, spirituality is not otherworldly. The Holy Spirit does not try to convert us from this life to something more than life, but rather from something less than life to the possibility of full life itself. "Do not be conformed to this world," thunders St. Paul. Formed by God, we must be nonconformists, our souls unbribed by even the most seductive, beguiling aspects of this world. But as "the earth is the Lord's and the fulness thereof," we are also not escapists. Our job is not to conform but to transform, to transform this world by helping God make humanity more human, more whole and more holy, freer, more loving and imaginative. So spirituality is this-worldly. We are not *of* this world, but we are *in* this world.

Well, so much for starters. I hope they have suggested our need for radical self-knowledge. Scratch the smoothest looking surface of any human life and you will uncover a maze of complexities and contradictions, all fed by insecurity. Everyone in this world is insecure. And all of us spend an inordinate amount of time trying to secure ourselves against our insecurities.

Recently I read of a little girl being tucked into bed in one more in too long a line of foster homes, by yet another foster mother. The girl asked the foster parent to take off her wedding ring so she could look at it. Surprised, but wanting to be responsive, the woman did so. She was startled when the little girl clutched the ring tightly and thrust her fist under the pillow, saying, "There. Now you won't leave me while I'm sleeping."

Notice how many central issues of life are in that story: belief and doubt, promise and betrayal, power and powerlessness, belonging and exclusion, suffering and hope. And the child knew the ring was precious to the adult. Why? Because of the ring's power to touch an adult's experience of the same things—belief and doubt, promise and betrayal, power and powerlessness, belonging and exclusion, suffering and hope. That's why the theologians say, "Anxiety is the precondition of sin"; "Anxiety is the serpent in the garden of life." That's why the Bible says that the opposite of love is not hate, but fear: "Perfect love casts out fear."

If we are not one in love with each other and with the Russians and with everybody else in the world, at least we are one in anxiety and sin. And that's a wonderful bond, because it precludes the possibility of separation through judgment. That's the meaning of the scriptural injunction, "Judge not that ye be not judged." All are anxious, all have fallen short, all have sinned, all of us have fears.

There are three things you can do with your fears: you can act them out, you can deny them, or you can turn them over to God. It's clear which solution spirituality requires. But don't you often find it easier to confess to God than to confess to someone else? Whenever I find that to be the case, I know I'm kidding myself. I'm not praying, I'm blowing down my shirt front. I'm not confessing to anyone beyond myself. It's time for me to find somebody to hear my confession. For only when I have experienced the pain of honesty do I know that I have owned up to my fears and the sins they prompt, and truly turned them over to God.

I like the way we have been talking to one another during the past few weeks after the service. I like the climate of acceptance that's been established. Some folks have even begun to express to one another what we all need to confront and confess concerning our frailty. Were that to happen all across the church, we would find one another to be a source of virtually unlimited consolation. This church would become a communion of the Holy Spirit.

Repression, I said, is the Devil's work, liberation the Spirit's. But let's be clear: we are freed *from* something *for* something. We are freed *from* fear *for* love, from shackling selfishness to walk in the Spirit, to live by the Spirit, to become all God made and meant us to be—people who can make a gift of themselves to one another, even as God made a gift to us in the person of Jesus. If you can say with the psalmists: "God is our refuge and strength, a very present help in trouble; therefore [one of the great Biblical words!] will we not fear"; if you say with conviction the opening words to the hymn we will sing later on: "A mighty Fortress is"—not my wealth, not my power, not my nation, not my race, my sex or sexual preference, but "A mighty Fortress is our God, a Bulwark never failing," then with like conviction you can end that greatest of all hymns:

> Let goods and kindred go,
> This mortal life also;
> The body they may kill:
> God's truth abideth still;
> His Kingdom is forever.

For "perfect love casts out fear."

Earlier I described spirituality as being more human, freer—a state of being rather than a state of doing. To love is not only to do things for others, it is to be things for others. To be available to someone who is in grief or in great joy is a loving thing to be. Most of the time we aren't really present one to another, we just bump masks; "to rejoice with those who rejoice, and to weep with those who weep," as St. Paul puts it, is a deeply spiritual way of being. And we can be that way in the family circle, in the choir, in the subway, in the office. Suddenly there is a moment when someone needs you, and it's terrible if that moment comes and then passes, and you missed it.

By emphasizing being over doing, I do not mean be passive. I'm only repeating Luther's thought that while doing good works does not necessarily make a person good, a good person will of necessity do good works. Likewise, practicing charity will not make a church charitable, but a charitable church will surely practice charity.

But to make sure our spirituality is not escapist but truly contemporary, I think we have to look beyond individual piety and communal loyalty.

On December 7, 1967, Captain Angelo (Charlie) Liteky, a Roman Catholic chaplain in Vietnam, personally carried more than 20 wounded men to a landing zone where they could be evacuated—this despite heavy fire and personal wounds in his neck and in his foot. For his heroism he received from President Johnson's hand what he certainly deserved, the Congressional Medal of Honor. Nineteen years passed. On July 29 of this year he returned to Washington, and in a brief ceremony at the Capitol, he turned back his medal as a protest against American policy in support of the Contras in Nicaragua. He said, "I find it ironic that conscience calls me to renounce the Congressional Medal of Honor for the same basic reason I received it—trying to save lives."

Most people would consider Chaplain Liteky's turning in his medal an act far more political than his receiving it. But was it less conscientious? Because it was more political, was it less spiritual? Why did Gandhi say that those who claim the spiritual and the political can't mix understand neither? Why did St. Paul write the Galatians, "For we are not contending against flesh and blood, but against the principalities, against the powers, against the world rulers of this present darkness" (Eph. 6:12)?

I hardly need to remind you that, like individuals and churches, nations by their thoughts and deeds can either practice or assault conscience and sanity. They can save or destroy lives. Nations too need to move away from the fear that produces prejudice, hatred, and war toward a love where reconciliation, healing, and peace can begin. The whole globe needs to move "from fear to love, from death to life, from stagnation to rebirth, from living as rivals to living as people who belong to one human community" (Henri Nouwen).

I cannot imagine any member of a Christian church anywhere in the world not wanting to think for peace, to suffer for peace, to struggle for peace, as if the life of the whole world depended on it, which indeed it does.

Reformation Sunday is a good day to ask, "What is the center that pulls us together?" And the answer is indeed the Spirit that moves in our midst as once the Spirit of God moved over the face of the waters. And what is the mission and ministry of Riverside Church? To live by the Spirit, to walk in the Spirit as once Enoch walked with God. "Let us," in St. Paul's words, "have no self-conceit, no provoking of one another, no envy of one another." Let us rather strive to be more deeply human, more whole (and holy), liberated, more imaginative and loving. Let us remember that love is first and foremost a state of being, of being at one with each other and with all our sisters and brothers everywhere, for God "has made of one blood all the nations of the earth."

Luther understood how all this can happen. When at Leipzig in 1517 he was asked, "Where will you be, Brother Martin, when church, state, princes, and people turn against you? Where will you be then?" He answered, "Why, then as now, in the hands of Almighty God."

The Saints

NOVEMBER 2, 1986
Reading: John 4:34–38

Let us take as a text the line we just heard from St. John: "Others have labored, and you have entered into their labor." Today, the world around, churches (Catholic, Orthodox—such as the Eastern Ethiopian Orthodox church, which had its service here in Riverside already this morning—and Protestant) will celebrate All Saints' or All Souls' Sunday. At Riverside we read the names of church members who have died since All Souls' Sunday last year. While the rest of us weep, the choir sings "Shall We Gather at the River?" The congregation sings "For All the Saints" or "Jerusalem My Home." All of us praise God for that "invisible cloud of witnesses in the listening skies" who hear and encourage us, speak tenderly, and cry unto us that our warfare too one day will be accomplished. We pray, "Lord, to those who hunger give bread; to those who have bread give a hunger for justice." We break bread together. We share the cup of blessing and, after a final hymn of praise to our Lord and Savior and to God "for all those who from their labors rest," we go forth to celebrate their lives in our own.

It's an important Sunday in the liturgical year. After life itself, and the beauty of the earth, and the redemption of the world by our Lord

Jesus Christ, for what should Christians be grateful if not for the ten thousand times ten thousand in the world unseen, whose faith lives on in our hearts, whose knowledge lights our paths, and whose tasks have now fallen to our hands?

It's wonderful that we should have this service to end the series on the Recovery of the Spirit, for the Spirit unites not only those within the church, but also all sisters and brothers on the face of the earth and down the march of generations. It is proper that we should be receiving so many new members, and see in our midst so many new Christians being baptized, for we see here the fulfillment of Scripture: "One sows, another reaps; others have labored and [we] have entered into their labor."

It's easier to live as a slave than to live free, which is why St. Paul said, "For freedom Christ has set you free" (Gal. 5:1). It is hard to be truly free. But unless we have the courage to see that we are free and use that freedom to build a better world, we deny our vocation. The saints, those great spirits of yesterday we today recall, are those who fulfilled their vocation. Francis of Assisi did it by serving the poor. Thomas More did it with the courage of conviction; Albert Schweitzer, Mother Teresa, and Tom Dooley did it with healing; Peter and Paul did it with preaching; Mary Magdalene, Priscilla, Dorcas, and Phoebe did it with humility and charity. They heeded Paul's mandate: "Whatever you do, work at it with your whole being. Be slaves of Christ the Lord" (which means, "servant to none and of service to all").

These saints did not look at the harsh realities of life through the softening mist of sentimentality. They were fully aware of humanity's capacity for idiocy and brutality, yet they were steadfast in their love of people near and far. These are the saints; their souls go marching on.

Then there are those whose memorial is in the minds and hearts of each of us sitting here—people we have known and admired, people who have encouraged us when we felt our own lives to be little more than a fleck of foam on a breaking wave. Take a minute now to think of a parent, a teacher, or a friend, someone who has affirmed your humanity against all the forces of history that wanted to contradict it.

At her funeral yesterday in Southern California we celebrated the life of a Riverside member who is now among the cloud of witnesses. Her son said of her, "Mother insisted on things others wanted to postpone insisting on." She herself wrote: "A patriarchal culture from primitive times to the present has so manipulated religion as to provide a rationale, in the name of religion, for holding women in an inferior, submissive place. If religious sanction is given for holding down those you love and who love you, what limits are there to rationalizing exploitative treatment of others?" So wrote Anne Bennett, whom many here will recall. She and her husband, John, former president of Union Theological Seminary, were long-time members of Riverside before they retired to California.

The first time I met Anne Bennett was in the fall of 1949 during the orientation for new students entering Union Theological Seminary. By the luck of the draw, I was invited to the Bennetts' for an evening. I knew neither Anne nor John, although I had totally absorbed two of John Bennett's books. I don't know what I expected, but after four years with the American and Russian armies throwing back vodka and scotch with the best of them—and doing much the same for a few more years at Yale—I simply was not prepared for the marshmallow swimming in hot cocoa with which Anne Bennett presented me at the door of their apartment. Clearly God had taught Mrs. Bennett the things we can live without. Hers was hardly a world of caviar, truffles, pheasant under glass, white peaches, and champagne. But oh, what an intellectual feast we were offered that evening—ideas as numerous as bubbles in a champagne bottle. Clearly, too, Mrs. Bennett was less worried about people like me being stupefied by drink, than stupefied by hate, self-righteousness, and a lot of other nasty things. That evening, I concluded that Mrs. Bennett shared my deep belief that religious faith shouldn't make you achingly earnest; zest for life should not be dimmed by long immersion in Biblical studies.

In the thirty-seven years that followed, like many of you, and many more all over the country, I came to love and admire this fierce feminist who adored her husband and spoiled her sons as well as her daughters. She knew that poverty, not children, is the enemy of liberation. I came to love and admire this peacemaker who spoke truth to power but always in love, knowing that shrill accusations never move the sensitive of heart who are put off by violence in words as well as in deeds.

Thinking of Anne, I remembered these words of Bertolt Brecht: "There are people who struggle for a day, and they are good. There are others who struggle many years, and they are very good. Then there are those who struggle all their lives; these are the indispensable ones." I am sure no blow for equality or peace is ever wholly lost, but over decades Anne Bennett delivered innumerable and powerful blows for both. Uneasy with success, happy in struggle, she became indispensable: indispensable for women who, through her, learned of their own neglected dignity, and also indispensable to men who, like me, read what she had to say. Anne Bennett also became indispensable to the Church, because she knew that religious tradition did not preclude the Church having something in its future that it never had in its past—the way the Vatican is now trying to argue against the ordination of women and the human rights of homosexuals. (When is the Vatican—when are all God's children—going to recognize God's right to a pluralistic creation?)

Anne was also indispensable to the Church because she never separated God's consolation from God's truth. She had nothing but scorn for the pulpiteers whose religious content is like unto an aspirin tucked into a banana split. She agreed with another great feminist peacemaker (and how those two grew together in the sixties, seventies, and eighties!), Dorothee Sölle, who wrote: "God consoles by illuminating truth, not by abandoning truth."

Anne was sick for the last year and a half—bedridden, that is—and any time I had an engagement anywhere near Claremont, California, I always went to see her for my own inspiration. St. Paul must have had her in mind when he wrote, "Though our outer nature is wasting away, our inner nature is being renewed each day" (2 Cor. 4:16). She proved the senior years to be the formative years. She could do this because she was married to John and had a wonderful family and spectacular friends. In other words, even so independent and fierce a spirit knew that it is sometimes more blessed to receive than to give. At least it takes more humility.

Now let's think of all the spirits we thought of earlier, and the forty-two members whose names we read earlier in the service. Death fills all lovers of life with unutterable sadness, yet we recognize the impermanence of this world. Here we have no abiding city. We seek one that is to come, beyond history and beyond death. We are always strangers and sojourners. Our citizenship is in heaven. So let's call death less a retirement than a promotion. It is said that our Lord Jesus Christ wept when he brought back Lazarus from the dead because he knew from what joys he would be returning. Beethoven said, "I shall hear in heaven," as the blind receive their sight and the lame walk and the homeless live in many mansions. Were it not so, our Lord and Savior would have told us.

Let us, on this All Souls' Sunday, grieve—but, with the clarity of Anne Bennett, grieve for ourselves and not for our beloved departed. Let us resolve not to hold them close by grief, for they would not wish to be held close by grief. Rather, let us pray God for that hope which can absorb all despair and that love which binds all immortal and mortal life, so that we may do as they would have us do: return to fight the good fight—yea, to become more than conquerors, to endure until the end, until, with them, we are made partakers of God's eternal Kingdom.

"Continue in the Truth . . ."

NOVEMBER 9, 1986
Readings: 2 Timothy 3:14–17; Psalm 100

When one considers the many activities of many a Christian church, one can't help but recall St. Augustine's quip back in the fourth century: "You run well, but off the track." Or perhaps one recalls what the French general observed as he watched the Charge of the Light Brigade: "*C'est magnifique*" (It is magnificent), "*mais ce n'est pas la guerre!*" (but it is not war!).

What is frightening is how widely this criticism applies to so many human activities far beyond those of the churches. What is truly frightening is how many of these activities, pursued in the honest belief that they benefit not only ourselves but the common good, turn out in the end to be far more destructive than constructive.

Speaking here at the recent Fosdick Convocation, Arthur Miller had this to say on the subject of morality—which, as we all know, is always interested in the common good:

> I have no doubt that when the Marxist Pol Pot in Cambodia set about murdering two million of their fellow Cambodians, they were moved by high moral considerations of the greater good for which no sacrifice is ever too much. When Lyndon Johnson put a half-million men into Vietnam, it was for the greater good of the whole world. And when he told his lies about events there, and Nixon told his after him, it was always for the greater good that the truth could not be told.
>
> It seems that it is always for moral considerations—considerations of the greater good—that the truth can never be told in time to prevent great calamities from overtaking mankind. We now have an administration which knows no limits to what it

> will do for the greater good, including even inventing
> news that will discomfort not only our enemies, like
> Qaddafi, but our supposed friends like CBS, NBC,
> ABC, and the United States Congress. And of course
> the moral basis for disinformation is that it protects
> the American public from harm in the shape of the
> unnerving effects of truth.

If you think about what is being done today in the name of moral-ity, in the name of common good, in Northern Ireland, in Israel, in Iraq, Iran, and Lebanon, I'm sure you will agree with me that St. Paul had a point in asking his disciple Timothy to check out yet again the truth he really believed in. I suggest we do the same this Bible Sun-day: "Continue in the truth that you were taught and firmly believe" (2 Tim. 3:14). What were we taught? What do we firmly believe?—particularly about God, because the God we worship will determine our self-image and our worldview.

When I ask atheists to describe the God they have rejected they invariably describe a God I wouldn't believe in either. Always it's a God who represents something less than human love, as we know it, at its best. Ironically, what sensitive, thoughtful atheists believe generally meshes with, rather than contradicts, the message of Jesus. But instead of seeking and perhaps embracing the God "who so loved the world that he gave his only begotten son that whosoever should believe in him should not perish but have eternal life," these atheists are content to repudiate the God of some fundamentalist preacher they may have heard in their youth, a preacher who may have embraced Christianity but clearly was never converted to the Spirit of Christ.

This God of the fundamentalist preacher, this God the sensitive, thoughtful atheists reject, resembles no one so much as a Marine ser-geant who has been handed a bunch of hopeless recruits. In this view of God, human passions and human enthusiasms are suspect. Love is a beautiful word Jesus used frequently, but the day-to-day driving force to keep our depraved natures under control and to herd us for-ward in the path of virtue is not love, but love's very opposite, fear. So life, instead of being one of unbroken joy in the Lord—"Sing to the Lord, all the world"—"Worship the Lord with joy"—"Come before God with happy songs," as the children just finished reading—is dominated by duty. Duty calls when love fails to prompt. Instead of a voyage of discovery and adventure, life becomes a matter of being escorted on a well-charted course by expert pilots. These pilot-preachers see their primary purpose to persuade people of the dangers and wickedness of the world, from which they must be saved. Their message is a triumph of law over love, a parody of Christ's message. Believing that all things worth knowing are already known, these fundamentalist preachers create an atmosphere of cultivated ignorance which guarantees that mediocrity will be a virtue.

Why am I so hard on fundamentalist preachers, so lacking in Christian charity? Because some fundamentalists have a hold on their convictions so fierce and clear as to make some of you feel your own are muddy and tentative. This is Bible Sunday, and I want to remind everybody that Biblical inerrancy is not upheld in Scripture. Belief in the inerrancy of Scripture has nothing to do with salvation. Salvation is a matter of repentance and of faith in Christ Jesus. There is no domino theory in faith. Loss of one belief doesn't lead automatically to the loss of a second; it makes the second possible with greater integrity.

It is right to be stabbed by doubt. "Commitment is healthiest where it is not without doubt, but in spite of doubt" (Rollo May). It is wrong to be clearer than clarity warrants, to write off intellectual and moral ambiguities simply because you haven't the security to live with uncertainty. It's wrong to require certitude to the point of blind stupidity. And it is dangerous. If God is like a Marine sergeant who has been handed a bunch of hopeless recruits, then those who believe in such a God will become like soldiers prepared to do almost anything they're told, no matter what, no matter to whom. To me, that is diametrically opposed to Jesus, whose central theme it was that there is something intrinsically sacred, intrinsically deserving of respect, intrinsically calling for and entitled to love in every human being. Seekers of truth can build communities of love. Possessors of truth have too much enmity toward those who don't possess the truth, or possess some other truth.

But let's move on. Most of us here, in our minds at least, have rejected a God of fear in favor of a God whose love is something more, rather than something less, than human love as we know it at its best.

But what about a tribalistic, nationalistic God in whose name so many kill and die today in Iran and Iraq and Lebanon, in Israel and Northern Ireland? Do we worship a God who loves other nations, even our enemies, just as surely as She loves us? I read in a James Carroll novel the other day that on the helmets of German soldiers in World War I were inscribed the words "*Mit Gott, für König und Vaterland*" (With God, for King and Fatherland). In subtle ways, don't we sometimes act as if Jesus Christ were our Secretary of Defense? It is almost as deeply rooted in our tradition as in Israel's to think of ourselves as specially chosen.

In Boris Pasternak's novel *Doctor Zhivago*, a character contrasts the mindset of ancient Rome with that of early Christianity:

> Rome was a flea market of borrowed Gods and conquered peoples, a bargain basement on two tiers— earth and heaven—slaves on one, gods on the other. . . .
>
> And then, into this tasteless heap of gold and marble, he came, light-footed and clothed in light, with his marked humanity, his deliberate Galilean provincialism, and from that moment there were neither gods nor peoples, there were only human beings . . . people whose names do not sound in the least proud, but who are sung in lullabies and portrayed in picture galleries the world over.

Just as the faithful use the infidels to confirm them in their fidelity, so we have seen hatred of other tribes and nations become a test of patriotism.

Do you see what is beginning to emerge? A Marine-sergeant God is concerned with sins of weakness, a God of love far more with sins of malice. Which sins concern you more?

A God of love or a God of fear. A God of all or a God only of some. Finally, do we believe in a God of things as they are, or a God of things as they are going to be—if we care a little more? Is your God above you, within you, or ahead of you? I think it is virtually impossible for Christians who profit by the status quo to believe that God is really against it. So we don't, most of us, not in our heart of hearts. We comfort ourselves with the thought that because our intentions are good (nobody gets up in the morning saying, "Whom can I oppress today?") we do not have to examine the consequences of our actions. We acknowledge injustices, are even eager to respond to them, just as long as we don't have to confront their causes and our own complicity therein.

When the God we worship is a God of the status quo, then the Church serves the state as a kind of ambulance service. Picture, if you will, an intersection where people keep getting run over. A church will nurse their wounds, will even build a hospital right on the corner. But most churches are reluctant to go down to City Hall and demand a change, a stop light, for that would be politics, and religion and politics don't mix.

Actually the illustration is trivial and inaccurate, for church members *would* go to City Hall to demand a stop light. What they would not do—if theirs is a God of the status quo, would be to go to the federal government to demand that a stop light be placed in the path of an economic "progress" that leaves behind so many victims.

"Continue in the truth that you were taught and firmly believe." We have distributed Bibles this Bible Sunday because we believe with St. Paul that Holy Scripture is able to give us the wisdom that leads to salvation through faith in Jesus Christ. The Bible is a wellspring of wisdom. It shows us both the green pastures and the paths of righteousness. It sings praises to a God who bruises our egos but mends our hearts. It demonstrates that active faith will arouse official discontent, and it assures us of the security that comes with the knowledge that God will ferret us out of any hiding place: "Adam . . . where art thou?" "What doest thou here, Elijah?"

But the Bible is a signpost, not a hitching post. It points beyond itself, saying, "Pay attention to God, not me." And the God of the prophets, who saw God ahead of them altogether as much as above and within them; the God of our Lord Jesus Christ; the God of Mary who sang the Magnificat and of Mary Magdalene, whose sins were those of weakness but certainly not of malice; the God of Peter and Paul was, is, and ever shall be a God of love surpassing human telling, a God of all, not of some, and a God who wants us to continue the work of creation until one day children such as these we have in our midst today will live in a world without famine, a world, in effect, without borders, a world at last at one and at peace.

How right these children were to recite: "Sing to the Lord, all the world! Worship the Lord with joy; come before God with happy songs! . . . For the Lord is good; and God's love is eternal and God's faithfulness lasts forever" (Ps. 100).

A Neighborhood as Wide as God's Heart

NOVEMBER 23, 1986
Reading: Luke 10

Every now and then, when reading Scripture, you come across a passage that attempts to epitomize, to express the heart of scriptural truth, to get at the spirit behind all the words. For example, in Ezekiel 18 you read: "if a [person] is righteous and does what is lawful and right . . . , does not defile his neighbor's wife . . . , does not oppress any one, but restores to the debtor his pledge, commits no robbery, gives his bread to the hungry and covers the naked with a garment, does not lend at interest or take any increase, withholds his hand from iniquity, executes true justice between [people], walks in my statutes, and is careful to observe my ordinances—[such a one] is righteous, [such a one] shall surely live, says the Lord God."

These attempts to epitomize are great scriptural guidelines, because they agree in what they emphasize. Take Micah 6:8: "What does the Lord require of you but to do justice, to love mercy, and to walk humbly with your God?" All the rest is commentary.

In the New Testament, among these attempts to epitomize we would have to select the Beatitudes, much of the Sermon on the Mount, 1 Corinthians 13, and surely the parable of the Good Samaritan. For better than any other, and more lyrically than any statement, this parable makes the point that love of God and love of neighbor are absolutely inseparable. Nowhere in literature, religious or other, is there to be found a simpler and more profound definition of a neighbor.

"And behold, a lawyer"—or scribe, a religious leader—"stood up to put him to the test, saying, 'Teacher, what shall I do to inherit eternal life?'" To which Jesus answers, "'What is written in the law? How do you read?'"

You know how Gentiles complain to Jews: "The trouble with you Jews is that every time someone asks you a question, instead of answering, you ask another question." To which the Jews reply, "Why not?" Yet I dare say that in this instance Jesus would not have answered the lawyer's question with another had the lawyer been more like the rich young ruler who, in another instance, asked the same question. But when the young ruler asked, "What must I do to inherit eternal life?" his question clearly came from a heart full of despair. Here was a man who knew that his life had missed many important turns. By contrast, the lawyer was trying to score points, and Jesus must have caught the undercurrent of his motives moving counter to the surface current of his words.

Nevertheless, the lawyer answers well. He may have read the words from the leather bands that pious Jews to this day wear around their wrists, or he may have known them by heart. In any case, he combined what the Jews call the "sh'ma Israel" from Deuteronomy (6:5), "Thou shalt love the Lord thy God with all thy soul and with all thy strength, and with all thy mind," with words from Leviticus (19:18), "Thou shalt love thy neighbor as thyself." There is another epitome, those two commandments put together. Jesus answers, "You have answered right; do this and you will live."

Did you notice how Ezekiel ends his attempt to epitomize—
"[Such a one] is righteous, [such a one] shall surely *live*." Likewise
Jesus said: "Do this and you will *live*." We don't live in order to love,
we love in order to live. To love is the expression of our aliveness.
Only by love do we escape the sarcophagus of the self. As it is written in the letter of John, "we pass out of death into life because we
love our brother and sisters."

"But the lawyer, desiring to justify himself" (the undercurrent is
now surfacing), "said, 'And who is my neighbor?'" That joins the issue,
doesn't it? To the lawyer, "neighbor" was undoubtedly "Jew" writ large,
just as it so often seems to be in the minds of certain Israeli leaders like
Ariel Sharon or Rabbi Kahane. Palestinians are not their neighbors.
There is a sad irony in this, because the Palestinians are Hitler's last
victims; Palestinians are the victims of the victims of the Nazis.

We Americans can understand this narrowing of the meaning of
neighbor. We like to think of ourselves as a melting pot, but we're not;
a pressure cooker is more like it. I'm sure when the first British landed
here on Manhattan Island the Stuyvesant family exclaimed, "Dagonnit,
there goes the neighborhood." Americans like to think that the demand
for community, the intimacies of a community, and the demand for
equality for all, pull in tandem. But they don't; they never have. The
Lincoln-Douglas debates were about this very issue, with Lincoln
arguing that the essence of democratic government was "the equality
of all men" derived from natural law, while Douglas insisted it was "the
principle of popular sovereignty," the right of American communities
to determine fundamental issues, like slavery, for themselves. Ultimately, force of arms held the nation together, but the tug of war
between equality and community persists to this day.

And here is Jesus in this parable arguing that international equality
is the sole basis for community. He's saying that nationalism at the
expense of another nation is as wicked as racism at the expense of
another race.

And listen to this: The lawyer asks about neighbor as object—
"Who is my neighbor?"—and Jesus answers by defining neighbor as
subject. At the end of the parable, he asks, "Which proved neighbor
to the man?" The question is not "Who is my neighbor?" but "Are you
a neighbor?" The truth epitomized is that you have to be a neighbor
in a neighborhood as wide as God's heart.

"A man was going down from Jerusalem to Jericho, and he fell
among robbers, who stripped him and beat him, and departed, leaving him half dead." After the mugging takes place, we can picture the
poor man unconscious, his face in the dirt. "Now by chance a priest

was going down that road; and when he saw him he passed by on the other side." I think it would be a mistake to write off that priest as being merely callous. Hearers of Jesus would have known that in the nineteenth chapter of Numbers it is written, "He who touches the dead body of any person shall be unclean for seven days." Had the man been as dead as he looked, and had the priest rolled him over to make sure, the priest would not have been able to perform his temple duties for a week. How many of you, by a kindly deed, have jeopardized your job for a week?

I like to think of the priest as a nice guy who probably felt sorry for the man and a little guilty about doing nothing—guilt being such a wonderful substitute for responsibility. In any case, it is clear that for the priest, the claims of liturgy, his temple duties, were greater than those of charity. A nice guy, but not a good man. Instead of going to the inn, he went to church!

"So likewise a Levite, when he came to the place and saw him, passed by on the other side." I like to think of the Levite as smart. He knew that robbers used decoys, so why take chances? But I may be wrong. Maybe the Levite was hurrying by because he was late for a meeting to discuss better security measures to protect travelers as they went from Jericho to Jerusalem.

"But a Samaritan, as he journeyed, came to where he was; and when he saw him, he had compassion, and went to him and bound up his wounds, pouring on oil and wine"—which he was probably carrying for his lunch. "Then he set him on his own beast"—which meant that the Samaritan was now on foot, more vulnerable—"and brought him to an inn, and took care of him." And that's really the heart of the parable, and of all Scripture. Caring is the greatest thing. Caring matters most.

To the children here, let me say that learning is so important, but love is even more important. Love is also much more important than the laws Jesus talked about in the beginning of the story, for love goes beneath the laws, getting at the question of motives. Love goes between the laws, filling in the cracks. And love goes beyond the law. Laws are more restraining, but love is more demanding. Laws are more irritating, but love is more costly.

This morning I want to pay tribute to some of the Good Samaritans who do what they can. They may not think it much, but we all should remember:

> If I can stop one heart from breaking,
> I shall not live in vain:

If I ease one life the aching,
   Or cool one pain,
. . . .
I shall not live in vain.
                                    Emily Dickinson

Those of you who have worked in our Shelter program, kindly
stand up. All of you who have worked in our Food Pantry, which gives
a hundred thousand dollars' worth of food away each year, please
stand up. All of you who work with Ruth Hermann in the clothing
department, please stand up. You are Good Samaritans and the church
is infinitely grateful to you, not to mention the hundreds of people
who have felt your reaching hands and seen the smile in your eyes.

I am sure those who stood up will agree with my closing thought.
All of you have heard me frequently be critical of charity as a substitute for justice. You've heard me suggest that giving without receiving is a downward motion. But in this story, the Samaritan receives
something in return. The Samaritan, when you stop to think of it,
receives his identity. The other two fellows never found out who they
were. But the Good Samaritan was called into being and accepted the
invitation. Had there not been that poor man beaten at the side of the
road, he might never have found out who he was. Ponder the fact that
those conspicuously called people—like Moses—have been called by
the sorrows of the poor. The prophets responded to the voices of the
oppressed. Think, then, what we receive when we accept the invitation to become Good Samaritans. We receive our identity. We receive
our life, because we do not live to love, but love in order to live. "We
pass out of death into life *because* we love the brothers and sisters."
Indeed, as St. Francis said, "It is in giving that we receive." We receive
our essential status in God's world, which is to be a neighbor in a
neighborhood as wide as God's heart.

The Promise of an Unpromising World

NOVEMBER 30, 1986
Readings: Isaiah 2:1–5; Romans 13:11–14

There is an ancient rabbinic saying that for the world to survive it
must hold fast to three things: to truth, to justice, and to peace.
To no one of these three have the peoples of the world ever held fast

with anything approaching a white-knuckled grip. The result: "a world of brilliance without wisdom, of power without conscience; we know more about war than we do of peace, more about killing than we know about living." As those words are even more applicable today than when they were first spoken by General Omar Bradley in 1948, the prospects for humanity are bleak.

On another occasion General Bradley said we Americans were becoming "a nation of nuclear giants and ethical midgets." I thought of that description this week as I watched with uneasy fascination the unraveling of the administration's covert operations. But I was less distressed by the president's ignorance or arrogance (take your choice!) than I was by the failure of any member of the press corps to ask, "Mr. President, how many dead Iraqis would be morally justified for the release of one live American hostage?" We are a nation of nuclear giants and ethical midgets cultivating an atmosphere of moral ignorance.

So what are good Christians to do—wear a sense of futility like a crown of thorns? The temptation is real. Yet did we not, just a few minutes ago, carry down the center aisle in front of the choir a giant banner with that gorgeous seven-letter word *PROMISE* written across it? Were we clutching at an eroding hope? Were we seeking consolation by abandoning the truth? How can we talk of promise in so unpromising a world?

For the answer, let us turn to the Old Testament reading for this first Sunday in Advent and to its author (or compiler), that man of the world who in the eighth century BC served four successive kings of Judah. No prophet, not even Amos or Jeremiah, more realistically and vividly described the greed, the ostentation, the self-indulgence of the rich and the powerful. Nor did he sentimentalize the poor. Isaiah understood what Lord Acton failed to note, that it is not only power that tends to corrupt, and absolute power absolutely; powerlessness does the same. It produces lives dreary with self-hatred and stingy with hope.

About his beloved Israel, which he describes as "a sinful nation, a people laden with iniquity," Isaiah writes:

> The whole head is sick,
>   and the whole heart faint.
> From the sole of the foot even to the head,
>   there is no soundness in it,
> but bruises and sores
>   and bleeding wounds;

they are not pressed out, or bound up,
or softened with oil.

Isa. 1:5–6

You'd think a prophet so aware of such heart-wrenching stuff would have a bottomless pessimism about the future. But not at all. Not in the 2,600 years since he died has anyone written more lyrically than Isaiah about "the latter days," when

[God] shall judge between the nations,
and shall decide for many peoples;
and they shall beat their swords into plowshares,
and their spears into pruning hooks;
nation shall not lift up sword against nation,
neither shall they learn war any more.

How could Isaiah talk of God's promise to a generation as faithless as his? For his words, which should have awakened faith, fell on deaf ears. The signs that should have made the truth visible were held up before blind eyes.

The answer is simple. No matter how unpromising the world, God's promises are sure. We say, "I never promised you a rose garden." But God says, in effect, "I promise you a rose garden. I will give you seed and sun and soil. Go to it, and I promise you that the wilderness you inhabit will flourish like the rose." And can anyone doubt, any more than did Isaiah, that if we all did "go to it," we would live in a rose garden, a world of truth, of justice, and of peace?

The other day I heard how the Great Peace March, just ended, got started. It started with a man whose life could be characterized as remarkable primarily because there was nothing remarkable about it. He was a lawyer in a small town in Oregon. He wasn't involved in causes; in fact, to hear him talk, he wasn't involved in much of anything until his wife gave birth to a baby daughter. Then, for the first time, he began to think about the future his daughter's future. For the first time he really took in what he had read about the dangers of nuclear fallout, which could reach even his out-of-the-way town. He began to worry, to the point that he realized his daughter would become terminally ill and began to imagine ways in which he might put her out of her misery. Then, like the prodigal son, he "came to himself." "This is a crazy way to be thinking," he told himself. "This must never happen. I must find some way to prevent it." So he took six months off from his practice (thereby losing a lot of money) and hiked across the country telling his story to every parent in the land who would listen.

If every father and mother across the face of the earth cared that much about the future of their every child—cared enough to do something comparable, cared as much as God cares—the landscape today would be dotted with rose bushes.

You see what I'm getting at? It's not the world that's unfriendly; it's we who are unfriendly. It isn't the UN that has failed the peoples of the world, it's the peoples of the world who have failed the UN. It's not God who doesn't believe in us, it's we who are a faithless generation. In a world of brilliance without wisdom, of power without conscience, where arms-control talks are designed not to reduce weapons but only to allay people's fear of nuclear annihilation, we, a faithless generation, settle down dully in the grooves we cut when we were young. We are caught in the tentacles of circumstance.

And we are fearful. Love seeks the truth, but fear seeks safety. And safety lies not in exaggerating the obstacles yet ahead—which would be difficult—but in underestimating our ability to deal with them.

Shakespeare was right: "Our doubts are traitors / And make us lose the good we oft might win / By fearing to attempt." And Stephen King is right: "We're not really afraid of ghosts, goblins, witches, warlocks and monsters. What really paralyzes us, what sends chills up our spines is—reality. We read horror stories to forget reality."

I don't know how I can persuade you by mere words that mere words are never enough. I don't know what, if not God's promise shining bright, can burn through the crust of humanity's ancient passivity: "Nation shall not lift up sword against nation, neither shall they learn war any more."

People in this century have risen up to knell the death of empires upon which the sun never set (nor, we might add, did the blood ever dry). Why can't the people rise up again now, to demand foreign policies fit for their children? Why can't they think for peace, struggle for peace, suffer for peace, as if peace were God's greatest promise to humanity, which it most certainly is; as if the very lives of our children depended on peace, as they most certainly do?

The fact is, we can—if we will. It's not enough to wish for peace; we have to will it. We have to claim the freedom Jesus proclaimed was the birthright of his followers. We have to believe in God's power to fulfill God's promise through us. The question is not whether we can; the only question is whether we will.

Let us listen again to St. Paul:

Besides this you know what hour it is, how it is full time now for you to wake from sleep. For salvation is nearer to us now than when we first believed; the night is far gone, the day is at hand. Let us then cast off the works of darkness and put on the armor of light.

The Fear of Christmas

DECEMBER 7, 1986
Reading: Matthew 3:1–10

Let's talk of John the Baptist, as is indicated by the designated reading for the second Sunday in Advent. He'd hardly head your Christmas party guest list. His garment of camel hair would not blend with the clothes of your friends. And he probably would not wish to wash down his locusts and honey with your eggnog. Christmas parties are supposed to be fun; no one ever accused John the Baptist of being the life of the party!

But if he is not fun, John is important. Remember that for 400 years before his birth there had been no prophet in the land of Israel. In the words of that day, "There was no voice, nor any that answered." The life of the average Israelite reeked with misery, yet the skies above seemed silent. Then suddenly they filled again with the sound of God's voice. No wonder we read, "Then went out to him Jerusalem and all Judea, and all the region around the Jordan, and they were baptized by him in the river Jordan, confessing their sins."

Remember too that John was single-minded. The compass needle of his will never oscillated. He was also fearless, denouncing evil wherever he found it, whether among church leaders mired in ritualistic formalism or among ordinary people whose lives reflected no sense of God's presence, or in the unlawful marriage contracted by King Herod.

Now that President Reagan is down, many are stomping on him. But where were they when he was up, when it was so important to dispel the illusion that the president did not mean the meanness of his policies? Said Diogenes, "He who never offended anyone, never did anyone any good." It was said of a journalist who never quite fulfilled his promise, "He was not easily enough disturbed." We are too like him, too unlike John the Baptist, who never tolerated the intolerable. We forget that to lower our anger at the oppressor also diminishes our love for the oppressed. What John the Baptist and all prophets teach is that love and anger work in harness.

But I am more interested today in those who went to be baptized, the shopkeepers and farmers, the rogues and rascals, the religious leaders too, folks like you and me, who by the thousands poured forth from "Jerusalem and all Judea and all the region around the Jordan." I am impressed both by their numbers and by their realization that judgment is inescapable. That's why we're asked to study this story in Advent. The darkness is always something we would rather ignore. But the Advent truth is: no darkness, no light; no denunciation, no annunciation. As Karl Barth once said: "Christmas without fear carries with it fear without Christmas."

Judgment is inescapable. Let's approach this unfashionable Advent truth in contemporary fashion. Psychiatrists have a nice way of characterizing certain statements as "true but not helpful," a variation on St. Paul's injunction to "speak the truth *in love.*" Well, John Walker, our beloved organist and choirmaster, once said something that was both true and helpful. In preparation for a recital in which I was to accompany two choir members, Cynthia Madison and Irwin Reese, I was practicing in his studio, and getting exasperated. "This isn't that difficult; I can play it. Why," I asked John, "am I so nervous?" "Bill," he said, "it's because you have so much more respect for music than you do for preaching."

He was right; and so was I, in a way, to be nervous. For any pianist who thinks he or she has mastered Mozart lacks respect. Any singer who doesn't feel inadequate approaching the lieder of Schubert, Schumann, and Hugo Wolf, Verdi's *Requiem*, or Handel's *Messiah*, lacks respect. And believe me, I'm not cavalier about preaching. Preachers, after all, are supposed to be convinced and convincing proclaimers of the Word of God, and for that very reason educators in faith, servants and teachers of revealed truth, especially the truth about Christ. If any think that's a piece of cake, they lack respect. And how about the callousness that is calculated? Think of the builders and industrialists who injure creation, harm its balance and harmoniousness, turn what is beautiful into what is ugly. Don't they lack respect for the source of all our humanity, the earth? And all of us who are too preoccupied with putting off death, or with piling up wealth, so much so that we can no longer savor life's simple and nonelitist pleasures, we too lack respect for life and its Giver.

One scholar tells us that for St. Francis salvation meant "enchanted existence." If we are not enchanted with our own existence we lack respect for it, and that should make the point—judgment is inescapable. For all of us lack respect. Our callousness is real, whether naive or calculated. None of us make of our lives all that our Maker intended. So what is crucial is not our successes, but how we bear our failures. Do they stretch our minds? Do they widen our hearts? Do they teach us the grace of dependence—how we all depend on one another and God for continuing love and forgiveness? We can learn from our failures so much more than we can from our successes. Our successes may benefit others, but our failures benefit ourselves. It was, after all, their failures that brought the thousands to the river Jordan, to John to be baptized. And it is *our* failures that bring us again and again to God to be forgiven, to be reconverted, which should always be viewed as being changed not from what we were but toward what we really are—generous, wise, loved and loving children of a Creator whose mercy ever exceeds our sin.

It is probably worth noting some special words of John the Baptist: "And do not presume to say to yourselves, 'We have Abraham as our father'; for I tell you, God is able from these stones to raise up children to Abraham." John was exposing the understandable but inexcusable yearning to live off the spiritual capital of the past, as if a heroic history could save a degenerate age. He was attacking a patriotism rooted in pride instead of in the hope that Abraham's successors might be worthy of their forebear.

Garry Trudeau has commented that in recent years our country has changed from one that wanted to *be* good to one that wanted to *feel* good. Now that's no longer possible. Now we can only feel bad. But if our hurt stems not from wounded pride but rather from genuine penitence, then feeling bad might help us be better. It could root our patriotism in hope, rather than in pride, in the hope that we could end our self-deception. We Americans have not been creating and enjoying peace; we have been creating power and loving it. Peace does not come through strength. Strength comes through peace. Theologically understood, hope is what's still there when your worst fears have been realized. Hope is what lives when optimism dies. The prophets preached destruction until the people saw the truth in their warnings. At that very moment, they started to preach hope. If we can appreciate the denunciation, we can hear the annunciation:

> There shall come forth a shoot from the stump of Jesse,
> and a branch shall grow out of his roots.
> And the Spirit of the Lord shall rest upon him.
>
> Isa. 11:1–2a

> Every valley shall be exalted
> and every mountain and hill made low.
>
> Isa. 40:4

If we can fear Christmas, as did the shepherds abiding in the fields, we can hear, as did they, "Fear not, for behold I bring you good tidings of great joy."

On this second Sunday in Advent let us make straight in our hearts a highway for God. Like the thousands who 2,000 years ago flocked to the river Jordan, let us confess our sins and await the coming of him who, as promised by John the Baptist, will baptize us with the Holy Spirit and with fire, that fire from heaven which alone can warm, illumine, and purify our lives.

The Rebirth of Hope, the Hope of Rebirth

DECEMBER 21, 1986
Readings: Isaiah 9:2–7; Luke 2:8–20

Advent celebrates the rebirth of hope. Hope is no mere morning mist hanging over a marshland waiting to be dissipated by the harsh heat of the rising sun; no, hope is the ultimate optimism that takes into account all the evil and sorrow that pushes thinking people toward pessimism. Hope is the certainty that God will make good the promise of life. Hope is an acorn dreaming its future; it is the image of the ultimate potential in any particular form of life. Hope is the reflection of the future while the future is still in the womb of potentiality. Mary was not wrong to expect so much from the child in her womb, any more than Bishop Desmond Tutu is wrong to say, "There is no doubt we are going to be free—for the God we worship is the Exodus God who leads his people always out of bondage into freedom." Faith puts us on the road, but hope keeps us there. Hope sustains in our minds the image of the promised time ahead—"and it shall come to pass in the latter days." Hope sees God ahead of us altogether as much as above and within us. Hope fires in our hearts a passion for the possible. Advent celebrates the rebirth of hope.

And Christmas celebrates the hope of rebirth, for Christ is born that we might be born anew. First, however, we must see our need to be saved by a Savior God. The bloodletting these days in Lebanon, the threatened "Lebanonization" of Israel, the slaughter of the innocents in El Salvador, Nicaragua, and South Africa—these cruelties, which are really as old as this ancient earth, are not attributable to God; they are our own doing. God doesn't discriminate against blacks—that's the work of white heartlessness. God doesn't persecute Palestinians—Israelis do that, along with other Arabs. God doesn't make people poor—rich folks do. And how many times do we have to repeat that God doesn't go around with his foot to the floorboard, his fist wrapped around knives, his finger on triggers? God doesn't abuse women and small children. And God certainly does not make Trident submarines!

Living as we do under the heavy hammerings of history should prompt all of us, in the manner of the long-suffering ancient Israelites, to lift our eyes to heaven with the psalmist's anguished question, "How long, O Lord, how long?"

The longing for a Messiah from beyond the earth should be the deepest hunger of every thinking person. To me, that is obvious. What is less obvious is that the Savior we seek will save us by love, never by force. Every Christmas we have to remember the difference between what we want and what God wants, the difference between what we want and what we need. We want God to be strong so that we can be weak, but at Christmas we see that God wants to be weak so that we can be strong. We want God to be God, but at Christmas we see that God wants to be human. We want to be protected by God's power, but at Christmas we see that God wants to support us with her love. In fact, God wants *us* to do the protecting—and for good reason. Suppose you had been one of the shepherds come to Bethlehem, and Mary had suddenly stood up and said to you, "Here, hold the baby for a minute." And there you were, holding in your arms all that unguarded goodness, God's love in person on earth. Wouldn't that have melted all those horrible defenses of yours? Could anything better disarm you or make you feel more responsible?

I think God comes to earth as a child so that you and I can finally grow up. You remember how Amahl, once he is cured, gives to the infant Jesus his crutch? That's the Christmas present we should all bring to the manger: our crutches, our way of making God responsible for all the thinking and doing we should be undertaking on our own, in response to everything God has done for us. For "God was in Christ reconciling the world unto himself" (2 Cor. 5:19). "God so loved the world that he gave his only begotten Son that whosoever believeth in him should not perish but have eternal life" (John 3:16). It is all love, and no force.

Let's consider those first followers of Jesus, the shepherds. (We're such snobs; we give the three kings all the attention!) You remember how Luke introduces them: "And there were in that same country shepherds abiding in the field, keeping watch over their flocks by night." Don't you love the vagueness of it all? No one knows the exact grazing grounds of those sheep, nor, for that matter, the exact spot where Jesus was born. It's as if God knew for sure that there would be people intent on commercializing every sacred spot in sight, and God wanted to make it clear that no one spot on earth was any nearer heaven than any other. And to show that all lives are also equally close to God may well be the reason the shepherds were chosen to hear "the good tidings of great joy which shall be to all people."

Actually, the shepherds were not only poor, they were despised by orthodox religious leaders, since, far out in the wilderness, they were unable to wash regularly and observe other ceremonial laws. At the same time they were needed, very much so by the authorities of the Temple who, according to their laws, twice a day had to sacrifice to God an unblemished lamb. These authorities actually owned flocks of sheep, and with the flocks went the shepherds. It's nice to think that those who looked after the sacrificial Temple lambs should have been the first to hear the news about the true Lamb of God "that taketh aways the sins of the world."

And here's another nice touch: "And suddenly there was with the angel a multitude of the heavenly host praising God and saying, 'Glory to God in the highest, and on earth peace, goodwill to all.'" Whenever a child was born in ancient Palestine, it was customary for local musicians to gather at the parents' house to sing God's praises. As no Bethlehem musicians heard the news of Jesus' birth, heavenly hosts had to take over. The first acclamations came from the sky itself—a host of angels singing "*Gloria in excelsis Deo.*"

And when the angels went away, what did the shepherds do? Did they sit around like a bunch of good intellectuals nursing their doubts, debating the pros and cons of going to Bethlehem? No, they acted immediately. No roadblocks to commitment in their minds! They knew they and the world needed a Savior. And that may be the real reason the revelation came to the shepherds: they were ready. Their hearts were up, high as the mountains among which with their flocks they wandered, those peaks that are always the first to receive the light of dawn.

And here's what impresses me most: When they found the babe "lying in a manger," the humility of the scene in no way destroyed their faith. They knew no place in this world is too lowly to kneel. They instinctively understood what so many of us two thousand years later still find difficult to comprehend: that greater than Caesar Augustus, the man worshipped as a god, was their God become a man. Better than all the armies of Caesar, this Lamb of God could bring peace to a warring world. For peace doesn't come through strength; strength comes through peace—at least that's what the prophecy says.

> For unto us a child is born
> Unto us a son is given;
> and the government shall be upon his shoulder,
> and his name shall be called
> "Wonderful Counsellor, Mighty God,
> Everlasting Father, Prince of Peace."
> Of the increase of his government
> and of peace
> there will be no end.

After their Bethlehem experience, the shepherds apparently felt no need to rush off to seminaries. Rather, they returned to their sheep, and a good thing for the sheep they did. But they didn't return to business as usual. It was to business as never before. For in the birth of the Christ Child they had experienced their own rebirth. They were themselves as they had never been before. They understood that Christ became like us so that we might become more like him.

Advent celebrates the rebirth of hope, and Christmas the hope of rebirth. If we can but realize our need for a Savior, that we are going to be saved by love, not force, then the shepherds' story can become our own. Wouldn't it be wonderful to be born anew, to hear the angel voices, to sing to God our own Glorias? For all the saving grace for all humanity is in that wee babe lying in a manger.

New Year's Eve Meditation

DECEMBER 31, 1986

Time does a lot of things. According to an old saying, it heals all wounds; if you find it doesn't quite heal all of them, at least it affords you the opportunity to improve the quality of your suffering, which sometimes is more important than being free of pain.

A more recent saying, circulating around Washington, D.C., insists that time also wounds all heels. But I don't want to expound on that beyond reminding you what St. Paul said of love: "it rejoices not in the wrong."

By dividing time into years, we designate certain moments to reflect on the past and to renew our hopes for the future. I want to do just that by considering one of the two people who, in the Christmas story, come off badly.

Herod, of course, is a real heel, deceiving the wise men and later killing countless innocent children. But what of the innkeeper, who, had he been of a more generous frame of mind, could easily have given his own room to a woman about to give birth? I picture him as less mean than hassled by all the guests in the inn and exhausted by the time Joseph's knocking woke him in the middle of the night. To his credit, he didn't tell Mary and Joseph to get lost; he led them instead to his stable, and maybe he left them a blanket.

With so many guests in the inn, the innkeeper had little time for the family in the stable, even after the baby arrived. When the shepherds came (whom he took to be relatives), he was glad the family was in the stable; shepherds can smell up an inn like a skunk in a woodshed. And when abruptly the family left for Egypt, fleeing the authorities (he heard), he was doubly grateful he had not allowed them in his inn.

But what interests me is whether the innkeeper ever realized his horrendous error, what an important turn in his life he had missed. Did he ever find out that the Messiah long awaited by devout Jews had come to him personally, and he had been too busy even to recognize him?

I like to think of the innkeeper as prospering in the thirty years after that first Christmas. With his brother he opened a second inn in Bethlehem and a third in Jericho. With the proceeds he was able to realize his life's ambition, which was to own a house in the capital city of Jerusalem. There I picture him one night talking with a friend up from Galilee, who asks him if he has heard of Jesus of Nazareth, whom some claim to be the Messiah. The innkeeper has—and is very impressed by all he has heard. Then the friend asks him (very gently) if he knows that thirty-three years ago Jesus had been born in the stable behind his inn.

"Oh, my God," groans the innkeeper, remembering now not only the child but also the star, the shepherds, and the wise men. A devout man, he knows that while tragic errors remain tragic, no tragedy has to remain pure tragedy, for as no sin is beyond God's forgiveness, the past is never beyond redemption. So, through his friend from Galilee, the innkeeper sends Jesus a message asking him to come to him a second time.

Verse seventeen of the twenty-sixth chapter of Matthew reads: "Now on the first day of Unleavened Bread the disciples came to Jesus, saying, 'Where will you have us prepare for you to eat the passover?' He said, 'Go into the city to such a one, and say to him, "The Teacher says, My time is at hand; I will keep the passover at your house with my disciples."' And the disciples did as Jesus had directed them, and they prepared the passover."

I like to think "such a one" was the innkeeper, that Jesus and his disciples celebrated the Last Supper in the same room where the innkeeper discovered his horrendous error. I like to picture him standing in the door watching Jesus break and distribute the bread. And when he saw Jesus take the cup, and heard him say that his blood would be poured out for the forgiveness of many, he shed tears of gratitude. The Messiah could not relieve him of the consequences of his sin, but could relieve him of the consequences of being a sinner.

If you missed Christmas this year, or other important times in your life, do not despair. Keep your heart alive with hope. Remember the innkeeper, remember that no sin is beyond forgiveness, no past beyond redemption—and have a happy New Year!

1987

Epiphany Meditation

JANUARY 4, 1987
Reading: Matthew 2:1–12

Someone said, "Christmas falls like a seed on soil exhausted by too many harvests." I'd say rather that Christmas falls like a seed on rocky ground, and, like the seed in Jesus' parable, it immediately springs up, since it has no depth of soil. But without roots it just as quickly withers away. More accurately, Christmas is a seed constantly trying to take root in souls whose soil is somewhere between rocky and fertile, because we are always of two minds about how much we really want to welcome the Christ Child into our hearts. We are a little bit like the innkeeper: we want the child around, but "maybe out back."

Epiphany I see less as a seed than as a flower, an expression of faith rather than a basis of faith. It's a mysterious flower because the story of the wise men—or are they kings?—appears only in the Gospel of Matthew. And, as it wasn't Matthew, who was it who decided that their number was three and that their names were Caspar, Balthazar, and Melchior?

This flower is as true and beautiful as it is mysterious. Think of the truths that Matthew manages to express in eleven short verses: the truth that people come from afar and by many ways to worship Christ; the truth that no place in this world is too lowly to kneel in; the truth that as knowledge grows, so also must reverence and love, lest too much learning dry the heart; the truth that wise men think as people of action and act as people of thought. And the Star over Bethlehem—what does God's sign set high in the night sky symbolize, if not the deepest longing of every thinking person, which is for a Savior from beyond a world too sin-sick to heal itself. Yet a sign is just that, only a sign, and the choice remains ours to journey toward it or to stay stuck wherever we are.

Another way of saying what was said earlier would be that we are of two minds about journeying to Bethlehem because we are of two minds about dedicating to Jesus the same gifts the three kings brought: for gold, frankincense, and myrrh, all three, are ours to give or ours to withhold.

Gold obviously represents our worldly substance. Few members of Riverside are rich enough to be worry-free. Some of you, I know, live in constant dread of a hospital bill that could wipe out savings of a whole lifetime's work. Others of you are in anguish because you can't do more for your children, or for your aged parents no longer able to care adequately for themselves. Understandably, your favorite Biblical passage is not the one about the lilies of the field that "toil not, neither do they spin; yet Solomon in all his glory was not arrayed like one of these." You bristle when told, "Do not be anxious, saying, 'What shall we eat?' or 'What shall we drink?' or 'What shall we wear?'"

Yet those words were spoken by a man whose sole possession was a robe, words as serious as any Jesus spoke, and they are addressed to you, for it is true: "Where your treasure is, there will your heart be also" (Matt. 6:21).

We think rich people should turn over their treasure to Jesus, and so they should; but it is not money that poisons the soul, it is being anxious about it, for the seed of Christmas cannot grow in the soil of anxiety. So if you are of two minds about dedicating your meager earnings or savings to Jesus, take comfort from these words: "Peace I leave with you; my peace I give to you; not as the world gives do I give to you. Let not your hearts be troubled, neither let them be afraid" (John 14:27). Then join the wise men. Go to Bethlehem. Give to the Christ Child your two ounces of gold. Crown him again "King forever, ceasing never," and you will know a peace the world can neither give nor take away.

Frankincense symbolizes our innermost thoughts. University professors often talk of the pursuit of truth as if truth were evasive, like a rabbit, whereas much of the time it is we who dodge and hide from that truth, that innermost thought expressed so well by St. Augustine: "Thou hast made us for thyself, and our hearts are restless until they find their rest in thee."

I've never understood hearts that weren't restless. I have a hard time understanding bright, intelligent people who don't hunger for God. I can see doubting the quality of the bread—Lord knows we Christians misbake it regularly—but I can't see kidding yourself that you are not hungry, unless your soul is so shrunk and shriveled that you have no appetite left for what the ancients used to call the *mysterium tremendum*—a universe fraught with wonder and purpose.

If you're here today because your innermost thought tells you that you hunger for God, then come to Christ's Communion table, and receive the Bread of Life. Commit as much of yourself as you can to as much of God as you believe in—that's an honest commitment. And make that commitment not for your sake alone, but for the sake of your neighborhood, because Howard Beach is not the only neighborhood rife with racism. Make that commitment for your country: "Ill fares the land, to hastening ills a prey / Where wealth accumulates, and people decay" (Oliver Goldsmith). Make that commitment for the sake of a world destined to be in pieces if not soon at peace.

Because it is used in embalming, myrrh has come to stand for our suffering and sorrow, the hardest things perhaps to dedicate to Christ. So often when we lose a child through death or a spouse through divorce, or lose a long and happily held job, we think God has deserted us—when, in fact, God's heart is as broken as our own. There's a lot of inexplicable tragedy in this world, although to me the mystery of grace, of unmerited good, is far greater. But let's trust where we cannot see, not blame God for things we don't understand, and remember that if God can use our money and our innermost thoughts, how much added good to the world can God do with our suffering and our sorrow! And, of course, in handing over our broken hearts to God lies our best hope for their healing.

On this Epiphany Sunday, let us join the shepherds and wise men and go "even unto Bethlehem and see this thing which has come to pass." To the Christ Child let us bring our gold, frankincense, and myrrh, our worldly goods, our innermost thoughts, and our suffering hearts. May the seed of Christmas take root in fertile soil and flower. And may the promise, hope, love, and joy of Christmas accompany each and every one of you until once again we gather to celebrate the birth of our Savior.

The Beginning

JANUARY 11, 1987

Readings: Genesis 2:4–7, 18–25; Revelation 22:1–5

The beginning of the new year is a good time to contemplate all kinds of beginnings, such as those portrayed in Genesis (which itself means beginning). The opening words of the first chapter read, "In the beginning God created the heavens and the earth"—a theme taken up in the Gospel of John: "In the beginning was the Word, and the Word was with God." The beginning of the universe, of human history, the first individuals, tribes, and nations, the birth of conscience and communion with God—all these are found in what is altogether a very exciting book. But how we approach Genesis, especially the creation stories in the early chapters, has proved to be, to say the least, of critical importance.

When I first set eyes on Rodin's famous statue *The Thinker,* I thought to myself, this low-browed, naked man with his gnarled fist pressed against his lips is certainly not having deep thoughts. In fact, were he to tell me that he had a couple of things on his mind, I would have to conclude that things were getting crowded up there.

Yet the statue had enormous dignity. I realized then that the dignity of the statue was the dignity of the mind awakening. Rodin had portrayed yet another beginning: the birth of the desire to know.

The desire to know is the yeast of life. Shouldn't all of us want to know from whence come the moon and the stars, and beyond that, the reason why life is not better than it is, and the reason for the unrest all of us seem to feel, which contrasts so sharply with the purring cheerfulness of our cats? Old age, I know, is no place for weaklings. But if, despite the cost of upkeep, you can keep curiosity and compassion alive, the desire to know and the desire to love, you will not only survive, but thrive. Said Maya Angelou: "To survive is important, but to thrive is elegant."

Creation stories arise from the desire to know. The early Israelites, the even earlier people of the Neolithic and Paleolithic ages, all found themselves in a world full of living things. How did they come to be? Who made them?

But now we must be more precise: What was it they most wanted to know? Was it the answer to the "how" question or the answer to the "why" question? Let me put it to you: Are you more interested in the process of creation or in the purpose of creation? That question all of you will have to answer for yourselves. But what all of us need to remember is that for the authors of Genesis the "why" question was more important than the "how."

They were less interested in the process of creation (about which they had no scientific knowledge whatsoever) than in the purpose of creation (which they understood far better than most of us). They were less interested in what came first than in what is eternally true, not once and then but now and always. The point of all creation stories is the Creator. The real concern of all creation stories in all religions is the relation of the known world and universe to the unknowable God. The conclusion of all creation stories is that the unknowable determines the value of everything that flows from it. And the authors of creation stories, scientifically illiterate, use the daring of the poet to imagine what they cannot see.

If this is not God's world, the most frenzied arguments won't make it so. If it is God's world, we should not be afraid of anything it reveals. Whether we human beings evolved from below or devolved from above, whether the earth took billions of years to come into being or was made in six days, in no way affects the central truth of creation, which is that the universe did not come to be by chance. It is God who made us and the world we live in. This we know not by science, nor by cold reason, which can defend the existence of God but never discover it. This we know by what God has put into the human heart, by what our spirits tell us: namely, that human beings are made for someone grander than themselves; that this God is a mother/father force for everyone from the pope to the loneliest wino on the planet; that God is closer than breathing, nearer than hands and feet; therefore, "let everything that hath breath praise the Lord."

To insist on a literal interpretation of the creation stories in Genesis is to confuse the "how" and the "why" questions, to confuse facts and meaning (once all the facts are in, no one has the truth!); it is to pit science against religion, misunderstanding the intentions of both: for the focus of science is facts, while the focus of religion is values and meaning. Literalism splits rather than unifies our consciousness. Alas, as we have seen time and again in history, literalism leads to blind faith, the greatest cause of blind unbelief.

Let me offer an inadequate analogy. A guidebook to Venice, a Baedeker, will provide the exact details of every point of interest in the city. In Turner's painting of Venice not a single detail is exact, but oh, the mystery, the wonder and beauty of that city!

With such thoughts as background, let us turn now to the creation stories of human beings, of which, in Genesis, there are two. In the first, in chapter one, God created us, we are told, in his own image and both sexes at once: "Male and female created he them."

Of the second story (even when it is translated quite brilliantly into nonsexist inclusive language), what can we say except perhaps that God practiced on Adam, then turned out the greatest masterpiece of creation—woman. Alas, a literal understanding of first Adam and then Eve, of Eve as always a first mate, never a captain—that interpretation has proved devastating to women, even more disastrous to men, a flat denial of what the Holy Spirit is trying to tell us. It is an example of the corruption of power, how power corrupts, first of all, the logic of those it benefits.

But there are truths that still serve well in this story: an individual is not a speck of restless protoplasm; life is not time's fool. If God has made us, then, in contrast to our cats, we may be confused and dismayed, but only because we have not found our life's purpose, not because there's none to it. Here's another truth worthy of remembrance: We can fulminate endlessly about the depravity of human beings, but we can never despise the humanity God has made. Even insensitivity to humanity signifies spiritual death. I don't know for which I am more grateful to God, that God created us all equal, or that God created us all interesting.

And why are we so interesting, more so even than "beasts and all cattle, creeping things and flying fowl"? Because we human beings are nature *plus*—in modern parlance, psychosomatic. "And the Lord God formed man of the dust of the ground"—the body is necessary to our complete being—"and breathed into his nostrils the breath of life"—the power to think, the power to communicate, the power of self-transcendence, a passion for justice, a capacity to love, to see something beautiful every day, if only a glint of sunlight on a child's hair, or, in an adult's heart, a glimpse of courage breaking like sunlight through the common fog. "And man became a living soul." A soul is not a thing, it's a dimension of depth, something we lose when, in shallow fashion, we allow ourselves to become a "how generation," forgetting the "why" question, the purpose of creation. (Said Tolstoy, "Certain questions are put to us not so much that we should answer them, but that we should spend a lifetime wrestling with them.")

Moving on in the story we come to God's first recorded and ever-so-instructive words about human life: "It is not good that the man should be alone." There follows a parade of animals and birds like unto the one that trooped into Noah's ark. Adam got to name them all. "I name you tiger, I name you elephant"—what a field day Adam must have had! And what imagination to come up with names like "ocelot" and "hippopotamus," not to mention "yellow-bellied sapsucker" and "tufted puffin."

"But for Adam there was not found a partner for him. And the Lord God caused a deep sleep to fall upon Adam, and he slept: and God took one of his ribs, and closed up the flesh" (what attention God pays to detail—I would have been so excited I would have forgotten to sew him up).

"And the rib, which the Lord God had taken from the man, made he a woman, and brought her to the man."

"And Adam said" (or probably shouted for joy), "This is now bone of my bone and flesh of my flesh: she shall be called Woman because she was taken out of Man."

No question it would have been more becoming had Adam said, "I wonder, by my troth, what thou and I / Did til we loved?" or even, "Trip no further, pretty sweeting, / Journeys end in lovers' meeting."

But perhaps we can forgive chauvinist Adam's initial impulsive outburst, provided his first thoughts were not his last. Eve was very smart. She knew that wedlock's no padlock, that "marriage is one long conversation checquered by disputes," and she never backed off.

I like to picture a conversation, years later, in which Adam says, "Eve, I love you not only for what you are, but for what I am when I am with you." And Eve replies: "I love you, Adam, not only for what you have become (in part thanks to me), but for the part of me you bring out—all the beautiful, radiant things that only you would have looked hard enough to find."

We'll have to leave the beginning of sin for the next time. But I do not want to leave Adam and Eve inside the garden; we cannot identify with them until they have been ejected from Eden, their lost innocence. What attitude do you suppose they took toward that which they could not change?

The Bible doesn't say precisely, but the whole Bible insists that what is best in the history of the race has come from those who did not surrender to defeat, but went on to try to correct disastrous beginnings, and to put together something better out of the pieces of broken hopes and plans. Standing as we all do outside the Eden our pride has forfeited, we can learn of a second Adam through whose blood shed for our transgressions our past can be redeemed. And standing in the present we have, for our comfort, a vision of the last things set forth in the book of Revelation, just as the first things were set forth in the book of Genesis. In the beginning is a garden, in the end a city. Adam in Eden never ate of the Tree of Life, but the promise of Revelation, heard earlier, says this as well: In the midst of that great city, "the Holy Jerusalem descending out of heaven from God," there will be "the tree of life" whose leaves are for "the healing of the nations."

It all began gorgeously. It will end the same way. "The throne of God and the Lamb will be there, and his servants shall worship him; they shall see him face to face, and bear his name on their foreheads. There shall be no more night, nor will they need the light of lamp or sun, for the Lord God will give them light; and they shall reign for evermore" (Rev. 22:3–5).

The Beginning of Sin

JANUARY 25, 1987
Readings: Genesis 3:1–13; 2 Corinthians 4:1–6

Two weeks ago, we talked about creation stories, the beginning of the universe and the world, the first human beings. I said that the authors of Genesis were less interested in the process of creation than in the purpose of creation, less interested in the "how" than in the "why" question, less interested in what came first than in what is always, not once and then, but now and forever. A creation story, therefore, is not a scientific account but rather what is called a myth, which, like a great painting, is a story not literally true, but eternally true. The great German writer Thomas Mann said that the truth of a myth is a truth that is and always will be, no matter how much we try to say it was. This means that no scientific discovery can threaten a myth; only another myth can do that, another interpretation of the purpose of life.

Bearing all that in mind, let's talk of yet another beginning, the beginning of basic, all-purpose, durable sin.

Are there really only two possible causes for sin? Unexpectedly, I found both illustrated while reading to a child a story of Winnie-the-Pooh, that cheerful if not overly bright bear who was such a good friend of Christopher Robin.

The child and I were reading of the time when Pooh goes to see Rabbit, who, like all rabbits, lives in a hole in the ground. A hospitable little animal, he offers Pooh a jar of honey, commenting, "Isn't it funny that bears like honey?" Then, in surprise and shock, Rabbit watches Pooh finish the entire jar. (Aside from hibernating, there really isn't too much for a bear to do in a hole in the ground.) So, having finished the jar, Pooh says "Good-bye," starts up the hole, and gets stuck halfway out. Being prudent, Rabbit has a back door, which he uses to come around to the front. The picture shows Rabbit looking down and Pooh looking uncomfortable. This illustrative exchange takes place:

> *Rabbit*: What's the matter, Pooh?
>
> *Pooh*: The trouble is, Rabbit, your door is too small.
>
> *Rabbit*: The trouble is, Pooh, you've eaten too much.

Many secular humanists, and a considerable number of Unitarian-Universalists, would tend to line up with Pooh. The trouble is the environment. It needs fixing. Widen the doors of opportunity, and bears (and human beings) will get along just fine. Most Jews and Christians, on the other hand, and humanists with a profound and tragic sense of life, would side with Rabbit. Of course the environment needs improvement, and needs it urgently, especially for the sake of the very poor and the very rich, for we are all deeply conditioned by our environment. Still, we are not determined by it. And even in a perfect environment—in a garden of Eden, with all the fruit of almost all the trees to choose from—human beings prove greedy. Isn't it funny that human beings like money? Human beings always want more than what's good for them, and for all who live with them. Two weeks ago I read that 73 percent of last fall's entering freshman class stated as their primary goal that they wanted to be very well off financially. People want to be number one. They want to be the center of their universe, they want to preach themselves. And when the serpent comes along and says, "Surely you will be like God," the Adam and Eve in each of us jumps at the chance.

A typewriter repairman the other day told me that the key most in need of repair is the letter "I," not because it is used so much but because it is hit with a peculiar force.

Mind you, I like the rebellious instinct in Adam and Eve. I have trouble with people who are polite and obedient, not even potentially defiant. I don't like to hear "Moderation in all things." People who say that are "extremely" moderate, fearful, and rigid.

On the other hand, life teaches us that we cannot deify our own powers with impunity. We cannot believe that while our freedom may be limited in other respects, toward God our freedom is without limits. God has given us the freedom to choose or reject God. But if we as individuals, or as a nation, reject God and choose to make ourselves the center of our universe, then we can no longer lead this world toward redemption, only to further perdition. In short, I disagree with those who say, "Human beings are not fallen, they have only begun to rise." I believe in the Fall. I believe in Original Sin, only not understood literally, chronologically—"In Adam's fall / We sinned all"—but sin understood as something inherent in every one of us. It is too inevitable not to happen; from time to time we will be selfish. We will make ourselves the center of our universe. I firmly believe that you are my neighbor, to be loved as I love myself, but I don't always feel it that way. So I see Adam and Eve as you and me. The story may not be literally true, but it is eternally true.

Let's go back to the story, which is told not laboriously but with great imagination, with pictures more vivid than any careful pedantry.

It seems a bit unfair to pick on snakes, creatures who don't have a leg to stand on, but for whatever reason the association of serpents with guile is an ancient one. In the story of Adam and Eve, the serpent slithers up with a kind of insinuating grace, his arguments all plausible, for the essence of evil is disguise. We can't say it often enough: Doing an evil thing does not make a person evil; what makes a person evil is disguising the evil as good and believing the lie. The story of Adam and Eve and the serpent is a witch's brew of half-truths and whole lies.

The serpent says to the woman, "Did God say 'You shall not eat of any tree of the garden'?" The serpent knows perfectly well what God said and so does Eve, but listen to her answer: "We may eat of the fruit of the trees of the garden; but God said, 'You shall not eat of the fruit of the tree which is in the midst of the garden, neither shall you touch it, lest you die.'"

The original prohibition hasn't a single word in it about not touching. Eve is embroidering, and any embroidery of the truth not undertaken for purposes of illuminating the truth (said Picasso, "Art is a lie at the service of truth") is an opening wedge for sin.

Then the serpent says, "You will not die," which is an outright lie, but "you will be like God," which is a half-truth and, of course, the real temptation. But Eve wants to disguise her real desire, which is for power. Deceived by the serpent, she now deceives herself. She sees, we read, that the tree "is good for food" and "a delight to the eyes." All she wants, she tells herself, is to satisfy two legitimate desires, for food and beauty. What's so wrong with that? Moreover, the tree, we read, "was to be desired to make one wise." But clearly it wasn't the wisdom of God that Eve was seeking. Knowledge is power; it was God's power, not God's likeness, that Eve was after.

But Eve's activity quickly pales in comparison with Adam's passivity. The prospect of glory must have excited his imagination, but for any wrongdoing he wanted no responsibility. (From Eden to Washington is not very far!)

Now let's go beyond the morning lesson. When God comes inspecting his creation in the cool of the day and calls to Adam, "Where are you?" it is not because God doesn't know where Adam is, it is to open the way to repentance. But Adam, instead of saying, "I'm in deep trouble, Lord," turns up overflowing with excuses: "The woman *you* put at my side—*she* gave me of the tree and I ate." (Incidentally, it's not specified that the tree was an apple tree, but the Latin translation of the Hebrew word for bad is *malum*, which also means apple.) Then Eve, not to be outdone in buck-passing, says, "The serpent duped me, and I ate."

When the reasons begin to pile up, watch it. A friend of mine cut me off the other day: "Don't get defensive, it's not your style." He was right; it's not my style. Nor is it yours. Nor should it be anyone's.

Adam and Eve *did* have the decency to realize they were naked, not physically but religiously. But instead of squaring things with God they tried to hide their nakedness behind fig leaves which, when you think of it, are not all that big!

At the beginning I called sin basic, all-purpose, and durable. It is really less an act than a state of being, in which we put ourselves first and thereby alienate ourselves from God, from each other, and from our true, generous selves. Obviously a too-small ego can do this as well as one too large. Wrote a modern Russian, Eugenia Ginzburg, "The egotism of those who suffer is probably even more all-embracing than the self-regard of those who are happy." I think Narcissus, the Greek youth staring endlessly at his reflection in the pool, was responding to a sense of unworthiness with defiance.

There are many more things that could be said about the story: how the author felt that the earth shared in the guilt of Adam and Eve (as the rabbis wrote: "When human beings corrupt their ways the land is corrupted"); how the early Hebrews considered work more a curse than a blessing.

But the basic choice is clear for each one of us. You can point to the physical or spiritual poverty of your inheritance, the depressing circumstances of your life. You can say the world has made you what you are, and that if God wanted you different, God should have made a different world.

Or you can say, "My environment can only condition but never determine who I am—that's a matter between me and God." You can say with St. Paul, "We have renounced disgraceful, underhanded ways; we refuse to practice cunning or to tamper with God's word, but by the open statement of the truth we would commend ourselves to everyone's conscience in the sight of God." And when you fail, as most assuredly you will, you don't have to hide your religious nakedness behind pathetic fig leaves. When you hear God asking, "Where are you?" you can answer, "Here, Lord, standing in the need of prayer." And you will find, as so many of you have already, that God's mercy is to our sin as the sea to a drop of water.

When like Winnie-the-Pooh you have been greedy and are stuck on account of it, don't blame some poor creature smaller than you. Accept responsibility, ask for help—forgiveness if necessary. Life's too beautiful, too interesting, too important to miss because you're stuck in some hole.

We'll never get back into Eden. There's an angel with a flaming sword barring the way. We're all outside the garden wall, condemned to be human. And I, for one, prefer to know good and evil and die, than to live forever in complete innocence. But most of all I want to know my Lord, for I am persuaded that whatever is of good is of God, and that inside or outside Eden there is land to till, a creation to be preserved. Praise the Lord that life is so full of meaning and purpose.

Raising Cain

FEBRUARY 1, 1987
Readings: Genesis 4:1–8; Colossians 3:12–17

L ast Sunday we left Adam and Eve outside the garden gate. An angel with a flaming sword bars any return to Eden; henceforth, not innocence but holiness is the only human option. I said Adam and Eve is all of us. Every one of us, knowing the better, has chosen the worse. All of us, from time to time, have done the most irrational thing possible: we have made ourselves—one human being among three billion—the center of God's universe.

Before we leave Adam and Eve, notice what happens at the end of chapter three: "And the Lord God made for Adam and for his wife garments of skins, and he clothed them." That was not only kind of God; it was also a very symbolic thing to do, for those clothes not only say something about our personal relations, they also illumine our economic relations.

Before the Fall there was no private property, no clothes; neither were needed. But in a fallen world we all need a little distance from one another. In a fallen world there is the danger of imperialism—I identify you with me—or the danger of submissiveness—I identify myself with you. Private property, clothes—they give us space. But remember this: We are distanced to facilitate our coming together, not to keep us apart. If clothes and private property serve only to separate us further, we are badly misusing both.

Chapter four begins, "Now Adam knew Eve, his wife" (the Bible uses that verb so wonderfully), "and she conceived and bore Cain, saying, 'I have gotten a man with the help of the Lord.'" Scholars wonder whether "with the help of the Lord" might be a gloss, something added later, but I find it marvelous. Parents will bear me out: Nothing in life is quite as miraculous as your newly born first child—unless, of course, it be your newly born second child, which Eve also had.

"And again, she bore his brother, Abel." For all we know, Abel could have been a twin. Then—talk about symbolism!—the first instance of brotherly love ends in fratricide, and the first murder takes place with an act of worship.

It is not stated why the Lord had no regard for Cain's offering. Perhaps God was testing Cain for his own benefit. Interestingly enough, it will not be the last time the firstborn is passed over. Think of Esau and Jacob, Joseph and his older brothers.

What is clear is that Cain's capacity to be hurt far exceeded God's desire to do him harm, and that Cain hated Abel less for anything he did than because of what he was. Shakespeare buffs will remember Iago's classic description of Cassio: "He hath a daily beauty in his life that makes mine ugly." In Cain's eyes, Abel was God's favorite, just as Joseph's brothers thought their father considered them inferior to Joseph.

It may be that Cain had no intention of killing Abel. How could he know what it took to kill a man? It had never been done before. If so, we can only note once again how often the result outruns what the will intended. Whatever the case, the deed is done, the result, apparently, of jealousy, that most corrosive and most futile of all human emotions. (Of the seven so-called deadly sins, jealousy—envy—is the only one with no gratification whatsoever. That's the paradigm of human sin: when there's no gratification in it, and we still succumb.)

Maybe Cain was even convinced that the murder he committed was not only the first but also the last the world would see, just as people in World War I considered it the war to end all wars.

Black History Month, which begins today, reminds us that our world still raises Cain. Our world is not imperfect, it is diseased— sick with a violence to which Cain was only the first to resort. But violence is not only physical; violence is anything that violates human integrity. When children have to fight for scraps of bread and scraps of their mother's distracted affections, that's violence. When racial division all by itself breeds prejudice, then racial division all by itself is violent. When the poor can't stop being poor simply because the rich are unwilling to get even richer at a slower rate; when college students, according to a recent poll, show an increase in their desire to be affluent and a decrease in their social concerns and altruism, that violates everybody's integrity. When Riverside Church members retail poisonous gossip—not out of deep malice, perhaps, but for the relish of saying something exciting—that's violence, just as it is violent to kill joy by sullenness and to destroy marital devotion by merely perfunctory gestures of affection.

There are so many ways to inflict mortal wounds that all of us can without difficulty claim kinship with Cain. You remember Oscar Wilde:

> Yet each man kills the thing he loves,
> By each let this be heard,
> Some do it with a bitter look,
> Some with a flattering word;
> The coward does it with a kiss,
> The brave man with a sword.

When I think of Cain killing Abel, I also think of Pontius Pilate washing his hands of any responsibility. What's worse: having blood on your hands—or water, like Pilate? Cain's act was one of destructive self-indulgence, but physical violence undertaken to save another from harm, or slavery, or colonialism, can be an expression of love, albeit perhaps a distortion of it. Indifference, on the other hand, can only be the perfection of egoism.

I am sickened by the sanctimonious way the *Wall Street Journal*, the State Department, and other callous institutions and people in this country are scolding Oliver Tambo and the African National Congress for their espousal of limited physical violence in South Africa. Have these good Americans so quickly forgotten George Washington and the boys of '76, and the Declaration of Independence, which specifically endorses revolution? Why are the descendants of Thomas Jefferson, who loved justice, behaving like George III, who loved order? Time and again, history has borne out the prophets' claim that those who fear disorder more than injustice invariably produce more of both.

Of course, there is a better way, one for all of us: the way that seeks to avoid not only external violence but also internal violence of spirit; the way that seeks to defeat evil, not people victimized by it; the way that seeks not to defeat or humiliate an opponent, but to awaken a sense of moral shame. Violence simply cannot expose injustice so well as nonviolence, and it tends to obscure moral issues. But nonviolence is no method for cowards, because it resists altogether as much as does violent resistance. It was Gandhi's way, it was Martin Luther King Jr.'s way—and it was Jesus' way: Jesus who opposed injustice but never took up arms, a revolutionary "who did not become an extremist since he did not offer an ideology, only Himself" (Henri Nouwen).

For men and women in a nuclear world, when the human race has outgrown war but hardly knows it yet, Jesus more than ever is the best way to liberation, freedom, and peace. The hostility that churned up Cain, and that others throughout the centuries have sought to perpetuate, Jesus seeks to ground. That makes it our calling: to ground, not to perpetuate hostility. The violence stops here, with each one of us who claims Christ's holy name. The gossip, the false witness borne against a neighbor, the cold unconcern for warm human beings—all forms of violence, everything that violates human nature—stops with us.

There is no cause for Cain's jealousy; God loves us all equally. There is cause only to spread the love God bore to us in Christ, and that is done by being lightning rods to ground the world's hostility. That's what holiness is all about: "Whatever you do, in word or deed, do everything in the name of the Lord Jesus."

Controversy: The Lifeblood of Unity

FEBRUARY 15, 1987
Reading: Philippians 2:1–11

Let us read again the first sentence of chapter 2 of St. Paul's epistle to the Philippians: "So if there is any encouragement in Christ"—and obviously there is—"any incentive of love"—reviving you when your spirits grow weary—"any participation in the Spirit"— Spirit, *Parakletos* in Greek, meaning one whom you call to your side; in Latin *advocatus*, counsel for the defense; sometimes also called the Comforter, *conforteor*, the one who gives you fortitude—"any affection and sympathy"—cannot Christ sympathize with our weakness?—"complete my joy by being of the same mind, having the same love, being in full accord and of one mind."

Anyone who can write a sentence like that has to be some kind of pastor, as well as theologian. I suppose we can draw some comfort from the facts that the problem St. Paul is addressing, Christians bickering with one another, is as old as the churches themselves; and that among the Philippians the feuding factions were led by two women— in the early churches, leadership was genuinely shared.

"Complete my joy by being of the same mind, having the same love, being in full accord and of one mind." We cannot love God and not love one another. To do that puts something other than God in place of God when we worship God. Says Jesus in the Sermon on the Mount, "If you are offering your gift at the altar, and there remember that your brother has something against you, leave your gift before the altar, and go; first be reconciled to your brother, and then come and offer your gift" (Matt. 5:23–24).

I'm tempted to interrupt the service, suggest we go patch up our differences with one another, reconvene at four o'clock when the Inspirational Choir sings, and then, inspirited by the choir, continue our service, "being of the same mind, having the same love, being in full accord and of one mind."

When the world faces the choice of living in peace or in pieces, it is terrible that the churches manifest so little unity within and among themselves. Just think: Two-thirds of today's Christians are Greek Orthodox or Roman Catholic, yet they and Protestants have very little to do with each other. You'd think that if Christians can pray together they could take Communion together, but not so. I've been at interfaith meetings full of good talk and warm feelings, yet when time came for

Mass (or Communion), the Catholics went to one end of the church and the Protestants to the other. We literally turned our backs on each other.

Consider also that the eleven o'clock hour on Sunday morning is still the most segregated hour of the week, and you have to conclude that not enough can be said for "being of the same mind, having the same love, being in full accord and of one mind."

Yet now we must be careful—careful in the first place to recognize an old story: The greatest differences in the world are never between people who believe different things, but between people who believe the same things and differ in their interpretation. (Consider Freudians and Jungians and Adlerians. Or consider those Marxists who think that Stalinism is to Marxism as the Ku Klux Klan is to Christianity—I agree with that; it's a manipulation of the symbols in order to deny the reality.) Second, we must always remember that there is no virtue in unity in and of itself. Think of the herd mentality that dominates nations during wartime—Nazi Germany, Iran and Iraq today, or even our own nation during the Vietnam War. What is the point of unity if it is unity in cruelty and folly? It is as easy to have community without truth as it is to have truth without community, Christ crucified being the most poignant symbol of the last.

I contend that controversy is the lifeblood of unity, and to make the point we have only to consider the history of the ecumenical movement in this century. From the Edinburgh conference in 1910 through the Faith and Order Conference in Lausanne, Switzerland, in 1927 through the post–World War II conferences in Amsterdam in 1948 and in Lund, Sweden, in 1952, the ecumenical movement of the Protestant and Greek Orthodox churches was dominated by a kind of naive idealism. There was a lot of talk of church unity. Convergences were noted, and mergers actually took place. But on the whole the talk was pretty abstract, so much so that it never captured the imaginations of local congregations.

But then in the 1960s everything changed. The Russian Orthodox joined the World Council of Churches. Women began to get into the conversation, the handicapped too, and particularly Third World Christians, who by then made up half the Christians in the world. They all began to talk of liberation, and liberation means diversification. Liberation creates diversity. Soon American Christians were shuddering at the prospect of Marxist influences in the churches, while Third World Christians were shuddering at words like capitalism, neocolonialism, and transnational corporations.

How much diversity can you have within unity? The answer is: a lot. And unity is genuine only when diversities are authentic—that is, when they do not dissolve into each other.

Isn't that exactly what we have been discovering here at Riverside, as we have moved from an all-white to a white and black church, from an all-straight (or seemingly so) church to one of straights and gays and lesbians, from a male-dominated church to one that seeks to share power equally between men and women, from an Establishment church to one that seeks increasingly to question the assumptions of Establishment America? Haven't we been discovering that unity is genuine only when diversities are authentic, and therefore that controversy is the lifeblood of unity?

We're also learning that to achieve such unity we must heed St. Paul's injunction to the Philippians, "Do nothing from selfishness or conceit"—and that this is the hardest thing in the world to do, because it takes more than intelligence and will power. Intelligence can make selfishness reasonable, but it can never convert selfishness into unselfishness. Will power won't do it because our wills are too self-centered to overcome self-love.

What is required, according to Paul, is to "have this mind among yourselves which you have in Christ Jesus, who, though he was in the form of God, did not count equality with God a thing to be grasped, but emptied himself, taking the form of a servant, being born in the likeness of human beings."

Paul is talking about a disposition of mind. He seems to be saying that what is essential for Christians is not a creed or a rite or a sacrament, but a disposition of mind, one in which you do not count equality with God a thing to be grasped, as did Adam and Eve in Genesis, as did Satan in Milton's *Paradise Lost*, as do all of us when we think we're the center of all things.

It helps to remember that the word "heresy" comes from the Greek verb *hireo,* which means to grasp or to seize, as for example a town. The implication is clear: You seize for yourself, at someone else's expense. That's heresy. Christ did just the opposite; he emptied himself—of pride, that is—so as to be filled with God's love. In the old pietistic phrase, he let go and let God. That's humility. To enter the garden of heavenly love, you must stoop through the gate of humility. Humility is selflessness; it makes for objectivity. It is not self-abasement but self-effacement. Humility has no thirst for glory. "Love," says St. Paul to the Corinthians, "does not insist on its own way."

You can understand why Christ says the meek shall inherit the earth: they are the only ones who can. The fury of faith you can oppose; the assertions of knowledge you can question; the assumptions of prophetic interpretation you can dispute; but meekness, the clear voice of love, is the winning note of the final victory. In the end it is irresistible, measureless. Whenever you meet it, it is like a burst of sunlight after weeks of gloom. Love is the only disposition of mind that can create unity, because only selfless love is unthreatened by diversity.

It is also unthreatened by sinful diversity. A passionate black preacher asked me this week whether the ministers and deacons of Riverside Church would exclude a known racist from Communion. "No," I replied, "because too many of the racist's victims would be homophobic, and too many deacons male chauvinists." I agreed with him: Sinners must be called to account—racism must be exposed—but only by fellow sinners. Humility recognizes that if we are not yet one in love at least we are one in sin, which is no mean bond, because it precludes the possibility of separation through judgment.

In 1844, sixteen years before the Civil War, the Methodist Church split apart over the issue of slavery. Two senators who rarely saw eye to eye—Daniel Webster of New Hampshire and John C. Calhoun of South Carolina—realized that this was no way to do business. Both took to the floor of the senate to deplore such a separation of Christians.

Next Sunday and the Sunday following we will once again gather after the service to share our diverse experiences. I am pleased that here at Riverside we have taxed our unity. It is part of our strength that we have done so, for controversy is the lifeblood of unity. It is part of our weakness that we have yet to achieve among ourselves the mind which is ours in Christ Jesus. But it can be ours if we pray to the Spirit for that disposition of mind which was Christ's, who "did not count equality with God a thing to be grasped, but emptied himself, taking the form of a servant, being born in the likeness of human beings."

What better way to end than where we began, with Paul's pastoral word to the saints in New York City: "So if there is any encouragement in Christ, any incentive of love, any participation in the Spirit, any affection and sympathy, complete my joy by being of the same mind, having the same love, being in full accord and of one mind."

"And Who Will Go for Us?"

MARCH 1, 1987
Reading: Isaiah 6:1–8

In the year that King Uzziah died I saw the Lord sitting upon a throne, high and lifted up."

In contrast to the prophet Isaiah, most Americans these days are not looking up, at least not very high, and especially not for a God exalted in righteousness whose whole nature so burns with wrath toward sin that She is about to visit judgment upon a nation which, like Tyre of old, corrupted its wisdom for the sake of its splendor.

"Chance," said the great French scientist Louis Pasteur, "favors the mind prepared." Today few Americans have minds prepared for the kind of cardinal experience that produced in Isaiah a sea-change in his perception of things. But more Americans may soon be prepared for an experience similar to his, for the year that King Uzziah died was a time not unlike our own.

Not since Solomon brought the Queen of Sheba to the foot of his throne two centuries before had Judah's national pride run so high, or the nation's dreams of imperial influence touched such remote borders. But at the height of his popularity, blinded by his success and power, Uzziah overreached (in the manner of American presidents after landslide victories), tripped, fell, and died a leper. As the temper of the people had been bound up in the person of their monarch, an era of careless optimism came to an end, and bewildering times began.

It was in that moment of disillusionment and uncertainty that Isaiah had his vision—not of an earthly monarch, but of the King of Kings, God, "sitting upon a throne, high and lifted up."

"Above him stood the seraphim; each had six wings: with two he covered his face, with two he covered his feet, and with two he flew. And one called to another and said: 'Holy, holy, holy is the Lord of hosts; the whole earth is full of [God's] glory.'"

Quite a vision. And it could have been with Isaiah in mind that Einstein said, "Imagination is more important than knowledge." It is so easy to know more and more about less and less, until finally you know everything about nothing. Conversely, it is so difficult to imagine the almost unlimited possibilities of human experience, to imagine what Jesus meant when he said, "that they might have life and have it more abundantly"; to imagine what St. Paul had in mind writing to the Corinthians (quoting Isaiah), "Eye hath not seen, nor ear heard, nor the heart of [men and women] conceived, the things which God hath prepared for those who love [God]" (1 Cor. 2:9).

The revolution this country needs most is a revolution of the imagination. Today it's as if, listening to a recording of Liberace, most Americans think they're hearing Horowitz; reading *Reader's Digest*, they think it's *King Lear*. Plato said, "What is honored in a country will be cultivated there." We Americans have fantastic basketball players; no other country can boast a Michael Jordan or a Larry Byrd. But we also have, as our chief export, waste—scrap iron and scrap paper— and a legal system that protects freedom of speech more than the right to food. And a president who cannot remember when he forgot what he knew. What all American hearts and minds need today is the kindling power of the imagination. What all of us need is Isaiah's shuddering sense of the sublimity of the Divine Presence.

"And the foundations of the thresholds shook at the voice of him who called, and the house was filled with smoke"—as when fire and water mingle, as when holiness and sin touch each other. Isaiah refers to the obscurity that envelops a weak mind in the presence of a truth too great for it; of the darkness that falls on a diseased eye when exposed to the midday sun.

Face to face with a Presence one feels totally unfit to meet, the only proper response is Isaiah's "Woe is me! For I am lost." In the presence of the Lord of hosts, any other response would represent the old crime of lèse-majesté (a failure of respect). In the presence of Goodness itself, "Woe is me!" is a cry of self-discovery.

Then Isaiah says something wonderfully imaginative: "For I am a man of unclean lips, and I dwell in the midst of a people of unclean lips."

How do we recognize racism if not through speech, sexism if not through failure to use inclusive language? Lips are, as it were, the bloom of a person. It is in the blossom of a plant that the plant's defects become conspicuous. It is through speech that our faults surface.

"Then flew one of the seraphim to me, having in his hand a burning coal which he had taken with tongs from the altar. And he touched my mouth, and said, 'Behold: this has touched your lips; your guilt is taken away, and your sin forgiven.'"

It was the custom in those days in Judah to lay one's sin on an altar in the form of some sacrifice—a material offering for the sin of the soul. With a keener sense of his sin's inseparability from his person, Isaiah offers his own lips. And with a sacrament of fire, one of God's angels sets at peace the prophet's mind and conscience. Seven centuries later Jesus would put bread and wine on the lips of his followers as a symbol of their forgiveness.

Having experienced the sublimity of the Divine Presence, having confessed his sin and accepted his forgiveness, Isaiah is now ready for one of the most celebrated calls in religious history. I particularly want to celebrate some of the finer points that usually go uncelebrated. Notice that when Moses is called, it's an imperative: "Come, I will send you to Pharaoh." What Jeremiah hears is, "And whatever I command you, you shall speak."

But Isaiah gets no direct summons; no compulsion is laid on him. He hears the voice of God saying, "Whom shall I send, and who will go for us?" He hears God asking generally for messengers, and on his own responsibility he answers, for himself in particular. He hears from the divine lips of a divine need for help and concludes that he has sufficient heart to give himself to it: "Here am I! Send me." Isaiah's is a willing commitment of a free soul. It is we—not God—who make the decision. Don't wait around for God to call you! We are not passive, but active, and anything that renders us less than fully alive mars the sincerity of our commitment and makes for evil in our subsequent service to God. For premature submission represents repressed rebellion.

Isaiah had a superbly endowed nature, which he in no way sacrificed in his conversion experience. The angel with the burning coal flew in to take away his sin—not his mind or his backbone. Isaiah did not sacrifice or mutilate his personality, he consecrated it. In the year that King Uzziah died, he consecrated his talents to the service of God. Thereafter, though very much a public servant in the service of an earthly monarch, he spoke with the dignity and moral authority befitting an ambassador of the Most High. His orientation never changed. He put first things first and kept them there, despite the tendency of first things to slip into second, third, fourth, not to say fourteenth place. He held fast to truth, to justice, and to peace.

Turning again to our own situation: For six years the temper of the American people has been bound up in the person of President Reagan. The mood of the country has been one of careless optimism, overweening national pride, love of luxury, and an extraordinary indifference to the poor. Far from addressing the generous self in every citizen, the president has made the American people comfortable in their prejudices. And, as did King Uzziah at the height of his popularity, the president has overreached, tripped, and fallen, and with him every one of us. For he has represented us, if none too wisely, all too well.

In the year of the Tower Commission's report and similar subsequent investigations, it is time not to desert the president, but, like Isaiah, to look again to higher authority. It is time to seek again the beauty of holiness, to feel the Divine Presence in our lives and in our public life, for "the whole earth is full of God's glory."

It is time to confess our sins, which are manifold and grievous: our desire as a people to *feel* good rather than to *be* good, the eagerness of our government to pursue force when the need is to control force; our persistent racism (in this year of the 200th anniversary of the Constitution, let no one ask Blacks to celebrate unduly a document that defined their ancestors as two-thirds of a person); our sexism and heterosexism; the abundance of our poverty and the poverty of our abundance; our failure to keep first things first and to hold fast to truth, to justice, and to peace.

Then we must truly believe that there is more mercy in God than sin in us. And, finally, as forgiven sinners, we must hear again God's constant question, "Whom shall I send, and who will go for us?" Having heard it, many of you have already answered, "Here am I! Send me." I have in mind the group Witness for Peace, whose numbers, worshipping with us this morning, have been telling our government with their presence in Nicaragua that $100 million there are better spent feeding children and helping teachers than in killing them. (Why are we so ready to kill people with whom we do not agree?)

I have in mind a new member of the church who decided to stop talking to Rotary Clubs about hypertension and to help instead those brought low with AIDS. I have in mind a nonmember who is about to become a buddy to the children dying of AIDS in the hospitals of New York City. I have in mind a long-time member, a nurse, who comes off the night shift directly to Riverside to help prepare Communion. I have in mind a deacon of the church who is presently fasting in solidarity with people across the land in protest against capital punishment.

Friends, whether you be citizens of this country or of some other, members or visitors here, this is the moment for conversion experiences similar to Isaiah's, to serve this nation as ambassadors of the Most High. For it is a fact of life, made only clearer this week, that if we do not look to something above ourselves, we shall surely sink to something below ourselves.

"Whom shall I send, and who will go for us?" May that question ring in our ears until the answer rises from grateful hearts and we respond with burning and forgiven lips, "Here am I! Send me."

Going to the Mat with the Devil

MARCH 8, 1987
Reading: Luke 4:1–13

My wife, Randy, loves animals, so we have two: a dachshund named Low-life (we debated Underdog), and a cat called Max. They are bosom buddies, but between them are two outstanding differences. The first is that the cat never puts his tail between his legs. The fault is always yours; Max knows no guilt.

The second difference is that, unlike the cat, the dog has very little life of her own. Low-life plays with Max, romps with Randy and me and the kids, and can't wait to greet every two-legged or four-legged visitor who comes by, but she hates to be alone. To the dog, all life is common life. The result is that whereas the cat has a certain depth and mystery, even mystique, Low-life, although lovable in the extreme, is finally—I have to say it—less interesting.

There are people like Low-life, people who are more themselves when they are with others than when they are alone. Often they are beautiful people, the kind you see in glamor magazines—graceful like ships under full sail, but somehow you feel the centerboard isn't down. They go with the wind. They may be the life of the party, but it must be said of them, as Peter De Vries said of one of his characters: Deep down, they're shallow.

In contrast, consider Jesus, whose life with others enriched his solitude, and whose solitude contributed so much to his life with others. Note the rhythms in his life: now he is alone on the mountain or in Gethsemane, now in the villages with his followers; now he's praying, now he's teaching and healing; one hour, as during his baptism in the river Jordan, he's full of the Holy Spirit; the very next, he's wrestling with the devil. One minute he trusts God; the next his trust is being tested. A soul is not a thing; it is a dimension of depth. God wills that we be deep-down deep, and not shallow.

Notice that Jesus "was led by the Spirit into the wilderness." It was God who wanted him alone, God who wanted his trust tested. How do we become profound? It has little to do with formal education. It has far more to do with imagination (which is more important than knowledge), with being thoughtful, sensitive, vulnerable—with having some kind of life of our own, immune to the noise of history and the distractions of our immediate surroundings, with having faith and having that faith tested. "Religion," said the philosopher Whitehead, "is what people do with their solitude." Certainly the story of Jesus in the wilderness, led there by the Spirit, makes that point, which we should contemplate as we enter the Lenten season.

"And Jesus, full of the Holy Spirit, returned from the Jordan, and was led by the Spirit for forty days in the wilderness, tempted by the devil."

I suppose at least once a year we should introduce or even reintroduce the devil to the three or four in the congregation who think they have never met the devil. Let me say four things very briefly. First, the devil is pictured as a person because evil is experienced as an intensely personal power (just as God is personified because love is experienced in an intensely personal way). Second, the devil is given a separate existence not because evil arises outside of us, but because evil is experienced as something greater than us. (St. Paul put it classically: "The good that I would, I do not, and that which I would not, that I do" [Rom. 7:19].) Third, the devil is pictured as a fallen angel because evil does not arise in our so-called lower nature, but in our spiritual nature, seeking always to corrupt our freedom. Many of us who talk about freedom of choice have, in effect, lost our capacity to choose. And fourth, rarely does the devil suggest anything that doesn't sound eminently reasonable. Eve, after all, took the apple only when she saw that it was "good for food, pleasing to the eye, and much to be desired to make [people] wise."

Having fasted forty days and forty nights, Jesus was hungry. And the devil came to him and said, "If you are the Son of God"—the devil always attacks at the point of our greatest vulnerability, our identity—"*If* you are the Son of God, command these stones to become loaves of bread."

And Jesus replies, quoting Deuteronomy 8:3, "[No one lives] by bread alone." Obviously those words do not mean that anyone lives without bread, or that bread is not "spiritual." The central prayer of the Christian faith says, "Give us this day our daily bread." Too much bread for me may be materialistic, but for someone needy, what could be more spiritual? What could be more spiritual today than to feed the hundreds of thousands of Ethiopian children marginally alive, orphaned by the famine of 1984–86?

Conversely, what act could be *less* spiritual for a rich nation like ours than to allow 12 million of our children and 9 million adults—9 percent of the U.S. population—to be chronically short of the nutrients necessary for their growth and health? (And to think that we had the problem of hunger virtually licked in the 1960s and 1970s!)

But it's true, we do not live by bread alone. On Ash Wednesday I quoted Kierkegaard's entry in his journal: "O infinite majesty, even if you were not love, even if you were cold in your infinite majesty, I could not cease to love you; I need something majestic to love."

We all need something majestic to love, which is why Jesus says, "[No one lives] by bread alone, but *by every word that proceeds from the mouth of God.*" Fasting, strangely enough, can persuade you of that, for often you feel more alive in pain than in contentment. Those who have not lost their capacity to choose never choose happiness over pain, they choose life—over a thousand little deaths. They choose to have something majestic to love.

Then the devil takes Jesus up to a high place, and after showing him "all the kingdoms of the world in a moment of time" (what a phrase!), says to him, "To you I will give all this authority and their glory; for it has been delivered to me." That's the devil's view of worldly power—"it has been delivered to me."

Then the devil makes Jesus an offer he thinks Jesus can't refuse: "If you, then, will worship me, it shall all be yours." And Jesus, once again using Scripture as a sword to parry the thrusts of the devil, answers, "you shall worship the Lord your God, and him only shall you serve."

Years ago, preparing a sermon on this passage, I took a piece of paper and wrote on one side "service to the Lord," and on the other "Service to the devil." Then I asked myself: What is the bottom line? What is the *sine qua non*, the one thing you cannot be without if you're serious about serving the Lord on the one hand, or the devil on the other? On the Lord's side of the paper the matter resolved itself quickly: if we fail in love, we fail in all things else.

On the devil's side the question seemed more complicated. But rereading the temptation story, it occurred to me that the one thing you cannot be without, if you are serious about serving the devil, is power. The temptation is to seek status through power.

Suddenly it hit me. The devil has taken hundreds of millions of Americans and more hundreds of millions of Russians up to a high place, has shown us "all the kingdoms of the world in a moment of time," and is whispering in our ears: "Now let's see. You two nations between you have enough weapons to kill not only each other but everyone in the world many times over, and you're still turning out five or six nuclear warheads a day. That's terrific—you can always bounce the rubble. And it takes warheads fewer and fewer minutes to go door to door, so that the two of you will have to adopt what the Pentagon calls a 'launch-upon-warning' strategy, which gives over your personal decision-making power to the impersonal province of all those imperfect computers that make all those ghastly mistakes—wonderful! And you both are going for a first-strike capability. Marvelous! That should make everyone as nervous as a cat in a room full of rocking chairs. Just think, you Americans and you Russians: One of these days you may be able to *destroy* all the kingdoms of the world in a moment of time—**by accident!**"

There is an escalation in this world that goes: smart, smarter, smartest—stupid. And it has a corollary: powerful, more powerful, most powerful—powerless. It's all too obvious where those two escalations in the arms race have led us. We have to pray mightily that those negotiators in Geneva start turning things around, for God is not mocked: nations that seek status through power by power will be destroyed.

To seek dignity through power is different. That's a matter of justice. Blacks, Latinos, women, gays and lesbians—it is natural for the disenfranchised to seek power. But the struggle for power must be for the sake of justice and dignity, not status. You can tell the difference by how inclusive the struggle becomes, for justice is always inclusive. The other morning at a breakfast meeting to organize a giant rally that will be held in Washington at the end of April to protest U.S. policy in Central America and South Africa, Wendel Foster, a black minister and a City Council member, said he regretted that the flyer promoting the rally didn't put South Africa first, before Central America. Blacks, he said, feel South Africa is always brought in as a stepchild. It was a good statement, a fine reminder to all whites. But wouldn't it have been even finer if someone—preferably Wendel himself—had thought to add, "And speaking of stepchildren, let's not forget the Palestinians." That morning the newspapers had reported that Palestinians were starving in two camps in Lebanon.

Jesus refused the devil's offer because, as the Son of God, he wanted not to rule, to overpower, but to *empower*—to empower everyone, all God's disenfranchised, suffering, beloved children. That's a special role for the Body of Christ, the Universal Church, which is a superracial, supernational, and supertemporal community of grace.

Finally the devil sets Jesus on a pinnacle of the temple in Jerusalem and says to him, "If"—once again, that "if"—"If you are the son of God, throw yourself down, for it is written, 'He will give his angels charge over you.'" And Jesus answers, "You shall not tempt the Lord your God."

How often we look to God as to a great vindicator—"Come on, God, confound your enemies, prove yourself to be God"—as if God wanted to prove his existence through the power of his power, instead of through the power of his love! And how often we look to God as to a great magician, asking God for things that can never be ours, or that we should be seeking ourselves.

There's a nice story told of a rabbi and a priest playing golf. Before putting, the priest crosses himself. By the ninth hole he is nine strokes ahead. So the rabbi asks if the priest thinks it would be all right if he too crossed himself. "Sure, rabbi, go ahead," says the priest. "But it won't do you any good until you learn how to putt."

Lent is the season to follow Jesus' example and go to the mat with the devil. It is a season for searching questions, such as: How attached am I to material things? How much money do I really need? Am I seeking dignity or only status through power? Do I use such power as I have to overpower or to empower others with whom I live and work? And these questions: How often do I pray for things that are already mine, neglected and unappropriated? How often do I pray for things that can never be mine? And how often do I labor endlessly for things that can come to me only in prayer?

We need solitude to wrestle with the devil, time to answer these questions. It's often painful. But of two things we are sure: we will feel more alive, and when the forty days are over—as to Jesus, so to us—angels will come ministering.

Jesus and Nicodemus

MARCH 15, 1987
Readings: Genesis 12:1–8; John 3:1–17

R abbi, we know that you are a teacher come from God; for no one can do these signs that you do, [except by the power of God]."

Among the many miracles reported to Nicodemus, one was never mentioned. Jesus made the blind to see, the deaf to hear, the lame to walk; he healed the sick and cynical; he even brought Lazarus back from the dead. But he never made an old person young again. Never in the long history of the race—despite periodic and frantic attempts to find some Shangri-La or fountain of eternal youth—has any human being been given the chance to relive any part of his or her life. For some, it's excruciatingly painful, and for all it's true:

> The Moving Finger writes; and having writ,
> Moves on; nor all your Piety nor Wit
> Shall lure it back to cancel half a Line
> Nor all your Tears wash out a Word of it.
> Omar Khayyam

But if you can't be young again, you can be born again; and precisely because it *is* impossible to be young again, it is so important to be born again. Oh, I know, there are problems: the very term "born again" conjures up those born-again Christians who tend to have all the answers because they allow none of the questions. "Born again" brings to mind the Boston lady of high birth and infallible rectitude who said, "If you're born in Boston, you don't have to be born again." No wonder an ad recently appeared in a Wisconsin paper that read:

"The Episcopal Church welcomes you regardless of race, creed, color, or the number of times you've been born."

But as the Catholics say, and as I never tire of repeating, *Abusis non tollit usum*—abuse, or misuse, does not negate right use. So let's give a fresh hearing to the story of Nicodemus and Jesus.

What's amazing is that Nicodemus came to Jesus at all. We know that the common folk heard Jesus gladly, but Nicodemus was not one of them. He was a Pharisee, a ruler, a member of the highest governing body of the Jewish people, the Sanhedrin. Wouldn't he have a self-satisfied view of life? Why would he come?

Some would have it that he was seeking to entrap Jesus, for other Pharisees intent on doing just that had addressed Jesus in the same fashion: "Rabbi, we know that you are a teacher come from God." But I prefer to think of Nicodemus as a genuinely troubled person, a sensitive seeker—albeit a furtive one, coming as he does under cover of darkness (of course, for a Pharisee such stealth might be expedient). In any case, Jesus tells him, "Unless one is born anew, [one] cannot see the kingdom of God," and Nicodemus asks, "Can [one] enter a second time into [one's] mother's womb and be born?"

Again, there are those who think Nicodemus obtuse, but I think he's stalling. I think he understands perfectly, in fact all too well, what Jesus is talking about. Nicodemus had hoped that with a few minor alterations here and there in his life, he might end his troubles and find salvation. But Jesus is suggesting radical transformation.

"Unless one is born anew, [one] cannot see the kingdom of God." Hearing that, Nicodemus must have been as stunned as a father I once knew who struggled day and night to get his family where he thought they'd all be happy, namely in the suburbs, only to overhear his daughter explain to a city friend, "You have to grow up in Scarsdale to know how bad it is."

St. Augustine has a word for both the father and Nicodemus: "You run well, but off the track."

But never mind the parallels between the Scarsdale father and Nicodemus; all of us are like Nicodemus, at least most of the time. When like Nicodemus we find ourselves in distress, and when like him we seek guidance, we think we want to change. In fact, we want to remain the same, but to feel better about it. In psychological terms, we want to be more effective neurotics. We prefer the security of known misery to the misery of unfamiliar insecurity.

But unfamiliar insecurity—not having all the answers—is precisely what being born again is all about. No wonder we back off, especially if we're a success like the father in Scarsdale or Nicodemus in ancient Palestine, or like the rich young ruler who also came to Jesus for advice. When he heard, "Sell what you have, and give to the poor, and you will have treasure in heaven; and come, follow me," we read, "His countenance fell, and he went away sorrowful" (Matt. 19:21–22). Who wants to entertain the possibility that every word of the congratulations you receive upon the successes of your life may represent the pat on the back that sends you deeper into the quicksand? "You run well, but off the track."

I have a friend—very successful—who years ago toyed with the idea of becoming a minister. He went to see Richard Niebuhr, Reinhold's brother (who, incidentally, had the most beautifully lined face you've ever seen. Why do we want to be young again when a merely pretty or handsome face can become mysteriously beautiful when its wrinkles, its "credentials of humanity," manifest the history of a splendid personality? Did anyone ever suggest to Whistler that he should have painted his mother ten years earlier?).

"I told him I believed in God and Jesus and the Christian life," my friend reported, "but that somehow being a minister seemed to me a bit irrelevant, not part of the big show."

"What," I wanted to know, "did Dr. Niebuhr say?"

"He simply asked, 'What *is* the big show?'"

My friend's countenance fell, and he went away sorrowful.

To be born again means to reexamine old questions as though they had never been asked before. It means that what is of utmost importance occupies the most important place in your life. To be born again is to recognize, and then to live as if, the kingdom of God is not only the big show, but the only show. Christians work in the world, but they live in the kingdom, or rather the kingdom of God dwells within us. It is there we must be born again—and again, and again.

I said we prefer the security of known misery to the misery of unfamiliar insecurity, and that rebirth is all about the latter. Nicodemus was a Pharisee, a ruler, and male. In his day, as still in ours, masculinity was not just a fact of biology. It was, then as now, something that had to be proved and proved again, a continuing quest for some ever-receding male grail that had to do with being secure, confident, right, and tough.

Twenty years ago this winter a modern ruler, like Nicodemus a religious one, went from Washington to Boston to discuss his war policies in Vietnam with an audience of Harvard faculty and students. When he was in his car ready to leave, Secretary of Defense Robert McNamara found himself surrounded by milling students, furious at what they took to be his plastic explanations. Suddenly he got out of the car, and newspapers the next morning showed him standing on the hood, shouting, "I was tougher than you are then"—meaning in World War II—"and I'm tougher than you are now."

What made the scene so poignant was that the students were not questioning his toughness. Quite the opposite: they were questioning his sensitivity, his intelligence, his humanity.

In rebirth, machismo is stillborn. Only humanity lives, full of fear and trembling. In rebirth, boundaries widen without direction. For "the wind blows where it wills, and you hear the sound of it, but you do not know whence it comes or whither it goes; so it is with every one who is born of the Spirit." To be born again is to be born vulnerable. It is to be born twice as strong and twice as tender, as only the truly strong can be tender.

"Unless one is born anew, [one] cannot see the kingdom of God." Born anew, we see that in God's kingdom there is peace and freedom—peace between us, peace within us. We haven't all the answers, but in our doubts and confusions Jesus is our model. For us he models life in the kingdom, which is already within us.

Nicodemus apparently never accepted radical transformation, although he must have remained a troubled person, a sensitive seeker, for at the end he was there with ointment to embalm Jesus' crucified body.

In contrast, Abraham—a man whose face, like Richard Niebuhr's, was full of the credentials of humanity—was seventy-five when described in this fashion in Hebrews 11: "By faith Abraham obeyed when he was called to go out to a place which he was to receive as an inheritance; and he went out, not knowing where he was to go" (v. 8).

At seventy-five, he didn't stay put or follow the beaten path; he went where there was no path, and what a trail he left: Perhaps it was of him that Browning wrote:

> Grow old along with me!
> The best is yet to be,
> The last of life, for which the first was made:
> Our times are in His hand
> Who saith, "A whole I planned,
> Youth shows but half; trust God: see all nor be afraid."

You can't be young again, but you can be born again: born of the water, symbol of forgiveness, and of the Spirit, symbol of power. You don't have to move out, as did Abraham, but you do have to move, as

Nicodemus somehow could not, from the ranks of Jesus' admirers to the ranks of his followers, from the sideshows of the world to the big show of the kingdom, from the security of known misery (or the security of success) to the joy of vulnerability, the joy of not being sure, of availability—for "the wind blows where it wills, and you hear the sound of it, but you do not know whence it comes or whither it goes; so it is with every one who is born of the Spirit."

There's always a choice. Do you wish to be a Nicodemus, or an Abraham? An admirer of Jesus, or one who prays, "Precious Lord, take my hand, lead me on, lead me on"?

Think about it; Lent's the time.

Jesus and the Samaritan Woman

MARCH 22, 1987
Readings: Isaiah 55:1–13; John 4:1–26

Years ago, as I was just starting out on my ministry, I came across a prayer for strength to do spiritual battle. I've forgotten the author and most of the words. Those I do remember went, "And when the day goes hard, and cowards steal from the field, grant that my place may be found where the fighting is fiercest." I liked the prayer, for it seemed to me then, as it appears to me now, we Christians whine more than we fight. Few of us have a sticking point, a *causa confessiones* that makes us say with Luther, "Here I stand, I can do no other." All the prophets, from Amos to Oscar Romero—including Jesus, who was something more than a prophet, never anything less—and all the martyrs were fighters who not only fought for the right, but contended against wrong without becoming wrongly contentious. They opposed national self-righteousness without personal self-righteousness. Truly, that is admirable!

Yet in the story assigned by the church lectionary for this Sunday, we find Jesus walking away from a fight, leaving town—in fact, leaving a whole region. "Now when the Lord knew that the Pharisees had heard that Jesus was making and baptizing more disciples than John . . . he left Judea and departed again to Galilee"—apparently not to get embroiled in controversy. Apparently this was not a good fight, nor a good time. The true goal of his ministry would get lost in the mists of disputation.

And there's another lesson. If Christians whine too much and fight too little, we also argue too much and witness too little. The Gospel of Jesus Christ is stunning in its truth, unforgettable in its impact. We should proclaim it, live it, at home, at work, and in the world. It's atheistic to be embarrassed by God's presence in the office! Like Jesus we shouldn't waste energy, passion, and time in disputation. Ecclesiastes has it right: "For everything there is a season . . . a time to keep silence, and a time to speak" (3:1, 7b).

Ancient Palestine was all of 120 miles long, and the shortest route from Judea in the south to Galilee in the north ran through Samaria. There, near the town of Sychar, was a field and a well that Jacob had willed to his son Joseph. For some 1,200 years before Christ and for 1,900 years since, that well nourished all the people around it. It is over 100 feet deep, the kind of well into which water percolates and gathers. There Jesus, "wearied as he was with his journey," sat down. It was high noon, and mighty hot.

"There came a woman of Samaria to draw water. Jesus said to her, 'Give me a drink.'"

With Good Friday but days away, that request, "Give me a drink," cannot help but recall the so-called fifth word from the cross, the only two words any one of us might have said, the two that lay bare the utter humanity of Jesus and show that God shares the lot of the least of us. They are recorded in the same Gospel of John: "After this, Jesus, knowing that all was now finished, said, 'I thirst'" (19:28).

"I thirst" on the lips of the Son of God: there's the perfect expression of God; for as St. Paul says, "In him all the fullness of God was pleased to dwell."

Sometimes I think our problem is not that we human beings care too little, but that we care a lot, and are numbed by fear. As terrorist bullets fly and farms fail, as teenagers commit suicide and the national deficit soars to record heights, as the sky threatens to flare with a glow not from the sun, maybe we don't dare approach the great internal lake that is our inner feeling for the pain of this world, lest we fall in and drown. Our seeming apathy is in fact numbness, born not of callousness but of confusion: we don't know how to accept and deal with the pain of the world. That's why it's so important that our Savior not be a conquering hero riding his way to sure victory, but a man who, weary from a long journey, slumps down at high noon at the side of a well and asks a stranger for water.

Earlier the choir sang, "Come unto me all ye who are weary and heavy-laden, and I will give you rest." Had Jesus himself not labored and been himself heavy-laden, such an invitation could sound more irritating than convincing—like the Vatican's recent ruling on reproduction, to which so many Roman Catholics, rather snidely, are responding, "If you don't play the game, you don't make the rules."

Thomas Carlyle once likened Emerson, living in the placid, unvexed village of Concord, to a man on the beach who, staying well out of reach of the spray, throws chatty and cheerful bits of advice to a swimmer battling for life in huge and angry waves.

In contrast, Jesus is a companion, which literally means "sharer of the loaf." He shares our bread, our thirst, our happiness, which means that if we walk with Jesus as our closest companion, he can both double our joys and halve our sorrows. It is wonderful—and so important—that the Gospel of John, which more than any other Gospel glorifies Christ's divinity, also stresses Jesus' humanity to the full: "Give me a drink."

Obviously Jesus' conversation with the Samaritan woman was a long one. What John records are only, as it were, the minutes of the meeting. They are enough, however, to paint the picture of a soul lonely and lost, the kind that looks at the world and says, "Everything could have been so beautiful, and look what happened."

Their conversation follows the pattern of Jesus and Nicodemus, whose story we heard last week. Jesus says something, and it's always taken in the wrong sense. I must say it rather puts me off, for it makes Nicodemus and the Samaritan woman sound a bit obtuse, and Jesus unduly indirect. But I understand that John would have us see that there are certain truths you cannot really accept but have to discover for yourself, and that Jesus is constantly asking people to face and discover these truths for themselves.

The amazing thing is that the conversation took place at all, for between Jews and Samaritans there was enormous enmity. At least four centuries before, in captivity, the Jews of Samaria—unlike those of Judea and Galilee—had intermarried with their captors, thereby losing their religious and racial purity. That they could not be forgiven for that may sound strange to us, but it helps to remember that even to this day, in some strict Jewish households, if a son or daughter marries a Gentile, his or her funeral service is carried out. That's why the woman asks, "How is it that you, a Jew, ask a drink of me, a woman of Samaria?"

There was a further prohibition. Strict rabbis forbade rabbis to greet any woman in public, even a wife or sister. There were even Pharisees who shut their eyes when they saw a woman on the street.

With their eyes shut, they walked into so many walls and houses that they were called "the bruised and bleeding Pharisees."

We forget how many barriers Jesus broke down: barriers of class, of race, of religion, of sex. To quote again St. Paul, "In Christ there is neither Jew nor Greek, neither male nor female, neither bond nor free, for you are all one in Christ Jesus" (Gal. 3:28). In our eagerness to bond too tightly with our own kind, we forget that the aim of life is to do just the opposite. For God made us all one, and Christ died to keep us that way. At Jewish weddings I have heard rabbis remind the couple that they are as earth and water. Without earth, water flows without direction, while earth without water dries up and blows away. But together they make clay, from which are made bricks, from which are made houses, which become homes.

We should all be one to another as earth and water, not only husbands and wives but gay and straight, Russians and Afghans, Jews and Christians, Muslims and Hindus, black and white, yellow and red, Central Americans and *norteamericanos*. Together we should build a home out of this lovely, strife-torn planet. Today we celebrate One Great Hour of Sharing and Central America Week—reminders that the Christian church, to which most of us here belong, is a superracial, supernational, supertemporal community of grace.

We'll never build that vastly inclusive, harmonious home on earth unless we drink the living water of which Jesus spoke. But where, where in this prosaic, automated, routinized life is the thirst for this water? In this psychological age, deep longing for God may be the most repressed of all emotions.

In Lynne Sharon Schwartz's *Disturbances in the Field*, Lydia plays the piano in a trio with a shy, angular violinist named Jasper and a large, earthy cellist named Rosalie. During rehearsal breaks the women light up, and Jasper leaves because smoke makes him cough. Rosalie then continues "the ramifying story of the demise of her marriage. She was recently separated from a psychiatrist who appeared unobjectionable in public." Says Rosalie, "Everything I did, for fifteen years, he said it was acting out." Lydia asks what that meant, although she knew acting out is "outlandish behavior based on distorted images of reality."

"'Acting out,' says Rosalie bitterly, flicking ash from her small black cheroot, 'is what the rest of us call living.'"

The psychiatrist husband who "appeared unobjectionable in public" and probably was equally so in private would no doubt have agreed with Socrates that the unexamined life is not worth living. But is the examined life worth living, Doctor, if you dare not approach that vast lake of internal feeling fed by streams of living water? And how examined is a life that fails to unearth that longing for universal harmony, that thirst for God? Too many psychiatrists think living is acting out. Too many are as fearful of life as their patients.

You know how futile it usually is to tell children to be careful? You know the secret contempt children feel for caution? Well, we should never lose it. For only those who throw caution to the winds, who fear neither hurt nor failure, who long beyond the manageable for the mysterious, who read "devout" to mean "daring"—only such seekers shall find the living water which Christ offers us all.

Cried St. Paul, "For freedom Christ has set you free" (Gal. 5:1). The French philosopher Jean-Paul Sartre wrote, "We were never freer than during the German occupation." I hear him saying: We lived close to the edge, close to death, we were in touch with all our feelings, everything we did was for real; there was no time to fool around, life was full of meaning.

"I who speak to you am he," said Jesus to the woman. We can't end without noting once again how Christ reveals himself almost always to the hurt, the needy, like this Samaritan woman. The most unlikely people are the most likely Christians. Christ makes whales out of minnows! Centuries after this woman died there lived a giddy-headed youth, probably voted in school the most likely to go straight to the devil. But on the way, Christ revealed himself, and the man became Francis of Assisi. And who authored "Amazing Grace"? A wretch, the brutal captain of a villainous slave ship. John Newton composed 280 other hymns, and then at the age of 82 he wrote, "My memory is nearly gone, but I remember two things, that I am a great sinner, and that Christ is a great saviour."

I hope the Samaritan woman found that same savior in Christ. I hope we all do. But first we have to acknowledge our longing for God, our thirst. We have to ask of Jesus what he asked of the woman: "Give me a drink."

Now's the time. Spring is bustin' out all over. Fresh energy is pouring up out of the ground into every form of new growth. It's time for us too to bust out, to break the bonds of sinful or successful or merely just prosaic, ordinary, routinized living, to seek anew the source of life, to hear again the ancient cry, "Ho, everyone who thirsts, come to the water," the living water that will become in us "a spring of water welling up to eternal life." If Christ is our Savior, then we may be certain that the living water is the clearest, coolest, deepest, sweetest water there is.

Jesus and the Man Who Was Born Blind

MARCH 29, 1987

Reading: John 9:1–41

A few years ago a well-known movie maker convened a few of us around a table. We were cast in the role of reluctant advisors, for this wonderful man had in mind to try his hand at a movie about Jesus. Not a modern version, mind you—say, about a man who makes computer chips in Japan—but yet another movie about the historical Jesus. All of us were gravely skeptical. When the movie maker asked how the movie might begin, Jerry Shepherd, then an Old Testament professor at Union Theological Seminary, spoke up instantly. "I'd have the cameras zoom right in on the Master surrounded by his disciples, performing a miracle. And then about five minutes into the movie the audience would realize, 'Uh-oh—we got the wrong one.'"

What Shepherd wanted was to clear the air of any suspicion that messiahship might be based on anything that even hinted of magic. He knew there were many miracle workers in Jesus' day, healers of all kinds—many of whom, incidentally, frequently used spittle. Pliny, the famous Roman collector of what was then considered scientific information, has a whole chapter on the use of spittle, in which he records its effectiveness against snake bites, epilepsy, conjunctivitis, and cricks in the neck, not to mention its use in averting the evil eye. And if the efficacy of any treatment depends largely on a patient's faith in it, then, in using spittle in the Gospel story, Jesus was only doing what the blind man might well have expected him to do.

Whether the movie maker will make the movie is still a question. What is certain is that miracles do not a messiah make. In fact, in the Bible, miracles are an expression of faith more than they are a basis of faith. In the Gospel of John, miracles are never just incidents in Jesus' ministry; rather they are "signs" of something deep and mysterious and universal, which then is interpreted in rather lengthy speeches.

Bearing all this in mind, let's examine the story of the man born blind, which John tells in graphic detail.

"As [Jesus] passed by, he saw a man blind from his birth. And his disciples asked him, 'Rabbi, who sinned, this man or his parents, that he was born blind?'"

As you can imagine, behind that question linking suffering to sin there stretches a long history, right back to the dim beginnings of human thought. From earliest times, in a sin-infested world people have needed to see some harmony, some beauty, and especially some kind of order, some fundamental justice woven into the fabric of life. Wrote the early Hebrews, "The sins of the [parents] are visited upon the children," and indeed they are if the sins be those of racism, sexism, heterosexism, and superpatriotism. Life is consequential, and the consequences of our deeds and attitudes spread not only laterally across the face of one generation, but also vertically down the march of generations. The full quotation is, "The sins of the [parents] are visited upon the children and unto their children's children."

But to assert that all forms of suffering, including genetic defects, stem from sin is a case far harder to argue. In fact, it is an assertion, not an argument. Yet to this day people persist in linking suffering to sin—and, conversely, happiness to virtue—in ways absolutely untenable. Let me ask you: When you hear that misfortune has befallen someone else, don't you sometimes for a split second feel that somehow it didn't befall you because you're a little more sensible, a little more virtuous? One of the deepest, most treasured of all human notions—certainly middle-class notions—is that good behavior should and will be rewarded.

Like Job before him, Jesus rejects this whole line of argument. "It was not that this man sinned, or his parents, but that the works of God might be made manifest in him." Now that sounds just a little as if the man is a tool to be used rather than a person to be loved. But that's a bad reading. In the three other gospels miracles always result from Jesus' compassion. In John they always reflect God's glory. But what is God's glory if not Jesus' compassion? Is God's glory ever more fully manifested than in the revelation of God's mercy? Then too, in joy and in sorrow, don't we ourselves, as Christians, want to show God's glory?

> When peace, like a river, attendeth my way,
> when sorrows like sea billows roll,
> Whatever my lot, thou hast taught me to say,
> "It is well, it is well with my soul."
> Horatio Spafford

(I don't know why that hymn always moves me to tears, except that maybe, like so many of you, there have been times when it has been very hard to say, "It is well, it is well with my soul.")

Jesus then reminds us he is not the only "light of the world" (as John constantly refers to him). "*We*," he says, "must work the works of [the one] who sent me, while it is day; night comes, when no one can work."

Not only is life swiftly over, but—if you ask me—it is badly planned, in that experience comes at the wrong end of it, like a light upon a vessel's stern illuminating what is past, and only when it is passed.

But let's not be peevish, only keenly aware of the need to be about the works of the Lord, for "Like as the waves make toward the pebbled shore, / So do our minutes hasten to their end."

Then Jesus spits on the ground, makes clay of the spittle, anoints the blind man's eyes with the clay, and sends him to wash in the pool of Siloam. That strikes me as bizarre—and really rough. How would you like to be sent in such a messy state, with face daubed with dust and clay and spittle, tapping your way through crowded streets to a pool clear across town? How would you like to be made a spectacle, a fool (in St. Paul's words) for Christ's sake?

But "he . . . came back seeing," to which we can respond, as did a minor poet, "When the shore is won at last / Who will count the billows past?" (John Keble). Or in the words of a great theologian, "Therefore, my beloved, be ye steadfast, immoveable, always abounding in the work of the Lord, knowing that your labor is not in vain."

Clearly, what John wants us to see in this story is that we too need the light of the world because of our darkness. Much of the time we are ignorant through complacency. It was four years ago that the TWA plane was hijacked by terrorists who, before finally landing at Beirut, set down briefly in Tripoli to release the women and children aboard. When the press gathered around the released captives, one woman said, "For some reason they hate New Jersey." That was indeed strange. What could young Palestinian terrorists possibly have against the Garden State?

What the woman had forgotten—had she ever known—was that *New Jersey* was the name of the battleship that only weeks before had stood off the shores of Lebanon lobbing half-ton shells into the hapless mountain villages, killing hundreds of innocent civilians.

There's an old saying, "What you don't know won't hurt you." That's nonsense. What we Americans don't know is already killing others and may end up destroying all of us.

But we're not really talking of ignorance through complacency. We're talking now of blind spots we do everything in our power to keep blind. We don't want to know what our nation is up to. We don't want to know what's wrong with our marriage, with our relationship with our parents and children, why we share so little of ourselves with our friends, why we stay stuck in jobs that are so dull. Human beings believe what is convenient for them to believe. We alter history to make it tolerable. To guard our pride, to keep hidden our souls, we keep ourselves in the dark. Like the man blind from birth, who didn't ask to be cured, we neither ask for nor want the miracle. We are intimidated by a vision of regeneration. We stand dazed and cringing before an eternity of possibilities. We say with Job, "I have made my bed in darkness."

But Christ did not leave the man alone, and Christ will not pass us by. The man, at least, had the grace to respond to Christ's initiative, which raises the question, What do we do when the light of the world offers to cure our blind spots? Will we finally let go our pride, bare our souls, take criticism from Christ and our friends, surrender a vision of regeneration, to grace so amazing as to enable us one day to say, "I was lost, but now I'm found, was blind, but now I see"?

Once the man blind from birth did see, thanks to Christ's compassion, the inevitable trouble began. Virtue does not automatically bring happiness. In fact, in a sin-infested world, we have to say, "No good deed goes unpunished." The Pharisees in the story represent those in every age and place—Catholic, Protestant, or Jewish—who condemn anyone whose idea of religion is not theirs, who think theirs is the only way to serve God. What they never learn is that only those who own their blindness can ever learn to see; only those who confess their sin can ever be forgiven; only those who recognize their weaknesses can ever be honestly strong. Therefore, at the end of the story, the Pharisees hear Christ's judgment: "If you were blind, you would have no guilt; but now that you say, 'We see,' your guilt remains."

Typically, because their case is so weak, they turn to abuse, escalate to insult, and end up threatening and using force, ordering the man out of the synagogue.

Fearing retaliation, his parents say, in effect, "We love you, son, but we can't support you," thereby twisting the definition of love. If life is consequential, in it neutrality is no option. Pilate washed his hands and thereby plaited the crown of thorns. General of the Armies Omar Bradley said, forty years ago today, "Noninvolvement in peace means certain involvement in war." Said Burke two centuries before, "All it takes for evil to prevail is for a few good people to do nothing."

But notice that when the Pharisees persecute and his parents desert the man, Jesus comes back to find him. What John wants us to see is that if your witness to truth separates you from others, it also brings you nearer to Jesus. If you are true to him, Christ is even truer to you, so true that in the midst of persecution and desertion you can say again, "It is well, it is well with my soul." Last week we sang, "How Firm a Foundation," whose last verse goes:

The soul that on Jesus hath leaned for repose,
I will not, I will not desert to his foes;
That soul, though all hell should endeavor to shake,
I'll never, no, never, no, never forsake.

John Rippon

Notice finally an important progression that takes place in the course of the forty-one verses in this ninth chapter of John. In verse 11 the one born blind says that "the man called Jesus" opened his eyes. By verse 17 he is calling Jesus a prophet, and at the end of the chapter he acknowledges him to be the son of God. It is this progression that John wants most of all to urge on us, for us to claim for ourselves. He wants us to see that we too can rise from Job's bed of darkness to live by the brightness and in the warmth of the "light of the world." The blind spots we treasure as if they were the most precious things in our lives—they are dangerous, and they can be cured.

The miracle of life is that we can see and repair what's wrong in our relationships to our family, our friends, our nation, and world. We can cease fleeing reality and begin to change it; we can act on what Christ has shown us. To kneel to him, as did the man in the story, means not self-obliteration but self-fulfillment. The fatigue of despair can be transformed into the buoyancy of hope. So why live dimly? Why grope in the dark when you can live in the light? Why be vexed when all can be well with your soul?

God grant that we may respond as creatively and courageously as did the man in John's story to Christ's initiative. So may we say, as did John Newton, that brutal captain of a villainous slave ship,

Amazing grace, how sweet the sound,
That saved a wretch like me!
I once was lost, but now am found,
Was blind, but now I see.

Jesus, Mary, Martha, and Lazarus

APRIL 5, 1987
Reading: John 11:1–44

In what is probably the most awesome story in Scripture we read, "Now Jesus loved Martha and her sister and Lazarus."

How wonderful it is that the Son of Man who, as Luke records, had "nowhere to lay his head," could at least rest his weary feet, his overburdened mind, and his often broken heart in this home two miles from the city of Jerusalem.

Nowhere in Scripture is it recorded that Jesus went for rest to his own family. Perhaps at home there was insufficient understanding. But instead of resenting it, in the rather futile fashion that so many of us do, he found another home. I certainly hope all of you do the same, for everyone needs a place to put up his or her feet and "dump the mud," a place where nobody laughs at your dreams, where what you say in confidence is both understood and kept in confidence, where without question you are accepted and appreciated to such a degree that even your weaknesses are loved more than are the strengths of others. With these two sisters and their brother, Jesus had such a spiritual retreat. That's how I read the statement, "Now Jesus loved Martha and her sister and Lazarus."

On the other hand, how wonderful for Mary and Martha to know that it sufficed to send word that Lazarus was ill for Jesus to appear. They were wise to ask for help; so few do. So many people steel themselves against the hardships of life, especially against sickness and death, and thereby wall out the very support they need. The one thing a clenched fist cannot do is accept a helping hand. In their distress Mary and Martha extended an open hand, a supplicating hand, and—as he always does—Jesus took it.

But what about the phrase, "This illness is . . . for the glory of God, so that the Son of God may be glorified by means of it"? Doesn't that make Lazarus sound, as some doctors make you feel, like a very uninteresting appendage to a very interesting illness?

The theology and style of St. John are very different from those of the other three evangelists. He's a mystic, which is what makes his gospel so appealing to many Russian, Greek, and Ethiopian Orthodox, whose liturgies celebrate so much better than do most Protestant liturgies the mystery of God's love. Often in John there is a surface truth—for example, that the cure of Lazarus will show the glory of God in action—and beneath the surface another truth—for example, that the raising of Lazarus will hasten Christ's crucifixion, for the crucifixion, in John's view, is the glorification of God's love.

So read the phrase "that the Son of God may be glorified" as "that the Son of God may be crucified." And sure enough. If Christ could dismantle the powers of death, so reasoned the rulers of Israel, he could certainly dismantle their own power. In the Gospel of John it is the raising of Lazarus that precipitates Christ's crucifixion, which is why the story is read on Passion Sunday, and why the story is doubly moving: the victim of death can be saved only by one who volunteers to take his place. "Greater love hath no man than this, that he lay down his life for his friend" (John 15:13).

> So when [Jesus] heard that [Lazarus] was ill, he stayed two days longer in the place where he was. Then after this he said to the disciples, "Let us go into Judea again." The disciples said to him, "Rabbi, the Jews were but now seeking to stone you, and are you going there again?" Jesus answered, "Are there not twelve hours in the day? If any one walks in the day, he does not stumble, because he sees the light of this world. But if any one walks in the night, he stumbles, because the light is not in him."

"Are there not twelve hours in the day?" is a question that points to two experiences with which all of us are all too familiar: There are twelve hours, so what's the rush? and, There are only twelve hours; there's no time to spare. What tension there is in time between haste and waste! A splendid Italian expression goes, *Festina lente*: make haste, slowly. It's a fact—you can see it when you read the gospels—that Jesus never rushed, but he was always on time. What does that say about the serenity and wisdom and depth of that man's character?

> Thus he spoke, and then he said to them, "Our friend Lazarus has fallen asleep, but I go to awake him out of sleep." The disciples said to him, "Lord, if he has fallen asleep, he will recover." Now Jesus had spoken of his death, but they thought that he meant taking rest in sleep. Then Jesus told them plainly, "Lazarus is dead; and for your sake I am glad that I was not there, so that you may believe. But let us go to him." Thomas, called the Twin, said to his fellow disciples, "Let us also go, that we may die with him."

Marching orders for all Christians, past, present, and future: "Let us also go, that we may die with him." The disciples were sure Jesus was going to be stoned, as he all but was the last time he was in Judea. Yet they are ready to go, not because they are full of faith and confidence, but because they are loyal despite their fear. There is nothing wrong with fear. No one need be afraid of it, only afraid that because of it one will not do what is right. Courage never means denial; it means being well aware of the worst that can happen, and then doing the right thing anyway. Isn't that what Christ is doing throughout this story?

> Now when Jesus came, he found that Lazarus had already been in the tomb four days. . . . When Martha heard that Jesus was coming, she went and met him, while Mary sat in the house.

As in Luke so in John: it is Martha who acts and Mary who sits, no doubt on the floor of the house, in mourning. Martha goes out to meet Jesus and half-reproachfully—how could she help herself?—says, "If you had been here, my brother would not have died." In other words, "Why didn't you come sooner?"

It's so natural. Anger is always the first step in grieving. Yet with a kind of desperate hope she adds, "I know that whatever you ask from God, God will give you."

"Your brother will rise again," says Jesus. To which Martha replies, reflecting an Orthodox Jewish belief of the time, "I know that he will rise again in the resurrection at the last day."

Then Jesus corrects her, with a statement now written in the soft places of every believer's heart: "I am the resurrection and the life; he who believes in me, though he die, yet shall he live, and whoever lives and believes in me shall never die."

Eternal life begins not at the end of time, nor even at the funeral home, but right now; the death that comes is not the death that separates us from God. "Though he die, yet shall he live." "Whoever believes in me shall never die." St. Paul said much the same thing: "No one lives unto himself alone, and no one dies unto himself alone. If we live, we live unto the Lord; and if we die, we die unto the Lord. So whether we live or whether we die, we are the Lord's" (Rom. 14:7–8).

The abyss of God's love is deeper than the abyss of death. And she who overcomes her fear of death lives as though death were a past and not a future experience.

"Do you believe this?" asks Jesus. And Martha, on behalf of all believers, past, present, and future, answers, "Yes, Lord; I believe that you are the Christ, the Son of God."

> When Martha had said this, she went and called her sister Mary, saying quietly, "The Teacher is here and is calling for you." And when she heard it, she rose quickly and went to him. Now Jesus had not yet

come to the village, but was still in the place where
Martha had met him. When the Jews who were with
her in the house, consoling her, saw Mary rise
quickly and go out, they followed her, supposing that
she was going to the tomb to weep there. Then
Mary, when she came where Jesus was and saw him,
fell at his feet, saying to him, "Lord, if you had been
here, my brother would not have died." When Jesus
saw her weeping, and the Jews who came with her
also weeping, he was deeply moved in spirit and
troubled; and he said, "Where have you laid him?"
They said to him, "Lord, come and see." Jesus wept.

Mary, Martha, the mourners, and now Jesus too—all weeping. For
a moment few words, no deeds, only tears.

And why does Jesus weep? Is it with anger at the display of unbelief while in their midst stands one who is the resurrection and the
life? I doubt it. Is it with the same sadness with which Jesus viewed
the hungry multitudes, the lepers, the man with palsy or the one
born blind? I imagine so; his heart went out to all sufferers. But it is
possible that Jesus weeps because he remembers that death can be a
welcome release from the burdens of life, and because he knows from
what joys Lazarus will be returning. For here on earth we see through
a glass darkly; there it is face to face. Here there is crying and pain;
there God will wipe the tears from our eyes. Here we sit in chairs,
there on thrones, for "when the battle's over we shall wear a crown,
/ Yes, we shall wear a crown."

Then Jesus, deeply moved again, came to the tomb;
it was a cave, and a stone lay upon it. Jesus said,
"Take away the stone." Martha, the sister of the
dead man, said to him, "Lord, by this time there will
be an odor, for he has been dead four days." Jesus said
to her, "Did I not tell you that if you would believe
you would see the glory of God?" So they took away
the stone. And Jesus lifted up his eyes and said,
"Father, I thank thee that thou hast heard me." . . .
When he had said this, he cried with a loud voice,
"Lazarus, come out." The dead man came out, his
hands and feet bound with bandages, and his face
wrapped with a cloth. Jesus said to them, "Unbind
him, and let him go."

"Father, I thank thee that thou hast heard me." Jesus prayed, Lazarus is raised. "Miracles are just so many answered prayers."

I said last week that miracles do not a messiah make. But a messiah can do miracles. If you ask me if Jesus literally raised Lazarus from the dead, literally walked on water and changed water into wine, I will answer, "For certain, I do not know. But this I do know: faith must be lived before it is understood, and the more it is lived, the more things become possible." I can also report that in home after home I have seen Jesus change beer into furniture, sinners into saints, hate-filled relations into loving ones, cowardice into courage, the fatigue of despair into the bouyancy of hope. In instance after instance, life after life, I have seen Christ be "God's power unto salvation," and that's miracle enough for me.

This interweaving of Christ's life in our own leads to a last thought about this passage. We've read of a tomb that was a cave, of a stone that was rolled away, of grave clothes. A believer's mind cannot but move from Lazarus to Jesus' death, burial, and resurrection. As St. John must have had this in mind when writing the story, we cannot help reflecting that "when anyone's story and Jesus' story are so interwoven, it is not simply a literary display; it is a presentation of the Gospel" (Fred Craddock).

Palm Sunday: God's Pageant

APRIL 12, 1987
Reading: Luke 19:28–40

For the first four Sundays in Lent, following the assigned lectionary readings of the Bible, we found Jesus one on one: with the devil, with Nicodemus, with the Samaritan woman at the well, and with the man born blind. Last Sunday, the fifth in Lent, it was one on three: Jesus with Mary, Martha, and Lazarus. Almost all these scenes were intimate; the atmosphere was tense, the dialogues long, and the action sparse.

Today it's just the reverse. Palm Sunday is a crowd scene, with dense mobs of excited and enthusiastic folk. There's a happy climate, a lack of restraint, an air of abandon reminiscent of God's prodigality when God scatters flowers on the hillside and stars in the sky and spreads his mercy over sinners. Palm Sunday is God's pageant, if you will.

To catch this mood that mingles piety with pageantry, religion with politics, try first of all to picture Jerusalem as it was in those days. Try to hear the shrill cries of the traders, the clatter made by the barbers with their shaving utensils, the cobblers with the heels of slippers, the perfumers with their copper bowls. Try also to hear the mules groaning and the quarreling of the wagoneers. Imagine a company of Roman soldiers trying to make their way through the press of people. Imagine the medley of smells.

Then picture the pilgrims as they approach the city, two by two, three by three, whole villages at a time, multitudes of them from all over the country, all on holiday, and more than ready to celebrate the Passover, the deliverance of their forbears out of Egypt. Remember that they have fallen anew into servitude, which means they will show redoubled zeal in their tribute to the glorious days of old.

Finally, in the midst of these exultant pilgrims, find the Galileans, recognizable as such by their long hair. Their eyes sparkle, their shouts reverberate across the valley in the streets of Jerusalem; and in their midst, riding on an ass in the heat of the sun and of glory, our Lord and Savior. His reticence is gone. Often he has forbidden his disciples to proclaim his messiahship; now he knows his hour has come. He is doing what Jeremiah and Ezekiel and other prophets had done before him: when words could serve no further purpose or were of no effect, when people refused to understand the spoken message, the prophets took a dramatic action that turned their message into a picture no one could fail to see. Today, by riding into Jerusalem as king of peace in fulfillment of the prophesy of Zechariah, Jesus, in unmistakable fashion, is proclaiming himself the promised Messiah.

And don't the pilgrims know it: "Blessed is he that cometh in the name of the Lord. Peace in heaven and glory in the highest." These shouting, dancing pilgrims must have been swept away by the rapture of the world and of the moment. Never before that day had they felt themselves so bursting with hope and adoration. When they hit the city limits, they must have moved through those narrow, crowded, noisy, smelly streets like a roaring springtime torrent that has burst its banks.

The only sour note is struck by the Pharisees, come to investigate the seditious noise. "Teacher," they say, all wrapped up in their doctoral robes and infallible rectitude, "Teacher, rebuke your disciples." And Jesus, without a moment's hesitation, replies, "I tell you, if these were silent, the very stones would cry out"—the hot stones of the wilderness Jesus refused to turn into loaves of bread; the motionless stones he said God could raise up into sons and daughters of Abraham; the hostile stones which twice had been picked up to hurl at him; and these cobblestones of Jerusalem, which could not have been harder than the hearts of these religious leaders.

It is hardly surprising that the Pharisees are sullen and the crowd ecstatic. But the deepest contrast is between the crowds and Jesus. While they shout wildly, "Hosannah, blessed is he who comes in the name of the Lord, even the king of Israel," the king—instead of smiling and acknowledging the cheers—weeps.

"And when he drew near and saw the city"—that is, when Jerusalem burst into view, including the long line of city wall embracing, like the setting of a jewel, the polished marble and gilded pinnacles of Herod's palace glittering in the morning sun—the sight that caused pilgrims to catch their breath made Jesus weep. "Would that even today you knew the things that make for peace," he said.

The jubilant multitude fully believed that Jesus was sent by God, but they misapprehended entirely the purpose for which he was sent. The kingdom of their expectation was totally different from the kingdom Jesus meant to found. His warfare was not with the legions of Rome, against whom this Jewish patriotism and indomitable courage and easily aroused enthusiasm might well count for something. His was with principalities and powers a thousandfold stronger: the demons of hatred and jealousy, of racism and violence, of lust for money and power, of carnality and selfishness. So, though the sky on Palm Sunday seemed bright without a cloud, he knew the throne awaiting him was a cross, that his coronation would be his brow's reception of every thorn and sting and burden that human sin had brought into the world.

Yet—and this is truly remarkable—he never counted the world unworthy of his suffering. He loved people even when they were least lovable, which was frequently. He didn't expect righteousness, he taught it, and demanded it, knowing that love and sacrifice were personally more fulfilling and powerful than authority and warfare. When he wept, it was not for himself but for the city. He pictured Jerusalem in smoke-blackened ruins, its streets slippery with blood, because, as he said, "You did not know the time of your visitation." Over twenty years ago Martin Luther King Jr. said, right here in Riverside Church, "Over the bleached bones and jumbled residue of numerous civilizations are written the pathetic words, 'Too late.'"

Palm Sunday sermons, as a rule, fail to note that the triumphant procession had a destination. The account of the afternoon activities of that same day is more fully recorded in Matthew. "And Jesus entered the temple of God and drove out"—presumably with a whip snatched from a herdsman—"all who sold or bought in the temple, and he overturned the tables of the money-changers and the seats of those who sold pigeons. He said to them, 'It is written [in Jeremiah], my house shall be called a house of prayer, but you make it a den of robbers'" (Matt. 21:12–13).

It is not hard to picture Jesus' emotional state at the end of this confusing and tumultuous day. Nor should we forget the loss of sleep and appetite that must have accompanied the decision to leave a tranquil lakeside in Galilee for certain death in Jerusalem. At day's end, to be confronted with the oldest and worst form of corruption, religion become subservient to profit-making—not business become a god, but God become a business—that did it. This first recorded act of violence stemmed from Jesus' passion for justice. For what appalled him was not only that the buying and selling interfered with the dignity of worship; it was that the house of worship was being used to exploit the worshipers. The helpless poor were once again catching it in the neck—right next to the Holy of Holies, and from the priests themselves.

The upshot of this act of violence was the guarantee that there would be no second one. Jesus had wounded the ruling priests in their prestige and in their purses. More than that, he had driven out their associates, the bankers, and other traffickers in money. The two threatened ruling groups drew together more closely to do away with the dangerous intruder. Perhaps that very evening priests and merchants agreed on the purchase of a betrayer and a cross. The bourgeoisie would give the small amount of money necessary; the clergy would supply the religious pretext; the occupying power, eager to stay on good terms with both the middle class and the clergy, could be counted on to lend its soldiers. The stage was set for the events of Maundy Thursday and Good Friday.

When I think of the price that was on his head before Jesus even came to Jerusalem (in the eleventh chapter of John we read, "Now the chief priests and the Pharisees had given orders that if anyone knew where he was, he should let them know, so that they might arrest him"); and how he then rode into the city in such fashion that every eye was fixed on him; and how singlehandedly he took on virtually the whole establishment, secular and religious; when I recall how he never lost his love for the perpetrators and perpetuators of evil, nor his anger at all they did; when I think of the supreme courage, the depth of tenderness and passionate anger Jesus displayed on this one day alone, I realize why Palm Sunday is so important a church festival. At the very least, it should make all of us want to be people for whom words such as courage, tenderness, and passion still carry resonance.

Spring is a time for birth, and I've heard that the instinctive fear of being left behind has a newborn calf on its wobbly legs within an hour. Well, we don't waste time either following the herd. Yet Palm Sunday teaches that it is strength, not weakness, to reject a life someone else has chosen, whether that someone else be a whole society or one's beloved mother or father. Parents are born to be disappointed; we learn that from Jesus' life. Loneliness doesn't come with birth but with maturity, with a new role, one written just for you as a child of God. We learn also from Jesus' life that like Jesus, we need to be free to say what we think when we think it should be said.

The realm of grace is a realm of danger. Too many of us lose our faith and keep our jobs, when we should be losing our jobs and keeping our faith.

On Palm Sunday we see Christ's life become like the life of a wave, whose only truth is that it is going to break. But we also see that death is not the worst thing that can happen to us. Far worse is losing our fragile grip on meaning. Our job, as Christians, is to make the Word, as John calls Jesus, credible; and if we dared put ourselves in jeopardy, the Word would be credible everywhere, every day. Everyone in the world would shout, "Blessed be he that cometh in the name of the Lord." And there would be an end to hatred and jealousy, an end to racism and violence, an end to lust for money and power, an end to carnality and selfishness.

I am not counting on the world to vote in the kingdom of God. But I trust I will always remember the lesson of Palm Sunday: "One on God's side is a majority."

"Blessed be he that cometh in the name of the Lord."

Easter: The Authority of Love

APRIL 19, 1987
Reading: Matthew 28:1–10, 16–20

It's always a shame when even one cloud mars the blue of Easter skies. But take heart; the poet had it right:

> Light breaks when no sun shines;
> Where no sea runs, the waters of the heart
> Push in their tides.

On Easter the waters of the heart, in Dylan Thomas's image, are no wave on an inland lake, but a sea-tide, oncoming.

Easter, of course, is fun, what with all the food and finery, the chickens and the rabbits, the forsythia, magnolia, and especially the cherry "hung with bloom." But what makes Easter exciting is its cosmic aspect. For Easter has less to do with one person's escape from the grave than with the victory of seemingly powerless love over loveless power.

Let's take a tough text (they're the most rewarding). We have just heard the last words of Jesus, if not exactly as delivered, at least as recorded in the Gospel of Matthew. To the disciples who heard them, they must have been astounding. What do they say to us, two thousand years and five thousand miles away?

"All authority in heaven and on earth has been delivered to me." When we speak with one another, we talk from premises. If no premises are shared, no conversation is possible. That's why the weather is so important: everyone loves a sunny, cool day; everyone is depressed when it rains. These are marvelously shared premises.

What other, and perhaps more significant, premises do we share? We would all agree that it is bad to eat too much bitterness, to whimper away our gift of laughter, to feel that nothing we do makes the slightest dent. It is correct to say that nowhere in the world is cowardice admired, whereas courage is admired everywhere. Most people would resonate to Justice Learned Hand's imperative, "Thou shalt not ration justice"; and, although the words are worn water-smooth, to what St. Paul had to say about love in First Corinthians 13: "If I speak in the tongues of men and of angels, but have not love, I am a noisy gong or a clanging cymbal." Do you believe that, choir members, and all you other singers in the congregation? "And if I have prophetic powers, and understand all mysteries and all knowledge"—academics, your turn; "and if I have all faith so as to remove mountains"—evangelists, take heed; "and if I give away all I have to the poor"—listen to this, radicals; "and deliver my body to be burned"—the very stuff of heroism—"but *have not love*, I gain *nothing*."

Without doubt, that is the most radical statement on ethics ever written. And though not one of us lives this life of love down to the bone, still we believe in it. We believe we are as we love, that there is no smaller package in this world than that of a person all wrapped up in himself. In other words, love is not merely another shared premise; love has authority in our lives.

What about the authority of these words: "We, the peoples of the United Nations, determined to save succeeding generations from the scourge of war, which twice in our lifetime has brought untold sorrows to humanity, and to reaffirm faith in fundamental human rights, in the dignity and worth of the human person, in the equal right of men and women and of nations large and small . . . and for those ends to practice tolerance and live together in peace with one another as good neighbors . . . have resolved to combine our efforts to accomplish these ends."

Never mind that the horrors of colonialism are overlooked, that the preamble to the Charter, written in 1945, is racist in mentality if not in purpose; never mind that forty-two years later it's still "Sob, heavy world, / Sob as you spin, / Mantled in mist, remote from the happy"—those words from the preamble of the Charter of the United Nations nevertheless have authority in the national lives of the 159 signatories.

"All authority in heaven and earth has been delivered to me." That doesn't mean that Christ is authoritarian, coercive in some physical or psychological way. His whole life refutes that notion. It means simply that whatever in our souls we find worthy of undying regard, whatever on earth is heavenly, is embodied in the person of Jesus. On Good Friday we crucified him, the best among us, because we had crucified the best within us, and did not want to be reminded of it, in the time-honored tradition of ancient kings who killed the bearer of bad news. But the Easter message is that all that goodness, scourged and stretched out on the cross on Friday, is back again. Love is not powerless but eternal. Love has too much authority to die, either in the Son of God or in each of us.

It is fair to say that few of us are truly evil; the trouble is, most of us mean well—feebly. We are not serious. We carry around justice, love, and peace in our shopping carts, but along with a lot of other things that make for injustice, hatred, and war.

Easter is serious. Easter is a demand as well as a promise. Easter demands not sympathy for the crucified Lord but loyalty to the risen one; it demands an end to all our complicity in crucifixion. "All authority in heaven and earth has been delivered to me": If there's no apartheid in the afterlife, there can be none in the here and now. If there's no colonialism in heaven, there can be none on the West Bank, in Central America, or in South Dakota. If there's peace in heaven, the retribution that infuses our personal and national lives must die in our hearts.

This cruel world is no friend to grace. At the close of this service we shall sing our hearts out: "And he shall reign for ever and ever and ever." But for Jesus to reign, we have to get serious about the issue of authority. What in your lives is worthy of your undying regard, worth living for, and therefore worth dying for? What defines you? Who tells you who you are?

Imagine yourselves now as Simon Peter, semiliterate, fishing the only trade you know; you've never been beyond the borders of Judea, Samaria, and Galilee. You've just deserted your Lord in his hour of greatest need, and then you hear him say, "Go, therefore, and make disciples of all the nations . . . teaching them to observe all I have commanded you."

Imagine yourselves in St. Peter's sandals. You would be astounded; your reaction would be similar to that of Moses when God said to him, "Come, I will send you to Pharaoh, that you may deliver the children of Israel out of Egypt." Moses didn't fall on his knees; he reared up on his hind legs: "Who am I that I should go to Pharaoh?" It's little comfort to realize that in the Bible God rarely commissions people of outstanding ability, like the prophet Isaiah or St. Paul. God expects extraordinary things, but from ordinary people—like Simon Peter, like you and me.

How are we this Easter, two thousand years and five thousand miles away, to interpret Christ's commission to his disciples, "Go, therefore, and make disciples of all the nations"? My first reaction is, "Aren't there a lot of churches in the world already?"

But churches in our day are a bit like families: they tend to be havens in a heartless world, but they reinforce that world by caring more for its victims than by challenging its assumptions. Christ wants us to challenge the assumptions of our nation and world, just as he challenged those of his.

In New York City we see how poignantly true is the old adage, "When poverty comes in the door, love flies out the window." We also see how spiritually devastating it is for the financially fortunate to put the impoverished out of their thoughts and off their consciences. It's true that in pursuing our individual economic interests we are assimilating the dominant American ethic, but is the dominant American ethic the true American dream?

As a patriot, I hope not. And as a Christian, striving to be loyal to our risen Lord, I have to question an economic system that reverses the priorities of Mary's Magnificat, filling the rich with good things and sending the poor empty away. As Christians we cannot have an undying regard for money. Better to bear in our mind's eye the epitaph inscribed on a stone in an old country cemetery: "What I gave, I have; what I spent, I had; what I kept, I lost."

Just as the faith is economically demanding in its implications, it is also politically demanding; "Go, therefore, and make disciples of the nations" is a political statement. Christ today wants his disciples to tell the nations that their disastrous cult of power leads to the pretensions of the powerful and to the despair of the powerless, leaving all lovers of life filled with unutterable sadness.

The will to power so characteristic of nations is irrational. It uses reason, as ancient kings their court, simply to add grace to the enterprise. It is also loveless, producing ever more dangerous and devastating situations. When the Allies at the end of World War II insisted that unconditional surrender alone was acceptable, they made the bomb the weapon of choice.

But God is not mocked: in the nuclear age we see that progress toward power is simultaneously a march toward weakness. God is not mocked: today theology and politics stand or fall together. Today in international as well as in personal affairs, humility is strength, self-examination is preparedness. We have to be merciful when we live at each other's mercy. Blessed indeed are the meek, for only they *can* inherit the earth. God through Jesus Christ is saying to us, "Go and tell the nations that no country is at the center of this planet, no matter how glorious its past, how brilliant its future, how mighty its arms, how generous its people." This is not the American century; Henry Luce was shortsighted. Nor is this the Russian century, nor will it be the Chinese century—this century, pragmatically as eternally in God's sight, is the human century. The truth is that the survival unit in our time is the entire human race.

When Moses protested, "Who am I that I should go to Pharaoh?" God answered, "But I will be with you"—and that took care of everything. Christ says the same in commissioning his disciples, then and now: "And lo, I am with you always, to the close of the age."

The Easter demand is great, but no less so is the promise. St. Paul knew its truth: "If God be for us, who can be against us? Who shall separate us from the love of Christ? Shall tribulation, or distress, or persecution, or famine, or nakedness, or the sword?" (Rom. 8:31, 35)—all of which he had experienced in his personal life. Likewise Matthew could testify to Christ's presence amid the persecutions he and his fellow Christians faced in the Syrian church.

If you yourself have not known the truth and power of this promise, if your life is more Christ-haunted than Christ-centered, be patient. Commit as much of yourself as you can to as much of Christ as you believe in. Keep asking, "What would Jesus have me do?" His authority and his presence will grow. For Christ is first but a figure on a page, then a light against which all life is silhouetted, then finally a face and a presence. "Lo, I am with you always"—even in death, which is only a horizon, and a horizon is nothing save the limit of our sight. And do not fear death. Did we not sing, "Made like him, like him we rise; ours the cross, the grave, the skies"?

St. Paul says it best: "For this corruptible must put on incorruption, and this mortal must put on immortality. And when this corruptible shall have put on incorruption, and when this mortal shall have put on immortality, then shall be brought to pass the saying that is written: Death is swallowed up in victory. O death, where is thy sting? O grave, where is thy victory? . . . Thanks be to God, who gives us the victory through our Lord Jesus Christ. Therefore, my beloved, be steadfast, immoveable, always abounding in the work of the Lord, knowing that in the Lord your labor is not in vain" (1 Cor. 15:53–55, 57–58).

Redeeming the Routine

MAY 3, 1987
Readings: Psalm 103; John 21:1–14

This story is about the rehabilitation of Peter, Jesus' three questions corresponding to Peter's three denials on Good Friday.

But the story suggests so many other things besides. For example, at the beginning of John's Gospel, you may remember, Jesus first visits human beings in their joy, at a wedding feast at Cana. Whether or not you believe he turned the water into wine (and I've seen Jesus turn beer into furniture), you have to concede that by his presence he greatly enhanced the joy of the occasion. (And if he did change the water to wine, I must tell you Baptists that, conservatively estimated, it was a little less than a hundred gallons!)

When you think of that miracle, and of the multiplying of the loaves and the fishes, and of Jesus helping the disciples to catch fish, when you think how hard Jesus works for our happiness, you have to admit, joy is a neglected virtue. Sure, times are hard; the world is full of rebuffs and heartache and millions of folk who are wretchedly poor. Nevertheless, as Albert Camus reminds us, "there is in this world beauty as well as the humiliated, and we must strive, hard as it is, not to be unfaithful neither to the one nor to the other." Besides, whom do you serve, walking around so grim-faced that people would think you had been bred by a combination of a sparrow-hawk and a tomahawk?

But such thoughts arise at the beginning of John; we're now at the end, where the story is entirely different. If a wedding feast is a special—and an especially joyful affair—what could be more routine than breakfast? Usually it's the same food, with the same people, at the same time, in the same place, and all, if not at their worst, certainly at something less than their best. But breakfast with Jesus, even though it's only bread and fish—that's like having fresh waffles with Vermont maple syrup. This was the best breakfast the disciples ever had.

Let me recall two breakfast scenes from twentieth-century American literature. The first is from the third act of Thornton Wilder's *Our Town*. Emily Webb has recently died, at the age of twenty-six, and, against the advice of the older dead, she chooses to go back. It's allowed, but if you want to relive your life you have to watch yourself doing it. That's the condition laid down by the Stage Manager, who runs things in heaven and on earth. So Emily chooses to return on the morning of her twelfth birthday:

"Good morning, Mama," says twelve-year-old Emily.

"Well, now, my dear," says her mother, "very happy birthday to my girl, and many happy returns. There are some surprises waiting for you on the kitchen table. . . . But birthday or no birthday, I want you to eat your breakfast good and slow; I want you to grow up and be a good, strong girl."

The whole thing is going too routinely, and twenty-six-year-old Emily says with mounting urgency (only of course her mother can't hear her): "Oh, Mama. I married George Gibbs, Mama. Well, he's dead, too. His appendix burst on a camping trip to North Conway. We just felt terrible about it, don't you remember? But just for a moment now, we are all together. Mama, just for a moment we are happy, let's look at one another."

But it isn't working, and finally Emily says to the Stage Manager, "I can't go on. It goes so fast. We don't have time to look at one another." She breaks down. "I didn't realize. So all that was going on and we never noticed. Take me back up the hill to my grave. But first, wait, one more look. Good-bye, world. Good-bye, Grover's Corners, Mama and Papa. Good-bye to clocks ticking, Mama's sunflowers, food and coffee, and new ironed dresses, and hot baths, and sleeping and waking up. Oh earth, you are too wonderful for anybody to realize you."

She looks toward the Stage Manager and asks abruptly through her tears, "Do any human beings ever realize life while they live it, every, every minute?"

The Stage Manager replies, "No. The saints and poets, maybe; they do some."

"So all that was going on and we never noticed." But with Jesus, even the routine is redeemed. With Jesus, our hearts are full, our eyes are open; we begin to notice things that heretofore we had only seen. We are alive, we observe, and we judge. *We look at one another*. Most of all, we realize that the world doesn't lack for wonders, only for a sense of wonder, for "the earth is the Lord's and the fulness thereof, the world and they that dwell therein." And therein dwells no one who isn't superspecial. "Mama, let's look at one another"—whether at home, in school, in the factory, at the office.

Now suppose your routine is not just dreary, but misery itself. A friend of mine, a minister, told me this week how his home had become, in effect, a hospital. So mentally distraught was his son that for months neither he nor his wife had dared leave him alone, and often they had to sit up with him all night. Near the breaking point, my friend shared his anguish with the ministers he worked with. "We'll pray for you," they said. One of the ministers, who was dying of the worst form of leukemia, heard the story in the isolation ward in the hospital. Said he, "I've little else to do until I die; I'll pray for you all the time."

Just as the water turned to wine and the sea filled with fish so miraculously, so despair gave way to hope. All three—father, son, and mother—are doing much better. Such is the power of prayer; and what is prayer if not talking to Jesus, who is right there listening, working always for our greater happiness?

That leads to the second breakfast scene. It concerns a man to whom befell every misfortune imaginable. His wife died, his children never called, his house burned down, his job disappeared—everything he touched turned to dust. Nonetheless, he always remained cheerful, always returning good for evil. His name, of course, was Sholem Aleichem.

Finally he died. Word of his imminent arrival at Heaven's gate caused the angels to gather. Even the Lord was there, so great was this man's fame. And when he arrived and stood with downcast eyes, the Prosecuting Angel arose and, for the first time in the memory of Heaven, said, "There are no charges." Then the Angel for the Defense arose and rehearsed all the hardships and recounted how in all circumstances this servant of God had remained cheerful, always returning good for evil.

When the angel was finished the Lord said, "Not since Job have we heard of a life such as this one." Turning to the man he said, "Ask, and it shall be given unto you."

The old man raised his eyes from the ground and said, "If I could start every day with a hot buttered roll . . ." And at that the Lord and all the angels wept.

It wasn't so much the modesty of the request as the understanding of the preciousness of what he was asking for. Sunshine should always be more important to us than another acquisition. We don't need all things to enjoy life; we have been given life to enjoy all things. Happiness lies in discerning the value of the things we have. And if we have only fish and bread—and Jesus—any routine is redeemed. So "Bless the Lord, O my soul, and forget not all his benefits."

So much for the first part of the story in John's Gospel. The second relates the most tender confrontation of which I've ever read. There is such poignancy in the question, "Simon, son of John, do you love me more than all else?" And such love in the imperative, "Feed my lambs."

"My lambs." Jesus is always thinking of children. For him every year is the Year of the Child. It's as if he is asking us, "Why don't the children of the world excite you at least as much as do its rulers?"

"A second time he said to him, 'Simon, son of John, do you love me?' He said to him, 'Yes, Lord, you know that I love you.' He said, 'Feed my sheep.'"

Now he's talking of the grown-ups. But from the image he uses, it's clear Jesus has in mind the sick, the frail, the old, the poor—those hardly less vulnerable than the children. "Feed my sheep." *Homo homini lupus*, goes the old Latin saying: People are as wolves to each other. But Jesus is saying, "*Homo homini pastor*"—Be as shepherds to each other. Feed my sheep, don't kill them. And if our Lord and Savior said these words to Peter, then "Feed my sheep" is not a human option, it is a divine imperative.

"He said to him yet a third time, 'Simon, son of John, do you love me?' Peter was grieved because he said to him the third time, 'Do you love me?' And he said to him, 'Lord, you know everything; you know that I love you.' And Jesus said to him, 'Feed my sheep.'"

The point is made. Peter is restored. And his restoration can be ours, for promise-making, promise-breaking Peter is all of us. To all of us Jesus says, "I know that you have denied me. But if you keep believing in me the way Peter did, you will understand how much I believe in you. If you love me, you will never hate again. I tell you, any one of you can be resurrected to new life, become a pastor, a shepherd, and feed my lambs and sheep."

The disciples had their last breakfast with Jesus—bread and fish. Today we again celebrate their last supper—bread and wine. In a way it's the same. *Ubi caritas et amor*—where charity and love are found—it really doesn't matter where you are, for *Deus ibi est*, there is God. The simplest things take on infinite meaning when we share them with each other, and when Christ blesses both them and us with his presence.

"Do any human beings ever realize life while they live it—every, every minute?"

To paraphrase the Stage Manager: "No; but with Jesus, you can come pretty close!"

"This Night Your Soul Is Required of You"

MAY 17, 1987
Readings: Deuteronomy 8; Luke 12:13–21

As some of you are DINKs (double income, no kids) and still others SINKs (single income, no kids), and many more of you tomorrow morning will set forth for the office "dressed for success," I had better say quickly that in my humble opinion indigence is not a prerequisite for discipleship. I say that because Jesus did not indiscriminately condemn wealth. As a matter of fact, many of his first followers came from homes of considerable comfort, and they and Jesus alike enjoyed the hospitality of similar homes, like the one in Bethany that belonged to Mary and Martha and Lazarus. It's true, of course, that to the rich young ruler Jesus did say, "Sell all that you have and give to the poor." But he seemed to be prescribing individual surgery, for he never said anything similar to rich Nicodemus or to other wealthy people. In other words, as regards the complicated matter of money, the anathemas of the moralists are always easy, often thoughtless, and sometimes insincere.

Furthermore, as any of you who work in our food pantry can see, an endless struggle for daily bread saps not only the body but the mind and spirit as well. There's merit to the old saying, "When poverty walks in the door, love flies out the window," for just about everybody needs a certain level of financial security to enhance their freedom, including the freedom to love. Exceptions there are, of course—Franciscan friars for example—but the fact that Diogenes was happy living in a barrel is no answer to the problems of the homeless, who need and deserve freedom from sordidness.

But when someone who has been living hand-to-mouth begins to earn some income, watch carefully, for that person has reached a critical fork in the road: thereafter he or she will be either a stronger, freer person, or a fool living the folly of an acquisitive life.

"And one out of the multitude said unto him, 'Teacher, bid my brother divide the inheritance with me.' But he said unto him, 'Who made me a judge or divider over you?'"

Jesus didn't come to be that kind of magistrate, and more than that, he disclaims the relevance of the request: "Take heed, keep yourselves from all covetousness, for people's lives do not consist in the abundance of things they possess." With an insight uniquely his, Jesus sees that at issue is not injustice but greed. The man has superficial problems because deeper ones are unresolved.

(It is interesting to note that whenever in the Gospels anyone complains to Jesus about someone else, he always waves aside the complaint. It's as if he is saying, "Before God you can only confess, never complain—not about anyone else." Before God we are all confessers; no one is a complainant.)

And then he tells them all a parable, which has been defined as "an earthly story with a heavenly meaning." Unlike some inside traders we could mention, the man in the parable came by his wealth honestly. There's no mention of adding field to field through exploitation, of devouring widows' houses by fraud. His farm simply yielded good crops. Moreover, he's no miser: "Soul, take thine ease, eat, drink, and be merry." He's farsighted and practical: "I will pull down my barns and build larger ones." Without doubt, almost any American today would call this man eminently successful. So why does a man most of us would admire end up being called by God a fool?

In the first place, the man is an incredible egotist. His sixty-one-word soliloquy contains six "I's" and six "mine's" (including the "thine" addressed to himself). He has no thought of God. He talks of "my fruits" and "my grain" as if he could command the sap in the trees and the fertility of the soil, as if he could guarantee the faithfulness of the seasons, cause the rain to fall and the sun to shine. Psalm 14 begins, "The fool says in his heart 'There is no God.'" A biblical fool is anyone who by word or deed denies the existence of God. The man in this parable is a practical atheist.

Heedless of God, he is also bereft of fellow feeling. He didn't plough alone, reap by himself, or build barns single-handedly. He just got rich single-handedly, forgetting that wealth is more a social than an individual achievement. (Like the folks in Massachusetts, we should all live in a "commonwealth.") And when he wonders where to store his excess grain, he shows no concern for those who have none at all.

"A face devoid of love and grace, / A hateful hard successful face" (Emily Dickinson). Though rich, the man is a spiritual pauper. Though "dressed for success," success will fit him like a shroud. "This night your soul is required of you": when his breathing stops, that will be but a belated announcement of an earlier demise. For this man died while he lived—like a tree dying from the top down.

It is to the whole multitude that Jesus speaks this parable, and most of them were not rich. So he is also warning the poor, those poor in every generation who long and strive only for the luxuries in which the rich have found no peace. He is saying to them, "Affluence doesn't buy morale." He is telling all of us, "You have been given freedom not to throw your lives away, but to give them away." And he is telling us we had better get our spiritual lives in order quickly, because this very night our souls, too, might be required of us.

This parable convicts the mercenary and ostentatious generation we have allowed ourselves to become. When PTL stands for "Pass the Loot," and Christians continue to contribute to it because they have allowed themselves to become, in effect, spiritual survivalists, seeking to save themselves rather than to transcend or forget themselves, the Christian community in this country is in trouble.

But so too are the universities, which naively believe that the humanities still humanize, when in fact they generally only neutralize; they are little more than cultural icing on an economic cake. When 73 percent of freshmen state that their primary goal is to be financially very well off, it's time for university presidents to join the Catholic bishops and Protestant leaders in lobbying for greater economic justice—not just for the sake of the wretchedly poor who make up the vast majority of the world's population, but also for the well-being of their own students and alumni.

"For people's lives do not consist in the abundance of their possessions." If the only truly renewable resources are intellectual and spiritual, and if it is easier for a camel to pass through the eye of a needle than for a rich man to enter the kingdom of heaven, then just as the poor should not be left at the mercy of their poverty, so the rich should not be left at the mercy of their riches. In the Bible, judgment of the rich spells mercy not only for the poor but finally for the rich as well. It is a gracious reminder of one of the Bible's most profound questions: "For what shall it profit a man if he gain the whole world and lose his soul?"

All this means that on a personal level we must cease the endless game of trying to possess our souls by possession of something outside them. We must draw a line between us and ours, clear a space between ourselves and our possessions, not love things and use people, but love people and use things, remembering that we are never more in possession of ourselves than when lost in one another. For our lives consist in the abundance of our love.

As for the nation, it had better heed the words from Deuteronomy we heard earlier: "Beware lest you say in your heart 'My power and the might of my hand have gotten me this wealth.' And if you forget the Lord your God and go after other gods and serve them and worship them, I solemnly warn you this day that . . . like the nations that the Lord God made to perish before you, so shall you perish" (8:17–20).

I believe that warning. God is not mocked. And I believe further that from the very beginning America has been torn between two philosophies, two visions of itself, both well described in 1981 by the National Council of Churches in a perceptive message sent to all the churches.

> From the first, there were those who saw America as a rich treasure waiting to be exploited for the benefit of those daring enough and strong enough to take it. . . . In this vision of America, the fittest survive and prosper, and there is little room for public purpose since it interferes with private gain. Compassion is a weakness in the competitive struggle of each against all, and charity is the voluntary option of individuals. Government is at best a necessary evil which must be strong enough to protect privilege from assault but kept too weak to impose public responsibility on private prerogative. In this vision, America is seen principally as Empire—"Manifest Destiny," "54–40 or Fight," "Remember the Maine"—with a mission to extend its power and commerce throughout the continent, the hemisphere, the world.

But, as the Council points out,

> [A]nother vision of America has been present from the beginning also. This second alternate vision has deep roots in religious faith and biblical images of divine intent and human possibility. The precious possession of pilgrims and padres, it was a vision of creating in the New World a new model of human community— the New Jerusalem—free from the oppression and misery that entrenched power and privilege perpetuated in the Old World they had fled.
>
> In this America, it was envisioned, government would promote the common welfare and secure the blessings of liberty for all. The dignity and worth of

each person would be respected and protected as a matter of policy as well as piety, and each person's potential would be developed to the fullest. Justice and compassion would reign in alabaster cities that stretched from sea to shining sea, and the bountiful resources of a favored land would be thankfully received and gladly shared with the whole human family, as the nurturing providence of the Creator meant them to be. This America would be known in the world for its compassion, its deep desire for peace and justice, its commitment to human rights and decency. It would stand as a beacon and a model, a city set on a hill, its power stemming from the irresistible example of a just, caring and peaceful people sharing life and treasure generously with all the people of the earth.

Never realized, this second vision of America has also never been abandoned. It is the real America, the essential America, America the beautiful, the one to which our better selves pledge allegiance. So let Christians renew their resolve to urge America toward care and compassion, not away from them. Let us lift up our hearts to the God who exalts those of low degree, the God who reminds us that our lives do not consist in the abundance of our possessions.

If some night in this Eastertide our souls were required of us, would it not be wonderful to be remembered not as the farmer in Jesus' parable, but as E. B. White described his wife, Katherine, at her death: "a member of the resurrection conspiracy, the company of those who plant seeds of hope under dark skies of grief or oppression, going about their living and dying until, no one knows how, when or where, the tender Easter shoots appear and a piece of creation is healed."

Psychosclerosis

MAY 24, 1987
Reading: Mark 5:23–41

As next Sunday we celebrate our annual Peace Sabbath, and as our preacher will be one of Great Britain's ablest advocates of peace, Monsignor Bruce Kent, I have decided this Memorial Day weekend only to recall, but not to dwell on, "those who will not grow old as we who are left grow old."

I am tempted to dwell on nuclear weapons, if only because nuclear war is so much more conceivable than nuclear disarmament. There is something about those evil weapons that seems unbudgeable, which prompted a sharp observer, Martin Amis, to write last month, "What is the only provocation that could bring about the use of nuclear weapons? Nuclear weapons. What is the priority target for nuclear weapons? Nuclear weapons. How do we prevent the use of nuclear weapons? By threatening to use nuclear weapons. And we can't get rid of nuclear weapons, because of nuclear weapons. The intransigence, it seems, is a function of the weapons themselves."

But instead of preaching on nuclear weapons, I'm going to return to one of my favorite New Testament stories, on which I haven't preached a sermon for almost ten years. (If any of you say, "Oh, that sounds familiar," it simply proves that a sermon isn't just a "pot of message.")

Let's first rehearse again the role of Scripture in our lives. If it's a mistake to sharpen our minds by narrowing them, then it's a mistake to look to the Bible to close a discussion. The Bible opens, widens, and deepens discussion. It is not an oracle to be consulted for specific advice on specific occasions, it is a well of wisdom about the glories and horrors, the ambiguity and insolubility of the human situation. It sings praises to a God who bruises our egos but mends our hearts. It shows us both the green pastures and the paths of righteousness. It demonstrates that an active faith will arouse official discontent, and that God will ferret us out of any hiding place we choose: "What doest thou here, Elijah?" "Adam . . . where art thou?"

(I thought of Adam this week as I listened to the president tailor his defense according to the latest revelation! Actually in the original, unedited version of Genesis, Adam says to God, "Did I eat the apple? I can't remember. But if I did, it was because the woman—whom you made—gave it to me. And if she gave it to me, it was because it was my idea to begin with, and if it was my idea to begin with, it was because the commandment not to eat the apple didn't apply to me.")

But I don't want to talk any more about Adam. I want to recall the woman who for twelve years bled internally. For twelve years she sought a cure, unsuccessfully. It's hard to believe that her illness wasn't in part emotional, particularly because in those days to hemorrhage in this fashion was thought to be unclean. So for twelve years, invisible to the public eye, she suffered her illness and her guilt.

It would be easy for each of us to say, "I see myself there reflected," for all of us have secret guilts, and not all of them are neurotic; many are the product of a healthy understanding of reality. We have fallen short as parents, as grandparents, and as children; as husbands, wives, and lovers. As American citizens we have strewn every continent with our blunders. Lord knows we often fail in our vocational life. And because to an extraordinary degree we are our memories—that is, our memories shape us altogether as much as do our genes—the memory of what we have done or have neglected to do, like the woman's hemorrhaging, has enormous secret power over our lives, draining them of vitality and joy.

It would be easy to say something like that, but what would be the point? For the story is not about the woman's sickness, it's about her cure. She hears what people are saying about Jesus; she says to herself, "If I touch even his clothes I will be cured"; she makes her way through the crowd, touches his robe, and instantly is well again.

I suspect at this point in the story we see ourselves mirrored more in the crowd than in the woman. As Christians we are pressing in around Jesus all right, so much so that some people, like the disciples in the story, think we are actually touching him. But he knows differently. No power has gone out of him. He knows a lot of us are keeping our hands to ourselves. In short, unlike the woman who for twelve long years sought a cure, we, after perhaps a comparable time, have come to terms with our bleeding. Our wounds are now familiar; we have accepted them. We have become almost comfortable with them, and some of us have even learned to use them to coerce others. Having reached a truce with our guilt, we now don't want to touch Jesus. We fear the cure more than the illness.

Have you ever heard yourself, or anyone else, say sentences like these:

"I think I'm just going to keep my mouth shut and endure my marital problems."

"One of these days I'm going to have to sit down and have a good long talk with the kids."

"I know my job is boring, and it certainly isn't useful to anybody, but it pays well—and I guess these days you're lucky to have any job at all."

"Too bad Congress keeps funding those darn Contras. Too bad that nice Young American engineer got killed in Nicaragua. I guess we just have to hope for the best."

Such sentences are symptoms of the advanced state of a disease Ashley Montagu has called "psychosclerosis," a hardening not of the arteries, as in arteriosclerosis, but of the spirit, in which the mind cannot embrace new ideas nor the heart stay vulnerable. Psychosclerosis staunches the bleeding, but it does not heal the wound. It's a way of deadening yourself against life, of selling your freedom as the price of your self-perpetuation. You also strike a deal with your conscience: in order not to feel too bad about some things, you promise not to feel too good about anything. To avoid judgment, which demands a new way of life, you decide to seek punishment, which, by assuaging your guilt, makes your old way of life bearable anew. (The best way to avoid judgment is always to seek punishment.)

The trick in life is obviously to die young, as late as possible. But sufferers of psychosclerosis seek spiritual death as early as possible. It's a frighteningly common disease.

People are right to fear the cure, for being healed means changing your ways. Healing brings the courage and freedom not to endure marital problems, which is easy, but to face and resolve them, which is difficult. To be healed means to talk to the kids right now, perhaps to change jobs, and certainly to do all in your power to change the course of your nation if you deem it disastrous.

Every time I hear Americans berating atheistic communism, it strikes me that the heresy of rejecting Christ is small potatoes compared to the heresy of remaking Christ into something he never was, still isn't, and never will be. You can't come to church and pretend that Christ is not a healer. You can't come to church just to crowd around him and keep your hands behind your back. We come to church to touch him, to feel his power coming into us, to heal our wounds, to forgive our sins, to make us again responsible—responseable, able to respond—to God, to each other, and to the world at large. And how it prefigures the cross to picture power coming out of Jesus to heal our bleeding! "He was wounded for our transgressions, he was bruised for our iniquities; . . . and with his stripes we are healed" (Isa. 53:5).

While it is true that without Christ the woman could not have been healed, what the woman did, she did entirely on her own. She didn't ask Jesus' permission, she didn't tell him what she was going to do, nor did she plan to tell him about it afterwards. In other words, she made herself totally responsible for her own cure—which is why she was healed. Christ didn't say, "My power has healed you"; he said, "Your faith has cured you." His power was there, but she had to want that power, to take it, to use it, which she did so audaciously as to recall words of Emily Dickinson to her sister-in-law: "Cherish power. It stands in the Bible between the kingdom and the glory, because it is wilder than both."

After Jesus has turned around, and after the woman explains why she touched him and how she was instantly cured, in Luke's version the Greek word for "crowd" changes to the word for "people" or "community." By her willingness to become deeply human, this woman humanizes all around her, changing a faceless multitude into a community of warm human beings. To touch Jesus is to be put in touch with one another.

Maybe this is a Memorial Day sermon after all, for the choice these days is to touch one another the world around, or to kill one another the world around. It's a choice between arms that embrace or arms that incinerate. The same holds true for our spiritual health. To be healed and strengthened we need only to touch Christ—and by the power that comes out of him and into us, we are put in touch with one another.

"Shine, Perishing Republic"

JULY 5, 1987
Readings: Numbers 13:25–33; 14:1–10; 2 Corinthians 4:7–10

The Old Testament lesson speaks to the nation on this fifth of July in the bicentennial summer of our country's constitution.

After a long and tear-stained trek, the Children of Israel finally reach the borders of the Promised Land. Spies are sent out, and when they return they give a majority report and a minority report. The minority report, submitted by Joshua and Caleb, is prophetic, saying, in effect, "Let's go ahead; we can make it if only we do not lose hope," which we can define as "a passion for the possible." The majority report, by contrast, is pragmatic. The prudence it counsels thinly veils the cowardice of those submitting it. It speaks of giants in the land— the sons of Anak (literally "the long-necked one"): "And we seemed to ourselves like grasshoppers, and so we seemed to them."

Predictably, because they are like most people, the Children of Israel accept the majority report. We read, "All the congregation raised a loud cry; and the people wept that night. And all the people of Israel murmured against Moses and Aaron; the whole congregation said to them, 'Would that we had died in the land of Egypt! . . .' And they said to one another, 'Let us choose a captain, and go back to Egypt.'" When Aaron and Moses remonstrate, and Caleb and Joshua get up once again and say, "The Lord is with us," all the congregation can think to do is to stone them.

"We seemed to ourselves like grasshoppers" reflects everyone's constant enemy—that nasty four-letter word, fear. The opposite of love is not hate, but fear; as Scripture says, "Perfect love casts out fear." The story shows that while love seeks truth, fear seeks safety. And fear distorts the truth not by exaggerating the ills of the world (which would be difficult), but by underestimating our ability to deal with them—"We seemed to ourselves like grasshoppers." The Children of Israel exemplify the protective strategy of deliberate failure: You can't lose any money if you don't place any bets; you can't fall out of bed if you sleep on the floor. Further, if you think other people—those giants—are responsible for making you a failure, you don't have to feel so bad about being one. And finally, if you think those trying to wean you from your sense of failure—the Calebs and Joshuas of the world—are only trying to push you around, you can, with good conscience, stone them.

"Let us choose a captain, and go back to Egypt." The Children of Israel look at the future, lose their nerve, and vote to return to the past. Hasn't this nation done much the same, not once but twice in this century, first in the 1920s and then again in the 1980s? The parallels are striking.

Riversiders will recall that in the 1920s Harry Emerson Fosdick led the fight against a resurgent Fundamentalism seeking to eliminate the teaching of evolution in the public schools. In the 1920s the Ku Klux Klan, lynch laws, and Jim Crow reached the zenith of their power. In the 1920s New York politicians were looting the city, while the federal government under President Harding reached a level of corruption unequaled since the days of President Grant. President Coolidge dispatched the Marines to Nicaragua, Bolshevism was enemy number one, and the free market was the most trustworthy ally of progress.

Even as the stock market continued to climb—endlessly, it seemed—the spiritual crisis deepened. Conscience and compassion were cauterized as sordid poverty lived check-by-jowl with flamboyant luxury. As usual, it was the poets who saw things most clearly. At the end of the decade Robinson Jeffers wrote his famous poem "Shine, Perishing Republic," which reads in part:

While this America settles in the mold
　　of its vulgarity, heavily thickening
　　to empire,
And protest, only a bubble in the
　　molten mass, pops and sighs out, and
　　the mass hardens,
I sadly smiling remember that the
　　flower fades to make fruit, the
　　fruit rots to make earth.
Out of the mother; and through the
　　spring exultances, ripeness and
　　decadence; and home to the mother.

You making haste haste on decay, not
　　blameworthy; life is good, be it
　　stubbornly long or suddenly
A mortal splendor; meteors are not
　　needed less than mountains: shine,
　　perishing republic.
But for my children, I would have them
　　keep their distance from the
　　thickening center; corruption
Never has been compulsory, when the
　　cities lie at the monster's feet
　　there are left the mountains.

And, we might add, the sea, to which Jeffers retreated in the 1930s, to Carmel, California, where, as a kid on a bicycle, every morning at seven o'clock I threw over his fence the daily newspaper.

It took the great Crash of 1929—as much a moral as an economic event, revealing as it did the hypocrisies of the land—to make Americans forget the fleshpots of Egypt, to turn their faces once again toward the future. I suspect a similar disaster awaits us at the end of this decade, if only because God is not mocked.

But let us hope that God has not condemned Americans in the 1980s to repeat the rake's progress of the 1920s. Let us hope that Christians at least, in large numbers, will in the manner of the Prodigal Son come to themselves and realize anew, with Caleb and Joshua, that nations, like individuals, must keep becoming, must stay always in transition, faces forward, eyes ahead—for God is ahead of us altogether as much as God is above and within us. And God wants all God's children to continue their Exodus toward the Promised Land.

It is written in Scripture, "Without a vision the people perish" (Prov. 29:18), and if God be ahead of us the vision must always be progressive, generous, and practical. What will it take for our republic to survive, for our land "long to be light with freedom's holy light"?

Let me suggest that it is not sufficient to put just enough money in our urban and rural ghettos to keep them from exploding. The nation must genuinely help its needy poor. It must give them what in the eyes of God they so richly deserve—decent education, decent housing, decent health care, and jobs.

God wants the whole world to become a safer and more humane place for all its people. I suggest that to prevent the pent-up forces of the world from exploding into costly and chaotic violence, we must unblock the development of the Third World. That's absolutely crucial. Real wages in the Third World must rise. Protectionism may be wrong, but so too is free trade unless it be for fair pay. Why pick on the Japanese? Consumer boycotts and punitive tariffs, not to say total embargos, should be aimed not at their products, but at products not made under decent conditions, often by American businesses exploiting cheap labor abroad. We must extend the Fair Employment Practice concept. We need a world minimum wage.

> America, America, God mend thine every flaw;
> Confirm thy soul in self-control,
> Thy liberty in law.

I love America for its freedom and decency, not for its power. If we go back to the politics of President Coolidge and send our troops once again into Central America, the results will be misery and slaughter for the folks down there, a legacy of hatred throughout Latin America, and at home the most unpopular war in our history, for we are bound by proximity, culture, and religion far more to Latin America than we were to Vietnam. The only case the government could make would be in terms of power and national interest, not justice.

Finally, as we have to keep reminding ourselves, nuclear energy has brought humanity to the point where physical and spiritual salvation are no longer separable. We can't save our skins without saving our souls—and we can't save our souls without saving everybody's skin. Pleading with his fellow Christians, psychiatrist M. Scott Peck writes, "The arms race is against everything Christianity supposedly stands for. It stands for nationalism; Jesus practiced internationalism. The arms race stands for hatred and enmity; Jesus preached forgiveness. It stands for pride; Jesus said, 'Blessed are the poor in spirit.' It is supported by the weapons manufacturers and the bellicose; Jesus said, 'Blessed are the peacemakers.' Its central dynamic is the search for invulnerability; Jesus exemplified vulnerability"—as we are about to recall in the Communion service.

So enough of this "back to Egypt" talk. Enough complaints about the giants ahead. After all, what are giant obstacles if not brilliant opportunities brilliantly disguised as giant obstacles? Besides, we too can become giants, Anaks—simply by sticking out our necks, which is exactly what Christians are expected to do. Fear is the only enemy, and it is always conquered by that other four-letter word, love, the love of God we see so clearly and movingly in Jesus Christ our Lord.

So let us conclude on this national holiday weekend that we may be perplexed, but not driven to despair; struck down, but not destroyed. Most of all, let us resolve to carry in our bodies the death of Jesus so that the immortal life of Jesus may also be made manifest in our mortal flesh.

Soft Individualism

JULY 12, 1987
Readings: Psalm 148; 1 Corinthians 1:26–31

Today I want to talk of something for which we all yearn, but of which we have so little. In our homes, whose family ties are often strained, in our sinfully divided churches and politically divided nation and world, we all want and desperately need genuine community. Whenever we sing, "Praise the Lord, God's glory show," or hear a psalm like the 148th, praising God for all God's glories, I always think that one of God's greatest glories is the incredible variety of human beings God has created.

Recently (for reasons I'd as soon not disclose) I found myself in the waiting room of the Bureau of Motor Vehicles. I was not alone—far from it. I tell you, we were no bland mush of humanity; rather, we were a salad of every kind of varied ingredients and textures. Some of us in that room looked like the cream of the intellectual crop, while others of us looked as if we had been scraped off the bottom of the gene barrel. If you want to celebrate the pluralism of God's creation, don't visit a bus depot, don't get on a New York City subway car; go straight to the Bureau of Motor Vehicles.

I know a lot of you visitors from out of town have come to this adrenaline capital of the world to see some of the varied and vibrant life of which we New Yorkers boast. So let me tell you one of my favorite New York stories. When Paddy Chayefsky, of blessed memory, first met his fellow playwright Arthur Miller, he asked, "Is it true, Mr. Miller, that you live in the country?" "Yes," said Mr. Miller, "in Connecticut." "Do you like it?" "Yes, I like it fine." "Well, but tell me—what do you do when you want to take a walk?"

What Chayefsky understood so well was how imperative it is for black and white, female and male, Latino and Anglo, gay and straight, to realize that God has brought into being a creation far more pluralistic than any of our poor imaginations can grasp; that each of us is unprecedented and irrepeatable; that none of us, therefore, can march to canned music, but each to his or her own drummer; that only actors and actresses have any business trying to be other than who they are; that the rest of us must shun pretension, facades, and empty routines, and be genuinely as God made and meant us to be, for there can be no authentic community except among authentic individuals.

If all this sounds like an argument for good old-fashioned rugged individualism, it is not. I know a lot about rugged individualists. Lieutenant Colonel Oliver North is only the latest to be nurtured in it (and somebody left out of his education the importance of independent thinking). The trouble with rugged individualism is that it encourages us to hide our weaknesses and failures, to be ashamed of our limitations. Rugged individualism means it is not safe to be anxious, afraid, depressed, in doubt—in other words, it's not safe to be yourself. Rugged individualists tend to have acquaintances by the droves, but very few intimate friends. In fact, intimacy is the big threat; rugged individualists neither desire nor trust intimacy. So it is clear that there can be nothing rugged about authentic individualism.

So let's try "soft individualism," as suggested by Scott Peck, a Christian psychiatrist, in his latest book, *The Different Drum*. He describes soft individualism as understanding that "we cannot be truly ourselves until we are able to share freely the things we most have in common: our weakness, our incompleteness, our imperfection, our inadequacy, our sins, our lack of wholeness and self-sufficiency." Years ago a book was published called *I'm OK, You're OK*. Immediately I wanted to write another, which I would entitle *I'm Not OK, You're Not OK—and That's OK*. It would have been far more biblical, based on St. Paul's claim, "For when I am weak, then I am strong" (1 Cor. 12:10b). When I have no blind sides, I can see straight. When I'm not uptight, or upright (generally they're the same) I am more open, candid, and honest. And only when you are the same way can you and I communicate, can we have real community between us. Otherwise, all we're doing is bumping masks.

I know somebody who reminds me of nothing so much as an island on a lake with heavy trees and bushes coming all the way down to the shoreline. Where do you land the canoe? I know somebody else whose cheerfulness would be her most engaging trait were it not so sinister. Whenever I meet her, she seems to throw a bridge across the moat so I may come across and visit her in her fortress. But as I approach the bridge, lo, I find that—full of cheer—she has rushed across it herself to make sure I don't cross it.

Don't all of us always push our best foot forward when it's the other one that needs the attention? All human relations are based on need. Community, like the charity it requires, begins at home, with a willingness to be the unique selves we are, with all our strengths and weaknesses, wisdom and foolishness (and without being too clear about which is which). For "God chose what is foolish in the world to shame the wise, God chose what is weak in the world to shame the strong, God chose what is low and despised in the world, even things that are not, to bring to nothing things that are" (1 Cor. 1:27–28).

But we still haven't mentioned the most important thing. We need community for mutual support, obviously, but most of all we need community for meaning. For while all human beings are wondrously different, we all have one fundamental purpose. We human beings are in part as we eat because we are part nature. We are in part as we think because the life of the mind is so important. But most of all we are as we love. As Scripture says, "We pass out of death into life, because we love the brothers and sisters" (1 John 3:14).

Descartes was wrong. *Cogito, ergo sum*—I think, therefore I am: that's off the target. *Amo, ergo sum*—I love, therefore I am, that's on target. And that's why we need community: to be who we are, to affirm life's meaning.

When I was sitting there—endlessly, it seemed—in the Bureau of Motor Vehicles, I tried not to do what most people do in the Bureau of Motor Vehicles, or in a subway car or a bus depot: withdraw and isolate themselves, or look at one another with hard eyes. I tried to look at everybody with soft eyes. I tried to picture how much each had suffered. I tried to be visionary in the manner of Jesus, and see the butterfly in every caterpillar, the eagle in every egg, the saint in every sinner. It was a good spiritual exercise. But I wondered if we couldn't be even bolder in what we attempt to see when we look at each other. Here's a story that Scott Peck uses to open his book on community building. He calls it "The Rabbi's Gift."

> The story concerns a monastery that had fallen upon hard times. Once a great order, as a result of waves of antimonastic persecution in the seventeenth and eighteenth centuries and the rise of secularism in the nineteenth, all its branch houses were lost and it had become decimated to the extent that there were only five monks left in the decaying mother house: the abbot and four others, all over seventy in age. Clearly it was a dying order.
>
> In the deep woods surrounding the monastery there was a little hut that a rabbi from a nearby town occasionally used for a hermitage. . . . It occurred to the abbot at one such time to visit the hermitage and ask the rabbi if by some possible chance he could offer any advice that might save the monastery.
>
> The rabbi welcomed the abbot at his hut. But when the abbot explained the purpose of his visit, the rabbi could only commiserate with him. "I know how it is," he exclaimed. "The spirit has gone out of people. . . . Almost no one comes to the synagogue any more." So the old abbot and the old rabbi wept together. Then they read parts of the Torah and quietly spoke of deep things. The time came when the abbot had to leave. They embraced each other. "It has been a wonderful thing that we should meet after all these years," the abbot said, "but I have still failed in my purpose for coming here. Is there nothing you can tell me, no piece of advice you can give me that would help me save my dying order?"
>
> "No, I am sorry," the rabbi responded. "I have no advice to give. The only thing I can tell you is that the Messiah is one of you." . . .
>
> In the days and weeks and months that followed, the old monks pondered this and wondered whether there was any possible significance to the rabbi's words. The Messiah is one of us? Could he possibly have meant one of us monks here at the monastery? If that's the case, which one? Do you suppose he meant the abbot? Yes, if he meant anyone, he probably meant

Father Abbot. He has been our leader for more than a generation. On the other hand, he might have meant Brother Thomas. Certainly Brother Thomas is a holy man. Everyone knows that Thomas is a man of light. Certainly he could not have meant Brother Elred! Elred gets crotchety at times. But come to think of it, even though he is a thorn in people's sides, when you look back on it, Elred is virtually always right. Often very right. Maybe the rabbi did mean Brother Elred. But surely not Brother Phillip. Phillip is so passive, a real nobody. But then, almost mysteriously, he has a gift for somehow always being there when you need him. He just magically appears by your side. Maybe Phillip is the Messiah. Of course the rabbi didn't mean me. He couldn't possibly have meant me. I'm just an ordinary person. Yet supposing he did? Suppose I am the Messiah? O God, not me. I couldn't be that much for You, could I?

As they contemplated in this manner, the old monks began to treat each other with extraordinary respect on the off chance that one of them might be the Messiah. And on the off, off chance that each monk himself might be the Messiah, they began to treat themselves with extraordinary respect.

Because the forest in which it was situated was beautiful, it so happened that people still occasionally came to visit the monastery to picnic on its tiny lawn, to wander along some of its paths, even now and then to go into the dilapidated chapel to meditate. As they did so, without even being conscious of it, they sensed this aura of extraordinary respect that now began to surround the five old monks and seemed to radiate out from them and permeate the atmosphere of the place. . . . They began to bring their friends to show them this special place. And their friends brought their friends.

Then it happened that some of the younger men who came to visit the monastery started to talk more and more with the old monks. After a while one asked if he could join them. Then another. And another. So within a few years the monastery had once again become a thriving order and, thanks to the rabbi's gift, a vibrant center of light and spirituality in the realm.

When family ties are strained and the nation is divided, when the whole human race stands at the brink of self-annihilation, this story is a good one for all of us to ponder.

Statement of Resignation to the Congregation

JULY 19, 1987
Readings: Isaiah 40:1–5, 9–11; Matthew 25:13–29

It was my heart's deep desire that you should hear first from me, dear Riversiders, of any change in our relationship. Alas, the press doesn't always honor such desires. That being the case in this instance, I have decided, in place of a sermon, to give you (in semisermonic form) some reasons for a decision I reached this week and, more importantly, to tell that wherever I am, I shall always love you.

How do any of us decide what to do with our lives? Obviously, in an ideal world, who we are should determine what we do. As philosophers say, "Being precedes doing." The trouble is that no matter at what stage of life we ask, "Who am I . . . really?" the answer has to be, "I'm not absolutely sure." In his forthcoming autobiography Arthur Miller writes, "I would be twenty before I learned how to be fifteen, thirty before I knew what it meant to be twenty, and now at seventy-two I have to stop myself from thinking like a man of fifty who has plenty of time ahead."

We all know what Miller is talking about. Chesterton was right: "The ego is more distant than any star." Aristotle was also right: "Life begins with wonder." Only he should have added, "and ends with wonder, too." In short, the minimum thing we can all say about our lives is that they never lose their mystery. For that, God be praised!

(I suppose we could add that most of us are not all we claim to be, and that none of us is what we were taught we are supposed to be— which may be merciful!)

If we go on to ask, as believers should, "What does God want me to do?" again we have to guard against absolute certainty. Christians who lionize Lieutenant Colonel Oliver North probably also view the Crusaders of the Middle Ages as the epitome of nobility. What they overlook is that to this day Arabs still curse them, as do Jews, so many of whom the Crusaders killed on their way to redeem Jerusalem. The lesson of history is clear: People never do evil so cheerfully as when they do it from religious conviction!

God is no idol, by which I mean that while idols tell us exactly what to believe and do, God presents us with choices we have to make ourselves. An idol has nothing but dependent children, but the children of God are simultaneously burdened and liberated by a call to participate in the decisions of an ongoing creation. I believe God calls each of us to be a co-creator, to help make the crooked straight and the rough places plain, to help exalt the valleys and not be deterred by high mountains. For what is an insuperable obstacle but a brilliant opportunity brilliantly disguised as an insuperable obstacle?

Just as the waves make toward the pebbled shore, so time ripples on. Change is as inevitable as death and taxes. Those who deny it, or, like Colonel North, resist all change not to their liking, are as the caterpillar who said, looking up at the butterfly, "You'll never find me flying around in one of those crazy things."

To obey the Creator is to live creatively: to invest, not bury our talents. And this creativity, like the parable Jesus spoke, has not primarily to do with money. Jesus is not urging us to pile up treasure that rusts, but rather to give ourselves to God and to one another and so to receive the reward of loving, which is to be able to love even more. In this sense it is true: "Unto him who hath shall more be given."

Christian life is love in search of form. And the search goes on—and on. "Though our outer nature is wasting away," says St. Paul, "our inner nature is being renewed each day" (2 Cor. 4:16). It is inconceivable that the saints and martyrs—and with his mother present among us today, let us include among the martyred Ben Linder, the young American killed in Nicaragua—it is inconceivable that all the saints and martyrs, and Christ himself, who ventured the Cross for the betterment of all, could ever bless a staid stagnation. Normalcy, to a good Christian, Jew, or Muslim, is a no-no. Normalcy is the name of the buried talent.

Obviously, then, to some degree the world we live in has to set the agenda for each of us. Recently I read what Luciana Castellina, a leader of the Italian peace movement, had to say about political parties: "In political parties the tendency is to think that what is rational already exists, so it becomes impossible to even conceive of a different world." I think that describes American as well as Italian parties.

The tragedy Castellina was getting at is that what exists is anything but rational. It is not rational that ghettos be crammed full of pain and misery—especially in this country, which should be big enough and strong enough to offer a fair break to everyone. It is not rational that since 1945, 20 million people have been killed in some 150 wars—that's more people than all the soldiers killed in World War II. It is not rational that for every soldier today the average world military expenditure is $20,000, while for every school-age child the average public education expenditure is $380. (I am giving you U.N. figures.) And it certainly is not rational that the shadow of Doomsday continues to darken every life on the planet.

By contrast, what *is* rational, and decent, and accords with my understanding of God's will, is for all of us to wage peace in the name of love and children. What is rational is to conceive of a different world; to offer every American a vision challenging far beyond what is currently being served up by either political party (not to mention inside arms controllers and most political candidates); to see, as did Walter Reuther in the 1930s and King in the 1950s and 1960s, common action as the way out of impossible conditions.

And that's what SANE/FREEZE, the two merging peace and social justice organizations—the oldest and the newest—want to do. They want to talk to Middle America, but in the name of a future America preferable to the predictable America. So when yesterday they asked me to be their primary spokesperson, their first president, I saw the invitation as representing for me a full-time peace and social justice ministry. I didn't see myself leaving the church, if only because I'm convinced that within a year we could double the present 180,000 membership out of the religious community alone.

So I accepted the invitation. At 9:30 this morning I submitted to the leadership of the church my resignation, effective December 31, 1987. That will give me lots of time to tell you how much I love you, how much the ten years mean to me during which I have been your senior minister.

It's not easy—in fact, it's heart-wrenching—to leave. While it is impossible to gauge the importance of one's own life in the lives of others, it is easy for me to measure the importance of your lives to mine. Still, like Abraham, one has to move on if one thinks that's what God wants one to do. And I know, and so do you, that the true shepherd, the one who "feeds the flock and gathers the lambs in his arms," is never a senior minister, only God.

Coming to Work on Sunday

SEPTEMBER 20, 1987
Reading: Luke 8:9–14

You won't believe this, but just before the service a couple of parishioners pleaded with me to include another Vermont story in my homecoming sermon, as they remembered I did last year. Well, I wasn't planning to, but if that's the expectation I'm happy to comply, provided it is understood that I tell stories only to illustrate profound truths. Humor should arise out of a situation, not be poured on top.

A Texan was driving in the back country of Vermont when he came upon an old farmer beside the road hoeing his land. Bringing his Mercedes to a halt, the Texan pressed the button to lower the window and stuck out his head. "Friend," he inquired of the farmer, "how much land do you own?" The farmer looked up. "Well," he said, "you see that ridge you're about to come to? Just let your eye follow the stream up the mountainside 'til you come to that stone wall. Then follow the stone wall over to that line of trees you just passed, and then down here to this road. That's my land." The Texan said, "Friend, what would you say if I were to tell you that I can get up before sunup and get in my car and start driving, and by sundown I haven't gotten around all my land?" The old farmer chuckled. "Yep, had a car like that myself once."

Come to think of it, that's not a bad story for yuppies and DINKs (double income, no kids) and SINKs (single income, no kids) who live in this adrenaline capital of the world—but of course it doesn't apply to Riverside, "where the women are strong and the men are good-looking and all the children are above average."

As the two parishioners recognized, today is Homecoming Sunday. Perhaps the idea of homecoming at the end of September is a bit obsolete and only persists because, as we all know, obsolete ideas never die, only those who have them, and rather slowly at that. Or maybe that's not quite a proper picture of the world. Maybe it's more accurate to say, with Abba Eban, "Human beings do the right and wise thing, but only after exhausting all alternatives."

That's why we're going to have a missile pact, thank God, which hopefully is a first step and not a sidestep in arms reduction. Never mind that the president is going to claim all the credit. It is part of the Divine Comedy of history that political parties take credit for championing ideas that they once did their best to stifle and then to betray.

So let us rejoice and be exceeding glad—bitterness is a diminishing emotion—and let us take fresh courage, because the future might change quite rapidly.

In any case, whether obsolete or not, "homecoming" properly designates a Sunday designed to remind us why we come to church, and why we do what we do when we come here.

I want to talk once again about the liturgy, which is Greek for "the work of the people" or "the work people do" (it once meant the work that they do anyplace; there was nothing sacred about it). What is it we do when we come to "work" on Sunday at Riverside Church?

When we enter, we see what people see in almost any Christian sanctuary: the lectern where the Word of God is read; across the way a pulpit, where the Word of God is "divided," to use the old Calvinist word for preaching; and centrally the altar, where the Word of God is sacrificed. It is the altar we all face. It is to the altar that the choir streams, as a river to its ocean home. The altar is central to Christian worship (worship meaning "worth-ship," the worthiness of God), because the altar tells us even more vividly than does the lectern, or certainly than the pulpit, that God not only created but so loved the world "that he gave his only begotten Son, that whosoever believeth in him should not perish, but have everlasting life."

If that's true, then Wesley was right: "O, for a thousand tongues to sing My dear Redeemer's praise." And Blake was right: "Exuberance is beauty"; "The road of excess leads to the palace of wisdom." For if only one-tenth of what Christians claim to believe is true, we ought to be ten times as exuberant as we are.

Were life indeed "but a tale told by an idiot, full of sound and fury, signifying nothing," then we could weep like a willow and mourn like a dove. But if creation has a Creator who will love us until the stars grow old and the sun grows cold, then what can we do but sing praise and thanksgiving, which is what the opening hymn is always about. Naturally, it's almost always in a major key, and appropriately this morning the opening hymn was in the key of D major, which Van Gogh characterized as an eleven-o'clock-in-the-morning color, as opposed, for example, to A major, which he characterized as a bright sunset color.

To sing praises to God is not to ignore how much of the world created by God is now controlled by sin. Nor is it to overlook the mystery of pain and death. But it does remind us of the mystery of unmerited good. I mean, what did you and I, who do wrong and compound it by the good we leave undone, ever do to deserve maple trees in the fall season?

Lord, I do fear
Thou'st made the world too beautiful this year.
Prithee, let no bird call,
Let no leaf fall.

What did you and I, who do not care for the destinies of others so much as we care for our own, ever do to deserve the beauty of music from Bach to the Beatles, to deserve the taste of food and drink, the smell of flowers, the very air we breathe—not to mention each other, neighbors with whom to walk and talk, love and laugh, and learn that in giving is receiving, and all is grace?

Even those of you who mourn, do you not mourn someone dear, whom God created just for you, just as those of you who are sick grieve the health that once, wonderfully, was yours? So even the shadow is finally the proof of the light.

So "bless the Lord, O my soul, and forget not all God's benefits." Forget not that even your highest, most satisfactory achievement, of which you have every right to be proud, stems from gifts—something for nothing. Gratitude is the most important and most profound of all religious emotions, and probably our primary purpose in coming to church is to unfetter that emotion, again and again.

But once you see the top of the mountain, you immediately become acutely aware of the floor of the valley on which you stand. It is a natural progression from a hymn of praise or thanksgiving to the prayer of corporate confession.

Whenever I watch TV evangelists, I am reminded that one of the great troubles of the world is that the stupid are cocksure, while the intelligent are full of doubt. But it's intelligent to have doubts; it's stupid not to. It is especially intelligent to have doubts about whether God is as pleased with you as you are with yourself. In fact, the world is made up of sinners who think they are saints, and saints who know they are sinners. Guilt is not always neurotic; far from it. Not to feel guilt at all is a failure of the imagination, and I hardly need remind you that it is precisely the failure to imagine that daily threatens to kill us all. In the Bronx Zoo is a sign, "This way to the most dangerous species." People approach expecting to see some fearsome wild beast, only to be surprised by a mirror.

I said earlier that the world created by God is now controlled by sin. The reason is simple. Robert McAfee Brown writes, "Christ is simply himself so fully that God can be seen through who he is and what he does." Sin, then, is not being fully the selves God made and meant us to be. Made and meant to love one another, we don't—not even in Riverside Church. Sin is praying today "Thy Kingdom come," and tomorrow barring its way. Sin is putting asunder what God himself has joined together. It is erecting barriers to the oneness to which God calls all his children, the world around: barriers like nuclear weapons, like economic systems based on greed, like privileges for the few based on self-concern.

Of course, the world has always been plagued by sin. But at least in the old days, in Europe, good Christians called the world evil and sought to leave it, or they called the world evil and sought to reform it. Today in America we have a Catholic Church largely without monastic orders and Protestantism largely without Reformation. Rarely do American Christians resist by confession, let alone confess by resistance.

So we come to church not only to unfetter our gratitude to God for all she has done for us, we come also to confess how much more we might have done for God and for each other had we only cared more. We come to church to sing praises to God, and to be as candid as possible about ourselves.

Gratitude opens the way for confession, and confession opens the way for even more gratitude. In the New Testament parable we just heard, what was wrong with the Pharisee, this pillar of the church, this ardent patriot respected in his community as a citizen of the highest character? In the first place, he was cocksure, and that's dumb. Second, he measured himself by the tax collector, forgetting that a mountain shames a molehill until both are measured by the stars. Most of all, what was wrong with him is that there was so little room in him for gratitude. Pride eliminates gratitude, while humility makes room for it.

Of course, there is that pride that apes humility. Nietzsche—keen, mean observer of Christians that he was—twisted the last line of the parable to read, "He who humbles himself wills to be exalted."

But let's assume that "Lord, be merciful to me, a sinner" is a sincere self-assessment and a sincere plea for forgiveness. Wonderful as that parable is, representing as it does a staggering assault on middle-class and religious respectability, what interests me most is what is not in it. Did the tax collector accept the forgiveness that Jesus assures us God offered him? He was humble, but did he have enough humility to give up his own opinion of himself and accept God's? For guilt is the last stronghold of pride; guilt represents my opinion of myself, while forgiveness represents yours, and God's: Do I have the humility to allow someone else to do for me what I cannot do for myself? (Sometimes it's more blessed to receive than to give; at least it takes more humility.)

And did the tax collector realize that to accept forgiveness meant a radical transformation of his life? Forgiveness is much harder than punishment, because forgiveness demands a new way of life, while punishment, by assuaging a bit the guilt, makes the old way of life bearable anew. Could the man, forgiven, have gone on collecting Roman taxes in a day when his fellow Israelites dreamed constantly of their freedom?

To me, the most awesome part of the liturgy comes between the prayer of confession and the assurance of pardon—if you know all that God's pardon entails. Let's be a bit Hegelian. In the opening hymn of praise we have a thesis: creation has a Creator whose steadfast love for us is as great as the heavens are high above the earth. In the general confession, we have an antithesis: the beauty of God's world is disfigured by sin. All of us have sinned and fallen short. The assurance of pardon, then, represents the synthesis we all need in order to go on. But it demands that Christians, in accepting the forgiveness that is always there, be more like Christ, who "is simply himself so fully that God can be seen through who he is and what he does."

Are you ready for the synthesis, the assurance of pardon?

I told you liturgy meant the work of the people. And it's hard work—but of the most rewarding kind. Wouldn't you say?

The Stages of Spiritual Development

SEPTEMBER 27, 1987
Reading: 2 Corinthians 4:7–18

I want to wrestle further with the question posed last week—Why come to church?—because I am convinced people come not only with differing motives but for motives that are totally opposite. Christian psychiatrist M. Scott Peck, author of *The Road Less Traveled, Children of the Lie,* and other books, insists that to grasp religious pluralism you must understand the degree to which people find themselves in different stages of spiritual development. He differentiates four such stages.

In stage one everything is chaotic. People are antisocial; they don't give a darn about anyone else. A lot of criminals are found in stage one.

Then, dramatically, they may get religion. And the religion to which they are converted may be rigid, for that is exactly what they are looking for—order, a God who is a kind of benevolent cop-in-the-sky. In stage two, people are apt to behave as model prisoners in very authoritarian churches; because it is not so much the essence as the form of the religion that has saved them from chaos, they don't take lightly people who seem to be fooling around with the rules. A lot of fundamentalists are found in stage two.

In stage three, doubt is recognized as important. Skepticism is affirmed. The bumper sticker "Question authority" refers not only to the government but also to the churches, which are often perceived by folk in stage three as having all the answers because they deny all the questions. People in stage three are frequently nonbelievers—but spiritually, Peck insists, they are more developed than those content to remain in stage two. Although more individualistic, they are not antisocial. A lot of academics are in stage three.

But then some of these stage three people begin to get restless. They sense there must be something more. They don't want to sacrifice intellect, but they do want to oppose its presumptions. They want to feel as well as think, intuit as well as reason, imagine, not just know. They want to laugh more, cry more, bleed, and especially dare to dream. They continue to mock the Knight of La Mancha, dear Don Quixote, but at the same time they realize that "there is no disaster so great as when the spirit is denied its journey—when the Knight loses his horse, spear and cause—for when that happens a terrible meaninglessness invades life."

Such people are ready for stage four, for a God who mysteriously infuses life with purpose and beauty. They are ready for a mystical experience of God, which is generally accompanied by a deeply communal view of the world. Believing that God provides maximum support but minimum protection, they have an awesome sense of human freedom and of the personal responsibility it entails. They pray, "O God, grant not that I be sheltered from dangers but fearless in facing them; I pray not for the stilling of my pain but for a heart to bear it. Grant me the blessings of success, but even more let me find the grasp of your hand in my failures."

In stage four are a lot of Riversiders—or so I'd like to think. They take seriously our text for today from St. Paul, "Though our outer nature is wasting away, our inner nature is being renewed every day." They know that life is a journey that starts in the physical world and continues in the spiritual world, where the journey is one of becoming more and more the selves God intends us to be. It is a journey for which God daily gives us what Ezekiel calls "a new spirit and a heart of flesh," a journey that only death finally grants permission to end. And who knows how it may continue thereafter? For death is only a horizon, and a horizon is nothing save the limit of our sight.

Yesterday, amid much weeping and mourning, we laid to rest the body of Clarence Lorick, Vicki and Ben Lorick's dear father. As we gathered around the grave amid all the tears, I remembered the words of that early English king who on his deathbed said, "Weep not, for I shall not die, and as I leave the land of the dying, I trust to see the blessings of the Lord in the land of the living."

Everything in life seems to be journeying on, starting with the earth itself. I love to read books by paleontologists, the folk who fuss with fossils—fossils which tell us that long before vegetable and animal life appeared, before the waters started to dream of fish and fish of human beings, the earth had been evolving for millions of years. I can still remember the day in the fifth grade when Mr. Hale told us wide-eyed kids that the length of human history compared to the life of the earth was as a nickel on the top of the Empire State Building. I think that was the first time that my life was put, as they say, "in perspective."

But human history itself is also a journey. Cro-Magnon and Pilt-down man, whose jaw muscles relaxed just in time to allow their eyes to widen and so to zero in on the objects their hands brought before them, produced all those nomads following the seasons to the ends of the earth, unimaginable hardships notwithstanding. Those were times when a capacity to journey was as vital to people as the air they breathed and the food they ate. And I remember learning in high school how whole races of indigenous people perished because foreign civilizations deprived them of their freedom of movement: Native Americans, for example, and Australian aborigines, whose "walka-bouts" were abruptly restricted by the impositions of civilization.

Human history can come to a very abrupt end. Our physical survival, as never before, depends on our spirits' capacity to continue the journey, to discover a whole new world greater than that discovered by Colum-bus or any other sailor of the seven seas. "No more shall be heard in it the sound of weeping, and the cry of distress. No more shall there be in it an infant that lives but a few days, or an old man who does not fill out his days" (Isa. 65:19–20). The prophets always saw that new world.

We talk of a world free of nuclear weapons, but we're talking here of one free of violence and hatred, fear and suspicion. "And it shall come to pass in the latter days . . ." The prophets were always taking a dim view of the present only because they held such a bright view of the future.

I hope that's why Riversiders come to church. Of course we come for comfort in sorrow, for reassurance in all our anxieties. But most of all I hope we come to realize all the unrealized being in ourselves, to ask God and each other's help to divest our minds and spirits of the vested interests that hem us in, that prevent our moving together on behalf of a more fully just and decent and lovely world.

I hope we come to church because, as we earlier confessed, we have allowed the present age to mold us and left untapped the power of the age to come.

I hope we come to church because, as we have just sung, "Jesus calls us from the worship of the vain world's golden store." Years ago an old white hunter in Africa said, "The difference between the white man and the black man in Africa is that the white man 'has' and the black man 'is.'" Possession is no substitute for being, and on the spiritual journey to which Jesus calls us, it is easier, like the disciples, to travel light.

In stage four, Christians are a pilgrim people who have decided never to arrive. It's an exhausting thought, yet one true to life where change is as insistent as sin and taxes. And it is true to our faith, for ours is a God who declares, "Behold, I create a new heaven and a new earth." Ours is a God of history—a history characterized by an Exodus; one that proclaims a New Testament, that describes a New Jerusalem, anticipates a new song and new wine, and promises that we shall become new beings. "If anyone is in Christ, she is a new creature; the old has passed away, behold, the new has come" (2 Cor. 5:17).

You've heard me say many a time, "God is ahead of us as much as above and within us." God gives us the "growth choice" as opposed to the "fear choice," to use Maslow's terms; God gives us a present with a future, and a future right up to the end of our days, "for though our outer nature is wasting away, our inner nature is being renewed each day."

There is a predictable world. Toward the end of Shaw's *Caesar and Cleopatra* Caesar says, "And so to the end of history murder shall breed murder, always in the name of right and honor and peace, until the gods are tired of blood and create a race that can understand."

And in contrast to the predictable world, there is a preferable world. It can be created by people in stage four of their spiritual development, who understand, as did Karl Barth, "To clasp hands in prayer is the beginning of an uprising against the disorder of the world."

I hope we come to church to clasp hands in prayer to God, and to clasp hands with one another, that we may continue our spirits' journey, this pilgrim life of ours, moving together on behalf of a more fully just and decent and lovely world.

It's tough. Imagination comes harder than memory, and faithfulness is more demanding than success. But it is possible. "For though our outer nature is wasting away, our inner nature is being renewed every day. . . . We look not to the things that are seen but to the things that are unseen; for the things that are seen are transient, but the things that are unseen are eternal."

The Wrong Look in Our Eyes

OCTOBER 4, 1987
Reading: Mark 10:17–22

If, after hearing the story of the rich young ruler, some of you are expecting a sermon on the evils of wealth (said the German playwright Bertolt Brecht, "What's robbing a bank compared to owning one?"), or if you thought you were going to hear a sermon on the need to be generous (said the German layman Baron von Hugel, with his dying breath, "Caring is the greatest thing, caring matters most"), in either case you're going to be disappointed—or pleased, as the case may be. True, in a week or two, as our annual canvass gets underway, I want to tell you that while making money can be fun, and spending it even more so, there is nothing like the joy of giving money away! But today I selected the New Testament lesson, the story in the tenth chapter of Mark, only because of a lovely line, which seemed appropriate for a Worldwide Communion Sunday sermon: "And Jesus, looking upon him, loved him."

I find it touching the way Jesus' heart warms instantly to this stranger—obviously a hundred times richer than he as the world measures riches. And I'm impressed that Jesus' love prompts him, without further ado, to lay upon this stranger a heavy burden: "You lack one thing; go, sell what you have and give to the poor, and you will have treasure in heaven; and come, follow me."

Jesus never withholds the telling blow if only the telling blow will serve. Never does he sacrifice friends for the sake of their friendship for him. Rather, he risks his friendship for the sake of his friends. He probably knew the man would requite his love with rejection of his advice. Nevertheless, "Jesus, looking upon him, loved him."

Let me tell you another story. Shortly after World War II the Dutch leaders in Java realized that their empire, the third largest in the world, was tumbling down about them. The Indonesians really wanted them out of their lovely emerald islands. Said the Governor General to Laurens van der Post, "I cannot understand it. Look what we have done for them. Look at the schools and hospitals we have given them. A hundred years ago the population was only a few millions, today it is nearly 60 millions. We have done away with malaria, plague and dysentery and given them a prosperous, balanced economy. Everyone has enough to eat. We have given them honest and efficient administration and abolished civil war and piracy. Look at the roads, the railways, the industries—and yet they want us to go. Can you tell me why they want us to go?"

Answered van der Post: "I am afraid it is because when you spoke to them you never had the right look in your eye."

When Jesus looked at that rich young ruler, or at the woman caught in adultery, or the Canaanite woman, or any one of the many children that were brought to him to bless, his eyes shone not only with love but with respect, as for equals. Jesus never looked down on anyone. But because in the eyes of so many of their European colonizers Asians and Africans represented, in Kipling's words, "lesser breeds without the Law," these empire builders of earlier centuries after World War II were blown out of one country after another— Asia, Africa, and the Middle East. God is not mocked!

And today it is our turn. Because we Americans have the wrong look in our eyes, and speak of Central America as our backyard, anti-American winds are gusting all over Latin America: "Yanqui go home!" The basic message of Sandinismo is, "We're not taking orders any longer from the U.S. ambassador." And because our Yankee pride can't stand it, we attack them and then blame them for being aggressive. Once again, in the metaphor of a former president of Guatemala, "The North American shark is feeding on the sardines of Latin America." Rarely do leaders and citizens of superpowers put themselves out to understand people of smaller nations. They think they can afford to be provincial.

"What do you call a person who speaks three languages?"
"Trilingual."

"What do you call a person who speaks two languages?"
"Bilingual."

"What do you call a person who speaks one language?"
"An American."

Yesterday was Yom Kippur, the holiest of holidays for Jews, their day of confession. Let Christians on Worldwide Communion Sunday be no less contrite. Is our country really a melting pot, or only a pressure cooker? Is New York Fun City, or more nearly Nineveh as described by the prophet Nahum, "a bloody city, full of lies and booty—no end to the plunder"?

What look in the eye have whites in New York City when they look at blacks? And blacks at Latinos, and black and white gentiles at Jews, and all of them at those overachieving Asians outscrambling everybody else?

St. Paul writes, "In Christ there is neither Greek nor Jew, neither slave nor free, neither male nor female" (Gal. 3:28), and we can add "neither gay nor straight, black nor white, yellow nor red, rich nor poor," because, as St. Paul concludes, "You are all one in Christ Jesus." To look down on anyone is to have the wrong look in the eye. If you can't treat others as equals, don't bleat fatuously about your love for them. To look down on anyone is downright unchristian.

So too is looking back. Said Jesus, "No one who puts his hand to the plow and looks back is fit for the kingdom of heaven" (Luke 9:62). Few things in this world are more unproductive than nostalgia—or, for that matter, more deceptive. To long for the good old days is to engage in selective amnesia, for the old days weren't that good, certainly not for a lot of people other than ourselves. I suspect that when older people look back on the springtime of their lives and sigh, "Ah, those were the days," what they are missing are not days but selves that were better— more generous, more caring, more alive.

In any case, however old we are, God wants us looking ahead, not back. Worldwide Communion Sunday calls us to labor on, as, in the stifling August heat, did the fifty-eight members of the Constitutional Convention two hundred years ago; but our task is to form a more perfect union *of the world*, to establish justice and to promote the general welfare of *everybody*. Our job is to planetize humanity, for we are all one on this planet. That's the way God made us; Christ died to keep us that way. Our sin is only that we are constantly putting asunder what God has joined together.

So enough of senseless strife and ruinous wars. Enough of thinking, "The future will have to be faced, but it isn't upon me yet." Said the manager of the Toronto Blue Jays after the team lost to the Tigers and had one game left: "There ain't many tomorrows left, are there?" There are even fewer for all of us. If we do not look ahead right now, our children will pay an awesome price for our backward looks.

We cannot look down on one another: "In Christ there is no East or West, there is no South or North." We cannot look backward: Jesus said, "Let the dead bury the dead," by which he meant, "and not the living."

Where then can we look? Obviously, up. Up, as did Jesus as he blessed the loaves and the fishes; up, as did Jesus before healing the lame, the halt, and the blind; up, as did Jesus before giving his disciples the cup, saying, "Drink of it, all of you, for this is my blood of the covenant, poured out for many for the forgiveness of sins." If, with Christ's disciples, we stand at the foot of the cross and look up, and realize as did they that we too are Christ's enemies, yet he forgives us, we can love our enemies. If we look up to God, to Jesus on the cross, God's heart laid bare for all to see, we can no longer look at anyone with the wrong look in our eyes. For just as Jesus drove the money changers out of the temple, so in our hearts, the true temple of God, God's love will drive out fear and prejudice, egotism and hatred. Having looked up to God and to Christ on the cross, we shall look at one another, and at all God's beloved children, as did Jesus the rich young ruler: "And Jesus, looking upon him, loved him."

"And God Remembered Noah"

OCTOBER 11, 1987
Readings: Genesis 6:5–8:12 (selected verses); 1 Peter 5:6–11

Never mind for the moment the New Testament lesson; let's stick with the story of Noah (so beautifully acted out by our Sunday School kids). Because legends of an early universal flood are as legion as they are seemingly physically impossible, we must conclude that the story of Noah is mostly myth. But as we all know by now, while not literally true, a myth may be eternally true. In fact, the myth of Noah is a parable of a terrible reality. The story of God and Noah, of God and Noah's neighbors, and that zoo of gorgeous and something-less-than-gorgeous animals and birds reflects both the cruel darkness and the magnificent light that seem eternally to be at the heart of divine-human encounters.

What would you have done, had you been God, and were being bugged continually by Gabriel, who just couldn't wait to blow the trumpet of final judgment? Remember:

All things bright and beautiful,
All things both great and small,
All things wise and wonderful,
[You had] made them all.

Not only had you created them, you had sustained them as well. Everywhere on earth your presence was a beneficent one. You had made an incredibly pluralistic, multicolored creation, including human beings with spirits as free, flowing, and smiling as mountain brooks. But now these free spirits had become mean-spirited. Of the original brothers, one had died at the hand of the other. While Enoch had "walked with God," his son had exhibited so little imagination that his whole long life could be summed up in a single sentence: "All the days of Methuselah were nine hundred and sixty-nine years; and he died."

It had been your intention that all should live as one big happy family, but few wanted to identify with more than one small fraction of it. As a result the world was filled with violence. The physical violence was now grosser than Cain's, for it was committed without Cain's remorse, while the psychological violence was getting mighty subtle—as when a man would do anything to please his wife, but didn't have the nerve to please himself, so she couldn't stop thinking that he was thinking something she couldn't understand.

Faced with this situation, what would you have done, had you been God?

Had the choice been mine, I think I would have engaged in what psychiatrists call "premature closure." I'd have told Gabriel, "Go ahead, blow your horn. I'm sick of this miscellaneous irresponsibility, this general rowdiness, this downright wickedness and willful ignorance. I'm bringing down the curtain on the whole show."

But that's me speaking, not God. Because in Genesis we read, "But Noah found favor in the eyes of the Lord." God always finds exceptions to our angry little human rules. There's always a Noah, a Moses, a Mary, a Martin, or a Sojourner, and so many others whose names we shall never know. Had there been ten righteous people, Sodom would have been saved; and Jews to this day believe that as long as there are thirty-six righteous people alive somewhere, the world will be saved.

"Noah found favor in the eyes of the Lord. . . . Noah was a righteous man, blameless in his generation." No doubt he made faith in God not only his religion but also his business. No doubt he sought to be faithful rather than successful. Instead of worrying, no doubt he cast all his anxieties on God, knowing how God cared for him.

How Noah contrasts with his neighbors, of whom Jesus said, "In those days before the flood they were eating and drinking, marrying and giving in marriage, until the day Noah entered the ark, *and they did not know until the flood came*" (Matt. 24:38–39a).

Can't you hear those neighbors: "Noah, look at the sky. The weather's promising!"

Said Jesus, "You know how to interpret the appearance of the sky, but you cannot interpret the signs of the times" (Matt. 16:3). In other words, "You know all about the way the wind is blowing in your little world, but you are totally oblivious to the mighty gale about to smash that little world to bits."

Why is it in human history that a crisis is never a crisis until it is validated by disaster?

"But Noah found favor in the eyes of the Lord." He didn't care about the big parade; he marched to a different drum. So he built the ark, collected the animals, two by two, and shut the door of the ark—and the rain began to fall.

Imagine what it must have been like inside the ark for the next five months. Outside, nothing but curtains of pitiless rain, gray days and black nights, empty waters, and a sky devoid of sun and moon and stars and hope.

And inside—well, an eighteenth-century British bishop once compared the church to Noah's ark, for, as he said, only the storm without could make bearable the stench within.

What impresses me even more is the thought of Noah making the daily rounds, reassuring the animals; like St. Francis putting his hand on their creased foreheads, reteaching each its loveliness, promising all that their freedom of movement, as vital to them as food and drink, would one day be restored. And we read, "God remembered Noah and all the beasts and all the cattle that were with him in the ark. And God made a wind blow over the earth, and the waters subsided; the fountains of the deep and the windows of the heavens were closed, the rain from the heavens was restrained, and the waters receded from the earth continually."

It wasn't until the tenth month that the tops of the mountains could be seen. On her second flight out, the dove returned holding in her mouth a freshly plucked olive leaf. That leaf stood for all things on earth, even for things that do not put forth leaves. That leaf vindicated Noah's trust in God. It was an olive leaf of peace, a laurel leaf of victory. And to top it all, a rainbow in the clouds signified God's promise that "the waters shall never again become a flood to destroy all flesh."

I love that rainbow. And as Noah didn't make it, but God hung it there, it signifies that all our hope is founded on God. When Noah saw that rainbow, he must not have known on what foot to dance!

God will never again destroy the earth. We know for sure the birds and the animals won't, which leaves only us. We certainly don't have God's authority to do so, but we do have the power. And we probably shall destroy the earth, most likely by accident, because we still haven't learned that retribution for revolt against God is built into the system. God doesn't have to send the rain; we human beings can bring on ourselves a flood of blood and tears. Sometimes the deluge continues not for five months but on through dragging decades, as we have seen in this cruelest of centuries. We shall probably destroy the earth because while we make peace our goal, we don't make it our business.

I want to end on what might best be called a sobering thought. When it was all over, and Noah became the first tiller of the fresh soil, he got drunk. He got drunk not to celebrate the end of a long and successful voyage, nor to escape its painful memories. He got drunk to escape not the past, but the future, the responsibilities of rebuilding life, this time a more just and peaceful one.

Today is no time to be drunk with the pride of power, or with the foolish optimism of Noah's neighbors, or with the sweet wine of self-pity. Now is the time to remember Noah as he was before the flood, and time for the words found in the New Testament lesson in the fifth chapter of first Peter:

"Humble yourselves therefore under the mighty hand of God, that in due time God may exalt you. Cast all your anxieties on God, for God cares about you. Be sober, be watchful. Your adversary the devil prowls around like a roaring lion, seeking some one to devour. Resist him, firm in your faith, knowing that the same experience of suffering is required of your sisters and brothers throughout the world. And after you have suffered a little while, the God of all grace, who has called you to his eternal glory in Christ, will himself restore, establish, and strengthen you. To God be the dominion for ever and ever. Amen."

A Famine of Truth

OCTOBER 18, 1987
Reading: Galatians 5:1–6

For freedom Christ has set us free; stand fast therefore and do not submit again to a yoke of slavery."

Ringing words, those, but what do they mean? Who's free, and according to whose definition of slavery?

Last Thursday, on my way to visiting a parishioner in a New Jersey hospital, I came up behind a pickup truck on the George Washington Bridge. Its bumper sticker read: GOD, GUNS, AND GUTS.

"Doesn't sound like a free spirit," I mused to myself. "I'll bet he's white, and I'll bet he's male." Half-hoping to see my stereotypes confounded by a black woman driver, I passed the truck. No such luck. He was white, thick-necked, and low-browed, and by his expression I would guess had not dedicated his life to making the world safe for its differences.

God, guns, and guts. I was reminded of another sticker popular in the days of the Victnam War: AMERICA—LOVE IT OR LEAVE IT. Which really meant, "America—obey it or leave it," or, more accurately yet, "America—obey it or it will leave you, bereft of the support all citizens naturally want from their country."

Later, on Route 4 in New Jersey, I came up behind an old Volvo. You could hardly see it for all the stickers, not only on the bumper, but all over the back, this time of the other kind:

QUESTION AUTHORITY

ARMS ARE FOR HUGGING

SPLIT WOOD, NOT ATOMS

ONE NUCLEAR BOMB CAN RUIN YOUR WHOLE DAY

Do you think this driver was freer? Demonstrably more imaginative, but less hostile, more loving? I'm not sure, for in my experience the political left loves humanity at large but not necessarily the nearest neighbor; whereas conservatives are pretty good with the folks next door, their problem being that they think society is but a figment of the socialist imagination.

So who's free, according to whose definition of slavery?

In the Gospel of John Jesus says, "And you shall know the truth and the truth shall set you free" (John 8:32). The implication is clear: if you can't face the truth—any kind of truth—you can't be free.

Writing in October's *Atlantic Monthly*, President Nixon's Secretary of Commerce, Peter Peterson, describes and derides what he calls "an enduring, bipartisan principle of American political life which in the 1980s has become gospel: never admit the possibility of unpleasantness—especially when it appears inevitable."

The unpleasant truth Mr. Peterson finds Americans unwilling to face is that in a few short years we have transformed ourselves from the world's largest creditor into the world's largest debtor; that supply-side economics means "foreigners supply most of the goods and all of the money"; that middle- and upper-class greed has become so colossal that while "in every previous decade we consumed slightly less than 90 percent of our increase in production, since the beginning of the 1980s we have consumed 325 percent of it."

According to Mr. Peterson, "We're standing tall on bended knees."

Like Felix Rohaytan a few months ago, Mr. Peterson is sure we're going to get our economic comeuppance. But who's listening? The American people don't want to hear; they're still at the movies, drinking beer and singing, "Who says you can't have it all?"

Twenty-seven hundred years ago the prophet Amos spoke truth both to power and to the people. The crafty priest Amaziah, recognizing that prophecy can exacerbate as much as illuminate a situation, correctly analyzed the result: "The land is not able to bear all his words" (Amos 7:10b). Amaziah knew there was a certain unacceptability about unpleasant truth, and that if the liberating truth were unpleasant—which it almost always is—most people would rather choose the yoke of deception.

Back to the present, and New York City, where Professor Marilyn Young teaches New York University students a course on the war in Vietnam. Her students, she says, know only the horrors American veterans had to endure, most of which they've learned through the movies. These movies, says Professor Young, show the how of the war but carefully avoid the why. In fact, they recall the war in such fashion as to allow us to forget it.

And now to stonewall the truth still further comes the television series *Tour of Duty*. In it, of course, the platoon is beautifully integrated (into a burning house, as James Baldwin would say): black, white, hillbilly, intellectual, even an antiwar GI. In the heat of battle this soldier stabs and kills a Vietnamese officer. Full of remorse, he cries out, "I killed a man!"

Sergeant: No, you saved our lives.

Antiwar GI: But this war is wrong.

Sergeant: Maybe, but that's not the point.

"And you shall know the truth and the truth shall set you free."

"The land is not able to bear all his words." But the land must hear the prophet's words, for if there's any way to the better, it lies in taking a full look at the worst. Without despair, there is no hope, no repentance, no forgiveness, no judgment, no salvation. There is no other way.

All this is no less true of our church life, where time and again we have to admit we are neither blameless nor helpless. "All have sinned and fallen short," says St. Paul, which is why we have to confess both to God and to one another, because if we cannot confess to one another, we're kidding ourselves that we're really confessing to God.

What do we have to confess at Riverside? A racism that persists, as do homophobia and sexism; and classism, for class is an even tougher nut to crack than race. It's understandable; we bring all these things into the church from outside. It's understandable, but it's still inexcusable. Some of us have also to confess the way we compensate for failures outside the church by seizing and holding turf within it, thereby making church life more competitive than loving.

I said, "Neither blameless *nor helpless*." We can be free. Truth seen and spoken is liberating. It's healing: "Sunshine is the best disinfectant."

Truth is "error burnt up," as Norman Brown once reminded us. Truth is only possible after our make-believe world is in ashes. Truth can reign in our national, church, and personal lives only after the power of the Holy Spirit has overturned our beloved self-protecting lies, has rejected the secret flatterings of self-importance, has pulled the rug from under ambition's tower of blocks.

I dwell on this because there is a famine of truth in the land. Few are those ready to face the truth of our consumption, never more conspicuous; the truth about our homeless, our poor, and especially our poor children; the truth about this nation's bullying behavior in Central America and now in the Persian Gulf, where we seem intent only on stirring things up and then doing everything to save our mythical faces instead of our very real soul. Only where truth is actively sought, known, proclaimed, and *abided by*, only there is freedom found. So let the truth make us free, remembering, "For freedom Christ has set us free."

Actually, Paul's meaning here is slightly different. The yoke of slavery he refers to is the religious law from which the spirit of Christ has set us free. But, like the Israelites under Moses, some of us waver and long for the easier life of a slave, where some external authority tells us what is right and wrong. It's not that the law is wrong, only limited. Religious law is like the stick on which a tomato vine grows. Without the stick and without the law, neither vine nor humans would get off the ground. But just as there's nothing in the stick that gives life to the tomato vine, which receives its life from a combination of sun and soil, so there's nothing in the law that gives us life, which comes from a combination of God and community, from the Holy Spirit emanating from God and moving among us.

"For freedom Christ has set us free" really means, "For love Christ has set us free": free from the letter that killeth, free for the Spirit that giveth life, free from slavery to self, freedom for others, freedom from fantasy, freedom for the truth—for error derives not so much from the mind as from impurities of the heart.

Friends, we have designated this Laity Sunday to install new officers and to salute gratefully the work of so many devoted members of Riverside Church. But I want to remind all officers and parishioners that their most important work lies outside this church. "For God so loved"—not Riverside nor any other church—"God so loved *the world* that he gave his only begotten son that whosoever should believe in him should not perish but have eternal life." We are here for those who suffer as we, *and far more*. We are here for those not here. We are a servant church, serving the world by proclaiming, wherever we are, the liberating truth, by demonstrating in all manner of ways the love of God which alone can overcome the enemies of God. For if there is one thing we have learned, it is that while it is difficult to overcome evil with good, it is even harder—nay, impossible—to overcome evil with evil.

Not all of us need bumper stickers to tell others what we think (and what we think of them), but all Christians need Jesus to keep us thinking, loving, and free. "For freedom Christ has set us free; stand fast therefore and do not submit again to the yoke" of deception, of hatred, "of slavery."

The paradox is real and true: God's service alone is perfect freedom.

Finding Something Worth Doing

NOVEMBER 8, 1987
Readings: Psalms 33:13–22; Matthew 8:14–17

In the Moffatt translation of the New Testament, the opening sentence of today's Scripture lesson reads, "On entering the house of Peter, Jesus noticed that his mother-in-law was down with fever."

"On entering the house"—immediately, at once—"Jesus noticed . . ." Very little passed Jesus unobserved. In the milling crowd, he sensed that somebody had touched his robe; when he stood before Pilate—his great moment of truth before the most powerful figure in the land—he intuited that there was no point in answering a single word to Pilate's question, "What is truth?" Jesus sensed, picked up on, intuited, noticed, more than anyone else. But his eyes didn't only take in; they took things apart and put them back together in a wonderful new way. No sooner had Jesus noticed that the woman was sick than "he touched her hand, and the fever left her." And so it went that day, on into the night: "That evening they brought to him many who were possessed with demons; and he cast out the spirits with a word, and healed all who were sick."

It's one of those short episodes that packs quite a message. To me, it says that my job in this world is less to make something of myself than to find something worth doing and lose myself in it. But in this competitive society, we are not daily encouraged to make a gift of ourselves. Harry Emerson Fosdick used to quote a character description from a novel contemporary to his time: "Edith was a small country bounded on the north, south, east, and west by Edith." Robert McCracken, Fosdick's successor, loved the ad in the Midwestern paper that read, "I am 58 years old. Would like to marry a woman of 30 who has a tractor. Please send a picture of the tractor." These days, I like Woody Allen: "If only God would give me some clear sign! Like making a large deposit in my name at a Swiss bank."

From reading of the death of little Elizabeth Steinberg, and all the other stories of abused children, we know that in this city, state, and country a lot of people lead vicious lives. But no one will argue that the vicious ones outnumber the trivial ones, nor that loss of perspective—which is what a trivial life represents—does not stem from loss of conscience. The details may be blurred, but the outline is clear, of what's wrong with our country. Shallow morality has wed deep materialism. "The true voodoo economic principle," says Professor Larry Rasmussen of Union Theological Seminary, "is that private vice makes public virtue, and that the public domain exists for the enhancement of the private." In New York City we daily witness the decay of everything not connected with profit-making.

Our business in life is less to make something of ourselves than to find something worth doing and lose ourselves in it. "On entering the house of Peter, Jesus noticed that his mother-in-law was down with fever. And he touched her hand, and the fever left her."

There are three things that seem to me to need eyes as observant as those of Jesus and hands altogether as tender and healing.

The first is the whole globe. In Fosdick's and McCracken's day, we worried that one part of the globe couldn't protect itself from another part. Today, it's the whole that can't protect itself from the parts. In World War II the nations at war targeted one another; today, the whole world lives on the target of World War III. We live in the shadow of an active volcano—all of us. "The war horse is a vain hope for victory and by its great might it cannot save." The psalmists and prophets were always right, but today they are right with a new urgency, for humanity has outlived war but doesn't know it yet. Our task, then, particularly in the Christian community, is to create a warless world—and if that sounds utopian, that may simply reflect how far we have slipped in the schedule we should have kept, had we been serious about saving the planet.

It's good that the military parade yesterday in Red Square celebrating the 70th anniversary of the Soviet Revolution was toned down. It's good that the INF treaty soon will be signed and hopefully ratified by the Senate. But our job is to make sure it is quickly followed by deep cuts in both nuclear and conventional weapons, and by sharp reductions in the pain and misery of urban and rural ghettos at home and abroad. It can never be said enough: disarmament is for development.

I look to the religious community to persuade open-minded Americans that the Cold War, always bad for warm hearts, is dangerous, expensive, and today obsolete. I look to the religious community in America to persuade Americans that we have sold our birthright of freedom and justice for a mess of national security. National security—which says, "I can only preserve the security of my country by threatening the security of yours"—must give way to something a little more in tune with the religious vision: common security, which insists no one is safe unless all are safe.

And I look to the business community to tell it like it is, to state the central emerging reality of our time, that geoeconomics is replacing geopolitics. We have only to look at Japan, which since the end of World War II has never tested a bomb, never even bared a bayonet, to realize that economic and not military might is what determines a nation's power and influence.

It's pathetic that Americans feel they are standing tall occupying Grenada when the whole world knows we were too scared to take on Cuba. It's pathetic for us to think it was courageous to bomb Libya when the whole world knows Syria was much more responsible for the terrorism we said we were avenging. Needless to say, this macho pride in national strength stems from profound self-doubt, reflecting a shallow faith in God Almighty.

I look to the religious and business communities to be a defining force in the debates taking place. I look to Washington only to ratify what it can no longer resist.

"On entering the house of Peter, Jesus noticed that his mother-in-law was down with fever. And he touched her hand, and the fever left her." Let's be imaginative. "On entering the world of 1987, Jesus noticed that it had achieved more brilliance than wisdom, more power than conscience, that it knew less about living than it did about killing. And he touched the hands of all who made and applauded weapons, and the war fever left them."

We say we have to begin at home; not so. We have simultaneously to act locally and globally—if we care for our children. Because we are all living in the shadow of an active volcano, international relations needs daily eyes as watchful as those of Jesus and hands as tender and healing.

And so also do race relations. As I wind up my ten-year ministry among you, I confess that I feel that I personally have not done enough about race relations, neither in the church nor, particularly, in the city. I'm pleased with what we have accomplished in the disarmament field; I'm glad we became a sanctuary church. I'm proud that we struck a blow against homophobia, that we pulled out of Citibank and divested, that we took three busloads of Riversiders to be arrested in Washington in protest against apartheid. But I wish I personally had recognized that, in New York City, while color is only skin deep, racism cuts to the bone. I would not have thought, ten years ago, that we could witness as racially divided a vote as we saw in Philadelphia this week. Ten years ago I would not have guessed that in Howard Beach people would be trying to blame the man driving the car for the death of the black who had been chased out in the street by clubs. Life in New York City so often appears like the Hudson River, sparkling clearly in the sun, while beneath the surface lurks the muck. And sinful, prejudicial muck it is when 55 percent of black children in New York City live below the poverty line, and 75 percent of black children don't finish high school, especially when five out of six jobs in this city demand a high-school degree.

It's going to be a long, hard fight to end racism, compounded as it is by class. And "fight" is a word I use advisedly when I'm talking about tenderness and healing, for while there are conflicts that can be reconciled, there are others that cannot be appeased without taking sides. Not to take sides is effectively to weigh in on the side of the stronger. Jesus never tolerated the intolerable, and neither should we. Racism is intolerable.

So I can only give you my word that in the future I will make the best of the lesson I have learned, and I will fight harder against racism. I'm sure this church will too.

But while we must fight racism in Riverside Church, we must never forget that the heavier suffering lies elsewhere. As Gardner Taylor yesterday warned the New York Baptists, "Black folk have been watching whites so long and so closely, and white folks have been watching blacks so long and so closely, that other folks are now running the country."

Our business in life is less making something of ourselves than finding something worth doing and losing ourselves in it. I know I wouldn't be here, and I daresay you wouldn't either, if we didn't think the work of this church was something worth doing. More than anything else, I'm going to miss this Sunday service, which means at least as much to me as it does to any of you. But I'll also miss the concerts, like the Mahler concert this afternoon; the workshops, such as the weekend one just ended on racism; the clothing service, which yesterday, thanks to so many of you who volunteered, raised $15,000 for the Social Services department; the work of the Food and Justice Task Force, the folks who go out in front of Sloan's and run up the Riverside sign and come back with over a thousand, sometimes even two thousand dollars' worth of food and money; the AIDS education, gay/lesbian, prison, and all the other task forces; the two language programs, presently teaching hundreds of immigrants from fifty-nine countries; the youth and older adults ministries, the Food Pantry, the men's shelter, both Carillons—if this sermon didn't have to end soon, I could go on for a long time.

In the worst times churches are always called on to do the best things. This is the season for pledging, and this is no time to trim donations if you can possibly help it. I personally would feel deeply distressed if, when I left Riverside, others left too. One monkey never stopped a show, and this show is too good not to go on and on.

I am going to ask all the hosts and hostesses here present who will invite the rest of you in small groups to their homes in the coming weeks to stand. With numbers like that, it's clear: "There's no hidin' place down here." But who wants to hide? These people are community builders who want your opinions and concerns as well as your pledge. Don't be embarrassed to talk about money. If there are two things that say a lot about our character, they are money and how we spend it. Too much for ourselves may be materialistic, as is also too little for others, but being generous is a religious activity.

And so too is intuiting, sensing, picking up on things, as did Jesus. I think we really come to church to be sensitized anew, to be reminded of the caring selves we really are.

I've mentioned international relations, race relations, and the financial needs of this church, but there are so many other things in this world that need observing eyes and tender, healing hands—enough, really, to overwhelm us. But let us act on the poet's insight: We are always undefeated because we go on trying. "For us, there is only the trying. The rest is not our business." Let us never forget that just as God pulls us down when we're too high, God pulls us up when we're too low. And always there is the love and support—and the example—of our Lord and Savior, who, "on entering the house of Peter, noticed that his mother-in-law was down with fever. And he touched her hand, and the fever left her."

The Moral Mediocrity of Midian

NOVEMBER 11, 1987
Readings: Exodus 3:1–12a; Matthew 4:18–22

The major decisions we reach about our lives we make on instinct rather than reason. And often, quite unconsciously, these decisions ripen over a long period of time so that major changes then become as easy as opening doors. I wonder if that wasn't so with Moses. Certainly, herding sheep in the wilderness of Horeb would have given him ample time to mull over his future, so that he was primed to see that bush flaming like a Vermont maple in October, and to hear the voice calling, "Moses, Moses."

But maybe not. It's more than possible that hearing that call was the last thing in the world Moses either expected or wanted. After all, he had barely escaped alive from Egypt; he had gone to Midian, where he had married, had a fine boy, and entered into his father-in-law's business. In short, after a period of youthful rebellion that included killing an Egyptian guard—for which act today we'd call him a terrorist (does that term ever need desegregation!)—Moses had settled down. And now, suddenly, in the midst of all that hard-won security, he hears, "Moses, Moses . . . Come, I will send you"—right back into the thick of everything he had tried so hard to escape.

Moses' mindset will always remain a mystery (at least until we see him face to face—I can hear him saying, "Well, I don't rightly remember, because time, like the Sinai sands, has silted over so many things"; heaven is going to be very frustrating to those of us who want things cleared up!). But this we can say with certainty: while God's call to Moses, as to Jeremiah, to Isaiah, and to almost all other biblical prophets entailed doing something, the call of God is fundamentally to *be* someone. Moses was called to be Moses, to be fully Moses, for, like all the rest of us, Moses was too insecure to dare his full capacity. That's why upon receiving his marching orders, far from falling on his knees, he reared up on his hind legs: "Who am I that I should go to Pharaoh?" ("You can get the slaves out of Egypt, but you can never get Egypt out of the slaves!") Likewise Jeremiah: "Ah, Lord God, behold I do not know how to speak, for I am only a youth." What we so fear in the world is not the evil in it, nor even the evil in ourselves; far more fearful is the good in ourselves, that good being so demanding. Even Christians, who believe that God can call forth a people from dry bones, sons and daughters from the stones at their feet, babes from barren wombs, and life from the tomb, don't believe, or don't want to believe, that they too—any one of them— could become a Moses or a Jeremiah, human beings fully human.

That's what the call of God is trying to call forth—our full humanity—for we are all too scared to dare our full capacity. God's call is a call into being, because if our being is right, our doing will take care of itself. Said Martin Luther: "Doing good works doesn't make a person good, but a good person will do good works."

Obviously no two of us are called to be alike, nor is any one of us called to be the same person in childhood as in old age. So before turning again to Moses—halfway between childhood and old age— let's take a moment to consider our calling in old age.

We say we are growing old. But, as May Sarton suggests, rightly done, we grow into old age, "into the final flowering and meaning of our lives." Instead of being dragged into it, instead of whimpering into it, we should try to grow into old age. "Though our outer nature is wasting away, our inner nature is being renewed each day" (2 Cor. 4:16). And we grow into old age by letting go "the driver, the implacable wanter and demander," and by letting loose the child in each of us available for every delight. I think in old age we should be free to enjoy without needing to possess. For there is always so much in the air for those who have the imagination to catch it.

I mentioned earlier the bush flaming like a Vermont maple. For myself the model of old age is autumn leaves blazing away in defiance against the onslaught of time, at their very best just before they drop.

Let's leave old age, but before getting back to Moses, let me make one comment about middle age. I'm against overeating, as I am against too much money; both tend to take the edge off perception. But why do we pretend that middle-aged spread is not a real phenomenon? Isn't trying to fight it a little like the old Chinese practice of trying to force women's feet into tiny shoes as a sign of breeding and beauty? To quote May Sarton once more: "I am not so much interested in being a dazzling model as in being comfortable in myself. And that I am." Would that all of us in middle age were so comfortable!

Now back to Moses and to our common insecurity, which prevents us from daring our full capacity.

It's always easier to pull in our horns, to play it safe, to obey what we might call the eleventh commandment—"Don't climb out on a limb"—the commandment on which are "hanged" all the law and the prophets. It's always easier to stay in Midian, to bury ourselves in our ongoing lives. And this, of course, is also true of churches. Even Riverside might decide to play it safe. But the fact of the matter is, Moses simply couldn't be Moses in Midian, only in Egypt. He was in Midian merely for what psychologists would call "a period of consolidation." Now his life needed again to expand. He needed despair, frustration, headaches of one kind or another to keep him in fighting form.

Most of all, he needed to be in Egypt because he had to keep open the channels of pain. "I have seen the affliction of my people who are in Egypt, and have heard their cry because of their taskmasters." God's call was embedded in a cry of pain, and Moses was called to alleviate that pain by sharing it. And when he chose to heed the call, I'll bet he felt a joyful sense of released power. I think the decision had been ripening a long time; after all, he called that fine boy of his Gershon, which means, "I am a sojourner in a foreign land."

Moses couldn't be Moses in Midian; only in Egypt. And when God said, "I will be with you," God didn't mean "I will be with you in Midian." God did not mean "I will be with you in Midian or in Egypt, whatever you elect." When God said "I will be with you," he meant "only in Egypt," because it was in Egypt that Moses belonged, where he would always make himself available to the power that came from God.

We think that wherever or whoever we are, whether in Midian or in Egypt, whether we side with the slaves or side with Pharaoh, it makes no difference, God is always on our side, with "strength for today and bright hope for tomorrow." Likewise, Americans tend to believe God cannot do without America, whereas it is precisely the reverse: America cannot do without God.

Do you know what I fear more than anything else? It's the moral mediocrity which is the glue of every society, and of all too many churches; the moral mediocrity that keeps people stuck in Midian while the pain throbs on in Egypt; the moral mediocrity that keeps people from being their fully human selves.

"Must then a Christ perish in torment in every age to save those who have no imagination?"

In this bright city, this adrenaline capital of the world, we today have so little imagination because we allow our heads, hands, and feet to outrun our hearts. So a pearl of a city has become Babylon-by-the-Sea, malnutrition, drugs, and violent death destroying its poorest people.

We have so little imagination that we drowse our way toward the end of the world, put to sleep by the vocabulary of dispassionate terror: missiles called Peacemakers and a submarine that can destroy 190 cities christened with the name of Christ.

"Must then a Christ perish in torment in every age to save those who have no imagination?" Later in that same play about St. Joan, Shaw puts these words in the mouth of the Bishop of Beauvais, now an old man: "I did a cruel thing once because I did not know what cruelty was like. I had not seen it, you know. That is the great thing. You must see it."

Yes, as God does: "I have seen the affliction of my people who are in Egypt." We must let pain penetrate our consciousness so that we can truly experience it, otherwise we'll stay stuck in the moral mediocrity of Midian. We'll never be a Moses or a Jeremiah; we'll never even be our own true selves. And we'll never know God's "own dear presence to cheer and to guide."

If I've made all this sound impossibly difficult, I want to correct the impression.

> Jesus calls us o'er the tumult
> Of our life's wild restless sea.
> Day by day his sweet voice soundeth,
> Saying, "Christian, follow me."
> Cecil Alexander

Jesus calls us by being something irresistible, not by demanding something impossible. Peter and Andrew, James and John—they simply had no choice. Never in their lives had they seen or heard the likes of this man, a person of such vision and clarity of purpose, a man tender as only the truly strong can be tender.

People who assert their religion are rarely religious in their being and in their actions; they are more assertive than loving. But Jesus was just the opposite. He was love incarnate, packed down and overflowing. That's why I say he calls us by being something irresistible, not by demanding something impossible. You know that wonderful poster that reads, "Dear God, remind me that nothing can possibly happen today that between us we can't handle"?

It doesn't take an enormous effort to follow Jesus. You just have to stop exhausting yourself by denying the attraction!

"Moses, Moses" . . . "Mary" . . . "John" . . . "Our Lady of Sorrows" . . . "Riverside Church." There is no question that the air is full of calls, for lives are full of pain in the city, nation, and world. The only question is which of us, and which of our churches, tired of staying stuck in Midian, will have the imagination and grace to reply, "Here am I" . . . "Here are we."

For the Joy, Pleasure, and Satisfaction
That Is Riverside

NOVEMBER 22, 1987
Reading: Luke 19:1–9a

Zacchaeus was short of stature. But as was said of St. Francis of Assisi, where he stopped physically, he was just getting underway. Something similar might be said of Zacchaeus; he obviously was a dime among nickels. Bound and determined to see Jesus, he ran ahead of the crowd blocking his view, found a sycamore tree, and scrambled up it. Literally and figuratively, he stood above the crowd. And Jesus, who never missed a thing, spied him up there and called out, "Zacchaeus, make haste and come down; for I must stay at your house today."

That, of course, is what Jesus says to all of us who come to see him. But not all who come to see come to receive. Some would like nothing better than to take out permanent membership in the association of life's bystanders. Not Zacchaeus, however. He "made haste and came down, and received him joyfully."

Several years ago a young Jewish woman applied for membership in Riverside Church. I was wary; it's no simple matter for a Jew to be converted to a Christian. The problem for St. Paul was to allow Gentiles to become Christians without becoming Jews; today the problem is to allow Jews to become Christians without becoming Gentiles—a severe indictment of gentility! So I said, "What's the matter, are you anti-Semitic?" "No, no," she replied. "I wasn't brought up in a synagogue. Jesus doesn't displace a thing; he just fills everything." So I suggested, "Why don't you, in the course of this week, take some time and write me a few pages about what Jesus means to you?" "I'll do it right now," she said. She went into the next room, and about fifteen minutes later she came back with pages of lyrical prose about what Jesus meant in her life. She, like Zacchaeus, received Jesus joyfully. After finishing the membership class, she was baptized, on her face an expression of bliss that I have not seen before or since.

Joy, of course, stems from appreciation. You can't enjoy what you don't appreciate. Zacchaeus appreciated what Jesus meant to him, as did Mary, the sister of Lazarus, who anointed Jesus with ointment and wiped his feet with her hair; as did the woman in the house of Simon the leper, who poured an alabaster flask of very expensive ointment on Jesus' head. They did not take him for granted. They appreciated Jesus, who went into the homes of the soul-sick like Zacchaeus, and of Simon the leper, leprosy being in those days the equivalent of AIDS.

Today I want to ask how deeply we appreciate the church. Do we do anything to the church, the body of Christ, comparable to Mary's wiping Jesus' feet with her hair, comparable to the woman's pouring expensive ointment on Jesus' head? Do we just go to church, or do we receive the church joyfully in our hearts?

As December 20, the last Sunday in Advent, will be my last Sunday in this pulpit, I can tell you I have given a lot of thought to the question of appreciation. I really appreciate Riverside, especially this service, which I have always felt was the heart of our life together. I will be preaching in many churches, but where else will I hear such celestial singing, such soaring organ tones? In what other church will I find a congregation so mixed, or one so large and so attentive? What other church will have a Social Service Department comparable to ours? A comparable Pastoral Counseling Center? So many varied task forces? What other church teaches English to hundreds of newly arrived immigrants, and within days has a national conference on low-intensity conflict (hardly low-intensity for its victims) and presents with full orchestra and bulging chorus Mahler's *Resurrection Symphony*? Does any other church try harder to be both a life raft for the shipwrecked and a beacon of light to a nation stumbling in gross darkness?

I can even appreciate what has been so hard for me to experience—for example, the dissolution of the hegemony of the white male. (Ah, the things I could have done had I been black, or a woman!) Not to mention the Riverside way of arguing it out, side by side, in what William Blake called "the severe contentions of friendship."

I'm leaving this place, so I can appreciate it. I hope those of you who are staying can do the same and will never take Riverside Church for granted.

Now back to Zacchaeus. He stood, we read, because he appreciated the importance of the moment and of what he was going to say. He stood and did not say, "Behold, Lord, I am now going to go regularly on retreats, read Scripture daily, and have a rich prayer life"—important as these things are. No, he rose to say, "Behold, Lord, the half of my goods I will give to the poor."

Zacchaeus was very rich, and I assume that he appreciated not only Jesus, but all that he was about to give away. We should never sacrifice without appreciating deeply the value of what we are sacrificing; otherwise, our giving is not sacrificial. In other words, we should appreciate not only the church but all the non-church-related things in our lives that give us such pleasure—eating out, movies, trips, vacations, nice clothes, perfume, concerts and theater, sports and hobbies.

Then, as wisely suggested by two Riverside members, we should tally up as best we can what we spend on these pleasures and compare that sum to what we give "for the joy, pleasure, and satisfaction that is Riverside."

The result is predictable: most of us will be shocked and ashamed, which is a sign of good spiritual health. Now we are in a position to negotiate with ourselves, to decide how much we want to decrease one sum in order to increase the other.

Zacchaeus decided to even up the two sums, to split what he had fifty-fifty. Either I am not as rich, or have more dependents, or am not as good a Christian—probably all three—because for the ten years I have been here I have pledged to the church, the body of Christ, only 10 percent of my salary. But I take some satisfaction in having given to the church over ten years some $50,000.

Lou Gropp, in his letter, is suggesting 5 percent of our gross annual income, or $10 for every $200 we earn. That's a weekly offering of $10 if your annual income is $10,000 and $100 a week if your annual income is $100,000. That doesn't strike me as excessive, provided Riverside means something to you.

I'm only giving you three examples: Zacchaeus', my own, and Lou Gropp's suggestion—50 percent, 10 percent, 5 percent. Obviously the decision is eminently yours to make. I can only remind you of the story that comes two chapters later in Luke: "Jesus looked up and saw the rich putting their gifts into the treasury; and he saw a poor widow put in two copper coins. And he said, 'Truly I tell you, this poor widow has put in more than all of them; for they all contributed out of their abundance, but she out of her poverty put in all the living that she had'" (Luke 21:1–4).

In other words, what counts is not how much you give, but how much is left after you give.

Let me make two final points. The chairperson of the Budget Committee, Jim Tsang, wrote in the "Carillon": "We have a responsibility to whomever we call to our pulpit as new senior minister to set our financial house in order so that she or he can concentrate on the task of helping this congregation perform its ministry. To require that person to devote valuable time and energy during his or her first months trying to set our financial house in order would be irresponsible."

I agree with that. You don't want a finance minister; you want a preaching minister.

Lastly, I want to go back to the fact that Zacchaeus did all this joyfully. He received Jesus gladly, and when he stood to announce his intention to give half his goods to the poor, I assume he did not do so with a long face and in a choking voice. No, he gave as joyfully as he received. And he did so because he knew that to give is not to give up, but to gain. Those who lose their lives will find them. We sacrifice for spiritual gain, for the only truly renewable resources.

As a life raft and as a beacon of light, Riverside is needed in this city and nation perhaps as never before. And none of us wants to be as those superpatriots who love America but don't want to pay to support it. We want to support what we love; we want to be generous. If like Zacchaeus we have joyfully received Jesus, we want as joyfully to follow Zacchaeus' example in giving. Like him, in appreciation of the importance of this moment and of the significance of your pledge, you, the members of the church, will shortly be invited to rise as did Zacchaeus.

I hope that when you do rise, you will feel some of that sense of incredible satisfaction that must have filled Zacchaeus when he rose to say, "Behold, Lord, the half of my goods I will give to the poor." And may salvation come to your house also.

Leaving Riverside

DECEMBER 13, 1987
Readings: Isaiah; Matthew 1:18–25

Before turning to the sermon, I want to turn toward all you my dearly beloved parishioners, and thank you again for Friday night. Thanks to John and David, Sherril Milnes, Clamma Dale, and David Schilling (whose singing isn't quite in the same category, but very fine never the less), and especially, I guess, Fran Massey and Marcia Martin and Mary Kay Coffin, and Heidi Campbell.

The invitations were too close for comfort, but the love shown was comfort itself.

If, to you visitors, I look (and I must say, feel) a little like Stravinsky's *Firebird*, it is because I am wearing this farewell robe and stole, that was given to me by this Church. It was not explained on Friday, but Pat Agea, who made this beautiful stole (and I want to thank you particularly), tells me that the parts of the stole come from China, India, Africa, literally from all over the world—which will be a constant reminder to me to keep stretching my mind, and more important yet, my heart.

So I do thank you. It was terrific.

Now, let as take as our text for this third Sunday in Advent, that line we just heard:

> "His name shall be called Emmanu-el
> (which means, God with us)."

In troubled times, like ours, when Cold War propaganda is still trying to destroy humanity's instinct for survival; when we seem regularly to forget Churchill's warning that "the stone age may return on the gleaming wings of science"; in times like our own where common integrity is made to look like courage, so that only those firm of faith stand firm, while others bend, shake and break like trees in a high wind; when famine revisits Ethiopia and when in our own country the religious crisis deepens even as Americans turn more desperately to religion because the religion to which they turn is devoid of prophetic fervor—in such times it is understandable that sensitive believers should cry to seemingly empty skies: "How long, O Lord, how long?"

"By some mighty act, prove your existence! Bring us to our senses!" "You are the Savior, so save!" It is, as I say, natural. We just

heard the prediction for every "boot of the tramping warrior in battle tumult and every garment rolled with blood will be burned as fuel
for the fire" (Isa. 9:5).

Last week, from the same prophet, we heard "God shall smite the
earth with a rod of his mouth, and with the breath of his lips shall he
slay the wicked" (Isa. 11:4).

In Jeremiah we read: "Is not his word like a hammer that breaketh
a rock into pieces?" (Jer. 23:29).

Yet I think that Isaiah and Jeremiah both knew, as well as any other
profoundly religious person, that the "Word of the Lord generally hits
the world with the force of a hint."

Often, it takes the form of a question: "Adam, where are you?"
God's eternal question. Spoken eternally to each of you: "James,
Mary, where are you?"

Remember Elijah's question: "What are you doing here?" Here
instead of there—where you should be. In the story of Elijah, you
will remember, "The Word of the Lord was not in the earthquake, the
wind or the fire, but in the still small voice." At Christmas, the Word
of the Lord is a very pretty little baby.

It is very interesting, and it is very touching and it is very unsatisfactory! How could it be otherwise? To say: "God, prove your existence, and so bring us to our senses," is really to pray "Please, God,
give us some evidence, so we can make some intelligently selfish decisions." But God is not in the business of trying to overcome our selfishness by appealing to selfish motives. God takes the freedom God
has given us ten times as seriously as do we. So God doesn't hit us
over the head so much as God tugs at our sleeves, or should we say,
at the strings of our heart.

Christ is the Prince of Peace, not because Christ is some benign
despot ordering us to lay down our arms, but because Christ disarms
us, coming as he does, as one of us. Jesus disarms us by being totally
vulnerable, unguarded goodness, lying in a manger, fragile as a rose
in winter.

As I have asked you to do before: picture yourself at the manger,
as one of the shepherds at the side of the crib. Suddenly, Mary looks
up and says: "Here, hold the baby for a minute." There you are, God's
love in person on earth in *your* arms. Instead of protecting yourself,
you are protecting the Baby Jesus. That is the personal responsibility
of Christmas we have all been given: the freedom to assume or not to
assume.

Each of us, I guess, has her favorite Christmas carol, and probably a
favorite Christmas story, many of whose heroes not surprisingly are

children like Tiny Tim and Amahl. As some of you know, my favorite is a Søren Kierkegaard story of "The King and the Maid." I know he didn't tell it as a Christmas story, but then the melody of "The Star-Spangled Banner" was originally a British drinking song—you can picture that— and the melody of Dvorak's "Going Home" was designed by Dvorak himself to go at twice the tempo that we now play it. In other words, authors are entitled to everything their hearers hear.

So, once upon a time, a King fell in love with a Maid. An old and wonderful theme of how love overcomes all barriers—race, class, nationality. But for all its beauty, the King did not see the matter easily resolved. Racking his mind and heart was the question, "How to declare his love?" Unable to find an answer, he summoned all the wise people in his realm to his palace and put the question to them. As one, they responded: "Sire, nothing could be easier. All your majesty has to do is to appear in all your glory before her humble abode, and instantly the maid will fall at your feet and be yours."

It was precisely that thought that so troubled the King. In return for his love, he wanted hers, not her fears that might lead to her submission. He wanted her glorification, not his. Oh, what a dilemma— when to declare your love is the death of your beloved, and not to declare it spells the death of love.

Night after night, the King paced the floor of his palace, pondering, until at last he saw love's truth: "*Freedom for the beloved demands equality with the beloved.*"

So, late one night, when all the councillors and courtiers had retired to their chambers, he stole out of a side door to the palace, and appeared before the maid's humble abode, dressed in the garb of a servant. "He came to us as one of us." Indeed, it is a Christmas story.

But it is maddening, as well as touching, this solution, so satisfying to the King, and to Kierkegaard. Had I been the Maid, I am not sure that I would have found it satisfactory at all. I would have wanted to know more about this young man of unspectacular appearance, about his future—and mine. "Were the two of us going to be stuck forever in this miserable hovel?" "Why couldn't he be more forthright?" "I wouldn't mind marrying a King!"

What makes the story irritating is that while we want a king to be a King, he wants to be a servant. *While we want him to be strong, so that we can be dependent, protected, and a little bit spoiled, He wants to be as weak as we, so that we can be as strong as he.* Christ became like one of us so that we might become more like him.

We want the King to prove himself. He asks us, "What do you want? Proof or Freedom?"

God is love's description—not might, not magic, not a foolproof formula or dogma. That means that the revelation of God is in the *relationship with God*. "And you will be called Emmanuel (which means, God *with us*)."

God is known devotionally, not dogmatically. "God is love" does not so much clear up old mystery as it discloses new mystery. "God is love" is not a truth we can master, it is only one to which we can surrender.

Christian faith is being grasped by the power of love. It is being captivated, enthralled, so the perfect self-expression of all-mighty God has to be in human form.

"Late one night he stole out of a side door of the palace, and appeared before the humble abode of the maid, dressed in the garb of a servant." Why should the Maid, why should any of us, open the door? Because, although we behave like frightened virgins, we know that it is in self-abandonment, not in self-improvement, that lies self-fulfillment.

We should open the door because although God has given us freedom of choice, most of us have lost our ability to choose. We need, once again, to be set free. Free *from* fear. Free *for* love. Free *from* self. Free *for* God and each other!

We need to open the door because we need to turn from things that are shallow, to things that are significant, from things that are apparent, to those that are real. We need to open the door, because too many of us think failure is final, and have shut the door on Grace and Forgiveness.

Most of all, we should open the door, because to enhance the plight of the poor, the predicament of the powerless, to avoid the planet's final defeat, brightly to deal with the earth's sins and needs, we need to have the help of One from heaven. And, because we know William Blake was right:

> We are put on earth a little space
> That we may learn to bear the beams of love.

As Christmas approaches, dear parishioners and dear visitors, let me suggest that this week, once or twice in the morning, and once or twice in the afternoon, as well as in the evening—several times a day—we pray to Jesus. Only we must pray to Him as God's Love in Person, on earth, Emmanuel, which means "God with us!" a totally beneficent presence everywhere.

Speak to Him as One more wonderful than upright; less law than love-abiding; yet pray to Him as One who can make our souls steady, as well as hardened, for love is a long-distance runner. "We are put on earth a little space that we may learn to bear the beams of love."

Like Kierkegaard's Maid, we live in a small space, and but for a little time. Yet, like St. Teresa, taking her turn in the kitchen, found Jesus easily among the pots and pans, so we can find him in the dreariest stretches of our experience.

Will we be stuck forever in this miserable hovel? Who is to say? In talking with Jesus, we learn the transporting power of prayer with a folding of hands and the spreading of wings. In a palace, or in a hovel, we can, through self-abandonment to the Servant King, find the fulfillment of citizens of heaven. You remember the old hymn:

> O Jesus, Thou art standing
>   Outside the fast-closed door,
> In lowly patience waiting
>   To pass the threshold o'er.
>   William How

I hope the Maid opened that door. And I hope this Christmas *we* open it too and as we open it sing or say the last words of the hymn:

> "Open now the door;
>   Dear Savior, enter, enter,
>   And leave us nevermore."